Lecture Notes in Computer Science

Lecture Notes in Artificial Intelligence 16099

Founding Editor

Jörg Siekmann

AF173765

Series Editors

Randy Goebel, *University of Alberta, Edmonton, Canada*
Wolfgang Wahlster, *DFKI, Berlin, Germany*
Zhi-Hua Zhou, *Nanjing University, Nanjing, China*

The series Lecture Notes in Artificial Intelligence (LNAI) was established in 1988 as a topical subseries of LNCS devoted to artificial intelligence.

The series publishes state-of-the-art research results at a high level. As with the LNCS mother series, the mission of the series is to serve the international R & D community by providing an invaluable service, mainly focused on the publication of conference and workshop proceedings and postproceedings.

Kai Sauerwald · Matthias Thimm
Editors

Symbolic and Quantitative Approaches to Reasoning with Uncertainty

18th European Conference, ECSQARU 2025
Hagen, Germany, September 23–26, 2025
Proceedings

Springer

Editors
Kai Sauerwald
FernUniversität in Hagen
Hagen, Germany

Matthias Thimm
FernUniversität in Hagen
Hagen, Germany

ISSN 0302-9743 ISSN 1611-3349 (electronic)
Lecture Notes in Artificial Intelligence
ISBN 978-3-032-05133-2 ISBN 978-3-032-05134-9 (eBook)
https://doi.org/10.1007/978-3-032-05134-9

LNCS Sublibrary: SL7 – Artificial Intelligence

This Springer imprint is published by the registered company Springer Nature Switzerland AG
The registered company address is: Gewerbestrasse 11, 6330 Cham, Switzerland

Preface

The biennial ECSQARU conferences (www.ecsqaru.org/) constitute a major forum for advances in the theory and practice of reasoning under uncertainty, with a focus on bringing symbolic and quantitative aspects together. Contributions come from researchers interested in advancing scientific knowledge and from practitioners using uncertainty techniques in real-world applications. The scope of the ECSQARU conferences encompasses fundamental issues, representation, inference, learning, and decision-making in qualitative and numeric uncertainty paradigms. Previous ECSQARU events have been held in Arras (2023), Prague (2021), Belgrade (2019), Lugano (2017), Compiègne (2015), Utrecht (2013), Belfast (2011), Verona (2009), Hammamet (2007), Barcelona (2005), Aalborg (2003), Toulouse (2001), London (1999), Bonn (1997), Fribourg (1995), Granada (1993), and Marseille (1991).

The call asked for regular papers reporting on novel technical contributions. We received 48 submissions and the committee decided to accept 34 papers. Each submission received three reviews. In total, our Program Committee members delivered 142 reviews. The review process was single-blind, with reviewer names unknown to the authors. We organized bidding on papers to ensure that reviewers received papers within their field of expertise.

We would like to thank all those who submitted papers, the members of the Program Committee and the external reviewers for their valuable reviews, the organizers of the associated workshops and tutorial, as well as the members of the local Organizing Committee, for all their support and contributions to the success of the conference. In addition to the main program of paper presentations, ECSQARU 2025 hosted two workshops: (i) The First International Workshop on Inconsistency Measurement (IM'25) and (ii) The First European Workshop on Argumentation and Uncertainty (ArgU'25). We were also very delighted to host the tutorial StaRAI: From a Probabilistic Propositional Model to a Highly Compressed Probabilistic Relational Model. ECSQARU 2025 also included invited talks by outstanding researchers in the field: Claudia d'Amato (University of Bari, Italy), Vanina Martinez (Artificial Intelligence Research Institute, Spain), and Tommie Meyer (CAIR, University of Cape Town, South Africa).

Finally, we are thankful for the financial and logistic support we received from the FernUniversität in Hagen, Deutsche Forschungsgemeinschaft (DFG, German Research Foundation), and the Journal of Artifical Intelligence. We are also thankful to Springer Nature for funding the Best Paper Award and collaborating smoothly on the proceedings.

September 2025

Kai Sauerwald
Matthias Thimm

Organization

Program Chairs

Kai Sauerwald	FernUniversität in Hagen, Germany
Matthias Thimm	FernUniversität in Hagen, Germany

Steering Committee

Salem Benferhat	CRIL - CNRS, University of Artois, France
Vanina Martinez	IIIA - CSIC, Spain
Giovani Casini	CNR - ISTI, Italy
Matthias Thimm	FernUniversität in Hagen, Germany
Sebastien Destercke	CNRS, UMR Heudiasyc, France
Lluis Godo	IIIA - CSIC, Spain
Anthony Hunter	University College London, UK
Weiru Liu	University of Bristol, UK
Henri Prade	IRIT - CNRS, France

Program Committee

Nahla Ben Amor	University of Tunis, Tunisia
Alessandro Antonucci	IDSIA, Switzerland
Jonathan Ben-Naim	IRIT - CNRS, LILaC, France
Salem Benferhat	CRIL - CNRS, University of Artois, France
Florence le Ber	ICube, Université de Strasbourg/ENGEES, France
Inés Couso Blanco	Oviedo University, Spain
Tanya Braun	University of Münster, Germany
Cory Butz	University of Regina, Canada
Serafín Moral Callejón	University of Granada, Spain
Andres Cano	University of Granada, Spain
Federico Cerutti	University of Brescia, Italy
Andrea Cohen	Universidad Nacional del Sur, Argentina
Giulianella Coletti	Università di Perugia, Italy
Fabio Cozman	University of São Paulo, Brazil
Thierry Denoeux	Université de Technologie de Compiègne, France
Sebastien Destercke	CNRS, UMR Heudiasyc, France

Dragan Doder	Utrecht University, The Netherlands
Patricia Everaere	CRIStAL-University Lille, France
Eduardo Fermé	Universidade da Madeira, Portugal
Tommaso Flaminio	IIIA - CSIC, Spain
Laura Giordano	Università del Piemonte Orientale, Italy
Jonas Philipp Haldimann	University of Cape Town, South Africa
Hykel Hosni	University of Milan, Italy
Anthony Hunter	University College London, UK
Nebojša Ikodinović	University of Belgrade, Serbia
Souhila Kaci	LIRMM, France
Gabriele Kern-Isberner	TU Dortmund, Germany
Sébastien Konieczny	CRIL - CNRS, France
Christophe Labreuche	Thales Research and Technology, France
Marie-Christine Lagasquie-Schiex	IRIT - Université de Toulouse, France
Helge Langseth	Norwegian University of Science and Technology, Norway
Joao Leite	Universidade Nova de Lisboa, Portugal
Philippe Leray	Polytech Nantes, France
Jean-Guy Mailly	IRIT, France
Maria Vanina Martinez	IIIA-CSIC, Spain
Jérôme Mengin	IRIT - University of Toulouse, France
David Mercier	University of Artois, France
Enrique Miranda	University of Oviedo, Spain
Ralf Möller	Universität Hamburg, Germany
Davide Petturiti	University of Perugia, Italy
Frédéric Pichon	University of Artois, France
Nico Potyka	Cardiff University, UK
Henri Prade	CNRS, France
Benjamin Quost	Université de Technologie de Compiègne, France
Silja Renooij	Utrecht University, The Netherlands
Jandson Ribeiro	Cardiff University, UK
Tjitze Rienstra	Maastricht University, The Netherlands
Regis Riveret	Data61, Australia
Florence Dupin de Saint-Cyr	University of Toulouse, France
Laurent Garcia	University of Angers, France
Leon Van der Torre	University of Luxembourg, Luxembourg
Matthias Troffaes	Durham University, UK
Ivan Varzinczak	Université Sorbonne Paris Nord, France
Srdjan Vesic	Université d'Artois, France
Jirka Vomlel	Czech Academy of Sciences, Czech Republic
Renata Wassermann	University of São Paulo, Brazil

Marco Wilhelm	Federal Institute for Occupational Safety and Health, Germany
Nic Wilson	University College Cork, Ireland
Stefan Woltran	TU Wien, Austria
Bruno Zanuttini	Université de Caen Normandie, CNRS, ENSICAEN, France

Contents

Game Theory and Social Choice

Conditionals, Inference, Change

Bayesian Networks

Inverse Marginalisation for Safely Expanding Bayesian Networks

Johan Kwisthout[1(✉)] and Silja Renooij[2]

[1] Radboud University, Nijmegen, The Netherlands
johan.kwisthout@donders.ru.nl
[2] Utrecht University, Utrecht, The Netherlands
s.renooij@uu.nl
https://www.socsci.ru.nl/johank/index.html,
https://www.uu.nl/staff/SRenooij

Abstract. After clinical decision support systems are validated and deployed, one is often reluctant to update the model with new insights or data, especially if this means that re-certification is required. In this paper we address this issue in updating Bayesian networks with new domain knowledge. More specifically, we introduce and study the concept of safe inverse marginalisation, an operation that allows for adding new variables to a network without affecting the distribution over the original variables. As such, the additional efforts required for validation and certification can be limited, re-using as much as possible the analyses and documentation from the original model. To support the process of safely extending a Bayesian network, we present an algorithm that flags potentially unsafe updates.

Keywords: Bayesian networks · Marginalisation · Safe expansion

1 Introduction

In the past decades a variety of clinical decision support systems (CDSSs) based on Bayesian networks have been proposed (see the overview in [8]). Bayesian networks are white-box AI models that encode uncertain relations using stochastic variables and include intuitive graphical structures and associated conditional probabilities. They are typically developed using a combination of expert knowledge and data. Firstly, variables of interest are selected; secondly, the structure of the network is learned or hand-crafted, and finally, the conditional probabilities are learned or elicited [5]. Once the network is validated and deployed (particularly if this deployment requires certification procedures) one is typically reluctant to change the network when new insights emerge or new data sets become available to avoid going over this long and arduous phase again. This hinders maintenance and update of Bayesian networks and puts them at risk of being outdated soon.

K. Sauerwald and M. Thimm (Eds.): ECSQARU 2025, LNAI 16099, pp. 3–16, 2026.
https://doi.org/10.1007/978-3-032-05134-9_1

New information, however, can sometimes significantly improve decisions made using the model. A motivating example can be found in the ENDORISK model [12] (see also Fig. 1). ENDORISK is a Bayesian network-based CDSS that allows oncologists to preoperatively estimate the risk of lymph node metastasis; this allows for risk stratification and the avoidance of unnecessary removal of the lymph nodes in low-risk patients, considerably improving their post-operative quality-of-life. On the basis of this network, a decision support tool (see www.endorisk.eu) can be used by gynaecological oncologists to enter available information (test results, biomarkers, preoperative tumour grade) and estimate the probability of lymph node metastasis for this patient. The CDSS's use was tested using focus groups with professionals and interviews with patients [4,17], and currently a prospective implementation study is initiated. Simultaneously, challenges in the implementation of ENDORISK in the clinic are being addressed: keeping the network up-to-date with new knowledge and additional patient data, and dealing with the EU regulation for clinical use of the tool, in particular CE marking and assessment according to the In Vitro Diagnostic Medical Devices Regulation (IVDR), simultaneously with the implementation trial.

During this whole trajectory, several new clinical insights have emerged[1]. In the current network model, myometrial invasion is established post-operation using microscopy. However, in recent clinical practice MRI scans can already indicate the depth of the tumour pre-operation. In addition, two molecular mutations (so-called POLE and MSI mutations) have been established that are strongly related to the tumour grade and risk of lymph node metastasis. In the presence of the POLE mutation the risk of metastasis is very low, in the presence of MSI mutations it is intermediate. Observations of these biomarkers considerably change the outcomes and the decisions and thus improve the model. However, the changes to the model need to be assessed to see whether they would alter the existing (part of the) model and thus require reassessment. This is particularly the case when, upon marginalisation of the added variables, the original model would be changed. In that case, the addition effectively alters the existing model; for example, by introducing conditional dependences.

In this paper, we systematically address the issue of updating networks with new domain knowledge. We study in more detail when marginalisation, i.e., summing out variables, preserves the chain rule factorisation, respectively the graphical depiction of the conditional independences (i.e., the I-map). We introduce the concept of *safe inverse marginalisation*, that is, adding variables to a network such that the original conditional independences in the network are preserved. Based on the identified properties, we present an algorithm that allows for flagging potentially unsafe expansion of Bayesian networks.

The remainder of this paper is structured as follows. After offering some preliminaries in Sect. 2, we further develop the concept of inverse marginalisation and its role in safe network expanding in Sects. 3 and 4. We introduce an algorithm for safe expansion in Sect. 5, and conclude the paper in Sect. 6.

[1] C. Reijnen (Radiotherapist, RUMC), personal communication, March 5, 2025.

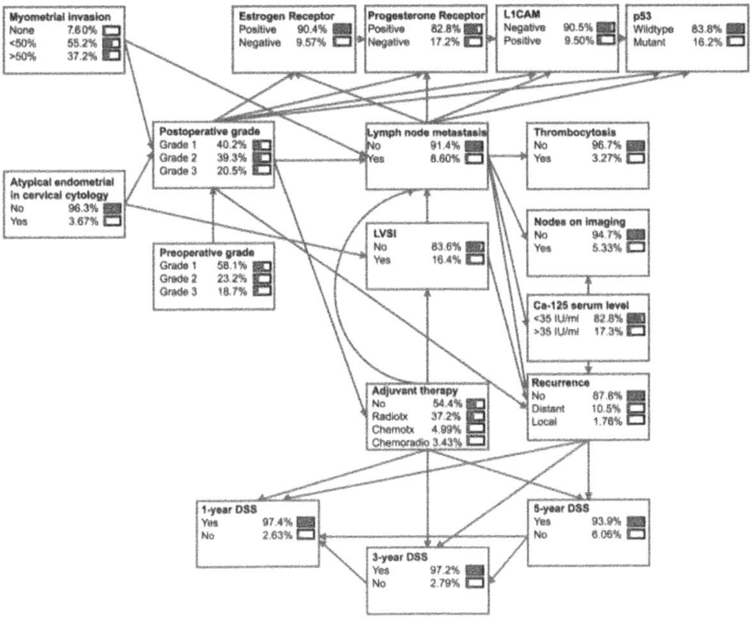

Fig. 1. The ENDORISK model for predicting lymph node metastasis and 5-year disease-specific survival in endometrial cancer [12, Figure 2a (copied with permission)].

2 Preliminaries

In this paper we assume a joint distribution Pr over a set $\mathbf{W}$ of discrete random variables. Upper case letters will denote individual variables, using a bold face to denote sets; lower case letters will denote value assignments to variables, bold-faced when referring to joint value assignments to sets of variables. $\boldsymbol{\Omega}(W)$ captures the domain of a variable W; this notation is extended to joint value assignments to a set of variables: $\mathbf{w} \in \boldsymbol{\Omega}(\mathbf{W})$.

We will consider Bayesian networks over subsets $\mathbf{V} \subseteq \mathbf{W}$ of random variables. A Bayesian network $\mathcal{B}$ captures a factorisation of a joint distribution over $\mathbf{V}$, by exploiting the independences among $\mathbf{V}$ [11]. An acyclic directed graph (DAG) $G_{\mathcal{B}} = (\mathbf{V}, \mathbf{A})$ models the variables as nodes and conditional independences through (absence of) arcs. More specifically, independences are read from the graph by means of *d-separation*[2]. $\mathcal{B}$ in addition includes a set of node probability tables (NPTs), one for each node $V_i \in \mathbf{V}$. A NPT for V_i describes a set of conditional probability distributions over the associated variable, conditioned on its parents $\pi_G(V_i)$ in the graph $G_{\mathcal{B}}$. We use $\sigma_G(V_i)$ to denote V_i's children, $\boldsymbol{\Delta}_G(V_i) = \{V_i\} \cup \sigma_G(V_i)$ to denote 'Donna con bambini', a node with all its

[2] Two sets of nodes $\mathbf{X}$ and $\mathbf{Y}$ are d-separated by a set $\mathbf{Z}$ if every chain between an $X \in \mathbf{X}$ and a $Y \in \mathbf{Y}$ contains a $Z \in \mathbf{Z}$ with at most one incoming arc on the chain, or a node not in $\mathbf{Z}$ with 2 incoming arcs that has no descendants in $\mathbf{Z}$.

children, and $\rho_G(V_i) = \pi_G(\sigma_G(V_i)) \setminus \mathbf{\Delta}(V_i)$ to denote the non-child co-parents of V_i. Finally, we use $\pi^+_G(V_i)$ to denote the set of ancestors of V_i, and $\sigma^+_G(V_i)$ to capture all its descendants. These definitions also generalise to sets of nodes. For example, for $\mathbf{Z} \subset \mathbf{V}$: $\pi_G(\mathbf{Z}) = \cup_{Z_i \in \mathbf{Z}} \pi_G(Z_i)$.

A Bayesian network now defines the joint distribution $\Pr_G(\mathbf{V})$ as follows:

$$\Pr_G(\mathbf{V}) = \prod_{i=1}^{|\mathbf{V}|} \Pr_G(V_i \mid \pi_G(V_i)) \tag{1}$$

Note that the graph is consistent with the factorisation: from the graph we can determine the factorisation, but we can also draw the graph based upon the factorisation.

Computing marginal or conditional probabilities from a joint distribution requires the use of *marginalisation*, a standard operation in probability theory that amounts to summing out one or more variables from a distribution. Marginalisation of joint distribution $\Pr(\mathbf{W})$ over a set $\mathbf{X} \subset \mathbf{W}$ results in a distribution over $\mathbf{V} = \mathbf{W} \setminus \mathbf{X}$:

$$\sum_{\mathbf{X}} \Pr(\mathbf{W}) = \sum_{\mathbf{X}} \Pr(\mathbf{V}, \mathbf{X}) = \sum_{\mathbf{x} \in \Omega(\mathbf{W} \setminus \mathbf{V})} \Pr(\mathbf{V}, \mathbf{x}) = \Pr(\mathbf{V})$$

We note that the joint distribution $\Pr(\mathbf{V})$ is in fact a marginal distribution computed from $\Pr(\mathbf{W})$. We will say that $\Pr(\mathbf{V})$ *agrees with* $\Pr(\mathbf{W})$.

Algorithms for exact inference in Bayesian networks typically try to perform marginalisation locally on the network-factorisation or the graph, to prevent having to compute the complete joint distribution. *Variable elimination* (VE) [3, 19] works on the factorisation, first multiplying all NPTs that involve a to be eliminated variable, and then summing it out from the product. The intermediate factor thus constructed is always a conditional probability table (a CPT, not a NPT), but does not necessarily agree with the joint [2,6]. *Arc-reversal* (AR) [10, 14] performs marginalisation directly on the graph by removing leaf nodes. Arc-reversals are used to turn children of nodes-to-be-removed into parents. Upon arc-reversal, the nodes between which the arc is reversed inherit each other's parents, thereby preventing the loss of possible dependencies.

3 Safe Marginalisation

Kwisthout [7] proposed the idea of *inverse marginalisation* for adding nodes to a Bayesian network in such a way that removing them again would result in the original network. Algorithms like VE and AR show that marginalisation directly on the factorisation or the graph can suffer from local loss of information. This is not surprising since DAGs, and therefore the associated factorisation, are not closed under marginalisation [13]. To be able to define an inverse marginalisation operator with the desired effect, we first introduce and analyse some new concepts related to the marginalisation operator.

3.1 Factorisation-Safe Marginalisation

Reconsider our joint distribution $\Pr(\mathbf{W})$, with $\mathbf{W} = \{W_1, \ldots, W_m\}$. Assume a linear order $\prec$ on $W_i \in \mathbf{W}$ such that $W_1 \prec \ldots \prec W_m$. The distribution $\Pr(\mathbf{W})$ can now be factorised according to $\prec$ by the *chain rule*:

$$\Pr(\mathbf{W}) = \prod_{i=1}^{m} \Pr(W_i \mid \mathbf{W}_{\prec i})$$

where $\mathbf{W}_{\prec i} = \{W_1, \ldots, W_{i-1}\}$ is the set of variables ordered lower than W_i. The conditioning set $\mathbf{W}_{\prec i}$ for each W_i can be further reduced by exploiting information about conditional independences.

We now introduce the concept of *factorisation-safe marginalisation.*

Definition 1. *Consider the chain rule factorisation of* $\Pr(\mathbf{W})$ *with respect to an order* $\prec$ *over* $\mathbf{W}$. *Marginalising out* $\mathbf{X} \subset \mathbf{W}$ *from* $\Pr(\mathbf{W})$ *is* factorisation-safe with respect to $\prec$, *if the chain rule factorisation of* $\Pr(\mathbf{W} \setminus \mathbf{X})$ *according to* $\prec$, *preserves the original factorisation over* $\mathbf{W} \setminus \mathbf{X}$.

Example 1. Let $\mathbf{W} = \{W_1, \ldots, W_5\}$ and let $\Pr(\mathbf{W})$ be factorised as follows:

$$\Pr(\mathbf{W}) = \Pr(W_5 \mid W_4, W_3) \cdot \Pr(W_4 \mid W_3) \cdot \Pr(W_3 \mid W_1, W_2) \cdot \Pr(W_2) \cdot \Pr(W_1)$$

Then marginalising out $\mathbf{X} = \{W_5, W_4\}$ from this factorisation gives

$$\sum_{\mathbf{X}} \Pr(\mathbf{W}) = \Pr(W_3, W_2, W_1) = \Pr(W_3 \mid W_1, W_2) \cdot \Pr(W_2) \cdot \Pr(W_1)$$

We conclude that this marginalisation is factorisation-safe. □

Factorisation-safe marginalisation preserves the factorisation over the remaining variables. We can always find an ordering for which marginalisation is factorisation-safe.

Proposition 1. *For any* $\mathbf{X} \subset \mathbf{W}$ *there exists an ordering* $\prec$ *on* $\mathbf{W}$ *such that marginalising* $\Pr(\mathbf{W})$ *over* $\mathbf{X}$ *is factorisation-safe with respect to* $\prec$.

Proof. The factorisation over variables that form the initial segment of the ordering always represents a marginal distribution over these variables [15]. Hence,

$$\Pr(\mathbf{W}) = \prod_{i=k+1}^{m} \Pr(W_i \mid \mathbf{W}_{\prec i}) \cdot \prod_{i=1}^{k} \Pr(W_i \mid \mathbf{W}_{\prec i}) \tag{2}$$

$$= \prod_{i=k+1}^{m} \Pr(W_i \mid \mathbf{W}_{\prec i}) \cdot \Pr(W_k, \ldots, W_1) \tag{3}$$

$$= \Pr(W_m, \ldots, W_{k+1} \mid W_k, \ldots, W_1) \cdot \Pr(W_k, \ldots, W_1) \tag{4}$$

As a result, we can marginalise out $m - k$ variables in a factorisation-safe way by choosing an ordering $\prec$ such that these variables are the top-ordered ones. □

The proposition above states that we can always do factorisation-safe marginalisation, provided that we can choose our own ordering. In Bayesian networks, a *topological ordering*[3] $\prec_G$ on the nodes in the graph G underlies the unique factorisation of its distribution in Eq. (1) [11]. As such, there is no guarantee that marginalising out variables from this distribution can be done in a factorisation-safe way. Nonetheless, we can identify cases in which marginalisation on $\Pr_G$ is factorisation-safe.

The following proposition states that marginalisation of barren[4] nodes, i.e. leaf nodes or nodes that have only barren descendants, is factorisation-safe.

Proposition 2. *Consider a Bayesian network $\mathcal{B} = (G_\mathcal{B}, \Pr_G(\mathbf{W}))$. Let $\mathbf{X} \subset \mathbf{W}$ be such that $\sigma_G(\mathbf{X}) \subset \mathbf{X}$. Then for any topological ordering $\prec_G$ for G, marginalisation over $\mathbf{X}$ is factorisation-safe with respect to $\prec_G$.*

Proof. Consider the network factorisation over $\mathbf{W} = \mathbf{V} \cup \mathbf{X}, \mathbf{V} \cap \mathbf{X} = \emptyset$:

$$\Pr_G(\mathbf{W}) = \prod_{i=1}^{|\mathbf{X}|} \Pr_G(X_i \mid \pi_G(X_i)) \cdot \prod_{i=1}^{|\mathbf{V}|} \Pr_G(V_i \mid \pi_G(V_i))$$

Since each X_i either has no children, or only children in $\mathbf{X}$, none of the $V_i \in \mathbf{V}$ can be conditioned on an X_i. The X_i are therefore the top-ordered nodes in any $\prec_G$ and the nodes in $\mathbf{V}$ form the initial segment of the ordering. Following the proof of Proposition 1, we can safely marginalise out $\mathbf{X}$. □

Example 2. Consider the ENDORISK network in Fig. 1. Marginalisation over $\mathbf{X} = \{$1-year DSS, 3-year DSS, 5-year DSS$\}$ is factorisation safe, since $\sigma(\mathbf{X}) = \{$1-year DSS, 3-year DSS$\} \subset \mathbf{X}$. □

3.2 Graph-Safe Marginalisation

Factorisation-safe marginalisation preserves the factorisation over the remaining variables. We similarly define graph-safe marginalisation, which preserves the graph structure.

Definition 2. *Consider a Bayesian network $\mathcal{B} = (G_\mathcal{B}, \Pr_G(\mathbf{V}))$. Marginalising out $\mathbf{X} \subset \mathbf{V}$ from $\Pr_G(\mathbf{V})$ is* graph-safe *if there exists a factorisation of* $\Pr(\mathbf{V} \setminus \mathbf{X})$ *that is consistent with the subgraph of $G_\mathcal{B}$ induced by $\mathbf{V} \setminus \mathbf{X}$.*[5]

Factorisation-safe marginalisation is a sufficient condition for graph-safe marginalisation, since the graph is consistent with the factorisation.

[3] A DAG G allows for a topological ordering $\prec_G$ of its nodes such that for every arc $V_i \to V_j$ we have that $V_i \prec_G V_j$. Although these constraints often allow for multiple orderings, we will use $\prec_G$ to refer to any such ordering.

[4] Barren nodes are actually defined to be barren relative to a target node T and evidence $\mathbf{E}$ in the context of inference; barren nodes cannot include T and $\mathbf{E}$. Our current context does not consider any target or evidence nodes.

[5] $G' = (\mathbf{V}', \mathbf{A}')$ is the *subgraph* of $G = (\mathbf{V}, \mathbf{A})$ *induced by* $\mathbf{V}' \subset \mathbf{V}$, if $\mathbf{A}' = (\mathbf{V}' \times \mathbf{V}') \cap \mathbf{A}$.

Proposition 3. *Consider a Bayesian network* $\mathcal{B} = (G_{\mathcal{B}}, \Pr_G(\mathbf{W}))$. *Let* $\prec_G$ *be a topological order over the nodes in* $G_{\mathcal{B}}$. *Then marginalising out* $\mathbf{X} \subset \mathbf{W}$ *is graph-safe if it is factorisation-safe with respect to* $\prec_G$.

Corollary 1. *Marginalising out* $\mathbf{X} \subset \mathbf{W}$ *such that* $\sigma_G(\mathbf{X}) \subset \mathbf{X}$ *is graph-safe.*

Note that, by Proposition 1, we can always construct a graph G^* that corresponds to a topological order $\prec_G^*$ that would allow for factorisation-safe and, hence, graph-safe marginalisation. Even though the joint distributions $\Pr_G(\mathbf{W})$ and $\Pr_{G^*}(\mathbf{W})$ may be the same, because of the different graphs we would consider these two different Bayesian networks over $\mathbf{W}$.

We will now consider further conditions under which marginalisation is graph-safe. It is obvious that a root node with only one child can be marginalised out and then simply removed from the graph [5]. We can generalise this property to a root "cluster" that has at most one outgoing arc to the rest of the graph.

Proposition 4. *Consider a Bayesian network* $\mathcal{B} = (G_{\mathcal{B}}, \Pr_G(\mathbf{W}))$. *Let* $\mathbf{X} \subset \mathbf{W}$ *be such that* $\pi_G(\mathbf{X}) \subset \mathbf{X}$ *and let* $\sigma_G(X_j) \subseteq \mathbf{V}$, $\mathbf{V} = \mathbf{W} \setminus \mathbf{X}$, *for at most one* $X_j \in \mathbf{X}$. *If* $|\sigma_G(X_j)| = 1$, *then marginalisation over* $\mathbf{X}$ *is graph-safe.*

Proof. With only a single connection between nodes in $\mathbf{X}$ and nodes in $\mathbf{V}$, there exists a topological order $\prec_G$ over the nodes in $G_{\mathcal{B}}$ such that all nodes in $\mathbf{X}$ form an initial segment in $\prec_G$. Hence [15],

$$\prod_{i=1}^{|\mathbf{X}|} \Pr_G(X_i \mid \pi_G(X_i)) = \Pr_G(\mathbf{X}) = \Pr_G(X_j \mid \mathbf{X} \setminus \{X_j\}) \cdot \Pr_G(\mathbf{X} \setminus \{X_j\})$$

Let $\sigma_G(X_j) = \{V_j\}$. Since $\mathbf{V}$ is independent of $\mathbf{X} \setminus \{X_j\}$ given $\{X_j\}$, and $\pi_G(V_i) \setminus \{X_j\}$ is independent of X_j, after marginalising $\Pr_G(\mathbf{W})$ over $\mathbf{X} \setminus \{X_j\}$, we are left with

$$\begin{aligned} &\prod_{i \neq j} \Pr_G(V_i \mid \pi_G(V_i)) \cdot \sum_{X_j} \Pr_G(V_j \mid X_j, \pi_G(V_j) \setminus \{X_j\}) \cdot \Pr_G(X_j) \\ &= \prod_{i \neq j} \Pr_G(V_i \mid \pi_G(V_i)) \cdot \Pr_G(V_j \mid \pi_G(V_j) \setminus \{X_j\}) \end{aligned}$$

The latter is a factorisation over the subgraph of G induced by $\mathbf{V}$. □

We now consider marginalisation of a single node X that is neither a leaf, nor a root with a single child.

Proposition 5. *Consider a Bayesian network* $\mathcal{B} = (G_{\mathcal{B}}, \Pr_G(\mathbf{W}))$. *Let* $X \in \mathbf{W}$ *be such that*

(1) there exists a topological order $\prec_G$ *for* G *in which* X *and* $\sigma_G(X)$ *are ordered consecutively, and*
(2) for each $C_i \in \sigma_G(X)$, $(\pi_G(X) \cup \mathbf{C}_{\prec_G i} \cup \pi_G(\mathbf{C}_{\prec_G i})) \subset \pi_G(C_i)$, *where* $\mathbf{C}_{\prec_G i} \subset \sigma_G(X)$ *is the set of child nodes that precede* C_i *in* $\prec_G$.

Then marginalisation over X *is graph-safe.*

Proof. Let $\mathbf{V} = \mathbf{W} \setminus \{X\}$. The joint distribution $\Pr_G$ then factorises over $G_\mathcal{B}$ as follows:

$$\Pr_G(\mathbf{V}, X) = \tag{5}$$
$$\Pr_G(X \mid \pi_G(X)) \cdot \prod_{V_i \in \sigma_G(X)} \Pr_G(V_i \mid \pi_{G'}(V_i), X) \cdot \prod_{V_i \in \mathbf{V} \setminus \sigma_G(X)} \Pr_G(V_i \mid \pi_G(V_i))$$

where $\pi_{G'}(V_i) = \pi_G(V_i) \setminus \{X\}$.

From condition (1) we have that

$$\Pr_G(X \mid \pi_G(X)) \cdot \prod_{V_i \in \sigma_G(X)} \Pr_G(V_i \mid \pi_{G'}(V_i), X)$$
$$= \Pr(X, \sigma_G(X) \mid \pi_G(X), \rho_G(X))$$

where the latter CPT agrees with $\Pr_G$ [1]. Then, after marginalising out X, the above results in

$$\Pr_G(\mathbf{V}) = \Pr_G(\sigma_G(X) \mid \pi_G(X), \rho_G(X)) \cdot \prod_{V_i \in \mathbf{V} \setminus \sigma_G(X)} \Pr_G(V_i \mid \pi_G(V_i))$$

Now consider factorising the CPT over $\sigma_G(X)$ according to the ordering $\prec_G$:

$$\Pr_G(\sigma_G(X) \mid \pi_G(X), \rho_G(X)) = \prod_{C_i \in \sigma_G} \Pr_G(C_i \mid \mathbf{C}_{\prec_G i}, \pi_G(X), \rho_G(X))$$

where $\mathbf{C}_{\prec_G i}$ is the set of child nodes preceding C_i in the ordering. Using condition (2), with $\pi_{G'}(C_i) = \pi_G(C_i) \setminus \{X\}$ for all $C_i \in \sigma_G(X)$, we now obtain a factorisation of $\Pr_G(\mathbf{V})$ over the subgraph G' of G induced by $\mathbf{V}$. □

We note from the above proof that to ensure graph-safe marginalisation, we in fact need to establish that for each $C_i \in \sigma_G(X)$, C_i is *independent* of $\mathbf{C}_{\prec_G i} \cup \pi_G(X) \cup \rho_G(X)$ given $\pi_G(C_i) \setminus \{X\}$ in $\Pr_G$. Condition (2) of the proposition guarantees that each C_i is *d-separated* from $\mathbf{C}_{\prec_G i} \cup \pi_G(X) \cup \rho_G(X)$ given $\pi_G(C_i) \setminus \{X\}$. This is a slightly weaker assumption (unless we can assume faithfulness), but can be easily verified from the graph alone.

Example 3. Consider the two Bayesian network graphs in Fig. 2. In both graphs we have the following topological ordering: $V_1 \prec_G V_2 \prec_G X \prec_G V_3 \prec_G V_4$. Therefore, condition (1) holds in both graphs. In Fig. 2(a), for child nodes V_3 and V_4 of X, condition (2) trivially holds. Marginalisation over X is therefore graph-safe:

$$\sum_X \Pr_G(V_1) \cdot \Pr_G(V_2) \cdot \Pr_G(X) \cdot \Pr_G(V_4 \mid V_1, V_2, V_3, X) \cdot \Pr_G(V_3 \mid X)$$
$$= \Pr_G(V_1) \cdot \Pr_G(V_2) \cdot \sum_X \Pr_G(X, V_3, V_4 \mid V_1, V_2)$$
$$= \Pr_G(V_1) \cdot \Pr_G(V_2) \cdot \Pr_G(V_3) \cdot \Pr_G(V_4 \mid V_3, V_1, V_2)$$
$$= \Pr_G(V_1, V_2, V_3, V_4)$$

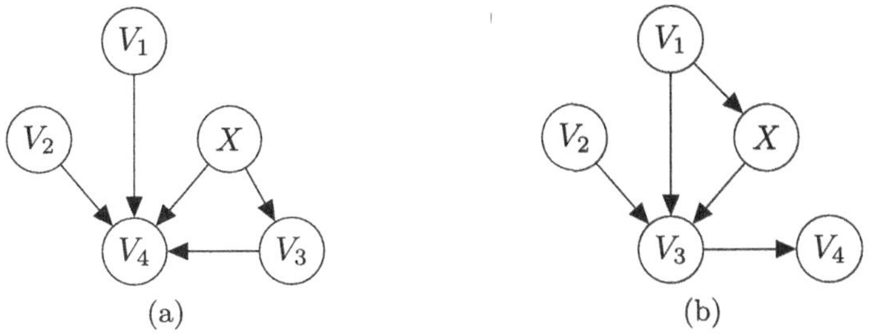

Fig. 2. Two example Bayesian network graphs.

Likewise in Fig. 2(b), condition (2) of the proposition clearly holds. Marginalisation over X is therefore also graph-safe:

$$\begin{aligned}
&\sum_{X} \Pr_G(V_1) \cdot \Pr_G(V_2) \cdot \Pr_G(X \mid V_1) \cdot \Pr_G(V_3 \mid V_1, V_2, X) \cdot \Pr_G(V_4 \mid V_3) \\
&= \Pr_G(V_1) \cdot \Pr_G(V_2) \cdot \Pr_G(V_4 \mid V_3) \cdot \sum_{X} \Pr_G(X, V_3 \mid V_1, V_2) \\
&= \Pr_G(V_1) \cdot \Pr_G(V_2) \cdot \Pr_G(V_3 \mid V_1, V_2) \cdot \Pr_G(V_4 \mid V_3) \\
&= \Pr_G(V_1, V_2, V_3, V_4)
\end{aligned}$$

□

4 Inverse Marginalisation

The idea behind inverse marginalisation is to extend a Bayesian network with variables $\mathbf{X}$ without changing the graph and distribution over the original set of variables. In this section we propose a formalisation of the inverse marginalisation operation and study its properties in the context of Bayesian network extensions.

We first define the inverse marginalisation operator $\sum_{\mathbf{X}}^{-1}$ to extend a distribution with variables $\mathbf{X}$ such that subsequent marginalisation of $\mathbf{X}$ returns the original distribution.

Definition 3. *Consider a joint distribution* $\Pr(\mathbf{V})$ *over variables* $\mathbf{V} \subset \mathbf{W}$ *and a set* $\mathbf{X} \subset \mathbf{W}$, $\mathbf{X} \cap \mathbf{V} = \emptyset$. Inverse marginalisation $\sum_{\mathbf{X}}^{-1}$ *on* $\Pr(\mathbf{V})$ *is defined as*

$$\sum_{\mathbf{X}}^{-1} \Pr(\mathbf{V}) = \Pr(\mathbf{V}, \mathbf{X}) \text{ such that } \sum_{\mathbf{X}} \Pr(\mathbf{V}, \mathbf{X}) = \Pr(\mathbf{V})$$

Given the motivation for this work, we are mainly interested in inverse marginalisation where subsequent marginalisation returns not only the original distribution, but the original Bayesian network, including the original graph.

In the remainder of this section, we assume an original Bayesian network $\mathcal{B} = (G, \Pr_G)$ with graph $G = (\mathbf{V}, \mathbf{A})$. We extend this network by inverse marginalisation with variable(s) $\mathbf{X}$, resulting in the Bayesian network $\mathcal{B}' = (G', \Pr_{G'})$

with graph $G' = (\mathbf{W}, \mathbf{A}')$, $\mathbf{W} = \mathbf{V} \cup \mathbf{X}$. We further assume that G is the subgraph of G', induced by $\mathbf{V}$, and that all NPTs except for those of the children $\sigma(\mathbf{X}) = \bigcup_i \sigma(X_i), X_i \in \mathbf{X}$, of the newly added nodes $\mathbf{X}$ remain the same.

Definition 4. *Let* $\Pr_G(\mathbf{V})$, $\mathbf{X}$ *and* $\Pr_{G'}(\mathbf{W})$ *be as defined above.* Inverse marginalisation $\sum_{\mathbf{X}}^{-1}$ *on* $\Pr_G$ *is said to be* safe *if marginalising out* $\mathbf{X}$ *from* $\Pr_{G'}(\mathbf{W})$ *is graph-safe.*

To create a full Bayesian network upon inverse marginalisation, we need to specify NPTs for all added nodes, as well as for all original nodes that obtained additional parents. Below we provide the constraints to which these NPTs have to adhere in order to be able to obtain the original Bayesian network upon marginalisation, if any.

Proposition 6. *Consider a Bayesian network* $\mathcal{B} = (G_\mathcal{B}, \Pr_G(\mathbf{V}))$. *Inverse marginalisation on* $\Pr_G$ *with* $\mathbf{X}$ *such that* $\sigma_{G'}(\mathbf{X}) \subset \mathbf{X}$, *is safe regardless of the choice of* NPTs *for* $X_i \in \mathbf{X}$.

Proof. This follows directly from the proof of Proposition 2. □

With root-clusters we require a constraint for the 'bridge' to the rest of the graph.

Proposition 7. *Consider a Bayesian network* $\mathcal{B} = (G_\mathcal{B}, \Pr_G(\mathbf{V}))$. *Inverse marginalisation on* $\Pr_G$ *with* $\mathbf{X}$ *such that* $\pi_{G'}(\mathbf{X}) \subset \mathbf{X}$ *and for at most one* $X_j \in \mathbf{X}$ $\sigma_{G'}(X_j) \subseteq \mathbf{V}$, *is safe if* $\sigma_{G'}(X_j) = \{V_j\}$ *and the* NPT *of* V_j *is updated such that* $\Pr_G(V_j \mid \pi_G(V_j)) = \sum_{X_j} \Pr_{G'}(V_j \mid \pi_{G'}(V_j)) \cdot \Pr_{G'}(X_j)$.

Proof. This follows directly from the proof of Proposition 4. □

For inverse marginalisation of a node X in general, we have the following sufficient condition.

Proposition 8. *Consider a Bayesian network* $\mathcal{B} = (G_\mathcal{B}, \Pr_G(\mathbf{V}))$. *Inverse marginalisation on* $\Pr_G$ *with* $\mathbf{X}$ *such that*

(1) there exists a topological order $\prec_{G'}$ *for* G' *in which* X *and* $\sigma_{G'}(X)$ *are ordered consecutively, and*
(2) for each $C_i \in \sigma_{G'}(X)$, $(\pi_{G'}(X) \cup \mathbf{C}_{\prec_{G'} i} \cup \pi_{G'}(\mathbf{C}_{\prec_{G'} i})) \subset \pi_{G'}(C_i)$

is safe if the NPT *of* X *is constructed such that* $\Pr_{G'}(X) = \sum_{\pi_{G'}(X)} \Pr_{G'}(X \mid \pi_{G'}(X)) \cdot \Pr_G(\pi_{G'}(X))$ *and the* NPT *of each* C_i *is updated such that* $\Pr_G(C_i \mid \pi_G(C_i)) = \sum_X \Pr_{G'}(C_i \mid \pi_{G'}(C_i)) \cdot \Pr_{G'}(X \mid \pi_G(C_i))$.

Proof. This follows from the proof of Proposition 5. □

Example 4. Reconsider the two Bayesian network graphs G' in Fig. 2, which are the result of inverse marginalisation in which node X is added to graph G. Suppose that X is binary-valued and that domain knowledge gives us the assessments $\Pr(X = 1) = 0.8$ and $\Pr(X = 0) = 0.2$. In Fig. 2(a), the NPTs for nodes V_3 and V_4 are updated (e.g., using constraint optimisation methods) such that $\Pr_G(V_3) = \Pr_{G'}(V_3 \mid X = 1) \cdot 0.8 + \Pr_{G'}(V_3 \mid X = 0) \cdot 0.2$ and $\Pr_G(V_4 \mid V_1, V_2, V_3) = \Pr_{G'}(V_4 \mid V_1, V_2, V_3, X = 1) \cdot 0.8 \cdot \Pr_{G'}(V_3 \mid X = 1)/\Pr_G(V_3) + \Pr_{G'}(V_4 \mid V_1, V_2, V_3, X = 0) \cdot 0.2 \cdot \Pr_{G'}(V_3 \mid X = 0)/\Pr_G(V_3)$.

Likewise in Fig. 2(b), the NPTs for nodes X and V_3 are updated such that $0.8 = \sum_{V_1} \Pr_{G'}(X = 1 \mid V_1) \cdot \Pr_G(V_1)$, $0.2 = \sum_{V_1} \Pr_{G'}(X = 0 \mid V_1) \cdot \Pr_G(V_1)$, and $\Pr_G(V_3 \mid V_1, V_2) = \Pr_{G'}(V_3 \mid V_1, V_2, X = 1) \cdot \Pr_{G'}(X = 1 \mid V_1) + \Pr_{G'}(V_3 \mid V_1, V_2, X = 0) \cdot \Pr_{G'}(X = 0 \mid V_1)$. □

We now illustrate the use of the graphical conditions from Proposition 8 to investigate potentially (un)safe additions to the ENDORISK network.

Example 5. Tumour size is reported to impact the risk of recurrence in endometrial cancer [16], to impact the risk of myometrial invasion [18], as well as to have an effect on the predictive power of the preoperative biopsy relative to the postoperative tumour grade [9]. In case the inclusion of tumour size would be considered relevant for decision support in the ENDORISK model, it is important to consider which of the above relations to include in the model, as some extensions are graph-safe while others are not. In particular, including arcs from tumour size to myometrial invasion and to postoperative grade, and given appropriate choices for the adjusted NPTs, is graph-safe: The relevant network fragment mimics Fig. 2(a), with X being tumour size, V_1 atypical cytology, V_2 preoperative tumour grade, V_3 myometrial invasion, and V_4 postoperative tumour grade (see Fig. 1). However, adding an arc from tumour size to recurrence is potentially unsafe, as the second condition in Proposition 8 is violated in this case.

5 Algorithm for Checking Safeness

Using Propositions 6, 7, and 8 we can establish when inverse marginalisation is guaranteed to be safe, and likewise, warn when it is (*potentially*) unsafe. To systematically assess safe inverse marginalisation, we propose an algorithm (Algorithm 1) for *iterative expansion* that can be integrated with network development tools. The algorithm takes as input a 'baseline' Bayesian network $\mathcal{B} = (G_{\mathcal{B}}, \Pr_G(\mathbf{V}))$, which is iteratively expanded by adding an unconnected variable or adding an arc (and adjusting NPTs). Prior to a user confirming a change, the algorithm checks whether the thus created network $\mathcal{B}' = (G'_{\mathcal{B}'}, \Pr_{G'}(\mathbf{W}))$ is graph-safe relative to $\mathcal{B}$, and issues a warning if safe extension cannot be guaranteed by the algorithm.

For procedural purposes, condition 1 of Proposition 8 is operationalised by the absence of nodes that are both a proper descendant and a proper ancestor of the set of X and its children, formalized as $(\pi^+_{G'}(\mathbf{\Delta}_{G'}(X)) \cap \sigma^+_{G'}(\mathbf{\Delta}_{G'}(X))) \setminus \mathbf{\Delta}_{G'}(X) = \emptyset$ [2]. Finding the ancestors and descendants of a node in a directed acyclic graph can be done in linear time using depth-first search assuming an adjacency list is used to represent the graph; checking the second condition of Proposition 8 can be done locally within the Markov Blanket of the node. The check in line 13 is performed as per the definitions in Propositions 6, 7, and 8.

Algorithm 1. Iterative network expansion algorithm

1: **procedure** ITERATIVEEXPANSION($\mathcal{B} = (G_{\mathcal{B}}, \Pr_G(\mathbf{V}))$)
2:     $\mathbf{X} \leftarrow \emptyset$ ▷ Set of variables added to $\mathbf{V}$
3:     **repeat**
4:         safe ← unknown
5:         **if** variable X added **then**
6:             $\mathbf{X} \leftarrow \mathbf{X} \cup X$
7:             safe ← true ▷ Unconnected variable
8:         **end if**
9:         **if** edge (U, V) added and NPT updated **then**
10:             **if** $U \in \mathbf{X}$ & $V \in \mathbf{X}$ **then**
11:                 safe ← true ▷ Not connected with original graph
12:             **else**
13:                 **if** $\sum_{\mathbf{X}} \Pr(\mathbf{V}, \mathbf{X}) \neq \Pr(\mathbf{V})$ **then**
14:                     safe ← false ▷ Def. 3
15:                 **else if** $V \in \mathbf{X}, \sigma(V) \subset \mathbf{X}$ **then**
16:                     safe ← true ▷ Prop. 6
17:                 **else if** $U \in \mathbf{X}, \sigma(\mathbf{X}) \setminus V = \emptyset$ **then**
18:                     safe ← true ▷ Prop. 7
19:                 **else if** $(\pi^+_{G'}(\mathbf{\Delta}_{G'}(X)) \cap \sigma^+_{G'}(\mathbf{\Delta}_{G'}(X))) \setminus \mathbf{\Delta}_{G'}(X) = \emptyset$ &
$\forall_{C_i \in \sigma_{G'}(X)} : (\pi_{G'}(X) \cup \mathbf{C}_{\prec_{G'} i} \cup \pi_{G'}(\mathbf{C}_{\prec_{G'} i})) \subset \pi_{G'}(C_i)$ **then**
20:                     safe ← true ▷ Prop. 8
21:                 **end if**
22:             **end if**
23:         **end if**
24:         **if** safe = true **then**
25:             print "Adding edge (U, V) is safe"
26:         **else**
27:             print "Warning: adding edge (U, V) is potentially unsafe"
28:         **end if**
29:     **until** User terminates extending $\mathcal{B}$
30: **end procedure**

---

6 Conclusions and Future Research

In this paper we propose a systematic way of establishing whether adding a variable (including connecting edges) to an existing network effectively changes the distribution underlying the existing network. A change to the underlying distribution potentially invalidates a certification of the network, which would require a re-assessment of the complete network, rather than only assessing the additions.

We introduced the notion of safe inverse marginalisation and provided conditions under which adding a variable is safe. Although we have not proven, and do not claim, that the set of 'safe cases' we present is exhaustive, we did not yet succeed in finding more of such cases. This requires further research, for now leaving open 'potentially unsafe additions' that may need be checked by hand. This is reflected in the pseudocode of the algorithm we propose for checking safeness. An implementation of this algorithm, coupled with a straightforward GUI, is currently under development.

We defined inverse marginalisation to be safe if it adheres to our notion of graph-safeness. There can be situations, however, in which it is reasonable to do inverse marginalisation while some existing arcs are removed upon introducing additional variables, In future, we would like to establish an additional notion of safeness that captures such cases.

Acknowledgments. This publication is part of the Personalised Care in Oncology programme with file number P21-03 of the research programme NWO Perspectief which is (partly) financed by the Dutch Research Council (NWO). This research was also supported by the Hybrid Intelligence Centre, a 10-year programme funded by the Dutch Ministry of Education, Culture and Science through NWO, https://hybrid-intelligence-centre.nl.

Disclosure of Interests. The authors have no competing interests to declare that are relevant to the content of this article.

References

1. Butz, C.J., Yan, W.: The semantics of intermediate CPTs in Variable Elimination. In: 5th European Workshop on Probabilistic Graphical Models, pp. 41–49 (2010)
2. Butz, C.J., Yan, W., Madsen, A.L.: On semantics of inference in Bayesian networks. In: van der Gaag, L.C. (ed.) ECSQARU 2013. LNCS (LNAI), vol. 7958, pp. 73–84. Springer, Heidelberg (2013). https://doi.org/10.1007/978-3-642-39091-3_7
3. Dechter, R.: Bucket elimination: a unifying framework for reasoning. In: 12th Conference on Uncertainty in Artificial Intelligence, pp. 211–219 (1996)
4. Grube, M., et al.: Improved preoperative risk stratification in endometrial carcinoma patients: external validation of the ENDORISK Bayesian network model in a large population-based case series. J. Cancer Res. Clin. Oncol. **149**(7), 3361–3369 (2023)
5. Kjærulff, U.B, Madsen, A.L: Bayesian Networks and Influence Diagrams: A Guide to Construction and Analysis. Springer, Cham (2008)
6. Koller, D., Friedman, N.: Probabilistic Graphical Models: Principles and Techniques. MIT Press, Cambridge (2009)
7. Kwisthout, J.: Expanding Bayesian networks. Presentation at the 34th Benelux Conference on AI (BNAIC), Lamot Mechelen, Belgium (2022)
8. Kyrimi, E., McLachlan, S., Dube, K., Neves, M.R., Fahmi, A., Fenton, N.: A comprehensive scoping review of Bayesian networks in healthcare: past, present and future. Artif. Intell. Med. **117**, 102108 (2021)

9. Lago, V., Martin, B., Ballesteros, E., Cárdenas-Rebollo, J.M., Minig, L.: Tumor grade correlation between preoperative biopsy and final surgical specimen in endometrial cancer: the use of different diagnostic methods and analysis of associated factors. Int. J. Gynecol. Cancer **28**(7), 1258–1263 (2018)
10. Olmsted, S.: On representing and solving decision problems. Ph.D. dissertation, Stanford University (1983)
11. Pearl, J.: Probabilistic Reasoning in Intelligent Systems: Networks of Plausible Inference. Morgan Kaufmann, Palo Alto (1988)
12. Reijnen, C., et al.: Preoperative risk stratification in endometrial cancer (ENDORISK) by a Bayesian network model: a development and validation study. PLoS Med. **17**(5), e1003111 (2020)
13. Richardson, T., Spirtes, P.: Ancestral graph Markov models. Ann. Stat. **30**(4), 962–1030 (2002)
14. Shachter, R.D.: Evaluating influence diagrams. Oper. Res. **34**(6), 871–882 (1986)
15. Shafer, G.: Probabilistic Expert Systems. Society for Industrial and Applied Mathematics, Philadelphia (1996)
16. Sozzi, G., et al.: Tumor size, an additional risk factor of local recurrence in low-risk endometrial cancer: a large multicentric retrospective study. Int. J. Gynecol. Cancer **28**(4), 684–691 (2018)
17. Vinklerová, P., et al.: External validation study of endometrial cancer preoperative risk stratification model (ENDORISK). Front. Oncol. **12**, 939226 (2022)
18. Ytre-Hauge, S., et al.: Preoperative tumor size at MRI predicts deep myometrial invasion, lymph node metastases, and patient outcome in endometrial carcinomas. Int. J. Gynecol. Cancer **25**(3), 459–466 (2015)
19. Zhang, N.L., Poole, D.: A simple approach to Bayesian network computations. In: 10th Canadian Artificial Intelligence Conference, pp. 171–178 (1994)

Classifying Control Room Operators' Performance Using Bayesian Networks

Houda Briwa[1(✉)], Anders L. Madsen[2,3], and Maria Chiara Leva[1]

[1] Technological University Dublin, Dublin, Ireland
d21127031@mytudublin.ie, mariachiara.leva@tudublin.ie
[2] HUGIN EXPERT A/S, Aalborg, Denmark
anders@hugin.com
[3] Aalborg University, Aalborg, Denmark

Abstract. One of the key uses of Bayesian networks in Human Reliability Assessment is to capture the probabilistic dependencies among the factors that influence human performance. Their ability to integrate uncertainty and contextual features makes them particularly suitable for safety-critical applications. In this study, we employ a data-driven Bayesian network approach to classify operator success in alarm management tasks using data from a formaldehyde plant simulator in which task complexity, alarm display configuration, and support level were experimentally controlled. Three classifiers, Naive Bayes, Tree Augmented Naive Bayes, and Pearl-Rebane augmented Naive Bayes, were evaluated under both constrained and unconstrained feature-selection approaches (mutual information filter versus greedy forward wrapper), incorporating both controlled variables and participant characteristics. Across 100 Monte Carlo cross-validation trials, the Pearl–Rebane model restricted to the three task-related features achieves a higher average AUC than both the Tree Augmented Naive Bayes model and the Naive Bayes model.

Keywords: Bayesian networks · Bayesian Classifiers · Human performance classification · Alarm management · Safety-critical systems

1 Introduction

Human Reliability Assessment (HRA) methods, originally developed within probabilistic safety assessment frameworks [1], estimate the likelihood of human error by modeling performance shaping factors (PSFs), which encompass personal, environmental, and organizational conditions [4]. Widely applied in nuclear energy, chemical processing, and aviation, where human error contributes to over half of reported incidents [2,3], HRA nonetheless struggles to represent interdependencies among PSFs explicitly [5]. Alarm management in control rooms highlights this challenge: operators must prioritize and respond to multiple alarms under time pressure and without direct process visibility [6], yet common survey-based evaluations lack the resolution for probabilistic modeling [7,8]. Moreover, empirical data in the process industry are often retrospective or adapted from the nuclear

K. Sauerwald and M. Thimm (Eds.): ECSQARU 2025, LNAI 16099, pp. 17–30, 2026.
https://doi.org/10.1007/978-3-032-05134-9_2

sector [5,9], limiting the ability of current approaches to capture the interactions among PSFs and thereby constraining model fidelity [10].

These challenges motivate the use of Bayesian networks (BNs), which offer a structured approach to modeling dependencies between a set of features such as, for instance, PSFs, allowing the representation of conditional relationships among human, technical, and organisational features. Their capacity to handle uncertainty and integrate expert input, simulation data, and observations makes them particularly valuable for human reliability modeling in data-limited contexts [11,12]. To support such data-driven modeling approaches, simplified simulators or microworlds have been proposed as a practical way to generate structured HRA data under controlled conditions. These tools allow for data collection with non-expert participants, such as students, making experimental studies more scalable [13]. While the generalisability of such data remains under investigation, this approach offers a practical response to ongoing data scarcity [14]. Although BNs are increasingly applied in HRA to estimate error probabilities and reveal PSF interactions [2], many studies provide limited detail on model validation procedures, and few address whether the learned structures generalize beyond the training data [15]. Moreover, the influence of BN structure on predictive performance remains underexplored in complex operational settings such as alarm management tasks, where dependencies between features are critical. In parallel, effective classification relies on selecting features that are both relevant and non-redundant [16], yet standard methods ignore domain expertise. Embedding constraints, drawn from physical laws or operational hypotheses, into feature selection can guide model induction, but the overall effect of such constraints on predictive performance has not been systematically evaluated [17].

In this study, we employ a data-driven BN approach to classify operator success in alarm management tasks using data from a formaldehyde plant simulator in which task complexity, alarm display configuration, and support level were experimentally controlled, and thereby quantify how these factors, participant characteristics and their interactions drive operator performance.

2 Theoretical Background

In this section, the theoretical background necessary to follow the rest of the paper is presented.

2.1 Bayesian Networks: Foundations

A Bayesian network $\mathcal{N} = (G, \mathcal{P})$ is a compact representation of a joint probability distribution $P(\mathcal{X})$ over random variables $\mathcal{X}$ where G is a directed acyclic graph (DAG) such that each vertex corresponds one-to-one with a variable $X \in \mathcal{X}$ and $\mathcal{P}$ is a set of conditional probability distributions. The set $\mathcal{P}$ is a factorized decomposition of the joint probability distribution $P(\mathcal{X})$ such that:

$$P(\mathcal{X}) = \prod_{P \in \mathcal{P}} P(X \mid \pi(X)), \qquad (1)$$

where $\pi(X)$ denotes the set of parents of X in G.

Inference in a BN is the task of computing the posterior probability distribution $P(X \mid \epsilon)$ where ϵ is the set of evidence for each $X \in \mathcal{X}$. We are only interested in the posterior distribution $P(AM \mid \epsilon)$ where AM represents whether the control operator is effective in alarm management and ϵ are PSFs.

2.2 Learning Bayesian Networks from Data

Inducing a BN from data involves two stages: structure learning, which identifies the DAG G connecting variables, and parameter estimation, which estimates the conditional probability tables associated with that DAG G [18]. Structure learning follows one of two paradigms. Constraint-based methods use statistical tests for conditional independence to assemble a graph satisfying those relations. Score-and-search methods assign each candidate DAG a goodness-of-fit score, such as BIC or a Bayesian Dirichlet metric, and traverse the space of structures via heuristics like greedy hill-climbing or tabu search [18,19].

In practical applications, classifiers differ in the assumptions they make about feature dependencies. Naive Bayes (NB) assumes conditional independence among features. Augmented Naive Bayes classifiers relax this assumption by introducing dependencies within constrained DAGs [35]). Tree-Augmented Naive Bayes (TAN) allows each attribute one additional parent [26,34], while Pearl-Rebane models allow polytree structures with multiple parents per attribute [27]. Although variants like Forest-Augmented Naive Bayes (FAN) exist [36], this study focuses on NB, TAN, and Pearl–Rebane for their balance of interpretability, efficiency, and capacity to capture complex dependencies.

The EM algorithm is applied for the parameter estimation [28]. The EM algorithm iteratively performs the Expectation (E-step) and Maximization (M-step) steps to update parameter estimates [20], making it useful for handling missing data and dealing with mixture models involving latent variables [18].

3 Case Study: Operator Control Room Simulation

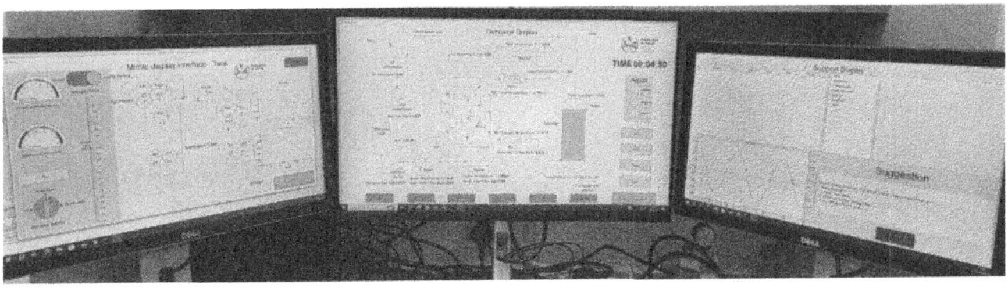

Fig. 1. Experiment setup

To support the development of data-driven human reliability models, an adapted version of the Formaldehyde Gas Production Simulator [21] was used to generate HRA data for our case study. Developed at Politecnico di Torino[1] as part of the LIVELAB3 initiative within the CISC consortium[2], the simulator replicates a control room environment for managing process disturbances in a formaldehyde production plant [22] The experiment included three scenarios, each simulating a distinct process failure: emergency shutdown, tank implosion, and reactor overheating, triggered in the absence of timely operator intervention following a critical alarm. Scenario conditions were varied along three controlled dimensions:

1. **Task complexity**, defined by the number of critical alarms requiring operator response. Scenarios 1 and 2 each involved a single critical alarm, while Scenario 3 introduced an alarm flood with more than ten alarms triggered within a 10-minute window, in line with EEMUA 191 guidance;
2. **Alarm display configuration**, which varied according to whether alarms were prioritised and colour-coded to differentiate critical alarms from nuisance alarms;
3. **Support system available**, determined by the format of the procedural guidance provided: either paper-based, screen-based, or screen-based with AI assistance.

All participants completed a standardised training session prior to the experiment to familiarise themselves with the simulator and task environment. Performance was recorded as a binary outcome (Effective/Failed), with success criteria encoded in the simulator logic. In Scenarios 1 and 2, success required resolution of a single low-pressure alarm and restoration of safe tank pressure. In Scenario 3, despite multiple concurrent alarms, participants were instructed to prioritize a high-temperature reactor alarm; success was defined by maintaining reactor temperature within safe limits during the final three minutes.

4 Methodology

In this section, we describe the methodology for training and evaluating three Bayesian-network classifiers on the experimental dataset. All models were implemented in Python using the HUGIN API[3]. The approach comprises three main stages, feature selection, network learning, and performance evaluation, each detailed in the subsections below.

4.1 Feature Selection (FS)

Both constrained and unconstrained approaches were employed. In the constrained approach, Task Complexity, Alarm Display, and Support Availability

[1] https://www.polito.it/.

[2] CISC is a Marie Curie Training Network funded by the European Commission under contract number 955901 www.ciscproject.eu.

[3] https://www.hugin.com.

were included a priori; in the unconstrained approach, no features were forced. Two approaches were considered:

Mutual Information Filter. was performed using scikit-learn's *mutual_info_classif*, which estimates the dependency between each feature and the AM (Alarm Management) outcome via k-nearest-neighbor entropy estimation [23]. Features were ranked in descending MI score and then added one at a time for the unconstrained feature selection and to the task-related features in the constrained selection; at each step, all three classifiers (NB, TAN, PR) were retrained on the expanded feature set and evaluated on the held-out data, providing an interpretable measure of each feature's individual contribution.

Greedy Forward Wrapper. Wrapper methods assess feature subsets by their joint effect on model accuracy rather than individual relevance [24,25]. In our implementation, we start from the initial feature set (constrained or empty), we iteratively add the feature whose inclusion maximizes cross-validated AUC. At each step, candidates are evaluated via three-fold CV on the training data, and the top performer is permanently included. The process stops when no remaining feature improves AUC.

Both mutual information (MI) ranking and the greedy forward wrapper were applied independently across 100 Monte Carlo iterations. While MI ranking provides a stable order of feature relevance, repeating the process allowed evaluation of classifier performance variability at each inclusion step. The wrapper method's repetition further quantified feature selection stability and joint predictive power. Results reported are aggregated averages over these iterations.

4.2 Learning BN Classifiers

Three Bayesian-network classifiers were trained under each feature-selection scenario:

- **Naive Bayes (NB):** A star-structured model in which the target node (AM) is the sole parent of each attribute node [26].
- **Tree-Augmented Naive Bayes (TAN):** Extends NB by first constructing a conditional Chow–Liu tree over the non-target features, using conditional mutual information given AM as edge weights, and then adding AM as an additional parent to every feature [26].
- **Pearl–Rebane (PR):** Generalizes the Chow–Liu approach to produce a polytree, allowing each feature to have multiple parents provided no directed cycles are introduced [27].

After fixing the structure of the BN, the conditional probability tables for all models were initialized with uniform priors and Laplace smoothing to prevent zero probability entries, and parameters were then estimated sequentially using the EM algorithm on the training data [28].

4.3 Model Validation and Statistical Testing

Cross Validation. Model performance was estimated via 100 repeats of Monte Carlo cross-validation (MCCV) with stratified 80%–20% train - test trials. For forward-wrapper selection only, each training partition was further subjected to nested 3-fold inner CV to guide feature inclusion. MCCV performs M random splits of the data into training and test sets, and averages the resulting performance metrics, yielding low-variance, approximately unbiased estimates despite overlapping test samples. In contrast, v-fold CV uses v disjoint folds, cycling each as test exactly once, where leave-one-out ($v = n$) minimizes bias at the cost of high variance [29].

Performance Metric. Model accuracy was quantified by the mean area under the ROC (Receiver-operating characteristic) curve (AUC) and its standard deviation across MCCV repeats. Following Hanley and McNeil (1982), AUC ranges from 0.5 (random performance) to 1.0 (perfect discrimination) [30].

Statistical Comparison. Paired AUC distributions were compared using the Wilcoxon signed-rank test, a nonparametric alternative to the paired t-test that assumes only symmetric differences and is robust to outliers. Zero differences were excluded; remaining nonzero differences were ranked (ties averaged), with a normal-approximation applied when more than 25 observations were available and exact permutation p-values otherwise [31].

5 Experimental Design and Results

5.1 Data From Control Room Simulation

The dataset analyzed in this study comprises 519 complete observations, collected from 176 participants who each performed the three predefined alarm-handling scenarios. Although the total expected sample size was 528, nine instances were removed during pre-processing due to missing values or corrupted log entries. A subset of the initial data batch published by [32,33], is publicly available.

Alarm management performance was encoded as a binary outcome (AM: Effective vs. Failed) according to the simulator's success criteria (see Sect. 3) and served as the target for all Bayesian classifiers. The predictor features are grouped into 2 categories: Task-related features, which were experimentally controlled and participant-related which contains both demographic characteristics and training scores. All features were used in their original categorical or ordinal form, except for Age, which was discretized using expert-defined bins (18–25, 26–35, >35 years) to reflect typical educational and career stages.

A summary of all features collected and used in BN modeling is presented in Table 1.

Table 1. Summary of features used for BN modeling.

Category	Feature	Description	Values/Range
Task-related	Alarm Display Support (ADS)	Whether alarms were color-coded by priority or not	Basic/Advanced
	Complexity (C)	Number of critical alarms in the scenario	Low/High
	Support System Availability (SSA)	Type of procedural support provided	Paper/Screen/AI
Participant-related	**Demographic**		
	Age	Age of participant (discretized)	[18, 25, 35, ∞[
	Degree	Highest or current level of education	Bachelor/Master/PhD/Other
	Course	Field of study	Engineering/IT/...
	Training assessment		
	T_scale	Ability to adjust a scale	1 (Low) – 5 (High)
	T_section	Ability to identify plant section	1 (Low) – 5 (High)
	T_ack	Ability to Acknowledge alarms	1 (Low) – 5 (High)
	T_procedure	Ability to locate procedures	1 (Low) – 5 (High)
	Know_Sim	Self-reported simulator knowledge	1 (Low) – 5 (High)
	Know_OP	Self-reported knowledge of operational procedures	1 (Low) – 5 (High)
Performance-related	AM	Alarm Management outcome (target feature)	Effective/Failed

5.2 Constrained Feature Selection Experiments

In the part of the experiment, models were conditioned on the three task-related features: Task Complexity, Alarm Display, and Support Availability, to determine whether subsequent changes in performance could be attributed to the remaining predictors. Sequential feature-selection was then performed using mutual-information (MI) based and wrapper-based approaches over 100 Monte Carlo trials. Figure 2 plots the resulting mean ROC AUC (± 1 SD) for NB, TAN, and PR against feature-set size.

(a) MI-based selection (3–12 features): all three classifiers begin at AUC ≈0.70 using the three task-related features, then decline nearly monotonically as more features are added; TAN and PR follow the same pattern. The overlapping error bars indicate that additional features introduce variance without improving discrimination.

(b) Wrapper-based selection (3–7 features): NB and PR each reach peak mean AUC ≈0.70 at three features, while TAN continues to improve until five features (peak AUC ≈0.70). Beyond these cutoffs, NB's AUC declines steadily to 0.67 by seven features, and PR and TAN drop to approximately 0.62 and 0.61 at six features (no variability is shown past their stopping points). The wrapper selection iteratively adds features until no further improvement in cross-validated AUC is observed within each iteration. Mean AUC values at each subset size are averaged only over iterations that reached that size, which accounts for values appearing beyond the average stopping point. These trajectories confirm that the wrapper criterion reliably identifies minimal feature subsets that preserve optimal performance before further inclusion induces rapid accuracy loss.

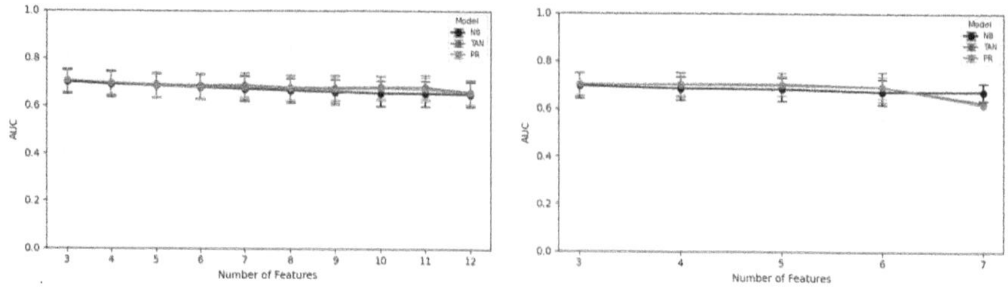

(a) MI-based selection (3-12 features)

(b) Wrapper selection (3–7 features)

Fig. 2. Mean AUC ± SD comparison across models and feature subset sizes over 100 trials, for (a) mutual-information-based selection and (b) wrapper-based selection.

Table 2. Mean AUC (± SD) of the three highest-performing model–feature configurations for each feature-selection method, based on 100 randomized trials.

FS method	Model	Features	Mean AUC (± SD)
MI	PR	3	0.7062 ± 0.0491
MI	TAN	3	0.7045 ± 0.0473
MI	NB	3	0.6989 ± 0.0505
Wrapper	TAN	5	0.7039 ± 0.0475
Wrapper	PR	3	0.7035 ± 0.0477
Wrapper	TAN	4	0.7033 ± 0.0485

Table 2 ranks the top three model–feature configurations under each selection method. The single best configuration is Pearl–Rebane with three features under mutual-information selection (AUC 0.7062 ± 0.0491), followed closely by TAN at three MI-chosen features (0.7045 ± 0.0473) and by TAN with five wrapper-selected features (0.7039 ± 0.0475). In the subsequent section, the statistical significance of these differences is evaluated using Wilcoxon signed-rank tests.

5.3 Pairwise Model Comparisons (Wilcoxon)

Table 3 presents the complete set of Wilcoxon signed-rank p-values for all pairwise AUC comparisons (NB vs. TAN, NB vs. PR, TAN vs. PR) at each feature count, under both MI and wrapper selection.

Under MI selection, PR significantly outperforms NB at three features ($p = 0.0383$) while the PR–TAN comparison does not reach significance. Under wrapper selection, PR outperforms both NB and TAN at three features ($p = 0.03096$). At four features, NB is outperformed by TAN($p = 5.30 \times 10^{-6}$) and PR ($p = 0.00021$).

Table 3. Wilcoxon signed-rank test p-values for pairwise AUC comparisons.

FS	Feature count	p-value		
		NB vs TAN	NB vs PR	TAN vs PR
MI	3	0.06308	**0.03830**	0.57632
Wrapper	3	0.20391	**0.03096**	**0.03096**
Wrapper	4	**5.30e-06**	**0.00021**	0.68495
Wrapper	5	0.15405	0.44446	0.71116

5.4 Learned Network Structures

In this section, the network topologies of the peak-performing configurations are examined. For each classifier (NB, TAN, PR), the single Monte Carlo trial with the highest AUC value was selected, regardless of feature selection method, and visualized its learned structure (Fig. 3).

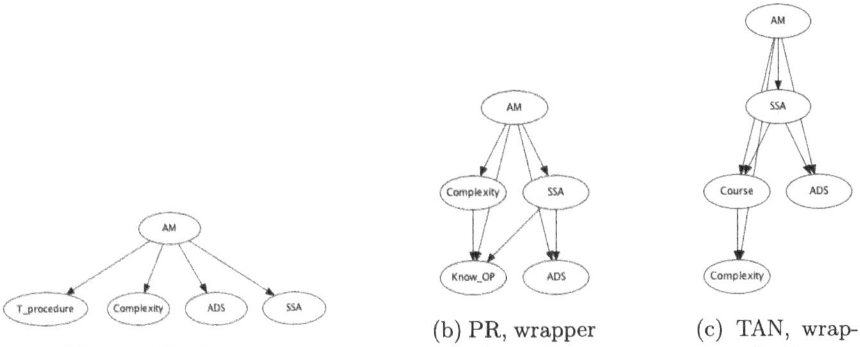

(a) NB, MI selection (b) PR, wrapper selection (c) TAN, wrapper selection

Fig. 3. Learned BN structures for the three highest-AUC model configurations.

NB always produces the familiar "star" topology, with every feature linked only to the target and no inter-feature edges. TAN augments this by adding exactly one parent among the features, yielding a single spanning tree that captures the strongest pairwise dependencies. PR, by contrast, often produces a richer, or at least differently organized-polytree structure: it may omit some TAN edges in favor of others with higher mutual information and can yield a more unbalanced tree.

5.5 Unconstrained Feature Selection Experiments

To gain insights on which predictors are most informative regardless of the classifiers, MI selection was applied to the full feature set without enforcing any fixed features over 100 Monte Carlo trials (Fig. 4).

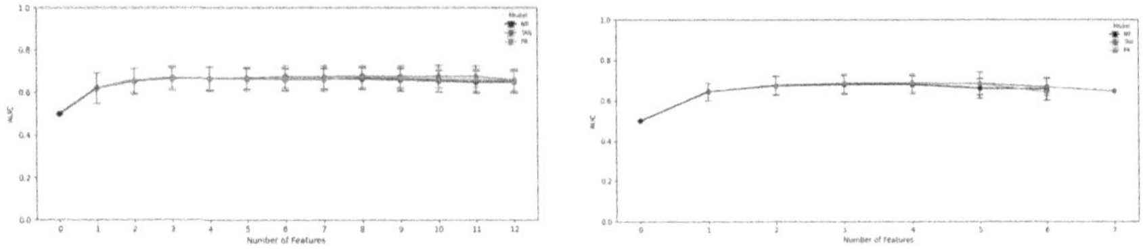

(a) MI-based selection (0-12 features) (b) Wrapper selection (0–7 features)

Fig. 4. Mean AUC ± SD comparison across models and feature subset sizes over 100 trials, for unconstrained mutual feature selection.

Figure 1 plots the resulting mean AUC (± 1 SD) for NB, TAN, and PR against feature-set size under uncontrained feature selection

(a) MI-based selection (0–12 features): all three classifiers, NB, TAN and PR, gain predictive power as features are added. NB, for instance, rises from an AUC of about 0.60 with its single highest-MI predictor, and each additional feature yields further improvement. However, after the first five or six features, the incremental gains fall within the ±1 SD error bars, indicating no reliable added predictive value.

(b) Wrapper-based selection (0–7 features): features are appended only while each addition increases cross-validated AUC; once no further gain is observed, the procedure stops. In our unconstrained trials, NB and PR both stopped at six features and TAN at seven. Across both MI and wrapper methods, TAN achieves the highest AUC values at its optimal feature counts.

Table 4. Mean AUC (± SD) of the three highest-performing model–feature configurations for each feature-selection method, based on 100 randomized trials.

FS method	Model	Features	Mean AUC (± SD)
MI	TAN	8	0.6785 ± 0.0507
MI	TAN	11	0.6774 ± 0.0504
MI	NB	10	0.6770 ± 0.0531
Wrapper	PR	4	0.6895 ± 0.0439
Wrapper	PR	3	0.6879 ± 0.0457
Wrapper	TAN	5	0.6862 ± 0.0562

Table 4 summarizes the three highest-performing model–feature configurations for each method. Here, wrapper selection yields uniformly higher AUCs than MI. The single best configuration overall is PR with four features (0.6895 ± 0.0439), followed by PR at three features (0.6879 ± 0.0457) and TAN at five features (0.6862 ± 0.0562).

These results suggest that, when features are chosen purely data-driven, the wrapper criterion more successfully identifies a small subset that maximizes test-set discrimination. Nevertheless, both unconstrained approaches underperform the constrained experiments (where expert-selected controls are forced in), indicating that domain knowledge still provides valuable guidance. In particular, in the unconstrained approach, the wrapper outperforms the MI approaches with just three features.

To reveal which feature dependencies drive these unconstrained outcomes, Fig. 5 depict the ten edges with highest empirical selection probability under MI-based and wrapper-based selection, respectively, across 100 Monte Carlo runs.

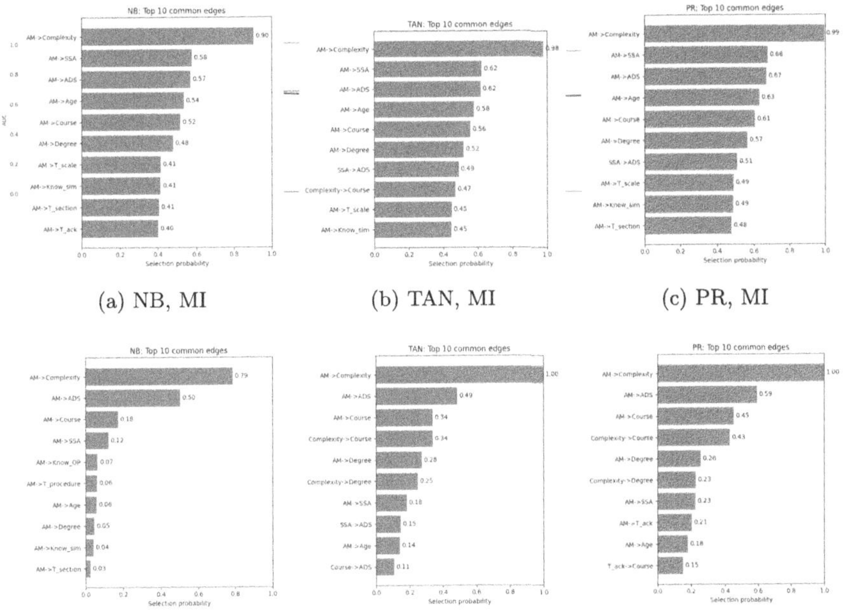

(a) NB, MI (b) TAN, MI (c) PR, MI

(d) NB, wrapper (e) TAN, wrapper (f) PR, wrapper

Fig. 5. Selection probabilities of the ten most frequent edges per classifier under unconstrained MI (top row) and wrapper (bottom row) selection across 100 Monte Carlo runs.

Figure 5 demonstrates that Complexity→AM is the most consistently recovered dependency across all classifiers and selection methods: under MI selection, it appears in over 90% of trials for NB, TAN, and PR; under wrapper selection, it is recovered in 100% of runs for TAN and PR and in 79% of runs for NB. In the MI regime, the next most frequent edges are AM→SSA (58–68%) and AM→ADS (57–67%). Wrapper selection elevates AM→ADS to the second position, with roughly 50% inclusion, while AM→SSA falls below 25%. The failure of unconstrained methods, particularly the wrapper, to consistently recover SSA (and, to a lesser extent, ADS) accounts for their lower AUC relative to the constrained feature selection, which guarantees inclusion of these critical features.

6 Discussion and Conclusion

In the constrained feature-selection experiments, where Task Complexity, Alarm Display, and Support Availability were enforced in every model, the addition of secondary predictors failed to yield consistent AUC improvements, and all classifiers performed comparably. Pearl–Rebane nevertheless demonstrated the strongest statistical significance under both MI and wrapper feature selection, reflecting its ability to capture the essential dependencies among the task-related features.

Under unconstrained mutual-information selection, the same three features, most prominently Complexity, were recovered in over 90% of trials, effectively marginalizing individual-difference predictors. Wrapper selection likewise placed Complexity first but elevated Alarm Display Support to second position ($\approx$50% inclusion), while Procedural Support fell below 25% recovery. This pattern explains the inferior performance of purely data-driven selection: mutual-information captures only marginal relevance, and wrappers, though optimized for AUC, may omit experimentally important factors.

From the perspective of human reliability assessment, these findings confirm that task complexity is the principal determinant of operator success, with alarm-display design and support systems exerting the next greatest influence. To reveal the contributions of demographic, training, and other human-factors features, future studies should replicate these analyses under reduced-complexity scenarios. Lowering baseline workload will allow subtler predictors to emerge, thereby supporting the development of more nuanced and interpretable Bayesian-network models of human reliability. Furthermore, forward wrapper selection was employed in this study for computational efficiency; however, backward elimination may be considered in future work to better capture complex feature interactions and avoid premature exclusion of relevant variables.

Acknowledgments. This research project has been supported by a Marie Skłodowska-Curie Innovative Training Network Fellowship of the European Commission's Horizon 2020 Programme under contract number 955901 CISC.

The authors would like to thank the anonymous reviewers for their valuable feedback, which improved the quality and clarity of this manuscript.

References

1. Hollnagel, E.: Human reliability assessment in context. Nucl. Eng. Technol. **37**(2), 159–166 (2005)
2. Paglioni, V.P., Groth, K.M.: Bridging the data-model gap for HRA: creating Bayesian networks from HRA data. In: 13th Nuclear Plant Instrumentation, Control & Human-Machine Interface Technologies (NPIC&HMIT 2023), Knoxville, TN (2023)

3. Wu, G., Mao, Y., He, Y., Yi, L., Jia, M., Shan, F.: Safety archetypes identification and behavior simulation for nuclear power plant operation human reliability improvement. Ann. Nucl. Energy **174**, 109189 (2022)
4. Liu, J., et al.: Analysis of dependencies among performance shaping factors in human reliability analysis based on a system dynamics approach. Reliab. Eng. Syst. Saf. **215**, 107890 (2021)
5. Ramos, M., Major, C., Ekanem, N., Malpica, C., Mosleh, A.: Human reliability analysis for oil and gas operations: analysis of existing methods. arXiv preprint arXiv:2109.14096 (2021)
6. Brazier, A.: Operations: A Control Room is Only a Component in a Complex System. Article of AB Risk Limited, Managing Risks of Control Room Operations (2010)
7. Dorgo, G., Tandari, F., Szabó, T., Palazoglu, A., Abonyi, J.: Quality vs. quantity of alarm messages-how to measure the performance of an alarm system. Chem. Eng. Res. Des. **173**, 63–80 (2021)
8. Briwa, H., Leva, M.C., Turner, R.: Alarm management for human performance. Are we getting better. In: Proceedings of the 32nd European Safety and Reliability Conference, pp. 3242–3251 (2022)
9. Liao, H., Groth, K., Stevens-Adams, S.: Challenges in leveraging existing human performance data for quantifying the IDHEAS HRA method. Reliab. Eng. Syst. Saf. **144**, 159–169 (2015)
10. Su, Y., Gao, X., Qian, H., Su, X.: Handling uncertainty in human cognitive reliability method for safety assessment based on DSET. CMES—Comput. Model. Eng. Sci. **132**(1) (2022)
11. Podofillini, L., Reer, B., Dang, V.N.: A traceable process to develop Bayesian networks from scarce data and expert judgment: a human reliability analysis application. Reliab. Eng. Syst. Saf. **230**, 108903 (2023)
12. O'Leary, J., Zhao, Y., Groth, K.: A Survey of Parameterization Techniques for Bayesian Network Models for Human Reliability Analysis (2023)
13. Park, J., et al.: A framework to collect human reliability analysis data for nuclear power plants using a simplified simulator and student operators. Reliab. Eng. Syst. Saf. **221**, 108326 (2022)
14. Bye, A., Julius, J.A., Boring, R.: Challenges for human reliability analysis in new nuclear power plant designs. In: 16th International Conference on Probabilistic Safety Assessment and Management (PSAM 2022) (2022)
15. Mkrtchyan, L., Podofillini, L., Dang, V.N.: Bayesian belief networks for human reliability analysis: a review of applications and gaps. Reliab. Eng. Syst. Saf. **139**, 1–16 (2015)
16. Dash, M., Liu, H.: Feature selection for classification. Intell. Data Anal. **1**(1–4), 131–156 (1997)
17. Bach, J., Zoller, K., Trittenbach, H., Schulz, K., Böhm, K.: An empirical evaluation of constrained feature selection. SN Comput. Sci. **3**(6), 445 (2022)
18. Kjærulff, U.B., Madsen, A.L.: Data-driven modeling. In: Bayesian Networks and Influence Diagrams: A Guide to Construction and Analysis, pp. 237–288 (2013)
19. Larrañaga, P., Karshenas, H., Bielza, C., Santana, R.: A review on evolutionary algorithms in Bayesian network learning and inference tasks. Inf. Sci. **233**, 109–125 (2013)
20. Koller, D., Friedman, N.: Probabilistic Graphical Models: Principles and Techniques. MIT Press, Cambridge (2009)

21. Demichela, M., Baldissone, G., Camuncoli, G.: Risk-based decision making for the management of change in process plants: benefits of integrating probabilistic and phenomenological analysis. Ind. Eng. Chem. Res. **56**(50), 14873–14887 (2017)
22. Amazu, C.W., Briwa, H., Demichela, M., Fissore, D., Baldissone, G., Leva, M.C.: Analysing 'human-in-the-loop' for advances in process safety: a design of experiment in a simulated process control room. In: Proceedings of the 33rd European Safety and Reliability Conference, Southampton, UK, pp. 3–7 (2023)
23. Kraskov, A., Stögbauer, H., Grassberger, P.: Estimating mutual information. Phys. Rev. E-Stat. Nonlinear Soft Matter Phys. **69**(6), 066138 (2004)
24. Kohavi, R., John, G.H.: The wrapper approach. In: Feature Extraction, Construction and Selection: A Data Mining Perspective, pp. 33–50. Springer, Boston (1998)
25. Chang, L.: Feature selection for grasp classification. Mach. Learn. (2006)
26. Friedman, N., Geiger, D., Goldszmidt, M.: Bayesian network classifiers. Mach. Learn. **29**, 131–163 (1997)
27. Rebane, G., Pearl, J.: The recovery of causal poly-trees from statistical data. arXiv preprint arXiv:1304.2736 (2013)
28. Lauritzen, S.L.: The EM algorithm for graphical association models with missing data. Comput. Stat. Data Anal. **19**(2), 191–201 (1995)
29. Smyth, P.: Clustering using Monte Carlo cross-validation. In: KDD, vol. 1, pp. 26–133 (1996)
30. Marzban, C.: The ROC curve and the area under it as performance measures. Weather Forecast. **19**(6), 1106–1114 (2004)
31. Benavoli, A., Corani, G., Mangili, F., Zaffalon, M., Ruggeri, F.: A Bayesian Wilcoxon signed-rank test based on the Dirichlet process. In: International Conference on Machine Learning, pp. 1026–1034. PMLR (2014)
32. Abbas, A.N., Amazu, C.W.: Human-in-the-Loop Decision Support in Process Control Room Dataset, Zenodo (2024). https://doi.org/10.5281/zenodo.10569181. https://zenodo.org/records/13984198
33. Amazu, C.W., et al.: Experiment data: human-in-the-loop decision support in process control rooms. Data Brief **53**, Article no. 110170 (2024)
34. Chow, C.K., Liu, C.: Approximating discrete probability distributions with dependence trees. IEEE Trans. Inf. Theory **14**(3), 462–467 (1968)
35. Sugahara, S.: Exact learning of augmented Naive Bayes classifiers. Doctoral thesis, Graduate School of Informatics and Engineering, The University of Electro-Communications (2023)
36. Lucas, P.J.F., Van der Gaag, L.C., Abu-Hanna, A.: Bayesian networks in biomedicine and health-care. Artif. Intell. Med. **30**(3), 201–214 (2004)

Wrong Data Detection in Electricity Distribution Grids Using Bayesian Networks

Anders L. Madsen[1,2](✉), Somesh Bhattacharya[3], Christian D. Jensen[4], Rasmus L. Olsen[4], and Hans-Peter Schwefel[3,4]

[1] HUGIN EXPERT A/S, Aalborg, Denmark
anders@hugin.com
[2] Department of Computer Science, Aalborg University, Aalborg, Denmark
alm@cs.aau.dk
[3] GridData GmbH, Anger, Germany
{somesh,schwefel}@griddata.eu
[4] Department of Electronic Systems, Aalborg University, Aalborg, Denmark
{christiandj,rlo,hps}@es.aau.dk

Abstract. Power grids depend on precise power measurements for various operational, economic, and security decisions. Wrong measurement data can lead to wrong or delayed decisions, ultimately wasting resources. This paper examines the detection of wrong data in active power measurements for distribution grids using Bayesian networks. Both supervised and unsupervised approaches are explored, where the supervised approach learns a Naive Bayes-type classifier from labeled active power measurements data, while the unsupervised method utilizes unlabeled data in conjunction with a surprise index (data conflict measure) to identify unusual data. An experimental analysis is conducted using a real-world dataset from a medium-voltage grid, where multiple types of anomalies are injected into the time series of active power data. The supervised model demonstrates high detection rates and short delays, while the performance of the unsupervised approach is promising.

Keywords: Bayesian networks · Wrong data detection · Electricity grids

1 Introduction

Anomaly detection in time-series data is a widely studied field, with the definition of an "anomaly" varying across application domains. In healthcare, it may indicate an unusual physiological condition; in banking, it often refers to fraudulent transactions; and in smart grids, it generally denotes irregular measurements, network faults or attempts on cyber attacks [15].

This paper builds on the anomaly detection framework proposed in [23], specifically targeting abnormal patterns in active power data received from measurement devices in Medium-Voltage (MV) substations. Utilizing the structure

K. Sauerwald and M. Thimm (Eds.): ECSQARU 2025, LNAI 16099, pp. 31–45, 2026.
https://doi.org/10.1007/978-3-032-05134-9_3

and methodology of the original framework, this work adapts and extends it through domain-specific modifications and experimental validations, informed by extensive analyses of power system anomalies and threats.

This paper presents a comparative perspective on each component—data description, feature selection, and evaluation results—highlighting both the continuity and innovation relative to [23]. It examines the detection of wrong data in active power measurements for distribution grids using Bayesian networks [7].

This study is part of the REDistXAI [1,13] project, which aims to enhance explainability and robustness in anomaly detection within electrical distribution networks. Therefore, within the framework of Digital Twin measurement head-ends, it is imperative that any wrong data or a possible anomaly is detected, and is localised.

This paper is organized as follows. Section 2 provides an overview of the state-of-the art related to anomalies and wrong data, in the power grid context. Section 3 provides preliminaries and introduces the notation used in the paper. Section 4 presents the electricity distribution grid case study and Sect. 5 describes the methodology applied in the case study while Sect. 6 presents the experimental design and Sect. 7 presents the experimental results and an evaluation of the results. Finally, Sect. 8 concludes the paper.

2 Electrical Background

Power grids utilize measurement devices to collect information about voltages, currents, and energy or power at different grid locations: in distribution grids, customer smart meters and measurements devices at transformer stations provide observations that can be used by advanced digital tools to estimate the distribution grid state. Depending on the measurement location, anomalous data from these measurement devices can lead to incorrect billing or, in a more concerning scenario for the distribution system operator, flawed conclusions on the operational state of the grid. In [22], a Long Short-Term Memory (LSTM) network-based detection mechanism was proposed to avoid incorrect relay tripping. In [21], a correntropy-based K-means clustering method was employed. That paper's main contribution was identifying distinct outliers that represent incorrect or anomalous data.

Several types of anomalies are mentioned in [18]. The primary categories include physical attacks, unintentional changes, natural disasters, and loss of IT. The paper also highlighted the importance of data sanitation. This process involves employing detection methods that utilize deviation-based analysis. One straightforward method is to disaggregate the smart meter data by appliance for a single household and analyze the final measurements from the devices. One such technique was developed in [5], where measurements across various appliances were assessed using a recurrent neural network. A similar approach for anomaly detection using smart meter data was proposed in [10]. The BILSTM autoencoder in this paper detected anomalies through reconstruction errors. However, the literature commonly assumes the unrestricted availability of smart meter data, which may not be ideal in scenarios such as when analysing a MV grid.

The use of Bayesian networks to examine the reliability of smart meters was presented in [19]. The paper offers real-time diagnosis and reliability prediction for smart meter components, thus enabling early anomaly detection. However, in MV systems, the measurements are collected via measurement devices, which are only sporadically spread across the MV network, and not all the transformation stations are measured. An approach to detect anomalies for MV networks in a Power Grid Digital Twin was established in [23]. The XGBoost method was used as a classifier in this case.

3 Preliminaries and Notation

3.1 Bayesian Networks

A Bayesian network is a probabilistic graphical model on a set of random variables $\mathcal{X}$ represented as nodes V in an acyclic directed graph (DAG) G [2,7,8,14] with directed edges E such that $G = (V, E)$ where there is one conditional probability distribution for each variable $X_i \in \mathcal{X}$. The set of conditional probability distributions represents a factorization of the joint probability distribution on $\mathcal{X}$:

$$P(\mathcal{X}) = \prod_{i=1}^{n} P(X_i \mid \pi(X_i)),$$

where $\pi(X_i)$ is the set of variables representing the parents of X_i (or the node representing X_i) in DAG G.

For the zero-day attack use case, an approach based on unsupervised learning of the Bayesian network was applied. The underlying idea of the approach is to use a sequence of non-faulty data to estimate a Bayesian network on variables representing active power measurements and a set of derived features. In [6], a measure to detect a possible conflict in a set of evidence ϵ that has been propagated in a Bayesian network was introduced. The conflict measure $\textsc{conf}(\epsilon)$ is defined as:

$$\textsc{conf}(\epsilon) = \log\left(\frac{\prod_{i=1}^{n} P(\epsilon_i)}{P(\epsilon)}\right),$$

where $\epsilon = \{\epsilon_1, \ldots, \epsilon_n\}$ is the set of evidence propagated in the Bayesian network. The assumption of this conflict measure is that the evidence is positively correlated. Thus, $\textsc{conf}(\epsilon) > 0$ can be interpreted as an indication of a possible conflict or surprise in the evidence (or data). The conflict measure is extended to the case of mixed continuous and discrete variables by using the value of the density function at the observed value in case of continuous variables. Continuous variables are assumed to follow a conditional linear Gaussian distribution. In [12], the conflict measure was used to implement an online alert system for production plants, while in [3] the conflict measure was used to detect anomalies in mixed tabular data. Hence, it is possible to use a Bayesian network estimated from *normal* operation data and the conflict measure $\text{CONF}(\epsilon)$ to continuously monitor the operation of a system and detect possible anomalies. In this paper, the approach is utilized to detect wrong data in a time series of active power measurements.

4 Case Study

This paper applies Bayesian networks and the conflict measure for wrong data detection in electricity distribution grids. The functionality is being integrated into a digital twin of the electricity grid.

4.1 Digital Twin of the Electricity Grid

In this paper, we use real measurements from distribution system operators (DSO) data as baseline for wrong data detection. This is achieved with the help of an advanced digital system, the GridData DigitalTwin. The latter is a software solution, with its exemplary structure illustrated in Fig. 1. A core component of the DigitalTwin is the Data Fusion Hub (DFH), which via customized interfaces receives structural information of the grid and measurement data from different sources, see examples in the bottom of the figure. The DFH then automatically and in real-time builds up a parameterized model of the distribution grid that can be used for a variety of monitoring and planning applications, see top of the figure.

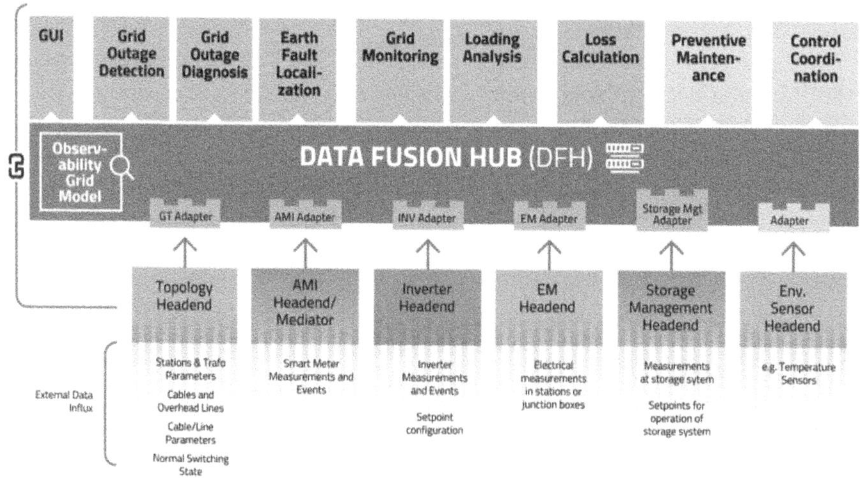

Fig. 1. GridData DigitalTwin used for baseline data access from operational grids

The grid monitoring function, as illustrated in Fig. 1 top, leverages voltage measurements and power measurements together with the grid structure and intelligent algorithms for pseudo-measurements to calculate voltage time-series behavior for all nodes in the grid. Similarly loading analysis calculates cable and transformer loadings covering measured as well as unmeasured transformers and cables.

Any wrong or anomalous measurement data coming from the remote measurement devices or from intermediate IT systems will affect the quality of the grid calculation. It is therefore imperative that the DFH has a mechanism to detect anomalies in the time series of the input data. The basic concept is to detect with the methods presented and assessed in this paper, which part of input data may be wrong. If such wrong data is detected, then the affected part of the input data is ignored and replaced by the smart algorithms for pseudo-measurements and forecasting within the GridData DigitalTwin. However, at this stage, the paper restricts itself to the actual anomaly detection, and the assessment of the correction strategies and their impact on DigitalTwin application results will be presented in future work.

4.2 Measurement Data Used as Baseline in the Case Study

As part of the REDistXAI project [1,13], the proposed method for detecting anomalies in time series data is applied to datasets having the following characteristics:

- Measurement data collected from 20 kV:4000 V transformer stations on a MV grid located in southern Germany - the measurement location can be either on the LV or MV side of the transformer, but will be harmonized by the DFH to appear as if it was an MV measurement.
- Measurements from four transformer stations within one MV feeder, consisting of approx 20 nodes, are utilized. These grid locations are referred to as Node IDs 28, 32, 34 and 36.
- The measurements contain multiple measurands as a 15min time series; this paper considers only the average active power (in kW) measured over each 15 min interval. Negative values represent power injected from the LV grid to the MV grid due to distributed local generation on the LV grid (mainly from photovoltaics in the considered stations).
- Data from Year 2024 is considered.

As mentioned above, the data contains the average active power over time, and the entire year of 2024 was taken into consideration, further averaged into one 'week' day of measurement. The resulting measurements for MV stations 28 and 36 are shown in Fig. 2. Section 6 contains further detailed analysis of the device measurements.

Structural similarity in the dataset can also be found in [23], where 15-minute measurements are used for other grids and utilizing energy values in kWh. The case study involved feature vectors' computation, described as "lag" and "moving average lag" of the 2, 5 and 10 past values. Additionally, feature vectors are night/day, weekend/weekday, and offpeak/onpeak. This results in a single observation of active energy with additional 9 features.

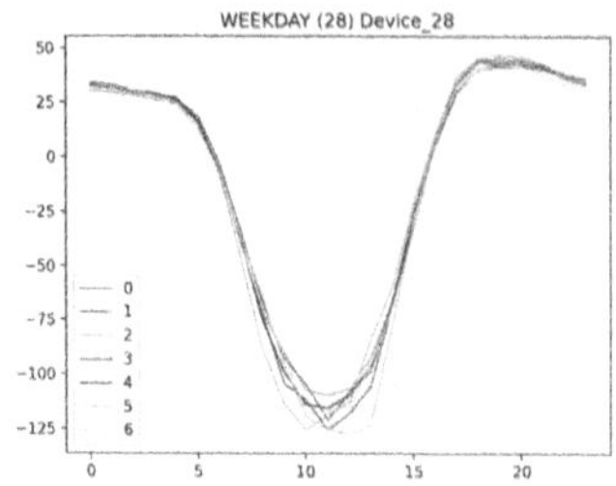

(a) Active power MV station 28.

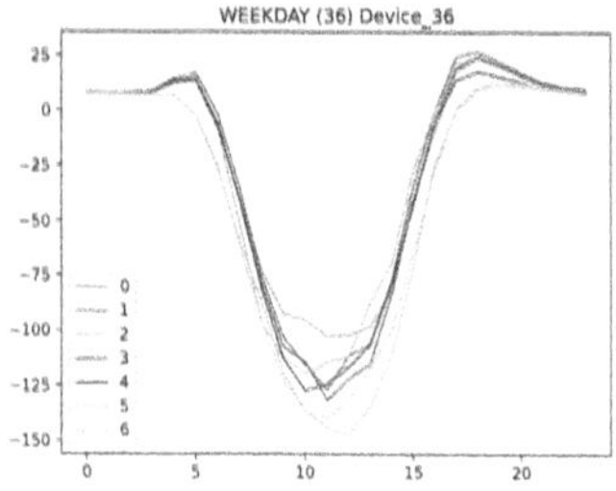

(b) Active power MV station 36.

Fig. 2. Active power measurements on two MV stations used in the case study

As an initial data analysis to determine the similarity of the four time series of data, the Spearman correlation coefficient r_s is calculated for the four devices from the raw data without injected errors. The coefficients are shown in Table 1. The Spearman correlation coefficient r_s suggests the strongest correlation between devices 32 and 34 and the weakest correlation between devices 28 and 36, which are the two grid elements farthest apart in the grid topology.

Table 1. Spearman correlation coefficients for the four devices.

Device pair	(28,32)	(28,34)	(28,36)	(32,34)	(32,36)	(34,36)
r_s	0.844	0.834	0.788	0.938	0.836	0.843

4.3 Wrong Data Types

A comprehensive discussion of power consumption anomaly types, based on a threat list developed by the European Union Agency for Cybersecurity (ENISA) is presented in [23]. This work has compressed and generalised all anomalies to six general types. Three of the six anomalies are listed in Table 2 where error type E2 sets the value of active power to zero for a period of time, error type E3 multiplies the active power by 0.5, and error type E4 multiplies the active power by 2. Notice that we consider active power, and not merely power consumption.

These three anomalies represent simple yet significant data integrity violations. Simple refers to the anomalies being controlled and interpretable in nature. Doubling or halving the power consumption can be caused if, e.g., a 2:1 transformer ratio is assumed to be a 1:1 transformer ratio. In addition, wrong installation as well as firmware and software bugs can also cause an error of this type, and even cyber attacks. Furthermore, if a load is physically disconnected from the grid or a false data injection has occurred, the power consumption would go to zero. These are some of the plausible causes which threatens to create the anomalies; however, this paper focuses mainly on the outcome, where further information on the causes and threats can be found in [23].

Table 2. Three difference types of wrong data injected.

Error type	Error description
E2	Setting active power to zero
E3	Multiplying active power by 0.5
E4	Multiplying active power by 2

5 Methodology

In this section the methodology to detect wrong data in active power measurements is described.

5.1 Features Derived from Active Power Measurements

The raw data from a measured device is a time series of the active power measurements of the device with a frequency of 15 min. To be able to detect wrong data in time series with errors (E2, E3, or E4) injected additional derived features are required. Following the approach of [23], a set of derived features $\mathcal{F}$ is constructed. The set $\mathcal{F} = \{F_1, \ldots, F_m\}$ consists of two discrete features (representing the weekday and the hour) and 20 continuous features derived from the active power measurements. The 20 continuous derived features are computed as the difference, the relative difference, and the relative difference to the moving average over i time steps for $i \in \{1, 2, 3, 4, 5, 10, 24, 96\}$ (no moving average over one timestep), see Fig. 7 for a model example where yellow nodes represent discrete variables and dark yellow nodes represent continuous variables. As examples the node *diff_t_5* represent the difference between the current power consumption and the power consumption five time steps before and *diff_ma_5* is the difference between the current power consumption and the moving average over five time steps.

5.2 Bayesian Network Models

Two different types of datasets are considered for the detection of wrong data. One type of dataset is labeled and includes the active power measurements and derived features as well as a class label indicating if a data sample is an anomaly (supervised learning) while the other type of dataset does not include the class label (unsupervised learning). For a labeled dataset, traditional structure-restricted Bayesian networks are appropriate. In this paper, we consider the Naive Bayes Model (NBM) [4] who cites [16] and the tree-augmented NBM (TAN) [4]. For the unlabeled dataset, a general Bayesian network structure learning algorithm [17] is applied in combination with the data conflict measure [6]. Since features $\mathcal{F}$ may have missing values, the EM algorithm [9] is used to estimate the probability distributions $\{P(X \mid \pi(X) : X \in \mathcal{X}\}$ from the incomplete data in both cases.

Supervised Learning. For the supervised learning, a NBM or TAN model with mixed discrete and continuous variables is created. The continuous variables represent the derived features while discrete variables represent the classification variable, weekday, and hour. For each device and each fault, a structure-restricted model is estimated to detect the type of fault. The model is evaluated on data from other devices in which the same error has been injected.

Unsupervised Learning. For the unsupervised learning, a Bayesian network over the feature variables only is created by learning from data. The Bayesian network over the feature variables is used in combination with the conflict measure to detect data conflicts. This approach detects data patterns that are considered in conflict with the model estimated from *normal* data. The model is not developed to detect specific types of abnormal patterns.

Thus, a Bayesian network with mixed discrete and continuous variables representing the features is constructed for the unlabeled data. The classification variable is not included in the model. For each device, a model is estimated from normal operation data. That is, the original data without errors injected. This model is evaluated on data from the other devices in which each type of error has been injected.

For learning the structure of the Bayesian network, the variant of the PC algorithm [17] presented by [11] is applied. The PC algorithm is a constrained-based structure learning algorithm.

6 Experimental Design

The experiments are designed to evaluate the performance of Bayesian networks as a method to detect wrong data in active power time series.

6.1 Wrong Data Injection

The data used in the experiment is described in Sect. 4.1 and an aggregated plot of the data for devices 28 and 36 is shown in Fig. 2a and Fig. 2b, respectively. The plots show the average hourly active power measurement by weekday (where zero represents Monday). The active power can be negative as it is the aggregated value of power consumption and generation (e.g., solar panels).

Anomalies are injected such that each sample has a 0.5% chance of starting a sequence of 12 anomalous samples (3 h of data being anomalous). To avoid overlapping anomalies, any new anomaly must begin at least 12 samples after the start of the previous anomaly. This ensures that no sample is affected by more than one anomaly. The average number of error sequences in a device time series is 165 with a range from 139 to 183.

This anomaly injection approach is significantly different from the approach of [23], which essentially injects anomalies randomly with intervals lasting from 5 to 50 subsequent observations throughout the time series.

6.2 Score Metrics

The experiment is designed to detect the presence of a sequence of errors in a time series of active power measurements. For each time series, a single type of error is injected. The score metrics considered are:

detection rate which is the number of sequences detected. A sequence is detected when the algorithm identifies at least one of the samples in the sequence as anomalous.
detection delay (or latency) which is the number of samples between the start of an anomalous event and the detection. The average detection delay is computed for the detected sequences only.
false positive rate (FPR) which is FP/(FP + TN) evaluated at sample level, where FP is false positives and TN are true negatives.
false positive per hour (FPH) which is $FP/(4 * n)$, where n is the number of 15-minute samples.
lift which is the ratio between model predictions and randomly generated predictions.

The conflict measure-based approach used on the unlabeled data does not produce a probability of data error. Instead, $\textsc{conf}(\epsilon_i)$ is computed for each data sample ϵ_i. If $\textsc{conf}(\epsilon_i) > 0$, this is considered an indication of an anomaly in the data sample. For the unlabeled data case, the lift, FPR, and FPH are used. To determine the lift an optimal threshold is computed for the cases with $\textsc{conf}(\epsilon_i) > 0$ normalized to be between 0 and 1 using Youden's J statistic ($J = \text{sensitivity} + \text{specificity} - 1$) [20].

As an alternative to using the full set of features, a forward feature selection method is applied. The forward feature selection is driven by the area under the Receiver Operator Characteristics curve (AUC) metric.

7 Experimental Results

The experimental results are presented in two separate sections corresponding to the supervised and unsupervised approaches.

7.1 Supervised Learning from Labeled Data

In the supervised approach, a NBM or TAN model is created for each device and each type of error. The model for one device and one type of error is evaluated on all time-series with the same error injected.

Figure 3 shows the structure of a TAN model for the case of device 28 and error E2 using forward feature selection. The top node *label* of the graph represents the class variable while the light yellow nodes represent discrete variables (hour and weekday) and the remaining nodes represent continuous variables. The features have been selected greedily using forward feature selection.

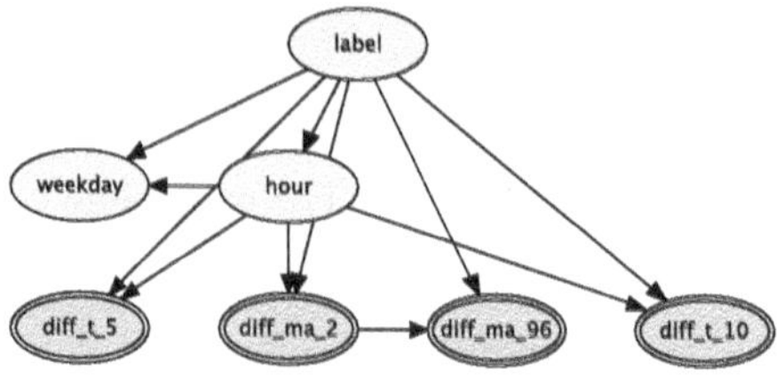

Fig. 3. The TAN structure created for device 28 and E2 using feature selection. (Color figure online)

The detection rate for error type E2 is high for all combinations of train and test devices, ranging from 0.99 to 1. Figure 4 shows a histogram of the detection delay for tests involving E2. The plots include both TAN and NBM models (e.g., "All Detection Rate" is for TAN with all features, while "N All Detection Rate" is for NBM, and "FS" is shorthand for feature selection). In the plot, the labels on the x-axis, for instance, E2-28-32, specify that the time series for device 28 was used as train data and the time series for device 32 was used as test data considering error E2. The detection rate for E2 is close to one for all cases, while there is a higher variation in the detection delay. The detection delay is between 1 and 2. Recall that E2 inject sequences where the active power is set to zero.

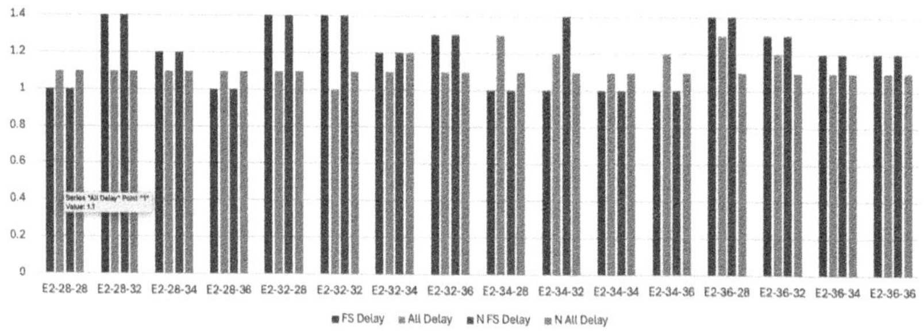

Fig. 4. E2 detection delay.

Figure 5 shows a histogram of the detection rate for tests involving error type E3. The detection rate for E3 varies between 0.5 and 1, but in most cases (50 out of 64 cases) are above 0.8 while there is a higher variation in the detection delay. It is the model with feature selection ("FS") that in most cases is lower than 0.8. The detection delay is between 1 and 4.5 and in most cases the TAN model combined with feature selection has the lowest detection delay. Recall that E3 injects sequences where the active power is multiplied by 0.5.

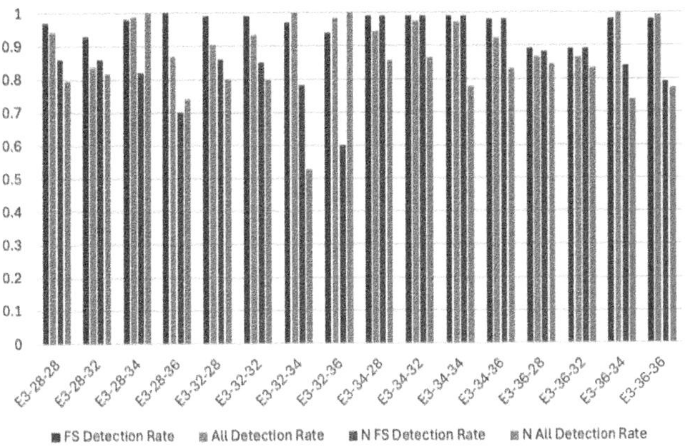

Fig. 5. E3 detection rate.

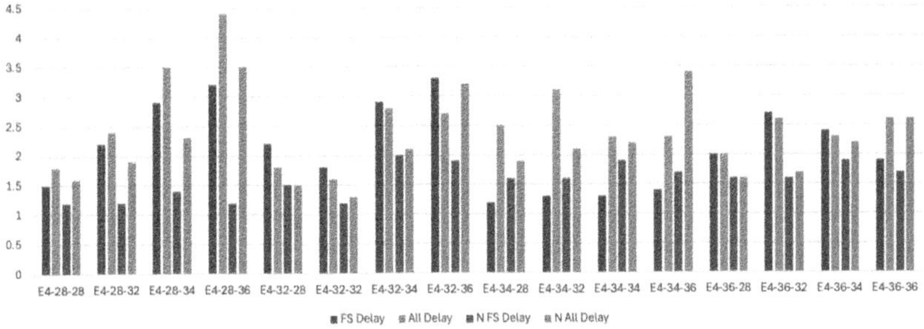

Fig. 6. E4 detection delay.

Figure 6 shows a histogram of detection delay for tests involving error type E4. For E4 there is a higher variation in the detection rate where in some cases the rate is below 0.3 for the NBM model with all variables. Overall, it appears that the NBM combined with feature selection has the highest detection rate (average 0.95). The detection delay ranges from 1 to 4.5.

From the plots, it is clear than performance as expected is high on the inside sample tests. The performance is also high on some of the outside sample tests, while in some cases the performance is useless. The correlation between the time series as measured using Spearmann's correlation coefficient (see Table 1) appears to be informative wrt. detection performance, see, e.g., the results using device 32 data for training and device 34 data for testing compared to device 28 data for training and device 36 data for testing. The first combination (with the highest correlation in the original time series) has better performance than the second combination for all models and error types except for the simplest NBM model with feature selection.

7.2 Unsupervised Learning From Unlabeled Data

Figure 7 shows the structure of a Bayesian network estimated from the unlabeled data for device 28 as an example. The graphs of other Bayesian networks have the same set of variables but different edges. Notice that the model does not contain the classification variable and that the graph is disconnected. Since the data in unlabeled, the same model is applied to detect all three error types. The Bayesian network is used in combination with the conflict measure $\text{CONF}(\epsilon)$ to identify potentially wrong data measurements in a single case ϵ, where ϵ typically has an observation on all variables in the model. If $\text{CONF}(\epsilon) > 0$, this may be an indication of an anomaly. Figure 8, 9 and 10 show the performance of the unsupervised approach on error types E2, E3, and E4, respectively, defined as the lift, FPR, and FPH. The figures show the lift of the model on the cases with a positive conflict measure, the lift on the top-1%, and the FPR and FPH.

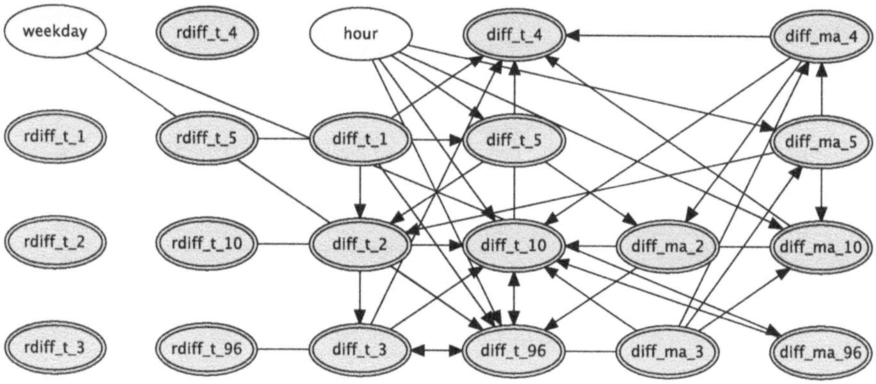

Fig. 7. The graph of the BBN model created for device 28. (Color figure online)

The lift (both on the positive conflict cases and the top-1%) is considerably better on E2 and E4. In some cases, the lift on E3 is less than one. This is the

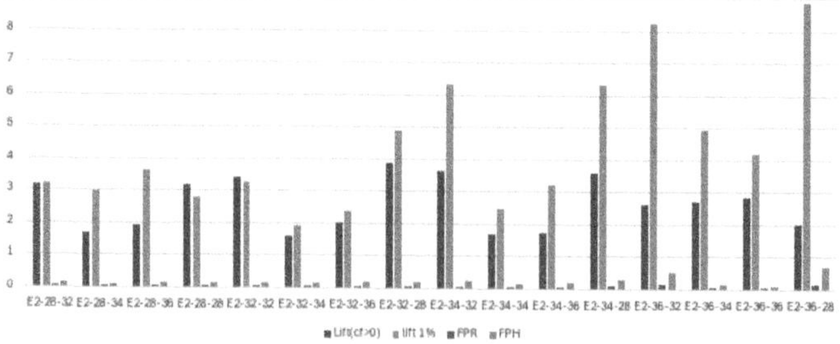

Fig. 8. E2 unsupervised approach.

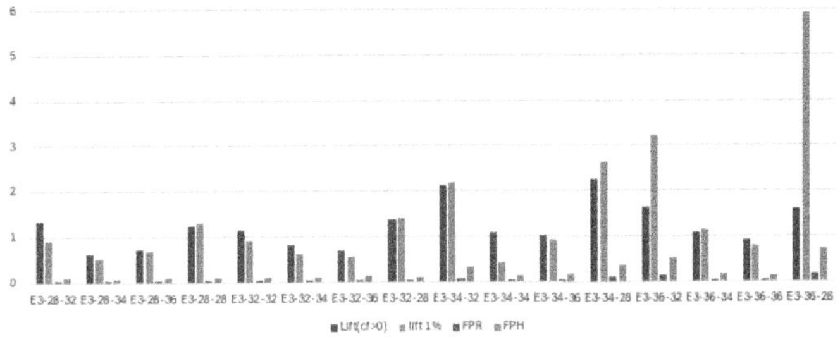

Fig. 9. E3 unsupervised approach.

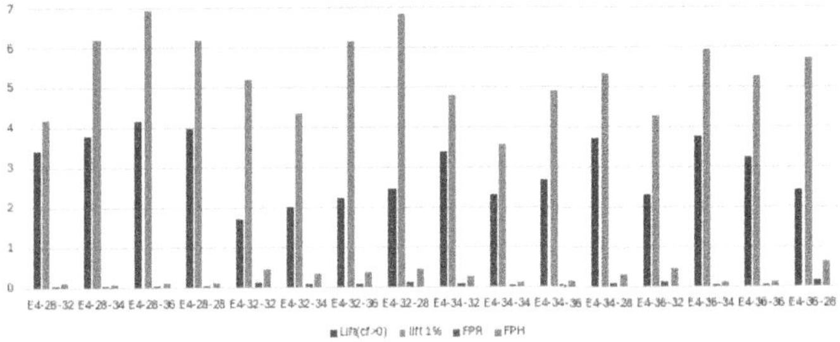

Fig. 10. E4 unsupervised approach.

case, e.g., for configuration E3-28-36 (the least correlated pair of devices). The FPH is in the range 0.06 to 0.71 (the latter is on the configuration E3-28-36, which are the two least correlated time series). The FPR is in the range 0.02 to 0.16 (again the worst performance is for configuration E3-28-36).

8 Conclusion

This paper has presented the application of Bayesian networks to the challenge of detecting wrong data in electricity distribution grids. Three different types of error sequences were randomly injected into active power measurements for four different devices. NBM and TAN models over a set of features derived from the active power measurements were developed from labeled data. The average detection rate was 0.95 with an average detection delay of 1.7 for the TAN. Thus, the detection rate is high and the detection delay is short.

In the case of unlabeled data, a general Bayesian network over the features was developed and applied in combination with the conflict measure. In this case, the lift, FPR, and FPH were computed. The lift range for the cases with $\text{CONF}(\epsilon) > 0$ on error types E2, E3, and E4 was 1.56 to 3.88, 0.63 to 2.25, and 1.73 to 4.17, respectively. For top-1% the lift ranges were 1.9 to 8.9, 0.4 to 5.9 and 4.2 to 7, respectively. These are considered promising results, but further research is needed to improve performance, and other features should be considered at least for the unlabeled data case.

Acknowledgements. This work is performed as part of REDistXAI, which is co-funded by the European Union under grant Eurostars E4748, the German Federal Ministry of Education and Research under grant 01QE2419A, and Innovation Fund Denmark under project no 3150-00040B. We thank the reviewers for valuable comments that have helped to improve the quality of the paper.

References

1. Aalborg University: REDistXAI Project (2023). https://vbn.aau.dk/en/projects/redistxai. Accessed 26 May 2025
2. Cowell, R.G., Dawid, A.P., Lauritzen, S.L., Spiegelhalter, D.J.: Probabilistic Networks and Expert Systems. Springer, Cham (1999)
3. Dufraisse, E., Leray, P., Nedellec, R., Benkhelif, T.: Interactive anomaly detection in mixed tabular data using Bayesian networks. In: Proceedings of the 10th International Conference on Probabilistic Graphical Models. Proceedings of Machine Learning Research, vol. 138, pp. 185–196. PMLR (2020)
4. Friedman, N., Geiger, D., Goldszmidt, M.: Bayesian Network classifiers. Mach. Learn. 1–37 (1997)
5. Hernandez, A., et al.: Detection of anomalies in daily activities using data from smart meters. Sensors **24**(2) (2024). https://doi.org/10.3390/s24020515. https://www.mdpi.com/1424-8220/24/2/515
6. Jensen, F.V., Chamberlain, B., Jensen, F., Nordahl, T.: Analysis in HUGIN of data conflict. In: Proceedings of the Sixth Conference on Uncertainty in Artificial Intelligence, pp. 546–554 (1990)
7. Kjærulff, U.B., Madsen, A.L.: Bayesian Networks and Influence Diagrams: A Guide to Construction and Analysis, 2nd edn. Springer, New York (2013)
8. Koller, D., Friedman, N.: Probabilistic Graphical Models—Principles and Techniques. MIT Press (2009)
9. Lauritzen, S.L.: The EM algorithm for graphical association models with missing data. Comput. Stat. Anal. **19**, 191–201 (1995)
10. Lee, S., et al.: Smart metering system capable of anomaly detection by bi-directional LSTM autoencoder. In: 2022 IEEE International Conference on Consumer Electronics (ICCE), pp. 1–6 (2022). https://doi.org/10.1109/ICCE53296.2022.9730398
11. Madsen, A.L., Jensen, F., Salmerón, A., Langseth, H., Nielsen, T.D.: A parallel algorithm for Bayesian network structure learning from large data sets. Knowl.-Based Syst. **117**, 46–55 (2017). https://doi.org/10.1016/j.knosys.2016.07.031. https://www.sciencedirect.com/science/article/pii/S0950705116302465, vol. Variety and Velocity in Data Science
12. Nielsen, T.D., Jensen, F.V.: On-line alert systems for production plants: a conflict based approach. Int. J. Approximate Reasoning **45**(2), 255–270 (2007)
13. Olsen, R.L., Schwefel, H.P., Madsen, A.L.: Reliable electricity distribution using a digital twin based on explainable artificial intelligence. In: 2024 IEEE International Conference on Communications, Control, and Computing Technologies for Smart Grids (SmartGridComm), pp. 84–85 (2024). https://doi.org/10.1109/SmartGridComm60555.2024.10738050
14. Pearl, J.: Probabilistic Reasoning in Intelligent Systems: Networks of Plausible Inference. Morgan Kaufmann, San Francisco (1988)

15. Samariya, D., Thakkar, A.: A comprehensive survey of anomaly detection algorithms. Ann. Data Sci. **8**(4), 829–850 (2021). https://doi.org/10.1007/s40745-021-00362-9
16. Spirtes, P., Glymour, C., Scheines, R.: Pattern Classification and Scene Analysis. Wiley, New York (1973)
17. Spirtes, P., Glymour, C., Scheines, R.: Causation, Prediction, and Search. Adaptive Computation and Machine Learning, 2nd edn. MIT Press (2000)
18. Sukhobok, D., Nikolov, N., Roman, D.: Tabular data anomaly patterns. In: 2017 International Conference on Big Data Innovations and Applications (Innovate-Data), pp. 25–34 (2017). https://doi.org/10.1109/Innovate-Data.2017.10
19. Wang, P., et al.: A reliability prediction method of smart meter based on dynamic Bayesian networks. In: 12th International Conference on Quality, Reliability, Risk, Maintenance, and Safety Engineering (QR2MSE 2022), vol. 2022, pp. 968–972 (2022). https://doi.org/10.1049/icp.2022.2995
20. Youden, W.J.: Index for rating diagnostic tests. Cancer **3**(1), 32–35 (1950)
21. Zhang, T., Qian, X., Zhou, Y., Xu, G., Wu, M.: Robust clustering and anomaly detection of user electricity consumption behavior based on correntropy. IET Gener. Transm. Distrib. **19** (2025). https://doi.org/10.1049/gtd2.70027
22. Zhou, M., Musilek, P.: Real-time anomaly detection in distribution grids using long short term memory network. In: 2021 IEEE Electrical Power and Energy Conference (EPEC), pp. 208–213 (2021). https://doi.org/10.1109/EPEC52095.2021.9621640
23. Zoppi, T., Bicchierai, I., Brancati, F., Bondavalli, A., Schwefel, H.P.: Deploying a generic threat model for detecting anomalies in a power grid digital twin. In: 2024 IEEE 29th Pacific Rim International Symposium on Dependable Computing (PRDC), pp. 208–215. IEEE, Osaka, Japan (2024). https://doi.org/10.1109/PRDC63035.2024.00039. https://ieeexplore.ieee.org/document/10858902/

Maximum Entropy-Based Quantification for Probability Elicitation in Bayesian Networks

Annet Onnes(✉) and Silja Renooij

Department of Information and Computing Sciences, Utrecht University, Utrecht, The Netherlands
{a.t.onnes,s.renooij}@uu.nl

Abstract. This paper proposes a quantification method to support the elicitation process for Bayesian network construction. The method aims at reducing the number of subjective modelling choices that need to be made to arrive at an initial quantification of a Bayesian network. Our method allows domain experts to express their knowledge in the form of probability constraints. Then, exploiting recent insights concerning the computation of entropy in Bayesian networks, it uses the Maximum Entropy principle to determine a single quantification that makes no assumptions beyond the information provided by the domain experts. The quantification can be used in an iterative probability elicitation process. We provide an overview of our maximum entropy-based quantification method, detail how to express experts' constraints for this technique for entropy maximisation and illustrate the method using an example.

Keywords: Bayesian Networks · Maximum Entropy · Qualitative Constraints · Idioms

1 Introduction

Bayesian networks (BNs) are compact graphical representations of discrete joint probability distributions that have established themselves to be useful for a wide variety of decision-making and prediction tasks, such as in healthcare through diagnostic systems [17] or in banking through fraud detection systems [3]. While they are proven to be versatile, the construction of Bayesian networks in data-poor domains is a challenge [14]. Assessing all point probabilities needed to quantify the complete network remains a labour intensive task, especially difficult to do in a timely manner, due to the often large number of probabilities and the difficulty for experts to communicate their knowledge directly in terms of the sought after numbers [10,24]. Without a complete network specification, however, inference cannot take place nor can the network's behaviour be studied, or only to a very limited extent.

Different approaches have been proposed to allow for studying aspects of the behaviour of a probabilistic model, based on a limited amount of information about the required probabilities. More robust qualitative information in the

K. Sauerwald and M. Thimm (Eds.): ECSQARU 2025, LNAI 16099, pp. 46–60, 2026.
https://doi.org/10.1007/978-3-032-05134-9_4

form of constraints on probabilities can be determined, instead of assessing all point probabilities. These approaches include qualitative probabilistic networks (QPNs), where qualitative signs indicate the direction of influence between variables [27], as well as semi-qualitative methods using intervals [25], which both come with dedicated inference algorithms. Other approaches use any available probabilistic information to constrain the space of all possible joint distributions that can fit a BN, and perform inferences over the resulting set of distributions [9], while credal networks directly allow for inference with imprecise probabilities [6]. In a different setting, to study inductive inference in objective Bayesian inductive logic, so-called *objective* BNs are generated using the maximal entropy principle, to represent a single joint distribution based on a logic statement, where the BN allows for performing the inference [30].

The maximum entropy principle has also be used in constructing Bayesian networks. Wiegerinck and Heskes [29], for example, use this principle in the context of probability elicitation for BNs to address the well-known general problem of finding a single joint distribution that adheres to constraints on its marginals and conditionals [7,8]. When maximising entropy in the joint distribution of a BN, the size of the optimisation problem is exponential in the number of network variables. Moreover, all probability constraints need to be stated in terms of constraints on the joint distribution, typically resulting in exponentially large constraints as well. Since ultimately they are not interested in a joint distribution, but in the Bayesian network parameters, i.e. the probabilities that make up the specification of the network, Wiegerinck and Heskes [29] propose to directly search the space of network parameters and to compute the entropy over the products of network parameters that define the joint distribution. To this end, they rephrase all constraints as constraints on the network parameters. As a result, the classical marginal and conditional probability constraints that they consider are no longer expressed as *linear* functions of joint probabilities, but typically become *non-linear* functions of network parameters. Moreover, the size of the problem remains exponential.

In this paper, we propose a new iterative method for network quantification that aims at producing a complete BN in every iteration, thereby focussing not on obtaining a joint distribution but on the parameters that define the network. Like Wiegerinck and Heskes [29], we employ the maximum entropy principle to arrive at a single network quantification. Contrary to Wiegerinck and Heskes, however, we exploit a BN-specific decomposition of the entropy function, which allows us to specify the optimisation problem directly in terms of the network's parameters, culminating in a more compact representation of many types of constraints and a more efficient computation of the entropy. The resulting network can be used by the domain experts to explore its current behaviour, as well as by modelling experts for further analysis, aiding in the iterative construction process. As such, we obtain a structured, reproducible methodology based on robust domain expert input, thereby creating more clarity and interpretability. Methodologies designed for domain experts to actively participate in the BN construction process, such as BARD [21], can benefit from this approach as it reduces the need for modelling experts and system developers to intervene.

This paper is organised as follows. Section 2 presents some preliminaries, followed by an overview of our quantification method in Sect. 3. In Sect. 4, we detail the technicalities of our optimisation problem, provide a proof of concept in Sect. 5 and conclude the paper with Sect. 6.

2 Preliminaries

In this section, we review Bayesian networks and the computation of entropy.

2.1 Bayesian Networks

A Bayesian network (BN) compactly represents a joint probability distribution $\Pr(\boldsymbol{V})$ over a set of discrete random variables [13]. Each variable $V \in \boldsymbol{V}$ can take on a value v from its domain $\Omega(V)$; in case of binary-valued variables we write v and $\bar{v}$ to denote the two outcomes. We use $\Omega(\boldsymbol{V})$ to denote all combinations of values $\boldsymbol{v}$ of variables $V \in \boldsymbol{V}$.

Formally, a BN $\mathfrak{B} = (G, \Pr)$ has two elements. Firstly, an acyclic directed graph (DAG) $G = (\boldsymbol{V}_G, \boldsymbol{A}_G)$ with nodes $\boldsymbol{V}_G = \boldsymbol{V}$ corresponding to the variables, and directed edges, or arcs, $\boldsymbol{A}_G$ describing the (in)dependences among $\boldsymbol{V}$. Secondly, the BN has local distributions $\Pr(V \mid \boldsymbol{Pa}(V))$ specified in conditional probability tables (CPTs) for each variable $V \in \boldsymbol{V}$, conditional on its parents $\boldsymbol{Pa}(V)$ in the graph G. As such, the BN defines a unique joint distribution that factorises over the graph G:

$$\Pr(\boldsymbol{V}) = \prod_{V \in \boldsymbol{V}} \Pr(V \mid \boldsymbol{Pa}(V)) \tag{1}$$

The set of all CPT-entries $\Pr(v \mid \boldsymbol{pa}(V))$, $v \in \Omega(V), \boldsymbol{pa}(V) \in \Omega(\boldsymbol{Pa}(V)), V \in \boldsymbol{V}$, together are referred to as the *network-* or *CPT-parameters* Θ. Any prior (or: marginal) probability from $\Pr(\boldsymbol{V})$ can be expressed as a multilinear polynomial in Θ, and any posterior (or: conditional) probability as a fraction of two such polynomials [1]; these probabilities can be efficiently computed [13].

Similar to the definition, the construction of BNs consists of two parts [13]. Firstly, the structure, i.e. a DAG G has to be constructed; the second part is the *quantification*, i.e. a probability assessment has to be determined for each parameter $\theta \in \Theta$. The structure and the quantification can be learned from data, when data is available. Manual construction, which is the focus of this paper, is most applicable when data is scarce, or of poor quality. Additionally, even in a data-rich domain there can be cases where we want to model parts of the domain that are not (yet) observable, such as when modelling experts' expectations about future or hypothetical situations in a monitoring context [23]. While not trivial, manually constructing a BN graph with the help of domain experts is considered doable; manually determining the quantification, however, is generally considered a daunting task [10].

2.2 Entropy and its Decomposition

The entropy of a distribution captures the amount of uncertainty in it [12] and is generally calculated over a joint probability distribution $\Pr(\boldsymbol{V})$ as follows:

$$H(\Pr) = E_{\Pr}(-\log \Pr(\boldsymbol{V})) = -\sum_{\boldsymbol{v} \in \Omega(\boldsymbol{V})} \Pr(\boldsymbol{v}) \cdot \log \Pr(\boldsymbol{v})$$

Computing the entropy of the joint distribution using this formula requires summing over a number of value combinations that is exponential in the number of variables. However, when the joint distribution is represented by a BN, we can exploit the factorisation over the conditional probability distributions from Eq. 1 to decompose the entropy calculations [15,26]:

$$H(\Pr) = \sum_{V \in \boldsymbol{V}} H(V \,|\, \boldsymbol{Pa}(V)) \tag{2}$$

where

$$H(V \,|\, \boldsymbol{Pa}(V)) = \sum_{\boldsymbol{pa}(V) \in \Omega(\boldsymbol{Pa}(V))} \Pr(\boldsymbol{pa}(V)) \cdot H(V \,|\, \boldsymbol{pa}(V)) \tag{3}$$

and

$$H(V \,|\, \boldsymbol{pa}(V)) = -\sum_{v \in \Omega(V)} \Pr(v \,|\, \boldsymbol{pa}(V)) \cdot \log \Pr(v \,|\, \boldsymbol{pa}(V)) \tag{4}$$

Note that with Eq. 4, we calculate the entropy for a single conditional distribution from its CPT-parameters alone. Using Eq. 3, a value is computed which summarises the entropy within the CPT, which is a set of distributions. Following this, in Eq. 2, the entropy within the whole BN and thus in the distribution it represents, is calculated. The total number of summations in this decomposition is linear in the number of variables and exponential only in the size of the parent sets.

Although the above decomposition has been known for some time, no efficient algorithm for its computation was available until recently [26]. The only term that is non-local to a CPT, and therefore potentially complex to compute, is $\Pr(\boldsymbol{pa}(V))$ in Eq. 3. Using the standard junction-tree algorithm for inference, nodes V and $\boldsymbol{Pa}(V)$ can always be found in a single clique, which allows for efficiently establishing the marginal $\Pr(\boldsymbol{pa}(V))$ [26].

3 Iterative Quantification Method

In this section, we motivate and present our iterative method for BN quantification based on limited information elicited from domain experts. There are two key elements to this proposed method: constraints as identified by the domain experts and optimising the distribution for maximum entropy. We consider domains in which domain experts are the main source of information. Since experts are a unique and valuable source of information, methods have been developed to utilise this information, as accurately as possible [20,24]. However, *eliciting all* information necessary for a complete probability distribution remains arduous [10]. Aside from eliciting accurately, there is the aspiration to ensure that any and all information that domain experts can provide *is represented* in the BN quantification. To do this, non-invasive methods are preferred, where information from the domain expert can be represented with minimal liaising of the BN engineers between the domain expert and the model [9]. The purpose is to allow experts to share their knowledge in various formats such as *"The probability of lung cancer is lower than that of a cold,"* or *"The probability of a cold is high, say* 90%*"*. All such information needs to be taken into consideration, regardless of the representation of constraints.

Our quantification method is based on using constraints to denote what the BN should represent according to the domain experts. There is a variety of ways to obtain such constraints. To begin, the graphical structure of a BN, which is generally considered easier to elicit from experts than the necessary quantification, can be annotated with qualitative signs (+, −) that in essence constrain the quantification. Such qualitative probabilistic networks (QPNs) are abstractions of Bayesian networks in which the CPTs are replaced by a set of *qualitative influences* and *synergies* (interaction patterns), all defined as CPT-constraints [27,28]. Additionally, in terms of the graphical structure, building blocks that formalise re-occurring reasoning patterns, *idioms* [19], have been developed for various domains, such a medicine [18] and law [11]. To accurately enforce intended reasoning patterns, idioms can be explicitly associated with constraints on the network's CPTs [22]. Idiom constraints can be QPN constraints, or other constraints on probabilities associated with variables in the idiom. Furthermore, to take into account any information provided, we also consider constraints on non-CPT probabilities, such as marginal or joint probabilities.

While the constraints restrict the possible different quantifications Θ, they will rarely provide a single, unique quantification. To determine a unique quantification we utilize the Maximum Entropy (MaxEnt) principle, as no assumptions or other information not evident from the domain expertise should be (accidentally) integrated into the BN through subjective modelling decisions. While maximising entropy in a distribution under constraints is a common optimisation problem and has previously been considered for expert systems [4], applying it for the purpose of quantifying Bayesian networks places additional restrictions on the specification of the problem. A key difference in our method with previous methods, including that by Wiegerinck et al. [29] is the use of a decomposed entropy function. Furthermore, we include different types of constraints further detailed in Sect. 4.1. An overview of our iterative method for MaxEnt-based probability quantification is given in Table 1.

During step (1) the initial network parameters for the optimisation that follows are chosen. In the following proposition, we show that prior to introducing constraints, CPTs with uniform distributions are the unique way to maximise entropy over the joint distribution:

Table 1. Overview Iterative MaxEnt-based Quantification Method

1.	Initialize the BN such that all local distributions are uniform
2.	Elicit constraints from the domain expert(s)
3.	Translate expert constraints into MaxEnt constraints (Definition 1)
4.	Update CPTs with the result of MaxEnt calculations (Problem 5)
Return	to step 2, if needed after testing

Proposition 1. *Consider a Bayesian network* $\mathfrak{B}$. *Then its* $\Pr(\boldsymbol{V})$ *is a uniform distribution if and only if all its conditional distributions* $\Pr(V \mid \boldsymbol{pa}(V))$, $V \in \boldsymbol{V}$, $\boldsymbol{pa}(V) \in \Omega(\boldsymbol{Pa}(V))$, *are uniform.*

Proof. Recall from Eq. 1 that every joint probability $\Pr(\boldsymbol{v})$ is a product of CPT-parameters, one from each CPT.
($\Leftarrow$) If all CPT distributions $\Pr(V \mid \boldsymbol{pa}(V))$ are uniform, then every product of CPT-parameters has the same outcome. Hence the joint distribution is uniform.
($\Rightarrow$) If not all CPT distributions are uniform, then there is at least one CPT distribution $\Pr(V \mid \boldsymbol{pa}(V))$ that is skewed such that one of its parameters $\Pr(v \mid \boldsymbol{pa}(V))$, $v \in \Omega(V)$, is larger than what would be the uniform probability value $1/|\Omega(V)|$, while, necessarily, another parameter $\Pr(v' \mid \boldsymbol{pa}(V))$, $v' \in \Omega(V)$, $v' \neq v$, is smaller than $1/|\Omega(V)|$. Given this, there is a product of CPT-parameters involving only all largest probabilities and another involving all smallest probabilities. Since the former must be larger than the latter, this results in a non-uniform joint distribution $\Pr(\boldsymbol{V})$. Hence, by contraposition, if the joint distribution is uniform, then all CPT distributions must be uniform. □

In step (2) information is elicited from the domain experts, and then formalised in terms of constraints for the MaxEnt optimisation problem in step (3). In Sect. 4.1, we discuss different forms of constraints and how these are formalised, while the MaxEnt optimisation problem itself is formulated in Sect. 4.2. After solving this optimisation problem, the CPTs are updated in step (4). This results in a complete BN quantification that adheres to the constraints provided by the domain expert(s), but contains no further information. Since it is a completely specified network, domain experts can test it to see if the behaviour matches their expectations. It is then also possible to execute a variety of analyses on the complete BN, such as sensitivity analyses [5]. Depending on the results of experimentation and analyses, it is possible to return to step (2) or to continue construction through other methods such as parameter tuning [2].

4 Technical Specification

In this section, we further detail how to transform different types of probability constraints into a form suitable for maximising entropy in its decomposed form.

4.1 Constraints

In this section, we consider different types of probability constraints that could be elicited from domain experts [2,9,27,29]: equality or inequality constraints on prior or posterior probabilities, or constraints on their ratio's or differences. Whereas previous research transformed such constraints into constraints involving functions of *joint probabilities* [9,29], we take the approach of transforming probability constraints into constraints involving functions of *network parameters*. The benefit of this is that many constraints can be more efficiently represented than when represented in terms of the exponentially sized joint distribution.

We discern two aspects that non-exhaustively help determine expert constraints that need to be taken into account. The first aspect that determines a constraint's form is whether it is qualitative or quantitative. When a probability needs to be (above or below) a specific probability value (e.g. $0 \leq \Pr(a) \leq 0.5$), this is a *quantitative* constraint. A *qualitative* constraint compares two probabilities (e.g. $\Pr(a) \geq \Pr(\bar{a})$, or $\Pr(b \mid a) \geq 2\Pr(b \mid \bar{a})$). The second aspect is the kind of probabilities it is expressed in: *network parameters* or *other non-parameter probabilities*. Both ultimately constrain the set of network parameters. Probability constraints on parameters (e.g. $\Pr(b \mid a) \geq \Pr(b \mid \bar{a})$, where $\boldsymbol{Pa}(B) = A$) can be trivially transformed into constraints on a function of those parameters. However, constraints expressed in terms of other probabilities, such as joint or marginal probabilities, require a more complex function, based on the network factorisation. Examples of such constraints are $\Pr(a, b) \geq \Pr(\bar{a}, b)$, where $\boldsymbol{Pa}(B) = A$ or $\Pr(b) \geq 0.7$, where $\boldsymbol{Pa}(B) \neq \emptyset$.

These aspects can be combined in four ways, for which Definition 1 defines transformations of the types of domain expert constraints under consideration, to constraints for the optimisation problem.

Definition 1 (Standardised constraints for optimisation). *Consider a BN $\mathfrak{B}$ with parameter set Θ and let $f^{\mathfrak{B}}_{\Pr(\boldsymbol{a} \mid \boldsymbol{b})}(\Theta)$ be a function that expresses a non-parameter probability $\Pr(\boldsymbol{a} \mid \boldsymbol{b})$, $\boldsymbol{a} \in \Omega(\boldsymbol{A}), \boldsymbol{b} \in \Omega(\boldsymbol{B}), \boldsymbol{A}, \boldsymbol{B} \subset \boldsymbol{V}$, in terms of network polynomials in Θ. Then*

1. *quantitative constraints on a parameter $\theta \in \Theta$ take the form $g(\theta) \geq 0$, with $g(\theta) = c_1 \cdot \theta - c_2, \quad c_1, c_2 \in \mathbb{R}$;*
2. *qualitative constraints between parameters $\theta, \theta' \in \Theta$ take the form $h(\theta, \theta') \geq 0$, with $h(\theta, \theta') = c_1 \cdot \theta - c_2 \cdot \theta' - c_3, \quad c_1, c_2, c_3 \in \mathbb{R}$;*
3. *quantitative constraints on a non-parameter probability $\Pr(\boldsymbol{a} \mid \boldsymbol{b})$ take the form $s(\Theta) \geq 0$, with $s(\Theta) = c_1 \cdot f^{\mathfrak{B}}_{\Pr(\boldsymbol{a} \mid \boldsymbol{b})}(\Theta) - c_2, \quad c_1, c_2 \in \mathbb{R}$;*
4. *qualitative constraints between non-parameter probabilities $\Pr(\boldsymbol{a} \mid \boldsymbol{b})$, $\Pr(\boldsymbol{d} \mid \boldsymbol{e})$ take the form $t(\Theta) \geq 0$, with $t(\Theta) = c_1 \cdot f^{\mathfrak{B}}_{\Pr(\boldsymbol{a} \mid \boldsymbol{b})}(\Theta) - c_2 \cdot f^{\mathfrak{B}}_{\Pr(\boldsymbol{d} \mid \boldsymbol{e})}(\Theta) - c_3, \quad c_1, c_2, c_3 \in \mathbb{R}$.*

Considering the first type of constraint in Definition 1, an example of a quantitative constraint on a parameter as provided by a domain expert would be $\Pr(b \mid a) \geq 0.6$, where $\boldsymbol{Pa}(B) = A$. While this notation is intuitive in accordance with the BN representation, it is not compatible with the formulation of an optimisation problem as in Sect. 4.2. For this, the constraint needs to be reformulated as a function that needs to be non-negative. This can be achieved by rewriting the (in)equalities such that one side is ≥ 0. For this example, $\Pr(b \mid a) \geq 0.6$ becomes $g(\Pr(b \mid a)) \geq 0$ for $g(\Pr(b \mid a)) = \Pr(b \mid a) - 0.6$. For quantitative constraints such as these, the specific probability value (here 0.6) is represented as a constant c_2. If this parameter should be below 0.6 rather than above it, we use $c_1 = -1$ and $c_2 = -0.6$. For the translation of constraints on non-parameter probabilities, such as for example the qualitative constraint $\Pr(b) > \Pr(\bar{b})$, where $\boldsymbol{Pa}(B) = A$, an additional function is required. The function $f^{\mathfrak{B}}(\Theta)$ computes non-parameter probabilities based on the network parameters. This can be done as a polynomial representation based on the network factorisation. To illustrate, consider two binary-valued nodes A and B such that A is the single parent of B, then constraint $\Pr(b) > \Pr(\bar{b})$ will become $t(\Theta) \geq 0$ with $t(\Theta) = f^{\mathfrak{B}}_{\Pr(b)}(\Theta) - f^{\mathfrak{B}}_{\Pr(\bar{b})}(\Theta)$, where e.g. $f^{\mathfrak{B}}_{\Pr(b)}(\Theta) = \Pr(b \mid a) \cdot \Pr(a) + \Pr(b \mid \bar{a}) \cdot \Pr(\mid \bar{a})$. Note that the latter expression contains only network parameters.

Considering that a uniform distribution maximises entropy, we have that our optimisation will try to find parameter values such that the (conditional) distributions in the CPTs are as close to uniform as the constraints allow. A side-effect of this can be that optimisation constraints that reformulate qualitative expert constraint will be satisfied by choosing (almost) equal probabilities, thereby diminishing the impact of the expert constraint. To prevent this, we can ask the domain expert to provide more detailed information, such as a minimal difference or ratio between the probabilities, thereby in essence providing more information about the strength of the relation. The different constants in the formulas from Definition 1 allow for expressing such strengths.

Although the constraints from Definition 1 allow for capturing many types of probability constraints, they are certainly not exhaustive. Consider for example the probability constraints that describe qualitative influences and synergies in QPNs [27,28]. A positive qualitative influence $S^{+}(A, B)$ associated with the arc $A \rightarrow B$ between two binary-valued variables A and B, for example, is defined as $\Pr(b \mid a\boldsymbol{x}) \geq \Pr(b \mid \bar{a}\boldsymbol{x})$ for all $\boldsymbol{x} \in \Omega(\boldsymbol{X})$, $\boldsymbol{X} = Pa(B) \setminus \{A\}$. Such an influence can be directly cast as a set of constraints on functions of type $h(\theta, \theta')$. For non-binary B, however, the definition for $S^{+}(A, B)$ involves cumulative distributions over B, requiring a more complex form of constraint. Moreover, if we include synergistic relations between the parents of a variable in the graph, so-called additive or product synergies, then we need to involve at least 4 CPT-parameters in the constraints. The required forms to capture such constraints are not covered by Definition 1, but they can be easily formulated in a similar fashion. In fact, we will employ a product synergy in our example in Sect. 5

4.2 Optimisation Problem Formulation

We present our formulation of the problem of entropy maximisation under various types of constraints specified for Bayesian networks, exploiting the entropy

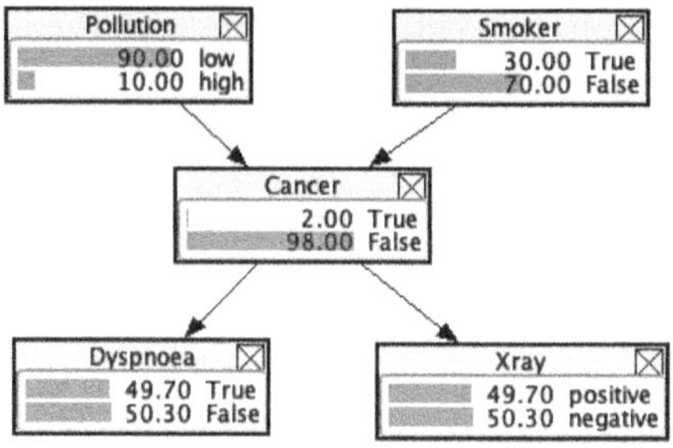

Fig. 1. CANCER-network with prior distributions, where the network quantification is based on constraints 1–8 from Table 2 (screenshot from Hugin GUI)

decomposition (see Sect. 2.2). To select a quantification Θ, we maximise the entropy function $H(\Theta)$ as in Eq. 2, under a set of constraints. The constraints take the reformulated form as in Definition 1. Let G, H, S and T be sets of constraints involving functions of type g, h, s and t, respectively. Moreover, let P be the set of regular probability constraints that ensure that each network parameter is between 0 and 1 and all parameters from the same distribution sum to 1. We then have the following optimisation problem:

$$\begin{aligned} \text{find } & \Theta \\ \text{maximising } & H(\Theta) \\ \text{subject to } & g(\theta) \geq 0, && \text{for all } g \in G \\ & h(\theta, \theta') \geq 0, && \text{for all } h \in H \\ & s(\Theta) \geq 0, && \text{for all } s \in S \\ & t(\Theta) \geq 0, && \text{for all } t \in T \\ & p(\Theta) \geq 0 && \text{for all } p \in P \end{aligned} \tag{5}$$

Since domain experts can provide as few or many constraints of each type, the optimisation can be subject to a list of constraints of any length. Furthermore, parameters, as well as non-parameter probabilities, can be subject to more than one constraint. This means that constraints might not be compatible with each other. In some cases this is obvious ($Pr(v) \leq 0.4$ and $Pr(v) \geq 0.7$), but in other cases this is more complex and beyond the scope of this paper.

5 Demonstration

In this section, we demonstrate the MaxEnt-based quantification method using an implementation of the concepts from previous sections. We aim at quantifying a small example network for diagnosing lung cancer, based on a variety of constraints. As a source of domain knowledge, we use the CANCER network as introduced in Korb & Nicholson [16] and available in the **bnlearn** repository.[1] We adopt the structure of this network, shown in Fig. 1.

[1] https://www.bnlearn.com/bnrepository/discrete-small.html.

Table 2. Overview of elicited constraints for the CANCER-network (all variables, represented by their first letter, are binary-valued)

1.	$S^+(P,C)$:	$\Pr(c \mid p, s_i) \geq \Pr(c \mid \bar{p}, s_i)$ for all $s_i \in \Omega(S)$	6.	$\Pr(\bar{s}) \geq 0.7$
2.	$S^+(S,C)$:	$\Pr(c \mid s, p_i) \geq \Pr(c \mid \bar{s}, p_i)$ for all $p_i \in \Omega(P)$	7.	$\Pr(p) \leq 0.1$
3.	$S^+(C,X)$:	$\Pr(x \mid c) \geq \Pr(x \mid \bar{c})$	8.	$\Pr(c) \leq 0.02$
4.	$S^+(C,D)$:	$\Pr(d \mid c) \geq \Pr(d \mid \bar{c})$		
5.	$X^-(\{P,S\},c)$:	$\Pr(c \mid p, s) \cdot \Pr(c \mid \bar{p}, \bar{s}) \leq \Pr(c \mid p, \bar{s}) \cdot \Pr(c \mid \bar{p}, s)$		

We extract information from the original network to simulate domain expert constraints (see Table 2). Constraints 1–4 capture reasoning patterns expected in the medical Risk Factor and Manifestation idioms, introduced by Kyrimi et al. [18], that actually fit the original example network: air pollution and smoking both *increase* the probability of lung cancer, while lung cancer *increases* the probability of the manifestations dyspnoea and a positive X-ray result. Such reasoning patterns correspond to positive qualitative influences S^+ [22,27].

Constraint 5 follows from another QPN constraint that captures explaining away between the two risk factors [28]. This negative synergy X^- indicates that when cancer is diagnosed and one of the risk factors is identified, the probability of the other also being present drops. Constraints 6 and 7 are quantitative constraints on the priors of the risk factors, which could be available as general statistics. Finally, for constraint 8, we consider that the marginal probability of lung cancer in the general population is rather slim, say less than 2%. Since the probability of cancer is not a CPT-probability in the network, we have a quantitative non-parameter probability constraint. Constraints 5–8 are again consistent with the information in the original network.

We now transform the constraints from Table 2 into constraints suitable for the optimisation as defined in Problem 5. For this example, we take a default strength for qualitative constraints to be a factor 1.2; for quantitative constraints there is no minimum difference. Following Definition 1, constraint 1, for example, results in two constraints of type $h(\theta, \theta') \geq 0$, with

$$h_1(\Pr(c \mid p, s), \Pr(c \mid \bar{p}, s)) = \Pr(c \mid p, s) - 1.2 \cdot \Pr(c \mid \bar{p}, s), \text{ and}$$
$$h_2(\Pr(c \mid p, \bar{s}), \Pr(c \mid \bar{p}, \bar{s})) = \Pr(c \mid p, \bar{s}) - 1.2 \cdot \Pr(c \mid \bar{p}, \bar{s})$$

Constraints 2–4 are transformed similarly.

Although Definition 1 does not directly provide a standard form for the negative synergy, we can build on the existing forms to formulate new constraint functions. For constraint 5, we define $e(\theta_1, \theta_2, \theta_3, \theta_4) = h(\theta_1 \cdot \theta_2, \theta_3 \cdot \theta_4) \geq 0$, with $e(\Pr(c \mid p, \bar{s}), \Pr(c \mid \bar{p}, s), \Pr(c \mid p, s), \Pr(c \mid \bar{p}, \bar{s})) =$

$$\Pr(c \mid p, \bar{s}) \cdot \Pr(c \mid \bar{p}, s) - 1.2 \cdot \Pr(c \mid p, s) \cdot \Pr(c \mid \bar{p}, \bar{s})$$

Note the inverted signs in the latter due to the original constraint being $\leq$. Constraints 6 and 7 transform into: $g_1(\Pr(\bar{s})) = \Pr(\bar{s}) - 0.7 \geq 0$ and $g_2(\Pr(p)) =$

Table 3. Overview of quantifications, given constraints from Table 2 and their resulting differences in performance (AUC) and divergence (KL)

Quantification Q:	original (P)	uniform	1–4	1–5	1–7	1–5, 8	1–8
AUC:	0.9458	0.5001	0.9090	0.9180	0.9159	0.9263	0.9260
KL(P, Q):	0	1.971	1.395	1.324	0.947	1.029	0.381

$0.1 - \Pr(p) \geq 0$. Constraint 8 concerns a non-parameter probability of the type $s(\Theta) \geq 0$ in Definition 1, where $s(\Theta) = -f^{\mathfrak{B}}_{\Pr(c)}(\Theta) + 0.02$ and $f^{\mathfrak{B}}_{\Pr(c)}(\Theta)$ is the polynomial that describes $\Pr(c)$ in terms of CPT-parameters.

Using existing Python implementations for optimisation and BN inference, we implemented our MaxEnt-based quantification method.[2] Using the structure of the original network, together with the transformed constraints, we applied the method and generated 5 different quantifications for five combinations of constraints from Table 2. As an example, Fig. 1 shows the prior distributions for all variables computed from one of these quantifications: the one given all constraints 1–8.

To analyse the five generated BNs, we tested their ability to predict the value of Cancer, given evidence in all other nodes. We generated a test data set consisting of 10,000 cases (combinations of value assignments to each of the networks variables) from the original network (108 cases with *Cancer*=*true*) and let each generated BN predict the value of *Cancer* given the rest of the values of the case. To determine the quality of the prediction we considered the area under the curve (AUC), which summarises the accuracy over all possible cut-off points for a successful prediction. Additionally, to give insight into the effect of adding constraints, we calculate the Kullback-Leibler (KL) divergence between the joint distributions based on each generated quantification (Q) and the original one (P). The quantification labelled as uniform is generated given no constraints.

The results are shown in Table 3 for each quantification, including the original one and the uniform one. We note that a decrease in KL-divergence does not necessarily coincide with an increase in performance.[3] We observe that the networks based on each of the quantifications generated with constraints by far outperform the one with a uniform distribution. Moreover, when the quantification is merely constrained by the positive influences resulting from the idioms (constraints 1–4), the performance already jumps to 0.9090. This shows how idioms extended with constraints can be used to generate a quantification that can already be insightful.

[2] For code see: https://git.science.uu.nl/ics/is/MEQ-PEBN/meq-peb. Libraries used include SciPy (https://scipy.org/) and pyAgrum (https://pyagrum.readthedocs.io/.

[3] While constraints 6 and 7 affect the values of the parameters in $\Pr(c \mid S, P)$ by weighing the entropy in the CPT during optimisation, variables S and P are initiated to test performance, thereby neutralising the effect of the priors on the prediction.

6 Discussion and Conclusion

The example in the previous section is a proof of concept for our method, where we use existing optimisation methods to demonstrate the ease with which multiple quantifications can be generated. It demonstrates how it creates opportunities for further analyses of a network's behaviour, as well as showing how this quantification method can enhance iterative elicitation methods. Getting a fully quantified network allows experts to test their intuitions about the model, which is especially beneficial for elicitation methods where the domain expert is the driver of the process, such as in the BARD method. The BARD method is an iterative, group elicitation method based on Delphi social processes that benefits from completed quantifications as they can help the domain experts in discussions about what behaviour they desire and expect [21].

Our MaxEnt-based quantification method combines several strategies, including using the decomposed entropy function and existing optimisation methods. The advantage of using the decomposition, is that the optimisation directly finds a quantification in terms of network parameters, rather than in terms of the joint probabilities that maximise entropy; the latter would require an additional step to determine the BN's network parameters, which is not trivial. Furthermore, with the network parameters as free variables in the optimisation problem, it allows many constraints to be directly and compactly expressed, such as QPN and idiom constraints. Moreover, it ensures that constraints on parameters are linear constraints in the optimisation problem.

When the generation of quantifications is used as part of an iterative elicitation method, the aim is to quickly and relatively easily quantify an entire network. With only linear constraints appropriately cast into functions for Problem 5, the optimisation can take place using more efficient convex optimisation solutions. This would to be the case when focussing on modular construction methods, for example when using idioms or other fragments in which parameter constraints are represented. A different approach to investigate, given only CPT-constraints, could be maximising the local entropy of the CPTs in topological ordering, thereby potentially fixing the $Pa(V)$ term in the entropy function during a local optimisation process.

We argued that domain experts should be able to provide information in a non-restricted way. Exploiting the decomposition ensures that local CPT-constraints, that were previously non-linear, are now expressed linearly. Given this, we broadened the types of probabilities that could be constrained. Even though non-linear constraints limit the available optimisation methods that we can employ, a straightforward implementation using existing libraries in Python, with the entropy function implemented according to Eq. 2, can easily handle the problem type and size we demonstrated in Sect. 5. Based on this proof of concept, future research can consider how optimisation methods can be further exploited to leverage characteristics that hold for Problem 5 and the BN factorisation. For example, to remove the need for inference in the network in the entropy computations, it is possible to opt for approximating the entropy function by leaving out the term $\Pr(\boldsymbol{pa}(V))$ in Eq. 3. Especially early on in the elicitation procedure, this is realistic, as it is equivalent to assuming the parents are uniformly distributed. Otherwise, as noted above, using the standard junction-tree algorithm, the marginal $\Pr(\boldsymbol{pa}(V))$ can efficiently be inferred [26].

In this paper, we introduced a quantification method that bridges the gap between domain experts' constraints and a full Bayesian network quantification. We exploit how entropy is calculated efficiently using the network factorisation through a decomposed entropy function, and the way maximum entropy imposes uniformity in all CPTs unless otherwise constrained. We presented how a wide variety of domain expert constraints are transformed into functions in the BN's parameters, such that they are suitable optimisation constraints. Finally, we showed how the combination of the decomposed entropy function and existing optimisation functions, allowed us to produce full quantifications based on many forms of constraints. Being able to produce these quantifications, with ease and requiring minimal modelling expertise, is valuable for human-centred, iterative elicitation processes where the end-users and stakeholders are the driving force for the BN construction.

Acknowledgments. This research was supported by the Hybrid Intelligence Centre, a 10-year programme funded by the Dutch Ministry of Education, Culture and Science through the Dutch Research Council (NWO), https://hybrid-intelligence-centre.nl.

Disclosure of Interests. The authors have no competing interests to declare that are relevant to the content of this article.

References

1. Castillo, E., Gutiérrez, J.M., Hadi, A.S.: Parametric structure of probabilities in bayesian networks. In: Froidevaux, C., Kohlas, J. (eds.) ECSQARU 1995. LNCS, vol. 946, pp. 89–98. Springer, Heidelberg (1995). https://doi.org/10.1007/3-540-60112-0_11
2. Chan, H., Darwiche, A.: When do numbers really matter? J. Artif. Intell. Res. **17**, 265–287 (2002). https://doi.org/10.1613/JAIR.967
3. Chandola, V., Banerjee, A., Kumar, V.: Anomaly detection: a survey. ACM Comput. Surv. **41**(3), 1–58 (2009). https://doi.org/10.1145/1541880.1541882
4. Cheeseman, P.: A method of computing generalized Bayesian probability values for expert systems. In: IJCAI'83: Proceedings of the Eighth International Joint Conference on Artificial Intelligence, vol. 1, pp. 198–202. Morgan Kaufmann Publishers, San Francisco, CA, US (1983)
5. Coupé, V., van der Gaag, L.C., Habbema, J.: Sensitivity analysis: an aid for belief-network quantification. Knowl. Eng. Rev. **15**, 215–232 (2000)
6. Cozman, F.G.: Credal networks. Artif. Intell. **120**(2), 199–233 (2000). https://doi.org/10.1016/S0004-3702(00)00029-1
7. Cramer, E.: Probability measures with given marginals and conditionals: i-projections and conditional iterative proportional fitting. Stat. Risk Model. **18**(3), 311–330 (2000). https://doi.org/10.1524/strm.2000.18.3.311
8. Csiszár, I.: I-divergence geometry of probability distributions and minimization problems. Ann. Probab. **3**(1), 146–158 (1975)

9. Druzdzel, M.J., van der Gaag, L.C.: Elicitation of probabilities for belief networks: combining qualitative and quantitative information. In: Besnard, P., Hanks, S. (eds.) Proceedings of the Eleventh Conference on Uncertainty in Artificial Intelligence (UAI'95), pp. 141–148. Morgan Kaufmann Publishers Inc., San Francisco, CA, US (1995)
10. Druzdzel, M.J., van der Gaag, L.C.: Building probabilistic networks: "where do the numbers come from?". IEEE Trans. Knowl. Data Eng. **12**(4), 481–486 (2000)
11. Fenton, N., Neil, M., Lagnado, D.A.: A general structure for legal arguments about evidence using bayesian networks. Cogn. Sci. **37**(1), 61–102 (2013). https://doi.org/10.1111/cogs.12004
12. Jaynes, E.: On the rationale of maximum-entropy methods. Proc. IEEE **70**(9), 939–952 (1982). https://doi.org/10.1109/PROC.1982.12425
13. Jensen, F.V., Nielsen, T.D.: Bayesian Networks and Decision Graphs, 2nd edn. Springer, Heidelberg (2007)
14. Kjærulff, U.B., Madsen, A.L.: Bayesian Networks and Influence Diagrams: A Guide to Construction and Analysis, Information Science and Statistics, vol. 22. Springer, New York (2013). https://doi.org/10.1007/978-1-4614-5104-4
15. Koller, D., Friedman, N.: Probabilistic Graphical Models: Principles and Techniques. MIT Press, Cambridge (2009)
16. Korb, K.B., Nicholson, A.E.: Bayesian Artificial Intelligence. CRC Press, Boca Raton (2011)
17. Kyrimi, E., McLachlan, S., Dube, K., Neves, M.R., Fahmi, A., Fenton, N.: A comprehensive scoping review of bayesian networks in healthcare: past, present and future. Artif. Intell. Med. **117**, 102108 (2021). https://doi.org/10.1016/j.artmed.2021.102108
18. Kyrimi, E., Neves, M.R., McLachlan, S., Neil, M., Marsh, W., Fenton, N.: Medical idioms for clinical bayesian network development. J. Biomed. Inform. **108**, 103495 (2020). https://doi.org/10.1016/j.jbi.2020.103495
19. Neil, M., Fenton, N., Nielson, L.: Building large-scale bayesian networks. Knowl. Eng. Rev. **15**(3), 257–284 (2000). https://doi.org/10.1017/S0269888900003039
20. Nunes, J., Barbosa, M., Silva, L., Gorgônio, K., Almeida, H., Perkusich, A.: Issues in the probability elicitation process of expert-based Bayesian networks. In: Enhanced Expert Systems. IntechOpen (2018). https://doi.org/10.5772/intechopen.81602
21. Nyberg, E.P., et al.: Bard: a structured technique for group elicitation of bayesian networks to support analytic reasoning. Risk Anal. **42**(6), 1155–1178 (2022). https://doi.org/10.1111/risa.13759
22. Onnes, A., Dastani, M., Dobbe, R., Renooij, S.: Extending idioms for Bayesian network construction with qualitative constraints. In: Lesot, M.J., Vieira, S., Reformat, M.Z., Carvalho, J.P., Batista, F., Bouchon-Meunier, B., Yager, R.R. (eds.) Information Processing and Management of Uncertainty in Knowledge-Based Systems. LNNS, vol. 1174, pp. 415–426. Springer, Cham (2024). https://doi.org/10.1007/978-3-031-74003-9_33
23. Onnes, A., Dastani, M., Renooij, S.: Bayesian network conflict detection for normative monitoring of black-box systems. In: The International FLAIRS Conference Proceedings, vol. 36 (2023). https://doi.org/10.32473/flairs.36.133240
24. Renooij, S.: Probability elicitation for belief networks: issues to consider. Knowl. Eng. Rev. **16**(3), 255–269 (2001). https://doi.org/10.1017/S0269888901000145
25. Renooij, S., van der Gaag, L.C.: From qualitative to quantitative probabilistic networks. In: Darwiche, A., Friedman, N. (eds.) Proceedings of the Eighteenth Conference on Uncertainty in Artificial Intelligence, pp. 422–429 (2002)

26. Scutari, M.: Entropy and the kullback-leibler divergence for bayesian networks: computational complexity and efficient implementation. Algorithms **17**(1), 24 (2024). https://doi.org/10.3390/a17010024
27. Wellman, M.P.: Fundamental concepts of qualitative probabilistic networks. Artif. Intell. **44**(3), 257–303 (1990). https://doi.org/10.1016/0004-3702(90)90026-V
28. Wellman, M., Henrion, M.: Explaining 'explaining away'. IEEE Trans. Pattern Anal. Mach. Intell. **15**(3), 287–292 (1993). https://doi.org/10.1109/34.204911
29. Wiegerinck, W., Heskes, T.: Probability assessment with maximum entropy in Bayesian networks. In: Lucas, P., van der Gaag, L.C., Abu-Hanna, A. (eds.) AIME'01 Workshop Bayesian Models In Medicine, pp. 71–80 (2001)
30. Williamson, J.: Where do we stand on maximal entropy? In: Hosni, H., Landes, J. (eds.) Perspectives on Logics for Data-driven Reasoning, vol. 35, pp. 39–61. Springer, Cham (2024). https://doi.org/10.1007/978-3-031-77892-6_3

Involving Uncertainty in Bayesian Network Tuning

Janneke H. Bolt[1,2(✉)], Arjen Hommersom[2], and Silja Renooij[1]

[1] Department of Information and Computing Sciences, Utrecht University, Utrecht, The Netherlands
j.h.bolt@uu.nl

[2] Department of Computer Science, Open University of the Netherlands, Heerlen, The Netherlands

Abstract. Parameter tuning in Bayesian networks is the process of adapting network parameters in order to enforce a predefined query response. Existing approaches select and adapt parameters based on their values in the partial derivatives of the query response. This approach is based on the assumption that a minimal change in parameters is preferred. In this paper we argue for including the uncertainty in the current parameter estimates in the selection and adaptation of the parameters. We propose a new evaluation criterion, for networks with binary-valued variables, together with new tuning heuristics that take this higher-order uncertainty into account. We evaluate our proposal and observe in our experiments that two of the proposed heuristics that take this additional uncertainty into account consistently outperform tuning based on gradients alone.

Keywords: Bayesian networks · Parameter tuning · Uncertainty-based

1 Introduction

Bayesian network tuning is the adaptation of the parameters of a Bayesian network to enforce some desired query response [1–3,5,6]. In tuning, choices have to be made with respect to which parameters to adapt and, if more than one parameter is to be adapted, with respect to the relative amount of the individual parameter changes. An often used criterion for judging parameter adaptations is the minimality of the total amount of necessary change of the parameter values. With this criterion, the partial derivatives of the query response, as expressed in the network's parameters, with respect to these parameters can be used to guide the tuning. More specifically, (a subset of) the parameters with the highest local effect are selected, and subsequently adapted proportional to their individual local effects [2,6]. This heuristic approximates locally the minimal parameter changes needed. In the rest of this paper we will call this the *gradient-tuning* heuristic, or also standard tuning.

A focus on minimal parameter changes, however, may result in adapted parameter values that are not most likely given the available knowledge. The

K. Sauerwald and M. Thimm (Eds.): ECSQARU 2025, LNAI 16099, pp. 61–74, 2026.
https://doi.org/10.1007/978-3-032-05134-9_5

parameters of a Bayesian network often will just be estimates computed from a limited amount of data or based on the assessments of an expert. The uncertainty in the parameter estimates thus may differ between the different parameters, depending on the data or on the knowledge of the expert. We advocate that the uncertainty in the parameter estimates also constitutes a reasonable ground for network tuning; it is reasonable to apply a larger change to parameters that have a high degree of uncertainty than to those that are more certain. In this paper, therefore, we explore the possibility of involving the uncertainty of the network's parameters in network tuning. First we propose an evaluation criterion for judging a single parameter change, and two derived criteria for judging multiple parameter changes, that involve the uncertainty of the parameters. We then give some new tuning heuristics that take the uncertainty of the parameters into account, and investigate the performance of these heuristics with respect to the proposed evaluation criteria.

2 Preliminaries

2.1 Bayesian Networks

A Bayesian network is a concise representation of a joint probability distribution Pr over a set of discrete stochastic variables that consists of an acyclic directed graph and a set of (conditional) probability tables (CPTs) [9,11]. In the sequel we will indicate single variables by uppercase letters (V); lowercase letters (v_i) indicate a value assignment to one of V's values in $\boldsymbol{\Omega}(V)$. In this paper we restrict ourselves to binary variables, writing v and $\overline{v}$ to denote the two possible instantiations of a variable V. For sets of variables we will use bold face letters. The nodes of the graph represent the variables of the modelled distribution[1] and the structure of the graph captures, as far as possible, the independences of this distribution according to the d-separation criterion. The joint distribution now factorises over the CPTs associated with the nodes in the graph. Each CPT-row consists of the conditional probabilities $\Pr(v_i \mid \pi_j^V)$, $v_i \in \boldsymbol{\Omega}(V)$, of a variable V given a specific value assignment π_j^V to its parents in the graph. Note that the parameter values of a CPT-row sum to 1. The probability of a joint value assignment $\mathbf{v}$ to $\mathbf{V}$ now equals

$$\Pr(\mathbf{v}) = \prod_{V \in \mathbf{V}} \Pr(v_i \mid \pi_j^V) \tag{1}$$

where v_i and π_j^V are compatible with $\mathbf{v}$. Using this formula, any probability of interest of the distribution can be computed. In this paper we consider a probability of interest $\Pr(h \mid \mathbf{e})$ that some hypothesis H is true given observations for a, possibly empty, set of variables $\mathbf{E}$. This probability equals:

$$\Pr(h \mid \mathbf{e}) = \frac{\sum_{\mathbf{w}} \Pr(\mathbf{w}, h, \mathbf{e})}{\sum_{\mathbf{w}, h_i} \Pr(\mathbf{w}, h_i, \mathbf{e})} \tag{2}$$

[1] We will use the terms nodes and variables interchangeably.

with $\mathbf{W} = \mathbf{V}\backslash(\{H\} \cup \mathbf{E})$, and $\Pr(\mathbf{w}, h_i, \mathbf{e})$ factorising according to Eq. 1.

The CPT-entries required for a Bayesian network are often more generally referred to as network *parameters*. To quantify the network, estimates for these parameters must be obtained from data and/or through expert elicitation. Typically, these estimates are uncertain. In this paper, we make the common assumption that the parameters are in essence random variables, θ, that follow a beta-distribution, which is the special case of a Dirichlet distribution for binary variables [8]. A beta distribution is continuous on the 0–1 interval and is fully characterized by its shape parameters α and β. Its mean $\mathbb{E}[\theta]$ and variance $\mathrm{Var}[\theta]$ are:

$$\mathbb{E}[\theta] = \frac{\alpha}{\alpha+\beta}, \quad \mathrm{Var}[\theta] = \frac{\alpha \cdot \beta}{(\alpha+\beta)^2 \cdot (\alpha+\beta+1)}$$

In this paper we now assume that we know $\mathbb{E}[\theta]$ and $\mathrm{Var}[\theta]$ of all network parameters θ, either obtained through (Bayesian) learning from data, or elicited from experts[2]. The mean $\mathbb{E}[\theta]$ is used as value for the corresponding CPT-entry, which we will indicate by θ^o (with $\boldsymbol{\theta}^o$ the set of all CPT-entries); slightly abusing notation, we will indicate the parameter of the same CPT-row as θ by $\overline{\theta} = 1 - \theta$. The probability distribution of θ is stored outside the network.

2.2 Network Tuning

Network tuning is one of the tools used to fine-tune a Bayesian network in the final stages of construction [6]. Suppose some query output of interest $\Pr(h \,|\, \mathbf{e})$ should equal q_t according to a domain expert, whereas the actual query response of the network equals q_o. The network can then be tuned by adapting one (one-way tuning) or more (more-way tuning) CPT-entries in order to achieve q_t as output. Note that when the value of a CPT-entry is changed, the entries in the same CPT-row have to be co-varied, to ensure that they add up to one. For multivalued variables, parameters are usually co-varied proportionally; for binary variables co-variation is trivial since $\overline{\theta} = 1 - \theta$.

Every probability that can be computed from a Bayesian network, can be written as a function of CPT-entries [4]. As such, Eq. 2 can be expressed as a function $f_{\Pr(h \,|\, \mathbf{e})}(\mathbf{x})$, where all CPT-entries in the factorisation are replaced by $\mathbf{x}$. All co-varying CPT-entries of $x_i \in \mathbf{x}$ are expressed as a function of x_i, thereby guaranteeing that CPT-rows still add up to 1 after tuning.

The function $f_{\Pr(h \,|\, \mathbf{e})}(\mathbf{x_s})$ specifies how $\Pr(h \,|\, \mathbf{e})$ will change if the $x_i \in \mathbf{x_s} \subseteq \mathbf{x}$ deviate from their values in the CPTs, while all CPT-entries associated with $\mathbf{x}\backslash\mathbf{x_s}$ remain fixed. This function is important for tuning, since from this function we can determine combinations of values $\mathbf{x}_\mathbf{s}^*$ for $\mathbf{x_s}$ such that the network would return $\Pr(h \,|\, \mathbf{e}) = q_t$ if $\mathbf{x}_\mathbf{s}^*$ were used as CPT-entries instead. Note that each CPT-entry in $\mathbf{x_s}$ acts as a variable x_i for function f, whereas at the same time its initial value is the mean θ_i^o of the stochastic variable θ_i that we associate with

[2] Note that this implies that we also know the α and β of these distributions, and vice versa.

the CPT-entry. To avoid confusion as much as possible, we will use the index i such that e.g. θ_1 and x_1 relate to the same CPT-entry.

In tuning, choices have to be made about which CPT-entries to adapt and, if more than one entry is adapted, about the relative amount of the individual CPT-entry changes applied. In an existing tuning approach, the goal is to keep the total amount of change applied to CPT-entries as low as possible [2,5].

A heuristic to achieve this goal is based on the gradient of $f_{\Pr(h\,|\,\mathbf{e})}(\mathbf{x})$. Various algorithms exist to compute such partial derivatives from a Bayesian network efficiently [7,10]. Note that the complexity of these algorithms is the same as the complexity of algorithms for network inference, which is in worst-case exponential in the treewidth of the network. For the choice which CPT-entries to adapt, first the gradient of $f_{\Pr(h\,|\,\mathbf{e})}(\mathbf{x})$ at $\boldsymbol{\theta}^o$ is computed. This gradient is used to select, in n-way tuning, the n CPT-entries that, at $\boldsymbol{\theta}^o$, have the strongest effect on $\Pr(h\,|\,\mathbf{e})$. These CPT-entries are then selected as the actual variables $\mathbf{x_s}$. The relative amount of change applied to these variables is proportional to their contribution to the gradient of $f_{\Pr(h\,|\,\mathbf{e})}(\mathbf{x})$ at $\boldsymbol{\theta}^o$. We will call this the *gradient tuning* heuristic, which is defined in more detail below [1,2].

Definition 1 (gradient tuning). *Let $\Pr(h\,|\,\mathbf{e})$ be a query response of a Bayesian network that is to be tuned to q_t, let $\nabla_i f(\boldsymbol{\theta}^o) = \partial/\partial x_i\ f_{\Pr(h\,|\,\mathbf{e})}(\boldsymbol{\theta}^o)$ be the partial derivative of $f_{\Pr(h\,|\,\mathbf{e})}(\mathbf{x})$ with respect to x_i at $\mathbf{x} = \boldsymbol{\theta}^o$ and let $\mathbf{x_s} = \{x_1, \ldots, x_n\}$ (not necessarily ordered) be the n variables in $\mathbf{x}$ with n-highest values $|\nabla_i f(\boldsymbol{\theta}^o)|$. Then in n-way gradient tuning all $x_i \in \{x_2 \ldots x_n\}$ of $f_{\Pr(h\,|\,\mathbf{e})}(\mathbf{x_s})$ are expressed in x_1 by*

$$x_i = \frac{\nabla_i f(\boldsymbol{\theta}^o)}{\nabla_1 f(\boldsymbol{\theta}^o)} \cdot (x_1 - \theta_1^o) + \theta_i^o$$

with θ_i^o the original value of the CPT-entry that is replaced by x_i. The tuned parameter values $\mathbf{x_s^*}$ are now found by solving

$$f_{\Pr(h\,|\,\mathbf{e})}(x_1) = q_t$$

In the above heuristic, the dimension of the problem is reduced to one by linking the change in all x_i, $i > 1$, to the change in x_1 [2]. Note that in general the equation $f_{\Pr(h\,|\,\mathbf{e})}(x_1) = q_t$ is too complex to be expressed and computed explicitly. The value of x_1^*, however, can be found by linear optimization using a single network computation per iteration.

3 Involving Uncertainty in Parameter Tuning

As described in Sect. 2.1, the parameters of a Bayesian network can be viewed as random variables themselves with, in the binary case, a beta distribution over their values. This implies that the variance in the parameter estimates may differ between the different parameters. We propose to involve this uncertainty in parameter tuning, since it is reasonable to apply a larger change to parameters that have a high degree of uncertainty than to those that seem more certain. To involve the uncertainty we need criteria to judge whether some parameter change is preferred over another parameter change that includes this uncertainty. To the best of our knowledge no such criteria exist. In the next section, therefore, we define such criteria. First we define a criterion for single parameter changes, and then we give two criteria based on this single parameter criterion for judging multiple parameter changes. In Sect. 3.2 we propose three tuning heuristics that are aimed at finding the best tuning with respect to the proposed criteria.

3.1 Uncertainty-Based Evaluation Criterion

A straightforward and feasible option for a criterion to compare single parameter adaptations that involves the parameter uncertainty, is to use the cumulative distribution function F_θ of θ. Let x^* be a value proposed for θ. If $x^* < \theta^o$, then determine $F_\theta(x^*)$, the probability that θ equals x^* or is even lower; if $x^* > \theta^o$ then determine $1 - F_\theta(x^*)$, the probability that θ equals x^* or is even higher. Higher values of this criterion thus are preferred. The definition is given below.

Definition 2 (evaluation criterion $ucr(x^*)$). *Let θ be a binary network parameter with $\theta^o = \mathbb{E}[\theta]$, let F_θ be the cumulative distribution over θ, and let $x^* \neq \theta^o$ be a proposed value of θ then*

$$ucr(x^*) = \begin{cases} F_\theta(x^*) & \text{if } x^* < \theta^o \\ 1 - F_\theta(x^*) & \text{if } x^* > \theta^o \end{cases}$$

Note that $ucr(x^*)$ depends only on the parameter θ and not on which query response is tuned.

The ucr-value of the co-varying parameter equals the ucr-value of the varying parameter, as is substantiated in the proposition below.

Proposition 1. *Let θ be a parameter of a binary Bayesian network, $\overline{\theta} = 1-\theta$ the complementary parameter in the same CPT-row, x^* a value of θ and $\overline{x}^* = 1-x^*$ the associated co-adapted value of $\overline{\theta}$. Then, $ucr(x^*) = ucr(\overline{x}^*)$.*

Proof. First, consider $x^* > \theta^o$. Then $1 - x^* < 1 - \theta^o$ and thus $\overline{x}^* < \overline{\theta}_o$. By definition therefore, $ucr(x^*) = 1 - F_\theta(x^*)$ and $ucr(\overline{x}^*) = F_{\overline{\theta}}(\overline{x}^*)$.

We have that the probability density function pdf($\overline{\theta}$) equals pdf($1-\theta$). We thus find that pdf($\overline{\theta}$) is equal to the reflection of pdf(θ) in $\theta = 0.5$ which implies that $F_{\overline{\theta}}(\overline{x}^*) = 1 - F_\theta(x^*)$. We thus find $ucr(x^*) = ucr(\overline{x}^*)$. Proof for the case $x^* < \theta^o$ is analogous. □

We thus do not have to consider the ucr-value of the co-varying parameter separately, since it will always be equal to the ucr-value of the varied parameter.

With the criterion ucr, unlike in standard tuning, a larger change of a parameter with a higher variance may be preferred over a smaller change of a parameter with a lower variance, as demonstrated in the example below.

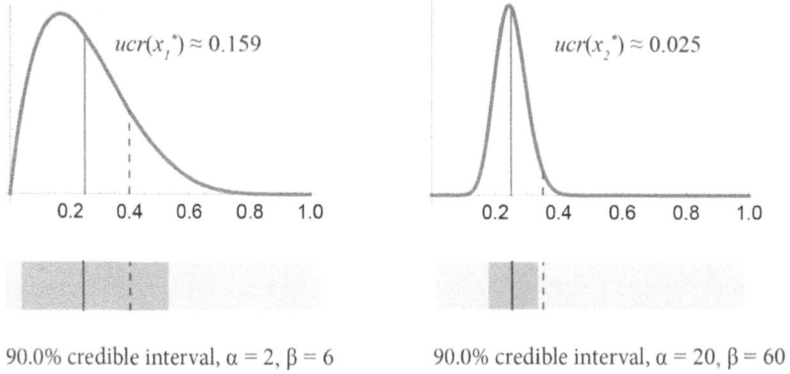

Fig. 1. The beta distributions and 90% credible intervals of Example 1.

Example 1. Figure 1 shows the beta distributions of parameters θ_1 (left) and θ_2 (right) with respectively $\alpha = 20$ and $\beta = 60$, and $\alpha = 2$ and $\beta = 6$. Both parameters have a mean value of 0.25. Now suppose that for some output $\Pr(h \mid \mathbf{e})$ we find that $|\nabla_1 f(\theta_1^o, \theta_{2_o})|$ is lower than $|\nabla_2 f(\theta_1^o, \theta_{2_o})|$, and that $\Pr(h \mid \mathbf{e})$ can be tuned by changing θ_1^o to $x_1^* = 0.4$ or, alternatively, by changing θ_{2_o} to $x_2^* = 0.35$. The change of θ_1^o is larger, however, we find that $ucr(x_1^*) \approx 0.159$ and that $ucr(x_2^*) \approx 0.025$. A change of θ_1^o therefore is preferred by the criterion. Figure 1 also shows, for further illustration of the preference for adapting θ_1, for both parameters their symmetric 90.0% credible intervals. $ucr(x_1^*)$ lies well within this interval while $ucr(x_2^*)$ lies outside. □

Evaluating n-Way Tuning. In the above example we considered one-way tuning where the ucr-values of two proposed changes to a single parameter were compared. In n-way tuning, a proposal for simultaneously adapting all parameters $\mathbf{x}_\mathbf{s}^* = \{x_1^*, \ldots, x_n^*\}$ needs to be evaluated. Below we give two options for assessing a combined ucr-value from the ucr-values for the n proposed individual changes.

One option is to take the lowest ucr-value of the n proposed individual changes. The lowest values of different heuristics can then be compared, thereby preferring the heuristic for which the worst individual change is best. We will indicate the lowest ucr-value by $ucr^1(\mathbf{x_s}^*)$ as defined below.

Definition 3 (evaluation criterion $ucr^1(x^*)$). *Let $\mathbf{x}_\mathbf{s}^* = \{x_1^*, \ldots, x_n^*\}$ be the proposed parameter adaptations in network tuning then:*

$$ucr^1(\mathbf{x}_\mathbf{s}^*) = \min_i ucr(x_i^*), \;\; x_i^* \in \mathbf{x}_\mathbf{s}^*$$

Another option is to multiply the ucr-outcomes of a heuristic. Since the parameters in $\mathbf{x}_\mathbf{s}^*$ are all from different conditional distributions, they are independent. The product of their ucr-values therefore equals the probability that *all* parameters equal their proposed values x_i^*, or are even higher cq. lower. This option combines the results for the individual parameters. We will indicate the product of the *ucr*-outcomes by $ucr^n(\mathbf{x_s^*})$, as defined below.

Definition 4 (evaluation criterion $ucr^n(x^*)$). *Let* $\mathbf{x_s^*} = \{x_1^*, \ldots, x_n^*\}$ *be the proposed parameter adaptations in network tuning then:*

$$ucr^n(\mathbf{x_s^*}) = ucr(x_1^*) \cdot \ldots \cdot ucr(x_n^*)$$

The example below illustrates the use of $ucr^1(\mathbf{x_s^*})$ and $ucr^n(\mathbf{x_s^*})$.

Example 2. Consider two-way tuning of a network output and suppose that in order to achieve the desired result, we can choose between the following options: option 1 is to adapt θ_2 and θ_5 with $scr(x_2^*) = 0.2$ and $ucr(x_5^*) = 0.03$, and option 2 is to adapt θ_2 and θ_7 with $ucr(x_2^*) = 0.1$ and $ucr(x_7^*) = 0.04$. We find $ucr^1(x_2^*, x_5^*) = 0.03$ for option 1, and $ucr^1(x_2^*, x_7^*) = 0.04$ for option 2. Using ucr^1 for comparison, option 2 is thus considered best. We moreover find that $ucr^2(x_2^*, x_5^*) = 0.2 \cdot 0.03 = 0.006$ for option 1 and $ucr^2(x_2^*, x_7^*) = 0.1 \cdot 0.04 = 0.004$ for option 2. Using ucr^2 for comparison, option 1 is thus considered best. □

3.2 Uncertainty-Involving Tuning Heuristics

The gradient tuning heuristic is designed to find parameter adaptations that minimize the change in parameter values compared to their original values. As illustrated in Example 1, using just the gradient values $\nabla_i f(\boldsymbol{\theta}^o)$ to guide the tuning may, however, result in suboptimal choices with respect to $ucr(x^*)$, the evaluation criterion based on the uncertainty in the parameters. When the goal is to find the best tuning with respect to $ucr(x^*)$, the gradient values will have to be weighted against the uncertainty in the parameters.[3] The most obvious way to do so is to multiply the gradient values $\nabla_i f(\boldsymbol{\theta}^o)$ by the standard deviations, i.e. by the square root of the variances $\sqrt{\mathrm{Var}[\theta_i]}$ and to use this product instead of $\nabla_i f(\boldsymbol{\theta}^o)$ in the tuning heuristic given in Definition 1. This $\sqrt{\mathrm{Var}[\theta]}$ weighted option is motivated by the fact that the standard deviation is measured on the same scale as the parameter. An alternative is to weigh the gradient by the variances $\mathrm{Var}[\theta_i]$, and yet another alternative is to weigh the gradient by the cube root of the variances, $\sqrt[3]{\mathrm{Var}[\theta_i]}$. These alternatives assign respectively, more and less relative weight to uncertainty than the weighting by the standard deviation.

The proposed heuristics are detailed in the definitions below.

Definition 5 (VAR-weighted tuning). *Let* $\Pr(h \mid \mathbf{e})$, q_t, $\nabla_i f(\boldsymbol{\theta}^o)$ *and* θ_i^o *be as before and let* $\mathbf{x_s} = \{x_1, \ldots, x_n\}$ *be the* n *variables in* $\mathbf{x}$ *with* n*-highest values*

[3] Note that tuning based on just the uncertainty is not a good choice: a parameter with a high degree of uncertainty may have no effect at all on the tuned output.

$|\nabla_i f(\boldsymbol{\theta}^o)| \cdot \text{Var}[\theta_i]$ *(not necessarily ordered). Then in* VAR*-weighted tuning all* $x_i \in \{x_2 \ldots x_n\}$ *of* $f_{\Pr(h \mid \mathbf{e})}(\mathbf{x_s})$ *are expressed in* x_1 *by*

$$x_i = \frac{\nabla_i f(\boldsymbol{\theta}^o) \cdot \text{Var}[\theta_i]}{\nabla_1 f(\boldsymbol{\theta}^o) \cdot \text{Var}[\theta_1]} \cdot (x_1 - \theta_1^o) + \theta_i^o$$

The tuned parameter values $\mathbf{x_s^*}$ *are now found by solving*

$$f_{\Pr(h \mid \mathbf{e})}(x_1) = q_t$$

Definition 6 (SD-weighted tuning). *Let* $\Pr(h \mid \mathbf{e})$*,* q_t*,* $\nabla_i f(\boldsymbol{\theta}^o)$ *and* θ_i^o *be as before and let* $\mathbf{x_s} = \{x_1, \ldots, x_n\}$ *be the* n *variables in* $\mathbf{x}$ *with* n*-highest values* $|\nabla_i f(\boldsymbol{\theta}^o)| \cdot \sqrt{\text{Var}[\theta_i]}$ *(not necessarily ordered). Then in* SD*-weighted tuning all* $x_i \in \{x_2 \ldots x_n\}$ *of* $f_{\Pr(h \mid \mathbf{e})}(\mathbf{x_s})$ *are expressed in* x_1 *by*

$$x_i = \frac{\nabla_i f(\boldsymbol{\theta}^o) \cdot \sqrt{\text{Var}[\theta_i]}}{\nabla_1 f(\boldsymbol{\theta}^o) \cdot \sqrt{\text{Var}[\theta_1]}} \cdot (x_1 - \theta_1^o) + \theta_i^o$$

The tuned parameter values $\mathbf{x_s^*}$ *are now found by solving*

$$f_{\Pr(h \mid \mathbf{e})}(x_1) = q_t$$

Definition 7 ($\sqrt[3]{\text{VAR}}$-weighted tuning). *Let* $\Pr(h \mid \mathbf{e})$*,* q_t*,* $\nabla_i f(\mathbf{x})$ *and* θ_i^o *as before and let* $\mathbf{x_s} = \{x_1, \ldots, x_n\}$ *be the* n *variables in* $\mathbf{x}$ *with* n*-highest values* $|\nabla_i f(\mathbf{x})| \cdot \sqrt[3]{\text{Var}[\theta_i]}$ *(not necessarily ordered). Then in* $\sqrt[3]{\text{VAR}}$*-weighted tuning all* $x_i \in \{x_2 \ldots x_n\}$ *of* $f_{\Pr(h \mid \mathbf{e})}(\mathbf{x_s})$ *are are expressed in* x_1 *by*

$$x_i = \frac{\nabla_i f(\boldsymbol{\theta}^o) \cdot \sqrt[3]{\text{Var}[\theta_i]}}{\nabla_1 f(\boldsymbol{\theta}^o) \cdot \sqrt[3]{\text{Var}[\theta_1]}} \cdot (x_1 - \theta_1^o) + \theta_i^o$$

The tuned parameter values $\mathbf{x_s^*}$ *are now found by solving*

$$f_{\Pr(h \mid \mathbf{e})}(x_1) = q_t$$

4 Experiments

In this section we compare the weighted tuning heuristics from Definitions 5, 6, and 7 with the gradient tuning heuristic from Definition 1, using *ucr* to judge their performances.

4.1 Experimental Setup

In all experiments we use Bayesian networks with the graph from Fig. 2 and assume that the independences captured by the graph are those of an underlying ground truth distribution. We subsequently perform the following steps:

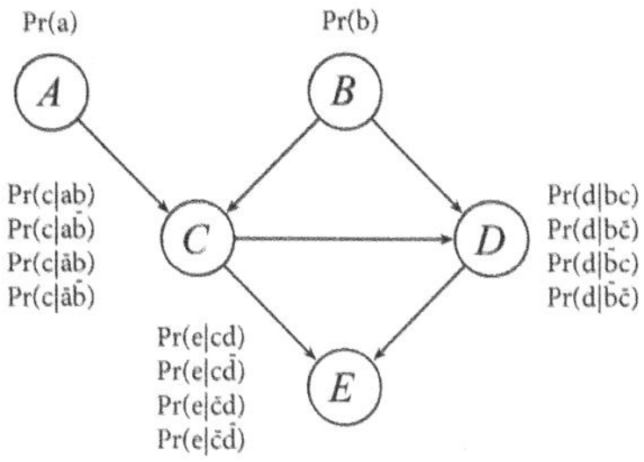

Fig. 2. The graph of the Bayesian networks of the experiments with the associated probabilities required for the CPT-entries.

1. We construct a ground truth distribution by generating random values for the parameters of the network. For each experiment, we generate 1000 parameter sets (and thus 1000 different Bayesian networks). The experiments are performed with ground truth parameters generated from a uniform distribution and with ground truth parameters biased towards 0 and 1, by drawing from the distribution with a probability density function defined by $(x-0.5)^2$.
2. From each ground truth network, we generate 75 data points (joint value combinations of the variables) by forward sampling.[4]
3. The generated data are then used to estimate the CPT-entries of a network that will be subjected to tuning; we apply standard Laplace smoothing.
4. Each heuristic is applied to tune the output value $\Pr(d \mid e)$ of each learned network, with as tuning goal the value $q_t = \Pr(d \mid e)$ as computed from the ground truth distribution. The choice of tuning $\Pr(d \mid e)$ is motivated by the fact that parameters of all CPT rows in all CPTs of the network are involved in the computation of this output. Note that for our small example network it is doable to express $f_{\Pr(d \mid \mathbf{e})}(x_1) = q_t$ explicitly in terms of the network parameters and can therefore be solved analytically.
5. The proposed adaptations are evaluated by their *ucr*-values.

In the first set of experiments we use one-way tuning and in the second set we use two-way tuning. When a heuristic does not find a valid solution, that is, when its solution includes a value x_i^* outside the interval $[0,1]$, the respective value of x_i^* is set to 0. This value yields an *ucr*-value of 0, regardless of the actual distribution over the parameter.

4.2 Results and Discussion

One-Way Tuning. Table 1 shows, for both uniform and biased generated ground truth parameters, the number of networks in which the heuristics introduced in Sect. 3.2 performed the same (*ucr*: =), better (*ucr*: >) and worse (*ucr*:

[4] The experiments were also performed with 150 generated data points per network. These experiments yielded results comparable results.

<) than gradient tuning, plus the net gain (*ucr*: > − *ucr*: <), given one-way tuning of $\Pr(d \mid e)$. To determine whether there is a significant difference between the number of times the heuristic is better or worse than gradient-tuning, a binomial test was conducted.

In one-way tuning, equal performance of heuristics is found when they propose the same parameter to adapt. Equivalence between the gradient heuristic and a weighted heuristic will be found more often when the relative weight of the uncertainty in the heuristic is lower, as illustrated in the following example.

Example 3. Suppose the option is to tune a network with either θ_1 or θ_2 and that $\mathrm{Var}[\theta_1] = 0.04$, $\nabla_1 f(\boldsymbol{\theta}^o) = 4$, $\mathrm{Var}[\theta_2] = 0.09$ and $\nabla_2 f(\boldsymbol{\theta}^o) = 2$. The gradient heuristic then chooses to adapt θ_1, since $4 > 2$. The SD-weighted heuristic uses that the product $\sqrt{0.04} \cdot 4 = 0.8$ of θ_1 is higher than the product $\sqrt{0.09} \cdot 2 = 0.6$ of θ_2 and chooses, like the gradient heuristic, to adapt θ_1. The VAR-weighted heuristic, however, uses that the product $0.04 \cdot 4 = 0.16$ of θ_1 is lower than the product $0.09 \cdot 2 = 0.18$ of θ_2 and thus chooses to adapt θ_2. □

Table 1. Number of networks in which the heuristics from Sect. 3.2 performed the same (*ucr*: =), better (*ucr*: >) and worse (*ucr*: <) than gradient tuning, in one-way tuning of $\Pr(d \mid e)$, and the net gain (*ucr*: > − *ucr*: <). All (negative) gains are significant with $p < 0.05$; highly significant gains ($p < 0.001$) in bold.

heuristic	uniform				biased			
	ucr: =	*ucr*: >	*ucr*: <	gain	*ucr*: =	*ucr*: >	*ucr*: <	gain
VAR-W	240	345	415	−70	267	278	455	**−177**
SD-W	599	324	77	**247**	680	277	43	**234**
$\sqrt[3]{\text{VAR}}$-W	741	221	38	**183**	796	185	19	**166**

Table 2. Number of networks in which different heuristics propose a parameter value outside the interval $[0, 1]$ in one-way tuning of $\Pr(d \mid e)$. Differences between gradient-tuning and proposed heuristics are all significant ($p < 0.01$) according to a χ^2-test.

	gradient	VAR-weighted	SD-weighted	$\sqrt[3]{\text{VAR}}$-weighted
uniform	73	121	36	41
biased	195	305	134	143

We indeed observe that the numbers of '*ucr*: =' increase with a decreasing weight of the uncertainty for both networks with uniform and with biased generated ground truth parameters.

We further observe that the net gain of including a weight factor is negative for the VAR-weighted heuristic and is highest (and positive) for the SD-weighted heuristic, given both networks with uniform and biased generated ground truth parameters. The negative result for the VAR-weighted heuristic indicates that this heuristic assigned an inappropriately high weight to uncertainty in this experiment.

In the 'biased' experiments we observe a slight increase in the numbers '*ucr*: ='. This might be caused by a larger number of networks that could not be tuned in all heuristics (see Table 2). Since the biased parameter values are on average closer to 0 and 1, this increases the chance that a proposed adaptation is outside the interval $[0, 1]$. More remarkable is that using the SD-weighted and $\sqrt[3]{\text{VAR}}$-weighted heuristics, the network could be tuned more often than using the gradient heuristic. An explanation might be that parameters with a higher uncertainty more often will be closer to 0.5 and thus will stay more often in $[0, 1]$ even when they are adapted more.

We conclude that, in our experiments, of all three weighted heuristics the SD-weighted heuristic is the best performing alternative to the gradient heuristic for one-way tuning.

Table 3. Number of networks in which the heuristics from Sect. 3.2 performed the same (ucr^1: =), better (ucr^1: >) and worse (ucr^1: <) than gradient tuning, comparison by ucr^1, in two-way tuning of $\Pr(d \mid e)$, and the net gain (ucr^1: > − ucr^1: <). All gains are significant with $p < 0.05$; highly significant gains ($p < 0.001$) in bold.

heuristic	uniform				biased			
	ucr^1: =	ucr^1: >	ucr^1: <	gain	ucr^1: =	ucr^1: >	ucr^1: <	gain
VAR-weighted	2	610	388	**222**	59	505	436	69
SD-weighted	8	738	254	**484**	83	637	280	**357**
$\sqrt[3]{\text{VAR}}$-weighted	20	747	233	**522**	128	619	253	**366**

Table 4. Number of networks in which the heuristics from Sect. 3.2 performed the same (ucr^2: =), better (ucr^2: >) and worse (ucr^2: <) than gradient tuning, comparison by ucr^2, in two-way tuning of $\Pr(d \mid e)$, and the net gain (ucr^2: > − ucr^2: <). All gains are highly significant ($p < 0.001$), indicated in bold.

heuristic	uniform				biased			
	ucr^2: =	ucr^2: >	ucr^2: <	gain	ucr^2: =	ucr^2: >	ucr^2: <	gain
VAR-weighted	2	565	433	**132**	59	535	406	**129**
SD-weighted	8	741	251	**490**	83	683	234	**449**
$\sqrt[3]{\text{VAR}}$-weighted	20	772	208	**564**	128	640	232	**408**

Table 5. Number of networks in which different heuristics propose a parameter value outside the interval $[0, 1]$ in two-way tuning of $\Pr(d \mid e)$. Differences between gradient-tuning and proposed heuristics are all significant ($p < 0.02$) according to a χ^2-test.

	gradient	VAR-weighted	SD-weighted	$\sqrt[3]{\text{VAR}}$-weighted
uniform	61	25	9	19
biased	184	142	91	133

Two-Way Tuning. In our two-way tuning experiments we used both ucr^1 and ucr^2 to compare the different heuristics. Tables 3 shows for uniform, respectively, biased parameter generation which of the heuristics from Sect. 3.2 performed the same (ucr^1: =), better (ucr^1: >) and worse (ucr^1: <) than gradient tuning, plus the net gain (ucr: > − ucr: <), given two-way tuning of $\Pr(d \mid e)$ as judged by ucr^1. Table 4 shows these results as judged by ucr^2.

In two-way tuning, due to the proportional adaptation of the chosen parameters, a weighted heuristic will only perform the same as the gradient heuristic when either an invalid solution is found in both heuristics, or when the same parameters are selected by both heuristics and those parameters moreover have the same variance. We indeed observe that far less often than in one-way tuning the result '=' occurs. Still, as in one-way tuning, higher numbers of '=' are found given lower relative weight of the uncertainty, and higher numbers of '=' are found in the biased case compared to the uniform case. Note that in case of '=', ucr^1 yields the same results as ucr^2. The highest net gain is, judged by ucr^1, found given the $\sqrt[3]{\text{VAR}}$-weighted heuristic, both in the uniform and in the biased case. Judged by ucr^2, the highest net gain is found given the $\sqrt[3]{\text{VAR}}$-weighted heuristic in the uniform case and given the SD-weighted heuristic in the biased case. The gain for the VAR-weighted heuristic, unlike in one-way tuning, is positive but still is considerably lower than in the other two heuristics both judged by ucr^1 and by ucr^2.

Table 5 shows for all four heuristics the number of times that $\Pr(d \mid e)$ could not be tuned with the selected parameters since a parameter value outside the interval $[0, 1]$ would be needed to do so. We observe that compared to one-way tuning less often invalid solutions are found. This was to be expected, since by tuning with two parameters smaller changes will be needed than by tuning with one parameter. The general trends, however, are the same as in one-way tuning.

We conclude that both the SD-weighted and $\sqrt[3]{\text{VAR}}$-weighted heuristic are well-performing alternatives to the gradient heuristic for two-way tuning in our experiments.

5 Conclusions

The standard assumption in parameter tuning in Bayesian networks is that minimal parameter changes are best. The standard approach to select parameters for adaptation is the gradient tuning heuristic, based on partial derivatives. In this paper we argued for involving the uncertainty in parameter estimates in selecting and adapting the parameters in tuning.

We proposed an evaluation criterion, *ucr*, based on the cumulative distribution function over a parameter, for judging one-way tuning, plus two derived criteria ucr^1 and ucr^n for judging n-way tuning. In addition, we proposed three heuristics that balance the partial derivatives with the uncertainty in the parameter estimates, and evaluated their performance in terms of *ucr*.

In our experiments we observe that, judged by the net gain compared to the standard heuristic, for one-way tuning the SD-weighted heuristic is the best of the considered alternatives, whereas in two-way tuning the $\sqrt[3]{\text{VAR}}$-weighted heuristic is best, except for the biased case judged by ucr^2 where, as in one-way tuning, the SD-weighted heuristic performed best. In view of the number of networks that could be tuned, in all experiments the SD-weighted heuristic is the best alternative. Future research is necessary to study how these results generalise to n-way tuning for larger n, and to gain more understanding of when to use which heuristic.

Although performance for uncertainty-weighted heuristics is in many cases the same as the gradient heuristic there is, compared to the gradient based heuristic, little additional computational cost involved in taking the uncertainty into account. The uncertainty-weighted heuristics just need additionally an uncertainty estimation which can be computed in time linear to the number of parameters. If the uncertainty in the parameter estimates is known, for example because a Bayesian approach was used to learn the parameters from data, we suggest to take that uncertainty into account in network tuning.

In this paper we considered networks with binary variables. The proposed heuristics generalize readily to multi-valued variables given some scheme for co-variation. For the generalization of the evaluation criterion *ucr* to this setting, we observe that the marginal distributions of single parameters still follow a beta distribution from which an *ucr*-value can be computed. A detailed elaboration of the generalization of *ucr* and the related concepts and an evaluation of the heuristics in networks with multivalued variables is for future research.

Acknowledgments. This publication is part of the Personalised Care in Oncology programme with file number P21-03 of the research programme NWO Perspectief which is (partly) financed by the Dutch Research Council (NWO).

Disclosure of Interests. The authors have no competing interests to declare that are relevant to the content of this article.

References

1. Bolt, J.H.: Bayesian networks: a combined tuning heuristic. In: Antonucci, A., Corani, G., Campos, C.P. (eds.) Proceedings of the 8th International Conference on Probabilistic Graphical Models. Proceedings of Machine Learning Research, vol. 52, pp. 37–49. PMLR, Lugano (2016)

2. Bolt, J.H., Renooij, S.: Local sensitivity of Bayesian networks to multiple simultaneous parameter shifts. In: van der Gaag, L.C., Feelders, A.J. (eds.) PGM 2014. LNCS (LNAI), vol. 8754, pp. 65–80. Springer, Cham (2014). https://doi.org/10.1007/978-3-319-11433-0_5
3. Bolt, J.H., van der Gaag, L.C.: Balanced sensitivity functions for tuning multi-dimensional Bayesian network classifiers. Int. J. Approximate Reasoning **80**, 361–376 (2017). https://doi.org/10.1016/j.ijar.2016.07.011
4. Castillo, E., Gutiérrez, J.M., Hadi, A.S.: Parametric structure of probabilities in Bayesian networks. In: Froidevaux, C., Kohlas, J. (eds.) Proceedings of the European Conference on Symbolic and Quantitative Approaches to Reasoning and Uncertainty, pp. 89–98. Springer, Heidelberg (1995)
5. Chan, H., Darwiche, A.: Sensitivity analysis in Bayesian networks: from single to multiple parameters. In: Halpern, J., Meek, C. (eds.) Proceedings of the 20th Conference on Uncertainty in Artificial Intelligence, pp. 67–75 (2004)
6. Chan, H., Darwiche, A.: When do numbers really matter? J. Artif. Intell. Res. **17**, 265–287 (2002). https://doi.org/10.1613/JAIR.967
7. Darwiche, A.: A differential approach to inference in Bayesian networks. J. ACM **50**(3), 280–305 (2003). https://doi.org/10.1145/765568.765570
8. Heckerman, D.: A tutorial on learning with Bayesian networks. In: Jordan, M.I. (ed.) Learning in Graphical Models, pp. 301–354. Springer, Dordrecht (1998). https://doi.org/10.1007/978-94-011-5014-9_11
9. Jensen, F.V., Nielsen, T.D.: Bayesian Networks and Decision Graphs, 2nd edn. Springer, Heidelberg (2007)
10. Kjærulff, U.B., van der Gaag, L.C.: Making sensitivity analysis computationally efficient. In: Boutilier, C. : Goldszmidt, M. (eds.) (ed.) Proceedings of the Sixteenth Conference on Uncertainty in Artificial Intelligence : UAI'00, pp. 317–325 (2000)
11. Pearl, J.: Probabilistic Reasoning in Intelligent Systems: Networks of Plausible Inference. Morgan Kaufmann (1988)

Learning and Probability

Discrete Minimax Probabilistic Classifier Chains for Multi-label Classification Under Label Imbalance

Salvador Madrigal(✉), Cyprien Gilet, Vu-Linh Nguyen, and Sébastien Destercke

Université de technologie de Compiègne, CNRS, Heudiasyc, Compiègne, France
{salvador.madrigal,cyprien.gilet,vu-linh.nguyen, sebastien.destercke}@hds.utc.fr

Abstract. In multi-label classification (MLC), each instance can be assigned to none, one or multiple labels from a predefined label set, and the task is to predict the relevant subset of labels for each new instance. A common challenge in MLC is class imbalance, which often leads to biased classifiers that underestimate rare labels. In this paper, we propose a framework that combines probabilistic classifier chains (PCC) with a minimax learning strategy based on the Discrete minimax classifier. PCC allows us to model label dependencies and optimize various loss functions, including the subset 0/1 loss, Hamming loss, and F1-measure, while the minimax learning strategy mitigates the class imbalance problem by minimizing and balancing the class conditional risks. We conduct experiments on ten benchmark datasets using multiple models of different learning strategies. Our analysis focuses on the ability of models to optimize a loss function while also reducing the false positive and false negative rates. To this end, we use two complementary metrics designed to measure imbalance in class-conditional accuracies.

Keywords: Multi-label classification · Label imbalance · Minimax classifier · Probabilistic classifier chains · Class-conditional risk minimization

1 Introduction

Multi-label classification (MLC) is a supervised learning problem where each instance can be associated with none, one, or multiple labels. MLC has been applied in a wide range of applications, such as fault detection [27,28] and medical diagnosis [16]. Despite a well-established literature, MLC remains a challenging problem, especially when balancing scalability and expressivity is critical. The challenge is further amplified by the issue of label imbalance, which is often encountered in applications of MLC [17,24].

Probabilistic classifier chains (PCCs) proposed in [6] are members of the family of chain rule-based discriminative classifiers [11,20], which achieve a compromise between scalability and model expressiveness. Moreover, they are

K. Sauerwald and M. Thimm (Eds.): ECSQARU 2025, LNAI 16099, pp. 77–91, 2026.
https://doi.org/10.1007/978-3-032-05134-9_6

multi-purpose probabilistic classifiers that allow the computation of expectation-optimal predictions (EOPs), which are also referred to as Bayes-optimal predictions, of multiple target loss functions at the prediction time [9,18,25]. However, to our knowledge, handling label imbalance in PCCs is largely underexplored.

Motivated by the promising results of the Discrete Minimax Binary Relevance Classifier (DMBRCs) in reducing false positive and negative rates when the Binary Relevance Classifier is employed to solve the MLC problem [17], in this paper, we propose Discrete Minimax Probabilistic Classifier Chains (DMPCCs), in which Discrete Minimax Classifiers (DMCs) [12,13] are used to reduce false positive and negative rates when PCCs are employed to solve the MLC problem.

As refinements of PCCs, DMPCCs are multi-purpose probabilistic classifiers that allow the computation of EOPs of multiple target loss functions at the prediction time, while inheriting the capacity of handling imbalanced data of DMCs. We would like to emphasize that while the notion of DMPCCs is intuitive, our work on seeking sound ways to couple DMCs with PCCs stems from a thorough investigation of both DMCs and PCCs, and how they can complement each other.

Specifically, our thorough empirical study suggests that DMPCCs own a promising ability to balance the false positive and negative rates, and the predictive performance under label imbalance (*c.f.* Fig. 3). In the cases of low imbalance, DMPCCs slightly/moderately improve the balancing scores at the expense of a slight/moderate reduction in the predictive performance. More interestingly, in the cases of high imbalance, DMPCCs significantly improve the balancing scores but only slightly/moderately degrade the predictive performances.

The remainder of this paper is organized as follows. In the next section, we recall notable MLC approaches and discuss related work on robustifying them under label imbalance. Our proposal, namely DMPCCs, is presented in Sect. 3. An extensive empirical study on the potential (dis)advantages of DMPCCs is described in Sect. 4, followed by discussions on the results. Finally, Sect. 5 concludes this work and sketches out potential follow-up works.

2 Multi-label Classification Under Label Imbalance

2.1 Multi-label Classification

General Setting. Multi-label classification (MLC) is a supervised learning problem in which each instance is associated with a subset of labels from a predefined label set $\Lambda = \{\lambda_1, \ldots, \lambda_K\}$. Each instance is represented by a D-dimensional feature vector $\boldsymbol{x} \in \mathcal{X} \subset \mathbb{R}^D$ and the corresponding label subset can be encoded as a binary vector, $\boldsymbol{y} \in \mathcal{Y} := \{0,1\}^K$, where, for any $1 \leq k \leq K$, the $k-$th component $y^k = 1$ indicates that the label λ_k is relevant (present) while $y^k = 0$ indicates it is irrelevant. We shall denote by $\mathbf{X} = \{X^1, \ldots, X^D\}$ and $\mathbf{Y} = \{Y^1, \ldots, Y^K\}$ the sets of features and label variables. Given a training data set $\mathbf{D} = \{(\boldsymbol{x}_n, \boldsymbol{y}_n)\}_{n=1}^N$, the goal of MLC is to learn a multi-label classifier $\delta_\theta : \mathcal{X} \rightarrow \mathcal{Y}$ that optimizes a given training function $\ell : \mathcal{Y} \times \mathcal{Y} \longmapsto \mathbb{R}$.

There are three main scalable approaches to address the MLC problem [11,20,25]: algorithm adaptation, problem transformation, and chain rule-based discriminative approach. In the algorithm adaptation approach, existing algorithms are adapted to handle the multi-label data. Notable examples of the algorithm adaptation approach are multi-label k-nearest neighbors [30]. The problem transformation approach converts the multi-label problem to one or more binary or multiclass problems, allowing the use of standard algorithms to solve the task. Notable examples of the problem transformation approach are the binary relevance classifier and label powerset classifier.

The chain rule-based discriminative approach relies on the chain rule of probability to factorize the joint conditional probability $\mathsf{P}(\boldsymbol{y}|\boldsymbol{x}) = \prod_{k=1}^{K} \mathsf{P}(y^k|\mathrm{pa}(y^k), \boldsymbol{x})$, where $\mathrm{pa}(Y^k) \subset \mathbf{Y} \backslash \{Y^k\}$ and the collection $\{\mathrm{pa}(Y^k), k = 1, \ldots, K\}$ forms a directed acyclic graph (DAG) [8,11,20]. Notable examples of the chain rule-based discriminative approach are PCCs [8], Recurrent Bayesian Classifier Chains [11], and probabilistic multi-dimensional classifiers [20]. The binary relevance classifier can also be seen as a specific chain rule-based discriminative classifier with an empty DAG.

Probabilistic Classifier Chains. PCCs are specific chain rule-based discriminative classifiers whose DAGs are fully connected [8]. It is known that PCCs achieve a compromise between scalability and model expressiveness. Its expressiveness stems from the non-uniqueness of the chain rule of probability [20]. While PCCs can have complex DAGs, their training phase is typically more scalable than other chain rule-based discriminative classifiers that also try to optimize DAG structures.

PCCs factorize the joint conditional probability $\mathsf{P}(\boldsymbol{y}|\boldsymbol{x}) = \prod_{k=1}^{K} \mathsf{P}(y^{(k)}| \mathrm{pa}(y^{(k)}), \boldsymbol{x})$, where $\mathrm{pa}(Y^{(k)}) = \{Y^{(1)}, \ldots, Y^{(k-1)}\}$ and $(1), \ldots, (K)$ is any ordering on the K label variables that should be fixed before proceeding with the training phase.

Training Phase. The parameter set $\boldsymbol{\theta}$ of the chosen PCC $\delta_{\boldsymbol{\theta}}(\boldsymbol{x})$, specified by the ordering $(1), \ldots, (K)$, are chosen to optimize the joint conditional log-likelihood:

$$\ell(\delta_{\boldsymbol{\theta}}|\mathbf{D}) = \log\left(\prod_{n=1}^{N}\prod_{k=1}^{K} \mathsf{P}_{\boldsymbol{\theta}_{(k)}}(y_n^{(k)}|\mathrm{pa}(y_n^{(k)}), \boldsymbol{x}_n)\right) = \sum_{k=1}^{K}\sum_{n=1}^{N} \log\left(\mathsf{P}_{\boldsymbol{\theta}_k}(y_n^{(k)}|\mathrm{pa}(y_n^{(k)}), \boldsymbol{x}_n)\right),$$

which can be done by independently selecting the optimal parameter set $\boldsymbol{\theta}_{(k)}$ of the binary classifier $\delta^{(k)}_{\boldsymbol{\theta}_{(k)}}$, $k = 1, \ldots, K$, which optimizes

$$\ell(\delta^{(k)}_{\boldsymbol{\theta}_{(k)}}|\mathbf{D}) = \sum_{n=1}^{N} \log\left(\mathsf{P}_{\boldsymbol{\theta}_{(k)}}(y_n^{(k)}|\mathrm{pa}(y_n^{(k)}), \boldsymbol{x}_n)\right),$$

Prediction Phase. Once the PCC $\delta_{\boldsymbol{\theta}}$ is trained, it predicts for each query instance $\boldsymbol{x}$ a joint conditional probability distribution

$$\delta_{\boldsymbol{\theta}}(\boldsymbol{x}) = \mathsf{P}_{\boldsymbol{\theta}}(\mathcal{Y}|\boldsymbol{x}) := \left\{\mathsf{P}_{\boldsymbol{\theta}}(\boldsymbol{y}|\boldsymbol{x}) = \prod_{k=1}^{K} \mathsf{P}_{\boldsymbol{\theta}_{(k)}}(y^{(k)}|\mathrm{pa}(y^{(k)}), \boldsymbol{x})|\boldsymbol{y} \in \mathcal{Y}\right\}, \quad (1)$$

which provides the necessary information to find an EOP of any target function $\mathcal{L} : \mathcal{Y} \times \mathcal{Y} \longmapsto \mathbb{R}$ (which can differ from the training function ℓ) [8,9,18,25]:

$$\hat{\boldsymbol{y}}_{\mathcal{L}} \in \underset{\bar{\boldsymbol{y}} \in \mathcal{Y}}{\operatorname{argmin}} \, \mathbb{E}_{\mathcal{Y}|\boldsymbol{x}} \left[\mathcal{L}(\bar{\boldsymbol{y}}, \boldsymbol{y})\right] = \underset{\bar{\boldsymbol{y}} \in \mathcal{Y}}{\operatorname{argmin}} \sum_{\boldsymbol{y} \in \mathcal{Y}} \mathcal{L}(\bar{\boldsymbol{y}}, \boldsymbol{y}) \mathsf{P}_{\boldsymbol{\theta}}(\boldsymbol{y}|\boldsymbol{x}). \tag{2}$$

It is known that different target functions $\mathcal{L}$ can have different EOPs [8,9, 18,25]. Moreover, the computational complexity of finding EOPs can greatly depend on the choice of $\mathcal{L}$. Let $[\![\cdot]\!]$ be the indicator function, i.e., $[\![A]\!] = 1$ if the predicate A is true and $= 0$ otherwise. EOPs of the commonly used subset 0/1 loss $\mathcal{L}_{\text{Sub}}$ and Hamming loss $\mathcal{L}_{\text{Ham}}$

$$\mathcal{L}_{\text{Sub}}(\hat{\boldsymbol{y}}, \boldsymbol{y}) = [\![\hat{\boldsymbol{y}} \neq \boldsymbol{y}]\!], \quad \mathcal{L}_{\text{Ham}}(\hat{\boldsymbol{y}}, \boldsymbol{y}) = \frac{1}{K} \sum_{k=1}^{K} [\![\hat{y}^k \neq y^k]\!] \tag{3}$$

are the joint mode of the distribution $\mathsf{P}_{\boldsymbol{\theta}}(\mathcal{Y}|\boldsymbol{x})$, i.e.,

$$\hat{\boldsymbol{y}}_{\text{Sub}} \in \underset{\bar{\boldsymbol{y}} \in \mathcal{Y}}{\operatorname{argmax}} \, \mathsf{P}_{\boldsymbol{\theta}}(\bar{\boldsymbol{y}}|\boldsymbol{x}) \tag{4}$$

and the marginal mode $\hat{\boldsymbol{y}}_{\text{Ham}} = (\hat{y}^1, \ldots, \hat{y}^k)$, where

$$\hat{y}^k \in \underset{\bar{y}^k \in \{0,1\}}{\operatorname{argmax}} \sum_{\boldsymbol{y} \in \mathcal{Y}; y^k = \bar{y}^k} \mathsf{P}_{\boldsymbol{\theta}}(\boldsymbol{y}|\boldsymbol{x}). \tag{5}$$

Finding an EOP $\hat{\boldsymbol{y}}_{\text{F1}}$ of the $F1-$measure

$$\mathcal{L}_{\text{F1}}(\hat{\boldsymbol{y}}, \boldsymbol{y}) = \frac{2 \sum_{k=1}^{K} \hat{y}^k \cdot y^k}{\sum_{k=1}^{K} \hat{y}^k + \sum_{k=1}^{K} y^k}, \tag{6}$$

can be done by first extracting/estimating $K^2 + 1$ probabilistic scores from the distribution $P_{\boldsymbol{\theta}}(\mathcal{Y}|\boldsymbol{x})$ and then run efficient algorithms to find an EOP. We refer to [25] for a thorough discussion on this problem. Finally, we emphasize that to achieve a promising level on a given target function $\mathcal{L}$, it is recommended to determine its EOPs (2) at the prediction time [8,9,25].

2.2 Handling Label Imbalance

Notable attempts in handling label imbalance in MLC can be divided into five categories [17,24]: resampling methods [2,14], classifier adaptation [23,29], ensemble methods [15,21], cost-sensitive approaches [7,26], and minimax-based approach [17]. We refer to [17] for a deeper discussion on these approaches. As a remark, we note that those solutions to imbalance have been employed/developed to robustify the algorithm adaptation and problem transformation approaches, but not the chain rule-based discriminative approach yet.

The large empirical study in [17] suggests that, compared to other approaches, minimax learning gives promising results in bringing closer false positive and negative rates when the Binary Relevance Classifier is employed to solve the MLC problem. This is expected, as a Binary Relevance Classifier (BRC) is essentially a collection of K independent binary classifiers. Therefore, implementing BRCs with Discrete Minimax Classifiers (DMCs), which are designed to equate false positive and negative rates in multi-class classification, as binary classifiers is a natural solution.

To our knowledge, there is a lack of a thorough study on robustifying the chain rule-based discriminative approach [8,9,11,20] under label imbalance. This might restrict its application domain, despite its capacity for balancing the scalability and expressivity. As a first attempt on this topic, we propose to employ DMCs as the base classifiers $\delta^{(k)}_{\boldsymbol{\theta}_{(k)}}$, $k = 1, \ldots, K$, when PCCs are employed to solve the MLC problem to balance the false positive and negative rates. The resulting multi-label classifiers, namely Discrete Minimax Probabilistic Classifier Chains (DMPCCs), are presented in the next section.

3 Discrete Minimax Probabilistic Classifier Chains (DMPCCs)

Discrete Minimax Classifiers [12] are members of the family of input space partitioning methods (see [20, Appendix B.5] and references therein). They are typically constructed in a two-stage manner: partition the input space into a finite number of regions, and construct for each region a local classifier. DMCs are specifically designed to optimally tackle imbalanced classes in multi-class classification.

DMCs are constructed on top of Minimax Classifiers (see [12] and references therein). From a statistical decision theory [1,10,22] viewpoint, Minimax Classifiers are Bayes optimal classifiers seeking minimized and balanced risks between the classes. Despite their theoretical properties, fitting minimax classifiers, which is usually done by maximizing the Bayes risk with respect to the priors, is practically challenging. This is because the conditional distributions of the features in each class are necessary to analytically calculate the Bayes risk. DMCs [12] overcome this challenge by partitioning the input space into a finite number of regions, which allows analytical calculation of the Bayes risk over the simplex. This, in turn, allows efficient computations of the priors for which the minimax classifier is obtained.

Besides their promising ability to handle imbalanced classes, DMCs are also robust in the presence of covariate noise [5]. This makes DMCs promising base classifiers $\delta^{(k)}_{\boldsymbol{\theta}_{(k)}}$, $k = 1, \ldots, K$, when implementing PCCs. This is because the base classifiers have to simultaneously handle imbalanced classes, which come from the imbalanced labels, and noisy input at the prediction time (since the augmented features $Y^{(1)}, \ldots, Y^{(k-1)}$ are predicted).

In the following, we briefly recall key building blocks of DMCs when being employed as the base classifiers of PCCs: input space partitioning, and constructing local Bayes-optimal classifiers.

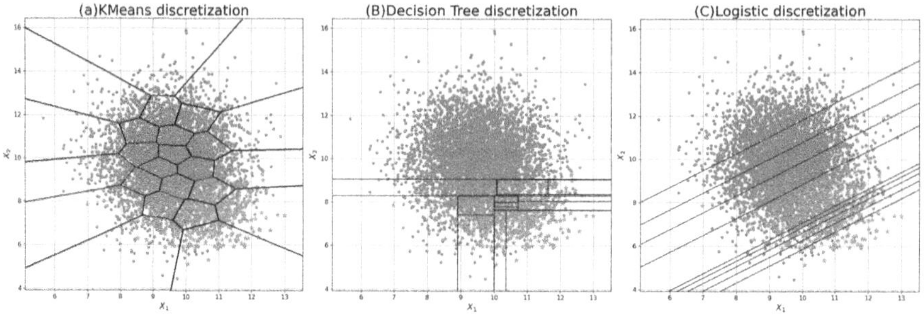

Fig. 1. Visualization of different discretization strategies (KMeans, Decision Tree, and Logistic Regression).

3.1 Input Space Partitioning

For any $k = 1, \dots, K$, for any $(\boldsymbol{x}, \boldsymbol{y}) \in \mathcal{X} \times \mathcal{Y}$, let $\boldsymbol{x}^{(k)} = (y^{(1)}, \dots, y^{(k-1)}, x^1, \dots, x^D)$. For any $k = 1, \dots, K$, let $\mathcal{X}^{(k)} = \mathcal{Y}^{(1)} \times \dots \times \mathcal{Y}^{(k-1)} \times \mathcal{X}$ and $\mathbf{D}^{(k)} = \{(y_n^{(k)}, \boldsymbol{x}_n^{(k)}), n = 1 \dots, N\}$. For any $k = 1, \dots, K$, the first step in constructing the DMC $\delta_{\boldsymbol{\theta}_{(k)}}^{(k)}$ is to partition $\mathcal{X}^{(k)}$ into T regions, which shall be referred to as discrete profiles, denoted by $\mathcal{X}_t^{(k)}$, $t = 1, \dots, T$. Different ways to construct the discrete profiles will result in different variants of DMCs as illustrated in Fig. 1. For example, in [12], Voronoi cells derived from a K-means algorithm are used for discretization (*c.f.* Fig. 1(a)), while in [13], leaves of a decision tree are used (*c.f.* Fig. 1(b)). Often, the discrete profiles are estimated using the training data $\mathbf{D}^{(k)}$. To seek meaningful discrete profiles, the hyper-parameters are typically selected using nested cross-validation. We refer to Sect. 4.1 for different ways to construct the discrete profiles used in this paper.

3.2 Constructing Local Bayes-Optimal Classifiers

Once the discrete profiles $\mathcal{X}_t^{(k)}$, $t = 1, \dots, T$, are given, DMCs equip each profile with a local Bayes-optimal classifier [12]. Let $\mathbb{S}$ be the probability simplex consisting of all the vectors $\pi \in [0,1]^2$ with $\pi_0 + \pi_1 = 1$. Assume the prior distribution $\pi = (\pi_0, \pi_1) = \big(\mathsf{P}(y^{(k)} = 1), \mathsf{P}(y^{(k)} = 0)\big) \in \mathbb{S}$ is given. Let

$$f_{ct}(\pi, \boldsymbol{x}) := \sum_{q \in \{0,1\}} L_{qc} \sum_{t=1}^{T} \frac{\pi_q \, \hat{p}_{qt}^{(k)}}{\sum_j \pi_j \, \hat{p}_{jt}^{(k)}} [\![\boldsymbol{x} \in \mathcal{X}_t^{(k)}]\!], c \in \{0,1\},$$

$$\hat{p}_{ct}^{(k)} := \frac{1}{N_c} \sum_{n=1; y_n^{(k)} = c}^{N} [\![\boldsymbol{x}_n \in \mathcal{X}_t^{(k)}]\!], c \in \{0,1\}, t = 1, \dots, T,$$

where N_c is the number of training instance with $y_n^{(k)} = c$, and L_{qc} is the cost of predicting class q while the true class is c. In the remainder of this paper, we will adopt the 0/1 cost, where $L_{qc} = [\![q \neq c]\!]$.

Based on [5], for each discrete profile $\mathcal{X}_t^{(k)}$, the corresponding local classifier predicts for all instances $\boldsymbol{x}^{(k)} \in \mathcal{X}_t^{(k)}$:

$$\mathsf{P}_{\pi}\left(y^{(k)} = c|\boldsymbol{x}^{(k)}\right) = \frac{f_{ct}(\pi, \boldsymbol{x})}{f_{1t}(\pi, \boldsymbol{x}) + f_{0t}(\pi, \boldsymbol{x})}, \quad c \in \{0, 1\}. \tag{7}$$

Since the shared parameter vector π of the local classifiers is unknown, DMCs fit it by maximizing the optimal empirical Bayes risk:

$$r^{(k)}(\pi) = \sum_{c=0}^{1}\sum_{t=1}^{T}\sum_{z=0}^{1} L_{cz}\, \pi_c\, \hat{p}_{ct}^{(k)} \left[\!\left[\sum_{j\in\{0,1\}} L_{jz}\pi_j\hat{p}_{jt}^{(k)} = \min_{q\in\{0,1\}} \sum_{j\in\{0,1\}} L_{jq}\pi_j\hat{p}_{jt}^{(k)} \right]\!\right].$$

Similarly to [12], the desired discrete minimax classifier minimizing and balancing the class risks is obtained by computing the least favorable priors $\bar{\pi}$ that maximize $r^{(k)}(\pi)$ over the simplex $\mathbb{S}$. This optimization problem

$$\bar{\pi} = \underset{\pi\in\mathbb{S}}{\operatorname{argmax}}\, r^{(k)}(\pi) \tag{8}$$

can be solved using the projected subgradient algorithm [12] for which the convergence is established.

Once the optimal prior distribution $\bar{\pi}$ is found, for each discrete profile $\mathcal{X}_t^{(k)}$, the corresponding local classifier predicts for all instances $\boldsymbol{x}^{(k)} \in \mathcal{X}_t^{(k)}$ the probabilistic prediction $\mathsf{P}_{\bar{\pi}}\left(\mathcal{Y}^{(k)}|\boldsymbol{x}^{(k)}\right) = \left(\mathsf{P}_{\bar{\pi}}\left(y^{(k)} = 1|\boldsymbol{x}^{(k)}\right), \mathsf{P}_{\bar{\pi}}\left(y^{(k)} = 0|\boldsymbol{x}^{(k)}\right)\right)$. Finally, $\mathsf{P}_{\bar{\pi}}\left(\mathcal{Y}^{(k)}|\boldsymbol{x}^{(k)}\right)$, $k = 1\ldots, K$, are used to find EOPs (2).

4 Experiments

In this section, we compare DMPCCs with other families of PCCs, implemented with the base classifiers $\delta_{\theta_{(k)}}^{(k)}$, where $(k) = k$, $k = 1, \ldots, K$, which either do not explicitly account for imbalance, or handle it through following cost-sensitive/resampling approaches (when those are available). The prediction phase of all the PCCs covered in our experiments is the same, i.e., for each target function, which is either the Hamming loss, or Subset 0/1 loss, or F1-measure, its EOPs (2) are computed using $P(\mathcal{Y}|\boldsymbol{x})$ as described in Sect. 2.

4.1 Experimental Setting

We evaluate the performance of DMPCCs on ten benchmark datasets with varied numbers of instances, features, and labels, obtained from the Cometa repository [3]. An overview of the datasets is presented in Table 1, where MeanIR and CVIR [2] are used to assess the imbalance level of the datasets. The imbalance ratio of each label is defined as the fraction of the relevance frequency of the most frequent label over the frequency of the considered label: MeanIR is then the average imbalance ratio over the labels, while CVIR is the coefficient of variation of the imbalance ratios between labels. Higher imbalance ratios indicate more imbalance situations.

Table 1. Overview of datasets used in the experiments.

Dataset	Instances	Features	Labels	MeanIR	CVIR
GpositivePseAAC	519	444	4	3.86	4.44
Image	2000	294	5	1.19	0.15
CHD_49	555	49	6	5.77	1.75
Emotions	593	72	6	1.47	0.24
Scene	2407	294	6	1.25	0.13
VirusPseAAC	207	446	6	4.04	3.34
Flags	194	19	7	2.25	1.59
GnegativePseAAC	1392	440	8	18.44	24.06
Foodtruck	407	21	12	7.09	4.69
PlantPseACC	978	440	12	6.69	4.56

DMPCCs Implementation. We employ four types of discretization strategies for the base of DMPCC: Kmeans, Kmeans-class-wise, Decision tree leaves and logistic regression decision boundaries. The resulting DMPCCs are denoted as DMPCC-KMs, DMPCC-KMsU, DMPCC-DT, and DMPCC-LR.

DMPCC-KMs, detailed in [17], uses the Voronoi cells generated by a Kmeans algorithm to form the discrete profiles, see Fig. 1(a). The Kmeans-based discretization employs a global discretization strategy, i.e., the discrete profiles are class-independent. While such an approach can give good results [17], the global nature of the partitioning can negatively impact loss metrics. To address the limitations observed with standard Kmeans, we propose a class-aware Kmeans-based discretization, denoted as DMPCC-KMsU, where the Kmeans partitioning is applied to samples of each class separately. The final discrete profiles are then defined as the Voronoi cells formed by the union of centroids issued from both partitionings. This strategy ensures that the partitioning process is sensitive to class distributions, potentially improving performance on loss metrics while maintaining risk balance.

The DMPCC-DT employs decision tree (DT) leaves to define discrete profiles, see Fig. 1(b). In this method, the leaves of a fitted decision tree represent the distinct partitions of the feature space. Finally, we introduce DMPCC-LR, in which the decision boundary of a logistic regression (LR) is shifted to generate the discrete profiles, as illustrated in Fig. 1(c).

To determine the optimal number of discrete profiles (T) for the DMPCC, we perform a grid search with three-subfold cross-validation using the Discrete Bayesian Classifier (DBC). Fifteen candidate values for T, ranging from #instances/30 to #instances/4, are evaluated, and the one with the highest accuracy is selected. Note that DBC serves two roles in our study: it is used as the base classifier in one of the competitor methods (PCC-DBC), and also as a model for hyperparameter selection in DMPCC. Finally, for each class, the number of centroids is defined proportionally to its frequency in the training data.

Competitors. To provide a complete evaluation, we compare DMPCCs against 3 families of PCCs, which only differ in the base classifiers $\delta^k_{\boldsymbol{\theta}_k}$, $k = 1, \ldots, K$.

- PCCs: PCC-LR, PCC-DT and PCC-DBC are PCCs implemented with LR, DT and DBC, respectively.
- Cost-sensitive based PCCs: PCC-WLR and PCC-WDT are PCCs implemented with weighted LR and weighted DT, respectively.
- Resampling-based PCCs: PCC-LR-ROS, PCC-DT-ROS and PCC-DBC-ROS are PCCs implemented with the multi-label random over-sampling (ROS) [4] option combined with LR,DT and DBC.
- Minimax-Binary relevance: DMBRC, the binary relevance strategies with minimax approach that we use in [17]

In combination with the two types of DMPCCs, we include in total thirteen types of PCCs in our empirical study.

Evaluation Metrics. We follow a stratified 5-fold cross-validation strategy to ensure robust results, and report the average scores. For each train-test split, and for each target function, we assess the predictive performance of each PCC δ using the corresponding average score on the test set, where EOPs (2) of the target function are computed. We also assess the balancing ability of each PCC δ using four complementary metrics, namely, $\rho_{\max}$, ρ_{avg}, $\psi_{\max}$, and ψ_{avg}:

$$\rho_{\max}(\delta) = \max_{\lambda \in \Lambda} \left| R_0^\lambda(\delta) - R_1^\lambda(\delta) \right|, \qquad \rho_{\text{avg}}(\delta) = \frac{1}{|\Lambda|} \sum_{\lambda \in \Lambda} \left| R_0^\lambda(\delta) - R_1^\lambda(\delta) \right| \tag{9}$$

$$\psi_{\max}(\delta) = \max_{\lambda \in \Lambda} \left(\max \left\{ R_0^\lambda(\delta), R_1^\lambda(\delta) \right\} \right), \quad \psi_{\text{avg}}(\delta) = \frac{1}{|\Lambda|} \sum_{\lambda \in \Lambda} \max \left\{ R_0^\lambda(\delta), R_1^\lambda(\delta) \right\} \tag{10}$$

where $R_0^\lambda(\delta)$ and $R_1^\lambda(\delta)$ respectively, denote the false negative rate and the false positive rate associated with the label λ.

All these metrics are "the lower the better", where lower values indicate a better balancing ability. Let us note that $\rho_{\max}$, ρ_{avg} are normalized metrics. Furthermore, $\rho_{\max}$ (ρ_{ave}) reaches 0 and 1 when the false negative rates are equal and maximally different on at least one label (all the labels), respectively, while $\psi_{\max}$, ψ_{avg} take values in $[0.5, 1]$. By definition, we have $\rho_{\max} \geq \rho_{\text{avg}}$ and $\psi_{\max} \geq \psi_{\text{avg}}$. Moreover, $\psi_{\max}$ (ψ_{avg}) and $\rho_{\max}$ (ρ_{avg}) reach their bounds for the same extreme situations.

We report the results for 3 target functions: The Hamming loss, the Subset 0/1 loss, and the F1-measure. All the code, implementations, and the full results for the experiments made in this paper are available in our public GitHub repository[1], which is developed on top of existing implementations of DMCs[2] and PCCs[3].

4.2 Results

The average scores and (the lower the better) average ranks of the classifiers over 10 data sets are given in Table 2. A ✓ indicates that the Friedman test on the average ranks across methods is statistically significant with respect to the evaluation metric for the corresponding EOP. We summarize the average ranks of all the classifiers on radar charts in Fig. 2.

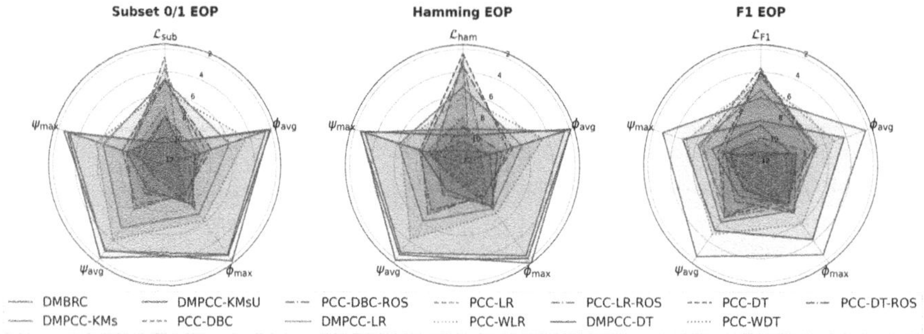

Fig. 2. Radar chart illustrating the average rank of the different classifiers. KmeansU family is represented in blue, decision tree family in red, and logistic regression family in green. Line styles indicate the imbalance handling approach: solid lines (—) for the DMPCC approach, dotted lines (···) for cost-sensitive methods, dashed lines (- -) for standard models, and dash-dotted lines (—·—) for resampling techniques. (Color figure online)

Overall, PCC-LR provides the most promising predictive performance, but its balancing scores are often worse than other classifiers specifically designed to handle imbalanced data: DMBRC, DMPCC-KMs, DMPCC-KMsU, DMPCC-LR, and PCC-WLR. The results of these classifiers are given in gray to facilitate further discussions.

The Case of Subset 0/1 Loss. DMBRC, DMPCC-KMs, DMPCC-KMsU provide the most promising balancing scores, but the least promising predictive performance. Among these classifiers, DMPCC-KMsU provides the most promising balance-performance trade-off. PCC-WLR provides less promising balancing

[1] https://github.com/SalvadorMC/Discrete_Minimax_Probabilistic_Classifier_Chains.git.

[2] https://github.com/cypgilet/discrete_box_constrained_minimax_classifier.

[3] https://github.com/hxtruong6/inference_probabilistic_mlc/tree/main.

Table 2. Average scores and ranks: A ✓ indicates that the Friedman test is significant.

Subset 0/1 EOP

Model	$\mathcal{L}_{sub}$ ✓	ρ_{avg} ✓	ρ_{max} ✓	ψ_{avg} ✓	ψ_{max} ✓
DMBRC	.759 (10.2)	.247 (2.5)	.562 (2.5)	.446 (2.8)	.709 (3.0)
DMPCC-KMs	.815 (12.1)	.193 (2.1)	.432 (1.8)	.427 (2.9)	.635 (2.5)
DMPCC-KMsU	.756 (10.2)	.231 (2.0)	.542 (2.4)	.436 (2.1)	.691 (2.9)
PCC-DBC	.682 (4.6)	.420 (8.2)	.768 (8.9)	.544 (7.7)	.820 (8.1)
PCC-DBC-ROS	.685 (4.8)	.418 (7.7)	.760 (9.0)	.547 (7.3)	.820 (8.4)
DMPCC-DT	.755 (9.7)	.401 (9.2)	.734 (7.9)	.581 (9.4)	.830 (8.5)
PCC-DT	.726 (7.9)	.428 (9.9)	.749 (7.4)	.597 (10.7)	.839 (9.5)
PCC-WDT	.718 (6.9)	.441 (10.8)	.746 (8.8)	.597 (11.2)	.822 (9.0)
PCC-DT-ROS	.724 (7.9)	.419 (8.8)	.749 (8.4)	.583 (9.0)	.839 (9.9)
DMPCC-LR	.694 (4.7)	.344 (6.0)	.665 (6.8)	.515 (5.3)	.773 (6.2)
PCC-LR	.656 (2.7)	.471 (10.6)	.777 (11.2)	.585 (9.6)	.829 (8.9)
PCC-WLR	.699 (5.6)	.314 (4.4)	.662 (6.2)	.487 (4.0)	.753 (5.5)
PCC-LR-ROS	.665 (3.7)	.460 (8.8)	.761 (9.8)	.578 (9.0)	.821 (8.5)

Hamming EOP

Model	$\mathcal{L}_{ham}$ ✓	ρ_{avg}✓	ρ_{max}✓	ψ_{avg}✓	ψ_{max}✓
DMBRC	.247 (8.9)	.247 (2.5)	.562 (2.4)	.446 (2.7)	.709 (3.0)
DMPCC-KMs	.294 (11.9)	.195 (1.9)	.455 (1.6)	.427 (2.5)	.650 (2.5)
DMPCC-KMsU	.249 (9.5)	.230 (1.9)	.537 (2.1)	.435 (1.9)	.689 (2.5)
PCC-DBC	.190 (2.4)	.421 (7.8)	.770 (8.8)	.544 (7.3)	.820 (8.1)
PCC-DBC-ROS	.194 (3.5)	.418 (7.4)	.761 (8.9)	.547 (6.8)	.820 (8.2)
DMPCC-DT	.263 (10.8)	.408 (8.8)	.734 (7.7)	.583 (9.5)	.829 (8.2)
PCC-DT	.234 (10.0)	.428 (9.5)	.749 (7.4)	.597 (10.7)	.839 (9.1)
PCC-WDT	.225 (7.9)	.441 (10.4)	.746 (8.2)	.597 (10.9)	.822 (8.6)
PCC-DT-ROS	.227 (8.7)	.419 (8.4)	.749 (7.7)	.583 (9.0)	.839 (9.8)
DMPCC-LR	.217 (5.3)	.374 (6.5)	.691 (7.5)	.529 (6.1)	.784 (6.1)
PCC-LR	.185 (2.8)	.492 (11.4)	.804 (11.7)	.598 (10.3)	.848 (9.4)
PCC-WLR	.231 (6.1)	.325 (4.5)	.690 (7.0)	.491 (4.2)	.775 (6.3)
PCC-LR-ROS	.190 (3.2)	.477 (10.0)	.786 (10.2)	.589 (9.1)	.839 (9.2)

F1 EOP

Model	$\mathcal{L}_{F1}$ ✓	ρ_{avg} ✓	ρ_{max}✓	ψ_{avg}✗	ψ_{max}✗
DMBRC	.533 (6.2)	.247 (2.2)	.562 (2.5)	.446 (2.3)	.709 (2.9)
DMPCC-KMs	.518 (8.6)	.435 (9.1)	.751 (7.9)	.566 (8.8)	.814 (7.5)
DMPCC-KMsU	.520 (8.2)	.317 (4.2)	.682 (4.2)	.503 (5.1)	.777 (4.8)
PCC-DBC	.566 (4.1)	.409 (7.1)	.753 (8.3)	.540 (6.6)	.814 (8.1)
PCC-DBC-ROS	.563 (3.9)	.411 (7.0)	.759 (9.1)	.541 (6.5)	.816 (8.5)
DMPCC-DT	.478 (11.0)	.442 (8.7)	.803 (7.9)	.610 (9.5)	.878 (9.2)
PCC-DT	.486 (11.3)	.428 (8.8)	.748 (7.0)	.598 (9.6)	.839 (8.7)
PCC-WDT	.494 (10.0)	.441 (9.7)	.746 (7.8)	.597 (10.2)	.822 (8.2)
PCC-DT-ROS	.493 (9.7)	.419 (7.9)	.749 (7.0)	.583 (8.2)	.839 (8.8)
DMPCC-LR	.547 (5.5)	.393 (6.9)	.711 (7.2)	.540 (6.0)	.790 (6.2)
PCC-LR	.574 (3.6)	.420 (7.6)	.730 (8.6)	.549 (7.0)	.783 (6.5)
PCC-WLR	.559 (4.5)	.360 (5.1)	.688 (5.8)	.508 (4.7)	.769 (5.0)
PCC-LR-ROS	.566 (4.4)	.403 (6.7)	.729 (7.8)	.543 (6.5)	.787 (6.7)

scores than these classifiers, but more promising predictive performance. However, PCC-WLR provides slightly worse predictive performance compared to DMPCC-LR, which also provides reasonably promising balancing scores.

The Case of Hamming Loss. Similar trends are observed in this case (*c.f.*. Table 2 and Fig. 2. Moreover, a detailed examination (*c.f.*. Figure 3) on the pair of DMPCC-KMsU, which might provide the most promising balancing scores, and PCC-LR which might be the most promising candidate in seeking predictive performance (concerning the three target losses) suggests that DMPCC-KMsU often provides moderate to significant gains on balancing scores at the expense of small to moderate reductions in the Hamming loss.

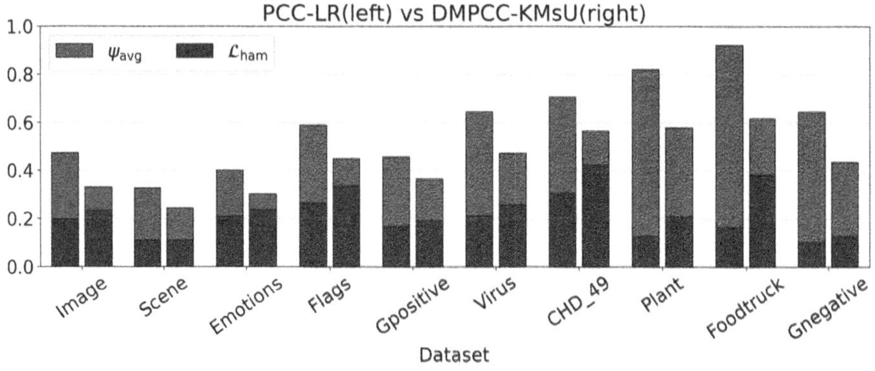

Fig. 3. Hamming loss and maximum class-conditional risk for PCC-LR (left) and DMPCC-KMsU (right) across different datasets. Datasets are sorted in increasing order of the mean imbalance ratio.

The Case of F1 Measure. PCC-WLR indeed provides a promising balance-performance trade-off in this case. However, it is still slightly worse than DMPCC-KMsU regarding balancing scores. Interestingly, DMBRC provides an impressive balance-performance in this case. This indeed complements the existing empirical findings on the promising performance of BRCs concerning F1 measure [19] despite their simplicity. This also suggests a worthy follow-up work on investigating scenarios where DMPCCs and DMBRCs may be more advantageous.

DMPCCs vs DMBRCs and Standard PCCs. For each pair of target function and evaluation criterion, we compare the average difference of three pairs: DMPCC-KMsU and PCC-DBC, DMPCC-DT and PCC-DT, and DMPCC-LR and PCC-LR. The results given in Table 3a reconfirm that, in the cases of Hamming and subset 0/1 losses, DMPCCs can provide significant improvements on balancing scores at the expense of small/moderate reductions in the predictive performance, compared to standard PCCs. In the case of F1-measure, the improvements on balancing scores are less significant, but still visible.

Table 3. Average improvements (in %) for the losses and risk-based metrics.

(a) DMPCCs vs standard PCCs: **EOP**

	Zero–one	Hamming	F1
$\mathcal{L}$	-4.66 ± 1.05	-4.03 ± 1.13	-2.72 ± 0.93
ρ_{avg}	11.44 ± 2.74	10.95 ± 2.33	3.47 ± 1.65
$\rho_{\max}$	11.77 ± 3.01	12.02 ± 3.09	1.17 ± 1.97
ψ_{avg}	6.50 ± 1.49	6.43 ± 1.30	1.14 ± 0.95
$\psi_{\max}$	6.49 ± 1.83	6.87 ± 1.97	-0.24 ± 1.25

(b) DMPCC-KMsU vs DMBRC : **EOP**

	Zero–one	Hamming	F1
$\mathcal{L}$	0.28 ± 1.09	-0.23 ± 0.57	-1.32 ± 1.31
ρ_{avg}	1.52 ± 0.91	1.65 ± 0.96	-7.06 ± 2.76
$\rho_{\max}$	2.03 ± 2.11	2.53 ± 2.39	-12.00 ± 5.25
ψ_{avg}	0.98 ± 0.85	1.13 ± 0.91	-5.69 ± 1.83
$\psi_{\max}$	1.84 ± 1.51	2.06 ± 1.76	-6.73 ± 2.60

The results given in Table 3b complement our above discussions with rather clear evidence on the promising ability of DMPCC-KMsU in seeking the balance-performance trade-off in the cases of the Hamming and Subset 0/1 losses, compared to DMBRC. Moreover, they reconfirm the strength of DMBRCs in the case of F1-measure.

5 Conclusion

We present DMPCCs, which inherit the multi-purpose nature of PCCs that allow the computation of EOPs of multiple target loss functions at the prediction time, and the capacity of handling imbalanced data of DMCs. Our thorough empirical study suggests that DMPCCs own a promising ability to balance the false positive and negative rates, and the predictive performance under label imbalance. As a potential follow-up work, one might think of conducting a thorough investigation on scenarios where DMPCCs and DMBRCs may be more advantageous. One could also think of generalizing DMPCCs to robustify other chain rule-based discriminative approaches in MLC [11] and multi-dimensional classification [20].

References

1. Berger, J.O.: Statistical Decision Theory and Bayesian Analysis. Springer Series in Statistics, 2nd edn. Springer, New York (1985)
2. Charte, F., Rivera, A., Jesus, M.J., Herrera, F.: A first approach to deal with imbalance in multi-label datasets. In: Pan, J.-S., Polycarpou, M.M., Woźniak, M., de Carvalho, A.C.P.L.F., Quintián, H., Corchado, E. (eds.) HAIS 2013. LNCS (LNAI), vol. 8073, pp. 150–160. Springer, Heidelberg (2013). https://doi.org/10.1007/978-3-642-40846-5_16

3. Charte, F., Rivera, A.J., Charte, D., del Jesus, M.J., Herrera, F.: Tips, guidelines and tools for managing multi-label datasets: The mldr.datasets R package and the Cometa data repository. Neurocomputing (2018)
4. Charte, F., Rivera, A.J., Jesus, M.J., Herrera, F.: Addressing imbalance in multilabel classification: measures and random resampling algorithms. Neurocomputing **163**, 3–16 (2015)
5. Chen, W., Gilet, C., Quost, B., Destercke, S.: Robust discrete Bayesian classifier under covariate and label noise. In: Destercke, S., Martinez, M.V., Sanfilippo, G. (eds.) SUM 2024. LNCS, vol. 15350, pp. 100–114. Springer, Cham (2024). https://doi.org/10.1007/978-3-031-76235-2_8
6. Cheng, W., Hüllermeier, E., Dembczynski, K.J.: Bayes optimal multilabel classification via probabilistic classifier chains. In: Proceedings of the 27th International Conference on Machine Learning (ICML), pp. 279–286 (2010)
7. Daniels, Z., Metaxas, D.: Addressing imbalance in multi-label classification using structured Hellinger forests. In: Proceedings of the AAAI Conference on Artificial Intelligence, vol. 31 (2017)
8. Dembczynski, K., Waegeman, W., Cheng, W., Hüllermeier, E.: An exact algorithm for f-measure maximization. In: Advances in Neural Information Processing Systems, vol. 24 (2011)
9. Dembczyński, K., Waegeman, W., Cheng, W., Hüllermeier, E.: On label dependence and loss minimization in multi-label classification. Mach. Learn. **88**, 5–45 (2012)
10. Ferguson, T.: Mathematical Statistics : A Decision Theoretic Approach. Academic Press (1967)
11. Gerych, W., Hartvigsen, T., Buquicchio, L., Agu, E., Rundensteiner, E.: Recurrent Bayesian classifier chains for exact multi-label classification. In: Proceedings of the 35th Conference on Neural Information Processing Systems (NeurIPS), pp. 15981–15992 (2021)
12. Gilet, C., Barbosa, S., Fillatre, L.: Discrete box-constrained minimax classifier for uncertain and imbalanced class proportions. IEEE Trans. Pattern Anal. Mach. Intell. **44**(6), 2923–2937 (2020)
13. Gilet, C., Guyomard, M., Barbosa, S., Fillatre, L.: Adjusting decision trees for uncertain class proportions. In: ECML/PKDD 2020 Tutorial and Workshop on Uncertainty in Machine Learning, Ghent, Belgium (2020). https://hal.science/hal-03624100
14. Giraldo-Forero, A.F., Jaramillo-Garzón, J.A., Ruiz-Muñoz, J.F., Castellanos-Domínguez, C.G.: Managing imbalanced data sets in multi-label problems: a case study with the SMOTE algorithm. In: Ruiz-Shulcloper, J., Sanniti di Baja, G. (eds.) CIARP 2013. LNCS, vol. 8258, pp. 334–342. Springer, Heidelberg (2013). https://doi.org/10.1007/978-3-642-41822-8_42
15. Liu, B., Tsoumakas, G.: Making classifier chains resilient to class imbalance. In: Asian Conference on Machine Learning, pp. 280–295. PMLR (2018)
16. Liu, M.C., et al.: Sensitive and specific multi-cancer detection and localization using methylation signatures in cell-free DNA. Ann. Oncol. **31**(6), 745–759 (2020)
17. Madrigal, S., Nguyen, V.L., Gilet, C., Destercke, S.: Discrete minimax binary relevance classifier for imbalanced multi-label classification. In: Destercke, S., Martinez, M.V., Sanfilippo, G. (eds.) SUM 2024. LNCS, vol. 15350, pp. 281–296. Springer, Cham (2024). https://doi.org/10.1007/978-3-031-76235-2_21
18. Nguyen, V.L., Hoang, X.T., Huynh, V.N.: Inference problem in probabilistic multi-label classification. In: Honda, K., Le, B., Huynh, V.N., Inuiguchi, M., Kohda, Y.

(eds.) IUKM 2023. LNCS, vol. 14376, pp. 3–14. Springer, Cham (2023). https://doi.org/10.1007/978-3-031-46781-3_1

19. Nguyen, V.-L., Hüllermeier, E., Rapp, M., Loza Mencía, E., Fürnkranz, J.: On aggregation in ensembles of multilabel classifiers. In: Appice, A., Tsoumakas, G., Manolopoulos, Y., Matwin, S. (eds.) DS 2020. LNCS (LNAI), vol. 12323, pp. 533–547. Springer, Cham (2020). https://doi.org/10.1007/978-3-030-61527-7_35
20. Nguyen, V.L., Yang, Y., de Campos, C.: Probabilistic multi-dimensional classification. In: Proceedings of the Thirty-Ninth Conference on Uncertainty in Artificial Intelligence (UAI), pp. 1522–1533 (2023)
21. Pakrashi, A., Mac Namee, B.: Stacked-MLkNN: a stacking based improvement to multi-label k-nearest neighbours. In: First International Workshop on Learning with Imbalanced Domains: Theory and Applications, pp. 51–63. PMLR (2017)
22. Poor, H.V.: An Introduction to Signal Detection and Estimation, 2nd edn. Springer, New York (1994)
23. Sun, K.W., Lee, C.H.: Addressing class-imbalance in multi-label learning via two-stage multi-label hypernetwork. Neurocomputing **266**, 375–389 (2017)
24. Tarekegn, A.N., Giacobini, M., Michalak, K.: A review of methods for imbalanced multi-label classification. Pattern Recogn. **118**, 107965 (2021)
25. Waegeman, W., Dembczyński, K., Jachnik, A., Cheng, W., Hüllermeier, E.: On the bayes-optimality of F-measure maximizers. J. Mach. Learn. Res. 3513–3568 (2014)
26. Wu, G., Tian, Y., Liu, D.: Cost-sensitive multi-label learning with positive and negative label pairwise correlations. Neural Netw. **108**, 411–423 (2018)
27. Yuan, Y., Liu, X., Ding, S., Pan, B.: Fault detection and location system for diagnosis of multiple faults in aeroengines. IEEE Access **5**, 17671–17677 (2017)
28. Zhang, K., Hu, X., Liu, Y., Lin, X., Liu, W.: Multi-fault detection and isolation for lithium-ion battery systems. IEEE Trans. Power Electron. **37**(1), 971–989 (2021)
29. Zhang, M.L., Li, Y.K., Yang, H., Liu, X.Y.: Towards class-imbalance aware multi-label learning. IEEE Trans. Cybern. **52**(6), 4459–4471 (2020)
30. Zhang, M.L., Zhou, Z.H.: ML-KNN: a lazy learning approach to multi-label learning. Pattern Recogn. **40**(7), 2038–2048 (2007)

Noise-Robust Weighted Logistic Regression Based on Outlier Detection with Expectation Maximization

Serafín Moral-García[1], Rafael Cabañas[2], and Antonio Salmerón[2](✉)

[1] Department of Computer Science and Artificial Intelligence, University of Granada, Granada, Spain
seramoral@decsai.ugr.es

[2] Department of Mathematics and Centre for the Development and Transfer of Mathematical Research to Industry (CDTIME), University of Almería, Almería, Spain
{rcabanas,antonio.salmeron}@ual.es

Abstract. Logistic regression (LR) is one of the most commonly used classification models in Machine Learning. Even though LR was shown to be asymptotically the best linear classifier, it can typically be at the cost of high variance when the sample size is small compared to the number of predictive variables. Moreover, LR models are extremely sensitive to outliers. The influence of outliers has traditionally been handled by using weighted LR so that data points considered not to be outliers have a weight equal to 1, whilst those considered outliers are assigned a lower weight, which is typically computed from some distance measure over the training data. In this paper, we propose a novel iterative procedure for estimating the parameters of an LR model that automatically accounts for the presence of outliers by following an expectation maximization (EM) approach. During the expectation step, each training data point is weighted according to its probability of being an outlier; in the maximization step, the parameters of the LR model and the outlier probabilities are updated. We have experimentally validated our proposal using a set of well-established benchmark datasets for classification. The results of the experiments show that, in addition to being computationally tractable, our new method outperforms both plain LR and several outliers detection methods, in terms of accuracy and logarithmic loss.

Keywords: Logistic regression · Expectation maximization · Outlier detection

1 Introduction

In Machine Learning, Logistic regression (LR) is one of the most commonly used classification models. LR was shown to be asymptotically the best linear classifier [5]. However, it is also known that its variance can be high, especially

K. Sauerwald and M. Thimm (Eds.): ECSQARU 2025, LNAI 16099, pp. 92–103, 2026.
https://doi.org/10.1007/978-3-032-05134-9_7

if the sample size is small in relation to the number of predictive variables [11]. Furthermore, the estimation procedure for LR models is extremely sensitive to outliers [7]. The influence of outliers has traditionally been handled by using weighted LR, so that data points that are not considered outliers are given a weight equal to 1, while those considered outliers are assigned a lower weight, which is typically computed through some distance measure over the training data [9,12]. The benefits of removing or weighting outliers for LR in terms of classification accuracy have also been studied [6].

Consequently, anomaly detection algorithms are often applied during pre-processing to identify outliers before fitting the model. In this context, various approaches have been proposed. One of the simplest methods is the *Elliptic Envelope* [8], which fits a robust multivariate Gaussian distribution to the data. Outliers are then identified as observations that fall outside the estimated elliptical contour. *Local Outlier Factor* [1] is a density-based method that evaluates the local density deviation of a data point with respect to its neighbors. Points with substantially lower density than their surrounding data are identified as outliers. *One-Class SVM* [10] is a kernel-based method that learns a decision boundary around training data in a high-dimensional space, separating it from the origin. *Isolation Forest* [4] detects anomalies by recursively partitioning the data using randomly selected features and split values. Outliers tend to be isolated with fewer splits, resulting in shorter path lengths in the tree ensemble.

In this work, we propose a novel iterative procedure for estimating the parameters of an LR model that automatically accounts for the presence of outliers by following an *expectation maximization* (EM) approach. During the expectation step, each training instance is weighted according to its probability of being an outlier, and, in the maximization step, the parameters of the LR model and the probability of outlier are updated. Hence, our proposed method uses individual weights for the instances that indicate the probability of each instance being an outlier. Such weights may represent quite useful information to learn the model and predict the probabilities of the class values for new instances.

An experimental analysis has been conducted to check the performance of our presented EM-based algorithm. Such an analysis has highlighted that our proposal outperforms the original LR method and three outlier detectors applied before using LR in terms of Accuracy and Logarithmic Loss.

The remainder of this paper is structured as follows. Section 2 provides an overview of the existing methods related to Logistic Regression. Our proposed Expectation-Maximization algorithm for Logistic Regression is introduced in Sect. 3. Section 4 details our experimental study. Conclusions and ideas for future work are provided in Sect. 5.

2 Background

Let C denote the class variable and $\{c^1, c^2, \ldots, c^K\}$ its possible values. Let N be the number of instances in the training set. Let $\mathbf{X} = \{X_1, \ldots, X_m\}$ denote a set of predictive attributes. Let $\mathbf{x_i}$ be the set of predictive attribute values of the i-th training instance and c_i its class value, $\forall i = 1, 2, \ldots, N$.

Given the class variable C and the predictive variables $\mathbf{X}$, an LR classifier [5] for C given $\mathbf{X}$ is a discriminative model that represents the corresponding conditional probability as

$$P(C = 1|\mathbf{x}) = \frac{\exp\{\mathbf{x}^\top \boldsymbol{\beta}\}}{\exp\{1 + \mathbf{x}^\top \boldsymbol{\beta}\}}, \tag{1}$$

where $\mathbf{x} = (1, x_1, \ldots, x_m)^\top$ encodes a possible value of $\mathbf{X}$ and $\boldsymbol{\beta} = (\beta_0, \ldots, \beta_m)^\top$, β_0 being the intercept and β_j, $1 \leq j \leq m$, is the coefficient corresponding to the j-th predictive variable.

The parameters are usually estimated from the training set by maximizing the conditional likelihood as

$$\boldsymbol{\beta}_{\text{LR}} = \arg \max_{\boldsymbol{\beta} \in \mathbb{R}^{m+1}} \prod_{i=1}^{N} P(c_i|\mathbf{x}_i, \boldsymbol{\beta}). \tag{2}$$

Equation (2) assumes that all elements in the sample are equally representative. Nevertheless, it is possible to learn LR models if the elements of the sample are assigned a weight $w_i \in [0, 1]$, so that in this case the parameters of the model are approximated as

$$\boldsymbol{\beta}_{\text{WLR}} = \arg \max_{\boldsymbol{\beta} \in \mathbb{R}^{m+1}} \prod_{i=1}^{N} (w_i P(c_i|\mathbf{x}_i, \boldsymbol{\beta})). \tag{3}$$

The impact of outliers in LR has previously been addressed via Weighted Logistic Regression [12], using an iterative procedure that divides the sample into outliers and non-outliers, assigning a weight equal to 1 to the non-outliers and $w < 1$ to outliers.

Our proposal consists of individually accounting for the contribution of each element in the sample by assigning individual weights that are iteratively updated.

3 Expectation-Maximization for Handling Outliers in Logistic Regression

The Expectation Maximization (EM) algorithm for LR proposed here weights the instances for the LR model so that those with higher probabilities of being outliers have lower weights. In addition, it regularizes the probabilities predicted by LR that each instance has each class value by considering the probability that the instance is an outlier. Two steps are iteratively repeated until convergence conditions are reached:

1. **Expectation:** The weight of each instance is computed. This weight indicates the probability that the instance is an outlier.

2. **Maximization:** An LR model is learned with the computed weights. The probability distribution of the class variable for outliers is estimated, as well as the probability of an instance being an outlier, which is determined via the average of the instance weights.

In order to describe our introduced EM algorithm, the following notation is employed:

- $P(c_i|\mathbf{x_i})$: Probability that the i-th training instance has the class value c_i, $\forall i = 1, 2, \ldots, N$.
- $P(O = 1)$ ($P(O = 0)$): General probability of an instance being an outlier (non-outlier).
- $P(c_i|\mathbf{x_i}, O = 1)$ ($P(c_i|\mathbf{x_i}, O = 0)$): Probability that the i-th training instance has the class value c_i given that the instance is an outlier (non-outlier).
- w_i: weight of the i-th training instance, which corresponds to the probability of that instance being a non-outlier.

The algorithm initially considers $P(O = 0) = 0.95$ (or equivalently, $P(O = 1) = 0.05$), as well as a uniform probability distribution on the class variable for outlier instances, that is, $P(c^j|O = 1) = \frac{1}{K}$, $\forall j = 1, 2, \ldots, K$. We select these values, which may be arbitrary, because it might make sense to consider that the majority of the instances are not outliers and assume the maximum uncertainty about the class distribution for outlier instances.

In the first step, all instances have the same probability of non-outlier (0.95). Hence, an LR model is learned with uniform weights. Such a model predicts the probability of each class value for each instance conditioned on that instance is a non-outlier, that is, $P(c_i|O = 0)$, $\forall i = 1, 2, \ldots, N$.

Using the law of total probability, the probability of c_i for each training instance $\mathbf{x}_i$, $i = 1, \ldots, N$, is corrected as

$$P(c_i|\mathbf{x_i}) = P(O = 0)P(c_i|\mathbf{x_i}, O = 0) + P(O = 1)P(c_i|O = 1). \quad (4)$$

Considering the sum of the logarithms of these probabilities, a score is obtained for this first iteration:

$$old\_score = \sum_{i=1}^{N} \log P(c_i|\mathbf{x_i}). \quad (5)$$

Then, the probabilities of each instance being a non-outlier (the instance weights) are updated via Bayes' theorem:

$$w_i = \frac{P(O = 0) \cdot P(c_i \mid \mathbf{x_i}, O = 0)}{P(c_i \mid \mathbf{x_i})}, \quad \forall i = 1, 2, \ldots, N, \quad (6)$$

where each $P(c_i \mid \mathbf{x_i})$ is computed via Eq. (4).

The general probability of an instance being a non-outlier is updated by means of the average of the new weights:

$$P(O = 0) = \frac{\sum_{i=1}^{N} w_i}{N}, \quad P(O = 1) = 1 - P(O = 0). \tag{7}$$

Now, the probability of each class value conditioned on an instance being an outlier is computed via the sum of the probabilities of outliers of the training instances that have such a class value and a regularization parameter s:

$$P(c^j \mid O = 1) = \sum_{i \mid c_i = c^j} 1 - w_i + \frac{s}{K}, \quad \forall j = 1, 2, \ldots, K. \tag{8}$$

These probabilities are normalized as follows:

$$P(c^j \mid O = 1) = \frac{P(c^j \mid O = 1)}{\sum_{k=1}^{K} P(c^k \mid O = 1)}, \quad \forall j = 1, 2, \ldots, K. \tag{9}$$

An LR model is learned with the new weights w_i. This model is used to predict $P(c_i \mid \mathbf{x_i}, O = 0)$. Again, $P(c_i \mid \mathbf{x_i})$ is computed using the total probability theorem (Eq. (4)), $\forall i = 1, 2, \ldots, N$.

These estimated probabilities lead to a new score for the current iteration:

$$new\_score = \sum_{i=1}^{N} \log P(c_i \mid \mathbf{x_i}). \tag{10}$$

The procedure is repeated iteratively until the score for an iteration is close enough to the score corresponding to the previous one or a maximum number of iterations is reached. Algorithm 1 summarizes our presented EM algorithm for handling outliers in LR.

When a new instance $\mathbf{x}$ is needed to be classified, the probability of each class value c^j for that instance conditioned on the instance is a non-outlier, namely, $P(c^j \mid \mathbf{x}, O = 0)$, is estimated via the learned model. Such a probability is corrected taking into account the probability of that class value for outlier instances, $P(c^j \mid, O = 1)$.

Then, the probability of each class value c^j for the instance to classify is computed via the law of total probability, similar to Eq. (4):

$$P(c^j \mid \mathbf{x}) = P(O = 0)P(c^j \mid \mathbf{x}, O = 0) + P(O = 1)P(c^j \mid O = 1), \quad \forall j = 1, 2, \ldots, K. \tag{11}$$

The output class value for the instance is the one with the highest predicted probability according to Eq. (11).

We may note that while other outlier detectors completely remove the instances that might be outliers, our proposed EM algorithm estimates the probability of each instance being an outlier and utilizes such probabilities to compute the probability of each class value for that instance through the LR method. Therefore, our proposed EM method may be quite suitable for LR to handle errors in a classification dataset. This point is corroborated via an experimental analysis conducted in Sect. 4.

Expectation-Maximization (threshold for the convergence ϵ, maximum of iterations max_it, regularization parameter s)
1. $P(c^j \mid O = 1) = 1/K, \quad \forall j = 1, 2, \ldots, K.$
2. $w_i = 0.95, \quad \forall i = 1, 2, \ldots, N.$
3. $P(O = 0) = 0.95, \quad P(O = 1) = 0.05.$
4. Learn an LR model with uniform weights.
5. Use the learned model to predict $P(c_i \mid \mathbf{x_i}, O = 0), \quad \forall i = 1, 2, \ldots, N.$
6. Using the Total Probability theorem, predict:
$P(c_i \mid \mathbf{x_i}) = P(O = 0)P(c_i \mid \mathbf{x_i}, O = 0) + P(O = 1)P(c_i \mid O = 1),$
$\forall i = 1, 2, \ldots, N$
7. Obtain $old\_score = \sum_{i=1}^{N} \log P(c_i \mid \mathbf{x_i})$
8. Update the weights through Bayes's theorem:
$w_i = \frac{P(O=0)P(c_i|\mathbf{x_i},O=0)}{P(c_i|\mathbf{x_i})}, \quad \forall i = 1, 2, \ldots N.$
9. $Convergence = False$
10. $num\_it = 1$
while *Not Convergence and* $num\_it < max\_it$ **do**
  11. $P(O = 0) = \frac{\sum_{i=1}^{K} w_i}{N}.$
  12. $P(c^j \mid O = 1) = \sum_{i|c_i=c^j} 1 - w_i + \frac{s}{K}, \quad \forall j = 1, 2, \ldots, K.$
  13. $P(c^j \mid O = 1) = \frac{P(c^j|O=1)}{\sum_{k=1}^{K} P(c^k|O=1)}$ (Normalization)
  14. Learn an LR model with the new weights w_i.
  15. Using the learned model, predict $P(c_i \mid \mathbf{x_i}, O = 0), \quad \forall i = 1, 2, \ldots, N.$
  16. $P(c_i \mid \mathbf{x_i}) = P(O = 0)P(c_i \mid \mathbf{x_i}, O = 0) + P(O = 1)P(c_i \mid O = 1), \quad \forall i = 1, 2, \ldots, N$
  17. $new\_score = \sum_{i=1}^{N} \log P(c_i \mid \mathbf{x_i})$
  if $|new\_score - old\_score| < \epsilon$ **then**
    18. $Convergence$ = True
  end
  else
    19. old_score = new_score
    20. Update the weights $w_i = \frac{P(O=0)P(c_i|\mathbf{x_i},O=0)}{P(c_i|\mathbf{x_i})}, \quad \forall i = 1, 2, \ldots, N.$
    21. num_it += 1.
  end
end

Algorithm 1: Proposed Expectation-Maximization procedure for Logistic Regression.

4 Experiments

4.1 Experimental Settings

For our experimental study, we have considered 23 well-known classification datasets, which can be downloaded from the *UCI Machine Learning Repository* [3]. Table 1 presents the most relevant characteristics of each dataset: number of instances, number of attributes (continuous and discrete), and number of class values. We may note that the datasets utilized are diverse concerning these issues.

Table 1. Datasets used in this experimental study. N is the number of instances, N_F indicates the number of predictive attributes, 'Cont' and 'Disc' mean, respectively, the number of continuous and discrete attributes, and K is the number of class values.

Dataset	N	N_F	Cont	Disc	K
Annealing	798	38	6	32	6
Balance scale	625	4	4	0	3
Breast cancer	286	8	0	8	2
Car	1728	6	0	6	4
Credit approval	690	15	6	9	2
Dermatology	366	34	1	33	6
Heart disease	303	13	6	7	2
Ionosphere	351	34	34	0	2
Iris	150	4	4	0	3
Letter	20000	16	16	0	26
Lung cancer	32	56	0	56	2
Nursery	12960	8	0	8	4
Post-operative patient	90	9	0	9	3
Solar flare	1389	12	9	3	3
Soybean	683	35	0	35	19
Spectrometer	531	101	100	1	48
Waveform	5000	40	40	0	3
Wine	178	13	13	0	3
Yeast	1484	8	8	0	10
Zoo	101	16	1	15	7
Website phishing	235795	54	50	4	2
Covid surveillance	14	7	0	7	2
Taiwanese bankruptcy	6819	95	95	0	2

Since LR only works with numerical predictive variables, all discrete attributes (except the class variable) have been transformed into dummy variables, that is, for each variable X with possible values $\{x_1, x_2, \ldots, x_t\}$, where $t \geq 3$, $t-1$ binary variables are created, $X_2, \ldots, X_t$, in such a way that, for a given instance, $X_j = 1$ if $X = x_j$ and 0 otherwise, $\forall j = 2, \ldots, t$. The functionality available in the Python library *sklearn* for this purpose has been employed. We must remark that we aim to highlight the performance of the proposed EM method with the presence of errors in the dataset. In consequence, for each dataset, a 10% of noise has been introduced as follows: 10% of the instances have been selected and, for each one of these instances, its class value has been changed randomly to another class value. This preprocessing has been applied to the training sets and then translated to the test sets.

We have employed the LR algorithm, the EM method introduced in Sect. 3, and three combinations of an outlier detection method followed by LR[1]. The outlier detectors employed are Elliptic Envelope [8], Isolation Forest [4], and Local Outlier Factor [1]. The implementation available in *sklearn* for LR has been utilized, and the necessary structures and methods for using EM have been added. We have also used the implementations available in sklearn for the mentioned outlier detectors, adding the required functionality for removing the instances detected as outliers.

For each preprocessed dataset and classifier considered in these experiments, a 5-fold cross-validation procedure has been conducted. The same partitions have been considered for all algorithms.

In order to check the performance of the algorithms employed here, the Accuracy and Logarithmic Loss metrics have been used.

For statistical comparisons, we have followed the indications given in [2] when there are three or more algorithms on many datasets. Hence, the Friedman test has been used with a significance level of 0.05 to compare the performance of the algorithms considered here in both Accuracy and Logarithmic Loss. This statistical test is nonparametric and ranks the algorithms separately on each dataset.

4.2 Results and Discussion

Tables 2 and 3 show the results obtained by each algorithm on each dataset in Accuracy and Logarithmic Loss, respectively. The average Friedman ranks of the methods in both evaluation measures can be seen in Table 4. In all tables, we use bold (italic) fonts to mark the best (second-best) results.

We may note that, for both evaluation metrics, our proposed EM method achieves the lowest average Friedman rank, the difference being more notable in Logarithmic Loss (2.1729 vs. 1.413). This point can also be observed in the results obtained per dataset: in Logarithmic Loss, EM achieves the best result in 16 datasets, whereas, in Accuracy, it gets the best performance in 13 datasets.

It can also be appreciated that for both evaluation metrics, the three outlier detectors considered here obtain the highest average Friedman ranks. Moreover, we may observe that LR obtains the best or second-best result in most datasets for both evaluation metrics. Thereby, it can be stated that LR performs better than LR with the three outlier detectors considered in these experiments. Within such detectors, in the Friedman ranks obtained in both Accuracy and Logarithmic Loss, it can be noted that Elliptic Envelope attains the worst results, followed by Isolation Forest and Local Outlier Factor. Again, the differences are more notable in Logarithmic Loss than in Accuracy. It might seem counter-intuitive that LR with the outlier detectors obtains worse results than a single LR model. Investigating in detail the reason for this issue is a pending task for future research. It is known that LR does not perform well with errors in the

[1] The outlier detectors are applied to the complete dataset rather than separately to each class.

Table 2. Accuracy results

Dataset	LR	EM	Elliptic Envelope	Isolation Forest	Local Outlier Factor
Annealing	0.6992	0.6992	0.6992	0.6992	0.6992
Balance scale	0.8032	**0.808**	0.7968	*0.8048*	0.8
Breast cancer	**0.7132**	**0.7132**	0.7131	0.6713	0.6852
Car	0.7691	**0.7847**	0.757	0.7483	*0.7755*
Credit approval	*0.6217*	0.6087	0.613	0.6101	**0.6333**
Dermatology	*0.7953*	0.7871	0.776	*0.7953*	**0.8005**
Heart disease	0.5675	*0.5708*	0.5644	0.5677	**0.5874**
Ionosphere	**0.7835**	*0.7834*	0.7721	0.7778	0.755
Iris	0.8	**0.86**	**0.86**	0.8533	**0.86**
Letter	*0.7449*	**0.7538**	0.7221	0.7365	0.7439
Lung cancer	0.619	0.619	**0.6476**	0.5476	**0.6476**
Nursery	*0.8262*	**0.8285**	0.8217	0.8206	0.8257
Post-operative patient	**0.6111**	**0.6111**	0.5889	**0.6111**	0.5889
Solar flare	0.8956	0.8956	0.8956	0.8956	0.8956
Soybean	*0.7755*	**0.7787**	0.694	0.7203	0.7396
Spectrometer	*0.7752*	*0.7752*	0.7714	**0.7863**	0.7639
Waveform	0.7834	**0.788**	*0.7848*	0.7816	0.7844
Wine	0.8141	**0.8198**	0.8084	*0.8143*	*0.8143*
Yeast	0.5155	**0.5216**	0.5135	0.5081	*0.5202*
Zoo	**0.8419**	**0.8419**	0.8229	0.8214	0.7829
Website phising	*0.7761*	0.7746	0.7709	**0.7776**	0.7724
Covid surveillance	**0.4667**	**0.4667**	0.3333	**0.4667**	0.4
Taiwanese bankrupcy	0.8678	0.8668	0.8674	**0.8749**	*0.8707*

data. The experimental results allow us to deduce that directly removing the instances detected as outliers might not be a good idea. Instead, it is probably better to take into account the outliers through lower weights, and this is done by our proposal.

To summarize, we can state that the three outlier detectors considered here obtain poor performance when they are used before applying LR. In fact, they perform worse than a single LR method. Our proposed EM method for handling outliers outperforms a single LR algorithm, unlike the outlier detectors mentioned. It might be because, unlike the outlier detectors, our proposal does not remove the instances that are likely to be outliers. Instead, it considers the probability that each instance is an outlier and uses that probability to estimate the probability of each class value for that instance. In this way, our proposed method may employ more useful information than the outlier detectors to address errors in the data.

Table 3. Logarithmic Loss results

Dataset	LR	EM	Elliptic Envelope	Isolation Forest	Local Outlier Factor
Annealing	*1.111*	**1.047**	1.1358	1.1178	1.1224
Balance scale	*0.6414*	**0.6303**	0.7241	0.7069	0.765
Breast cancer	*0.6024*	**0.5996**	0.6025	0.6181	0.6125
Car	*0.6838*	**0.6435**	0.7909	0.72	0.8237
Credit aproval	0.6765	0.6771	*0.674*	0.6753	**0.6564**
Dermatology	*0.9984*	1.0044	1.0404	1.0364	**0.9681**
Heart disease	*1.1547*	**1.149**	1.1739	1.1621	1.1656
Ionosphere	*0.5193*	**0.5042**	0.5354	0.5429	0.5816
Iris	*0.7587*	**0.6489**	0.8595	0.8647	0.8252
Letter	*1.3041*	**1.1694**	1.3816	1.3358	1.3548
Lung cancer	**0.8542**	*0.8577*	0.8634	0.9896	0.9261
Nursery	*0.6744*	**0.6159**	0.8693	0.6875	0.9845
Post-operative patient	*1.0522*	**1.0423**	1.0776	1.0678	1.0611
Solar flare	*0.4137*	**0.4108**	0.4239	0.4285	0.4186
Soybean	*1.1327*	**1.115**	1.4878	1.3796	1.3679
Spectrometer	0.5528	**0.5413**	0.5614	0.5625	*0.5479*
Waveform	*0.6838*	**0.6007**	0.6872	0.6917	0.6853
Wine	0.6329	**0.6178**	*0.6304*	0.6387	0.6394
Yeast	*1.4555*	**1.4405**	1.4627	1.4778	1.4668
Zoo	*0.7465*	*0.7465*	0.8023	0.7799	**0.7438**
Website phising	*0.6427*	**0.6369**	0.6587	0.6509	0.6577
Covid surveillance	1.1971	*1.1879*	1.2806	**1.1546**	1.2237
Taiwanese bankrupcy	*0.4123*	**0.3852**	0.4156	0.4164	0.4134

Table 4. Average Friedman Ranks in Accuracy and Logarithmic Loss.

Algorithm	Friedman rank Accuracy	Friedman rank Logarithmic Loss
LR	*2.6522*	*2.1957*
EM	**2.1739**	**1.413**
Elliptic Envelope	3.8696	4.0435
Isolation Forest	3.3261	3.8696
Local Outlier Factor	2.9783	3.4783

The differences are more notable in Logarithmic Loss than in Accuracy. This might happen because the former metric reflects better the improvements in the estimated probabilities than the latter. Actually, in many cases, improvements in the computed probabilities do not affect the predicted class values. However, if we consider the results obtained across many datasets, an improvement in the predicted probabilities tends to imply, on average, an improvement in the output class values.

5 Conclusions and Future Research

In this work, we have presented an Expectation-Maximization (EM) procedure to handle outliers in Logistic Regression (LR). This procedure iteratively estimates the probability that each instance is an outlier in two steps. In the expectation step, each instance is weighted according to the probability that such an instance is an outlier. In the maximization step, an LR model is learned with the computed weights, and the probability distribution of the class variable for outliers and the probability of outlier for each instance are updated. In this way, our presented model uses weights for the instances in LR according to the probability that each instance is an outlier, unlike other outlier detectors, which only determine whether an instance is an outlier.

An experimental analysis conducted has highlighted that our proposal performs notably better than a single LR method and LR applying previously other outlier detection methods to remove outlier instances. The satisfactory performance achieved by our introduced EM-based method suggests that it is appropriate for handling errors in classification datasets.

Future work might include deeper experimentation with a fine calibration of the parameters of the proposed EM algorithm: the initial probability of non-outliers and the initial probability distribution of the class variable for outliers. Moreover, as said before, it would be convenient to study in detail why the outlier detectors considered here perform worse than plain LR, which may be counter-intuitive. We also plan to design a Bayesian version of the presented algorithm.

Acknowledgments. RC and AS acknowledge Grant PID2022-139293NB-C31 funded by MICIU/AEI/10.13039/501100011033 and by ERDF "A way of making Europe". RC and AS acknowledge the University of Almería Research and Transfer Programme funded by "Consejería de Universidad, Investigación e Innovación de la Junta de Andalucía" through the European Regional Development Fund (ERDF), Operation Programme 2021–2027. Programme: Research and Innovation 54.A. RC was also supported by "Plan Propio de Investigación y Transferencia 2024–2025" from University of Almería under the project P_LANZ_2024/003.

This research has been supported by the Project PID2022-139293NB-C33, funded by MICIU/AEI/10.13039/501100011033/and the European Regional Development Fund (ERDF/EU), and by the "FEDER/Junta de Andalucía-Consejería de Transformación Económica, Industrial, Conocimiento y Universidades" under Project DGP_PID I_2024_00396.

Disclosure of Interests. The authors have no competing interests to declare that are relevant to the content of this article.

References

1. Breunig, M.M., Kriegel, H.P., Ng, R.T., Sander, J.: LOF: identifying density-based local outliers. In: Proceedings of the 2000 ACM SIGMOD International Conference on Management of Data, pp. 93–104 (2000)
2. Demšar, J.: Statistical comparisons of classifiers over multiple data sets. J. Mach. Learn. Res. **7**, 1–30 (2006)
3. Kelly, M., Longjohn, R., Nottingham, K.: The UCI machine learning repository. https://archive.ics.uci.edu
4. Liu, F.T., Ting, K.M., Zhou, Z.H.: Isolation forest. In: 2008 Eighth IEEE International Conference on Data Mining, pp. 413–422. IEEE (2008)
5. Ng, A., Jordan, M.: On discriminative vs. generative classifiers: a comparison of logistic regression and naïve Bayes. In: Advances in Neural Information Processing Systems, pp. 841–848 (2002)
6. Nurunnabi, A., West, G.: Outlier detection in logistic regression: a quest for reliable knowledge from predictive modeling and classification. In: IEEE 12th International Conference on Data Mining Workshops (ICDMW), pp. 643–652 (2012)
7. Pregibon, D.: Logistic regression diagnostics. Ann. Stat. **9**, 705–724 (1981)
8. Rousseeuw, P.J., Driessen, K.V.: A fast algorithm for the minimum covariance determinant estimator. Technometrics **41**(3), 212–223 (1999)
9. Rousseeuwa, P.J., Christmann, A.: Robustness against separation and outliers in logistic regression. Comput. Stat. Data Anal. **43**, 315–332 (2003)
10. Schölkopf, B., Platt, J.C., Shawe-Taylor, J., Smola, A.J., Williamson, R.C.: Estimating the support of a high-dimensional distribution. Neural Comput. **13**(7), 1443–1471 (2001)
11. Tan, Y., Sherwood, B., Shenoy, P.P.: A naïve Bayes regularized logistic regression estimator for low-dimensional classification. Int. J. Approximate Reasoning **172**, 109239 (2024)
12. Venter, J.H., Rey, T.: Detecting outliers using weights. S. Afr. Stat. J. **41**, 127–160 (2007)

From RBMs to BN2A Models: Parameter Transformation for Interpretable Educational Diagnostics

Iván Pérez[1,2,3(✉)], Jiří Vomlel[1], and Patrícia Martinková[2]

[1] Institute of Information Theory and Automation, Czech Academy of Sciences, Prague, Czechia
{cabrera,vomlel}@utia.cas.cz
[2] Institute of Computer Science, Czech Academy of Sciences, Prague, Czechia
martinkova@cs.cas.cz
[3] Faculty of Mathematics and Physics, Charles University, Prague, Czechia

Abstract. Restricted Boltzmann Machines (RBMs) are bipartite graphical models with binary latent and observed variables that have shown promise for representation learning. However, their lack of interpretable parameters limits their utility in domains requiring explainability, like educational assessment. Despite extensive RBM research, non-negativity constraints on weights—essential for monotonicity in educational contexts—remain largely unexplored. To address this, we propose a method to translate RBMs into a specialized class of bipartite Bayesian networks, which we term BN2A networks, characterized by strict 2-layer separation (hidden and observed variables), Noisy-AND conditional probability tables, and directly interpretable parameters for educational models. Our work establishes a mathematical transformation from RBM weights to BN2A's interpretable parameters (leak and penalty probabilities), theoretical analysis showing BN2A's constrained connectivity is a subset of RBM architectures, and empirical evidence that the transformation preserves model fidelity under realistic conditions. By bridging these paradigms, our method leverages RBM's representational power while achieving BN2A's interpretability, opening new possibilities for adaptive learning systems and diagnostic tools.

Keywords: Restricted Boltzmann Machines · BN2A models · Educational Assessment · Interpretable machine learning

1 Introduction

Bayesian networks (BNs) [8,9,13] are a widely used framework for modeling probabilistic relationships between random variables. This paper develops an analytical framework for a specific subclass of BNs that we termed BN2A [15]: BNs with 2-layer structure and noisy-AND interactions. In this model, the top layer comprises mutually independent hidden (unobservable) binary variables, while the bottom layer consists of observed binary variables that depend exclusively on the hidden layer. These dependencies are characterized by conditional

K. Sauerwald and M. Thimm (Eds.): ECSQARU 2025, LNAI 16099, pp. 104–117, 2026.
https://doi.org/10.1007/978-3-032-05134-9_8

probability tables (CPTs) based on noisy-AND models, a well-established family of canonical CPT representations [2,6]. Figure 1 illustrates the directed bipartite graph structure of a BN2A model.

The BN2A framework is particularly relevant in psychometrics [14], where it is applied to cognitive diagnostic modeling of students. Here, hidden variables represent latent skills, while observed variables correspond to test responses. A key feature of this domain is that correct answers typically require mastery of all relevant skills, though compensatory mechanisms may exist (e.g., alternative knowledge compensating for a missing skill). The Noisy-AND model naturally captures this "conjunctive" relationship between skills and responses.

Restricted Boltzmann Machines (RBMs) [7,18] represent another two-layer architecture widely used for unsupervised learning. Like BN2A models, RBMs consist of visible and hidden units with restricted connectivity, enabling them to learn complex data distributions [4]. A key distinction, however, is that RBM connections are undirected rather than directed. Recent studies have demonstrated their potential in psychometrics, particularly for modeling latent traits and response patterns [10].

Despite nearly four decades of research on RBMs, there is limited literature addressing non-negativity constraints on RBM weights. This gap is particularly relevant in educational contexts where monotonicity properties (a direct consequence of non-negativity constraints) are essential, students with higher skill levels should have higher probabilities of correct responses.

Although prior work has explored connections between BNs and neural networks [1], studies specifically linking RBMs to BNs interpretations are limited. This work demonstrates how constrained RBMs with non-negative weights can be effectively applied to educational diagnosis, and more importantly, how their parameters can be directly interpreted through transformation to BN2A parameters, bridging the gap between representational power and interpretability in cognitive diagnostic modeling.

The paper is organized as follows: Sect. 2 introduces RBMs and their mathematical formulations, while Sect. 3 formally defines BN2A models and their educational testing applications. In Sect. 4, we establish conditions linking BN2A models and RBMs, alongside a modified Contrastive Divergence (CD) algorithm for RBMs parameter learning. Experimental results are presented in Sect. 5, followed by conclusions in Sect. 6.

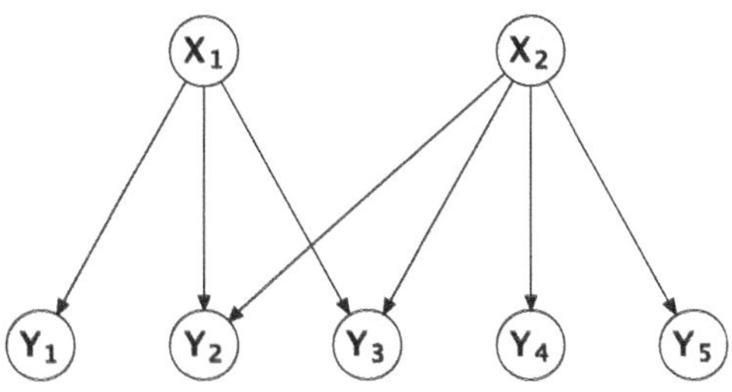

Fig. 1. An example of a BN2A model structure.

2 RBM Model

RBMs have emerged as powerful generative neural networks with applications spanning computer vision, recommendation systems, and educational assessment [7].

2.1 Definition and Structure

An RBM is a bipartite undirected graphical model consisting of two distinct layers. The visible layer ($\mathbf{v}$) contains binary observed variables, where $v_i \in \{0, 1\}$. The hidden layer ($\mathbf{h}$) comprises binary latent variables ($h_j \in \{0, 1\}$) that capture underlying latent features. The model exhibits *restricted connectivity*, meaning there are no intra-layer connections between visible-visible or hidden-hidden units (Fig. 2).

This architecture enables the model to learn latent representations through symmetric connections between layers. The bipartite structure ensures that units within the same layer are conditionally independent given the state of the other layer, simplifying inference procedures.

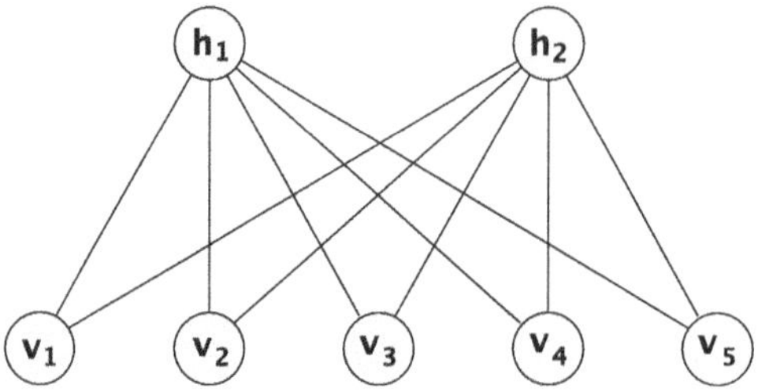

Fig. 2. Architecture of an RBM with 5 visible and 2 hidden units.

2.2 Mathematical Formulation

The model defines a probability distribution through an energy function that captures the compatibility between visible and hidden unit configurations:

$$E(\mathbf{v}, \mathbf{h}) = -\sum_i b_i v_i - \sum_j c_j h_j - \sum_{i,j} v_i W_{ij} h_j, \tag{1}$$

where b_i and c_j are biases for visible and hidden units respectively, and W_{ij} represents the weight connecting visible unit i to hidden unit j.

Lower energy configurations correspond to higher probability states. The joint probability distribution follows a Boltzmann distribution:

$$P(\mathbf{v}, \mathbf{h}) = \frac{1}{Z} e^{-E(\mathbf{v}, \mathbf{h})}, \quad Z = \sum_{\mathbf{v}, \mathbf{h}} e^{-E(\mathbf{v}, \mathbf{h})}. \tag{2}$$

The partition function Z ensures normalization but is generally intractable to compute. Due to the bipartite structure, conditional probabilities take sigmoid forms:

$$P(h_j = 1|\mathbf{v}) = \sigma\left(c_j + \sum_i v_i W_{ij}\right), \tag{3}$$

$$P(v_i = 1|\mathbf{h}) = \sigma\left(b_i + \sum_j h_j W_{ij}\right), \tag{4}$$

where $\sigma(x) = 1/(1+e^{-x})$ is the logistic function. These conditional independence properties enable efficient sampling through alternating Gibbs sampling between layers.

3 BN2A Model

Let $\mathbf{X}$ denote the vector $(X_1, \ldots, X_K)$ of K hidden variables, and similarly let $\mathbf{Y}$ denote the vector $(Y_1, \ldots, Y_L)$ of L observed dependent variables. The hidden variables are also called attributes or skills in the context of cognitive diagnostic models (CDMs) [19], and observed dependent variables are usually called items or questions in the same context. All variables are assumed to be binary, taking states from $\{0, 1\}$. The state space of the multidimensional variable $\mathbf{X}$ is denoted $\mathbb{X}$ and is equal to the Cartesian product of the state spaces of $X_k, k = 1, \ldots, K$:

$$\mathbb{X} = \times_{k=1}^{K} \mathbb{X}_k = \{0, 1\}^K. \tag{5}$$

Similarly, the state space of multidimensional variable $\mathbf{Y}$ is denoted $\mathbb{Y}$ and is equal to the Cartesian product of state spaces of $Y_\ell, \ell = 1, \ldots, L$:

$$\mathbb{Y} = \times_{\ell=1}^{L} \mathbb{Y}_\ell = \{0, 1\}^L. \tag{6}$$

The basic building blocks of a BN2A model are conditional probability tables (CPTs) specified in the form of a Noisy-AND model. Let Y_ℓ be an observed dependent variable and $pa(Y_\ell)$ be the subset of indices of related variables from $\mathbf{X}$. They are referred to as the parents of Y_ℓ.

Definition 1 (Noisy-AND model).
A conditional probability table $P(Y_\ell|\mathbf{X}_{pa(Y_\ell)})$ represents a Noisy-AND model if

$$P(Y_\ell = y_\ell|\mathbf{X}_{pa(Y_\ell)} = \mathbf{x}_{pa(Y_\ell)}) = \begin{cases} q_{\ell,0} \cdot \prod_{i \in pa(Y_\ell)} (q_{\ell,i})^{(1-x_i)} & \textit{if } y_\ell = 1 \\ 1 - q_{\ell,0} \cdot \prod_{i \in pa(Y_\ell)} (q_{\ell,i})^{(1-x_i)} & \textit{if } y_\ell = 0. \end{cases} \tag{7}$$

Note that if $x_i = 1$ then $(q_{\ell,i})^{(1-x_i)} = 1$ and if $x_i = 0$ then $(q_{\ell,i})^{(1-x_i)} = q_{\ell,i}$. The interpretation is that if $X_i = 1$, then this variable definitely enters the AND relation with the value 1. If $X_i = 0$, then there is still a probability $q_{\ell,i}$ that it enters the AND relation with value 1. The model also contains an auxiliary parent X_0 which is always 0 and thus enters the AND relation with probability $q_{\ell,0}$ for the value 1. This probability is traditionally called *leak* probability and allows non-zero probability of $Y_\ell = 0$ even if all parents of Y_ℓ have value 1. In educational diagnosis, the leak parameters $q_{\ell,0}$ represent the probability of answering question ℓ correctly when the student masters all required skills, while the parameters $q_{\ell,k}$ represent penalty factors for lacking the k-th skill when answering question ℓ. In the area of psychometrics, this model belongs to CDMs and is known as the Reduced Reparametrized Unified Model (RRUM) [5].

The prior probability of the hidden skill for $k = 1, \dots, K$ is defined as

$$P(X_k = x_k) = (p_k)^{x_k}(1 - p_k)^{(1-x_k)}, \tag{8}$$

which means that if $x_k = 1$ then it is p_k and if $x_k = 0$ then it equals $1 - p_k$.

Now we are ready to define a special class of BNs models with hidden variables, called BN2A model.

Definition 2 (BN2A model).
A BN2A model is a pair (G, P), where G is a directed bipartite graph with its nodes divided into two layers. The nodes of the top layer correspond to the hidden variables $X_1, \dots, X_K$ and the nodes of the bottom layer correspond to the observed variables $Y_1, \dots, Y_L$. All edges are directed from a node of the top layer to a node of the bottom layer. The symbol P refers to the joint probability distribution over the variables corresponding to the nodes of the graph G. The probability distribution is parameterized by a vector of model parameters $(\mathbf{p}, \mathbf{q})$:

$$(\mathbf{p}, \mathbf{q}) = \left((p_k)_{k\in\{1,\dots,K\}}, (q_{\ell,k})_{\ell\in\{1,\dots,L\},k\in\{0\}\cup pa(Y_\ell)}\right). \tag{9}$$

The bipartite graph G of a BN2A model can also be specified by an incidence matrix, in the context of CDM, traditionally denoted by $\mathbf{Q}$. A $\mathbf{Q}$-matrix is an $L \times K$ binary matrix, with entries $\mathbf{Q}_{\ell,k} \in \{0, 1\}$ that indicate whether or not the ℓth observed dependent variable is linked to the kth hidden variable:

$$\mathbf{Q}[\ell, k] = \begin{cases} 1 \text{ if } X_k \in pa(Y_\ell) \\ 0 \text{ otherwise.} \end{cases}$$

Monotonicity in BN2A

In the context of BNs, the concept of monotonicity constraint has been discussed in the literature for a long time [3,20]. More recent papers in this topic are [17], [12] and [16].

BNs model the probabilistic influences between its variables. Considering binary variables X and Y, a positive qualitative influence of a variable X on a variable Y along an arc $X \to Y$ in the network means that the occurrence of X increases the probability of Y occurs, assuming that the values of the other parents of Y remain the same. It means that

$$P(Y = 1|X = 1, \mathbf{z}) \geq P(Y = 1|X = 0, \mathbf{z}),$$

for any combination of values $\mathbf{z}$ for the set of parents of Y other than X [11,12]. In the context of educational testing, a positive influence is commonly assumed since mastering the skill X increases the probability of answering correctly the question Y.

BN2A models inherently satisfy the monotonicity property through their positive qualitative influences. Consider a variable Y with parent set $pa(Y)$ and two parent configurations $\mathbf{x}_{pa(Y)}$ and $\mathbf{x}'_{pa(Y)}$ that differ only in one skill: $x_i = 1$ in $\mathbf{x}_{pa(Y)}$ and $x'_i = 0$ in $\mathbf{x}'_{pa(Y)}$, while all other entries remain identical.

Using the Noisy-AND conditional probability from Eq. 7, for configuration $\mathbf{x}'_{pa(Y)}$ where $x'_i = 0$, the probability becomes:

$$P(Y_\ell = 1|\mathbf{x}'_{pa(Y_\ell)}) = q_{\ell,0} \cdot q_{\ell,i} \cdot \prod_{j \in pa(Y_\ell), j \neq i} q_{\ell,j}^{(1-x'_j)}. \tag{10}$$

The key difference is the additional penalty factor $q_{\ell,i}$ that appears when $x'_i = 0$. Since $0 < q_{\ell,i} \leq 1$ by model constraints, this factor can only reduce the probability. Therefore:

$$P(Y_\ell = 1|\mathbf{x}_{pa(Y_\ell)}) \geq P(Y_\ell = 1|\mathbf{x}'_{pa(Y_\ell)}). \tag{11}$$

4 Relation Between RBM and BN2A Models

While RBMs and BN2A models arise from different theoretical frameworks, neural networks and BNs, their two-layer architectures reveal intriguing parallels. Both models use hidden variables to influence observed responses, yet differ substantially in interpretability and parameter constraints.

The structural similarity becomes apparent when examining core components. BN2A models explicitly define hidden-observed relationships through prior probabilities $\boldsymbol{p}$ (analogous to RBM hidden activations $\mathbf{h}$) and structured parameters: leak probabilities and penalty parameters that, in educational contexts, determine how missing skills affect response probabilities. RBMs capture these relationships through a learned weight matrix $\mathbf{W}$ and bias terms, but without explicit cognitive interpretation.

The key difference lies in their design approaches. BN2A models prioritize interpretability and measurement consistency, constraining parameters to ensure meaningful relationships. In educational contexts, each penalty parameter $q_{j,k}$ directly represents the probability reduction when skill k is absent for question j, while $q_{j,0}$ represents success probability for question j when all required skills are present. RBMs optimize for representational flexibility, allowing weights to take any values that minimize reconstruction error, potentially sacrificing cognitive interpretability. This distinction leads to critical differences in monotonicity satisfaction. While BN2A models inherently satisfy monotonicity through constrained parameter spaces, RBMs require explicit modifications to ensure this fundamental property.

4.1 Lack of Monotonicity in Standard Binary RBMs

RBMs with binary units do not inherently satisfy the monotonicity property when interpreted in a cognitive diagnostic context, where hidden units represent latent skills and visible units correspond to test questions. In a binary RBM, the conditional probability of a visible unit v_i being active given the hidden layer configuration $\mathbf{h}$ is defined in Eq. 4.

The fundamental issue arises from the fact that weights W_{ij} can take negative values in standard RBM formulations. When $W_{ij} < 0$, activating hidden unit j (i.e., mastering skill j) actually decreases the logit and consequently reduces the probability of correctly answering question i. This counterintuitive behavior violates the monotonicity assumption that acquiring additional skills should not decrease performance. Consider two skill mastery patterns $\mathbf{h}$ and $\mathbf{h}'$ where $\mathbf{h} \preceq \mathbf{h}'$ (meaning $h_j \leq h'_j$ for all j). If there exists at least one negative weight $W_{ij} < 0$ for a skill j where $h_j < h'_j$, then the contribution $W_{ij}(h'_j - h_j) < 0$ to the logit sum, potentially making $P(v_i = 1|\mathbf{h}') < P(v_i = 1|\mathbf{h})$, thus violating monotonicity.

4.2 Ensuring Monotonicity Through Non-negative Weight Constraints

Monotonicity can be guaranteed in binary RBMs by imposing non-negative constraints on the weight matrix, i.e., $W_{ij} \geq 0$ for all i, j. Under this restriction, the model becomes monotonic with respect to hidden unit activations. Formally, for any two hidden layer configurations $\mathbf{h}$ and $\mathbf{h}'$ such that $\mathbf{h} \preceq \mathbf{h}'$, we have:

$$\sum_j W_{ij} h'_j + b_i \geq \sum_j W_{ij} h_j + b_i.$$

This inequality holds because $W_{ij} \geq 0$ and $h'_j \geq h_j$ for all j, ensuring that $\sum_j W_{ij}(h'_j - h_j) \geq 0$. Since the sigmoid function $\sigma(\cdot)$ is strictly increasing, this logit ordering directly translates to probability ordering: $P(v_i = 1|\mathbf{h}') \geq P(v_i = 1|\mathbf{h})$. This constrained RBM formulation aligns with the cognitive interpretation where mastering additional skills should either maintain or improve test performance.

The non-negative weight constraint can be implemented during training through various approaches, including projected gradient methods, penalty functions, or weight reparameterization techniques. Among these alternatives, projection based methods offer computational efficiency and direct interpretability. In our approach, we implement this constraint within an algorithm by applying weight projection after each parameter update. Specifically, we enforce non-negativity through element-wise projection: $W \leftarrow \max(W, 0)$, ensuring that all weights remain non-negative throughout the training process.

4.3 From RBM to BN2A Parameters

Once we restrict the RBM model to non-negative weights, we can interpret the leak and penalty parameters of the BN2A model in terms of the biases of the observed variables and the weights connecting the hidden and observed layers in the RBM.

The relationship between both parameter sets can be derived from Eqs. 7 and 4.

$$q_{\ell,0} = \sigma\left(b_j + \sum_k W_{jk}\right), \tag{12}$$

$$q_{\ell,i} = \sigma\left(b_j + \sum_{k \neq i} W_{jk}\right) \cdot \frac{1}{q_{\ell,0}}, \tag{13}$$

where $\sigma(x) = 1/(1 + e^{-x})$ is the logistic function.

4.4 Algorithm

A key motivation for this research was the observation that RBM and BN2A models share very similar structures. Initially, we applied the well-established Contrastive Divergence (CD) [4,7] algorithm to data generated from a BN2A model (Sect. 5), but the resulting RBM exhibited some negative weights. We were unable to find a meaningful interpretation connecting these negative weights, or combinations thereof, to the parameters of the original BN2A model. This limitation motivated us to propose a modification to the CD algorithm.

The proposed approach extends the original CD algorithm for RBMs by incorporating two domain-specific constraints critical for educational testing: structural correspondence and non-negativity of weights.

Model structure: The algorithm enforces a binary mask (Q-matrix) that defines permissible connections between observed questions and hidden skills. During initialization, weights $\mathbf{W}$ are element-wise multiplied ($\odot$) by the Q-matrix $\mathbf{Q}$, ensuring zero weights for prohibited connections. This masking operation is reapplied after each weight update, maintaining the predefined structure throughout training.

Non-Negativity: Weights are constrained via $\max(\mathbf{W}, 0)$ to guarantee non-negative values, ensuring monotonicity between skill mastery and correct response probability, a cognitive assumption stating that higher skill proficiency cannot decrease the probability of correct responses.

The training process follows these key phases for each mini-batch:

Positive Phase: Computes hidden unit activations $\mathbf{h}_{\text{prob}}$ from observed data using the sigmoidal function σ, followed by stochastic binarization.

Negative Phase: Reconstructs visible units $\mathbf{V}_{\text{recon}}$ from sampled hidden states, then recomputes hidden activations.

Gradient Update: Adjusts parameters using the difference between positive and negative phase statistics, scaled by the learning rate η. Biases $\mathbf{b}$ and $\mathbf{c}$ are updated via gradient estimates [4].

This constrained approach maintains the computational efficiency of standard RBMs ($O(NLK)$ per epoch for N samples, L questions, K skills) while

Input : $\mathbf{V} \in \{0,1\}^{N \times L}$ – Binary observed data
K – Number of hidden units
$\mathbf{Q} \in \{0,1\}^{L \times K}$ – Mask matrix (Q-matrix)
T – Number of epochs
B – Batch size
η – Learning rate
Output: $\mathbf{W} \in \mathbb{R}_{+}^{L \times K}$ – Non-negative weights
$\mathbf{b} \in \mathbb{R}^{L}$ – Visible layer biases
$\mathbf{c} \in \mathbb{R}^{K}$ – Hidden layer biases

Initialize $\mathbf{W} \leftarrow |\mathcal{N}(0, 0.01)| \odot \mathbf{Q}$;
Initialize $\mathbf{b} \leftarrow \mathbf{0}$, $\mathbf{c} \leftarrow \mathbf{0}$;
for *epoch* $t \leftarrow 1$ **to** T **do**
  for *each batch* $\mathbf{V}_{batch} \subset \mathbf{V}$ *(size B)* **do**
    Positive phase:;
      $\mathbf{h}_{\text{prob}} \leftarrow \sigma(\mathbf{V}_{\text{batch}} \mathbf{W} + \mathbf{1}\mathbf{c}^T)$;
      $\mathbf{h}_{\text{states}} \leftarrow \text{Bernoulli}(\mathbf{h}_{\text{prob}})$;
    Negative phase:;
      $\mathbf{V}_{\text{recon}} \leftarrow \sigma(\mathbf{h}_{\text{states}} \mathbf{W}^T + \mathbf{1}\mathbf{b}^T)$;
      $\mathbf{h}_{\text{prob}}^{\text{neg}} \leftarrow \sigma(\mathbf{V}_{\text{recon}} \mathbf{W} + \mathbf{1}\mathbf{c}^T)$;
    Parameter update:;
      $\Delta\mathbf{W} \leftarrow \eta(\mathbf{V}_{\text{batch}}^T \mathbf{h}_{\text{prob}} - \mathbf{V}_{\text{recon}}^T \mathbf{h}_{\text{prob}}^{\text{neg}})/B$;
      $\mathbf{W} \leftarrow (\mathbf{W} + \Delta\mathbf{W}) \odot \mathbf{Q}$; `// Restrict structure`
      $\mathbf{W} \leftarrow \max(\mathbf{W}, 0)$; `// Enforce non-negativity`
      $\mathbf{b} \leftarrow \mathbf{b} + \eta \cdot \text{mean}(\mathbf{V}_{\text{batch}} - \mathbf{V}_{\text{recon}})$;
      $\mathbf{c} \leftarrow \mathbf{c} + \eta \cdot \text{mean}(\mathbf{h}_{\text{prob}} - \mathbf{h}_{\text{prob}}^{\text{neg}})$;
  end
end

Algorithm 1: Modified CD algorithm with Non-Negativity and Structure Constraints.

producing interpretable parameters that respect cognitive diagnostic requirements. The non-negativity constraint particularly differentiates it from conventional RBMs, guaranteeing plausible monotonic relationships.

5 Experiment

To demonstrate how we can learn RBM model parameters using Algorithm 1 and make these parameters interpretable by showing their relationship with BN2A model parameters, we conducted an experiment using a model with three hidden variables representing skills and 12 observed variables representing test questions. We used the structure shown in Fig. 3. In this model, note that some questions require only one skill, while the other questions require two skills to be answered correctly.

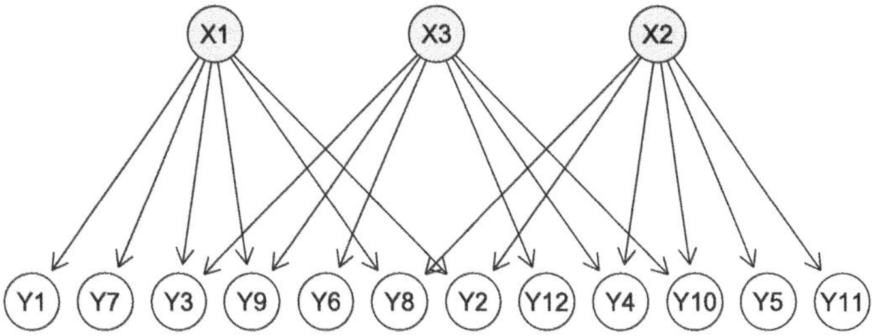

Fig. 3. BN2A model with three hidden variables and 12 observed variables.

As in any knowledge domain, some skills are easy to master and others are difficult; thus, tests typically require skills of varying mastery prevalence in the population. In our experiment, the simulated proportion of skill mastery (prior probabilities of mastering the skills) was set as $p_1 = 0.8$, $p_2 = 0.6$, and $p_3 = 0.4$. The leak parameters $q_{\ell,0}$ were selected to range from 0.6 to 0.95, and the penalty parameters $q_{\ell,k}$ were selected in the range of 0.1 to 0.4. These ranges are considered realistic for datasets where BN2A models are used in educational diagnosis [5]. The parameters of the model used in our experiment are presented in Table 1.

With the structure in Fig. 3 and the above parameters, we randomly generated a dataset $\mathbf{V}$ of size $n = 10^4$, a feasible sample size for large-scale standardized tests [14].

Table 1. True parameter values used to generate synthetic data for the BN2A model (structure shown in Fig. 3): leak and penalty parameters (left), and prior probabilities (right).

ℓ	$q_{\ell,0}$	$q_{\ell,1}$	$q_{\ell,2}$	$q_{\ell,3}$
1	0.900	0.400	-	-
2	0.800	0.200	0.100	-
3	0.700	0.100	-	0.300
4	0.600	-	0.200	0.100
5	0.700	-	0.200	-
6	0.800	-	-	0.300
7	0.950	0.300	-	-
8	0.850	0.400	0.200	-
9	0.750	0.300	-	0.200
10	0.650	-	0.200	0.400
11	0.750	-	0.100	-
12	0.850	-	-	0.200

p_1	p_2	p_3
0.800	0.600	0.400

5.1 RBM Parameters

We ran Algorithm 1 using dataset **V** in two different ways. First, using a single constraint: non-negativity on the weights **W**; and subsequently, using two constraints: non-negativity on the weights **W**, and the structure in Fig. 3 encoded in the Q-matrix **Q**.

Table 2 presents the RBM model parameters obtained with one and two constraints. Interestingly, the non-negativity constraint alone is sufficient to learn the model parameters. In Table 2(a), we highlight the **W** values that are close to zero, which indicate that those hidden variables have very little or no influence on the activation of the corresponding observed variables. Upon closer inspection, these near-zero values correspond to the 0 entries in Table 2(b). That is, Algorithm 1 is also useful for learning the model's structure—i.e., the relationships between latent and observed variables [10].

Table 2. RBM parameters learned using Algorithm 1: without Q-matrix constraint (left) vs. with Q-matrix constraint (right).

Question	b	$\mathbf{W}_1$	$\mathbf{W}_2$	$\mathbf{W}_3$
Y1	-0.518	2.782	**0.008**	**0.027**
Y2	-4.147	1.975	3.238	**0.003**
Y3	-3.553	2.225	**0.000**	1.806
Y4	-4.470	**0.005**	1.897	2.810
Y5	-1.598	**0.018**	2.523	**0.016**
Y6	-1.083	**0.033**	**0.028**	2.532
Y7	-0.763	3.777	**0.006**	**0.014**
Y8	-2.743	1.306	2.847	**0.000**
Y9	-3.068	1.350	**0.021**	2.592
Y10	-2.950	**0.013**	2.017	1.278
Y11	-2.163	**0.003**	3.232	**0.018**
Y12	-1.522	**0.018**	**0.016**	3.230

Question	b	$\mathbf{W}_1$	$\mathbf{W}_2$	$\mathbf{W}_3$
Y1	-0.602	2.825	0	0
Y2	-4.163	1.984	3.257	0
Y3	-3.783	2.494	0	1.806
Y4	-4.532	0	1.903	2.812
Y5	-1.617	0	2.470	0
Y6	-1.113	0	0	2.516
Y7	-0.867	3.882	0	0
Y8	-2.785	1.330	2.921	0
Y9	-3.138	1.394	0	2.553
Y10	-2.945	0	2.037	1.322
Y11	-2.112	0	3.191	0
Y12	-1.447	0	0	3.272

Section 4 established that RBMs capture the relationship between hidden and observed variables through learned weight matrices **W** and bias terms, but without explicit cognitive interpretation. Below, we show how to transform the parameters to make them interpretable.

5.2 BN2A Parameters

As mentioned in Sect. 3, BN2A models can be applied in educational assessment. A particular advantage of these models is their interpretability.

Using the Eqs. 12 and 13, we can transform the parameters of the RBM model (Table 2) into the parameters of a corresponding BN2A model. The results are shown in Table 3.

Table 3. BN2A parameters derived from RBM model: without Q-matrix constraint (left) vs. with Q-matrix constraint (right).

ℓ	$q_{\ell,0}$	$q_{\ell,1}$	$q_{\ell,2}$	$q_{\ell,3}$
1	0.909	0.420	**0.999**	**0.997**
2	0.745	0.387	0.138	**0.999**
3	0.617	0.240	**1.000**	0.339
4	0.560	**0.998**	0.286	0.127
5	0.723	**0.995**	0.239	**0.996**
6	0.819	**0.994**	**0.995**	0.323
7	0.954	0.338	**1.000**	**0.999**
8	0.804	0.654	0.239	**1.000**
9	0.710	0.547	**0.994**	0.218
10	0.589	**0.995**	0.272	0.484
11	0.748	**0.999**	0.140	**0.995**
12	0.851	**0.997**	**0.998**	0.216

ℓ	$q_{\ell,0}$	$q_{\ell,1}$	$q_{\ell,2}$	$q_{\ell,3}$
1	0.902	0.392	-	-
2	0.746	0.386	0.136	-
3	0.626	0.194	-	0.345
4	0.546	-	0.278	0.123
5	0.701	-	0.236	-
6	0.803	-	-	0.308
7	0.953	0.310	-	-
8	0.812	0.657	0.232	-
9	0.692	0.516	-	0.215
10	0.602	-	0.273	0.477
11	0.746	-	0.144	-
12	0.861	-	-	0.221

Table 3(a) shows the transformation of the RBM model parameters using only the non-negativity constraint. In this table, we can observe that the weights $W_{\ell,k}$ close to zero correspond to very low penalties (i.e., $q_{\ell,k}$ values very close to one). This makes sense, as all of these highlighted relationships are absent in the original model used to generate dataset $\mathbf{V}$, which can be confirmed by comparing these values with their corresponding entries in Table 3(b). In particular, we observe that the parameters of the model with and without the Q-matrix constraint are very similar, and are also comparable to the original parameters used to generate dataset $\mathbf{V}$ (Table 1).

Finally, with the RBM model parameters and Eq. 3, it is possible to compute the prior probabilities of mastering the three skills in the model (Table 4). These probabilities are quite similar whether the model is learned with or without the Q-matrix constraint, and they are also comparable to the true prior probabilities (Table 1).

Table 4. Comparison of prior probabilities for skill mastery: without Q-matrix constraint (left) vs. with Q-matrix constraint (right).

p_1	p_2	p_3
0.780	0.577	0.394

p_1	p_2	p_3
0.778	0.576	0.392

6 Discussion

This work addresses a fundamental limitation of RBMs in educational contexts: the lack of direct interpretability of their parameters. Our main contribution is the development of a mathematical framework that transforms RBMs into BN2A models, preserving representational capacity while obtaining direct interpretability of leak and penalty parameters essential for educational diagnosis. The key modification of the CD algorithm incorporates non-negativity constraints on weights, ensuring the monotonicity property expected in educational contexts. This constraint does not compromise the model's learning capacity and facilitates subsequent transformation to interpretable BN2A parameters. The validation experiment demonstrates that transformed parameters maintain high fidelity with the originals and that model structure can be effectively recovered. The transformation is mathematically sound and practically viable under realistic conditions. Our approach enables combining RBMs' representational power with BN2A interpretability, enabling granular diagnosis, computational scalability, and dynamic adaptability. This combination is especially valuable in intelligent tutoring systems where both predictive accuracy and explainability are crucial. Main limitations include restriction to controlled synthetic data and potential expressivity limitations due to non-negativity. Future research should validate the approach with real educational data, explore extensions to more complex architectures (Deep Boltzmann Machines), and evaluate applications in specific domains such as mathematics and language.

Acknowledgments. The authors acknowledge financial support for this work: the first author was supported by the Czech Science Foundation through the project No. 25-18070S, and the third author was supported by the project "Research of Excellence on Digital Technologies and Wellbeing CZ.02.01.01/00/22_008/0004583" which is co-financed by the European Union.

Disclosure of Interests. The authors have no competing interests to declare that are relevant to the content of this article.

References

1. Choi, A., Wang, R., Darwiche, A.: On the relative expressiveness of Bayesian and neural networks. Int. J. Approximate Reasoning **113**, 303–323 (2019). https://doi.org/10.1016/j.ijar.2019.07.008
2. Díez, F.J., Druzdzel, M.J.: Canonical probabilistic models for knowledge engineering. Technical report CISIAD-06-01, UNED, Madrid, Spain (2006)
3. Druzdzel, J., Henrion, M.: Efficient reasoning in qualitative probabilistic networks. In: Proceedings of the Eleventh National Conference on Artificial Intelligence, pp. 548–553 (1993)
4. Fischer, A., Igel, C.: Training restricted Boltzmann machines: an introduction. Pattern Recogn. **47**(1), 25–39 (2014). https://doi.org/10.1016/j.patcog.2013.05.025
5. Hartz, S., Roussos, L.: The fusion model for skills diagnosis: blending theory with practicality. ETS Res. Rep. Ser. **2008**(2), i–57 (2008). https://doi.org/10.1002/j.2333-8504.2008.tb02157.x

6. Henrion, M.: Some practical issues in constructing belief networks. In: Proceedings of the Third Conference on Uncertainty in Artificial Intelligence (UAI-87), pp. 161–173. Elsevier Science Publishers B.V. (North Holland) (1987)
7. Hinton, G.E.: A practical guide to training restricted Boltzmann machines. In: Montavon, G., Orr, G.B., Müller, K.-R. (eds.) Neural Networks: Tricks of the Trade. LNCS, vol. 7700, pp. 599–619. Springer, Heidelberg (2012). https://doi.org/10.1007/978-3-642-35289-8_32
8. Jensen, F.V., Nielsen, T.D.: Bayesian Networks and Decision Graphs. Information Science and Statistics, 2nd edn. Springer New York (2007). https://doi.org/10.1007/978-0-387-68282-2
9. Koller, D., Friedman, N.: Probabilistic Graphical Models: Principles and Techniques. The MIT Press (2009)
10. Li, C., Ma, C., Xu, G.: Learning large Q-matrix by restricted Boltzmann machines. Psychometrika **87**(3), 1010–1041 (2022). https://doi.org/10.1007/s11336-021-09828-4
11. Lucas, P.J.: Bayesian network modelling through qualitative patterns. Artif. Intell. **163**(2), 233–263 (2005). https://doi.org/10.1016/j.artint.2004.10.011
12. Masegosa, A.R., Feelders, A.J., Gaag, L.C.: Learning from incomplete data in Bayesian networks with qualitative influences. Int. J. Approximate Reasoning **69**, 18–34 (2016)
13. Pearl, J.: Probabilistic Reasoning in Intelligent Systems: Networks of Plausible Inference. Morgan Kaufmann Publishers Inc., San Francisco (1988)
14. Pérez, I., Vomlel, J.: Enhancing Bayesian networks with psychometric models. In: Kwisthout, J., Renooij, S. (eds.) Proceedings of The 12th International Conference on Probabilistic Graphical Models. Proceedings of Machine Learning Research, vol. 246, pp. 401–414. PMLR (2024). https://proceedings.mlr.press/v246/perez24a.html
15. Pérez, I., Vomlel, J.: On identifiability of BN2A networks. In: Bouraoui, Z., Vesic, S. (eds.) ECSQARU 2023. LNCS, vol. 14294, pp. 136–148. Springer, Heidelberg (2023). https://doi.org/10.1007/978-3-031-45608-4_11
16. Plajner, M., Vomlel, J.: Learning bipartite Bayesian networks under monotonicity restrictions. Int. J. Gen Syst **49**(1), 88–111 (2020). https://doi.org/10.1080/03081079.2019.1692004
17. Restificar, A.C., Dietterich, T.G.: Exploiting monotonicity via logistic regression in Bayesian network learning. Technical report, Corvallis (2013)
18. Smolensky, P.: Information processing in dynamical systems: foundations of harmony theory. In: Parallel Distributed Processing, Volume 1: Explorations in the Microstructure of Cognition: Foundations. The MIT Press (1986). https://doi.org/10.7551/mitpress/5236.003.0009
19. de la Torre, J., Minchen, N.: Cognitively diagnostic assessments and the cognitive diagnosis model framework. Psicología Educativa. Rev. los Psicól. Educ. (2014). https://www.redalyc.org/articulo.oa?id=613765435004
20. Wellman, M.P.: Fundamental concepts of qualitative probabilistic networks. Artif. Intell. **44**(3), 257–303 (1990)

Denoising the Future: Top-p Distributions for Moving Through Time

Florian Andreas Marwitz[1(✉)], Ralf Möller[1], Magnus Bender[2], and Marcel Gehrke[1]

[1] Institute of Humanities-Centered Artificial Intelligence, University of Hamburg, Hamburg, Germany
{florian.marwitz,ralf.moeller,marcel.gehrke}@uni-hamburg.de
[2] Department of Management, Aarhus University, Aarhus, Denmark
magnus@mgmt.au.dk

Abstract. Inference in dynamic probabilistic models is a complex task involving expensive operations. In particular, for Hidden Markov Models, the whole state space has to be enumerated for advancing in time. Even states with negligible probabilities are considered, resulting in computational inefficiency and increased noise due to the propagation of unlikely probability mass. We propose to denoise the future and speed up inference by using only the top-p states, i.e., the most probable states with accumulated probability p. We show that the error introduced by using only the top-p states is bound by p and the so-called minimal mixing rate of the underlying model. Moreover, in our empirical evaluation, we show that we can expect speedups of at least an order of magnitude, while the error in terms of total variation distance is below 0.09.

Keywords: Hidden Markov Model · Probabilistic Graphical Models · Language Models

1 Introduction

Inference in dynamic probabilistic graphical models (dynamic PGMs) [11] is a daunting task as it is in general NP-hard: The probability distribution over all states has to be advanced in time. However, certain future states are highly unlikely. Our goal is to reduce the inference time and denoise the future by only considering the events with a high probability mass. Suppose we have a simple weather model and the sun is shining. In the next time step, the conditions partly cloudy and light rain are much more probable than, e.g., heavy thunderstorm. In this paper, we propose to use only the *top-p* events, i.e., the most probable events with accumulated probability of at least p, for inference, where we only iterate about the more likely states. This way, we reduce the runtime while retaining control over the induced error by setting p appropriately. This approach can also be viewed as a generative AI approach, we generate one possible world, for which we have probability and error assertions.

K. Sauerwald and M. Thimm (Eds.): ECSQARU 2025, LNAI 16099, pp. 118–132, 2026.
https://doi.org/10.1007/978-3-032-05134-9_9

Let us shortly motivate the runtime savings with language models, e.g., Llama 3 [9]. In language models, we have multibillion parameters and more possible events to be generated than words in the English language. Now, take for example the words *The weather is*, then the probability of the next word being *rainy* or *sunny* is much more probable than *eating*. With our *top-p* approach, we can thus spare the iteration over lots of unlikely states. Let us dive a bit deeper into what we actually do by looking at a simple example: Going back to our initial weather model, when we have the weather condition *sunny*, the next ones could be *partly cloudy*, *light rain*, and *foggy* with relatively high probabilities while a direct transition to more extreme conditions like *heavy rain* or *thunderstorm* is less likely. For inference, we now skip the enumeration of *heavy rain* and *thunderstorm*. While this change may seem marginal for a minimalistic example at first, it is of great use for very large models: First, the savings are present in each time step, accumulating and reducing the overall time. Second, the model is made sparse, helping human understanding. Also, the obtained sparse HMM can be used in edge computing, where a full HMM may be too big to run.

In our approach, less likely transitions are ignored, leading to potential problems regarding minorities. We note here that the problems arising do not originate from our approach, but from the underlying model. Though, our approach amplifies biases present in the model, e.g., not allowing the switch from sunny to thunderstorm. We also highlight that in applications, where our approach can lead to problems regarding minorities, tools from the field of AI should not be used at all or at least with high caution, as they are prone to biases.

Contribution. In this paper, we propose using only the top-p events for inference in Hidden Markov Models (HMMs) as a representative for PGMs. We show that by using the top-p distributions to proceed in time, we (i) increase the ratio of zeroes in the transition probabilities in our empirical evaluation significantly to above 0.9, (ii) bound the theoretical error in terms of total variation by $\frac{1-p}{\gamma}$, where γ is a model-specific parameter, which we back up in our empirical evaluation by showing that (iii) the introduced error in our examples is only 0.09 for top-0.9 in terms of total variance, and (iv) reduce the runtime for inference by an order of magnitude.

Related Work. Rabiner introduces HMMs [16] and proposes to use the Forward-Backward algorithm [2] for inference. Zhang et al. distill a language model into an HMM [20]. HMMs can be extended to Dynamic Bayesian Networks (DBNs) [7], which can model interactions between different state variables. Inference is done by, e.g., the interface algorithm [14]. However, query answering in Bayesian networks [15] is NP-hard [6], giving rise to approximations. Boyen and Koller represent the distribution over the random variables with successors in the next time step as a product of marginals [5], which is extended by Murphy and Weiss to always use a factored representation [13]. Instead of instantiating a DBN for each time step, Gao et al. introduce a sliding window approach [8]. Murphy provides an overview over approximate inference [14]. Though, the focus in literature is on approximate inference in DBNs or approximation for learning HMMs, but not on approximate inference within HMMs, which we propose in this paper. Vithanage et al. [19] effectively use a top-k approach, i.e., the k most probable transitions, and show that this minimizes the Kullback-Leibler divergence if restricting to k transitions. Contrary, we provide a more fine-grained error assertion. Also, when fixing p, one indirectly fixes k, too.

Structure. The remainder of this paper is structured as follows: First, we introduce HMMs. Second, we explain our top-p model and how to use it. Third, we provide a theoretical analysis of the error and bound the error. Fourth, we provide an empirical evaluation.

2 Hidden Markov Models Generalizing Dynamic Models

In this section, we lay the foundation for our top-p modeling. We introduce HMMs as a representative of dynamic PGMs. An HMM consists of two random variables per time step: One for the state and one for the observation, e.g., the weather condition and whether we see a person wearing a raincoat. The probability of an observation depends only on the current state and the probability of the next state depends only on the current state:

Definition 1 (Hidden Markov Model [16]). *A Hidden Markov Model consists of two series of random variables $(S_t, O_t)_t$ over a set S of states and O of observations, where S_t denotes the state random variable in time step t and O_t the respective observation random variable. The probability $P(O_t \mid S_t)$ of an observation depends only on the current state. The probability distribution over the states is given as the temporal behavior $P(S_t \mid S_{t-1})$ and a prior $P(S_0)$. The semantics for a time step t is thus given by*

$$P(S_t \mid S_{t-1}) = \sum_{s_{t-1} \in S_{t-1}} P(S_t \mid s_{t-1}) \cdot P(s_{t-1}) \quad \textit{and} \tag{1}$$

$$P(O_t) = \sum_{s_t \in S_t} P(O_t \mid s_t) \cdot P(s_t), \tag{2}$$

where $P(S_t)$ is the distribution specifying the probabilities s_t for each state $s \in S$.

We illustrate the definition of an HMM with our introductory example:

Example 1. In each time step, the *state* is the weather condition. The *observation* is the probability of wearing a raincoat. Table 1 gives the state transition probabilities. The initial state distribution is uniform. The probability of wearing a raincoat is the sum over the *rainy* conditions light rain, heavy rain, and thunderstorm. When it is sunny, the probability of partly cloudy in the next time step is 0.3. The probability of wearing a raincoat when it is sunny is 0.35.

Now, the important part is that the sum in Eq. 1 goes over all possible states, rendering the equation inefficient for large state spaces, like in language models. Our goal is to reduce the number of states that have to be enumerated. While an HMM seems simple, it can be thought of as a generalized dynamic PGM: We

Table 1. State transition probabilities giving the probability of transitioning to the next state given the current state.

Next/current	Partly cloudy	Light rain	Foggy	Sunny	Heavy rain	Thunderstorm
Partly cloudy	0.3	0.2	0.3	0.3	0.1	0.1
Light rain	0.2	0.2	0.2	0.25	0.2	0.2
Foggy	0.1	0.1	0.2	0.15	0.1	0.1
Sunny	0.2	0.1	0.1	0.2	0.1	0.1
Heavy rain	0.1	0.2	0.1	0.06	0.2	0.3
Thunderstorm	0.1	0.2	0.1	0.04	0.3	0.2

have a, potentially complex, state S_t emitting observations O_t. Let us denote the distributions $P(s_t)$, $s_t \in S$, as *forward message* updating the state probabilities through time. DBNs [7] can be viewed as HMMs by treating the joint probability distribution over the interface [14] as state and all other random variables jointly as observation. Furthermore, GPT-based language models can be viewed as HMMs and learn the forward message in a highly complex state space. At their core, they can be viewed as HMMs, interpreting, analogous to DBNs, each possible complex internal state of the language model as a state of an HMM with respective transition and observation (or emission) probabilities. Generating sentences from language models is then the same as predicting states and sampling observations from HMMs, which leads to a noisy distribution in the far future without any observations.

Throughout this paper, we use HMMs as a representative for dynamic PGMs. The same ideas apply to Kalman filters [17] for continuos variables. But for illustrative purposes, we show the idea for discrete variables in an HMM setting. In the next section, we define the top-p approach for HMMs to reduce the space that has to be enumerated for the forward message.

3 Inference in Top-p Hidden Markov Models

Our goal is to denoise the future and reduce the runtime for inference by using only the top-p events, effectively reducing the number of enumerations by not accounting for values not included in the *top-p set*. Moreover, we focus on the highly probable transitions, denoising the lower ones. With HMMs as our probabilistic model, we present our top-p modeling approach: Given an HMM, we alter the probabilities of the next state given the current state. For all possible next states, we only keep those with the highest probability until we accumulated a total probability mass of p. We first formalize this for a single random variable and then extend it to HMMs.

Before we give the definition for top-p HMM, we give a helper definition to select the top probabilities:

Definition 2. (Top-p Set). *Given a probability distribution P with a set of events X, the* sorted order *of P is a sequence $Z \subseteq X$ with the events of X arranged descending according to $P(X)$. The* top-p set *of P is then the set $Y \subseteq X$ built from Z by taking events until their probabilities reach p.*

For events with equal probability, an arbitrary choice is made. The top-p set is the set of events, also called *top-p events*, whose probability will be kept and scaled later on, while the probability of events not in the top-p set will be set to zero. We illustrate the sorted order and top-p set with our introductory example:

Example 2. Let P denote the probability of the weather condition in the next time step given it is sunny in the current time step. Table 1 defines the probability distribution P. The sorted order of P is then: Partly cloudy, light rain, sunny, foggy, heavy rain and thunderstorm. For $p = 0.9$, the top-p set consists of partly cloudy, light rain, foggy and sunny. For $p = 0.91$, the top-p set additionally includes heavy rain.

Table 2. Top-p distribution for the state in the next time step given it is currently sunny for $p = 0.9$.

Weather condition	Probability
Partly cloudy	$\frac{1}{3}$
Light rain	$\frac{5}{18}$
Foggy	$\frac{1}{6}$
Sunny	$\frac{2}{9}$
Heavy rain	0
Thunderstorm	0

Building on the top-p set, we define the top-p distribution:

Definition 3 (Top-p Distribution). *Given a probability distribution P with a set of events X, the* top-p distribution *of P is another probability distribution Q over the same set of events X. Let Y be the top-p set of P for a given p. Then, $Q(X)$ is defined as*

$$Q(x) = \begin{cases} \frac{P(x)}{P(Y)} & x \in Y \\ 0 & otherwise \end{cases} . \tag{3}$$

In other words, events with high probabilities are promoted while events with low probabilities are ignored, effectively amplifying the differences. For Example 2 and $p = 0.9$, Table 2 shows the top-p distribution. As an HMM consists of conditional probability distributions, we independently apply the top-p distributions to them:

Algorithm 1. Apply the top-p approach according to Definition 3 to a vector

Require: $v \in [0,1]^d, p \in (0,1]$ ▷ *Input* probability distribution and p value
Ensure: $v' \in [0,1]^d$ is the top-p distribution of v

```
v' ← 0 ∈ ℝ^d
idx ← sort_indices_by_value_desc(v)          ▷ create sorted order of v
sum ← 0
for j in idx do                               ▷ j is an index for v and v'
    sum ← sum + v[j]
    v'[j] ← v[j]                              ▷ take events ...
    if sum ≥ p then                           ▷ ... until accumulated probability reaches p
        break
    end if
end for
v' ← v'/sum                                   ▷ scale to sum to one
```

Definition 4 (Top-p HMM). *Given an HMM H with a set S of states, a set O of observations, probability distributions over the states given by $P_H(S_0)$ and $P_H(S_{i+1} \mid s_i)$, for each state $s_i \in S$, and probability distributions $P_H(O_i \mid s_i)$, $s_i \in S$, over the observations, the* top-p HMM *of H is another HMM Q over the same set S of states and same set O of observations. The probability distributions of Q are the top-p distributions of the respective ones of H, that is, (i) $P_Q(S_0)$ is the top-p distribution of $P_H(S_0)$, (ii) $P_Q(S_{i+1} \mid s_i)$ is the top-p distribution of $P_Q(S_{i+1} \mid s_i)$, for each state $s_i \in S$, and (iii) $P_Q(O_i \mid s_i)$ is the top-p distribution of $P_H(O_i \mid s_i)$, $s_i \in S$.*

Algorithm 1 is pseudo-code for Definition 3 and returns the top-p distribution for a vector representing a probability distribution. For an HMM, Algorithm 1 is applied to (i) the initial state distribution,(ii) each next state distribution given the current state,(iii) and each observation distribution given the current state. We illustrate the top-p HMM on our running example:

Example 3. Table 3 shows the state transition probabilities for $p = 0.7$. For the observations, the probability of wearing a rain coat is one for heavy rain and thunderstorm and unaltered for all other states.

Having shifted the probability mass, we now exploit the new distributions for efficient inference without enumerating all states. Since the transition matrix still has the same dimensions, but is more spare, we use sparse matrices to only enumerate the non-zero entries. We explain how to perform inference, by (sparse) matrix multiplication, in a top-p HMM Q of an original HMM: (1) The top-p HMM Q is built according to Definition 4 by using Algorithm 1. (2) The obtained transition probabilities and observation probabilities are stored in a transition and observation matrix, respectively. (3) The two matrices are each transformed into *compressed row storage* [1]: For each row in the matrix, a tuple (c, x) for each non-zero entry, where c is the column number and x the value. (4) For inference, sparse matrix-vector multiplication [4] is used to proceed the

Table 3. Top-p state distributions for the simple weather HMM with $p = 0.7$.

Next/current	Partly cloudy	Light rain	Foggy	Sunny	Heavy rain	Thunderstorm
Partly cloudy	$\frac{3}{7}$	0.25	$\frac{3}{7}$	0.4	0	0
Light rain	$\frac{2}{7}$	0.25	$\frac{2}{7}$	$\frac{1}{3}$	$\frac{2}{7}$	$\frac{2}{7}$
Foggy	0	0	$\frac{2}{7}$	0	0	0
Sunny	$\frac{2}{7}$	0	0	$\frac{4}{15}$	0	0
Heavy rain	0	0.25	0	0	$\frac{2}{7}$	$\frac{3}{7}$
Thunderstorm	0	0.25	0	0	$\frac{3}{7}$	$\frac{2}{7}$

current state distribution in time and to get the observation distribution: The dot product between each row and the vector is calculated by summing the products of x and the entry c of the vector for each (c, x) tuple in the row. Sparse matrix-vector multiplication runs in time proportional to the number of non-zero entries [4] and is also available for GPUs [3].

Since we only keep the top-p events, our top-p HMM definitely introduces an error. For example, in Table 3 we see that we introduce an error by dropping the possibilities of transitioning from sunny to heavy rain or thunderstorm. Next, we show that the error induced by top-p modeling is bounded in terms of p.

4 Bounding the Approximation Error

When we use the top-p HMM, inference is done with altered distributions, dropping events of the original one. In this section, we bound the approximation error introduced by the top-p modeling. The bound can then be used to determine whether to apply the top-p approach or not. Throughout this section, we use the total variation distance to measure the approximation error: ss

Definition 5 (Total Variation). *The* total variation distance *between two discrete probability distributions P and Q over the same set of possible outcomes X is defined as*

$$\delta(P, Q) = \frac{1}{2} \sum_{x \in X} |P(x) - Q(x)| \,. \tag{4}$$

We choose the total variation distance, because it allows, in contrast to the Kullback–Leibler divergence [12], arbitrary probabilities being zero. Moreover, the absolute value can be more easily resolved than, e.g., square roots in the Helliner distance and the total variation fulfills the triangle equality. We first start by bounding the error of a single time step approximation and continue to bound the error over all time steps based on the result for one time step.

4.1 Approximation Error in a Single Time Step

We show that the error introduced by a top-p distribution is at most $1 - p$:

Theorem 1. *Given a probability distribution P and the top-p distribution Q of P, the total variation distance between P and Q is bounded by*

$$\delta(P, Q) \leq 1 - p. \tag{5}$$

Proof. Let us denote with Y the top-p set of P. We first assume that the probabilities kept exactly match p, i.e., $P(Y) = p$ and $Q(Y) = 1$. Moreover, for each $y \in Y$: $Q(y) = \frac{P(y)}{p}$. Now, we can start deriving the distance:

$$\begin{aligned}
\delta(P, Q) &= \frac{1}{2}\sum_{x \notin Y} |P(x)| + \frac{1}{2}\sum_{x \in Y} |P(x) - Q(x)| && (6)\\
&= \frac{1}{2}(1-p) + \frac{1}{2}\sum_{x \in Y} \left|P(X) - \frac{P(x)}{p}\right| && (7)\\
&= \frac{1}{2}(1-p) + \frac{1}{2}\sum_{x \in Y} \left|P(X)\left(1 - \frac{1}{p}\right)\right| && (8)\\
&= \frac{1}{2}(1-p) + \frac{1}{2}\sum_{x \in Y} |P(x)| \left|1 - \frac{1}{p}\right| && (9)\\
&= \frac{1}{2}(1-p) - \left(1 - \frac{1}{p}\right) \cdot \frac{1}{2}\sum_{x \in Y} |P(x)| && (10)\\
&= \frac{1}{2}(1-p) - \left(1 - \frac{1}{p}\right) \cdot \frac{1}{2}p = 1 - p. && (11)
\end{aligned}$$

Lifting the assumption of $P(Y) = p$, if the probabilities in the top-p set exceed p, i.e., $P(Y) = p' \geq p$, we have $\delta(P, Q) = 1 - p' \leq 1 - p$. □

Because the total variation distance is invariant to linear transformations and by the triangle inequality, we can give a first bound on multiple steps:

Corollary 1. *Given an HMM with a probability distribution P^k over the set of states for each time step k and a probability distribution Q^k, which is the top-p distribution of the previous Q^{k-1} and Q^0 is the top-p distribution from P^0, then the total variation distance is*

$$\delta(P^k, Q^k) \leq (k+1) \cdot (1-p). \tag{12}$$

Unfortunately, the bound in Eq. 12 quickly approaches the trivial bound of 1. Boyen and Koller show that the error in terms of Kullback-Leibler divergence is bounded [5]. However, the Kullback-Leibler divergence is not applicable to our top-p HMM, because we set probabilities to zero and the Kullback-Leibler divergence divides by probabilities. Nevertheless, we use the key idea of Boyen and Koller [5] to show the same bound for our total variance distance.

4.2 Overall Approximation Error

Boyen and Koller show for the Kullback-Leibler divergence that the error in each time step is at most $\frac{\epsilon}{\gamma}$, where γ is a parameter inherent to the specific HMM and ϵ is the error incurred in each time step [5]. The parameter γ of an HMM tells the minimum probability mass on which two different state distributions agree on after a single time step. While the bounded error result is promising, we cannot use their theorems directly, because of their use of the Kullback-Leibler divergence, which is not applicable in our case. The Kullback-Leibler divergence divides by probabilities and we set probabilities to zero, rendering the Kullback-Leibler divergence useless in our case. Therefore, we use the key idea from Boyen and Koller [5] to bound the error our top-p HMM in terms of our used total variation distance. We start by defining the parameter γ and continue by proving that an error incurred in one time step diminishes by a factor of $1-\gamma$ over the next time steps. Then, given that our error increases at most by $1-p$ in each time step (c.f. Corollary 1), we build a geometric series and prove that our overall approximation error in terms of total variation distance is at most $\frac{1-p}{\gamma}$ in each time step.

Let us first prove that an error introduced in one time step diminishes by a constant factor per time step. For this, we define the *minimal mixing rate* γ, which directly links to the diminishing factor of $1-\gamma$. The minimal mixing rate sets the minimum probability mass two different state distributions agree on after a single time step [5].

Definition 6 (Definition 3 from Boyen and Koller [5]). *For a Markov process with stochastic transition model Q with states ω_i, the* minimal mixing rate *of Q is*

$$\gamma := \min_{i_1, i_2} \sum_j \min\left\{Q\left(\omega_j \mid \omega_{i_1}\right), Q\left(\omega_j \mid \omega_{i_2}\right)\right\}. \tag{13}$$

For showing the diminishing factor of $1-\gamma$ for the error, we split the transition from one time step to the next into two transitions containing an intermediate state. We are primarily interested in the first transition, as we show later, using the following lemma, that this one diminishes the error.

Lemma 1 (Lemma 2 and Theorem 3 by Boyen and Koller [5]). *Fixing two state distributions φ and ψ, the transition of a stochastic process Q can be split into two steps: First, a transition defined by R^{Γ} from Ω to $\tilde{\Omega}$ and, second, a transition defined by R^{Δ} from $\tilde{\Omega}$ to Ω, where $\Omega = \{\omega_i\}_i$ is the state space of Q and $\tilde{\Omega} = \Omega \cup \{c\}$ with a new intermediate state c. The process R^{Γ} preserves its state with probability $1-\gamma$ and transitions to state c with probability γ. The process R^{Δ} transitions from ω_i to ω_j with probability $\frac{Q^{\Delta}_{i,j}}{1-\gamma}$. For state c, R^{Δ} transitions to state ω_j with probability $\sum_i \varphi(\omega_i)\frac{Q^{\Gamma}_{i,j}}{\gamma}$. The matrices Q^{Γ} and Q^{Δ} arise from an additive contraction decomposition $Q = Q^{\Gamma} + Q^{\Delta}$, where Q^{Γ} and Q^{Δ} are non-negative matrices such that, for all i, $\sum_j Q^{\Gamma}_{i,j} = \gamma$, and for all j, $\sum_i \varphi(\omega_i)Q^{\Gamma}_{i,j} = \sum_i \psi(\omega_i)Q^{\Gamma}_{i,j}$.*

We now show that the first transition diminishes the error by $1-\gamma$ and that the second one does not increase the error:

Theorem 2. *For two state distributions φ and ψ and their counterparts φ' and ψ' in the next time step as defined by a stochastic process Q:*

$$\delta(\varphi', \psi') \leq (1-\gamma)\,\delta(\varphi, \psi). \tag{14}$$

Proof. We fix φ and ψ. Using Lemma 1, let $\tilde{\varphi}$ and $\tilde{\psi}$ denote the respective distributions in the intermediate step. We show that our claim holds by showing the error $\delta(\tilde{\varphi}, \tilde{\psi}) = (1-\gamma)\delta(\varphi, \psi)$ in the intermediate step and the error $\delta(\varphi', \psi') \leq \delta(\tilde{\varphi}, \tilde{\psi})$ in the next time step. The last inequality holds because the total variation is invariant to linear transformations.

For showing $\delta(\tilde{\varphi}, \tilde{\psi}) = (1-\gamma)\delta(\varphi, \psi)$, we first note

$$\tilde{\varphi}(c) = \sum_i \gamma\varphi(\omega_i) = \gamma \quad \text{and} \tag{15}$$

$$\tilde{\varphi}(\omega_i) = (1-\gamma)\varphi(\omega_i), \tag{16}$$

which also hold for $\tilde{\psi}$. Then, we have

$$\delta(\tilde{\varphi}, \tilde{\psi}) = \frac{1}{2}\sum_i \left|\tilde{\varphi}(\omega_i) - \tilde{\psi}(\omega_i)\right| + \frac{1}{2}\left|\tilde{\varphi}(c) - \tilde{\psi}(c)\right| \tag{17}$$

$$= \frac{1}{2}\sum_i \left|(1-\gamma)\,\varphi(\omega_i) - (1-\gamma)\,\psi(\omega_i)\right| \tag{18}$$

$$= (1-\gamma)\,\delta(\varphi, \psi). \tag{19}$$

□

At this point, we have already shown that we (i) introduce an approximation error of $1-p$ when using the top-p distribution once (c.f. Theorem 1), (ii) the error introduced in one time step diminishes by a factor of $1-\gamma$ for each future time step (c.f. Theorem 2), which is $(1-p)(1-\gamma)^k$ for time step k, and (iii) in each time step we only add an additional error of at most $1-p$ (c.f. Corollary 1). We combine these results in our overall approximation guarantee by analyzing the induced geometric series:

Theorem 3. *The total variation distance between the state distributions for the top-p HMM Q and the original HMM P in each time step k is*

$$\delta(P^k, Q^k) \leq \frac{1-p}{\gamma}, \tag{20}$$

where γ is the minimal mixing rate of P.

Proof. We prove the claim by induction: In the first time step, the error is $1-p \leq \frac{1-p}{\gamma}$ by Theorem 1 and because of $\gamma \leq 1$.

Induction Step. In time step k, because of the triangle inequality, the error consists of the error from time step $k-1$ and an additional error of at most

$1-p$. However, the error of time step $k-1$ is, by Theorem 2, diminished by the factor $1-\gamma$. Therefore, the error in time step k is

$$(1-\gamma)\cdot\frac{1-p}{\gamma}+1-p=(1-\gamma)\cdot\frac{1-p}{\gamma}+\gamma\cdot\frac{1-p}{\gamma} \tag{21}$$

$$=(1-\gamma+\gamma)\cdot\frac{1-p}{\gamma}=\frac{1-p}{\gamma}. \tag{22}$$

□

We highlight that Theorem 3 helps an agent to decide whether to use the top-p approach beforehand based on the error bound. Moreover, the exact total variation can be calculated for individual HMMs. In the next section, we substantiate our theoretical margin of error empirically, show a reduced runtime for inference, and an increased sparsity.

5 Evaluation

We evaluate the top-p approach on three HMMs: One favoring our approach, one that is disadvantageous for the top-p approach, and a language model for a realistic application. We investigate the sparsity, the runtime with and without observations, and the total variation distance of the top-p model. We evaluate top-p for the p values 0.5, 0.7, and 0.9 and for the maximum time step 50. In the runtime evaluation, we solely report numbers for $p = 0,9$, as the three top-p approaches are mostly comparable. For the error investigation, we also report numbers for the other tested p values. We run all tests on a 13th Gen Intel(R) Core(TM) i5-1345U CPU with 1.60 GHz and 16 GB of RAM. We use NumPy [10] and SciPy [18] for matrix and sparse matrix operations, respectively.

For the different HMMs, we have trained a very simple language model (*LM HMM*) as an HMM with 7620 states. In practice, one would distill a larger model into an HMM [20]. However, in this evaluation, we focus on the runtime and not on the quality of the language model. We create a synthetic *Bell HMM*, which is designed to favor the top-p approach. The Bell HMM distributes, in each next-state distribution, a probability mass of 0.9 over five states and the remaining 0.1 over 795 states, favoring our approach by having lots of unlikely successor states. For a synthetic HMM disadvantageous for the top-p approach, we create a *Uniform HMM* consisting of uniform state distributions for a system of 800 states. The number of observations equals the number of states in all HMMs.

Sparsity: We define the sparsity as the ratio of zero-entries in the transition matrix. In the Bell HMM, all three top-p approaches lead to a sparsity of above 0.99. In the Uniform HMM, the sparsity is approximately $1-p$. And in the LM HMM, the sparsity is for all three top-p greater than 0.97.

Runtime for Inference: The top-0.9 HMM for the Bell HMM outperforms exact inference in the original HMM by a factor of more than 15. Moreover, all three top-p approaches are significantly faster than inference in the original HMM and are comparable fast. For the Uniform HMM, top-0.9 is around 3.39 times slower than the original HMM. Clearly, the lower p, the faster the inference. The reason for the slower runtime is the low sparsity: Sparse matrix multiplication only pays off for high sparsity, which increases with higher p. In the LM HMM, top-p is more than 18 times faster than the original HMM. Figure 1 shows the experiments for the three tested HMMs.

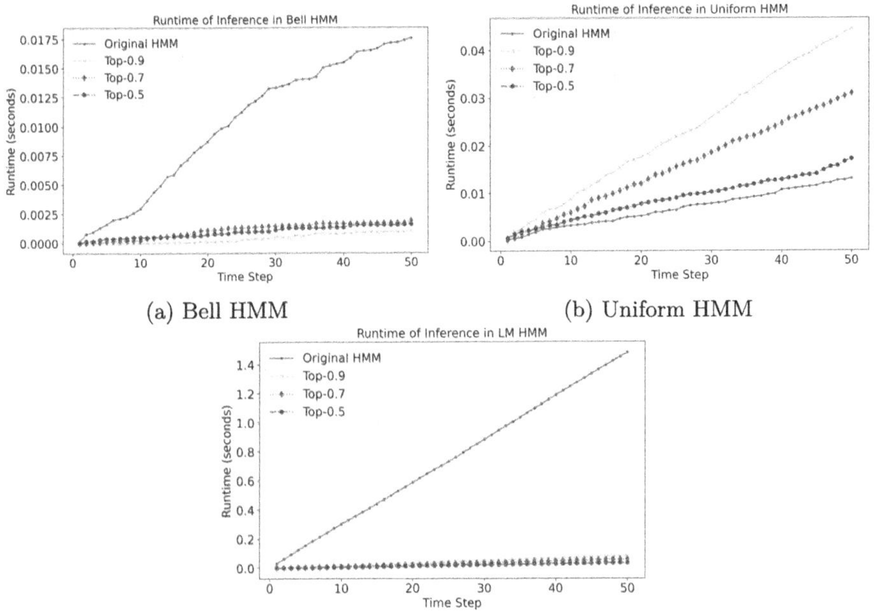

(a) Bell HMM

(b) Uniform HMM

(c) LM HMM

Fig. 1. Runtime for inference in the test HMMs. The blue line shows the runtime in the original HMM and the other three ones for different top-p ones. (Color figure online)

Runtime for Filtering: Before, we reported runtimes without observations. Now, we enter an observation every five time steps. We omit the LM HMM, since observation in text generation is not useful. In the Bell HMM, the top-0.9 approach is more than 77 times faster than filtering in the original HMM. In the Uniform HMM, in contrast to regular prediction, the top-0.9 approach is now more than 24 times faster than the original HMM, due to more probabilistic calculations helping the overhead induced by sparse matrices to pay off. Figure 2 shows the experiment for the two tested HMMs.

Total Variation Distance: The total variation in the Bell HMM is 0.086 for top-0.9, 0.285 for top-0.7 and 0.78 for top-0.5. In the Uniform HMM, the total variation distance is 0.099, 0.299 and 0.499 for top-0.9, top-0.7 and top-0.5,

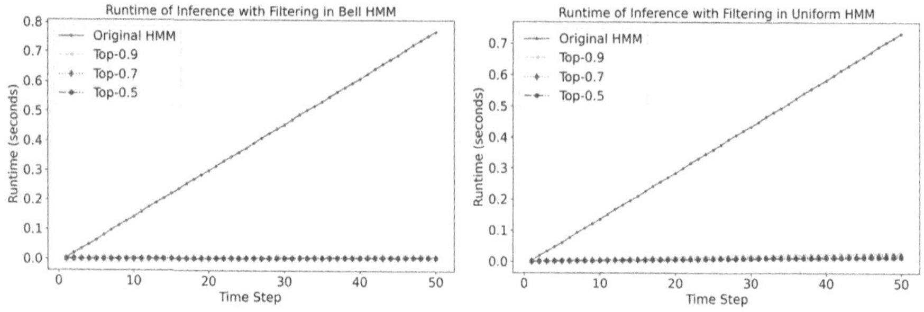

(a) Bell HMM with filtering (b) Uniform HMM with filtering

Fig. 2. Runtime for filtering in two test HMMs. The blue line shows the runtime in the original HMM and the other three ones for different top-p ones. (Color figure online)

respectively. In the LM HMM, the total variation distance is 0.059, 0.172 and 0.3 for top-0.9, top-0.7 and top-0.5, respectively.

Total Variation Distance for Filtering: With observations, the total variation in the Bell HMM is 0.095 for top-0.9, 0.491 for top-0.7 and 0.846 for top-0.5. The increased error compared to without filtering is because more approximations are made in the process. In the Uniform HMM, the total variation distance is the same as for no observations, since the model is uniform. We again omit the LM HMM, since observation in text generation is not useful.

Regarding which p to choose, our evaluation suggests to start with higher values like 0.9 and adapt them based on the requirements for runtime and total variation. Summing up, the top-p approach significantly increases sparsity to more than 0.9 for top-0.9. Moreover, top-p is at least an order of magnitude faster than the original HMMs, while the total variation distance for top-0.9 stays below 0.09.

6 Conclusion

Inference in large (dynamic) probabilistic models like HMMs, DBNs, or GPT-based language models like Llama 3, is a complex task involving expensive operations. In particular, the whole state space needs to be enumerated for advancing in time. We propose to only use the top-p events, i.e., the most probable events with an accumulated probability of p. Using only the top-p events and setting the probability for all other ones to zero, we can significantly speedup inference by at least an order of a magnitude. Moreover, the error introduced by the top-p HMM can be bound in terms of total variation distance. For a simple language model, the total variation distance is below 0.059 for top-0.9. Furthermore, an agent can decide whether to use the top-p approach by checking the error bound. In future work, the top-p approach can be utilized for first-order inference in DBNs. Moreover, the obtained sparse top-p HMM can be used in edge computing, where a full HMM may be too big to run on.

Acknowledgments. The research for this paper was funded by the Deutsche Forschungsgemeinschaft (DFG, German Research Foundation) under Germany's Excellence Strategy – EXC 2176 'Understanding Written Artefacts: Material, Interaction and Transmission in Manuscript Cultures', project no. 390893796. The research was conducted within the scope of the Centre for the Study of Manuscript Cultures (CSMC) at Universität Hamburg.

Disclosure of Interests. The authors have no competing interests to declare that are relevant to the content of this article.

References

1. Barrett, R., et al.: Templates for the Solution of Linear Systems: Building Blocks for Iterative Methods. Society for Industrial and Applied Mathematics (1994)
2. Baum, L.E., Petrie, T.: Statistical inference for probabilistic functions of finite state Markov chains. Ann. Math. Stat. **37**(6), 1554–1563 (1966)
3. Bell, N., Garland, M.: Efficient sparse matrix-vector multiplication on CUDA. Technical report, Nvidia Technical Report NVR-2008-004, Nvidia Corporation (2008)
4. Blelloch, G.E.: Programming parallel algorithms. Commun. ACM **39**(3), 85–97 (1996)
5. Boyen, X., Koller, D.: Tractable inference for complex stochastic processes. In: UAI, pp. 33–42 (1998)
6. Cooper, G.F.: The computational complexity of probabilistic inference using Bayesian belief networks. Artif. Intell. **42**(2–3), 393–405 (1990)
7. Dagum, P., Galper, A., Horvitz, E.: Dynamic network models for forecasting. In: UAI, pp. 41–48. Elsevier (1992)
8. Gao, X.G., Mei, J.F., Chen, H.Y., Chen, D.Q.: Approximate inference for dynamic Bayesian networks: sliding window approach. Appl. Intell. **40**, 575–591 (2014)
9. Grattafiori, A., et al.: The LLaMA 3 herd of models. arXiv preprint arXiv:2407.21783 (2024)
10. Harris, C.R., et al.: Array programming with NumPy. Nature **585**(7825), 357–362 (2020)
11. Koller, D., Friedman, N.: Probabilistic Graphical Models: Principles and Techniques. MIT Press (2009)
12. Kullback, S., Leibler, R.A.: On information and sufficiency. Ann. Math. Stat. **22**(1), 79–86 (1951)
13. Murphy, K., Weiss, Y.: The factored frontier algorithm for approximate inference in dbns. In: UAI, pp. 378–385 (2001)
14. Murphy, K.P.: Dynamic Bayesian networks: representation, inference and learning. University of California, Berkeley (2002)
15. Pearl, J.: Probabilistic reasoning using graphs. In: Bouchon, B., Yager, R.R. (eds.) IPMU 1986. LNCS, vol. 286, pp. 200–202. Springer, Heidelberg (1987). https://doi.org/10.1007/3-540-18579-8_19
16. Rabiner, L.R.: A tutorial on hidden Markov models and selected applications in speech recognition. Proc. IEEE **77**(2), 257–286 (1989)
17. Russell, S.J., Norvig, P.: Artificial Intelligence: A Modern Approach. Pearson Education, Inc. (2010)

18. Virtanen, P., et al.: SciPy 1.0: fundamental algorithms for scientific computing in python. Nat. Methods **17**, 261–272 (2020)
19. Vithanage, C.M., Andrieu, C., Piechocki, R.J.: Approximate inference in hidden Markov models using iterative active state selection. IEEE Signal Process. Lett. **13**(2), 65–68 (2006)
20. Zhang, H., Dang, M., Peng, N., Van den Broeck, G.: Tractable control for autoregressive language generation. In: ICML, pp. 40932–40945. PMLR (2023)

Distortions of Lower Probabilities as a Tool for Avoiding Conflict

David Nieto-Barba, Enrique Miranda(✉), and Ignacio Montes

Department of Statistics and Operations Research, University of Oviedo, Oviedo, Spain
{nietodavid,mirandaenrique,imontes}@uniovi.es

Abstract. This paper studies the use of distortions as a tool for addressing conflicts between a finite number of uncertainty models, in the general case where these initial models may not be precise, in particular a lower probability. We propose to distort the associated credal sets until the global conflict is removed, and to use the conjunction aggregation rule in that moment. We investigate this procedure in the case where the distortion is made using the total variation distance, and compare its properties with other aggregation rules from the literature. In addition, we also explore an alternative where the distortion is tweaked so as to enlarge the credal sets only in the directions where conflict is present.

Keywords: Distortion models · Aggregation rules · Conflict · Total variation distance

1 Introduction

In situations of ambiguous or missing information, *imprecise probabilities* [1,23] have emerged in the past decades as a robust alternative to probability theory. They include as particular submodels 2-monotone capacities [3], belief functions [19], possibility measures [5] or coherent lower previsions [23], just to name a few. Our focus in this paper is on *distortion models*, that are defined by considering a neighbourhood around a given probability measure. How the neighbourhood is defined once the radius is fixed is the basis for a number of different models in the literature, such as the ϵ-contamination [7], pari-mutuel [10,18,23] or total variation models [6]. A unified study of some of the most prominent distortion models can be found in [11,12].

Recently [16,17], we extended the idea of distortion models to the case where we start from a lower probability, or its associated *credal set*, instead of a probability measure. We focused on the case where the distortion was made using generalisations of the total variation distance, even though our ideas can be extrapolated to other models. The advantages of such a procedure are several: the starting model may be inherently imprecise, and we may still want to incorporate robustness into it; we may want to consider an outer approximation of a given model, in order to have a more conservative model that is at the same

K. Sauerwald and M. Thimm (Eds.): ECSQARU 2025, LNAI 16099, pp. 133–147, 2026.
https://doi.org/10.1007/978-3-032-05134-9_10

time easier to work with; or, as we shall do in this paper, we may want to deal with conflict in a context of aggregation [2].

Specifically, in this paper we consider a number of experts that provide their input about the uncertainty in an experiment by means of a lower probability, and we have the goal of systematically assembling a global model that represents the opinion of the group. This is the problem of *probabilistic opinion pooling*, for which a number of rules have been considered in the literature, such as the conjunction, disjunction, mixture or Pareto rules [14,20,22]. A number of different rules were analysed from the axiomatic point of view in [9]. One of them is the so-called *conjunction-disjunction*, that computes the intersection of the credal sets when the latter is non-empty and takes the convex hull of the union otherwise.

An empty intersection of the credal sets points towards a situation of (global) conflict between the sources, in the sense that there is no probability model compatible with all of them. However, considering the disjunction of the models in the case of conflict may be too crude a solution for such a scenario. One alternative would be to measure the conflict between the sources and enlarge the credal sets in a minimal way until compatibility is achieved. This is the approach we shall investigate in this paper: we distort the lower probabilities by means of the total variation distance until their associated credal sets have non-empty intersection, and then take the conjunction of the models we obtain. We shall study in detail the properties of this procedure, by making a comparison with the results from [9], and investigate the role of the minimal total variation as a conflict measure as well as a closely related extension of the total variation distance analysed in [16,17].

The paper is organised as follows: after giving some preliminaries about imprecise probability theory, distortion models and aggregation rules in Sect. 2, in Sect. 3 we define our aggregation procedure and analyse its properties. In Sect. 4 we discuss an alternative approach where the distortion takes into account the extent of the conflict between the experts on each event. Finally, Sect. 5 synthesises our contributions and provides some additional discussion. Due to the space limitations, proofs have been omitted.

2 Preliminary Concepts

2.1 Imprecise Probability Models

Let us briefly recall some aspects of imprecise probability theory in order to make the paper as self-contained as possible. We refer to [1] for a detailed account.

Consider a possibility space $\mathcal{X}$, that in this paper shall always be finite. Let $\mathcal{P}(\mathcal{X})$ denote its power set, and let $\mathbb{P}(\mathcal{X})$ be the set of probability measures on $\mathcal{X}$. Since $\mathcal{X}$ is finite, we may consider on $\mathbb{P}(\mathcal{X})$ the topology induced by the Euclidean distance on the mass functions associated with the elements of $\mathbb{P}(\mathcal{X})$. A convex and closed set $\mathcal{M} \subseteq \mathbb{P}(\mathcal{X})$ is called a *credal set* [8]. It can be used to determine a *coherent lower prevision* [21,23] on the set of *gambles* $\mathcal{L}(\mathcal{X})$ (i.e. real-valued functionals over $\mathcal{X}$), by means of $\underline{P}(f) := \min_{P \in \mathcal{M}} P(f)$ for all

$f \in \mathcal{L}(\mathcal{X})$, where $P(f)$ denotes the expected value of f with respect to P. The associated *conjugate upper prevision* is defined as $\overline{P}(f) := -\underline{P}(-f)$, where $-f$ is the gamble given by $(-f)(x) = -(f(x))$ for any $x \in \mathcal{X}$.

When the domain of a coherent lower prevision is the set $\{\mathbb{I}_A \in \mathcal{L}(\mathcal{X}) \mid A \subseteq \mathcal{X}\}$ of indicator functions of events, we refer to it as a *coherent lower probability*. More generally, a lower probability, not necessarily coherent, is a function $\underline{P} : \mathcal{P}(\mathcal{X}) \to [0, 1]$ satisfying: (i) $\underline{P}(\emptyset) = 0$ and $\underline{P}(\mathcal{X}) = 1$ (normalisation) and (ii) $A \subseteq B$ implies $\underline{P}(A) \leq \underline{P}(B)$ for each $A, B \subseteq \mathcal{X}$ (monotonicity). Its conjugate upper probability is thus given by $\overline{P}(A) = 1 - \underline{P}(A^c)$. We shall denote by $\mathbb{P}(\mathcal{X})$ the family of lower probabilities on $\mathcal{X}$.

The *natural extension* of a lower probability $\underline{P}$ is the functional $\underline{E}_{\underline{P}}$ given by $\underline{E}_{\underline{P}}(f) := \min\{P(f) \mid P \geq \underline{P}\}$ for all $f \in \mathcal{L}(\mathcal{X})$; in particular, if $\underline{P}$ is coherent $\underline{E}_{\underline{P}}$ is the smallest coherent lower prevision on $\mathcal{L}(\mathcal{X})$ that agrees with $\underline{P}$ on events.

A particular case of coherent lower probabilities that shall be of interest for this paper are those that are 2-*monotone*, meaning that

$$\underline{P}(A \cup B) \geq \underline{P}(A) + \underline{P}(B) - \underline{P}(A \cap B) \quad \forall A, B \subseteq \mathcal{X}.$$

While a coherent lower probability need not be 2-monotone, it is so when the possibility space has cardinality three. Furthermore, a particular case of 2-monotone lower probabilities are *belief functions*, that satisfy

$$\underline{P}(\cup_{i=1}^k A_i) \geq \sum_{\emptyset \neq I \subseteq \{1,\ldots,k\}} (-1)^{|I|+1} \underline{P}(\cap_{i \in I} A_i) \quad \forall k \in \mathbb{N}, A_1, \ldots, A_k \subseteq \mathcal{X}.$$

2.2 Distortions of Credal Sets

The second leg on which this paper stands are distortion models, that were considered for credal sets in the seminal work by Moral [13].

Take $P_0 \in \mathbb{P}(\mathcal{X})$ and $\delta \geq 0$, and let $d : \mathbb{P}(\mathcal{X}) \times \mathbb{P}(\mathcal{X}) \to [0, +\infty)$ be a continuous function that is quasi-convex with respect to its first argument. It determines [11, Prop.3.1] a credal set

$$B_d^\delta(P_0) := \{Q \in \mathbb{P}(\mathcal{X}) \mid d(Q, P_0) \leq \delta\}.$$

Our focus in this paper shall be on a particular instance of such function d, the *total variation distance* [6,12]:

$$d_{\mathrm{TV}}(P_1, P_2) := \max_{A \subseteq \mathcal{X}} |P_1(A) - P_2(A)| = \frac{1}{2} \sum_{x \in \mathcal{X}} |P_1(\{x\}) - P_2(\{x\})|. \quad (1)$$

We shall consider two extensions of the total variation distance to coherent lower probabilities. These are respectively given by

$$\begin{aligned} d_{\mathrm{TV}}^{\min}(\underline{P}_1, \underline{P}_2) :&= \min_{\substack{P_1 \in \mathcal{M}(\underline{P}_1)\\ P_2 \in \mathcal{M}(\underline{P}_2)}} d_{\mathrm{TV}}(P_1, P_2) = \min_{\substack{P_1 \in \mathcal{M}(\underline{P}_1)\\ P_2 \in \mathcal{M}(\underline{P}_2)}} \max_{A \subseteq \mathcal{X}} \big|P_1(A) - P_2(A)\big|, \\ &= \min_{\substack{P_1 \in \mathcal{M}(\underline{P}_1)\\ P_2 \in \mathcal{M}(\underline{P}_2)}} \max_{A \subseteq \mathcal{X}} \big(P_1(A) - P_2(A)\big), \end{aligned} \quad (2)$$

where last equality follows taking into account that $P_1(A) - P_2(A) = P_2(A^c) - P_1(A^c)$ for each $A \subseteq \mathcal{X}$, and

$$d'_{\mathrm{TV}}(\underline{P}_1, \underline{P}_2) := \max_{A \subseteq \mathcal{X}} \min_{\substack{P_1 \in \mathcal{M}(\underline{P}_1) \\ P_2 \in \mathcal{M}(\underline{P}_2)}} (P_1(A) - P_2(A)) = \max_{A \subseteq \mathcal{X}} (\underline{P}_1(A) - \overline{P}_2(A)),$$

where the last equality follows from the coherence of $\underline{P}_1, \underline{P}_2$. It can be checked that in the equations above the minima are indeed attained, using continuity arguments. In general, $d_{\mathrm{TV}}^{\min} \geq d'_{\mathrm{TV}}$ and the equality holds [15, Prop. 2] whenever $\underline{P}_1, \underline{P}_2$ are 2-monotone.

A coherent $\underline{P}_0 \in \underline{\mathbb{P}}(\mathcal{X})$, a function $d : \underline{\mathbb{P}}(\mathcal{X}) \times \underline{\mathbb{P}}(\mathcal{X}) \to [0, +\infty)$ and a positive real number $\delta \geq 0$ determine a neighbourhood by:

$$B_d^{\delta}(\underline{P}_0) := \{Q \in \underline{\mathbb{P}}(\mathcal{X}) \mid d(Q, \underline{P}_0) \leq \delta\}.$$

It turns out [17, Cor.1] that for both $d = d_{\mathrm{TV}}^{\min}$ and $d = d'_{\mathrm{TV}}$, this neighbourhood determines the coherent lower probability

$$\underline{Q}(A) := \max\{\underline{P}_0(A) - \delta, 0\} \quad \forall A \neq \emptyset, \mathcal{X}, \tag{3}$$

$\underline{Q}(\emptyset) := 0$ and $\underline{Q}(\mathcal{X}) := 1$. However, their lower envelopes on gambles do not necessarily coincide, although they do whenever $\underline{P}_0$ is 2-monotone [17, Thm.1].

2.3 Aggregation Rules

We shall use distortions of credal sets as a tool to adequately aggregate imprecise probability models. By the aggregation problem we understand here the elicitation of an imprecise model that represents the global opinion of the members of a group. We assume that their individual opinions are represented by means of coherent lower previsions $\{\underline{P}_i\}_{i=1}^n$, and denote the output of the aggregation rule by $\underline{Q}_{\mathrm{agg}}$.

There are many aggregation rules for imprecise probabilities in the literature (see [9] for a survey). Here we shall consider the following:

Conjunction: $\underline{Q}_{\mathrm{agg}}^C$ is the natural extension of $\max_i \underline{P}_i$, and gives a coherent lower prevision when $\cap_{i=1}^n \mathcal{M}(\underline{P}_i) \neq \emptyset$.
Disjunction: $\underline{Q}_{\mathrm{agg}}^D(f) := \min_i \underline{P}_i(f)$ for all $f \in \mathcal{L}(\mathcal{X})$.
Pareto: $\underline{Q}_{\mathrm{agg}}^P(f) := \min\{\max_i \underline{P}_i(f), \min_i \overline{P}_i(f)\}$ for all $f \in \mathcal{L}(\mathcal{X})$.
Mixture: $\underline{Q}_{\mathrm{agg}}^M(f) := \sum_i \alpha_i \underline{P}_i(f)$ for all $f \in \mathcal{L}(\mathcal{X})$ and for some fixed $\alpha_i \geq 0$ with $\sum_i \alpha_i = 1$.

The choice of the best rule for our purposes can be done by means of the rationality criteria they satisfy. A few of them are the following:

Coherence: The aggregated model $\underline{Q}_{\mathrm{agg}}$ is coherent.
Symmetry: Any permutation of $\{\underline{P}_i\}_{i=1}^n$ yields the same aggregated model.

Marginalisation: For each $A \subseteq \mathcal{X}$, $\underline{Q}_{\text{agg}}(A)$ depends merely on $\{\underline{P}_i(A)\}_{i=1}^n$.
Precise preservation: $\{\underline{P}_i\}_{i=1}^n \subset \mathbb{P}(\mathcal{X})$ implies $\underline{Q}_{\text{agg}} \in \mathbb{P}(\mathcal{X})$.
Monotonicity: If one of the sources $\underline{P}_i$ is replaced by certain $\underline{P} \leq \underline{P}_i$, then the resulting aggregate $\underline{Q}'_{\text{agg}}$ is also dominated by $\underline{Q}_{\text{agg}}$.
Total reconciliation: $\underline{Q}_{\text{agg}} \leq \min_i \underline{P}_i$.
Strong Pareto: $\underline{Q}_{\text{agg}}(f) \geq \min\{\max_i \underline{P}_i(f), \min_i \overline{P}_i(f)\}$ for each $f \in \mathcal{L}(\mathcal{X})$.
Unanimity: $\underline{Q}_{\text{agg}} \geq \min_i \underline{P}_i$.
Associativity: $\underline{Q}_{\text{agg}}$ coincides with the result of aggregating any $\underline{P}_i$ with the aggregation of the rest of the individuals.

Here, we shall consider the aggregation problem in situations of global conflict among the sources, i.e. when $\cap_{i=1}^n \mathcal{M}(\underline{P}_i) = \emptyset$. For this reason, some of the properties considered in [9] such as conjunction, indeterminacy, idempotence, vacuity preservation or relative ignorance are excluded from our discussion. We also exclude other interesting properties related to conditioning such as irrelevance or independence preservation and updating, due to space limitations.

3 Aggregation Under Conflict Through the Minimal TV

This core section of the paper establishes and analyses our pooling method for imprecise probability models in conflict. We do so by considering the minimal distortion of the initial models that permits to take their conjunction, where the distortion is performed via the generalisations of the total variation distance from Sect. 2.2. We determine in the first place some general features, and next investigate its relationship with other aggregation rules.

3.1 Distortion-Conjunction Aggregation Rule

The starting point of our procedure is a finite family $\{\underline{P}_i\}_{i=1}^n$ of coherent lower probabilities in conflict, which in this paper shall be understood as the non-existence of a probability measure that is compatible with all the sources, i.e., as $\cap_{i=1}^n \mathcal{M}(\underline{P}_i) = \emptyset$. Given a distorting function $d \in \{d_{\text{TV}}^{\min}, d'_{\text{TV}}\}$ and a radius $\delta > 0$, we consider the neighbourhoods in $\{B_d^\delta(\underline{P}_i)\}_{i=1}^n$. The idea is then to consider the minimum value of δ such that the distorted models avoid conflict in the sense above and then take the conjunction of the distorted models. This results in the following definition.

Definition 1. *Let $\{\underline{P}_i\}_{i=1}^n$ be a set of coherent lower probabilities such that $\cap_{i=1}^n \mathcal{M}(\underline{P}_i) = \emptyset$, $d \in \{d_{\text{TV}}^{\min}, d'_{\text{TV}}\}$ and $\underline{Q}_i$ be the lower envelope of $B_d^{\delta^*}(\underline{P}_i)$ where*

$$\delta^* := \min\{\delta \geq 0 \mid \cap_{i=1}^n B_d^\delta(\underline{P}_i) \neq \emptyset\}. \tag{4}$$

We define the aggregate lower prevision by distortion-conjunction as

$$\underline{Q}_{\text{agg}}(f) := \min\{P(f) \mid P \in \cap_{i=1}^n B_d^{\delta^*}(\underline{P}_i)\}. \tag{5}$$

By construction, it follows that:

$$\mathcal{M}(\underline{Q}_{\text{agg}}) = \mathcal{M}\big(\max_i \underline{Q}_i\big) = \cap_{i=1}^n B_d^{\delta^*}(\underline{P}_i),$$

whence $\underline{Q}_{\text{agg}}$ coincides with the natural extension of $\max_i \underline{Q}_i$. Moreover:

$$\mathcal{M}(\underline{Q}_{\text{agg}}) = \left\{P \in \mathbb{P}(\mathcal{X}) \mid \max_i d(P, \underline{Q}_i) = 0\right\},$$

since $d(P, \underline{Q}) = 0$ if and only if $P \in \mathcal{M}(\underline{Q})$, for any coherent $\underline{Q} \in \underline{\mathbb{P}}(\mathcal{X})$ and $P \in \mathbb{P}(\mathcal{X})$.

The idea behind the distortion-conjunction rule can be graphically seen in Fig. 1. In the left hand-side of the figure we have two credal sets in conflict (they are disjoint), and in the right hand-side we distort them until they have a non-empty intersection so we can apply the conjunction rule.

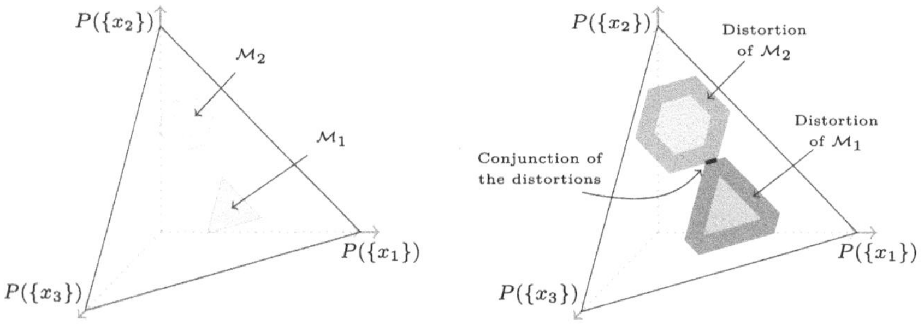

Fig. 1. Graphical representation of the rationale behind the distortion-conjunction aggregation rule.

3.2 Characterisation of the Distortion Factor

We begin our analysis by identifying the values of the parameter δ for which the intersection of the distorted models is indeed non-empty. We focus on the aggregation of two models, i.e., $n = 2$.

Proposition 1. *Let $\underline{P}_1, \underline{P}_2 \in \underline{\mathbb{P}}(\mathcal{X})$ be coherent and assume that $\mathcal{M}(\underline{P}_1) \cap \mathcal{M}(\underline{P}_2) = \emptyset$ holds. Consider $\delta \geq 0$, $d \in \{d_{\text{TV}}^{\min}, d'_{\text{TV}}\}$, δ^* as in Eq. (4) and denote $\overline{\delta} = d(\underline{P}_1, \underline{P}_2)$. Then, $B_d^\delta(\underline{P}_1) \cap B_d^\delta(\underline{P}_2) \neq \emptyset$ if and only if $\delta \geq \overline{\delta}/2$. As a consequence, $\delta^* = \frac{1}{2} d(\underline{P}_1, \underline{P}_2) = \frac{1}{2}\overline{\delta}$.*

The proof of this result for $d = d_{\text{TV}}^{\min}$ lingers on the fact that the restriction to precise probabilities of the minimum total variation satisfies the triangle inequality. Thus, the extension of this result to other distorting functions should take into account this property. It can also be checked that, whenever the initial models are 2-monotone, the value δ^* may be obtained directly from the lower probabilities without using the probability measures in the respective credal sets.

In the example presented above in Fig. 1, the right hand-side illustrates the minimum distortion so that the enlarged models have a non-empty intersection. We observe also that this intersection is included in the boundaries of the distorted credal sets. Our next result shows that, when aggregating two models, this feature is always satisfied: the credal set of the aggregated model equals the intersection of the boundaries of the respective neighbourhood models.

Proposition 2. *Let $\underline{P}_1, \underline{P}_2 \in \underline{\mathbb{P}}(\mathcal{X})$ be coherent and assume that $\mathcal{M}(\underline{P}_1) \cap \mathcal{M}(\underline{P}_2) = \emptyset$ holds. Consider $d \in \{d_{TV}^{\min}, d'_{TV}\}$ and $\delta = \delta^*$ as in Eq. (4). Then:*

$$B_d^\delta(\underline{P}_1) \cap B_d^\delta(\underline{P}_2) = \partial B_d^\delta(\underline{P}_1) \cap \partial B_d^\delta(\underline{P}_2),$$

where ∂ denotes the boundary of the set.

We may interpret the distortion factor δ^* as a measure of the discrepancy between the sources. Indeed, let us define the conflict of a precise probability $P \in \mathbb{P}(\mathcal{X})$ with the i-th piece piece of information among $\{\underline{P}_i\}_{i=1}^n$ as:

$$C_i(P) := \min_{P_i \in \mathcal{M}(\underline{P}_i)} d_{TV}(P, P_i) = d_{TV}^{\min}(P, \underline{P}_i).$$

Then, the maximal conflict of the given P according to the global, initial, group beliefs may be defined by:

$$C_{\text{group}}^{\max}(P) := \max_i C_i(P) = \max_i d_{TV}^{\min}(P, \underline{P}_i),$$

and we may interpret $C_{\text{group}}^{\max}(P)$ as a measure of group conflict with the precise model P, according to the individual initial beliefs. We then have that

$$\cap_{i=1}^n \mathcal{M}(\underline{P}_i) = \emptyset \Leftrightarrow \forall P \in \mathbb{P}(\mathcal{X}) \quad C_{\text{group}}^{\max}(P) \neq 0$$

and also that the model $\underline{Q}_{\text{agg}}$ given by Eq. (5) satisfies

$$\mathcal{M}(\underline{Q}_{\text{agg}}) = \left\{ Q \in \mathbb{P}(\mathcal{X}) \mid C_{\text{group}}^{\max}(Q) = \min_{P \in \mathbb{P}(\mathcal{X})} C_{\text{group}}^{\max}(P) = \delta^* \right\}.$$

In other words, after discounting by a factor δ^*, the probability measures in the aggregated model are consistent with the distorted beliefs of the group.

3.3 Properties as an Aggregation Rule

In this subsection we analyse the desirable properties that our procedure verifies, under the axiomatic lens considered in [9]. In first place, we observe that coherence and symmetry are satisfied by construction. However, as our next examples show, the other properties considered in Sect. 2.3 fail to hold. Note that in the majority of our examples we consider a possibility space of cardinality three, and then the 2-monotonicity due to coherence of $\underline{P}_1, \underline{P}_2$ means that we need not distinguish between $d_{TV}^{\min}$ and d'_{TV}.

We begin by showing that precise preservation, monotonicity and total reconciliation are not satisfied by our procedure.

Example 1. Let $\mathcal{X} = \{x_1, x_2, x_3\}$ and $\underline{P}_1 = P_1$, $\underline{P}_2 = P_2$ be the probability measures associated with the mass functions $(0.2, 0.2, 0.6), (0.4, 0.4, 0.2)$, respectively. Consider also the distortion of $\underline{P}_1$ with radius $\delta = 0.1$ using Eq. (3), which is given by $\underline{P}(A) = \max\{\underline{P}_1(A) - 0.1, 0\}$ for each $A \neq \emptyset, \mathcal{X}$. Then, clearly $\underline{P} \leq \underline{P}_1$. We observe that Eqs. (1), (2) yield the distortion parameter $\delta^* = 0.2$ for the aggregation $\underline{Q}_{agg}$ of $\underline{P}_1, \underline{P}_2$. If we now aggregate $\underline{P}, \underline{P}_2$, we obtain that the distortion parameter we must consider is

$$\delta^{*\prime} = \frac{d'_{TV}(\underline{P}, \underline{P}_2)}{2} = \frac{\underline{P}(\{x_3\}) - \overline{P}_2(\{x_3\})}{2} = 0.15,$$

using the values of $\underline{P}, \underline{P}_2$ given in Table 1.

Table 1. Lower probabilities involved in Example 1, showing that the procedure does not satisfy precise preservation, monotonicity nor total reconciliation.

A	$\{x_1\}$	$\{x_2\}$	$\{x_3\}$	$\{x_1, x_2\}$	$\{x_1, x_3\}$	$\{x_2, x_3\}$	$\mathcal{X}$
$\underline{P}(A)$	0.1	0.1	0.5	0.3	0.7	0.7	1
$\underline{P}_2(A)$	0.4	0.4	0.2	0.8	0.6	0.6	1
$\underline{Q}_1(A)$	0	0	0.4	0.2	0.6	0.6	1
$\underline{Q}_2(A)$	0.2	0.2	0	0.6	0.4	0.4	1
$\underline{Q}_{agg}(A)$	0.2	0.2	0.4	0.6	0.6	0.6	1
$\underline{Q}'_{agg}(A)$	0.25	0.25	0.35	0.65	0.6	0.6	1

To see that $\underline{Q}_{agg}$ takes the values reported in Table 1, we note that $Q \in B^{\delta}_{d_{TV}^{\min}}(\underline{P}_1) \cap B^{\delta}_{d_{TV}^{\min}}(\underline{P}_2)$ if and only if

$$Q(\{x_3\}) = 0.4 \text{ and } Q(\{x_i\}) \in [0.2, 0.4] \text{ for } i \in \{1, 2\}.$$

Therefore, $\underline{Q}_{agg}$ is imprecise, since its credal set contains the masses $Q_1 = (0.2, 0.4, 0.4)$ and $Q_2 = (0.4, 0.2, 0.4)$. Precise preservation is thus not satisfied. On the other hand, our aggregation procedure for $\underline{P}$, $\underline{P}_2$ leads to the coherent lower probability $\underline{Q}'_{agg}$ also given in Table 1, considering that $Q \in B^{0.15}_{d_{TV}^{\min}}(\underline{P}) \cap B^{0.15}_{d_{TV}^{\min}}(\underline{P}_2)$ if and only if

$$Q(\{x_3\}) = 0.35 \text{ and } Q(\{x_1\}), Q(\{x_2\}) \in [0.25, 0.4].$$

We observe that, although $\underline{P}_1 \geq \underline{P}$, $\underline{Q}_{\text{agg}} \not\geq \underline{Q}'_{\text{agg}}$: indeed, $\underline{Q}_{\text{agg}}(\{x_1\}) = 0.2 < 0.25 = \underline{Q}'_{\text{agg}}(\{x_1\})$. In other words, monotonicity fails to hold. Since in addition $\underline{Q}'_{\text{agg}}(\{x_1\}) \not\leq \underline{P}(\{x_1\})$, it follows that total reconciliation does not hold either in this example. ♦

As shown in [9], some of the most important aggregation rules such as the disjunction or convex mixtures do not satisfy strong Pareto. The next example shows that the proposed distortion-conjunction rule also violates this property. In addition, and somewhat surprisingly, the same example shows that our rule also violates unanimity.

Example 2. Let $\mathcal{X} = \{x_1, x_2, x_3, x_4\}$ and $\underline{P}_1, \underline{P}_2$ be the coherent lower probabilities given in Table 2. If we consider $d = d'_{\text{TV}}$, we obtain

$$\delta^* = \frac{d'_{\text{TV}}(\underline{P}_1, \underline{P}_2)}{2} = \frac{\underline{P}_1(\{x_1, x_2\}) - \overline{P}_2(\{x_1, x_2\})}{2} = 0.05.$$

The lower probabilities $\underline{Q}'_1, \underline{Q}'_2$ determined by $(\underline{P}_1, \delta^*), (\underline{P}_2, \delta^*)$ using Eq. (3) and their conjunction $\underline{Q}'_{\text{agg}}$, are also shown in Table 2.

Table 2. Lower probabilities involved in Example 2, showing that the procedure does not satisfy unanimity nor strong Pareto.

A	$\underline{P}_1(A)$	$\overline{P}_1(A)$	$\underline{P}_2(A)$	$\overline{P}_2(A)$	$\underline{Q}'_1(A)$	$\underline{Q}'_2(A)$	$\underline{Q}'_{\text{agg}}(A)$	$\min_i \underline{P}_i(A)$
$\{x_1\}$	0.25	0.5	0	0.2	0.2	0	0.2	0
$\{x_2\}$	0.25	0.5	0	0.2	0.2	0	0.2	0
$\{x_3\}$	0	0.25	0.3	0.5	0	0.25	0.25	0
$\{x_4\}$	0	0.25	0.3	0.5	0	0.25	0.25	0
$\{x_1, x_2\}$	0.5	1	0	0.4	0.45	0	0.45	0
$\{x_1, x_3\}$	0.5	0.5	0.5	0.5	0.45	0.45	0.45	0.5
$\{x_1, x_4\}$	0.5	0.5	0.5	0.5	0.45	0.45	0.45	0.5
$\{x_2, x_3\}$	0.5	0.5	0.5	0.5	0.45	0.45	0.45	0.5
$\{x_2, x_4\}$	0.5	0.5	0.5	0.5	0.45	0.45	0.45	0.5
$\{x_3, x_4\}$	0	0.5	0.6	1	0	0.55	0.55	0
$\{x_1, x_2, x_3\}$	0.75	1	0.5	0.7	0.7	0.45	0.7	0.5
$\{x_1, x_2, x_4\}$	0.75	1	0.5	0.7	0.7	0.45	0.7	0.5
$\{x_1, x_3, x_4\}$	0.5	0.75	0.8	1	0.45	0.75	0.75	0.5
$\{x_2, x_3, x_4\}$	0.5	0.75	0.8	1	0.45	0.75	0.75	0.5
$\mathcal{X}$	1	1	1	1	1	1	1	1

We see that

$$\underline{Q}'_{\text{agg}}(\{x_1, x_3\}) = 0.45 < 0.5 = \min_i \underline{P}_i(\{x_1, x_3\}),$$

hence the aggregation procedure determined by d'_{TV} does not satisfy unanimity. Since the aggregated model by $d_{\mathrm{TV}}^{\min}$ is never more precise than the one determined by d'_{TV}, we deduce from this example that it does not satisfy unanimity either. And since strong Pareto is a sufficient condition for unanimity, it follows that these two aggregation procedures do not satisfy this property either. ♦

We conclude this subsection by giving a counterexample of the associativity for $n = 3$ initial lower probabilities. By doing this, we also note that the value of δ^* in Eq. (4) may satisfy

$$\delta^* > \frac{1}{2} \max_{i,j} d(\underline{P}_i, \underline{P}_j).$$

In other words, although taking the value $\delta = {}^{\max_{i,j} d(\underline{P}_i, \underline{P}_j)}/_2$ gives a pairwise non-empty intersection of the discounted credal sets by Proposition 1, this does not guarantee that the distorted models are not in global conflict. Our counterexample uses precise probability measures, so in that case $d = d_{\mathrm{TV}}^{\min} = d'_{\mathrm{TV}} = d_{\mathrm{TV}}$.

Example 3. Let $\underline{P}_1 = P_1$, $\underline{P}_2 = P_2$ and $\underline{P}_3 = P_3$ be the precise probabilities associated with the probability mass functions $(0.5, 0.3, 0.2)$, $(0.5, 0.2, 0.3)$ and $(0.4, 0.3, 0.3)$, respectively. For each $i, j \in \{1, 2, 3\}$, denote $\delta^*_{ij} = {}^{d(P_i, P_j)}/_2$ and note that it holds $\delta^*_{ij} = 0.05$ for every i, j. It can also be verified that the pairwise intersections of the credal sets are singletons. Specifically:

$$B_d^{\delta^*_{12}}(\underline{P}_1) \cap B_d^{\delta^*_{12}}(\underline{P}_2) = \{P^*\}, \qquad B_d^{\delta^*_{13}}(\underline{P}_1) \cap B_d^{\delta^*_{13}}(\underline{P}_3) = \{Q^*\}, \text{ and}$$
$$B_d^{\delta^*_{23}}(\underline{P}_2) \cap B_d^{\delta^*_{23}}(\underline{P}_3) = \{R^*\},$$

where $P^* = (0.5, 0.25, 0.25)$, $Q^* = (0.45, 0.3, 0.25)$ and $R^* = (0.45, 0.25, 0.3)$. Then, the intersection of the three neighbourhoods is empty, which proves that

$$\delta = \frac{\max_{i,j} d(\underline{P}_i, \underline{P}_j)}{2} = 0.05$$

is not the minimum distortion parameter. In fact, it can be checked that this minimum value is $\delta^* = {}^2/_{30} = 0.0\overline{6}$. Table 3 gives the corresponding distorted models as well as the aggregated one, whose credal set is a precise probability.

Table 3. Lower probabilities $\underline{Q}_1, \underline{Q}_2, \underline{Q}_3$ in Example 3 together with $\underline{Q}_{\mathrm{agg}}$.

A	$\{x_1\}$	$\{x_2\}$	$\{x_3\}$	$\{x_1, x_2\}$	$\{x_1, x_3\}$	$\{x_2, x_3\}$	$\mathcal{X}$
$\underline{Q}_1(A)$	$13/30$	$7/30$	$4/30$	$22/30$	$19/30$	$13/30$	1
$\underline{Q}_2(A)$	$13/30$	$4/30$	$7/30$	$19/30$	$22/30$	$13/30$	1
$\underline{Q}_3(A)$	$1/3$	$7/30$	$7/30$	$19/30$	$19/30$	$8/15$	1
$\underline{Q}_{\mathrm{agg}}(A)$	$7/15$	$4/15$	$4/15$	$11/15$	$11/15$	$8/15$	1

On the other hand, the aggregation of $\underline{P}_1, \underline{P}_2$ gives another precise probability $\underline{Q}_{agg}^{\delta_{12}^*} = P^*$ and the aggregation of the latter with $\underline{P}_3$, denoted as $\underline{Q}'_{agg}$ (for which we must use the distortion parameter $\delta' = 0.05$), does not coincide with $\underline{Q}_{agg}$, as shown in Table 4.

Table 4. Lower probabilities $\underline{Q}_{agg}^{\delta_{12}^*}$, $\underline{Q}_{agg}^{\delta_{12}^*,\delta'}$, $\underline{Q}'_3$ and $\underline{Q}'_{agg}$ in Example 3.

A	$\{x_1\}$	$\{x_2\}$	$\{x_3\}$	$\{x_1, x_2\}$	$\{x_1, x_3\}$	$\{x_2, x_3\}$	$\mathcal{X}$
$\underline{Q}_{agg}^{\delta_{12}^*}(A)$	0.5	0.25	0.25	0.75	0.75	0.25	1
$\underline{Q}_{agg}^{\delta_{12}^*,\delta'}(A)$	0.45	0.2	0.2	0.7	0.7	0.2	1
$\underline{Q}'_3(A)$	0.35	0.25	0.25	0.65	0.65	0.55	1
$\underline{Q}'_{agg}(A)$	0.45	0.25	0.25	0.7	0.7	0.55	1

We conclude thus that $\underline{Q}'_{agg} \neq \underline{Q}_{agg}$, and therefore that our aggregation procedure is not associative. ♦

3.4 Comparison with Other Aggregation Rules

In this part of the work, we demonstrate the non-existence of a dominance relation between the aggregation rules proposed here and those presented in Sect. 2.3.

That our aggregation rule is not more precise than disjunction or Pareto in general can be deduced from Example 2. That these are not more precise than our rule either can be seen with Example 1. On the other hand, since in this paper we focus on the case where the original sources of information are in conflict, we have that the conjunction rule does not give a coherent output. Finally, we show, also by means of Example 1, that there is not a dominance relation between our rule and the mixture: for this, use the weights $(\alpha_1, 1-\alpha_1)$ with $\alpha_1 < \frac{1}{2}$ and $A = \{x_1, x_2\}$ for one inequality and with $\alpha_1 > \frac{1}{2}$ for the other.

4 Aggregation by Event-Dependent Distortions

Next we explore a proposal where the distortion is not uniform along all directions of the simplex, but is instead only made in those where the two credal sets are in conflict, and proportionally to it; a similar idea can be found in [2, Sect. 3.3.2]. This is in line with a subjacent philosophy of minimal change. Specifically, given a pair of coherent lower probabilities, $\underline{P}_1, \underline{P}_2 \in \underline{\mathbb{P}}(\mathcal{X})$, we let

$$\begin{aligned} \mathcal{A}^{=} &= \{A \subseteq \mathcal{X} \mid [\underline{P}_1(A), \overline{P}_1(A)] \cap [\underline{P}_2(A), \overline{P}_2(A)] \neq \emptyset\}, \\ \mathcal{A}^{1>2} &= \{A \subseteq \mathcal{X} \mid \underline{P}_1(A) > \overline{P}_2(A)\}, \\ \mathcal{A}^{2>1} &= \{A \subseteq \mathcal{X} \mid \underline{P}_2(A) > \overline{P}_1(A)\} \end{aligned} \tag{6}$$

and define the event-dependent distortion factor:

$$\delta_A = \begin{cases} \frac{1}{2}(\underline{P}_1(A) - \overline{P}_2(A)), & \text{if } A \in \mathcal{A}^{1>2}, \\ \frac{1}{2}(\underline{P}_2(A) - \overline{P}_1(A)), & \text{if } A \in \mathcal{A}^{2>1}. \end{cases} \quad (7)$$

We now define the distorted models as

$$\underline{Q}_i(A) = \begin{cases} \underline{P}_i(A), & \text{if } A \in \mathcal{A}^{=} \cup \mathcal{A}^{j>i}, \\ \underline{P}_i(A) - \delta_A, & \text{if } A \in \mathcal{A}^{i>j}, \end{cases} \quad (8)$$

for $i, j \in \{1, 2\}$, $i \neq j$. We observe that $\underline{Q}_i \leq \underline{P}_i$ by construction. The underlying idea is that $\underline{P}_1, \underline{P}_2$ are at conflict on an event A when one of the intervals $[\underline{P}_1(A), \overline{P}_1(A)]$, $[\underline{P}_2(A), \overline{P}_2(A)]$ is above the other, and then we decrease the lower limit of the one above so that they intersect. Note that we only need to do it in half of the distance, because our construction entails that we will increase the upper limit of the interval that is below. This is a consequence of the following proposition.

Proposition 3. *Let $\underline{P}_1, \underline{P}_2 \in \underline{\mathbb{P}}(\mathcal{X})$ be coherent and consider $\mathcal{A}^{=}, \mathcal{A}^{1>2}, \mathcal{A}^{2>1}$ as in Eq. (6). Then:*

(a) $A \in \mathcal{A}^{1>2} \Leftrightarrow A^c \in \mathcal{A}^{2>1}$ and $A \in \mathcal{A}^{=} \Leftrightarrow A^c \in \mathcal{A}^{=}$.
(b) $\delta_A = \delta_{A^c}$ for every $A \subseteq \mathcal{X}$, where δ_A is given in Eq. (7).
(c) If $\underline{Q}_1, \underline{Q}_2$ are defined by Eq. (8), then $[\underline{Q}_1(A), \overline{Q}_1(A)] \cap [\underline{Q}_2(A), \overline{Q}_2(A)] \neq \emptyset$ for each $A \subseteq \mathcal{X}$.

In spite of this, the above construction also has a number of issues: on the one hand, the lower probabilities $\underline{Q}_1, \underline{Q}_2$ it defines need not be coherent. And more importantly, the procedure does not entail that $\mathcal{M}(\underline{Q}_1) \cap \mathcal{M}(\underline{Q}_2)$ is non-empty. This is all illustrated in our next example:

Example 4. Let $\mathcal{X} = \{x_1, x_2, x_3, x_4\}$, $\underline{P}_1$ be the coherent lower probability with conjugate $\overline{P}_1$ and $\underline{P}_2 = \overline{P}_2 = P_2$ be the precise probability given in Table 5. In this case:

$$\mathcal{A}^{1>2} = \{\{x_1\}, \{x_1, x_3\}, \{x_1, x_3, x_4\}\}$$

and

$$\delta_{\{x_1\}} = 0.05, \qquad \delta_{\{x_1, x_3\}} = 0.08, \qquad \delta_{\{x_1, x_3, x_4\}} = 0.025.$$

Using Proposition 3 and Eq. (8), we obtain the lower probabilities $\underline{Q}_1, \underline{Q}_2$ given in Table 5. To see that $\underline{Q} := \max\{\underline{Q}_1, \underline{Q}_2\}$ does not avoid sure loss (and therefore that $\mathcal{M}(\underline{Q}_1) \cap \mathcal{M}(\underline{Q}_2) = \emptyset$), it suffices to see that $\sum_i \underline{Q}(\{x_i\}) > 1$ (see the last column in Table 5. We can also observe that $\underline{Q}_2$ is not a coherent lower probability since

$$\underline{Q}_2(\{x_2, x_3, x_4\}) = 0.85 < 0.9 = \underline{Q}_2(\{x_2, x_3\}) + \underline{Q}_2(\{x_4\}). \qquad \blacklozenge$$

In spite of this example, it is worth remarking that there are cases where taking distortions in preferential directions preserves coherence [4]. On the other hand, it is precisely when this preservation fails that the non-empty intersection of the probability bounds associated with each separate event is not equivalent to the non-empty intersection of the credal sets, in contradistinction with the similar approach considered in [2].

Table 5. Lower probabilities in Example 4, showing that the non-uniform distortion may not remove the initial conflict.

A	$\underline{P}_1(A)$	$\overline{P}_1(A)$	$P_2(A)$	$\underline{Q}_1(A)$	$\underline{Q}_2(A)$	$\max\{\underline{Q}_1(A), \underline{Q}_2(A)\}$
$\{x_1\}$	0.2	0.4	0.1	0.15	0.1	0.15
$\{x_2\}$	0.1	0.5	0.55	0.1	0.525	0.525
$\{x_3\}$	0.1	0.5	0.1	0.1	0.1	0.1
$\{x_4\}$	0.05	0.4	0.25	0.05	0.25	0.25
$\{x_1, x_2\}$	0.35	0.85	0.65	0.35	0.65	0.65
$\{x_1, x_3\}$	0.36	0.7	0.2	0.28	0.2	0.28
$\{x_1, x_4\}$	0.3	0.6	0.35	0.3	0.35	0.35
$\{x_2, x_3\}$	0.4	0.7	0.65	0.4	0.65	0.65
$\{x_2, x_4\}$	0.3	0.64	0.8	0.3	0.72	0.72
$\{x_3, x_4\}$	0.15	0.65	0.35	0.15	0.35	0.35
$\{x_1, x_2, x_3\}$	0.6	0.95	0.75	0.6	0.75	0.75
$\{x_1, x_2, x_4\}$	0.5	0.9	0.9	0.5	0.9	0.9
$\{x_1, x_3, x_4\}$	0.5	0.9	0.45	0.475	0.45	0.475
$\{x_2, x_3, x_4\}$	0.6	0.8	0.9	0.6	0.85	0.85
$\mathcal{X}$	1	1	1	1	1	1

5 Synthesis and Conclusions

In this paper, we have put forward an approach to aggregate a number of conflicting imprecise probability models, in two steps: first of all, we consider conservative approximations of the models so that their conflict becomes only partial; and secondly, we aggregate these approximations by means of some operator. Our procedure hinges on the choice of the distortion procedure used to remove the global conflict, that here has been done through generalisations of the total variation distance, and on the aggregation rule applied on the distorted models, that in our case has been made via the conjunction operator. For these choices, and for $n = 2$, we have given a formula of the minimal distortion parameter that is needed, and showed that the credal set that determines the aggregate model lies in the intersection of the boundaries of the neighbourhoods thus defined.

While our procedure satisfies some desirable properties on aggregation rules, such as coherence and symmetry, it also fails to verify others that may be of interest, even for small cardinality spaces; among these, perhaps the more striking is that the aggregation of precise models need not be precise or the lack of monotonicity and unanimity. It is also somewhat surprising that the output of our procedure is not always more informative than the one determined by the disjunction rule.

On the other hand, the attempt to replace the uniform distortion by a similar event-dependent one that acts only on the events where conflict is present shows that coherence preservation may be crucial; the approach should be further investigated in order to overcome some of its deficiencies.

As the main future lines of research, in addition to explore more deeply the connection of our distortion parameter with axiomatic measures of conflict, we would like to compare our approach with other alternatives, where a different distortion procedure or aggregation rule is put in place. It would also be worth exploring the option of removing first the pairwise conflicts and then applying the disjunction on the resulting sets. In such a case, the conflict would be only partially solved before the ulterior phase of the aggregation.

Acknowledgments. This contribution is part of grant PID2022-140585NB-I00 funded by MICIU/AEI/10.13039/501100011033 and "FEDER/UE". David Nieto-Barba is also supported by the Severo Ochoa predoctoral program by the Principality of Asturias (NAC-AT-PUB-ASV-2025 BP24-18).

Disclosure of Interests. The authors have no competing interests to declare that are relevant to the content of this article.

References

1. Augustin, T., Coolen, F., de Cooman, G., Troffaes, M. (eds.): Introduction to Imprecise Probabilities. Wiley Series in Probability and Statistics. Wiley (2014)
2. Cano, J., Moral, S., Verdegay-López, J.: Partial inconsistency of probability envelopes. Fuzzy Sets Syst. **52**, 201–216 (1992)
3. Choquet, G.: Theory of capacities. Ann. l'Inst. Fourier **5**, 131–295 (1953–1954)
4. Destercke, S.: A new contextual discounting rule for lower probabilities. In: Hüllermeier, E., Kruse, R., Hoffmann, F. (eds.) IPMU 2010. CCIS, vol. 81, pp. 198–207. Springer, Heidelberg (2010). https://doi.org/10.1007/978-3-642-14058-7_20
5. Dubois, D., Prade, H.: Possibility Theory. Plenum Press, New York (1988)
6. Herron, T., Seidenfeld, T., Wasserman, L.: Divisive conditioning: further results on dilation. Philos. Sci. **64**, 411–444 (1997)
7. Huber, P.J.: A robust version of the probability ratio test. Ann. Math. Stat. **36**, 1753–1758 (1965)
8. Levi, I.: The Enterprise of Knowledge. MIT Press, Cambridge (1980)
9. Miranda, E., Salamanca, J.J., Montes, I.: A comparative analysis of aggregation rules for coherent lower previsions. Int. J. Approximate Reasoning **185**(109474) (2025)
10. Montes, I., Miranda, E., Destercke, S.: Pari-mutuel probabilities as an uncertainty model. Inf. Sci. **481**, 550–573 (2019)
11. Montes, I., Miranda, E., Destercke, S.: Unifying neighbourhood and distortion models: part I- New results on old models. Int. J. Gen Syst **49**(6), 602–635 (2020)
12. Montes, I., Miranda, E., Destercke, S.: Unifying neighbourhood and distortion models: part II- New models and synthesis. Int. J. Gen. Syst. **49**(6), 636–674 (2020)
13. Moral, S.: Discounting imprecise probabilities. In: Gil, E., Gil, E., Gil, J., Gil, M. (eds.) The Mathematics of the Uncertain. Studies in Systems, Decision and Control, vol. 142, pp. 685–697. Springer, Cham (2018). https://doi.org/10.1007/978-3-319-73848-2_63

14. Moral, S., Sagrado, J.: Aggregation of imprecise probabilities. In: Bouchon-Meunier, B. (ed.) Aggregation and Fusion of Imperfect Information. Studies in Fuzziness and Soft Computing, vol. 12, pp. 162–188. Springer, Heidelberg (1998). https://doi.org/10.1007/978-3-7908-1889-5_10
15. Nieto-Barba, D., Miranda, E., Montes, I.: The total variation distance for comparing non-additive measures. International Journal of Uncertainty, Fuzziness and Knowledge-Based Systems. Accepted for publication (2025)
16. Nieto-Barba, D., Montes, I., Miranda, E.: Distortions of imprecise probabilities. In: Lesot, M.J., et al. (eds.) IPMU 2024. LNNS, vol. 1175, pp. 78–90. Springer, Cham (2025). https://doi.org/10.1007/978-3-031-74000-8_7
17. Nieto-Barba, D., Montes, I., Miranda, E.: The imprecise total variation model and its connections with game theory. Fuzzy Sets Syst. **517**, 109448 (2025)
18. Pelessoni, R., Vicig, P., Zaffalon, M.: Inference and risk measurement with the pari-mutuel model. Int. J. Approximate Reasoning **51**, 1145–1158 (2010)
19. Shafer, G.: A Mathematical Theory of Evidence. Princeton University Press, New Jersey (1976)
20. Stewart, R., Quintana, I.O.: Probabilistic opinion pooling with imprecise probabilities. J. Philos. Log. **47**(1), 17–45 (2018)
21. Walley, P.: Coherent lower (and upper) probabilities. Technical report 22, University of Warwick, Coventry (1981)
22. Walley, P.: The elicitation and aggregation of beliefs. Technical report 23, University of Warwick, Coventry (1982)
23. Walley, P.: Statistical Reasoning with Imprecise Probabilities. Chapman and Hall, London (1991)

Analogical Proportions Between Probabilities

Henri Prade(✉) and Gilles Richard

IRIT – CNRS, Université Paul Sabatier, 118, route de Narbonne, Toulouse, France
{Henri.Prade,Gilles.Richard}@irit.fr

Abstract. Analogical proportions are relations that link 4 items a, b, c and d and that are expressed as "a is to b as c is to d". These 4 items are often described by vectors of Boolean, nominal, or numerical values. Analogical proportions can however relate logical formulas. The article proposes a first study of analogical proportions between probabilities, whether they are simply between values, or between distributions (which requires the preservation of their normalization). The properties of definitions based on arithmetic proportion, or combining the latter with geometric proportion are studied, and potential uses are described. An appendix proposes a proof of the Pythagorean theorem in terms of geometric proportions.

Keywords: analogical proportion · probability · numerical proportions

1 Introduction

Analogies and probabilities are rarely considered together, although they can be both related to induction [17]. However, already in the 1930s, Janina Hosiasson-Lindenbaum [24], a formal philosopher, specialist of probabilistic reasoning and logician, considered the following analogical reasoning: if two conjectures f_1 and f_2 are consequences of the same hypothesis h, the observation of f_1 (which therefore becomes a fact) induces h and increases belief in conjecture f_2. She sought additional hypotheses allowing her a probabilistic justification for this increase in belief. Later, in the same spirit, Polya [13] will consider that f_1 and f_2 are analogous if they are implied by a common hypothesis.

In this article we are interested in another approach where analogies are expressed in the form of analogical proportions.[1] That is, statements of the form "a is to b as c is to d". Like Bayesian probabilistic inference, analogical proportions-based inference allows classification tasks to be performed successfully [3,5]. In classification, a, b, c, d are vectors of attribute values describing the examples and the items to be classified. The attributes can be Boolean, nominal, or numeric. However, analogical proportions can be extended to general representational frameworks such as propositional logic [18]. In this article, we consider the probabilistic framework.

[1] These two views of analogy are quite different. However, if a and b on the one hand, and c and d on the other hand are "analogous", one can argue that an analogical proportion "a is to b as c is to d" must hold. This is shown in [14] where "a analogous to b" is modeled, quite differently from Polya [13], by the non-monotonic consequence relations "if a generally b" and "if b generally a".

K. Sauerwald and M. Thimm (Eds.): ECSQARU 2025, LNAI 16099, pp. 148–163, 2026.
https://doi.org/10.1007/978-3-032-05134-9_11

This article[2] is divided into five main sections and two annexes. Section 2 provides background on Boolean and nominal analogical proportions as well as numerical analogical proportions, emphasizing the parallel between the three types of proportions. The latter type can be considered either in terms of arithmetic proportions or geometric proportions. Section 3 focuses on analogical proportions between probability values: these values represent the probabilities that an item has particular attribute values. Section 4 considers the possibility of defining analogical proportions between four probability distributions on a finite set. To this end, two definitions are specifically considered: one based on arithmetic proportions only, the other requiring both arithmetic and geometric proportions. This second definition is consistent with the preservation of the Kullback-Leibler divergence between pairs of distributions. Section 5 briefly considers the case of continuous probability density functions on the real line. Section 6 discusses potential applications of analogical proportions between probabilities. An appendix provides an illustration of the power of geometric proportions by showing an elegant proof of the Pythagorean theorem. Another appendix exhibits examples of analogical proportions between probabilities densities on the real line.

2 Background

An analogical proportion is a relation between four items a, b, c, d, denoted $a : b :: c : d$ that reads "a is to b as c is to d". This notion traces back to Aristotle [1], who proposed it, based on a parallel with numerical proportions studied a generation earlier by mathematicians such as Archytas of Tarentum and Eudoxus of Cnidus. It is supposed to obey the three foundational postulates (which are satisfied by the arithmetic and the geometric proportions):

- *reflexivity*: $a : b :: a : b$;
- *symmetry*: $a : b :: c : d \Rightarrow c : d :: a : b$;
- stability under *central permutation*: $a : b :: c : d \Rightarrow a : c :: b : d$.

As a consequence, $a : b :: c : d \Rightarrow b : a :: d : c$ (internal reversal). In this paper a, b, c, d are Boolean, categorical, or numerical values, or vectors thereof, or also function values.

When the items are represented by vectors of attribute values (e.g. $a = (a_1, \ldots, a_n)$, etc.), the analogical proportion $a : b :: c : d$ is defined componentwise:

Definition 1. *$a : b :: c : d$ holds iff $\forall i \in [1, n]$, $a_i : b_i :: c_i : d_i$ holds.*

In this section, we successively consider cases where the components i correspond to Boolean, nominal, and then numerical variables. In these subsections, we will omit the i subscripts to simplify the notation, given that we only focus on a single component.

2.1 Boolean Analogical Proportion

The minimal Boolean model of the three previous postulates is given in Table 1, where we present the 6 valuations of a, b, c, d that any model of the 3 postulates must contain. In this minimal model, the other 10 (= $2^4 - 6$) valuations are invalid. A logical expression that is true only for the quadruplets in Table 1 is given by the formula [11]:

[2] A preliminary version of this paper, in French, was presented in a national workshop [20].

$$a : b :: c : d = [(a \wedge \neg b) \equiv (c \wedge \neg d)] \wedge [(\neg a \wedge b) \equiv (\neg c \wedge d)] \quad (1)$$

This formula expresses precisely that "a differs from b as c differs from d, and b differs from a as d differs from c" (2 first lines of the Table 1) and "when a and b do not differ, c and d do not differ" (last 4 lines of the Table 1).

Boolean analogical proportions not only satisfy the three postulates, but also enjoy remarkable properties that are not consequences of the postulates:

- code independence [15]: $a : b :: c : d \Rightarrow \neg a : \neg b :: \neg c : \neg d$;
- transitivity [15]: $a : b :: c : d, c : d :: e : f \Rightarrow a : b :: e : f$;
- C-transitivity [2,22]: $a : b :: c : d, a : b' :: c' : d \Rightarrow b : b' :: c' : c$.[3] Note that, in agreement with internal reversal property, C-transitivity also yields $b' : b :: c : c'$.

Table 1. Analogy minimal model.

	a	b	c	d
1.	0	1	0	1
2.	1	0	1	0
3.	0	0	0	0
4.	1	1	1	1
5.	0	0	1	1
6.	1	1	0	0

Analogical inference is based on finding d given a, b, c and relies on the minimal model. Table 1 shows that if it exists, d is unique, but that there does not always exist x such that $a : b :: c : x$ is true. Indeed, there is no solution in $\{0, 1\}$ for $1 : 0 :: 0 : x$ and $0 : 1 :: 1 : x$.

The equation $a : x :: y : d$ true has 3 kinds of solution depending on the values of a and d; it corresponds to 3 types of patterns in the Table:

- if $a = d$ then $x = y = a = d$ (lines 3 and 4 in the Table);
- if $a \neq d$ then $x = a$ and $y = d$ (lines 5 and 6 in the Table),
- or $x = d$ and $y = a$ (lines 1 and 2 in the Table).

The formula (1) also applies to Boolean variables representing any propositional formulas. It states that for the proportion $a : b :: c : d$ to be satisfied, $(a \wedge \neg b) \equiv (c \wedge \neg d)$ and $(\neg a \wedge b) \equiv (\neg c \wedge d)$ must be satisfied. Consider the example of an analogical proportion that appears in [15] and that is also valid for any lattice structure [2]:

$$p \vee q : p :: q : p \wedge q$$

It can be easily checked that $(p \vee q) \wedge \neg p \equiv q \wedge \neg(p \wedge q) \equiv \neg p \wedge q$ and $p \wedge \neg(p \vee q) \equiv (p \wedge q) \wedge \neg q \equiv \bot$.

A propositional formula with n variables can be described over the 2^n interpretations of the language under consideration. For example, if we have two Boolean variables p and q, we have the interpretations pq, $p\neg q$, $\neg pq$, $\neg p \neg q$. Taking them in this order, p is encoded by 1100, $p \wedge q$ by 1000, $p \vee q$ by 1110, q by 1010, etc.

We can show that if these 4 logical formulas a, b, c, d involve a set of n variables, and that they are therefore representable by bit strings of size 2^n, this amounts to having an analogical proportion $a_i : b_i :: c_i : d_i$ on each component i of the bit strings that represent the formulas, that is to say for each possible interpretation [18] (note that i here refers to an interpretation, and not to a Boolean variable as in the Definition 1).

[3] This is easy to check. If $a = d = 1$ (resp. 0) then $b = c = b' = c' = 1$ (resp. 0) and then $b : b' :: c' : c$ holds. If $(a, d) = (0, 1)$ then $(b, c) = (0, 1)$ or $(b, c) = (1, 0)$, and $(b', c') = (0, 1)$ or $(b, c) = (1, 0)$, which yields 4 possible cases where it can be checked that $b : b' :: c' : c$ holds. The case $(a, d) = (1, 0)$ is similar.

Indeed, in the example above, we have 1110 : 1100 :: 1010 : 1000, component by component. Given three propositional formulas, we can find, if it exists, the propositional formula forming an analogical proportion with these three formulas; in the same way we can semantically verify whether four propositional formulas form an analogical proportion; see [18].

2.2 Nominal Analogical Proportions

Item descriptions can involve nominal attributes, that is, attributes with a finite domain whose cardinality can be greater than 2.

As pointed out in the previous subsection, the patterns that makes the analogical proportion true are of three types, namely $ssss$, $sstt$, and $stst$ (where s and t can take the values 0 or 1); the last two patterns are swapped by central permutation.

The Boolean analogy then easily extends to a nominal attribute $\mathcal{A}$ taking its values in a finite domain $\mathcal{D}_{\mathcal{A}}$. Then $a : b :: c : d$ is true for a nominal variable associated with an attribute $\mathcal{A}$ if and only if (as first suggested in [12]) :

$$(a, b, c, d) \in \{(s, s, s, s), (s, t, s, t), (s, s, t, t) | s, t \in \mathcal{D}_{\mathcal{A}}\} \tag{2}$$

where s, t are distinct values in the domain of the attribute $\mathcal{A}$. The condition (2) clearly generalizes the Boolean case. It guarantees the satisfaction of the postulates of analogical proportions. Nominal analogical proportions are also transitive and C-transitive.

2.3 Numerical Analogical Proportions

Among the numerical proportions, two proportions which involve the four elementary operations have an important place (a, b, c, d are real numbers here):

- the arithmetic proportion $a - b = c - d$;
- the geometric proportion $\frac{a}{b} = \frac{c}{d}$.

We will take the convention $\frac{0}{0} = 1$ considering that $\lim_{x \to 0} \frac{x}{x} = 1$.

It is easy to verify that these two proportions are indeed analogical proportions since they satisfy the three postulates recalled at the beginning of this section. They are also transitive and C-transitive. As in the Boolean case, they express the identity of the comparison results of a and b, and of c and d, either in terms of differences or in terms of ratios. We can also verify the agreement with the truth table of the analogical proportion: for the 6 patterns that makes it true, the equalities of the numerical proportions are satisfied (we take $\frac{1}{0} = +\infty$) and there are no equalities for the other possible quadruplets. Unlike the Boolean case, the number frame offers solutions for continuous analogical proportions of the form $a : m :: m : b$. Indeed, they lead to the definition of the arithmetic mean ($m = \frac{a+b}{2}$) and the geometric mean ($m = \sqrt{ab}$).

These proportions can also be written by combining the extremes and the means:

- $a + d = b + c$ (arithmetic proportion);
- $a \cdot d = b \cdot c$ (geometric proportion).

However, for geometric proportions, this allows us to have $0 \cdot 1 = 0 \cdot 0$, whereas $0 : 0 :: 0 : 1$ is certainly not an analogical proportion. We therefore see that the equivalence between the "quotient" and "product" forms excludes 0.

These two proportions are exchanged by a logarithmic/exponential transformation:
if $\frac{a}{b} = \frac{c}{d}$ then we have $\ln(a) - \ln(b) = \ln(c) - \ln(d)$,
if $a - b = c - d$ then we have $\frac{e^a}{e^b} = \frac{e^c}{e^d}$.

Finally, let us recall that the notation $a : b :: c : d$ was used (at least) until Gaspard Monge [16] to mean $\frac{a}{b} = \frac{c}{d}$ (the notation '::' was introduced by the English mathematician William Oughtred at the beginning of the 17th century). A proof of the Pythagorean theorem in terms of geometric proportions is given in Annex 1 to illustrate their expressive power.

On the one hand, there are multivalued extensions of the Boolean analogical proportion [7] that allow us to evaluate on $[0, 1]$ to what extent an analogical proportion between four numbers of $[0, 1]$ approximately holds. On the other hand general frameworks [10, 19] have recently been proposed to define whether or not an analogical proportion holds between four numbers of $[0, 1]$. These frameworks include arithmetic and geometric proportions as important special cases. Therefore, in the remainder of this article, we will only consider these two proportions.

We end this section by a proposition showing that numerical analogical proportions that are *both* arithmetic and geometric are highly constrained. However we shall see in Sect. 4 that this result still opens the possibility of an interesting definition of analogical proportions between probability densities.

Proposition 1. *Let a, b, c, d be four real numbers. Then these numbers are in* arithmetico-geometric *analogical proportion, denoted $a : b ::_{arigeo} c : d$ if we have $a - b = c - d$ and $\frac{a}{b} = \frac{c}{d}$. The only 4-tuples of real numbers a, b, c, d such that $a : b ::_{arigeo} c : d$ holds, are such that:*

- *case 1: either $a = b$ and $c = d$,*
- *case 2: or $a = c$ and $b = d$.*

and these are the only solutions.

Proof. Setting $a + d = s$ and $ad = p$, we obtain $d = s - a$, then $a(s - a) = p$, that is, $a^2 - s \cdot a + p = 0$. Thus, a must be a solution to the quadratic equation [19]: $x^2 - sx + p = 0$. Its discriminant is equal to $\Delta = s^2 - 4p = (b+c)^2 - 4b \cdot c = (b-c)^2$. The two solutions are therefore $a = \frac{s \pm \sqrt{\Delta}}{2} = \frac{b+c \pm (b-c)}{2}$. This gives $a = b$ or $a = c$. Thus, we should have $(a, d) = (b, c)$ or $(d, a) = (b, c)$. □

The arithmetico-geometric analogical proportions are thus valid for the same kind of patterns as Boolean or nominal analogical proportions.

3 Analogical Proportion Between Probability Values

In this section, and the next, we are interested in analogical proportions between real numbers which are probabilities, which therefore have values between 0 and 1.

For instance, consider the case of four probabilities that refer to four different populations and that concern a certain value of the same attribute for the elements of these four sets. a, b, c, d are then the probabilities that an element of a set A, respectively B, C, D takes e.g. the value v_i for attribute i. We can of course be interested in different attributes simultaneously. This is the case, for example, if we have a collection of examples and can perform statistics on the attribute values for four different data groups. In the following, we use the following notations $::_{ari}$ and $::_{geo}$ to distinguish between arithmetic and geometric analogical proportions.

The following property, which is straightforward to verify, ensures that if an analogical proportion holds between four probabilities, it also holds when considering their corresponding complementary events:

Property 1. *If* $a : b ::_{ari} c : d$ *holds then* $1 - a : 1 - b ::_{ari} 1 - c : 1 - d$ *holds.*

This desirable property is not true for $::_{geo}$. However, it does hold if the probabilities are also in arithmetic proportion.

Property 2. *If* $a : b ::_{ari} c : d$ *and* $a : b ::_{geo} c : d$ *hold then* $1-a : 1-b ::_{geo} 1-c : 1-d$ *holds.*

Proof. The equality $(1-a)(1-d) = (1-b)(1-c)$ holds if $ad = bc$ and $a + d = b + c$. □

This can be considered as the counterpart of the following implication, valid in Boolean logic: $a : b :: c : d \Rightarrow \neg a : \neg b :: \neg c : \neg d$, where a, b, c, d represent Boolean values.

As in the Boolean and nominal cases, there is not always x *such that* $a : b ::_{ari} c : x$ *is true.* Indeed

$$0 \leq a \leq 1, 0 \leq b \leq 1, 0 \leq c \leq 1 \not\Rightarrow 0 \leq x = b + c - a \leq 1.$$

Similarly, there is not always x such that $a : b ::_{geo} c : x$ holds, since

$$0 \leq a \leq 1, 0 \leq b \leq 1, 0 \leq c \leq 1 \not\Rightarrow 0 \leq x = \frac{bc}{a} \leq 1.$$

In both cases, if b and c are large then we must have a large, and if a is small, we must have b or c small for there to be a solution.

4 Analogical Proportion Between Probability Distributions

Instead of vectors as in Definition 1, we consider the case where a, b, c, d denote probability distributions over the same finite domain. The only difference with the vectors case, is that we impose $\Sigma_{i=1}^{n} a_i = 1$, etc. In that context, given an attribute A, a_i could be understood as $P(A = v_i)$ where v_i is a candidate value for attribute A and P a probability over the finite set of all these values.

We will examine several possible definitions of analogical proportions between probability distributions and study their properties.

4.1 Arithmetic Definition

Let us first consider a definition based on arithmetic proportion.

Definition 2. *Let a, b, c, d be four probability distributions on a finite domain $X = \{x_1, \ldots, x_n\}$. Then these distributions are in* arithmetic *analogical proportion, denoted $a : b ::_{ari} c : d$ if for all i we have $a_i - b_i = c_i - d_i$,*
where $a_i = a(x_i)$, $b_i = b(x_i)$, $c_i = c(x_i)$, $d_i = d(x_i)$.

It is clear that $::_{ari}$ satisfies the three postulates of analogical proportions. There exist probability distributions that satisfy this definition. Indeed we have:

Proposition 2. *Let a, b, c be three probability distributions, if $0 \leq c_i + b_i - a_i \leq 1$, $\forall i$, then there exists a unique probability distribution d such that $a : b ::_{ari} c : d$.*

Proof. The condition $0 \leq c_i + b_i - a_i \leq 1$ ensures that $0 \leq d_i \leq 1$. Since $\forall i, a_i - b_i = c_i - d_i$, member-by-member addition of these equalities shows that $\Sigma_{i=1,n} d_i = 1$ since $\Sigma_{i=1,n} a_i = 1$; $\Sigma_{i=1,n} b_i = 1$ and $\Sigma_{i=1,n} c_i = 1$. □

The condition $0 \leq c_i + b_i - a_i \leq 1$ is necessary for d to be a probability distribution, as the following counterexample shows.

Counterexample 1. *Let us take $n = 2$. $a_1 = 0.7, a_2 = 0.3$; $b_1 = 0.3, b_2 = 0.7$; $c_1 = 0.2, c_2 = 0.8$.*
We obtain $d_1 = -0.2, d_2 = 1.2$. □

The Definition 2 covers the deterministic case:

Observation 1. *In the deterministic case, the probability distributions are such that $\exists i, e_i = 1$ and $\forall j \neq i, e_j = 0$, for $e \in \{a, b, c, d\}$. There are then three possibilities for $a : b ::_{ari} c : d$ to hold:*

- *$\exists i, a_i = b_i = c_i = d_i = 1$;*
- *$\exists i, a_i = b_i = 1$ and $\exists j \neq i, c_j = d_j = 1$;*
- *$\exists i, a_i = c_i = 1$ and $\exists j \neq i, b_j = d_j = 1$.* □

Let us now give some examples, not extreme like the previous ones, of probability distributions for which we will obtain $a : b ::_{ari} c : d$.

Example 1.

1. Using the Property 1, we see that as soon as $\exists i, \exists j \neq i$, s. t. $a_i : b_i ::_{ari} c_i : d_i$, with $a_j = 1 - a_i, b_j = 1 - b_i, c_j = 1 - c_i, d_j = 1 - d_i$ and $a_k = b_k = c_k = d_k = 0, \forall k \neq i, j$, we have $a : b ::_{ari} c : d$.
2. In fact if $a_i : b_i ::_{ari} c_i : d_i$, for any real number λ we have $\lambda - a_i : \lambda - b_i ::_{ari} \lambda - c_i : \lambda - d_i$. Thus by taking positive values whose sum λ does not exceed 1, we can construct pairs$((a_i, b_i, c_i, d_i), (a_j, b_j, c_j, d_j))$ forming two arithmetic proportions s. t. $a_i + a_j = b_i + b_j = c_i + c_j = d_i + d_j = \lambda$, as in the following example where we have partial probability allocations $\lambda = 0.4$ and $\lambda' = 0.5$ completed by a quadruplet (a_k, b_k, c_k, d_k) of values all equal to $1 - \lambda - \lambda' = 1 - (0.4 + 0.5) = 0.1$ (here λ pertains to $i = 1, 2$, λ' to $i = 4, 5$, and $k = 3$):

$a_1 = 0.1; a_2 = 0.3; a_3 = 0.1; a_4 = 0.2; a_5 = 0.3.$
$b_1 = 0.3; b_2 = 0.1; b_3 = 0.1; b_4 = 0.3; b_5 = 0.2.$
$c_1 = 0.2; c_2 = 0.2; c_3 = 0.1; c_4 = 0.4; c_5 = 0.1.$
$d_1 = 0.4; d_2 = 0;\ d_3 = 0.1; d_4 = 0.5; d_5 = 0.$

We check that $a : b ::_{ari} c : d$ holds between probability distributions, all different.

3. For $a : b ::_{ari} c : d$ to be satisfied, it is not necessary to proceed as before, that is, to construct pairs of quadruplets whose term-by-term sum is constant. This is shown by the following two examples for $n = 3$ and $n = 4$:
   $a_1 = 0.3; a_2 = 0.2; a_3 = 0.5.$
   $b_1 = 0.5; b_2 = 0.1; b_3 = 0.4.$
   $c_1 = 0.4; c_2 = 0.2; c_3 = 0.4.$
   $d_1 = 0.6; d_2 = 0.1; d_3 = 0.3.$
4. $a_1 = 0.1; a_2 = 0.2; a_3 = 0.4; a_4 = 0.3.$
   $b_1 = 0.3; b_2 = 0.3; b_3 = 0.2; b_4 = 0.2.$
   $c_1 = 0.2; c_2 = 0.2; c_3 = 0.2; c_4 = 0.4.$
   $d_1 = 0.4; d_2 = 0.3; d_3 = 0; d_4 = 0.3.$ □

These examples show that there exist non-trivial distributions satisfying Definition 2. Of course, given three distributions a, b, c, there does not always exist a distribution d such that $a : b ::_{ari} c : d$ holds, since we must have the inequalities

$$\forall i, 0 \leq c_i + b_i - a_i \leq 1. \tag{3}$$

Observation 2. *Note, however, that given any two distributions a and b, it is always possible to find a distribution c such that the inequalities* (3) *are satisfied for each i. We can then find a distribution d in arithmetic analogical proportion with a, b, c.*

Remark 1. *It is natural to wonder what would happen to a definition similar to Definition 2 but in terms of geometric proportion, that is:*

Definition 3. *Let a, b, c, d be four probability distributions over a finite domain $X = \{x_1, \ldots, x_n\}$. Then these distributions are in* geometric *analogical proportion, denoted $a : b ::_{geo} c : d$ if for all i we have $\frac{a_i}{b_i} = \frac{c_i}{d_i}$,*
where $a_i = a(x_i)$, $b_i = b(x_i)$, $c_i = c(x_i)$, $d_i = d(x_i)$.
Unfortunately, as the following counterexample shows, the counterpart of Proposition 2 for geometric proportion is false. Having $\Sigma_{i=1}^n a_i = 1, \Sigma_{i=1}^n b_i = 1,\ \Sigma_{i=1}^n c_i = 1$ is not sufficient to guarantee $\Sigma_{i=1}^n d_i = 1$ when $a : b ::_{geo} c : d$ holds.

Counterexample 2. *Let us take $n = 3$. We have $a_1 + a_2 + a_3 = 1$, $b_1 + b_2 + b_3 = 1$, $c_1 + c_2 + c_3 = 1$, and $a_1 \cdot d_1 = b_1 \cdot c_1$, $a_2 \cdot d_2 = b_2 \cdot c_2$, $a_3 \cdot d_3 = b_3 \cdot c_3$, with the condition $b_i \cdot c_i \leq a_i$.*

- $b_1 = 0.2; b_2 = 0.3; b_3 = 0.5,\ c_1 = 0.4; c_2 = 0.3; c_3 = 0.3$ *thus* $b_1 \cdot c_1 = 0.08; b_2 \cdot c_2 = 0.09; b_3 \cdot c_3 = 0.15$. *We take* $a_1 = 0.3; a_2 = 0.4; a_3 = 0.3$. *This gives* $d_1 = \frac{4}{15}; d_2 = \frac{9}{40},; d_3 = \frac{1}{2}$, *and finally* $\Sigma_i d_i = 0.991666 < 1$
- $b_1 = 0.1; b_2 = 0.5; b_3 = 0.4,\ c_1 = 0.2; c_2 = 0.2; c_3 = 0.6$. *Thus* $b_1 \cdot c_1 = 0.02; b_2 \cdot c_2 = 0.10; b_3 \cdot c_3 = 0.24$. *Keeping the same a as above, we get* $d_1 = \frac{1}{15}; d_2 = \frac{1}{4}; d_3 = \frac{4}{5}$ *and then* $\Sigma_i d_i = 1.116666 > 1$.

Remark 2. *In the same spirit as for probabilities, one could ask the question of defining an analogical proportion between* possibility *distributions [6, 26] a, b, c, d, where the normalization is expressed by* $\max_i a_i = 1, \max_i b_i = 1, \max_i c_i = 1, \max_i d_i = 1$, *the* a_i, b_i, c_i, d_i *being between 0 and 1. Since a possibility distribution* e *can be seen in terms of its* α*-cuts* $e_\alpha = \{i \mid e_i \geq \alpha\}$ *which are nested subsets* $e_\alpha \subseteq e_\beta$ *if* $\alpha \geq \beta$, *we can reduce ourselves to the approach of the Boolean case for each* α*-cut [18].*

4.2 Definition Combining the Two Types of Numerical Proportions

In this subsection, we study a definition of the analogical proportion between probability distributions, more demanding than Definition 2 because it combines arithmetic and geometric proportions.

Definition 4. *Let* a, b, c, d *be four probability distributions over a finite domain* $X = \{x_1, \ldots, x_n\}$. *Then these distributions are in* arithmetico-geometric *analogical proportion, denoted* $a : b ::_{arigeo} c : d$ *if for all* i *we have* $a_i - b_i = c_i - d_i$ *and* $\frac{a_i}{b_i} = \frac{c_i}{d_i}$, *where* $a_i = a(x_i)$, $b_i = b(x_i)$, $c_i = c(x_i)$, $d_i = d(x_i)$.

It is clear that $::_{arigeo}$ satisfies the three postulates of analogical proportions. Due to Proposition 1, there exist vectors a, b, c, d, which can all be different, such that $a : b ::_{arigeo} c : d$ holds. Despite the restrictive nature of Definition 4, there exist non-trivial probability distributions that satisfy it.

Proposition 3. *If* a, b, c *represent probability distribution (i.e.* $\Sigma_{i=1}^n a_i = 1$, *etc.) on the same finite set* X, *then this is also the case for* d, *such that* $a : b ::_{arigeo} c : d$ *holds.*

Proof. Due to Proposition 1 a, b, c, d are such that for each component i,

- either $a_i = b_i$ and $c_i = d_i$,
- or $a_i = c_i$ and $b_i = d_i$.

Thus, we should have $(a_i, d_i) = (b_i, c_i)$ or $(d_i, a_i) = (b_i, c_i)$. So $a : b ::_{arigeo} c : d$ iff for each component i, we have ($a_i = b_i$ and $c_i = d_i$), or ($a_i = c_i$ and $b_i = d_i$).

Note that if $n \geq 2$, and $\exists j, a_j = b_j$, $c_j = d_j$, and $\exists k, a_k = c_k$, $b_k = d_k$ then a, b, c, d are all different.

Let $J = \{j \mid a_j = b_j\}$ and $K = \{k \mid a_k = c_k\}$.

Then
$$\begin{aligned}\Sigma_{i=1}^n d_i &= \Sigma_{j \in J} d_j + \Sigma_{k \in K} d_k \\ &= \Sigma_{j \in J} c_j + \Sigma_{k \in K} b_k \text{ (since } c_j = d_j \text{ if } j \in J \text{ and } b_k = d_k \text{ if } k \in K) \\ &= 1 - \Sigma_{k \in K} c_k + 1 - \Sigma_{j \in J} b_j \text{ (since } \Sigma_{i=1}^n b_i = \Sigma_{i=1}^n c_i = 1) \\ &= 1 - \Sigma_{k \in K} a_k + 1 - \Sigma_{j \in J} a_j \text{ (} a_j = b_j \text{ if } j \in J, a_k = c_k \text{ if } k \in K) \\ &= 1 \text{ (since } \Sigma_{i=1}^n a_i = 1)\end{aligned}$$

□

Here is an example of an analogical proportion between normalized probability distributions a, b, c, d, all different, obeying the Definition 4:

Example 2.

$$a_1 = 0.1, a_2 = 0.3, a_3 = 0.2, a_4 = 0.3, a_5 = 0.1$$
$$b_1 = 0.1, b_2 = 0.4, b_3 = 0.2, b_4 = 0.2, b_5 = 0.1$$
$$c_1 = 0.1, c_2 = 0.3, c_3 = 0.3, c_4 = 0.3, c_5 = 0$$
$$d_1 = 0.1, d_2 = 0.4, d_3 = 0.3, d_4 = 0.2, d_5 = 0$$

We can verify that $\Sigma_{i=1}^n a_i = 1$, $\Sigma_{i=1}^n b_i = 1$, $\Sigma_{i=1}^n c_i = 1$, $\Sigma_{i=1}^n d_i = 1$, and that for each i, we have both $a_i - b_i = c_i - d_i$ and $\frac{a_i}{b_i} = \frac{c_i}{d_i}$ (recall that we have taken the convention $\frac{0}{0} = 1$). Observe that for each component i we have three kinds of possible patterns for the probability values: (s, s, s, s), (s, t, s, t), and (s, s, t, t), these are precisely those already encountered for the nominal values in Subsect. 2.2. Note that the last two patterns must be present if we want to have distinct distributions, otherwise we have $a = b$ (and therefore $c = d$), or $a = c$ (and therefore $b = d$). The pattern (s, s, s, s) may be absent. A similar situation had already been observed in the Boolean case [4].

It is easy to find probability distributions a, b, c, d such that $a : b ::_{arigeo} c : d$ holds. Indeed, we have the following result.

Proposition 4. *Given two different probability distributions a and b, there always exist two probability distributions c and d such that $a : b ::_{arigeo} c : d$ holds. If there exists at least one i such that $a_i = b_i$, the four distributions can be different.*

Proof. Indeed, $a : b ::_{arigeo} c : d$ entails $a_i = b_i$ and $c_i = d_i$, or $a_i = c_i$ and $b_i = d_i$. If $a_i \neq b_i$, then $c_i = a_i$ and $d_i = b_i$. Note, since $\Sigma_{i \mid a_i = b_i} a_i = \Sigma_{i \mid a_i = b_i} b_i \triangleq \rho$, that $\Sigma_{i \mid a_i \neq b_i} a_i = \Sigma_{i \mid a_i \neq b_i} b_i = 1 - \rho$. So we also have $\Sigma_{i \mid c_i \neq d_i} c_i = \Sigma_{i \mid c_i \neq d_i} d_i = 1 - \rho$. For i such that $a_i = b_i$, we assign to $c_i = d_i$ parts of the remaining mass ρ so that $\Sigma_{i=1,n} c_i = \Sigma_{i=1,n} d_i = 1$. □

These probabilities a, b, c, d satisfying $a : b ::_{arigeo} c : d$ have, as we have just seen, a particular form; they satisfy a remarkable property in terms of Kullback-Leibler divergence, which, as we recall, evaluates the change between two distributions a and b by the expression $KL(a||b) = \Sigma_{i=1,n} a_i \log \frac{a_i}{b_i}$ (in the finite case). In general, $KL(a||b) \neq KL(b||a)$. Then, we can state the following result:

Proposition 5. *Let a, b, c, d be four probability distributions forming an arithmetico-geometric analogical proportion $a : b ::_{arigeo} c : d$. Then we have:*

$$KL(a||b) = KL(c||d)$$

where KL is the Kullback-Leibler divergence.

Proof. Since $KL(a||b) = \Sigma_{i=1,n} a_i \log \frac{a_i}{b_i}$ and $KL(c||d) = \Sigma_{i=1,n} c_i \log \frac{c_i}{d_i}$, let us look at the different terms i : $a_i \log \frac{a_i}{b_i}$ and $c_i \log \frac{c_i}{d_i}$; due to Proposition 1, we know that there are two cases:

- case (1): $a_i = b_i$ (and $c_i = d_i$): both terms are zero; case (2): $a_i = c_i$: then we have $a_i \log \frac{a_i}{b_i} = c_i \log \frac{c_i}{d_i}$ since $\frac{a_i}{b_i} = \frac{c_i}{d_i}$. Hence $KL(a||b) = KL(c||d)$. □

Since $::_{arigeo}$ satisfy the analogical proportion postulates, we also have

Property 3. If $a : b ::_{arigeo} c : d$ then i) $KL(a||c) = KL(b||d)$; ii) $KL(b||a) = KL(d||c)$; iii) $KL(d||b) = KL(c||a)$.

Proof. i) thanks to Proposition 5 and central permutation; ii) since $a : b ::_{arigeo} c : d \Rightarrow b : a ::_{arigeo} d : c$, by successive applications of the central permutation, symmetry, and again central permutation; iii) the last equality, which corresponds to the permutation of the extremes, can be obtained by applying the second equality to the first one. □

5 Towards Further Developments

In the previous section, the probabilities where associated with a finite set of values X without any particular structure. We may wonder if the previous results can be extended to other kind of probabilities, for instance, defined via continuous densities. In such a case, definitions extend straightforwardly: $a : b ::_{ari} c : d$ if for all $x \in X = \mathbb{R}$ we have $a(x) - b(x) = c(x) - d(x)$ where the four densities a, b, c, d obey $\int_{\mathbb{R}} a(x)dx = \int_{\mathbb{R}} b(x)dx = \int_{\mathbb{R}} c(x)dx = \int_{\mathbb{R}} d(x)dx = 1$. The geometrical proportion can be similarly extended in a pointwise manner. Some examples of an arithmetico-geometric analogical proportion between continuous distributions, defined using piecewise linear functions, are given in Annex 2.

An option for working with discrete or continuous distributions characterized by two parameters, such as binomial distributions B(n, p) or Gaussian distributions $\mathcal{N}(\mu, \sigma)$, is to define analogical proportions directly between their parameters (possibly with two different numerical proportions), rather than in a pointwise manner. For instance, consider a, b, c, d be four Gaussian probability density functions, with respective means $\mu_a, \mu_b, \mu_c, \mu_d$ and standard deviations $\sigma_a, \sigma_b, \sigma_c, \sigma_d$, and let us say that they form an arithmetico-geometric analogical proportion iff $\mu_a - \mu_b = \mu_c - \mu_d$ and their variances are such that $\sigma_a^2/\sigma_b^2 = \sigma_c^2/\sigma_d^2$. Then we have [23]

$$KL(a||b) = \frac{1}{2}[\frac{\sigma_a^2}{\sigma_b^2} - ln(\frac{\sigma_a^2}{\sigma_b^2}) + \frac{(\mu_a - \mu_b)^2}{\sigma_b^2} - 1],$$

then it is clear that $KL(a||b) = KL(c||d)$ only if $\sigma_b^2 = \sigma_d^2$. But due to the geometric constraint, we should also have $\sigma_a^2 = \sigma_c^2$, which limits the significance of the result.

When the set X can be equipped with structures such as order, and distance (this is the case if $X = \mathbb{N}$ or $X = \mathbb{R}$, or Cartesian products thereof), other comparison metrics such as Wasserstein distance may be used. Indeed, consider the case $X = \mathbb{R}$, and let us denote CDF_a the cumulative distribution of a, i.e.:

$$CDF_a(y) = \int_{-\infty}^{y} a(x)dx$$

If $a : b ::_{ari} c : d$, we have (by linearity of the integral):

$$\forall y \in \mathbb{R}, CDF_a(y) - CDF_b(y) = CDF_c(y) - CDF_d(y).$$

If we consider Wasserstein distance for $p = 1$, because we have [9,21]:

$$W_1(a,b) = \int_{\mathbb{R}} |CDF_a(y) - CDF_b(y)| dy,$$

we will have (using the $L1$ metric on $\mathbb{R}$) $W_1(a,b) = W_1(c,d)$.

The developments outlined above would require a more precise, detailed and complete investigation. This is left for further research.

6 Potential Applications

In this section, we suggest several potential applications of analogical proportions between probabilities. Since the results of Sect. 4 also apply to any collection of positive or zero numbers whose sum is 1, we conclude with an application to weighted sums in multi-criteria aggregation (since, as in a probability distribution, the sum of the coefficients is equal to 1).

We begin by recalling the principle of Bayesian classification. Bayes' theorem writes:

$$P(c|x)P(x) = P(x|c)P(c)$$

where x is a vector of attribute values describing an item, c is a class, and we assign to x, among the possible classes, the class c that maximizes $P(c|x)$. It is worth noticing that this equality is a geometric proportion:

$$P(x) : P(x|c) :: P(c) : P(c|x).$$

We can at least think of three ways of using analogical proportions in probabilities:

1. **Parallel analogy-probabilities**
   Just like the Bayesian approach, analogical proportions offer an application to classification [3,5]. This suggests drawing a parallel between the two. Consider four items a, b, c, d whose vector descriptions form an analogical proportion in the sense of Definition 1. Furthermore, we assume that these four items have been classified, on the one hand by the Bayesian method, and on the other hand by the method of analogical proportions. If the classes provided for a, b, c, d by the analogical classifier are themselves in analogical proportion, we can of course ask ourselves whether the two classifiers are in agreement, but also more generally, whether the probability distributions provided by Bayes' rule form an analogical proportion (at least approximately in the sense of the numerical gradual extension of analogical proportions between nominal values, called conservative extension in [7]).
2. **Uncertain attribute values**
   In a classification problem, some attributes may have uncertain values. Consider the case of a single uncertain attribute, whether Boolean or nominal. For a given item, each possible value of that attribute is associated with a probability. Suppose that four items corresponding to the most probable value of the attribute form an analogical proportion. If the associated probabilities also respect this proportion (at least approximately as above) and the analogical equation on classes allows us to infer a solution for the fourth item, then we could accept this solution with the corresponding probability.

3. **Analogical proportions between distributions**
   Recall that transfer learning can be seen as a kind of analogical reasoning performed at a meta-level (see for example [25]), since it involves taking advantage of what has been learned in a source domain in order to improve the learning process in a target domain related to the source domain. As the vocabulary suggests, the approach used for case-based reasoning is quite similar [8]. One might wonder whether analogical proportions between probability distributions,in the sense of Definitions either 2, or 4 (which is perhaps better), could allow for more sophisticated and controlled transfers, using Propositions 2, or 3 and 4.
   More simply, we could ask for two attributes of interest (age and sex in the example below), if the probabilities of being in a class $\mathcal{C}$
   - for a man under 40,
   - for a woman under 40,
   - for a man over 40,
   - for a woman over 40,

   form an analogical proportion for the probability distributions over the classes of each of the four populations.

Multicriteria Aggregation. Positive values that add up to 1 are not necessarily probabilities. They can also be the coefficients of a weighted sum. Thus, we can adjust coefficients d relative to other sets of coefficients a, b, c by solving an analogical equation $a : b :: c : x$ between coefficient distributions, as in the following example:

- a: coefficients of the subjects in the science stream at school 1,
- b: coefficients of the subjects in the literature stream at school 1,
- c: coefficients of the subjects in the science stream at school 2,
- d: coefficients of the subjects in the literature stream at school 2,

7 Conclusion

This article is likely the first to explore analogical proportions between probability distributions. In particular, it has been shown that it is possible to have a definition combining arithmetic and geometric proportions. This definition ensures, in the finite case, the invariance of the Kullback-Leibler divergence between the distributions forming the two pairs of the analogical proportion.

Because we define analogical proportion between finite probability distributions in a pointwise manner, the extension to the discrete or continuous case requires careful study, to better understand what are the possible situations (beyond some examples given in Appendix 2), and to know when the conservation of the Kullback-Leibler divergence associated with pairs is preserved. As suggested in the previous section, another way, worth of investigation, of defining analogical proportions between probability distributions for discrete or continuous distributions characterized by two parameters, is to directly define the analogical proportions on their parameters (possibly with two different numerical proportions). Besides, concrete applications remain to be developed.

Annex 1: Proof of Pythagorean Theorem by Geometric Proportions

Consider a right triangle ABC at C, and the height from C, as shown in the figure below. The angles $\widehat{HAC}$ and $\widehat{HCB}$ are equal because they have the same complement $\widehat{ACH}$. Triangles ABC, ACH and CBH are therefore similar.

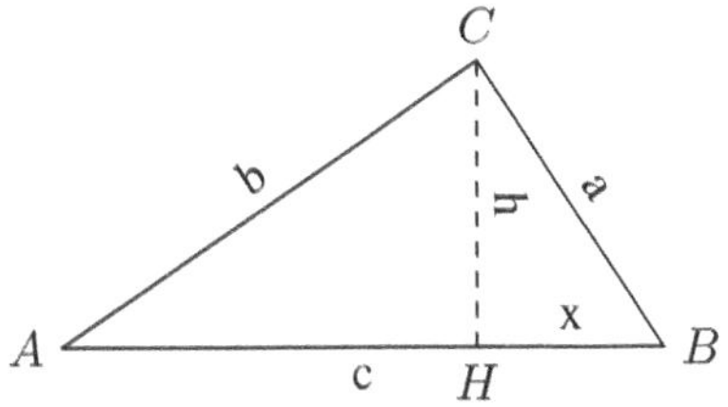

In this figure, two sides of one of the three right triangles are therefore proportional to the two corresponding sides of another right triangle, and therefore form a geometric proportion, in terms of lengths. Thus one can write $CA : AB :: AH : CA$, i.e., $b : c :: c - x : b$ which leads to $b^2 = c^2 - cx$.

But we also have $AB : CB :: CB : BH$, i.e., $c : a :: a : x$ and thus $cx = a^2$. Hence we obtain $c^2 = a^2 + b^2$.

Note the use of a continuous proportion ($c : a :: a : x$).

Annex 2: Examples of Analogical Proportion Between Continuous Distributions

We start from a parametric function $S_{x_0,a}$, defined on $[0, +\infty)$ and whose graph is displayed in plain line in the next figure, where point A has coordinates (x_0, y_0).

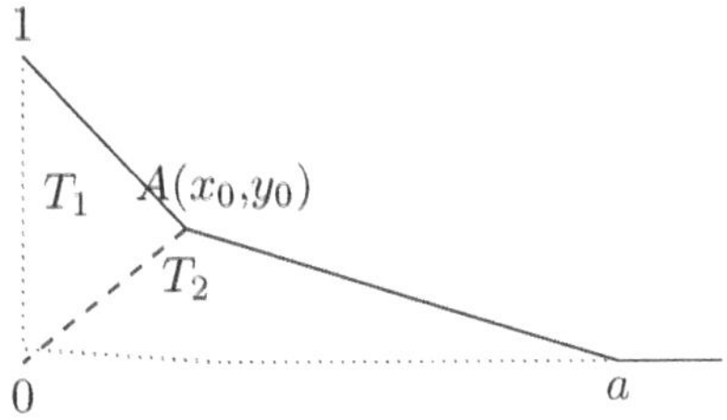

We can then build an example in the following way (where a, b, c, d are now probability density functions):

$$a(x) = p(x) \text{ on } (-\infty, +\infty)$$
$$b(x) = p(x) \text{ on } (-\infty, 0]\ ;\ b(x) = q(x) \text{ on } [0, +\infty)$$
$$c(x) = q(x) \text{ on } (-\infty, 0];\ c(x) = p(x) \text{ on } [0, +\infty)$$
$$d(x) = q(x) \text{ on } (-\infty, +\infty)$$

where:

$p(x) = S_{x_0,a}(x)$ on $[0, +\infty)$, $p(x) = S_{x_0,a}(-x)$ on $(-\infty, 0]$.
$q(x)$ is similarly defined with parameters x'_0 and a'.

Note that $p(0) = q(0) = 1$, then a, b, c, d are continuous. The area under $S_{x_0,a}$ is equal to $area(T_1) + area(T_2) = x_0/2 + ay_0/2$. To ensure the normalization of the distributions, this area should be equal to $1/2$, we have then to add the constraint that: $(x_0 + ay_0) = 1$ and $(x'_0 + a'y'_0) = 1$. In that context, we can easily check that $a : b ::_{arigeo} c : d$ and $KL(a, b) = KL(c, d)$.

Starting with the above example, and using parametric functions $S_{h,x_0,a}$ and $S_{h,x'_0,a'}$ similar to the previous ones, but such that $S_{h,x_0,a}(0) = S_{h,x'_0,a'}(0) = h$, one can build a complex example:

Let $p_1 < p_2$. Let $\lambda < 1/2$.

$$a(x) = p(x) \text{ on } (-\infty, p_1];\ a(x) = r(x) \text{ on } [p_1, p_2];\ a(x) = p(x) \text{ on } [p_2, +\infty)$$
$$b(x) = p(x) \text{ on } (-\infty, p_1];\ b(x) = r(x) \text{ on } [p_1, p_2];\ b(x) = q(x) \text{ on } [p_2, +\infty)$$
$$c(x) = q(x) \text{ on } (-\infty, p_1];\ c(x) = r(x) \text{ on } [p_1, p_2];\ c(x) = p(x) \text{ on } [p_2, +\infty)$$
$$d(x) = q(x) \text{ on } (-\infty, p_1];\ d(x) = r(x) \text{ on } [p_1, p_2];\ d(x) = q(x) \text{ on } [p_2, +\infty)$$

where $p(x) = S_{h,x_0,a}(x - p_1)$ on $[p_1, +\infty)$, $S_{h,x_0,a}(p_1 - x)$ on $(-\infty, p_1]$ and $q(x) = S_{h,x'_0,a'}(x - p_2)$ on $[p_2, +\infty)$, $S_{h,x'_0,a'}(p_2 - x)$ on $(-\infty, p_2]$,

$r(x)$ is such that $r(p_1) = r(p_2) = h$ (ensuring continuity of the 4 distributions) and $\int_{p_1}^{p_2} r(x)dx = 2\lambda$ (r may be taken, e.g., as uniform; in this case $h(p_2 - p_1) = 2\lambda$), with the constraints $(hx_0 + ay_0) = 1 - 2\lambda$, $(hx'_0 + a'y'_0) = 1 - 2\lambda$,

(for ensuring normalization of the 4 distributions).

Acknowledgments. The authors thank Giuseppe Sanfilippo for posing the question "Do analogical proportions apply to probabilities?" during the presentation of their article [19]. This article hopes to demonstrate that the question was fruitful. The authors would also like to thank Mathieu Serrurier for drawing their attention to the Wasserstein distance.

This research was supported by the ANR project "Analogies: from Theory to Tools and Applications" (AT2TA), ANR-22-CE23-0023.

Disclosure of Interests. The authors have no competing interests to declare that are relevant to the content of this article.

References

1. Aristotle: Nicomachean Ethics. Univ. of Chicago Press (2011), trans. by R. C. Bartlett and S. D. Collins
2. Barbot, N., Miclet, L., Prade, H.: Analogy between concepts. Artif. Intell. **275**, 487–539 (2019)
3. Bounhas, M., Prade, H.: Analogy-based classifiers: an improved algorithm exploiting competent data pairs. Int. J. Approx. Reason. **158**, 108923 (2023)
4. Bounhas, M., Prade, H.: Revisiting analogical proportions and analogical inference. Int. J. Approx. Reason. **171**, 109202 (2024)
5. Bounhas, M., Prade, H., Richard, G.: Analogy-based classifiers for nominal or numerical data. Int. J. Approx. Reason. **91**, 36–55 (2017)
6. Dubois, D., Prade, H.: Possibility Theory: An Approach to Computerized Processing of Uncertainty. Plenum Press, New York (1988)
7. Dubois, D., Prade, H., Richard, G.: Multiple-valued extensions of analogical proportions. Fuzzy Sets Syst. **292**, 193–202 (2016)
8. Fuchs, B., Lieber, J., Miclet, L., Mille, A., Napoli, A., Prade, H., Richard, G.: Case-based reasoning, analogy, and interpolation. In: Marquis, P., Papini, O., Prade, H. (eds.) A Guided Tour of Artificial Intelligence Research, pp. 307–339. Springer, Cham (2020). https://doi.org/10.1007/978-3-030-06164-7_10

9. Gibbs, A.L., Su, F.E.: On choosing and bounding probability metrics. Int. Stat. Rev. **70**, 419–435 (2002). arXiv:math/0209021 [math.PR]
10. Lepage, Y., Couceiro, M.: Analogie et moyenne généralisée. In: Actes des 18èmes Journées d'Intelligence Artificielle Fondamentale, La Rochelle, 1-3 July. pp. 114–124 (2024)
11. Miclet, L., Prade, H.: Handling analogical proportions in classical logic and fuzzy logics settings. In: Sossai, C., Chemello, G. (eds.) ECSQARU 2009. LNCS (LNAI), vol. 5590, pp. 638–650. Springer, Heidelberg (2009). https://doi.org/10.1007/978-3-642-02906-6_55
12. Pirrelli, V., Yvon, F.: Analogy in the lexicon: a probe into analogy-based machine learning of language. In: Proceedings of 6th International Symposium on Human Communiccation, Santiago de Cuba, p. 6 (1999)
13. Polya, G.: Mathematics and Plausible Reasoning-Vol.1: Induction and analogy in Mathematics, Vol.2: Patterns of Plausible Inference. Princeton Univ. Press, 2nd ed. 1968 (1954)
14. Prade, H., Richard, G.: Cataloguing/analogizing: a nonmonotonic view. Int. J. Intell. Syst. **26**(12), 1176–1195 (2011)
15. Prade, H., Richard, G.: From analogical proportion to logical proportions. Log. Univers. **7**(4), 441–505 (2013)
16. Prade, H., Richard, G.: Multiple analogical proportions. AI Commun. **34**(3), 211–228 (2021)
17. Prade, H., Richard, G.: Analogical proportion- based induction: From classification to creativity. J. Appl. Logics - IfCoLog J. Logics Appl. **11**, 51–87 (2024)
18. Prade, H., Richard, G.: Diagrammatic analogical reasoning. In: Lemanski, J., Johansen, M.W., Manalo, E., Viana, P., Bhattacharjee, R., Burns, R. (eds.) Proceedings of 14th International Conference on Diagrammatic Representation and Inference (Diagrams'24), Münster, Sept. 27 - Oct. 1. LNCS, vol. 14981, pp. 485–489. Springer, Cham (2024). https://doi.org/10.1007/978-3-031-71291-3_44
19. Prade, H., Richard, G.: Frank's triangular norms in Piaget's logical proportions. In: Destercke, S., Martinez, M.V., Sanfilippo, G. (eds.) Proceedings of 16th International Conference on Scalable Uncertainity Management (SUM'24), Palermo, Nov. 27-29. LNCS, vol. 15350, pp. 369–377. Springer, Cham (2024). https://doi.org/10.1007/978-3-031-76235-2_27
20. Prade, H., Richard, G.: Proportions analogiques entre probabilités. In: 19èmes Journées d'IA Fondamentale (JIAF'25), Plate-Forme Intelligence Artificielle (PFIA), Dijon, 2-4 Juil, pp. 38–47 (2025). https://pfia2025.u-bourgogne.fr/conferences/jiaf/
21. Ramdas, A., Trillos, N.G., Cuturi, M.: On Wasserstein two-sample testing and related families of nonparametric tests. Entropy **19**(2) (2017). arXiv:1509.02237 [math.ST]
22. Schockaert, S., Ibáñez-García, Y., Gutiérrez-Basulto, V.: A description logic for analogical reasoning. In: Zhou, Z. (ed.) Proc. 30th International Joint Conference on Artificial Intelligence (IJCAI'21), Virtual Event / Montreal, Canada, 19-27 Aug, pp. 2040–2046 (2021)
23. Soch, J., et al.: StatProofBook/StatProofBook.github.io: The Book of Statistical Proofs (2024), the Book of Statistical Proofs (Version 2023). Zenodo. https://doi.org/10.5281/ZENODO.4305949
24. Sznajder, M.: Janina Hosiasson-Lindenbaum on analogical reasoning: new sources. Erkenntnis **89**, 1349–1365 (2024)
25. Wang, H., Yang, Q.: Transfer learning by structural analogy. In: Burgard, W., Roth, D. (eds.) Proceedings of 25th AAAI Conference on Artificial Intelligence, (AAAI'11), San Francisco, Aug.7-11, pp. 513–518. AAAI Press (2011)
26. Zadeh, L.A.: Fuzzy sets as a basis for a theory of possibility. Fuz. Sets Syst. **1**, 3–28 (1978)

Robust Explanations: The Case of Prime Implicants

Chenrui Zhu(✉), Vu-Linh Nguyen, Marie-Hélène Masson, and Sébastien Destercke

Université de technologie de Compiègne, UMR CNRS 7253 Heudiasyc, Alliance Sorbonne Université, Compiègne, France
{chenrui.zhu,vu-linh.nguyen,marie-helene.masson, sebastien.destercke}@hds.utc.fr

Abstract. This paper studies the problem of quantifying the robustness level of explanations. In particular, we propose to quantify the robustness level of each given explanation as the maximum level of perturbation on the parameters of a classifier below which an explanation remains valid. We derive theoretical results on the computational complexity of determining the robustness level in the case of linear models, which underpin the design of a log-linear time algorithm. We then apply the proposed notion of robustness level to analyze the robustness of commonly used specific types of prime implicants, including the shortest and the most robust ones. The insights are then leveraged to construct guidelines on scenarios where each type of explanations may be more beneficial.

Keywords: Robust explanations · Prime Implicants · Linear Models

1 Introduction

Reliability and interpretability are critical components of Trustworthy AI, particularly in high-stakes applications such as cybersecurity, healthcare, finance, and autonomous systems [3,12]. In these domains, providing concise explanations for model decisions may be essential to build user trust and ensure regulatory compliance. Robustness is another expected feature of trustworthy explanations, especially in applications where data are scarce and/or noisy, and where the use of non-optimal models is unavoidable. Despite a well-established literature on explanation methods, ranging from feature attribution techniques [6,11] to rule-based approaches [7], research aiming at quantifying the robustness of explanations is still limited.

There are however some notable attempts in robustness analysis of explanations, which focus on LIME [16] and counterfactual explanations [4,5]. These attempts can be categorized into two primary approaches [9]: *model perturbation* and *data perturbation*. Both methods evaluate the sensitivity of explanations: (1) against variations in the model parameters; (2) under small perturbation in the input information. The former typically refers to the process of slightly altering the parameters of a trained model, such as retraining it with a different subset of

K. Sauerwald and M. Thimm (Eds.): ECSQARU 2025, LNAI 16099, pp. 164–177, 2026.
https://doi.org/10.1007/978-3-032-05134-9_12

the data or applying noise to its internal weights and then observing how the explanation of a prediction changes. If the explanation remains stable, it is considered robust to model perturbations. The latter involves making small changes to the input features of a given instance (e.g., modifying a patient's age by one year or slightly adjusting a lab value) and then analyzing whether the explanation of the prediction changes significantly. This captures the sensitivity of explanations to minor, potentially realistic input variations. Another notable attempt is to define the robustness level using consistency of explanations over repeated trials or minor data shifts [14]. However, we are not aware of any related work in the case of prime implicants or abductive explanations [2, 7], which shall be explored in this paper.

More precisely, we propose to define the robustness level of prime implicants [2, 7] following the *model perturbation* approach. In particular, we propose to quantify the robustness level of each given explanation as the maximum level of perturbation on the classifier below which that explanation remains valid. Similar to what has been done in [4], we define the perturbation level on the classifier as the size of the neighborhood around its parameter vector defined using L^p-norms. The problem of determining the robustness level is indeed not obvious since the notion of prime implicants is defined in a *data perturbation* manner. Therefore, determining the proposed robustness level calls for efficient algorithmic solutions to tackle the *model perturbation* and *data perturbation* simultaneously.

As the first attempt in this direction, we focus on the case of linear models, for which efficient algorithmic solutions for determining prime implicants (needed before analysing the robustness level) were developed in [7]. Specifically, we derive theoretical results on the computational complexity of determining the robustness level in the case of linear models where the neighborhood is defined using the L^∞-norm, which underpin the design of a log-linear time algorithm. We present empirical evidence confirming that the proposed notion of robustness level can indeed capture the robustness of prime implicants under perturbations on the classifier, where the linear model is the logistic regression [10].

The proposed notion of robustness level is then adopted to analyze the robustness of commonly used specific types of prime implicants, including the shortest and the most robust ones. In particular, we find that, while the shortest prime implicants are not necessarily the most robust ones, the longest prime implicants are often the least robust ones. Depending on the application, a conciseness-robustness trade-off has to be found. These insights are then leveraged to construct guidelines about this trade-off in a given scenario.

Section 2 discusses notable attempts in robustness analysis of explanations, followed by the formulation of our proposed notion of robustness level of explanations. Section 3 details the proposed notion of robustness level in the case of prime implicants. Section 4 focus on the case of linear models. Section 5 presents theoretical results on the computational complexity of determining the robustness level and efficient algorithmic solutions in the case of linear models, where the neighborhood is defined using the L^∞-norm. Section 6 presents empirical evidence illustrating properties and potential applications of the proposed notion of robustness level. Finally, Sect. 7 concludes this paper.

2 Formalizing Robust Explanations

In this section, we briefly discuss explanation methods and their robustness, and then formalize the concept of robust explanations for classifiers.

2.1 On the Robustness of Explanations

In the classification setting that we consider in this paper, and more generally in supervised learning, notable explanation methods can be categorized into local and global methods [12]. While global explanation methods typically quantify the global behavior of the model, local explanation methods aim to explain the local prediction of a specific instance. The local explanations can be categorized into statistical explanations and logical explanations.

A statistical explanation, for example SHAP [6], is usually defined as an importance scoring vector reflecting the contribution of the features to the prediction. Logical explanations can be defined in different forms. For example, a counterfactual explanation (CFE) is defined as the closest (valid) instance to the query instance, whose prediction differs from the one assigned to the query instance [15]. Another example is the notion of prime implicants (PIs), where each prime implicant is a minimal subset of features that should be fixed to ensure the prediction on the query instance [7].

One can, in principle, define the robustness level for statistical and logical explanations by analysing either the robustness under *model perturbation*, or *data perturbation*, or their combination. The robustness level of statistical explanations has been quantified as the minimal perturbation required to induce significant changes in the importance scoring vector, thereby offering a nuanced way to compare the stability of different techniques [1]. The robustness level of logical explanations has been quantified as the minimal perturbation required to invalidate the explanation [4,5].

As the primary focus of this paper is on prime implicants [7], which is defined in a *data perturbation* manner, defining the robustness level following the *data perturbation* approach might (overly) amplify the perturbation level, which may in turn degrade the discriminative ability of the robustness level in explanation selection. Therefore, in this paper, we propose to define the robustness level of prime implicants [2,7] following the *model perturbation* approach. Moreover, we propose to quantify the robustness level of each given explanation as the maximum level of perturbation on the classifier below which an explanation remains valid, as done in the related work on logical explanations [4].

Finally, we emphasize that our proposal also covers the practical setting where logical explanations are extracted from statistical explanations and presented to the end-user, such as top-ranked importance features provided by SHAP [6].

2.2 ϵ-Robustness

In this paper, we focus on the binary classification setting. Let $\mathbf{X} := \{X_1, \ldots, X_Q\}$ the set of Q features. Let Y be a binary class variable. For each feature X_q, let $\mathcal{X}_q$ be the set of possible values. The complete input space is given by $\mathcal{X} = \mathcal{X}_1 \times \mathcal{X}_2 \times \cdots \times \mathcal{X}_Q$. An instance is represented by a vector $\boldsymbol{x} \in \mathcal{X}$, and the class variable Y takes values in $\mathcal{Y} = \{0, 1\}$. A classifier is a function $h : \mathcal{X} \to \mathcal{Y}$ that maps each instance to a label. We assume that the decision $h(\boldsymbol{x})$ associated with instance $\boldsymbol{x}$ is defined based on a scoring function $g(\boldsymbol{x})$ which informs the relevance of the classes.

We associate each perturbation level ϵ with a set of neighbour models H_ϵ of h, where the cardinality of H_ϵ is controlled by ϵ. The way of defining the neighbourhood depends on the nature of the classifier. If the classifier is defined by a set of parameters, it is natural to define the neighbourhood of h through a distance between the parameters of the model. This point will be detailed in the next section. The following definition formalizes the notion of ϵ-robustness:

Definition 1. *An explanation of $h(\boldsymbol{x})$ is ϵ-robust if it is also an explanation for any model in H_ϵ.*

The notion of ϵ-robust explanations poses two technical problems: (1) checking whether an explanation is ϵ-robust; (2) finding an explanation which is ϵ-robust. Efficient solutions for these problems can be especially beneficial in applications where each instance can be associated with multiple explanations. The latter might be beneficial when, for each instance, at least one explanation of a certain robustness level should be presented to the end-user. The former might be beneficial in applications where, for each instance, explanations are constructed sequentially and only explanations of a certain robustness level should be presented to the end-user.

Note that the notion of ϵ-robust explanation given in Definition 1 is more general than the one studied in [4,5] for the particular case of CFEs, in the sense that it applies to any type of explanations.

Definition 2. *The robustness level of an explanation is the maximum value of ϵ for which the explanation remains a valid explanation for any member of H_ϵ.*

This definition poses the third technical problem: (3) finding the largest ϵ such that an explanation is ϵ-robust.

In the next sections, we detail the notions of ϵ-robust explanations and the robustness level of explanation presented in Definition 1 and 2 in the case of prime implicants as explanations.

3 Prime Implicants

3.1 Standard Prime Implicants

Our approach is grounded in earlier studies [8,13], which conceptualize explanations as abductive (factual) explanations, also known as prime implicants. These explanations are defined as subset-minimal sets of features that are sufficient to account for a model decision.

For any subset $E \subseteq I$, where $I = \{1, \ldots, Q\}$ denotes the complete set of feature indices, we denote the corresponding subspace as

$$\mathcal{X}_E = \bigtimes_{q \in E} \mathcal{X}_i.$$

Given an instance $\boldsymbol{x} \in \mathcal{X}$, the notation $\boldsymbol{x}_E \in \mathcal{X}_E$ represents its projection onto the features in E, while $\boldsymbol{x}_{I \setminus E} \in \mathcal{X}_{I \setminus E}$ refers to the projection onto the remaining features. We denote by $(\boldsymbol{x}_E, \boldsymbol{x}'_{I \setminus E})$ the completion of $\boldsymbol{x}_E$ with the values of $\boldsymbol{x}'$ for features in the set $I \setminus E$.

Definition 3. *Let $h : \mathcal{X} \to \mathcal{Y}$ be a classifier. A set $E \subseteq \{1, \ldots, Q\}$ is a* prime implicant explanation *for $h(\boldsymbol{x})$ if and only if:*

$$\forall \boldsymbol{x}'_{I \setminus E} \in \mathcal{X}_{I \setminus E}, \quad h(\boldsymbol{x}_E, \boldsymbol{x}'_{I \setminus E}) = h(\boldsymbol{x}) \tag{1}$$

and no proper subset of E satisfies this condition.

Note that all supersets of a prime implicant are implicants.

Example 1. Assume we are interested in predicting whether a customer will subscribe to a term deposit given her/his information: Age (A - X_1), Job (J - X_2), Marital status (M - X_3), Balance (B - X_4), Housing (H - X_5), Loan (L - X_6). A classifier that predicts for a particular customer with (A,J,M,B,H,L) = (45, Management, Married, 1000, Yes, No) that they will subscribe could have as prime implicant explanation the subset $E = \{2, 3\}$ corresponding to variables {Job = Management, Marital = Married}.

3.2 Robust Prime Implicants

This section presents the notions of ϵ-robust prime implicants and the robustness level of prime implicants.

Definition 4. *Let $\mathcal{H}$ be a hypothesis space of parametric models, i.e., each $h \in \mathcal{H}$. Let $h : \mathcal{X} \to \mathcal{Y}$ be a classifier, and $H_\epsilon := \{h' \in \mathcal{H}$ s.t. $d(h, h') \leq \epsilon\}$, where $d(h, h')$ is a distance between h and h', be a valid set of models in the neighbourhood of h and let $\boldsymbol{x} \in \mathcal{X}$. For a given robustness level ϵ, a set $E \subseteq I$ is said to be an* ϵ-robust implicant *if*

$$\forall h' \in H_\epsilon, \; \forall \boldsymbol{x}'_{I \setminus E} \in \mathcal{X}_{I \setminus E}, \quad h'(\boldsymbol{x}_E, \boldsymbol{x}'_{I \setminus E}) = h(\boldsymbol{x}). \tag{2}$$

Definition 5. *A set $E \subseteq I$ is said to be an ϵ-robust prime implicant if removing one attribute from E makes (2) invalid.*

Definition 6. *The level of robustness of an implicant is equal to the maximum value of ϵ for which equation (2) holds.*

The next proposition tells us that there is a monotonicity of the level robustness with respect to the inclusion of the neighbourhoods of h.

Proposition 1. *For any ϵ and ϵ', if $H_\epsilon \subset H_{\epsilon'}$ and if a set $E \subseteq I$ is an ϵ'-robust prime implicant, then E is an ϵ-robust implicant*

Example 2. As an illustration, consider a problem with $I = \{1, 2, 3, 4\}$. The lattice of the subsets of I is given in Fig. 1. The highest level of robustness for an unconstrained prime implicant is reached for the set $\{2, 3, 4\}$. If a minimum level of robustness of 0.1 is required, then $\{1, 2\}$ is no longer a prime implicant under this constraint, and $\{1, 2, 3\}$ becomes the prime implicant with the highest robustness level.

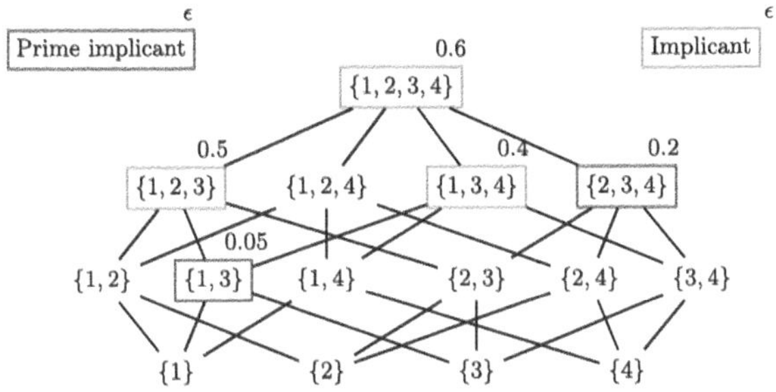

Fig. 1. Example of ϵ-robust implicants when 2^Q subsets $E \subset I$ is organized in the lattice structure. The implicants and prime implicants are respectively colored by green and *blue*, whose robustness levels are given in the superscript.

4 The Case of Linear Models

Let $\mathcal{X} \subset \mathbb{R}^Q$. A model is linear in $\boldsymbol{x}$ if the decision of the classifier $h : \mathcal{X} \longrightarrow \mathcal{Y}$ is based on a score function $f_w(\boldsymbol{x})$:

$$f_w(\boldsymbol{x}) = w_0 + \sum_{q=1}^{Q} w_q x_q, \tag{3}$$

where $\boldsymbol{w} = (w_1, ..., w_Q)$ denote a set of Q real-valued weights. Decisions are made by comparing the score function with a given threshold 0:

$$h(\boldsymbol{x}) = \begin{cases} 1 \text{ if } f_w(\boldsymbol{x}) \geq 0, \\ 0 \text{ else.} \end{cases} \tag{4}$$

A typical way to define a neighbourhood around a model h in this case is to consider that H_ϵ is composed of models defined by weights belonging to

$$\Delta_\epsilon = \{\boldsymbol{w}' : \|\boldsymbol{w} - \boldsymbol{w}'\|_p \leq \epsilon\}, \tag{5}$$

where $\|\cdot\|_p$ is an L^p-norm.

Since in this case each model h is specified by a weight vector $\boldsymbol{w}$, we shall use h and $\boldsymbol{w}$ interchangeably from now on. To simplify notations, we shall also equate Δ_ϵ and H_ϵ. In this and the next section, we shall focus without loss of generality on the case where $h(\boldsymbol{x}) = 1$, the treatment of the case $h(\boldsymbol{x}) = 0$ being similar. When $h(\boldsymbol{x}) = 1$, Definition 3 and 5 can be translated as follows:

Proposition 2. *Let $h_w : \mathcal{X} \to \{0, 1\}$ be a binary classifier with a score function $f_w : \mathcal{X} \to \mathbb{R}$. Let us consider without loss of generality an instance $\boldsymbol{x}$ such that $f_w(\boldsymbol{x}) \geq 0$. A subset $E \subseteq I$ is a prime implicant for $h(\boldsymbol{x})$ if and only if:*

$$\underline{f}_w(\boldsymbol{x}_E) = \inf_{\boldsymbol{x}'_{I\setminus E} \in \mathcal{X}_{I\setminus E}} f_w(\boldsymbol{x}_E, \boldsymbol{x}'_{I\setminus E}) \geq 0\,. \tag{6}$$

and no proper subset of E satisfies this condition.

Proof. Followed directly from the definition of linear model h (4).

Proposition 3. *Let $h_w : \mathcal{X} \to \{0, 1\}$ be a binary classifier with a score function $f_w : \mathcal{X} \to \mathbb{R}$. Let us consider without loss of generality an instance $\boldsymbol{x}$ such that $f_w(\boldsymbol{x}) \geq 0$. A prime implicant $E \subseteq I$ is said to be ϵ-robust if the following condition holds:*

$$\underline{f}_{\Delta_\epsilon}(\boldsymbol{x}_E) = \inf_{\boldsymbol{w}' \in \Delta_\epsilon} \inf_{\boldsymbol{x}'_{I\setminus E} \in \mathcal{X}_{I\setminus E}} f_{w'}(\boldsymbol{x}_E, \boldsymbol{x}'_{I\setminus E}) \geq 0. \tag{7}$$

By definition, if $\mathcal{X} = \mathbb{R}^Q$, for any linear model h with a score function f_w (3),

$$\inf_{\boldsymbol{x}'_{I\setminus E} \in \mathcal{X}_{I\setminus E}} f_w(\boldsymbol{x}_E, \boldsymbol{x}'_{I\setminus E}) = w_0 + \sum_{q\in E} w_q x_q + \sum_{q \in I\setminus E} \inf_{x'_q \in \mathcal{X}_q} w_q x'_q = -\infty$$

for any $E \neq I$. Therefore, for any $\boldsymbol{x} \in \mathcal{X}$, the only prime implicant is I if the variable domains are unbounded. In this paper, for ease of exposition and space reasons, we now proceed with the assumption of bounded normalized features $\mathcal{X} \subsetneq [0, 1]^Q$, or equivalently

$$\mathcal{X} := \bigtimes_{q\in I} \mathcal{X}_q := \bigtimes_{q\in I} [0, 1]\,. \tag{8}$$

5 Checking the Level of Robustness

The problems of finding a prime implicant and finding all the prime implicants has been studied in [7], to which the reader should refer to find algorithms. Based on those, we present an efficient algorithm to check the level of robustness of any given prime implicant.

To construct efficient algorithms to check if a given prime implicant E is ϵ-robust and compute the level of robustness of a given implicant, we shall first focus on the specific case of L^∞-norm.

$$\|\boldsymbol{w} - \boldsymbol{w}'\|_\infty = \max_{q \in \{1,\dots,Q\}} |w_q - w'_q|\,, \forall \boldsymbol{w}, \boldsymbol{w}'\,. \tag{9}$$

Under the L^∞-norm, we have

$$\Delta_\epsilon = \bigtimes_{q \in I} [w_q - \epsilon, w_q + \epsilon]\,. \tag{10}$$

We want to determine for which value ϵ^* the function $\underline{f}_{\Delta_\epsilon}(\boldsymbol{x}_E)$ goes from a positive to a negative value, i.e. we search ϵ^* such that $\underline{f}_{\Delta_{\epsilon^*}}(\boldsymbol{x}_E) = 0$. Considering the L^∞-norm, $\underline{f}_{\Delta_\epsilon}(\boldsymbol{x}_E)$ is equal to:

$$\underline{f}_{\Delta_\epsilon}(\boldsymbol{x}_E) = w_0 - \epsilon + \sum_{q \in E} (w_q - \epsilon) \cdot x_q + \sum_{q \in I \setminus E} \inf_{x'_q \in [0,1]} (w_q - \epsilon) \cdot x'_q$$

For any $q \in I \setminus E$, $\inf_{x'_q} \left[(w_q - \epsilon) \cdot x'_q\right]$ depends on whether $w_q - \epsilon$ is positive or negative: If $w_q - \epsilon > 0$, then the minimum is achieved when $x'_q = 0$; If $w_q - \epsilon < 0$, then the minimum is achieved when $x'_q = 1$. Thus, we have

$$\sum_{q \in I \setminus E} \inf_{x'_q \in [0,1]} (w_q - \epsilon) \cdot x'_q = \sum_{q \in I \setminus E} \begin{cases} w_q - \epsilon & \text{if } w_q - \epsilon < 0, \\ 0 & \text{otherwise.} \end{cases}$$

For any fix value $\epsilon \geq 0$, $\underline{f}_{\Delta_\epsilon}(\boldsymbol{x}_E)$ can thus be rewritten as

$$\underline{f}_{\Delta_\epsilon}(\boldsymbol{x}_E) = \inf_{\boldsymbol{w}' \in \Delta_\epsilon} \inf_{\boldsymbol{x}'_{I \setminus E} \in \mathcal{X}_{I \setminus E}} f_{\boldsymbol{w}'}(\boldsymbol{x}_E, \boldsymbol{x}'_{I \setminus E}) = A(\epsilon) - \epsilon B(\epsilon)\,, \tag{11}$$

$$\text{where } A(\epsilon) := w_0 + \sum_{q \in E} w_q \cdot x_q + \sum_{q \in I \setminus E, w_q - \epsilon < 0} w_q\,, \tag{12}$$

$$B(\epsilon) := 1 + \sum_{q \in E} x_q + \sum_{q \in I \setminus E, w_q - \epsilon < 0} 1 \tag{13}$$

It is easy to see that $A(\epsilon)$ and $B(\epsilon)$ are both piecewise constant functions, partitioned into several intervals defined by each positive value of w_q. Function $\underline{f}_{\Delta_\epsilon}(\boldsymbol{x}_E)$ is thus piecewise linear decreasing in ϵ on the same intervals.

The following Lemma shows that the function $g_\epsilon(\boldsymbol{x}_E)$ is a monotonically decreasing function of ϵ:

Lemma 1. *For any $\epsilon > \epsilon'$, for any $E \subset I$, we have*

$$g_\epsilon(\boldsymbol{x}_E) > g_{\epsilon'}(\boldsymbol{x}_E)\,. \tag{14}$$

Proof. The proof is trivial because, by Definition (5), we have $\Delta_\epsilon \subset \Delta_{\epsilon'}$.

Considering that $\underline{f}_{\Delta_0}(\boldsymbol{x}_E) > 0$ by assumption and that the limit of $\underline{f}_{\Delta_\epsilon}(\boldsymbol{x}_E)$ goes to minus infinity as ϵ goes to infinity, there exits a unique value ϵ^* such that $\underline{f}_{\Delta_{\epsilon^*}}(\boldsymbol{x}_E) = 0$. The next proposition tells us that finding ϵ^* can be done in $\mathcal{O}(Q \log(Q))$.

Proposition 4. *Let $S = [w_{(1)}, w_{(2)}, \ldots, w_{(Q^+)}]$ denote the sorted list of positive weights in increasing order, where Q^+ denote the number of positive weights. This sorting can be done in $\mathcal{O}(Q \log Q)$. Suppose there exists an index k such that $\underline{f}_{\Delta_{w_{(k-1)}}}(\boldsymbol{x}_E) \geq 0$ and $\underline{f}_{\Delta_{w_{(k)}}}(\boldsymbol{x}_E) < 0$. Then, the* maximum robustness level ϵ^* *is given by $\epsilon^* = A(w_{(k)})/B(w_{(k)})$. As a result, the worst-case computational complexity is $\mathcal{O}(Q)$ for identifying ϵ^*, and $\mathcal{O}(Q \log Q)$ overall.*

Figure 2 provides a graphical illustration of the process of determination of ϵ^*. The horizontal axis represents the sorted $w_{(q)}$. At a low perturbation level, $\underline{f}_{\Delta_\epsilon}(\boldsymbol{x}_E)$ is positive, indicating that the prediction remains stable. As ϵ increases, the function $\underline{f}_{\Delta_\epsilon}(\boldsymbol{x}_E) = A(\epsilon) - \epsilon\, B(\epsilon)$ decreases, and eventually, at a critical perturbation level ϵ^*, it crosses zero—this is the maximum robustness level beyond which the prediction would change. The interval around ϵ^* highlights the transition in the model response under perturbation. Before proceeding to experiments, note that the above procedure does not rely on the fact that E is prime, and can be used to assess the maximal robustness level of any implicant, meaning that it could compute the values for any subset (e.g., in Fig. 1, provide any number above the subsets).

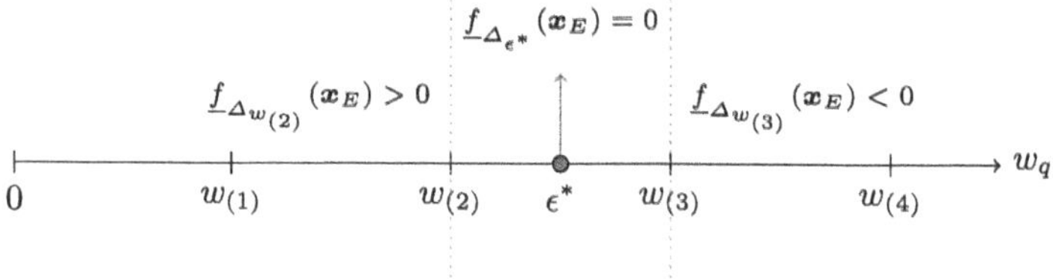

Fig. 2. Determination of ϵ^*

6 Experiments

In this section, we empirically show that the proposed notion of robustness level indeed captures the robustness of prime implicants under model perturbations. We also present its application in prime implicant selection.

6.1 Experimental Setting

We conduct experiments on 6 publicly available benchmark datasets, which are summarized in Table 1. Logistic regression [10] is employed in all the experiments. The features are normalized to [0, 1]. For each data set, we perform a 5-fold cross-validation and report the average results.

Robustness of Prime Implicants Under Model Perturbations. Two ways of introducing perturbations into the model are considered:

Table 1. Overview of Datasets

Datasets	Banknote	Diabetes	Rice	Gamma	Climate	Parkinsons
Features	4	8	7	10	18	22
Instances	1372	768	3810	19020	540	195

Perturbations Introduced by Direct Changes to the Weight Vectors : For each train-test split, we first partition the train set into 2 equally sized subsets, $\mathcal{D}_1$ and $\mathcal{D}_2$. Two models $\mathcal{M}_1$ and $\mathcal{M}_2$ are trained, using, respectively, $\mathcal{D}_1$ and $\mathcal{D}_2$. Model $\mathcal{M}_2$ is only used to compute a maximal perturbation level ϵ_{max} arbitrarily fixed according to the L^∞-norm between $\mathcal{M}_1$ and $\mathcal{M}_2$. We construct an increasing sequence of possible values of ϵ with equal step-size: $0 = \epsilon_0 \leq \ldots \leq \epsilon_{10} = \epsilon_{max}/5$, to concentrate on small to moderate levels of perturbations.

For each test instance $\boldsymbol{x}$, we sort its explanations associated with model $\mathcal{M}_1$ by robustness level ϵ^* in descending order and select the 50% top-ranked explanations. For each perturbation level ϵ_k, we compute the percentage of top-rank prime implicants that are ϵ_k-robust. The average scores over the test set are reported. We do the same test with the 50% shortest prime implicants. We also test all prime implicants for comparison.

Perturbations Introduced by Changes to the Training Data: For each train-test split, we first partition the train set into 2 equally sized subsets, $\mathcal{D}_1$ and $\mathcal{D}_2$. A model $\mathcal{M}_1$ is trained using only $\mathcal{D}_1$, and a second model $\mathcal{M}_2$ is trained on the entire training data set $\mathcal{D}_1 \cup \mathcal{D}_2$. For each test instance, we sort its explanations associated with model $\mathcal{M}_1$ by robustness level ϵ^* in descending order. Then, for each decile $\alpha \in \{10\%, 20\%, \ldots, 100\%\}$, we select the α top-ranked explanations. For each decile α, we compute the percentages of explanations that remain valid prime implicants of model $\mathcal{M}_2$. The average scores over the test set are reported. We do the same test with the shortest prime implicants and randomly sorted ones.

Application in Prime Implicant Selection. We also conduct experiments to illustrate the potential application of the proposed robustness level in prime implicant selection. For each instance $\boldsymbol{x}$, for each $q = 1\ldots, Q$, we define the robustness level of the cardinality q as the highest robustness level given by all the prime implicants of cardinality q. We then report the average robustness level over the test set of each possible cardinality q, $q = 1\ldots, Q$. This is designed to check the possible relation between the two interesting specific types of prime implicants: the shortest and the most robust prime implicants.

6.2 Results

Robustness of Prime Implicants Under Model Perturbations. The results suggest that the proposed notion of robustness level indeed captures the robustness of prime implicants under model perturbations.

Perturbations Introduced by Direct Changes to the Weight Vectors: One can see in Fig. 3 that robust prime implicants, as determined by our procedure, are indeed always more robust than the shortest ones, in the sense that more of them remain valid as perturbation increases, and this for all perturbation levels. However, the validity of shortest PIs remains high, compared to the whole set of PIs. This suggests a possible correlation between robustness and length of prime implicants. Moreover, the rapid and drastic reduction of the validity ratio on the Climate and Parkinsons data sets suggests that explanations for those are fragile, and that one should only focus on the most robust prime implicants.

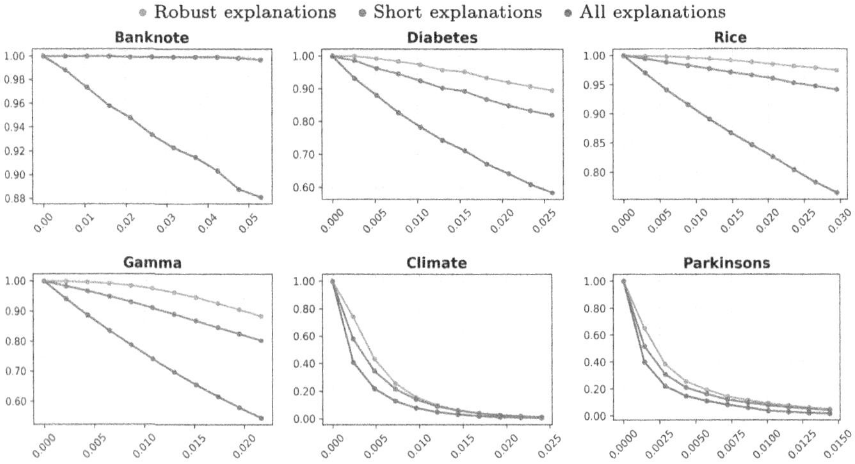

Fig. 3. Validity ratio for direct changes to weight vectors. X-axis: robustness level; Y-axis: average validity (in %).

Perturbations Introduced by Changes to the Training Data: The results given in Fig. 4 confirm that robust prime implicants are generally more stable to finite sampling bias, except for Gamma and Climate, where the short prime implicants perform slightly better with respect to model changes. Indeed, the results show that the validity of the top-ranked PIs for the first deciles remains very high even when changing the samples, except for Climate and Parkinson. Again, this suggests that it is preferable to focus on the most robust prime implicants.

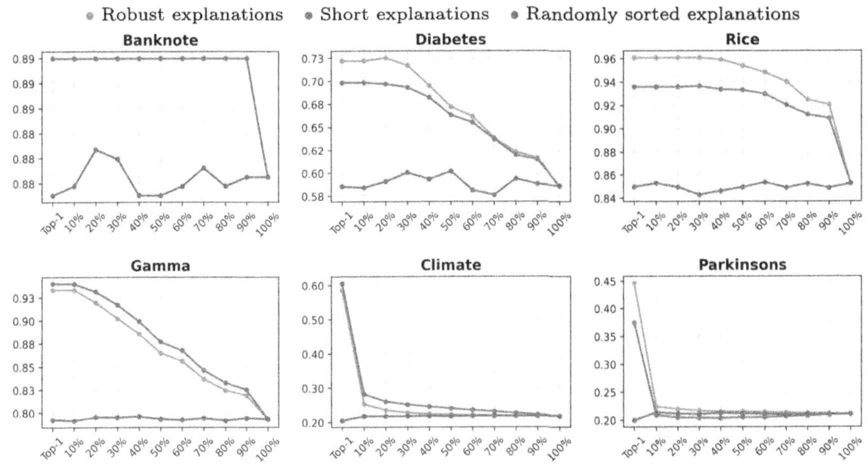

Fig. 4. Validity ratio in retrained models. X-axis: top-ranked explanations; Y-axis: average validity (in %).

Application in Prime Implicant Selection. The results given in Fig. 5 show that while the shortest prime implicants are not necessarily the most robust ones, the longest prime implicants are often the least robust ones. A conciseness-robustness trade-off must thus be found, depending mainly on the application. Luckily, we can see that longer prime implicants tend to be less robust, yet allowing for slightly longer prime implicants than the shortest ones may increase

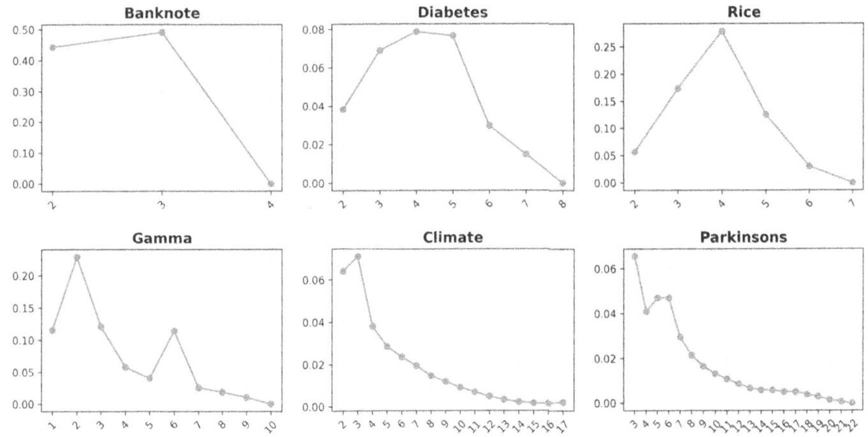

Fig. 5. Relationship between explanation length and robustness. X-axis: PI-explanation length; Y-axis: average robustness level.

robustness. There is therefore a trade-off to be found, but it is likely that one will not have to sacrifice shortness for robustness, or the other way around.

7 Conclusion

In this paper, we propose the notion of robustness in factual explanations through prime implicant (PI) explanations, with one main goal that is assessing the validity of explanations under model changes. We demonstrate that robust explanations perform better under such changes, suggesting their greater relevance in real-world applications. Given the large number of possible PI-explanations, robustness offers a principled way to filter out less stable explanations, thereby reducing the explanation space and improving interpretability for human users. Furthermore, we show that the shortest PI-explanation is not necessarily the most robust, highlighting an important distinction to consider in practice: it may be better to avoid the "simplest" explanation and consider a more robust explanation when it comes to critical decisions (questioning to some extent the famous "Occcam's razor" in XAI). As a potential direction for future work, one could explore ways to further reduce the number and the length of PI-explanations by incorporating feature-specific constraints, where certain feature values may be irrelevant to a given prediction. One could also extend this approach to categorical data to compare the related performance in different model settings.

Acknowledgments. This work was partially supported by the Junior Professor Chair in Trustworthy AI (Ref. ANR-R311CHD).

References

1. Burger, C., Walter, C.: Improving stability estimates in adversarial explainable AI through alternate search methods. arXiv preprint arXiv:2501.09006 (2025)
2. Darwiche, A.: Logic for explainable AI. In: 2023 38th Annual ACM/IEEE Symposium on Logic in Computer Science (LICS), pp. 1–11. IEEE (2023)
3. Guidotti, R., Monreale, A., Ruggieri, S., Turini, F., Giannotti, F., Pedreschi, D.: A survey of methods for explaining black box models. ACM Comput. Surv. (CSUR) **51**(5), 1–42 (2018)
4. Jiang, J., Leofante, F., Rago, A., Toni, F.: Interval abstractions for robust counterfactual explanations. Artif. Intell. **336**, 104218 (2024)
5. Jiang, J., Leofante, F., Rago, A., Toni, F.: Robust counterfactual explanations in machine learning: a survey. arXiv preprint arXiv:2402.01928 (2024)
6. Lundberg, S.: A unified approach to interpreting model predictions. arXiv preprint arXiv:1705.07874 (2017)
7. Marques-Silva, J., Gerspacher, T., Cooper, M., Ignatiev, A., Narodytska, N.: Explaining Naive Bayes and other linear classifiers with polynomial time and delay. Adv. Neural. Inf. Process. Syst. **33**, 20590–20600 (2020)

8. Marques-Silva, J., Ignatiev, A.: Delivering trustworthy AI through formal XAI. In: Proceedings of the AAAI Conference on Artificial Intelligence, vol. 36, no. 11, pp. 12342–12350 (2022). https://doi.org/10.1609/aaai.v36i11.21499, https://ojs.aaai.org/index.php/AAAI/article/view/21499
9. Mishra, S., Dutta, S., Long, J., Magazzeni, D.: A survey on the robustness of feature importance and counterfactual explanations. arXiv preprint arXiv:2111.00358 (2021)
10. Murphy, K.P.: Machine Learning: A Probabilistic Perspective. MIT Press, Cambridge (2012)
11. Ribeiro, M.T., Singh, S., Guestrin, C.: "why should i trust you?" Explaining the predictions of any classifier. In: Proceedings of the 22nd ACM SIGKDD International Conference on Knowledge Discovery and Data Mining, pp. 1135–1144 (2016)
12. Samek, W., Montavon, G., Vedaldi, A., Hansen, L.K., Müller, K.-R.: Explainable AI: Interpreting, Explaining and Visualizing Deep Learning. Springer, Cham (2019)
13. Shih, A., Choi, A., Darwiche, A.: A symbolic approach to explaining Bayesian network classifiers. arXiv preprint arXiv:1805.03364 (2018)
14. Slack, D., Hilgard, S., Jia, E., Singh, S., Lakkaraju, H.: Fooling lime and SHAP: adversarial attacks on post hoc explanation methods. In: Proceedings of the AAAI/ACM Conference on AI, Ethics, and Society, pp. 180–186 (2020)
15. Verma, S., Boonsanong, V., Hoang, M., Hines, K., Dickerson, J., Shah, C.: Counterfactual explanations and algorithmic recourses for machine learning: a review. ACM Comput. Surv. **56**(12), 1–42 (2024)
16. Visani, G., Bagli, E., Chesani, F., Poluzzi, A., Capuzzo, D.: Statistical stability indices for lime: obtaining reliable explanations for machine learning models. J. Oper. Res. Soc. **73**(1), 91–101 (2022). https://doi.org/10.1080/01605682.2020.1865846

Consensus in Motion: A Case of Dynamic Rationality of Sequential Learning in Probability Aggregation

Polina Gordienko[1(✉)], Christoph Jansen[2], Thomas Augustin[1], and Martin Rechenauer[3]

[1] Department of Statistics, Ludwig-Maximilians-Universität München, Munich, Germany
Polina.Gordienko@stat.uni-muenchen.de
[2] School of Computing and Communication, Lancaster University Leipzig, Leipzig, Germany
[3] Munich Center for Mathematical Philosophy, Ludwig-Maximilians-Universität München, Munich, Germany

Abstract. We propose a framework for probability aggregation based on propositional probability logic. Unlike conventional judgment aggregation, which focuses on static rationality, our model addresses dynamic rationality by ensuring that collective beliefs update consistently with new information. We show that any consensus-compatible and independent aggregation rule on a non-nested agenda is necessarily linear. Furthermore, we provide sufficient conditions for a fair learning process, where individuals initially agree on a specified subset of propositions known as the common ground, and new information is restricted to this shared foundation. This guarantees that updating individual judgments via Bayesian conditioning—whether performed before or after aggregation—yields the same collective belief. A distinctive feature of our framework is its treatment of sequential decision-making, which allows new information to be incorporated progressively through multiple stages while maintaining the established common ground. We illustrate our findings with a running example in a political scenario concerning healthcare and immigration policies.

Keywords: Probability aggregation · Judgement aggregation · Dynamic rationality · External Bayesianity · Fair learning · Probability logic · Sequential learning

1 Introduction

Traditional aggregation methods, such as majority voting, are notorious for producing collective judgments that are logically inconsistent and for failing to meet minimal rationality constraints. This shortcoming lies at the heart of the impossibility theorems that have emerged in judgment aggregation theory over the past two decades (e.g., [3,4,6,14–16,19,21–23]). Unlike social choice—where

K. Sauerwald and M. Thimm (Eds.): ECSQARU 2025, LNAI 16099, pp. 178–190, 2026.
https://doi.org/10.1007/978-3-032-05134-9_13

preferences involve ranking alternatives – the aggregation of judgments concerns interconnected issues that capture acts of assent or dissent. Despite numerous attempts to weaken constraints on aggregation functions in order to achieve logical consistency [20,24], prior research has focused mainly on static rationality.

In contrast, this paper advocates a shift toward a *dynamic* theory of collective decision-making in which both individual and collective beliefs update rationally in response to new information (see [5]). Motivated by the first impossibility result for dynamically rational judgment aggregation [10], our main contribution is a possibility result for dynamically rational collective decision-making on logically interconnected propositions. We introduce a framework of probability aggregation based on propositional probability logic that generalizes traditional approaches from both judgment and preference aggregation. Building on prior work in probability aggregation [1,2,7,9,12,17,18], our first theorem establishes that any *consensus-compatible* and *independent* aggregation rule on a *non-nested* agenda must be *linear*. Furthermore, we show that dynamically rational linear aggregation is attainable when the domain of the aggregation function is restricted to profiles in which all group members share the same probabilistic judgments for a specified subset of propositions—what we term the *common ground* (here understood in line with a broader notion of consensus)[1]. This common ground represents the set of propositions on which all individuals already agree, and by ensuring that new information is limited to this shared foundation—a process we call *fair learning*—all members benefit equally, preventing dynamically irrational outcomes arising from unequal starting beliefs. Importantly, we demonstrate that fair learning not only achieves dynamic rationality but also preserves the common ground across *sequential* updates.

The paper is organized as follows. In Sect. 2.1 and Sect. 2.2 we develop our framework of probability aggregation based on propositional probability logic. Section 2.3 introduces a running example from the context of political decision-making, which we use to illustrate our framework throughout the paper. Section 3 is divided into two parts: Sect. 3.1 presents our characterization result for the linear aggregation rule, and Sect. 3.2 introduces a Bayesian updating process that demonstrates dynamic rationality under a restricted domain. Section 4 concludes.

2 The Model of Probability Aggregation

2.1 Propositional Probability Logic

Let $\mathcal{L}$ be the set of all logically non-equivalent[2] formulas based on a propositional logic with a finite set A of atomic formulas. The variable ϕ is then a generic

[1] Throughout this paper, "consensus" is used in two senses: (i) as a broad notion of mutual agreement—here, synonymous with our technical term "common ground" and (ii) as "consensus compatibility," the requirement that if all individuals assign probability 1 to a proposition, then the collective judgment must also assign 1.

[2] Logical equivalence (i.e., $\phi \equiv \psi$ if and only if $\models \phi \leftrightarrow \psi$) is an equivalence relation. We select one finitary representative from each equivalence class so that no two distinct formulas in $\mathcal{L}$ are equivalent. Since A is finite, and we consider only finitary formulas, $\mathcal{L}$ is finite.

variable ranging over all well-formed formulas in $\mathcal{L}$, i.e., any expression that can be constructed from the atomic elements in A using the logical connectives $\neg, \wedge, \vee, \rightarrow, \leftrightarrow$.

Definition 1. *An* ***agenda*** *is defined as a finite subset* $X \subseteq \mathcal{L}$ *such that* $\forall\ \phi \in \mathcal{L}\colon \phi \in X \Rightarrow \neg\phi \in X$. *An agenda* X *is called* $\wedge$***-stable****, if* $\forall\ r \in \mathbb{N}$, $\forall \phi_1, ..., \phi_r \in X\colon \bigwedge_{j=1}^{r} \phi_j \in X$. *A* ***propositional probability*** *is a map* $P\colon \mathcal{L} \rightarrow [0,1]$ *such that the following holds:*

- $P(\phi) = 1$ *if* $\models \phi$ *(i.e.* ϕ *is a tautology);*
- *If* $\phi_1, \phi_2 ... \in \mathcal{L}$ *such that* $\models \neg(\phi_i \wedge \phi_j)$ *for all* $i \neq j \in \mathbb{N}$, *then*

$$P(\bigvee_{i=1}^{\infty} \phi_i) = \sum_{i=1}^{\infty} P(\phi_i).$$

2.2 The Framework of Probability Aggregation

Each individual $i \in N$ with $N = \{1, 2, \ldots, n\}$ holds a *probabilistic judgement* which is considered as a *degree of confidence* in the truth of the propositions in the agenda X that ranges from 0 (maximal doubt) to 1 (maximal confidence).

Definition 2. *The probabilistic judgement* J *is a function* $J\colon X \rightarrow [0,1]$. *The judgement* J *is called* ***probabilistically rational*** *if there exists a propositional probability* $P^*\colon \mathcal{L} \rightarrow [0,1]$ *on the whole set* $\mathcal{L}$ *such that* $\forall\ \phi \in X\colon J(\phi) = P^*(\phi)$. *A* ***probabilistic profile*** *on an agenda* X *is a tuple* $(J_1, ..., J_n)$, *where each of* $J_1, ..., J_n$ *is a probabilistically rational probabilistic judgement. The* ***probabilistic aggregation rule*** *is a function* $F\colon J(X)^n \rightarrow J(X)$, *where* $J(X)$ *is the collective set of all probabilistically rational probabilistic judgements on the agenda* X.

Note that the propositional probability P^* is an extension of the probabilistic judgement J. The probabilistic profile captures the landscape of beliefs across group members, while the aggregation rule consolidates these individual probabilities into a unified collective judgment that maintains probabilistic rationality.

2.3 A Running Example: A Political Scenario

To illustrate the concepts introduced in Sect. 2.2, consider a $\wedge$-stable agenda X that comprises the following atomic propositions along with their logical interconnections:

a: *Population ageing is straining the healthcare and pension systems.*
b: *It is necessary to implement new immigration policies to attract more skilled professionals who can contribute to the economy.*
c: *The current tax revenue is sufficient to meet the fiscal demands imposed by population ageing.*

Table 1 shows a sample *probabilistic profile* on the agenda X, where we have three individuals (denoted by J_1, J_2, and J_3). This example serves as our running example throughout the paper.

Table 1. A sample probabilistic profile on the agenda $X = \pm\{a, b, c, a \to b, a \wedge b, a \wedge c, b \wedge c, a \wedge b \wedge c\}$, where each individual assigns a degree of confidence (ranging from 0 to 1) to the propositions. Each entry is chosen so as to align with the relationships dictated by logical connectives, ensuring that bounds for probability assignments are satisfied. Note that since X is $\wedge$-stable, this agenda uniquely determines a single joint distribution over $\{a, b, c\}$.

Individual	a	b	c	$a \to b$	$a \wedge b$	$a \wedge c$	$b \wedge c$	$a \wedge b \wedge c$
J_1	0.7	0.8	0.4	0.9	0.6	0.3	0.3	0.25
J_2	0.7	0.5	0.4	0.8	0.5	0.3	0.25	0.15
J_3	0.7	0.4	0.4	0.6	0.3	0.3	0.15	0.1

3 Probability Aggregation

3.1 Static Rationality

Our first theorem is an adaptation of the characterization result from [9] on the linear pooling function. In order to state the theorem in our framework of probability aggregation, we need to introduce the following constraints on the agenda X, formulas $\phi \in \mathcal{L}$ and the probabilistic aggregation rule F.

Definition 3. *An agenda X is called* **nested**, *if there exist formulas $\phi_1, ..., \phi_r \in X$ such that the following holds:*

- $\forall\, j = 1, ..., r - 1{:}\ \models \phi_j \to \phi_{j+1}$;
- $X = \bigcup_{j=1}^{r} (\{\phi_j\} \cup \{\neg\phi_j\})$.

Otherwise the agenda X is called **non-nested**. *A formula $\phi \in \mathcal{L}$ is called* **contingent** *if neither $\models \phi$ nor $\models \neg\phi$. We denote the set of contingent elements of $Y \subset \mathcal{L}$ by $cont(Y)$.*

In the next step, we will show that it is possible to characterize linear probabilistic aggregation rules for a very large class of agendas – all non-nested agendas. In the setting of probabilistic opinion pooling, the agenda has been traditionally assumed to be a σ-algebra (i.e. closed under complementation and countable union of events). Dropping the assumption of a σ-algebra, [9] consider more general agendas. The constraint of nestedness implies that formulas $\phi_1, ..., \phi_r \in X$ are logically interconnected by material implication which corresponds to the subset-relations in a nested agenda X in the framework of [9]. Intuitively, non-nestedness means that there is no subagenda in X that comprises only propositions that are logically interrelated by material implications and that are closed under negation. Thus, the propositions under consideration can be probabilistically dependent (correlated) without being logically interrelated by material implication.

The intuition of consensus preservation requirements is well-known in the literature on collective decision theory: a proposition in the agenda should have a collective probability of 1 if every group member assigns it a probability of 1 (certainty). In judgement aggregation theory the analogue of this requirement is referred to as *unanimity preservation* criterion [19], and in probability aggregation theory it is often called *zero probability property* [18]. Here, we introduce a version of consensus preservation that holds even if group members' beliefs are not revealed in the process of decision-making, similarly to [9].

Definition 4. *We say a judgement is* ***consistent with truth of*** $\phi^* \in \mathcal{L}$*, if there exists a propositional probability* $P^*\colon \mathcal{L} \to [0,1]$ *such that the following holds:*

- $\forall\, \phi \in X\colon P^*(\phi) = J(\phi);$
- $P^*(\phi^*) = 1,$

where the propositional probability P^* *is an extension of the individual probabilistic judgement* J*. A probabilistic aggregation rule* F *is called* ***consensus compatible*** *if the following holds: For all* $\phi \in \mathcal{L}$ *and for all* $J_1, ..., J_n \in J(X)$*, if* $J_1, ..., J_n$ *are consistent with truth of* ϕ*, then also* $F(J_1, ..., J_n)$ *is consistent with truth of* ϕ*.*

Intuitively, Definition 4 implies that if there is a possibility that all group members assign the probability of 1 to a formula ϕ (though these beliefs may remain unrevealed), then the collective opinion must reflect this certainty in ϕ.

Definition 5. *A probabilistic aggregation rule* F *is called* ***independent*** *if for every* $\phi \in X$ *there exists a function* $S\colon [0,1]^n \to [0,1]$ *such that, for all* $J_1, ..., J_n \in J(X)^n$*,* $F(J_1, ..., J_n)(\phi) = S(J_1(\phi), ..., J_n(\phi))$*.*

The independence requirement asserts that the aggregate probability of each formula ϕ in the agenda X should depend only on the individual probability assignments to ϕ. In the literature on probability aggregation, this condition has been referred to as *weak setwise function property* [1].

Definition 6. *A probabilistic aggregation rule* F *is called* ***linear****, if for every profile of individual probabilistic judgements* $(J_1, ..., J_n)$ *and every formula* $\phi \in X$*, the collective probability for the proposition* ϕ *is the weighted average of individual values of probabilistic judgements for* ϕ*:*

$$F(J_1(\phi), ..., J_n(\phi)) = w_1 J_1(\phi) + w_2 J_2(\phi) + ... + w_n J_n(\phi),$$

where $w_1, \ldots, w_n$ *are fixed non-negative individual weights with sum-total of 1.*

The individual weights may vary, for instance, a *dictatorship* of individual i would imply that $w_i = 1$ and $w_j = 0$ for all other individuals $j \in N$ [8]. It can be shown that the following general characterization result for linear probabilistic aggregation rules holds in our framework.

Theorem 1. *Let $F\colon J(X)^n \to J(X)$ be consensus compatible and independent. Let X be non-nested. Let $|cont(X)| > 4$. Then F is linear.*

Proof. Let $S = \{0,1\}^{|A|}$ be the set of all truth assignments to the finite set of atomic propositions A. For every formula $\phi \in \mathcal{L}$ define $[\phi] = \{v \in S \mid v \text{ satisfies } \phi\}$. It is easy to show that the mapping $I : \mathcal{L} \to 2^S,\ \phi \mapsto [\phi]$ is bijective. Since I preserves the Boolean operations, i.e.,

$$I(\phi \wedge \psi) = I(\phi) \cap I(\psi), \quad I(\phi \vee \psi) = I(\phi) \cup I(\psi), \quad I(\neg\phi) = S \setminus I(\phi),$$

it is an isomorphism. For each truth assignment $v \in S$, let χ_v be a formula that is true only at v. Then define the set function $\mu : 2^S \to [0,1]$ on 2^S induced by the propositional probability $P : \mathcal{L} \to [0,1]$ via

$$\mu(M) = P\Big(\bigvee_{v \in M} \chi_v\Big),$$

for every $M \subseteq S$. Since P satisfies the Kolmogorov axioms, μ naturally defines a full probability measure on 2^S.

Since I is bijective, any non-nested agenda $X \subseteq \mathcal{L}$ with $|cont(X)| > 4$ is mapped to a non-nested set system $I(X)$ in 2^S with $I(cont(X)) = 2^S \setminus \{S, \emptyset\}$ and hence $|I(cont(X))| > 4$. Now let $F : J(X)^n \to J(X)$ be a consensus compatible and independent aggregation rule. Define the induced operator

$$\widetilde{F} : J(I(X))^n \to J(I(X)) \quad \text{by} \quad \widetilde{F}(I(J_1), \ldots, I(J_n)) = I\Big(F(J_1, \ldots, J_n)\Big).$$

Since I preserves truth values, consensus compatibility of F implies that if $J_i(\phi) = 1$ for all i then $\widetilde{F}(I(J_1), \ldots, I(J_n))(I(\phi)) = 1$. Therefore, $\widetilde{F}$ is consensus compatible in the sense of [9]. By Theorem 4a in Sect. 5.1 in [9], any consensus-compatible and independent aggregation rule on a non-nested agenda with $|I(cont(X))| > 4$ is linear; hence, F is linear. □

Table 2 demonstrates the resulting collective judgement in the running example using the linear aggregation rule. Note that the conditions of Theorem 1 (e.g. non-nestedness, number of contingent elements) are satisfied in our example. Intuitively, Theorem 1 does not exclude the possibility of non-dictatorial and probabilistically rational aggregation of individual attitudes in our framework. Non-dictatorship means there is no individual $i \in N$ such that, for every profile $(J_1, \ldots, J_n)$ in the domain of F and every formula $\phi \in X$, the collective judgement for ϕ is given by $F(J_1(\phi), \ldots, J_n(\phi)) = J_i(\phi)$. Linearity encompasses both the case of dictatorship (if one weight equals 1 and the others 0) and the possibility of non-dictatorial aggregation (if the weights are chosen otherwise).

Table 2. Collective probabilistic profile obtained via the linear aggregation rule with equal weights $\frac{1}{3}$ for each individual and values rounded to four decimals.

Individual	a	b	c	$a \to b$	$a \wedge b$	$a \wedge c$	$b \wedge c$	$a \wedge b \wedge c$
J_1	0.7	0.8	0.4	0.9	0.6	0.3	0.3	0.25
J_2	0.7	0.5	0.4	0.8	0.5	0.3	0.25	0.15
J_3	0.7	0.4	0.4	0.6	0.3	0.3	0.15	0.1
$F(J_1, J_2, J_3)$	0.7	0.5667	0.4	0.7667	0.4667	0.3	0.2333	0.1667

The possibility of non-dictatorial aggregation of individual attitudes on logically interrelated issues arises because the domain of the probabilistic aggregation rule F is extended in our model allowing for probabilistic individual attitudes, as compared to impossibility results from the standard framework of judgement aggregation (see e.g. [3,16,19]).

3.2 Dynamic Rationality

Now, suppose the group learns the truth of one of the propositions in the agenda of interest. This raises the question: How should the group update their beliefs in response to this new information? A convincing criterion for the quality of this updating process is dynamic rationality—the requirement that the outcome of belief revision should be invariant to the order in which updating and aggregation occur [10]. In other words, whether individuals first update their personal probabilistic judgements and then aggregate them, or first aggregate their personal probabilistic judgements and then update the collective judgement, the result should remain the same.

We define the updating process as follows. Initially, an individual holds a probabilistic judgement $J(\phi)$ with respect to formula ϕ as well as probability $J(\psi)$ for all other formulas $\psi \in X$. Later she learns the truth of ϕ and adopts a new probabilistic judgement $J^{\phi}(\psi)$. The updating process is formalized by an *update operator* which is a mapping $U : J(X) \times X \to J(X)$.

In this paper, we are interested in scenarios where group members initially agree on the probability assignments for a subset of propositions within the agenda, denoted as $\Phi \subseteq X$. To formalize this setup, we introduce the notion of a *common ground* within the agenda, referring to cases where individuals share identical probabilistic judgments on Φ. The learning process of the group then consists of successively learning the truth or falsity of the propositions in Φ and the group members having to adjust their probabilistic judgements about the remaining propositions in X accordingly.

Definition 7. *Assume X to be some $\wedge$-stable agenda of interest, and let $\Phi \subseteq X$ be $\wedge$-stable. We define the domain $\mathcal{D}_\Phi$ induced by Φ by setting*

$$\mathcal{D}_\Phi = \{(J_1, \dots, J_n) \in J(X)^n \mid \forall \phi \in \Phi\ \forall i, j\colon J_i(\phi) = J_j(\phi) \neq 0\}.$$

We call Φ the ***common ground*** *of our aggregation problem. A* ***Φ-aggregation operator*** *is a mapping $F : \mathcal{D}_\Phi \to J(X)$. We call an update operator U* ***common ground preserving*** *(or* ***Φ-preserving****), if for all $\phi, \psi \in \Phi$ and all $(J_1, \ldots, J_n) \in \mathcal{D}_\Phi$ it holds that*

$$U(J_1, \phi)(\psi) = \cdots = U(J_n, \phi)(\psi).$$

If F is a Φ-aggregation operator and if U is a Φ-preserving update operator, we call the pair (F, U) ***probabilistic dynamic rational w.r.t. Φ****, if for all $\phi \in \Phi$ and $\psi \in \mathcal{L}$ it holds that*

$$F(U(J_1, \phi), \ldots, U(J_n, \phi))(\psi) = U(F(J_1, \ldots, J_n), \phi)(\psi).$$

The requirement of probabilistic dynamic rationality is a plausible constraint, since it demands that the individual and collective probabilistic judgements are updated after learning the truth of ϕ in such a manner that it makes no difference whether they are updated before aggregation or after aggregation process. Thus, it intuitively corresponds to the requirement of *external Bayesianity* from the literature on probability aggregation [11] and to the condition of dynamic rationality in the judgement aggregation framework of [10]. The following result illustrates that the possibility of dynamically rational aggregation with a Φ-preserving update operator on the restricted domain $\mathcal{D}_\Phi$.

Theorem 2. *Assume X to be some $\wedge$-stable agenda of interest, and let $\Phi \subseteq X$ be $\wedge$-stable. If $F : \mathcal{D}_\Phi \to J(X)$ is linear and U is defined by*

$$U : J(X) \times X \to J(X), \quad (J, \phi) \mapsto J^\phi,$$

where $J^\phi(\psi) := \frac{J(\phi \wedge \psi)}{J(\phi)}$ for all $\psi \in J(X)$ is the ***Bayesian updated probabilistic judgement of ψ given the truth of ϕ****, then the pair (F, U) is probabilistic dynamic rational w.r.t. Φ and U is Φ-preserving.*

Proof. Assume that the group $N = \{1, 2, 3, ..., n\}$ learns the truth of formula $\phi \in \Phi$. Consider now the aggregation of updated individual judgements

$$F(U(J_1, \phi), \ldots, U(J_n, \phi))(\psi) = \frac{1}{n} \sum_{i=1}^{n} U(J_i, \phi)(\psi) = \frac{1}{n} \sum_{i=1}^{n} \frac{J_i(\phi \wedge \psi)}{J_i(\phi)}$$

and the updating of the aggregated collective judgement

$$U(F(J_1, \ldots, J_n), \phi)(\psi) = \frac{F(J_1, ..., J_n)(\phi \wedge \psi)}{F(J_1, ..., J_n)(\phi)} = \frac{\frac{1}{n} \sum_{i=1}^{n} J_i(\phi \wedge \psi)}{\frac{1}{n} \sum_{i=1}^{n} J_i(\phi)}.$$

By the definition of the domain $\mathcal{D}_\Phi$, where $\forall i, j \in N$: $J_i(\phi) = J_j(\phi)$ for all $\phi \in \Phi$, it follows that:

$$U(F(J_1, \ldots, J_n), \phi)(\psi) = \frac{1}{n} \sum_{i=1}^{n} \frac{J_i(\phi \wedge \psi)}{J_i(\phi)} = F(U(J_1, \phi), \ldots, U(J_n, \phi))(\psi).$$

Hence, the pair (F, U) is probabilistic dynamic rational w.r.t. Φ. Since $\forall i, j \in N$: $J_i(\phi) = J_j(\phi)$ for all $\phi, \psi \in \Phi$, we have:

$$U(J_i, \phi)(\psi) = \frac{J_i(\phi \wedge \psi)}{J_i(\phi)} = \frac{J_j(\phi \wedge \psi)}{J_j(\phi)} = U(J_j, \phi)(\psi)$$

Thus, the update operator U is Φ-preserving. □

Table 3. Updated probabilistic judgements after learning a, with values rounded to four decimals. The last row, denoted by $F(\square)$, displays the collective judgement resulting from updating individual judgements and aggregating them via the linear rule $F(U(J_1, a), U(J_2, a), U(J_3, a))$.

Individual	a	b	c	$a \to b$	$a \wedge b$	$a \wedge c$	$b \wedge c$	$a \wedge b \wedge c$
J_1^a	1	0.8571	0.4286	0.8571	0.8571	0.4286	0.3571	0.3571
J_2^a	1	0.7143	0.4286	0.7143	0.7143	0.4286	0.2143	0.2143
J_3^a	1	0.4286	0.4286	0.4286	0.4286	0.4286	0.1429	0.1429
$F(\square)$	1	0.6667	0.4286	0.6667	0.6667	0.4286	0.2381	0.2381

Table 4. Updated probabilistic judgments after learning $\neg c$, following the update on a, with values rounded to four decimals. The probabilities for b and $a \to b$ are computed as $J^{a,\neg c}(b) = J^{a,\neg c}(a \to b) = \frac{J^a(b \wedge \neg c)}{J^a(\neg c)} = \frac{J^a(b) - J^a(b \wedge c)}{J^a(\neg c)}$, and for $a \wedge b$ as $J^{a,\neg c}(a \wedge b) = \frac{J^a((a \wedge b) \wedge \neg c)}{J^a(\neg c)} = \frac{J^a(a \wedge b) - J^a(a \wedge b \wedge c)}{J^a(\neg c)}$, using the value $J^a(\neg c) = 0.5714$. Here, $F(*)$ abbreviates $F(U(J_1, a, \neg c), U(J_2, a, \neg c), U(J_3, a, \neg c))$.

Individual	a	b	c	$a \to b$	$a \wedge b$	$a \wedge c$	$b \wedge c$	$a \wedge b \wedge c$
$J_1^{a,\neg c}$	1	0.8750	0	0.8750	0.8750	0	0	0
$J_2^{a,\neg c}$	1	0.8750	0	0.8750	0.8750	0	0	0
$J_3^{a,\neg c}$	1	0.5000	0	0.5000	0.5000	0	0	0
$F(*)$	1	0.7500	0	0.7500	0.7500	0	0	0

Let us illustrate the dynamically rational aggregation on our running example. Here, the common ground Φ comprises the propositions a, c, and their conjunction $a \wedge c$—that is, the issues on which all individuals initially share equal confidence in the initial Table 1. The first learning iteration is shown in Table 3, in which all group members learn the truth of a. As a consequence, the updated probability for a is set to $J^a(a) = \frac{J(a \wedge a)}{J(a)} = 1$. The updated probability for each proposition $\psi \in X$ is computed as $J^a(\psi) = \frac{J(a \wedge \psi)}{J(a)}$, using the value $J(a) = 0.7$ from Table 1.

Note that when we update the individual first and then aggregate, we obtain the collective updated values shown in Table 3. When we aggregate first and then update, we compute the collective probability for propositions b and $a \rightarrow b$ with values from Table 2 as $\frac{F(J_1,J_2,J_3)(a \wedge b)}{F(J_1,J_2,J_3)(a)} = 0.6667$; for c and $a \wedge c$ as $\frac{F(J_1,J_2,J_3)(a \wedge c)}{F(J_1,J_2,J_3)(a)} = 0.4286$; and for conjunctions $a \wedge b$ and $a \wedge b \wedge c$ as $\frac{F(J_1,J_2,J_3)(a \wedge b \wedge c)}{F(J_1,J_2,J_3)(a)} = 0.2381$. Since both ways to proceed yield identical results for all propositions in the agenda, it is apparent that regardless of whether we first aggregate and then update or update each individual judgement and then aggregate, the final collective judgement stays the same.

Table 4 then illustrates the second learning iteration, in which, after having learned a, the individuals learn the falsehood of c (i.e. the truth of $\neg c$). Importantly, while the update on propositions that involve c (such as c, $a \wedge c$, $b \wedge c$, and $a \wedge b \wedge c$) drops to 0, the common ground is preserved: the judgments for a, c, and $a \wedge c$ remain identical over all individuals even after successive updates.

This *sequential decision-making process*—whereby new evidence is incorporated in stages while preserving the common ground—is a crucial aspect of our model. Not only does it demonstrate dynamic rationality (i.e. that the order of updating and aggregation does not affect the final collective judgment), but it also offers a promising approach to sequential collective decision-making, a topic that has received little attention in traditional judgment aggregation frameworks.

This perspective sheds new light on the significance of Theorem 2, which establishes that, on the restricted domain $\mathcal{D}_{\Phi}$, a linear aggregation rule achieves dynamic rationality for logically interconnected issues. Since our linear aggregation rule F satisfies consensus compatibility and independence (as shown in Theorem 1), our result demonstrates that—under these two constraints—a positive possibility for dynamically rational aggregation is attainable. It is important to note that Theorem 2 does not directly address the issues of dictatorship or oligarchy in the aggregation process. The collective outcome is determined by the individual weights assigned in the linear rule; hence, while the aggregation function could be dictatorial for certain weight choices, our result shows that non-dictatorial (and thus non-oligarchical) aggregation is possible with appropriate weight selection.

A key aspect of our model is the restricted domain $\mathcal{D}_{\Phi}$, which is justified by the notion of *fair learning*. Here, learning is deemed fair when group members can only update on propositions in the common ground $\Phi \subseteq X$, where all members have equal degrees of confidence (i.e., $\forall \phi \in \Phi$, $\forall i, j \in N : J_i(\phi) = J_j(\phi)$). Under fair learning, any Bayesian update on $\phi \in \Phi$ produces the same posterior shift in every individual's beliefs, thereby preserving dynamic rationality. Our epistemic notion of fairness is grounded in equal information processing, guaranteeing that no agent is advantaged or disadvantaged by newly received data.

It has been established in [10] that under standard aggregation axioms (e.g. universal domain, systematicity) no judgment aggregation rule can be dynamically rational with respect to any revision operator satisfying basic conditions on revision, if the propositions in the agenda are non-trivially interrelated. By contrast, when we recast the same agenda in our probabilistic framework – replacing "yes/no" verdicts with probability assignments over the logically interconnected propositions – and impose a common-ground domain restriction – weighted linear pooling both preserves collective coherence and commutes with Bayesian updating.

Thus, our result points out that impossibility theorems in dynamically rational judgment aggregation such as [10] arise when fair learning is absent – namely, when members begin with differing degrees of confidence. Our model not only supports fair learning but also underscores its necessity for maintaining rationality in dynamic collective decision-making.

Furthermore, while previous research (e.g., [11]) has shown that geometric pooling functions satisfy external Bayesianity and unanimity preservation, and [13] demonstrated that the linear opinion pool fails external Bayesianity unless it is dictatorial, our framework adopts a different perspective. In Theorem 2 we show that within our propositional probability logic framework, linear aggregation can be dynamically rational under suitable domain restrictions. This result does not conflict with earlier findings but rather highlights that linear averaging, when combined with our approach to belief updating, yields a dynamically rational aggregation rule – an insight that opens promising new avenues for research and applications in dynamic and sequential collective decision-making.

4 Concluding Remarks

Building on the implications of Theorem 2, we conclude that our framework generalizes classical judgment and preference aggregation approaches, offering new insights into dynamic and sequential collective decision-making. We demonstrated that under consensus compatibility and independence on a non-nested agenda, any aggregation rule must be linear. More importantly, when the domain is restricted to a common ground (i.e., under fair learning), dynamic rationality is achieved: Bayesian updating, whether performed before or after aggregation, yields the same collective judgment. A key contribution of our model is its emphasis on sequential decision-making, where common ground preservation across updates enables consistent multi-stage deliberation. Our result highlights the central role of fair learning in ensuring dynamic consistency and avoiding the impossibilities found in more general domains. While we do not directly address the normative choice of aggregation weights, our findings show that non-dictatorial and dynamically rational aggregation is possible under appropriate conditions.

Future work will explore relaxing the common ground assumption and extending our framework to more general classes of aggregation functions. We anticipate that our approach will not only enrich the theoretical foundations of collective decision-making but also inform practical applications in machine learning that require robust mechanisms for dynamically updating group beliefs.

Acknowledgements. Polina Gordienko gratefully acknowledges the support of the Friedrich-Ebert-Stiftung Academic Foundation. We would like to thank three anonymous referees for their helpful comments.

Disclosure of Interests. The authors have no competing interests to declare that are relevant to the content of this article.

References

1. Aczél, J., Wagner, C.: A characterization of weighted arithmetic means. SIAM J. Algebraic Discrete Methods **1**(3), 259–260 (1980)
2. Aczél, J., Wagner, C., Ng, C.T.: Aggregation theorems for allocation problems. SIAM J. Algebraic Discrete Methods **5**(1), 1–8 (1984)
3. Dietrich, F.: A generalised model of judgement aggregation. Soc. Choice Welfare **28**(4), 529–565 (2007)
4. Dietrich, F.: Aggregation theory and the relevance of some issues to others. J. Econ. Theory **160**, 463–493 (2015)
5. Dietrich, F.: Fully Bayesian aggregation. J. Econ. Theory **194**, 105255 (2021)
6. Dietrich, F., List, C.: Arrow's theorem in judgement aggregation. Soc. Choice Welfare **29**(1), 19–33 (2007)
7. Dietrich, F., List, C.: The aggregation of propositional attitudes: towards a general theory. Oxford Stud. Epistemology **3**, 215–234 (2010)
8. Dietrich, F., List, C.: Probabilistic opinion pooling. In: Hájek, A., Hitchcock, C. (eds.) Oxford Handbook of Probability and Philosophy. Oxford University Press, Oxford (2016)
9. Dietrich, F., List, C.: Probabilistic opinion pooling generalized. Part one: general agendas. Soc. Choice Welfare **48**(4), 747–786 (2017)
10. Dietrich, F., List, C.: Dynamically rational judgment aggregation. Soc. Choice Welf. **63**, 531–580 (2024)
11. Genest, C.: A characterization theorem for externally Bayesian groups. Ann. Stat. **12**(3), 1100–1105 (1984)
12. Genest, C.: Pooling operators with the marginalization property. Can. J. Stat. **12**(2), 153–163 (1984)
13. Genest, C., Zidek, J.: Combining probability distributions: a critique and an annotated bibliography. Stat. Sci. **1**(1), 114–135 (1986)
14. Jansen, C., Schollmeyer, G., Augustin, T.: A probabilistic evaluation framework for preference aggregation reflecting group homogeneity. Math. Soc. Sci. **96**, 49–62 (2018)
15. List, C.: The theory of judgement aggregation. Introductory Rev. Synthese **187**(1), 179–207 (2012)
16. List, C., Pettit, P.: Aggregating sets of judgements. An impossibility result. Econ. Philos. **18**(1), 89–110 (2002)
17. Madansky, A.: *Externally Bayesian Groups*, Technical report RM-4141-PR, RAND Corporation (1964)
18. McConway, K.J.: Marginalization and linear opinion pools. J. Am. Stat. Assoc. **76**(374), 410–414 (1981)
19. Mongin, P.: Factoring out the impossibility of logical aggregation. J. Econ. Theory **141**(1), 100–113 (2008)
20. Nehring, K., Pivato, M., Puppe, C.: The Condorcet set: majority voting over interconnected propositions. J. Econ. Theory, **151**(C), 268–303 (2014)
21. Nehring, K., Puppe, C.: The structure of strategy-proof social choice. Part I: general characterization and possibility results on median spaces. J. Econ. Theory, **135**(1), 269–305 (2007)

22. Nehring, K., Puppe, C.: Abstract Arrowian aggregation. J. Econ. Theory **145**(2), 467–494 (2010)
23. Pauly, M., van Hees, M.: Logical constraints on judgement aggregation. J. Philos. Log. **35**(6), 569–585 (2006)
24. Pivato, M.: Geometric models of consistent judgement aggregation. Soc. Choice Welfare **33**(4), 559–574 (2009)

Arithmetic Circuit Compilation Using Symbolic Probabilistic Inference and Indicator-Determined Buckets

Cory J. Butz[1(✉)], Camilla E. Lewis[1], Alejandro Santoscoy-Rivero[1], and Anders L. Madsen[2,3]

[1] University of Regina, Regina, SK S4S0A2, Canada
{cory.butz,cel806,asj799}@uregina.ca
[2] HUGIN EXPERT A/S, Aalborg, Denmark
anders@hugin.com
[3] Aalborg University, Aalborg, Denmark

Abstract. We propose compiling *Bayesian networks* (BNs) into *arithmetic circuits* (ACs) using *symbolic probabilistic inference* (SPI). Traditionally, ACs have been compiled from BNs using *variable elimination* (VE). A key advantage of SPI is its ability to combine product terms that VE would not. When the BN exhibits specific topological structures, SPI produces significantly smaller ACs than VE, addressing the core concern of circuit size in knowledge compilation. We also introduce the notion of *indicator-determined buckets* (IDBs) in ACs. These are sets of AC nodes that take on two exclusive values: zero or a fixed probability value. We present a method for identifying and leveraging them to construct more compact circuits. Experimental results on benchmark BNs demonstrate that combining SPI with IDB optimization yields a noticeable reduction in circuit size and in the time required for exact inference compared to inference using an AC compiled with VE.

Keywords: Arithmetic circuits · Symbolic probabilistic inference · Bayesian networks

1 Introduction

Probabilistic circuits (PCs) [6] are a broad term encompassing frameworks such as *arithmetic circuits* (ACs) [9], and equivalently [18], *sum-product networks* (SPNs) [17]. *Bayesian networks* (BNs) [10,12,16] are probabilistic graphical models that can be compiled into ACs for efficient inference. Inference time refers to the duration of propagation from the AC leaf nodes to the root after the indicators have been set. It does not include the time required to compile the AC. While exact marginal inference is linear in the size of the compiled AC (number of edges), circuit size can grow exponentially with the number of BN variables in the worst case. Special binary leaf nodes, referred to as *indicators*,

K. Sauerwald and M. Thimm (Eds.): ECSQARU 2025, LNAI 16099, pp. 191–204, 2026.
https://doi.org/10.1007/978-3-032-05134-9_14

are set per query, allowing or preventing the associated probability from contributing to the inference process. In particular, ACs remain important today as a recent rigorous empirical study [3] of eighteen techniques for computing a probabilistic graphical model's partition function showed that ACs solved the largest number of problems. Research continues today on optimizing AC inference, such as modifying the structure to run on GPUs [15].

Originally, ACs were compiled once from BNs and then reused for answering all future queries [4,8,9]. This process involves tracing the *variable elimination* (VE) inference algorithm [20]. Subsequently, they could also be indirectly compiled using logical optimizers [10]. Exploiting *determinism* [10] is also highly effective in simplifying an AC based on parameter-specific information such as 0/1 entries and equal parameters [5]. The above optimization techniques are incorporated into the ACE system [1], a state-of-the-art compiler that either compiles BNs using VE or represents BNs as logical formulas and then applies conditioning on these formulas. However, the inaugural choice of applying VE to compile ACs can be reconsidered.

In this paper, we propose directly compiling ACs from discrete BNs using *symbolic probabilistic inference* (SPI) [7,13], which is another BN inference algorithm [14]. The striking feature of SPI is that it is ideally suited for particular BN topologies, specifically those with nodes having two or more non-adjacent parents, known as *v-structures* [12], and can compile an AC with fewer nodes than when VE is applied. Second, we introduce the notion of *indicator-determined buckets* (IDBs) in an AC as those nodes that assume a predetermined value depending on a single indicator setting and can thereby be collapsed in the AC. Compared with VE without determinism, our preliminary experimental results on a set of BNs from the literature using randomly generated queries empirically show consistent noticeable improvements in size and time when exploiting SPI and IDBs. This paper will not consider determinism, as with the original VE compilation investigations.

The remainder of this paper is organized as follows. Background knowledge is reviewed in Sect. 2. Section 3 puts forth AC compilation with SPI. The introduction and exploitation of IDBs are established in Sect. 4. Section 5 describes experiments demonstrating the effectiveness of SPI and IDBs. Conclusions drawn and suggested future work are given in Sect. 6.

2 Background Knowledge

We briefly review *Bayesian networks* [16] and *arithmetic circuits* [10], referring the reader to [10] for a thorough discussion.

Variables will be denoted by uppercase letters from the start of the alphabet, and their values by lowercase letters. A *Bayesian network* (BN) consists of a *directed acyclic graph* (DAG) over a set of nodes (variables) U and a set of *conditional probability tables* (CPTs) $\{p(v_i|pa(v_i)) \mid v_i \in U\}$, where $\mathrm{pa}(v_i)$ denotes the parents (immediate predecessors) of v_i in the DAG. A CPT $p(v|pa(v_i))$ has the property that probabilities sum to one for each fixed configuration of $pa(v_i)$. The product of the BN CPTs is a joint probability distribution $p(U)$ over U.

One example BN is in Fig. 1 (i) over variables A, B, C, and D. The CPT probabilities are $p(a) = 0.1$, $p(b) = 0.15$, $p(c) = 0.2$, $p(d|a,b,c) = 0.25$, $p(d|a,b,\overline{c}) = 0.3$, $p(d|a,\overline{b},c) = 0.35$, $p(d|a,\overline{b},\overline{c}) = 0.4$, $p(d|\overline{a},b,c) = 0.42$, $p(d|\overline{a},\overline{b},c) = 0.44$, $p(d|\overline{a},b,\overline{c}) = 0.46$, and $p(d|\overline{a},\overline{b},\overline{c}) = 0.48$, where, without loss of generality, we assume binary variables and missing probabilities are determined from those given, for instance, $p(\overline{a}) = 0.9$.

(i) a v-structure BN. (ii) a BN to be compiled from [10].

Fig. 1. (i) a v-structure BN. (ii) a BN to be compiled from [10].

Let X, Y, Z be sets of variables. A *potential* [19] on X is a function ϕ over X such that $\phi(x) \geq 0$, for each configuration x in the domain of X. Shafer [19] calls the following property the *combination axiom*: if ϕ_1 is a potential on X and ϕ_2 is a potential on Y, then the marginalization of $\phi_1 \cdot \phi_2$ onto X is the same as ϕ_1 multiplied with the marginalization of ϕ_2 onto $X \cap Y$. For instance,

$$\sum_{Z} \phi_1(X,Y) \cdot \phi_2(Y,Z) \quad = \quad \phi_1(X,Y) \cdot \sum_{Z} \phi_2(Y,Z).$$

Variable elimination (VE) [20] eliminates a variable v_i from a set of probability potentials by multiplying together all potentials with v_i in the domain and then summing out v_i from the product. The order in which variables are eliminated is referred to as an *elimination order*, denoted π. *Bucket elimination* [11] organizes the CPTs of a BN into distinct buckets. Each bucket corresponds to a variable and contains exactly the probabilistic information required to eliminate that variable at the appropriate stage in the elimination process.

A BN can be compiled into an *arithmetic circuit* (AC) [10] (see §12.4.1) by eliminating all BN variables using VE. The circuit contains two types of leaf nodes: (i) *parameter nodes*, which represent the CPT entries of the BN, and (ii) *indicator nodes*, which are used to specify query variables. All non-leaf nodes are either multiplication or summation nodes, denoted $*(n, n')$ and $+(n, n')$, respectively, meaning that nodes n and n' are the two children of the said node.

Algorithm 1 states the method for compiling a BN into an AC using VE.

Algorithm 1: [10] Compile AC from a BN using VE following order π

Input: A BN $\mathcal{B}$, an elimination order π of the variables in $\mathcal{B}$
Output: An AC $\mathcal{C}$
foreach *CPT* $p(v_i|pa(v_i))$ *in* $\mathcal{B}$ **do**
  foreach *configuration* $v_i = \mu$ ***and*** $pa(v_i) = \omega$ **do**
    $\mathcal{C} \leftarrow *(I(v_i = \mu), p(v_i = \mu|pa(v_i) = \omega))$
$\mathcal{C} \leftarrow *(n, n')$ and $+(n, n')$ according to VE's elimination of all variables following π

Example 1. Let us run Algorithm 1 on the BN in Fig. 1 (i). The first step creates AC nodes: $n_1 = *(\mathbf{I}(\mathbf{a}), p(a))$ $n_2 = *(\mathbf{I}(\overline{\mathbf{a}}), p(\overline{a}))$ $n_3 = *(\mathbf{I}(\mathbf{b}), p(b))$ $n_4 = *(\mathbf{I}(\overline{\mathbf{b}}), p(\overline{b}))$, and similarly for $p(C)$ and $p(D|A, B, C)$, as illustrated in Fig. 2 where $\mathbf{I}(\mathbf{a})$ is illustrated as $\mathbf{a}$, for instance. The remainder of the AC construction adheres to VE's elimination of the variables following elimination order $\pi = (B, A, D, C)$ and is left to the reader to verify.

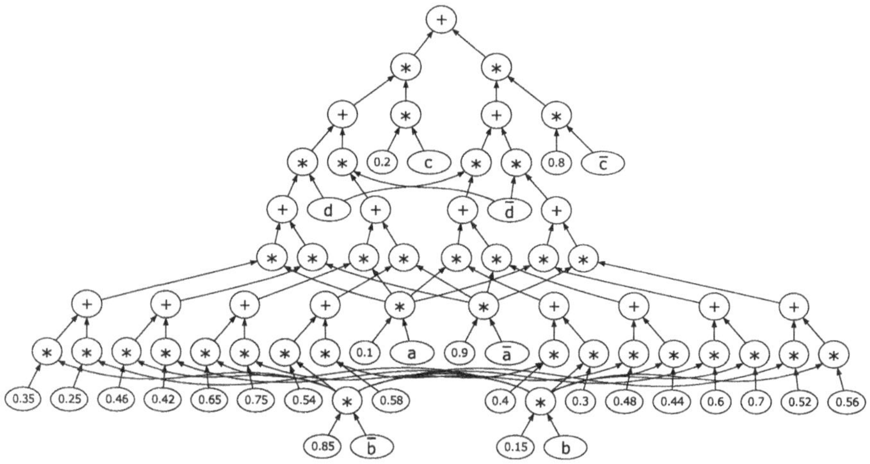

Fig. 2. The AC compiled from the BN in Fig. 1 (i) using Algorithm 1 (VE).

Example 2. More abstractly, VE could build the AC in Fig. 2 from the BN in Fig. 1 (i) using elimination order $\pi = (B, A, D, C)$ [1], by:

$$\sum_C \mathbf{I(C)} \cdot p(C) \cdot \sum_D \mathbf{I(D)} \cdot \sum_A \mathbf{I(A)} \cdot p(A) \cdot \sum_B \mathbf{I(B)} \cdot p(B) \cdot p(D|A, B, C), \quad (1)$$

where $\mathbf{I}(\mathbf{a})$ and $\mathbf{I}(\overline{\mathbf{a}})$, for instance, are denoted as $\mathbf{I}(\mathbf{A})$ for simplified notation.

We now review how AC inference is conducted for sets X and Y of variables. The marginal probability $p(X = x)$ can be computed with one upward pass. The conditional probability $p(X = x|Y = y)$ can be computed after two upward passes, namely, one for $p(X = x, Y = y)$ and another for $p(Y = y)$, followed by one division conducted after AC inference. A systematic downward pass, referred to as a *differentiation* pass, can efficiently compute many other marginal probabilities, including family marginals $p(v_i = \mu, pa(v_i) = \omega, X = x)$, with important applications to sensitivity analysis [9].

Inference can be run on an AC by setting all indicators incompatible with the query to 0 and the rest to 1. The indicator must not contradict (or be inconsistent with) the query to be compatible. Probability propagation is conducted across the entire network from the leaves to the root. The answer to a marginal query $p(X = x)$ is given as the value δ of the root node, i.e., $p(X = x) = \delta$.

Example 3. Consider answering the marginal query $p(d)$ posed to the AC in Fig. 2. Indicator $\mathbf{I}(\overline{\mathbf{d}})$ is set to 0 as it contradicts the query. All the other indicators are set to 1. Probability propagation then flows from the AC leaves to the root, performing numerical multiplication and summation as required.

3 Compiling ACs Using SPI

Here, we propose compiling BNs directly into ACs using an adjusted version of *symbolic probabilistic inference* (SPI), an inference algorithm that treats BN reasoning as a combinatorial optimization problem over potential functions [7, 13]. VE, which eliminates variables in a fixed order and relies heavily on the BN's graphical structure, SPI operates algebraically and selects the product of potentials that results in the smallest output dimension at each step.

This flexibility allows SPI to combine certain product terms earlier than VE, yielding multiplication combinations that VE would not compute—especially in the presence of v-structures, where nodes have two or more non-adjacent parents. To further leverage BN structure, we adjust SPI's heuristic to favour multiplying the smallest compatible potentials within the same bucket, particularly those involved in v-structures. This relaxed strategy yields more compact ACs compared to VE.

Example 4. Consider adjusting SPI to compile the BN in Fig. 1 (i) into an AC. SPI could compute the following, yielding the AC in Fig. 3:

$$\begin{aligned}
& \Sigma_A\ \Sigma_B\ \Sigma_C\ \Sigma_D\ \mathbf{I}(\mathbf{A}) \cdot p(A) \cdot \mathbf{I}(\mathbf{B}) \cdot p(B) \cdot \mathbf{I}(\mathbf{C}) \cdot p(C) \cdot \mathbf{I}(\mathbf{D}) \cdot p(D|ABC) \\
= {} & \Sigma_A\ \Sigma_B\ \Sigma_C\ \Sigma_D \phi(A) \cdot \phi(B) \cdot \phi(C) \cdot \mathbf{I}(\mathbf{D}) \cdot p(D|ABC) \\
= {} & \Sigma_A\ \Sigma_B\ \Sigma_C\ \Sigma_D \phi(AB) \cdot \phi(C) \cdot \mathbf{I}(\mathbf{D}) \cdot p(D|ABC) \\
= {} & \Sigma_A\ \Sigma_C\ \Sigma_D \phi(C) \cdot \mathbf{I}(\mathbf{D}) \cdot \Sigma_B \phi(ABCD) \\
= {} & \Sigma_C\ \Sigma_D \phi(C) \cdot \mathbf{I}(\mathbf{D}) \cdot \Sigma_A \phi(ACD) \\
= {} & \Sigma_C\ \phi(C) \cdot \Sigma_D\ \mathbf{I}(\mathbf{D}) \cdot \phi(CD) \\
= {} & \Sigma_C\ \phi(C) \cdot \Sigma_D\ \phi'(CD) \\
= {} & \Sigma_C\ \phi(C) \cdot \phi'(C) \\
= {} & \Sigma_C \phi''(C) \\
= {} & 1.
\end{aligned}$$

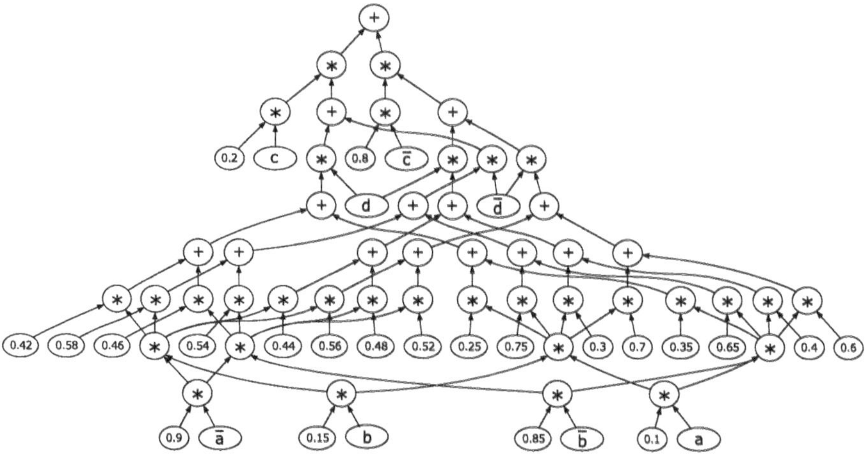

Fig. 3. The AC compiled from the BN in Fig. 1 (i) using SPI.

By taking the product $\phi(A) \cdot \phi(B)$, the key point from Example 4 is that the SPI AC in Fig. 3 contains four fewer multiplication nodes than the AC compiled using VE in Fig. 2. It is explicitly written in [4] that every operation saved makes the size of the resulting AC smaller, yielding more efficient inference.

4 Compressing ACs with Indicator-Determined Buckets

Here, we put forth a novel technique for compressing compiled ACs. This technique is especially effective when there is little to no determinism. Before introducing the central notions of a normal form AC and an indicator-determined bucket, let us first review how Algorithm 1 would build an AC in these situations.

Example 5. Consider the BN in Fig. 1 (ii) over binary variables A, B, C, and with CPT probabilities $p(a) = 0.8$, $p(b|\overline{a}) = 0.7$, $p(b|a) = 0.9$, $p(c|\overline{a}) = 0.2$, $p(c|a) = 0.6$, and using elimination order $\pi = (A, B, C)$. Because an indicator for variable v is immediately multiplied with the BN CPT for v, we have

$$\sum_C \sum_B \sum_A [\mathbf{I}(\mathbf{A}) \cdot p(A)] \cdot [\mathbf{I}(\mathbf{B}) \cdot p(B|A)] \cdot [\mathbf{I}(\mathbf{C}) \cdot p(C|A)]], \tag{2}$$

giving the AC in Fig. 4.

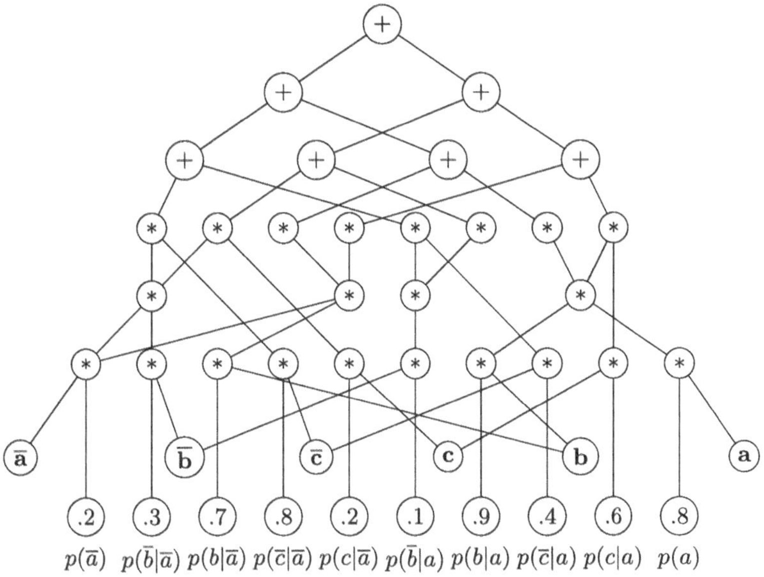

Fig. 4. The AC compiled from the BN in Fig. 1 (ii) using Algorithm 1 (VE).

We now introduce the key notion of normal form ACs.

Definition 1. *An AC for a given BN is in normal form if the last multiplication before the summation of variable v involves the indicator $I(v)$. That is, $I(v)$ is multiplied with the product of v's bucket as the last step prior to the marginalization of v.*

Every AC compiled from a BN using VE can be equivalently rewritten in normal form by applying the combination axiom and properties of multiplication.

Example 6. The AC in Example 5 can be rewritten in normal form by applying the combination axiom and properties of multiplication on Eq. (2):

$$\sum_{C} \mathbf{I(C)} \cdot \sum_{B} \mathbf{I(B)} \cdot \sum_{A} \mathbf{I(A)} \cdot [p(A) \cdot p(B|A) \cdot p(C|A)]. \qquad (3)$$

That is, the AC in Fig. 4 can be equivalently modified into normal form as illustrated in Fig. 5.

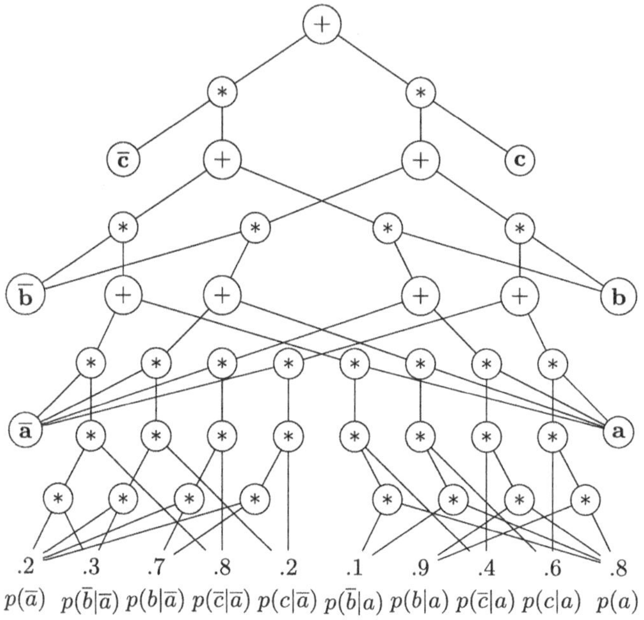

Fig. 5. Equivalently rewriting VE's AC in Fig. 4 into AC normal form.

We now introduce the fundamental notion of an indicator-determined bucket.

Definition 2. *Given a BN and an elimination order, uniquely assign the BN CPTs as bucket elimination prescribes for VE. If v does not appear in any CPT in any earlier bucket, the bucket for variable v is referred to as an* indicator-determined bucket *(IDB).*

Example 7. Given the elimination order $\pi = (A, B, C)$ for the BN in Fig. 1 (ii), to build an AC following Algorithm 1, bucket elimination would be initialized as follows:

$$A : [p(A), \mathbf{I(A)}, p(B|A), \mathbf{I(B)}, p(C|A), \mathbf{I(C)}],$$
$$B : [\,],$$
$$C : [\,].$$

Bucket A contains all three CPTs, while buckets B and C are empty. By definition, bucket A is an IDB.

The striking feature of an IDB is that its computation can be collapsed. The reason is that this AC computation gives either a zero or a constant, which, in turn, is entirely controlled by the value of the corresponding indicator. If the indicator is set to zero, this AC computation yields zero; otherwise, if the indicator is set to one, then this computation always yields the same constant.

Example 8. Regardless of how indicators are set for any given query, the computation $p(A) \cdot p(B|A) \cdot p(C|A)$ yields the constant $\phi(A, B, C)$ in the IDB for A in Example 7. Thus, the computation leading to $\phi(A, B, C)$ can then be replaced with the product itself, $\phi(A, B, C)$:

$$\sum_{C} \mathbf{I(C)} \cdot \sum_{B} \mathbf{I(B)} \cdot \sum_{A} \mathbf{I(A)} \cdot \phi(A, B, C). \tag{4}$$

Graphically, the normal form AC in Fig. 5 can be compressed as illustrated by the smaller AC in Fig. 6.

The important point in Example 8 is that the size of VE's AC in Fig. 4 has been reduced from 45 nodes down to 35 in Fig. 6 by requiring eight fewer multiplication nodes and two fewer probability nodes.

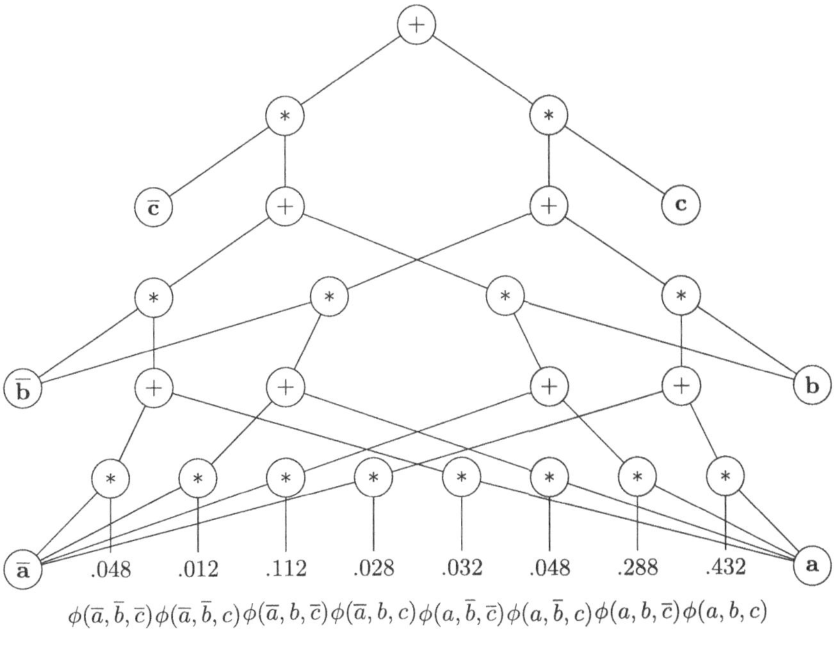

Fig. 6. Compressing the normal form AC in Fig. 5 by collapsing IDBs.

Algorithm 2 states a formal method for collapsing IDBs.

Algorithm 2: Normalize AC and Collapse IDBs

Input: A BN and an elimination order π
Output: An AC $\mathcal{C}$

1 Build an AC $\mathcal{C}$ using Algorithm 1 following π
2 Initialize bucket elimination uniquely following π
`/* Normalize the AC */`
3 **foreach** *outgoing edge* (S, N) *from a sum node* S **do**
4   Replace edge (S, N) with two edges $(S, *)$ and $(*, N)$
5   Add edge $(*, \mathbf{s})$ where $*$ is the introduced new vertex and $\mathbf{s}$ is the indicator for value s of S on edge (S, N)
6 Collapse adjacent multiplication nodes
7 Determine all IDBs
`/* Collapse all IDBs */`
8 **foreach** *IDB* $(v_i = \mu)$ **do**
9   Set all of $(v_i = \mu)$'s multiplication nodes to 1
10   **foreach** *probability node* p *of* $(v_i = \mu)$ **do**
11   **foreach** *parent multiplication node* m *of* p **do**
12             $m = m * p$
13   Delete edge (m, p)
14   Delete probability node p
15   **foreach** *multiplication node* m *of* $(v_i = \mu)$ **do**
16   Create a new leaf probability node n
17   Add edge (n, m)
18         $n = m$
19         $m = 1$

Example 9. Consider running Algorithm 2 on the AC in Fig. 4, which was constructed from the BN in Fig. 1 (ii) following elimination order $\pi = (A, B, C)$. Lines 3–6 provide the graphical operations to normalize this AC, yielding the normal form AC in Fig. 5. By Example 8, only bucket A is deterministic in line 7:

$$\overline{a} : [\mathbf{I}(\overline{\mathbf{a}}), p(\overline{a}), p(\overline{b}|\overline{a}), p(b|\overline{a}), p(\overline{c}|\overline{a}), p(c|\overline{a})],$$
$$a : [\mathbf{I}(\mathbf{a}), p(a), p(\overline{b}|a), p(b|a), p(\overline{c}|a), p(c|a)].$$

Lines 8–19 provide the graphical operations needed to collapse IDBs within the AC. Due to space limitations, we illustrate the effect of this graphical manipulation. Consider the IDB $(\overline{a})$ above. The probability value $p(\overline{a})$ is multiplied with the probability value $p(\overline{b}|\overline{a})$, i.e., 0.2 and 0.3 are multiplied, giving 0.06. This product value is then multiplied with the probability value $p(\overline{c}|\overline{a})$, that is, 0.06 times by 0.8, yielding 0.048. This deterministic value 0.048 is cached as a leaf node in AC in Fig. 6. The rest of the example follows similarly.

Lemma 1. *Algorithm 2 builds a sound AC from a given BN.*

Proof. Given a BN and an elimination order, Algorithm 1 constructs an AC with a leaf node for every indicator $\mathbf{I(v_i} = \mu)$ for every value of every variable v_i and a leaf node for every BN CPT probability. Line 3 of Algorithm 1 multiplies each indicator $\mathbf{I(v_i} = \mu)$ with each corresponding probability value $p(v_i = \mu|pa(v_i) = \omega)$. However, since multiplication is commutative and associative, multiplication can be done in any order. Thus, consider the multiplication as Algorithm 1 prescribes, but delay all multiplication with indicator nodes. By the combination axiom, the multiplication of every indicator node can be taken immediately before that variable's summation, that is, take each indicator multiplication as the last multiplication before summation. By definition, the organization of multiplication, sum, indicator, and probability nodes constitute a normal form AC. Furthermore, as the product of any two or more given BN CPT probabilities defines constants, these multiplications can be cached with their constant values. Therefore, the resultant AC root node value is unchanged.

Example 10. Recall how Algorithm 1 compiles an AC for the BN in Fig. 1 (ii) following elimination order $\pi = (A, B, C)$:

$$\sum_C \sum_B \sum_A [\mathbf{I(A)} \cdot p(A)] \cdot [\mathbf{I(B)} \cdot p(B|A)] \cdot [\mathbf{I(C)} \cdot p(C|A)]. \tag{5}$$

Since multiplication is commutative and associative, the parentheses can be omitted and the potentials rearranged:

$$\sum_C \sum_B \sum_A \mathbf{I(A)} \cdot \mathbf{I(B)} \cdot \mathbf{I(C)} \cdot p(A) \cdot p(B|A) \cdot p(C|A). \tag{6}$$

By the combination axiom [19], the indicators can be moved as follows:

$$\sum_C \mathbf{I(C)} \cdot \sum_B \mathbf{I(B)} \cdot \sum_A \mathbf{I(A)} \cdot p(A) \cdot p(B|A) \cdot p(C|A). \tag{7}$$

IDBs can then be collapsed as they yield constants:

$$\sum_C \mathbf{I(C)} \cdot \sum_B \mathbf{I(B)} \cdot \sum_A \mathbf{I(A)} \cdot \phi(A, B, C). \tag{8}$$

Lemma 1 ensures that a sound AC is constructed when exploiting IDBs. Henceforth, we compile ACs by utilizing SPI first, followed by collapsing IDBs, and denote this approach by SPI-IDB.

Theorem 1. *Given a BN, a sound AC is compiled by SPI-IDB.*

Proof. SPI is a sound inference algorithm [7,13]. Collapsing IDBs is correct as established in Lemma 1. As the techniques are applied sequentially, there is no conflict between the two methods. Thus, the claim immediately follows.

5 Experimental Analysis

In this section, we present a preliminary experimental analysis comparing AC construction methods using VE and SPI-IDB. The experiment involves eight BNs of different complexities taken from the literature [1]. The experimental analysis aims to investigate and compare the impact on circuit size and performance of using VE and SPI-IDB

Information on the 8 BNs can be found in Table 1 (columns one and two). Elimination orders were taken from prior work [2], ensuring comparison consistency.

The empirical evaluation was conducted on a laptop running Windows 11 Pro (version 23H2), equipped with a 3.3 GHz AMD Ryzen 5 5600H processor (six physical cores, twelve logical threads), integrated Radeon Graphics, and 64 GB of RAM. Computation time is measured as the elapsed (wall-clock) time in seconds and covers propagation from all leaf nodes to the root.

Table 1 also shows the AC size and inference time results. Circuit size results are given in columns three through five. Inference times for VE and SPI-IDB are provided in the last three columns. The average time is reported for answering a random query ten times. The query size is fixed at 5% of the VE circuit size, and an identical randomly generated query is used for both VE and SPI-IDB. The last column gives the time improvement as a percentage.

Table 1. Circuit size and inference time in seconds by VE and SPI-IDB.

BN	$\|U\|$	VE AC size	SPI-IDB AC size	Space savings	VE time	SPI-IDB time	Time savings
Water	32	12,807,648	12,515,924	2.28%	0.0472	0.0468	0.81%
Hepar2	70	8,480	8,293	2.21%	0.0061	0.0057	6.56%
Pathfinder	109	2,148,976	1,976,268	8.03%	0.0193	0.0176	8.81%
Pigs	441	1,160,578	1,078,246	7.09%	0.0373	0.0338	9.44%
Link	724	57,377,435	49,314,905	14.05%	0.3058	0.2473	19.12%
Munin2	1003	4,048,705	3,987,451	1.51%	0.0983	0.0892	9.31%
Munin3	1041	6,077,390	6,062,772	0.24%	0.1125	0.1121	0.39%
Munin4	1038	23,978,136	23,342,027	2.65%	0.1876	0.1702	9.28%

Inspection of the results in Table 1 reveals that SPI-IDB has a small but noticeable improvement over VE when constructing ACs from BNs. SPI-IDB always compiled smaller ACs without exception, ranging from 0.24% to 14.05%. Considering all networks, the ACs constructed by SPI-IDB were, on average. 4.73% smaller compared to VE. The inference time saved on SPI-IDB ACs ranged from 0.39% to 19.12% and averaged 7.97%.

Analysis of Table 1 reveals that circuit size compression does not necessarily result in a linear speedup for inference. This effect is likely due to the removal of predominantly multiplication nodes during the application of SPI and the collapsing of IDBs. Since multiplication can be a slower operation than addition, removing multiplication nodes is more important than eliminating other node types.

6 Conclusions

We proposed that SPI be used to compile BNs rather than VE. SPI and VE are competing approaches to BN inference [14]. One striking feature of SPI, compared to VE, is that SPI can take products that VE cannot. We have shown that SPI is especially effective in crafting smaller ACs when v-structures are present in the given BN. For example, the AC constructed by VE in Fig. 2 is larger than the SPI AC in Fig. 3.

We also propose identifying and collapsing certain portions of a compiled AC, which we refer to as *indicator-determined buckets* (IDBs). These sets of AC nodes take on two exclusive values: zero or a fixed probability value. Furthermore, each node value is determined entirely by an indicator node, which is set to zero or one depending on the input query. Thus, this fixed numeric computation does not need to be repeated every query and can instead be cached. For example, the AC in Fig. 4 constructed by VE can be equivalently modified to collapse IDBs by Algorithm 2 as depicted in the AC in Fig. 6. Lemma 1 formally establishes that this compression still yields a sound AC. The notions of SPI and IDBs taken together, denoted SPI-IDB, provide a sound approach to compiling BNs into ACs as guaranteed by Theorem 1.

Preliminary experimental results on eight real-world and benchmark BNs of various complexities show a consistent, noticeable compression on the size of the compiled ACs compared to using VE. In addition, the reported time savings of inference are slightly more substantial. Our analysis of these findings highlighted that SPI-IDBs tend to primarily remove multiplication nodes from an AC, which is beneficial as floating-point multiplication can be slower than floating-point addition.

Acknowledgments. This research was partially supported by the NSERC Discovery Grant Program (Grant No. 238880).

Disclosure of Interests. The authors declare that they have no known competing financial interests or personal relationships that could have appeared to influence the work reported in this paper.

References

1. Ace: Arithmetic circuit evaluator. http://reasoning.cs.ucla.edu/ace. Accessed 18 May 2025
2. Bayesian network repository. https://www.cs.huji.ac.il/~galel/Repository/. Accessed 18 May 2025

3. Agrawal, D., Pote, Y., Meel, K.: Partition function estimation: a quantitative study. In: Proceedings of the 30th International Joint Conference on Artificial Intelligence, pp. 4276–4285 (2021)
4. Chavira, M., Darwiche, A.: Compiling Bayesian networks using variable elimination. In: Proceedings of the 20th International Joint Conference on Artificial Intelligence, pp. 2443–2449 (2007)
5. Chen, Y., Darwiche, A.: Constrained identifiability of causal effects. arXiv preprint arXiv:2412.02869 (2024). https://arxiv.org/abs/2412.02869
6. Choi, Y., Vergari, A., Van den Broeck, G.: Probabilistic circuits: A unifying framework for tractable probabilistic models. Technical report UCLA (2020)
7. D'Ambrosio, B.: Symbolic probabilistic inference in belief networks. In: Proceedings of the Eleventh Annual Conference on UAI, pp. 98–107 (1989)
8. Darwiche, A.: A differential approach to inference in Bayesian networks. In: Proceedings of the 16th Conference on UAI, pp. 123–132 (2000)
9. Darwiche, A.: A differential approach to inference in Bayesian networks. J. ACM **50**(3), 280–305 (2003)
10. Darwiche, A.: Modeling and Reasoning with Bayesian Networks. Cambridge University Press, Los Angeles (2009)
11. Dechter, R.: Bucket elimination: a unifying framework for reasoning. In: Proceedings of the Twelfth Conference on UAI, pp. 211–219 (1996)
12. Koller, D., Friedman, N.: Probabilistic Graphical Models: Principles and Techniques. MIT Press, Cambridge (2009)
13. Li, Z., D'Ambrosio, B.: Efficient inference in Bayes networks as a combinatorial optimization problem. Int. J. Approximate Reasoning **11**(1), 55–81 (1994)
14. Madsen, A., Butz, C.: A comparison of different marginalization operations in simple propagation. In: European Conference on Symbolic and Quantitative Approaches to Reasoning with Uncertainty. LNCS, vol. 14208, pp. 172–182. Springer, Cham (2023). https://doi.org/10.1007/978-3-031-45608-4_14
15. Maene, J., Derkinderen, V., Zuidberg Dos Martires, P.: KLay: accelerating arithmetic circuits for neurosymbolic AI. In: Proceedings of the International Conference on Learning Representations (2025)
16. Pearl, J.: Probabilistic Reasoning in Intelligent Systems: Networks of Plausible Inference. Morgan Kaufmann, San Francisco (1988)
17. Poon, H., Domingos, P.: Sum-product networks: a new deep architecture. In: Proceedings of the Twenty-Seventh Conference on UAI, pp. 337–346 (2011)
18. Rooshenas, A., Lowd, D.: Learning sum-product networks with direct and indirect variable interactions. In: Proceedings of the Thirty-First International Conference on Machine Learning, pp. 710–718 (2014)
19. Shafer, G.: Probabilistic Expert Systems. Society for Industrial and Applied Mathematics, Philadelphia, PA, Philadelphia (1996)
20. Zhang, N., Poole, D.: A simple approach to Bayesian network computations. In: Proceedings of the Tenth Canadian Artificial Intelligence Conference, pp. 171–178 (1994)

Game Theory and Social Choice

Counting Agents in Partially Observable Stochastic Games

Nazlı Nur Karabulut(✉) and Tanya Braun

Computer Science Department, University of Münster, Münster, Germany
{nnur.karabulut,tanya.braun}@uni-muenster.de

Abstract. Multi-agent decision-making under uncertainty can be modelled using partially observable stochastic games (POSGs), with numerous agents, partial observability, stochastic dynamics, and individual goals. However, POSGs are notoriously difficult to solve due to their exponential dependence on the number of agents. In this work, we present counting POSGs using the lifting technique of counting to compactly encode symmetries in a POSG, which enables using representative policies. We exploit the encoding for a counting version of the multi-agent dynamic programming operator to solve such a POSG. Doing so reduces the exponential dependence on the number of agents to a polynomial one, making the problem tractable with respect to agent numbers.

1 Introduction

Multi-agent decision making is one of the most fundamental and challenging problems of artificial intelligence. Partially observable stochastic games (POSGs) formalise such problems, in which self-interested agents interact with an environment considered to be stationary and describable by a probabilistic transition model. The solution to a POSG is a set of policies, describing which actions to take to maximise agents' reward given their observation history. Solving a POSG is notoriously difficult, since the number of policies exponentially depends on the number of agents, i.e., the problem is intractable in the number of agents.

Over the years, researchers have worked on this scalability issue, focusing mainly on approximations [6,15,20,30,33] with few works on exact methods [18,19]. One way to make the problem tractable in the number of agents lies in making assumptions. So-called isomorphic POSGs use ideas from lifted probabilistic inference [26], assuming a partitioned agent set, where agents in each partition are considered *indistinguishable*, i.e., they share the same action and observation space, their behaviour is *symmetric* in the sense that permutations of their actions and observations lead to the same outcome, and the agents are conditionally independent within a partition [18]. These assumptions allow for working with representative agents in each partition, which is used in an adapted dynamic programming operator [14], reducing the model and runtime complexity to exponentially depend on the number of partitions instead, making the problem tractable in the number of agents assuming the number of partitions is much smaller than the number of agents.

K. Sauerwald and M. Thimm (Eds.): ECSQARU 2025, LNAI 16099, pp. 207–222, 2026.
https://doi.org/10.1007/978-3-032-05134-9_15

While the savings are impressive in isomorphic POSGs, the assumption of conditional independence is a strong one that highly restricts the expressivity of the POSG. Thus, in this paper, we present a fresh approach that no longer relies on the conditional independence assumption among agents, increasing the expressivity of the formalisation and its applicability in general. In particular, the contributions are twofold: (i) so-called counting POSGs that efficiently encode the symmetric behaviour of agents in a partition, which allows for counting representative policies in a partition, and (ii) a dynamic programming operator that works with counting POSGs. Using counting allows for reducing the model and runtime complexity to no longer exponentially depend on the number of agents but only polynomially, keeping the problem tractable in agent numbers (exponential in a horizon) while increasing the expressivity of the model compared to isomorphic POSGs. To the best of our knowledge, we are the first to apply counting to POSGs and demonstrate how it can be used.

The remainder of the paper is organised as follows: First, we recap POSGs, dynamic programming, and indistinguishability of agents. Then, we define counting POSGs and show how they allow for representative policies. Last, we present the counting dynamic programming operator and end on related work.

2 Preliminaries

In this section, we define POSGs and provide an overview of dynamic programming for POSGs as well as the assumptions for indistiguishability of agents. Definitions are based on [14,27], using a probabilistic inference lens: The state space is represented by a random variable S, which can take discrete values, referred to as range, $ran(S) = \{s_1, \ldots, s_n\}$. Actions form the range of so-called *decision random variables*. Assigning a variable V a value $v \in ran(V)$ is denoted as $V = v$ or v for short if V is clear from its context.

2.1 Partially Observable Stochastic Game

A POSG is a formal model designed to express interactions between a group of self-interested agents that each have their own reward function.

Definition 1. *A POSG M is a tuple $(\boldsymbol{I}, S, \boldsymbol{A}, \boldsymbol{O}, T, \boldsymbol{R})$, with*

- *$\boldsymbol{I}$ a set of N agents,*
- *S a random variable with a set of states as range,*
- *$\boldsymbol{A} = \{A_i\}_{i \in \boldsymbol{I}}$ a set of decision random variables A_i, each with a set of local actions as range, with $ran(\boldsymbol{A}) = \times_{i \in \boldsymbol{I}} ran(A_i)$ the set of* joint actions,
- *$\boldsymbol{O} = \{O_i\}_{i \in \boldsymbol{I}}$ a set of random variables O_i, each with a set of local observations as range, with $ran(\boldsymbol{O}) = \times_{i \in \boldsymbol{I}} ran(O_i)$ the set of* joint observations,
- *$T(S', S, \boldsymbol{A}, \boldsymbol{O}) = P(S', \boldsymbol{O} \mid S, \boldsymbol{A})$ a probability distribution denoting the probability of moving from state s with joint action $\boldsymbol{a}$ to state s' and making the joint observation $\boldsymbol{o}$, with $T(S_0, ., ., .) = P(S_0)$ referring to a state prior, and*

Algorithm 1. Multi-agent Dynamic Programming Operator

function MA-DP(set of policies Π_i^{t-1} for each agent $i \in \boldsymbol{I}$ with value vectors $\boldsymbol{V}_i^{t-1}$)
  $\Pi_i^t \leftarrow$ Perform exhaustive backup using Π_i^{t-1} for each agent $i \in \boldsymbol{I}$
  $\boldsymbol{V}_i^t \leftarrow$ Calculate new value vectors for each agent $i \in \boldsymbol{I}$
  while $\exists \pi_{i,j}^t \in \Pi_i^t$: Eq. (3) holds **do**
    $\Pi_i^t \leftarrow \Pi_i^t \setminus \{\pi_{i,j}^t\}$, $\boldsymbol{V}_i^t \leftarrow \boldsymbol{V}_i^t \setminus \{v_{i,j}^t\}$
  return $\{(\Pi_i^t, \boldsymbol{V}_i^t)\}_{i \in \boldsymbol{I}}$

- $\boldsymbol{R} = \{R_i(S, \boldsymbol{A})\}_{i \in \boldsymbol{I}}$ *a set of reward functions.*

We call T transition function. Optional are a finite horizon τ and a discount factor $\gamma \in [0,1]$ (default 1). With subscript $t_s{:}t_e$ denoting a sequence over a discrete time interval $[t_s, t_e]$, each agent $i \in \boldsymbol{I}$ has a local policy $\pi_i : ran((O_{i,0:t})) \mapsto ran(A_i)$ mapping observation histories $o_{i,0:t}, t \leq \tau - 1$, to actions a, with $\boldsymbol{\pi} = (\pi_i)_{i \in \boldsymbol{I}}$ a joint policy. *The set of policies for agent i is denoted by Π_i. Subscript $-i$ refers to a set or sequence of elements over all agents except i. $E_i \circ E_{-i}$ denotes adding an element E_i to a sequence of elements E_{-i} at the fitting position.*

We consider rooted trees as a local policy's representation with actions as nodes and observations as edge labels (see Fig. 1). An agent's belief $b_i(s, \boldsymbol{\pi}_{-i})$ is a probability distribution over the state space $ran(S)$ and the other agents' policies $\boldsymbol{\Pi}_{-i}$. The value V_i of b_i is defined by

$$V_i(b_i) = \max_{\pi_i \in \Pi_i} \sum_{s \in ran(S)} \sum_{\boldsymbol{\pi}_{-i} \in \boldsymbol{\Pi}_{-i}} b_i(s, \boldsymbol{\pi}_{-i}) V_i'(s, \pi_i \circ \boldsymbol{\pi}_{-i}) \tag{1}$$

where $V_i'(s, \pi_i \circ \boldsymbol{\pi}_{-i})$ refers to the value of acting according to joint policy $\boldsymbol{\pi} = \pi_i \circ \boldsymbol{\pi}_{-i}$ in state s:

$$V_i'(s, \boldsymbol{\pi}) = R_i(s, \boldsymbol{\pi}(\emptyset)) + \gamma \sum_{s' \in ran(S)} \sum_{\boldsymbol{o} \in \boldsymbol{O}} T(s', s, \boldsymbol{\pi}(\emptyset), \boldsymbol{o}) V_i'(s', \boldsymbol{\pi}.\boldsymbol{o}) \tag{2}$$

with $\boldsymbol{\pi}(\emptyset)$ denoting the joint action at the roots of the policy trees in $\boldsymbol{\pi}$ and $\boldsymbol{\pi}.\boldsymbol{o}$ denoting the remaining policy after observing $\boldsymbol{o}$. The next section summarises dynamic programming as a solution method for POSGs.

2.2 Dynamic Programming for POSGs

Since it is not possible to describe what an optimal policy in a POSG is, solution methods usually aim for a Nash equilibrium [24]. One such method combines pruning and dynamic programming [14] in a dynamic programming operator to solve a POSG with horizon τ, which keeps, for each agent, a set of policies that yield a maximum reward in some state given the policies of the other agents.

Algorithm 1 shows the dynamic programming operator. It takes a set of policies $\Pi_i^{t-1} = \{\pi_{i,j}^{t-1}\}_{j=1}^m$ of depth $t-1$ for each agent i. For each policy, there exists a value vector $v_{i,j}^{t-1}$ that denotes the value of that policy in each possible combination of state $s \in ran(S)$ and policies of the other agents $\boldsymbol{\pi}_{-i} \in \boldsymbol{\Pi}_{-i}^{t-1}$. We denote the set of corresponding value vectors by $\boldsymbol{V}_i^{t-1}$. The first step is called exhaustive backup, generating all possible policies of depth t given the policies of depth $t-1$, expanding all existing policies with all possible combinations of observations and actions. Then, the value of each policy of each agent is calculated. The last step is pruning, which involves finding policies that are very weakly dominated by other policies, meaning that over the complete space of $S \times \boldsymbol{\Pi}_{-i}^t$ there is always another policy with higher value. Formally, a policy $\pi_{i,j}^t$ is pruned if the following holds, which can be solved using a linear programme:

$$\forall s \in ran(S), \boldsymbol{\pi}_{-i}^t \in \boldsymbol{\Pi}_{-i}^t \exists \pi_{i,j'}^t \in \Pi_i^t : V_i'(s, \pi_{i,j}^t \circ \boldsymbol{\pi}_{-i}^t) \leq V_i'(s, \pi_{i,j'}^t \circ \boldsymbol{\pi}_{-i}^t), \quad (3)$$

The operator is called repeatedly with the set of policies previously returned as inputs until τ is reached.

2.3 Tractability Through Indistinguishability of Agents

POSGs are intractable in the number of agents due to their exponential dependence. One way to tame POSGs is by assuming a partitioned agent set, in which the agents of each partition are indistinguishable, which is based on three assumptions: The first assumption is a prerequisite, in which available actions, observations, and the reward function are the same for all agents in a partition:

$$ran(A_i) = ran(A_j) \wedge ran(O_i) = ran(O_j) \wedge R_i = R_j \quad (4)$$

The second assumption is that the transition function T and the reward functions R_i are symmetric, meaning that exchanging actions or observations between agents of a partition has no effect on the results of both transition and reward, which can be formally expressed for two agents as:

$$\begin{aligned} \forall \boldsymbol{a} \in ran(\boldsymbol{A}), \boldsymbol{a} = (a_i, a_j, \boldsymbol{a}_{-i,-j}), \boldsymbol{o} \in ran(\boldsymbol{O}), \boldsymbol{o} = (o_i, o_j, \boldsymbol{o}_{-i,-j}) : \\ T(s', s, a_i, a_j, \boldsymbol{a}_{-i,-j}, \boldsymbol{o}) = T(s', s, a_j, a_i, \boldsymbol{a}_{-i,-j}, \boldsymbol{o}) \\ T(s', s, \boldsymbol{a}, o_i, o_j, \boldsymbol{o}_{-i,-j}) = T(s', s, \boldsymbol{a}, o_j, o_i, \boldsymbol{o}_{-i,-j}) \\ R_h(s, a_i, a_j, \boldsymbol{a}_{-i,-j}) = R_h(s, a_j, a_i, \boldsymbol{a}_{-i,-j}), h \in \{i, j\} \end{aligned} \quad (5)$$

The third assumption regards conditional independence between agents of a partition. If two indistinguishable agents $i, j \in \boldsymbol{I}$ are conditionally independent, then actions a_i, a_j (observations o_i, o_j) are conditionally independent given the state and observations of other agents, which allows for factorising the transition and reward functions into factors and summands for each agent. Moreover, together with the second assumption, one can show that the factors and summands are identical for all agents of a partition. Thus, one can define a so-called isomorphic POSG, which is a highly compact encoding of a POSG, independent of the number of agents in its model complexity, and allows for using representative agents during computations for each partition, allowing for tractability. Please refer to [18] for more details including proofs.

The downside of this complexity reduction is the rather strict assumption of conditional independence among agents of a partition, which also means that certain interactions between agents of a partition cannot be modelled. Thus, in this paper, we lift the third assumption and present a counting POSG based on the first two assumptions.

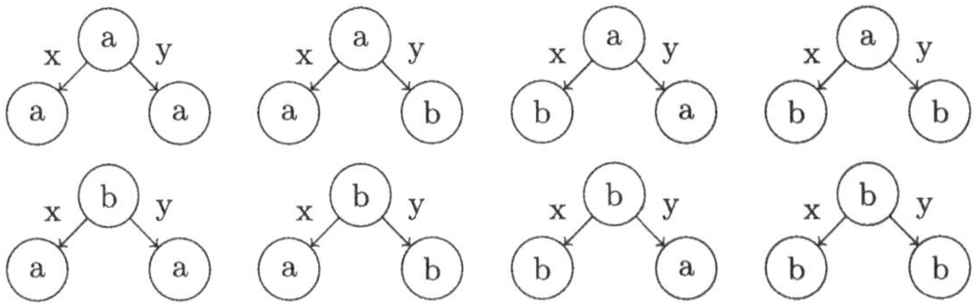

Fig. 1. Policies at horizon 1 available to agents with actions a, b and observations x, y

3 Counting POSGs

This section presents counting POSGs, which have Eq. (4) and Eq. (5) as fundamental assumptions, but first, we provide an intuition about counting in POSGs.

3.1 An Intuition About Counting in POSGs

Symmetric behaviour, formalised in Eq. (5), means that permutations of the same number of actions and observations within a partition map to the same probability or reward. To make that more clear, let us look at a small example: Imagine that there are $N = 12$ symmetric agents with two actions available, where 8 agents perform one action and the remaining 4 perform the other action. Then, there exist $\binom{12}{8} = \frac{12!}{8! \cdot 4!} = 495$ ways to get the 12 agents to perform the two actions, all leading to the same outcome (refer to [23] for details). As a result, for these input permutations, the transition and reward functions map to identical values, which is what Eq. (5) formalises. We can use a histogram that carries the counts of how many agents perform which action to encode this symmetric behaviour efficiently in the transition and reward function, i.e., $[4, 8]$. We can replace the 12 individual actions with this histogram, for all 495 mappings, meaning that these mappings become one.

Another effect of the same action and observation space as required in Eq. (4) is that these agents have the same possible policies available to them. Continuing the above example and assuming two possible observations, each of the 12 agents has 8 policies available to them at step $t = 1$, see Fig. 1. These 8 policies can be used as *representative policies* at $t = 1$, where we do not need to track, which agent follows which particular policy, only how many agents follow which policy. Again, this can be encoded using a histogram: All agents following the first policy is encoded by $[12, 0, 0, 0, 0, 0, 0, 0]$. One agent following the second policy while the other follow the first one is encoded by $[11, 1, 0, 0, 0, 0, 0, 0]$, which immensely reduces the number of joint policies to consider.

To summarise, due to the symmetric behaviour, we can count actions and observation as well as policies, moving the focus from individual agents to whole partitions of agents, in which we count agents' actions, observations, and policies, to store in histograms. Next, we formally define counting POSGs.

3.2 Definition of Counting POSGs

A counting POSG is a POSG with a partitioned agent set, in which each partition fulfils Eqs. (4) and (5). To formally define counting POSGs, we define histograms first, which equals distributing n balls (agents) into m urns (actions, observations, policies). Afterwards, we show that a counting POSG is equivalent to a *ground* POSG that fulfils Eqs. (4) and (5). To distinguish standard random variables from variables with histograms as range on a syntactic level, we use so-called counting random variables [23] for the latter.

Definition 2. *Given a set of n agents $\boldsymbol{I}$ and a set of m values $\boldsymbol{v}$ (actions, observations, policies), a* histogram *is given by $\{(v_l, n_l)\}_{l=1}^m$, with $\sum_{l=1}^m n_l = n$ and $v_l \in \boldsymbol{v}$. The shorthand notation is $[n_1, \dots, n_m]$ if $\boldsymbol{v}$ is clear from context. A* counting random variable *is a syntactic construct $\#_{\boldsymbol{I}}[V]$ with histograms $\{(v_l, n_l)\}_{l=1}^m$ that fulfil $\sum_l n_l = |\boldsymbol{I}|$ as ranges where $ran(V) = \boldsymbol{v}$.*

Definition 3. *A* counting POSG *$\bar{M}$ is a tuple $(\bar{\boldsymbol{I}}, \bar{S}, \bar{\boldsymbol{A}}, \bar{\boldsymbol{O}}, \bar{T}, \bar{\boldsymbol{R}})$, with*

- *$\bar{\boldsymbol{I}}$ a* partitioning *$\{\mathfrak{I}_k\}_{k=1}^K$ of N agents, $n_k = |\mathfrak{I}_k|$ and $|\bar{\boldsymbol{I}}| = \sum_k n_k = N$,*
- *$\bar{S}$ a random variable with a set of states as range as in Definition 1,*
- *$\bar{\boldsymbol{A}} = \{A_k\}_{k=1}^K$ a set of decision random variables A_k, one for each k,*
- *$\bar{\boldsymbol{O}} = \{O_k\}_{k=1}^K$ a set of random variables O_k, one for each k,*
- *$\bar{T} = \bar{T}(\bar{S}, \bar{S}', \#_{\mathfrak{I}_1}[A_1], \dots, \#_{\mathfrak{I}_K}[A_K], \#_{\mathfrak{I}_1}[O_1], \dots, \#_{\mathfrak{I}_K}[O_K])$ a transition function with counted actions and observations, and*
- *$\bar{\boldsymbol{R}} = \{R_k(\bar{S}, \#_{\mathfrak{I}_1}[A_1], \dots, \#_{\mathfrak{I}_K}[A_K]\}_{k=1}^K$ a set of reward functions.*

Theorem 1. *A counting POSG $\bar{M}$ is equivalent to a ground POSG M that fulfils Eqs. (4) and (5).*

Proof. A POSG $M = (\boldsymbol{I}, S, \boldsymbol{A}, \boldsymbol{O}, T, \boldsymbol{R})$ that fulfils Eqs. (4) and (5) can be turned into a counting POSG $\bar{M} = (\bar{\boldsymbol{I}}, \bar{\boldsymbol{S}}, \bar{\boldsymbol{A}}, \bar{\boldsymbol{O}}, \bar{T}, \bar{\boldsymbol{R}})$ by setting (i) for each k: $\mathfrak{I}_k = \{i, j \mid i, j \in \boldsymbol{I}, A_i = A_j, O_i = O_j, R_i = R_j, \text{Eq. (5) holds for } i, j\}$, $n_k = |\mathfrak{I}_k|$, (ii) $\bar{S} = S$, (iii) $\bar{\boldsymbol{A}} = \{A_k\}_{k=1}^K, A_k = A_i, i \in \mathfrak{I}_k$ (any i suffices), (iv) $\bar{\boldsymbol{O}} = \{O_k\}_{k=1}^K, O_k = O_i, i \in \mathfrak{I}_k$ (any i suffices), (v) $\bar{T} = T$, and (vi) $\bar{\boldsymbol{R}} = \{R_k\}_{k=1}^K, R_k = R_i, i \in \mathfrak{I}_k$ (any i suffices). The last two items do not yet encode the symmetric behaviour of Eq. (5) efficiently in counting random variables. To transform $\bar{T}$ and the R_k's into counting versions, we need to count the actions and observations in their mappings from input assignments to output and encode them in histograms, transforming the set of random variables

$\boldsymbol{A}_k = \{A_{k,1}, \ldots, A_{k,n_k}\}$, which have the same range values $ran(A_k)$ per Eq. (4), for each partition k into counting random variables $\#_{\mathfrak{I}_k}[A_k]$ in the inputs: Specifically, for each assignment $\boldsymbol{a}_k \in ran(\boldsymbol{A}_k)$, we count how often each range value $a_k \in ran(A_k)$ occurs in $\boldsymbol{a}_k$, building a histogram h_k of Definition 2 with $\boldsymbol{v} = ran(A_k)$ and $n = n_k$. We replace the inputs $\boldsymbol{A}_k$ with a single input $\#_{\mathfrak{I}_k}[A_k]$. Then, for each unique histogram h_k, we collect all assignments $\boldsymbol{a}_k \in ran(\boldsymbol{A}_k)$ yielding this histogram h_k and replace all mappings in $\bar{T}$ and R_k containing $\boldsymbol{a}_k$ with a mapping containing h_k, mapping to the same number as before. The same has to be done for observations $\boldsymbol{O}$. Doing so for each k leads to $\bar{T}$ and $\boldsymbol{R}$ of Definition 3.

Turning a counting POSG $\bar{M}$ into a POSG M essentially reverses the steps as given above: (i) $\boldsymbol{I} = \bigcup_{k=1}^{K} \mathfrak{I}_k$, (ii) $S = \bar{S}$, (iii) $\boldsymbol{A} = \bigcup_{k=1}^{K} \bigcup_{i \in \mathfrak{I}_k} \{A_{k,i}\}$, (iv) $\boldsymbol{O} = \bigcup_{k=1}^{K} \bigcup_{i \in \mathfrak{I}_k} \{O_{k,i}\}$, and (v) for each $k \in \{1, \ldots, K\}$, for all agents $i \in \mathfrak{I}_k$, $R_i = R_{k,i}$, with the last three items fulfilling Eq. (4). Regarding Eq. (5), we basically need to expand the counting random variables $\#_{\boldsymbol{I}_k}[A_k]$, which encode the agents of whole partitions, back into sets of random variables $\boldsymbol{A}_k = A_{k,1}, \ldots, A_{k,n_k}$, in $\bar{T}$ and $\bar{\boldsymbol{R}}$, in a way grounding the histograms. To do so, for each k, we replace the counting random variable $\#_{\mathfrak{I}_k}[A_k]$ with its set of random variables $\boldsymbol{A}_k$ it represents as inputs in T and $R_{k,i}$ (for all i). Then, we replace each mapping from h_k with a set of mappings from $\boldsymbol{a}_k$ to the same number as before, where the $\boldsymbol{a}_k$ yield h_k. Again, the same has to be done for the observations. This leads to a POSG of Definition 1 exhibiting the symmetry of Eq. (5) by construction. □

Theorem 1 means that the solutions of a counting POSG and its equivalent ground POSG are equivalent, with a counting POSG having a more compact encoding. Before we show how we can use the more compact encoding for more efficient calculations, we consider the model complexity of counting POSGs. We assume a fixed action and observation space and partition number as well as a much smaller number of partitions than number of agents, i.e., $K \ll N$.

Theorem 2. *The model complexity of a counting POSG $\bar{M}$ is polynomial in N.*

Proof. The histogram space of a counting random variable for partition k of size n_k has size $\binom{n_k+m-1}{m-1}$, which is bounded by n_k^m [23]. As we assume K is fixed and does not grow with the number of agents N, and that $K \ll N$, n and N have the same order of magnitude, thus, $n_k^m \leq N^m$. As such, due to the range sizes of their inputs, the sizes of the functions $\bar{T}$ and $\{R_k\}_{k=1}^{K}$ lie in $O(s^2 N^{Ka} N^{Ko})$ and $O(KsN^{Ka})$ with $s = |ran(S)|$, $a = \max_{i \in \boldsymbol{I}} |ran(A_i)|$, and $o = \max_{i \in \boldsymbol{I}} |ran(O_i)|$, making the dependence polynomial in N. □

In comparison, in the isomorphic case, we have an additional assumption, conditional independence, which leads to being able to use a representative *agent*. As such, the model complexity does not change with the number of agents N because each partition is represented by a representative agent, i.e., the dependence is exponential in K but independent of N. However, by releasing this assumption, it is necessary to keep track of the number of agents performing an action (or observation/policy) within each partition. As a result, the model can express more complex behaviour by being able to encode interactions between agents of the same partition but pays for it with a polynomial dependence on the number of agents. Thus, while isomorphic POSGs provide a simple representation, counting POSGs offer a more expressive modelling that results in a more computationally challenging structure that one needs to deal with during value computations as seen next.

3.3 Representative Policies

In this section, we show that we can use representative policies per partition and a policy space made of histograms for computing Eqs. (1) and (2) efficiently.

The set of policies for any two agents i, j of a partition k are built from the same set of actions $A_i = A_j = A_k$ and observations $O_i = O_j = O_k$, i.e., $\forall i, j \in \mathfrak{I}_k : \Pi_i = \Pi_j$. We refer to this set of policies as *representative policies* Π_k of partition k. In addition, these policies also carry the same value given the same state and policies of the other agents if policies are simply exchanged between agents of a partition. We first derive the counted value computation using representative policies before arguing for its correctness. We define the counted policy space using histograms of Definition 2 with $\boldsymbol{v} = \Pi_k$ and $n = n_k$:

Definition 4. *For a partition k of size n_k, the* counted policy space *H_k is given by all histograms $\{h_l\}_l^L$, $L = \binom{n_k+J-1}{J-1}$, with $h_l = \{(\pi_j, m_j)\}_{j=1}^J$ where $\pi_j \in \Pi_k$ and $J = |\Pi_k|$, such that $\sum_{j=1}^J m_j = n_k$. $\boldsymbol{H} = \times_{k=1}^K H_k$ denotes the counted joint policy space over all partitions, $\boldsymbol{H}_{-k} = \times_{l \neq k} H_l$ the counted policy space over all other partitions, and $\boldsymbol{H}_{-i}$ the counted policy space over all agents without some agent i of partition k, which is given by $H_k' \times \boldsymbol{H}_{-k}$, with H_k' equal to H_k but with $n_k - 1$ instead of n_k to account for one agent less.*

An element of $\boldsymbol{H}$ is a sequence of histograms, one for each partition, compactly encoding a joint policy as a *counted joint policy*. The value of an agent's belief $b_k(s, \boldsymbol{h}_{-i})$ in a partition k is a distribution over the state space $ran(S)$ and the counted policy space of the other agents $\boldsymbol{H}_{-i}$:

$$V_k^{\#}(b_k) = \max_{\pi_k \in \Pi_k} \sum_{s \in ran(S)} \sum_{\boldsymbol{h}_{-i} \in \boldsymbol{H}_{-i}} b_k(s, h_{-i}) V_k'^{\#}(s, \pi_k \oplus \boldsymbol{h}_{-i}) \tag{6}$$

with $\pi_k \oplus \boldsymbol{h}_{-i}$ denoting the addition of policy π_k to the corresponding count in the histogram of partition k in $\boldsymbol{h}_{-i}$, yielding a counted joint policy $\boldsymbol{h}$. Computing the value of a counted joint policy $\boldsymbol{h}$ in partition k needs to be adapted to a larger degree to be able to work with histograms. There are three items to consider: First, the R_i in Eq. (2) becomes R_k in the adapted equation with action histograms as inputs next to the state. The same holds for T becoming $\bar{T}$. We need to compute action histograms out of $\boldsymbol{h}$ for the actions that are carried out first. For a partition k with histogram $\{(\pi_j, m_j)\}_{j=1}^J$ in $\boldsymbol{h}$, the resulting action histogram $h_a = \{(a_l, m_l)\}_{l=1}^{|ran(A_k)|}$, $\sum_{l=1}^{|ran(A_k)|} m_l = n_k$ is given by

$$m_l = \sum_{\pi_j \in \Pi_k} m_j \mid \pi_j(\emptyset) = a_l. \tag{7}$$

That is, we add for each policy that starts with action a_l in the root the respective count in the policy histogram. Analogous to $\boldsymbol{\pi}(\emptyset)$ in Eq. (2), we use $\boldsymbol{h}(\emptyset)$ to denote this sequence of histograms of root actions in the policies of $\boldsymbol{h}$.

Second, for the recursive call to $V_k'^{\#}$ in the sum over joint observations, we need to find the counted joint policy of depth -1 given a joint observation. In the ground case, the joint observation specifies for each agent, which edge to follow from the root action to yield the subtrees that make up the joint policy of depth -1. With histograms, we no longer have this one-to-one correspondence between policy trees and observations. Therefore, we need to know for each policy π_j in a policy histogram $\{(\pi_j, m_j)\}_{j=1}^{J}$ for a partition k how many agents have which observation. Given observation counts for each π_j, we can determine how many agents follow which subtree for each π_j. Due to the Markov assumption, we do not need to keep track what agents did and observed as a consequence and thus can merge the subtree counts into one histogram for the whole partition again, building the fitting policy histogram of depth -1 by counting how many agents follow which subtree over all representative policies of partition k Given a policy histogram $\{(\pi_j, m_j)\}_{j=1}^{J}$ for a partition k, the joint observation part for k is encoded by a set of observation histograms $\boldsymbol{h}_k^o$, one histogram h_{k,π_j}^o for each representative policy π_j in k, i.e., $h_{k,\pi_j}^o = \{(o_j, n_j)\}_{j=1}^{|ran(O_k)|}$, with the counts n_j adding up to m_j. Thus, the sum over joint observations iterates over observation histograms for each policy count for each partition. We use $\boldsymbol{H}^o$ to denote this space of histograms over all partitions and representative policies in each partition and in analogy to the syntax used in Eq. (2) use $\boldsymbol{h}.\boldsymbol{h}^o$ to denote the policy histogram that emerges out of following $\boldsymbol{h}^o$ in $\boldsymbol{h}$.

The third item to consider is a consequence of the second one: With a joint observation encoded in histograms over representative policies per partition, we need to form an observation histogram on partition level as input for $\bar{T}$. Here, we need to take the set of observation histograms $\boldsymbol{h}_k^o$ per partition and, for the new histogram $h_k^{\#o} = \{(o_j, n_j')\}_{j=1}^{|ran(O_k)|}$ to use as input to $\bar{T}$, add up the counts n_j in the different histograms of $\boldsymbol{h}_k^o$ for each o_j to get n_j'. Taking these three items together, Eq. (2) becomes

$$V_k'^{\#}(s, \boldsymbol{h}) = R_k(s, \boldsymbol{h}(\emptyset)) + \gamma \sum_{s' \in ran(S)} \sum_{\boldsymbol{h}^o \in \boldsymbol{H}^o} T(s', s, \boldsymbol{h}(\emptyset), \boldsymbol{h}^{\#o}) V_k'^{\#}(s', \boldsymbol{h}.\boldsymbol{h}^o). \tag{8}$$

Given this derivation, we argue that V_i' and $V_k'^{\#}$ compute the same value:

Theorem 3. *Given a counting POSG $\bar{M}$ with a counted joint policy $\boldsymbol{h}$ and the equivalent ground POSG M with joint policy $\boldsymbol{\pi}$, $V_k'^{\#}(s, \boldsymbol{h}) = V_i'(s, \boldsymbol{\pi})$.*

Proof. Since there is a direct correspondence between the counted versions of joint policies, joint observations, and joint actions in histograms and their ground counterparts as inputs to $V_k'^{\#}$ and V_i' respectively as well as Eq. (5) meaning that in the ground version, permutations of an input map to the same output, which makes $\bar{T}$ and T as well as $\boldsymbol{R}$ and $\bar{\boldsymbol{R}}$ equivalent as shown in Theorem 1, $V_k'^{\#}$ and V_i' compute the same value. □

This counted computation allows for saving redundancy when calculating policy values and using the compact encoding of the transition and reward functions without having to ground the functions or the joint inputs at any point.

Note 1. The number of counted observations in Eq. (8) no longer depends exponentially on the number of agents.

With Theorem 3, we also know that we can compute policy values for representative policies of each partition and do not need to compute policy values for each agent, which leads to a reduction in the number of joint policies. Again, we assume the action and observation space and number of partitions to be fixed. An exponential dependence on the horizon is still present.

Corollary 1. *Since $V_k'^{\#} = V_i'$, it holds for two agents i, j of partition k that $V_k'^{\#}(s, \pi_k \oplus \boldsymbol{h}_{-i}) = V_i'(s, \pi_k \circ \boldsymbol{\pi}_{-i}) = V_j'(s, \pi_k \circ \boldsymbol{\pi}_{-j})$, which allows for computing $V_k'^{\#}$ on a representative policy level for each partition instead of each agent.*

Theorem 4. *The number of counted policies in a counting POSG $\bar{M}$ is polynomial in the number of agents N.*

Proof. The number of representative policies for each partition is $|\Pi_k| = \frac{a^{(o^T-1)}}{(o-1)}$ [24]. As a histogram can be used to compactly encode a joint policy if the agents exhibit symmetric behaviour, the number of histograms is given by

$$\binom{n_k + |\Pi_k| - 1}{|\Pi_k| - 1} = \binom{n_k + a^{\frac{o^T-1}{o-1}} - 1}{a^{\frac{o^T-1}{o-1}} - 1} \leq n_k^{\frac{a(o^T-1)}{o-1}} \leq N^{\frac{a(o^T-1)}{o-1}},$$

which is no longer exponential in the number of agents but only polynomial. □

Another direct consequence of Theorem 3 is that we can also check pruning for representative policies.

Corollary 2. *Given Corollary 1, Eq. (3) is identical for agents i, j of partition k given a representative policy π_k, which allows for checking π_k once per partition.*

Thus, formally, a representative policy π_k^t is pruned if the following holds, which can still be solved using a linear program:

$$\forall s \in ran(S), \boldsymbol{h}_{-i}^t \in \boldsymbol{H}_{-i}^t \exists \pi_{l \neq k}^t \in \Pi_k^t : V_k'^{\#}(s, \pi_k^t \oplus \boldsymbol{h}_{-i}^t) \leq V_k'^{\#}(s, \pi_l^t \oplus \boldsymbol{h}_{-i}^t) \quad (9)$$

Before we set up a dynamic programming operator for counting POSGss using the results of this section, we briefly discuss using histograms directly as actions and observations in policies.

Why Using Histograms Directly in Policies Fails. An alternative considered to our approach is to define a POSG with an agent for each partition and swapping histograms for joint actions and observations. Even if this strategy may seem more straightforward, it causes a huge explosion in the policy space: If histograms are used as nodes in policy trees, all the different combinations of all possible histograms need to be built in each iteration. Let us look at a simple example, consider a partition with 4 agents and 2 actions: the number of action histograms is 5 (i.e., $[4,0],[3,1],[2,2],[1,3],[0,4]$), the number of trees grows like a tree over histograms, not actions; this becomes unmanageable when building policy trees. Thus, the number of possible policies grows exponentially, along the lines of N^N, which is even worse original exponential complexity. This strategy has been discussed for the collaborative setting [4], which demonstrates this negative result. In contrast, our method counts representative policies, which makes the problem tractable in the number of agents.

4 Counting Dynamic Programming for Counting POSGs

In this section, we present the counting dynamic programming operator, which uses representative policies along with Eq. (8) for efficiently computing policy values in counting POSGs.

Algorithm 2 shows the counting version of the operator. For each representative policy, their corresponding value needs to be calculated according to Eq. (8) and pruning is checked according to Eq. (9). Next, we argue for correctness of Algorithm 2 based on the correctness of Algorithm 1 and show that the runtime of the operator no longer depends exponentially on the number of agents.

Theorem 5. *Using Algorithm 2 on a counting POSG $\bar{M}$ is equivalent to using Algorithm 1 on an equivalent POSG M, in which Eqs.* (4) *and* (5) *hold.*

Proof. The correctness of Algorithm 2 follows from the previous results: Given Theorem 3, Algorithm 2 computes the same values as Algorithm 1. Given Corollary 1, it is enough to compute those values for representative policies. Given Corollary 2, it is enough to check pruning for representative policies. Thus, Algorithm 2 only prunes policies that Algorithm 1 would prune. Thus, the solutions are equivalent. □

Algorithm 2. Counting Multi-agent Dynamic Programming Operator

function COUNTING-MA-DP(Set of representative policies with corresponding value vectors $\{(\Pi_k^{t-1}, \boldsymbol{V}_k^{\#,t-1})\}_{k=1}^K$)
  $\Pi_k^t \leftarrow$ Perform exhaustive backup using Π_k^{t-1} for each partition $\Im_k \in \bar{\boldsymbol{I}}$
  $\boldsymbol{V}_k^{\#,t} \leftarrow$ Calculate new value vectors for each representative policy for each $\Im_k \in \bar{\boldsymbol{I}}$
  while $\exists \pi_{k,l}^t \in \Pi_k^t$: Eq. (9) holds **do**
    $\Pi_k^t \leftarrow \Pi_k^t \setminus \{\pi_{k,l}^t\}$, $\boldsymbol{V}_k^{\#,t} \leftarrow \boldsymbol{V}_k^{\#,t} \setminus \{v_{k,l}^t\}$
  return $\{(\Pi_k^t, \boldsymbol{V}_k^{\#,t})\}_{k=1}^K$

Theorem 6. *Given a counting POSG $\bar{M}$, the runtime of Algorithm 2 depends polynomially on the number of agents N.*

Proof. The operator consists of three main steps. First, the representative policies for each partition are generated, of which exist $p = a^{\frac{o^T-1}{o-1}}$ as seen in Theorem 4. Second, each representative policy is evaluated, which depends on the number of states and the number of counted observations due to the sums. Computing the action and observation histograms is of minor cost. The number of counted histograms depends polynomial on N and p considering Note 1. Each representative policy is evaluated for each state and the policies of the other agents and partitions, of which there polynomially many given Theorem 4. The third step is pruning using a linear program, which depends polynomially on the number of variables and constraints [34], which again depends polynomially on the number of agents with the number of variables depending on s and the number of counted policies as of Theorem 4. Pruning is carried out for each representative policy in each partition, which is independent of the number of agents N. Thus, the runtime depends only polynomially on the number of agents. □

Theorem 6 again assumes a fixed action and observation space as well as number of partitions, with $K \ll N$. The exponential dependence on the horizon is still given.[1] As such, we have succeeded in setting up a POSG using counting to compactly encode symmetric behaviour enabling tractability in the number of agents. We briefly consider related work before we conclude the paper.

5 Related Work

We look at related work for POSGs as well as lifting in the context of Markov decision process (MDP)-based formalisms.

Despite POSGs being notoriously difficult to solve, with results including that the complexity of determining if one team has a positive-expected-reward strategy is complete for $\mathrm{NEXP}^{\mathrm{NP}}$ [13], researchers have worked on finding ways to solve POSGs efficiently. The dynamic programming operator [14] has been extended by approximate pruning techniques [21]. To further work on scalability, specific variants of POSGs have been considered such as zero-sum games (e.g., [15,33,36]), one-sided POSGs (e.g., [5,16,17]), and POSGs with common payoffs [6]. On a more practical level, partially observable game-theoretic Golog extends Golog with game-theoretic multi-agent planning in POSGs [8]. Using assumptions, isomorphic POSGs and the so-called lifted dynamic programming operator allow for tractable POSGs [18]. The work was inspired by the lifting of decentralised partially observable MDPs (DecPOMDPs) [4], which are POSGs with a joint reward function. The lifted variants of DecPOMDPs include an isomorphic version, with results similar to isomorphic POSGs. The counting version

[1] One could argue that for Algorithm 2 as well as a routine calling Algorithm 2 repeatedly until a horizon is reached, the horizon can be considered fixed as part of the input.

uses histograms of actions and observations in policies, which blows up the policy space and thus has not been used yet as the basis for a solution method as discussed above. The idea of grouping based on a notion of similarity for efficiency gains has also been used in other areas: GMAA*, which is a policy search algorithm based on multiagent A* (MAA*) [32], clusters action-observation histories of agents at the same stage if they have the same optimal Q-values in the game [25]. In a similar vein within the POSG framework, clustering of observation histories in an approximate way has been used for efficiency gains, proposing low-probability clustering and minimum-distance clustering of similar observation histories [7].

Lifting has been used to exploit a relational state description in (PO)MDPs: In first-order MDPs (FOMPDs) [3], the situation calculus [22] is used to describe the state space. In factorised FOMDPs, the state space representation is further factored [28]. In object-oriented POMDPs, the state space is similarly factorised based on objects in the state space [35]. In FO-POMDPs, lifting is applied to policies, pruning policies that are indistinguishable [29]. In open-universe FO-POMDPs, Bayesian logic is used as a basis, allowing for an open universe [31]. In lifted online decision making problems, a factored state space representation is extended with decision random variables and utility functions, encoding symmetries using logical variables, which allows for using representatives in calculations [1,2,9–12]. While somr og these models allow for concurrent actions, they do not solve a classical multi-agent decision making problem.

To the best of our knowledge, we are the first to apply the idea of counting to POSGs, using representative policies, allowing for solving POSG instances with a large number of agents.

6 Conclusion

This paper presents counting POSGs, a POSG with partitioned agent set that exhibits symmetric behaviour. It allows for compactly encoding the symmetries in the transition and reward functions to reduce the model complexity as well as using and counting representative policies per partition during policy value computation and pruning. The counting multi-agent dynamic programming operator is able to use the compact encoding of counting POSGs to efficiently compute a solution to a counting POSG. As such, we are able to reduce the exponential dependence of POSGs on the number of agents to a polynomial one for counting POSGs, making the problem tractable. Consequently, counting POSGs have great potential for applications that have a large number of agents.

Future research includes integrating of the concept of symmetry into the state space, which will further increase scalability. This extension will enable POSG counts to be applied to domains with large state spaces, allowing for even more reductions in the model complexity. In addition, we plan to apply the concept of representative policies to Dec-POMDPs.

References

1. Apsel, U., Brafman, R.I.: Extended lifted inference with joint formulas. In: UAI-11 Proceedings of the 27th Conference on Uncertainty in Artificial Intelligence, pp. 74–83. AUAI Press (2011)
2. Apsel, U., Brafman, R.I.: Lifted MEU by weighted model counting. In: AAAI-12 Proceedings of the 26th AAAI Conference on Artificial Intelligence, pp. 1861–1867. AAAI Press (2012)
3. Boutilier, C., Reiter, R., Price, B.: Symbolic dynamic programming for first-order MDPs. In: IJCAI-01 Proceedings of the 17th International Joint Conference on Artificial Intelligence, pp. 690–697. IJCAI Organization (2001)
4. Braun, T., Gehrke, M., Lau, F., Möller, R.: Lifting in multi-agent systems under uncertainty. In: UAI-22 Proc. of the 38th Conference on Uncertainty in Artificial Intelligence, pp. 1–8. AUAI Press (2022)
5. Carr, S., Jansen, N., Bharadwaj1, S., Spaan, M.T.J., Topcu, U.: Safe policies for factored partially observable stochastic games. In: RSS-21 Proceedings of Robotics: Science and Systems XVII, pp. 1–11. RSS Foundation (2021)
6. Emery-Montemerlo, R., Gordon, G., Schneider, J., Thrun, S.: Approximate solutions for partially observable stochastic games with common payoffs. In: AAAMAS-04 Proceedings of the 3rd International Joint Conference on Autonomous Agents and Multiagent Systems, pp. 136–143. IEEE (2004)
7. Emery-Montemerlo, R., Gordon, G., Schneider, J., Thrun, S.: Game theoretic control for robot teams. In: Proceedings of the 2005 IEEE International Conference on Robotics and Automation, pp. 1163–1169. IEEE (2005)
8. Finzi, A., Lukasiewicz, T.: Partially observable game-theoretic agent programming in Golog. Int. J. Approximate Reasoning **119**, 220–241 (2020)
9. Gehrke, M., Braun, T., Möller, R.: Lifted temporal maximum expected utility. In: Meurs, M.-J., Rudzicz, F. (eds.) Canadian AI 2019. LNCS (LNAI), vol. 11489, pp. 380–386. Springer, Cham (2019). https://doi.org/10.1007/978-3-030-18305-9_33
10. Gehrke, M., Braun, T., Möller, R., Waschkau, A., Strumann, C., Steinhäuser, J.: Towards lifted maximum expected utility. In: Proceedings of the First Joint Workshop on Artificial Intelligence in Health at the 27th International Joint Conference on Artificial Intelligence, vol. 2142, pp. 93–96. CEUR-WS.org (2018)
11. Gehrke, M., Braun, T., Möller, R., Waschkau, A., Strumann, C., Steinhäuser, J.: Lifted maximum expected utility. In: Koch, F., et al. (eds.) AIH 2018. LNCS (LNAI), vol. 11326, pp. 131–141. Springer, Cham (2019). https://doi.org/10.1007/978-3-030-12738-1_10
12. Gehrke, M., Braun, T., Polovina, S.: Restricting the maximum number of actions for decision support under uncertainty. In: Alam, M., Braun, T., Yun, B. (eds.) ICCS 2020. LNCS (LNAI), vol. 12277, pp. 145–160. Springer, Cham (2020). https://doi.org/10.1007/978-3-030-57855-8_11
13. Goldsmith, J., Mundhenk, M.: Competition adds complexity. In: NIPS-07 Advances in Neural Information Processing Systems 20, pp. 1–8. Curran Associates, Inc. (2007)
14. Hansen, E.A., Bernstein, D.S., Zilberstein, S.: Dynamic programming for partially observable stochastic games. In: AAAI-04 Proceedings of the 19th National Conference on Artificial Intelligence, vol. 4, pp. 709–715 (2004)
15. Horák, K., Bošanskỳ, B.: Solving partially observable stochastic games with public observations. In: Proceedings of the AAAI conference on Artificial Intelligence, pp. 547–552. AAAI Press (2019)

16. Horák, K., Bošanský, B., Kiekintveld, C., Kamhoua, C.: Compact representation of value function in partially observable stochastic games. In: IJCAI-19 Proceedings of the 28th International Joint Conference on Artificial Intelligence, pp. 350–356. IJCAI Organisation (2019)
17. Horák, K., Bošanský, B., Pěchouček, M.: Heuristic search value iteration for one-sided partially observable stochastic games. In: AAAI-17 Proc. of the 31st AAAI Conference on Artificial Intelligence, pp. 558–564 (2017)
18. Karabulut, N.N., Braun, T.: Lifting partially observable stochastic games. In: SUM-24 Proceedings of the 16th International Conference on Scalable Uncertainty Management, pp. 201–216. Springer (2024)
19. Koops, W., Jansen, N., Junges, S., Simao, T.D.: Recursive small-step multi-agent A* for Dec-POMDPs. In: IJCAI-23 Proceedings of the 32nd International Joint Conference on Artificial Intelligence, pp. 5402–5410. IJCAI Organization (2023)
20. Koops, W., Junges, S., Jansen, N.: Approximate Dec-POMDP solving using multi-agent A*. In: IJCAI-24 Proceedings of the 33nd International Joint Conference on Artificial Intelligence, pp. 6743–6751. IJCAI Organization (2024)
21. Kumar, A., Zilberstein, S.: Dynamic programming approximations for partially observable stochastic games. In: FLAIRS-09 Proceedings of the 22nd International Florida Artificial Intelligence Research Society Conference. AAAI Press (2009)
22. McCarthy, J.: Situations, Actions, and Causal Laws. Standford University, Technical report (1963)
23. Milch, B., Zettelmoyer, L.S., Kersting, K., Haimes, M., Kaelbling, L.P.: Lifted probabilistic inference with counting formulas. In: AAAI-08 Proceedings of the 23rd AAAI Conference on Artificial Intelligence, pp. 1062–1068. AAAI Press (2008)
24. Oliehoek, F.A., Amato, C.: A Concise Introduction to Decentralised POMDPs. Springer, Cham (2016)
25. Oliehoek, F.A., Whiteson, S., Spaan, M.T.: Lossless clustering of histories in decentralized POMDPs. In: AAMAS-09 Proceedings of the 8th International Conference on Autonomous Agents and Multiagent Systems, pp. 577–584. IFAAMAS (2009)
26. Poole, D.: First-order probabilistic inference. In: IJCAI-03 Proceedings of the 18th International Joint Conference on Artificial Intelligence, pp. 985–991. IJCAI Organization (2003)
27. Russell, S., Norvig, P.: Artificial Intelligence: A Modern Approach. Pearson (2021)
28. Sanner, S., Boutilier, C.: Approximate solution techniques for factored first-order MDPs. In: ICAPS-07 Proc. of the 17th International Conference on Automated Planning and Scheduling, pp. 288–295. AAAI Press (2007)
29. Sanner, S., Kersting, K.: Symbolic dynamic programming for first-order POMDPs. In: AAAI-10 Proc. of the 24th AAAI Conference on Artificial Intelligence, pp. 1140–1146. AAAI Press (2010)
30. Seuken, S., Zilberstein, S.: Memory-bounded dynamic programming for DEC-POMDPs. In: IJCAI-07 Proceedings of the 21st International Joint Conference on Artificial Intelligence, pp. 2009–2015. IJCAI Organization (2007)
31. Srivastava, S., Russell, S., Ruan, P., Cheng, X.: First-order open-universe POMDPs. In: UAI-14 Proceedings of the 30th Conference on Uncertainty in Artificial Intelligence, pp. 742–751. AUAI Press (2014)
32. Szer, D., Charpillet, F., Zilberstein, S.: MAA*: a heuristic search algorithm for solving decentralized POMDPs. In: UAI-05 Proceedings of the 21st Conference on Uncertainty in Artificial Intelligence, pp. 576–583. ACM (2005)
33. Tomášek, P., Horák, K., Aradhye, A., Bošanský, B., Chatterjee, K.: Solving partially observable stochastic shortest-path games. In: IJCAI-21 Proceedings of the

30th International Joint Conference on Artificial Intelligence, pp. 4182–4189. IJCAI Organisation (2021)
34. Vaidya, P.M.: Speeding-up linear programming using fast matrix multiplication. In: 30th Annual Symposium on Foundations of Computer Science, pp. 332–337. IEEE Computer Society (1989)
35. Wandzel, A., Oh, Y., Fishman, M., Kumar, N., Wong, L.L., Tellex, S.: Multi-object search using object-oriented POMDPs. In: ICRA-19 Proceedings of the 2019 International Conference on Robotics and Automation, pp. 7194–7200. IEEE (2019)
36. Wiggers, A.J., Oliehoek, F.A., Roijers, D.M.: Structure in the value function of two-player zero-sum games of incomplete information. In: ECAI-16 Proceedings of the 22nd European Conference on Artificial Intelligence, pp. 1628–1629. IOS Press (2016)

Expected Shapley Value is Shapley Value for Expected Utility Game

Pratik Karmakar[1,2], Antoine Gauquier[3], and Pierre Senellart[2,3,4,5](✉)

[1] National University of Singapore, Singapore, Singapore
[2] CNRS@CREATE Ltd., Singapore, Singapore
pierre@senellart.com
[3] DI ENS, ENS, PSL University, CNRS, Inria, Paris, France
[4] Institut Universitaire de France, Paris, France
[5] IPAL, CNRS, Singapore, Singapore

Abstract. The Shapley value provides a principled framework for attributing marginal contributions to players in coalitional games. While its axiomatic fairness guarantees have made it a cornerstone of value distribution in economics and multi-agent systems, recent computational advances have extended its applicability to data-driven domains. This paper bridges game-theoretic foundations with probabilistic reasoning by studying Shapley-like scores in stochastic environments. We prove that the *expected Shapley value* (EShap) – a player's average impact in a game with an independent probabilistic setting – coincides with the Shapley value of the game whose utility is the expected utility of the original game (ShapE). This equality, however, *fails* for other power indices, such as the Banzhaf index, underscoring the Shapley value's specificity of consistency in uncertain settings. We further identify that for a certain class of coefficients (including normalized Banzhaf indices) the equality persists, broadening the scope of reliable attribution mechanisms.

Keywords: Shapley value · probabilistic game · probabilistic database

1 Introduction

In coalitional games, the Shapley value [13] resolves a fundamental question: how to fairly distribute collective gains among players based on their marginal contributions. Its axiomatic foundation – efficiency, symmetry, linearity, and null-player invariance – has made it a gold standard for attribution in domains ranging from cost allocation in economics [12], to feature importance [9] and data valuation [5] in explainable AI. Central to its adoption is the ability to compute player-specific values that reflect their *average contribution* across all possible player orderings.

Modern applications increasingly demand reasoning under uncertainty, where players (or, in data-centric settings [2,7], data elements) participate stochastically. Consider a probabilistic coalitional game where each player i is available

K. Sauerwald and M. Thimm (Eds.): ECSQARU 2025, LNAI 16099, pp. 223–237, 2026.
https://doi.org/10.1007/978-3-032-05134-9_16

to join a coalition with independent probability p_i. In such a stochastic setting, the *expected* contribution of a player participating in a coalition can be estimated by the expected value (over all randomized subgames) of the Shapley value of this player, i.e., its *expected Shapley Value* [3,7] (EShap). Recent work [7] demonstrated that EShap and its Banzhaf variant (EBanz) can be computed in **polynomial time** when the utility of the game can be described by a Boolean function with specific characteristics (e.g., read-once, or admitting a deterministic and decomposable circuit decomposition), unlocking applications in scenarios ranging from reliability analysis in decentralized systems to responsibility attribution in probabilistic databases [14].

But another natural way of quantifying the contribution of a player in a stochastic environment is to compute the Shapley value of that player for the game whose utility function is the *expected utility* of that player in a coalition; we denote this alternate definition as ShapE. For example, in a probabilistic database setting such as that of [7,14], EShap is the expected Shapley value (over all possible sub-databases with their probabilities) of a tuple in making a query true, while ShapE represents the Shapley value of that tuple for the game whose utility is the probability a coalition satisfies the query.

While both EShap and ShapE measure influence, it is *a priori* unclear whether they are related – the former averages contributions across subgames, while the latter applies Shapley's axioms directly to expected utility.

Contributions. We resolve this question as follows:

- **Equality for Shapley values:** We prove EShap = ShapE (Sect. 4). This equality validates the consistency of Shapley-based attribution in probabilistic environments, from cooperative games to data management.
- **Non-equality for Banzhaf values**: Interestingly, this result is not just a consequence of the linearity of expected value. Indeed, we show that for some other Shapley-like values, such as Banzhaf values [1], equality doesn't hold (Sect. 5). However, for *normalized* Banzhaf indices, equality does hold, with a different proof as for Shapley values (Sect. 6).

After briefly describing related work in Sect. 2, we introduce in Sect. 3 all relevant notions. In Sect. 4, we prove the equality. In Sect. 5, we show that the equality does not hold in general for arbitrary Shapley-like scores (and in particular for Banzhaf values). In Sect. 6, we discuss other cases where equality holds. Before concluding, we discuss in Sect. 7 the setting of non-independent probabilistic games.

2 Related Work

The Shapley value has been widely studied for fair attribution in cooperative games, with extensions to probabilistic settings gaining recent attention. Borkotokey et al. [3] and Karmakar et al. [7] formally define the expected Shapley value in games where coalition participation is stochastic, showing it satisfies natural axioms and coincides with intuitive influence measures.

From a computational perspective, Deutch et al. [4] and Karmakar et al. [7] link Shapley value computation to probabilistic inference in databases, leveraging provenance circuits for tractable query evaluation. These approaches allow efficient computation of expected Shapley scores over some tractable Boolean functions under uncertainty.

Other game-theoretic works, such as those by Miranda and Montes [10] and Pongou and Tondji [11], reinterpret Shapley and Banzhaf values as expectations under different coalition distributions. In AI, Shapley values have been extended to uncertain environments for data and feature attribution [9], though such applications typically rely on sampling and heuristic methods.

Our work complements these by proving a formal equality: the expected Shapley value (EShap) equals the Shapley value of the expected utility (ShapE) (which, to the best of our knowledge has not been specifically studied so far). As a consequence, we inherit tractability results from [7].

3 Definitions

We begin by introducing the notion of marginal contribution through a class of player scoring functions based on coefficients, which we call *Shapley-like scores* as in [7]. Let $c : \mathbb{N} \times \mathbb{N} \to \mathbb{Q}$ be a function, referred to as a *coefficient function*, and let $v : 2^N \to \mathbb{R}$ be a utility function defined on coalitions of a finite set N of players, with $i \in N$. We define the *score of player i with coefficients c* in the game as:

$$\mathsf{Score}_c(v, N, i) \stackrel{\text{def}}{=} \sum_{C \subseteq N \setminus \{i\}} c(|N|, |C|) \times [v(C \cup \{i\}) - v(C)]$$

This generic formulation encompasses well-known coefficient functions from cooperative game theory:

- When $c(k, \ell) = c_{\text{Shapley}}(k, \ell) \stackrel{\text{def}}{=} \frac{\ell!(k-\ell-1)!}{k!} = \left[\binom{k-1}{\ell} \cdot k\right]^{-1}$, $\mathsf{Score}_c(v, N, i)$ corresponds to the classical *Shapley value*.
- When $c(k, \ell) = c_{\text{Banzhaf}}(k, \ell) \stackrel{\text{def}}{=} 1$, $\mathsf{Score}_c(v, N, i)$ corresponds to the *Banzhaf value*.
- The Penrose–Banzhaf index (a standard normalization of the Banzhaf value [8]) corresponds to $c(k, \ell) = 2^{-k+1}$.

In the context of this work, we consider a player-independent probabilistic game $\mathcal{G} = (N, (p_i)_{i \in N})$, where p_i is the probability that player i participates in a random instance of the game. See Sect. 7 for a discussion of the non-independent setting.

We also use the following notation: $\Pi_Z(C) \stackrel{\text{def}}{=} \prod_{j \in C} p_j \prod_{j \in Z \setminus C} (1 - p_j)$ for C and Z two sets of players.

For $i \in N$ and some utility function v (i.e., a function from coalitions of players to $\mathbb{R}$ indicating the utility of this coalition), $\mathsf{EShap}(v, \mathcal{G}, i)$ is the expected

Shapley value of player i for utility v in $\mathcal{G}$. The expectation is taken over all possible participating coalitions Z:

$$\begin{aligned}
\mathsf{EShap}(v,\mathcal{G},i) &\stackrel{\text{def}}{=} \sum_{Z\subseteq N, i\in Z} \left(\Pi_N(Z) \times \mathsf{Score}_{c_{\text{Shapley}}}(v,Z,i)\right) \\
&= \sum_{Z\subseteq N, i\in Z} \left(\Pi_N(Z) \times \sum_{C\subseteq Z\setminus\{i\}} c_{\text{Shapley}}(|Z|,|C|) \times [v(C\cup\{i\}) - v(C)]\right) \\
&= p_i \times \sum_{Z\subseteq N\setminus\{i\}} \left(\Pi_{N\setminus\{i\}}(Z) \times \sum_{C\subseteq Z} c_{\text{Shapley}}(|Z|+1,|C|) \times [v(C\cup\{i\}) - v(C)]\right) \\
&= p_i \times \sum_{C\subseteq N\setminus\{i\}} (v(C\cup\{i\}) - v(C)) \left(\sum_{C\subseteq Z\subseteq N\setminus\{i\}} c_{\text{Shapley}}(|Z|+1,|C|)\Pi_{N\setminus\{i\}}(Z)\right)
\end{aligned}$$

For a utility function v, a probabilistic game $\mathcal{G} = (N,(p_i)_{i\in N})$ and a player i, we now define $\mathsf{ShapE}(v,\mathcal{G},i)$ as the Shapley value of i in N with a value function that maps a coalition Z to *the expected value (under* $\mathcal{G}$*) of the utility* v:

$$\begin{aligned}
\mathsf{ShapE}(v,\mathcal{G},i) &\stackrel{\text{def}}{=} \sum_{Z\subseteq N\setminus\{i\}} c_{\text{Shapley}}(|N|,|Z|) \times (\mathbb{E}_{\mathcal{G}}(v(Z\cup\{i\})) - \mathbb{E}_{\mathcal{G}}(v(Z))) \\
&= \sum_{Z\subseteq N\setminus\{i\}} c_{\text{Shapley}}(|N|,|Z|) \left(\sum_{C_1\subseteq Z\cup\{i\}} \Pi_{Z\cup\{i\}}(C_1)v(C_1) - \sum_{C_2\subseteq Z} \Pi_Z(C_2)v(C_2)\right) \\
&= \sum_{Z\subseteq N\setminus\{i\}} c_{\text{Shapley}}(|N|,|Z|)\Big(\sum_{C_1'\subseteq Z} p_i\Pi_Z(C_1')v(C_1'\cup\{i\}) \\
&\qquad + \sum_{C_1''\subseteq Z} (1-p_i)\Pi_Z(C_1'')v(C_1'') - \sum_{C_2\subseteq Z} \Pi_Z(C_2)v(C_2)\Big) \\
&= \sum_{Z\subseteq N\setminus\{i\}} c_{\text{Shapley}}(|N|,|Z|)\Big(\sum_{C_1'\subseteq Z} p_i\Pi_Z(C_1')v(C_1'\cup\{i\}) - \sum_{C_1''\subseteq Z} p_i\Pi_Z(C_1'')v(C_1'') \\
&\qquad + \cancel{\sum_{C_1''\subseteq Z} \Pi_Z(C_1'')v(C_1'')} - \cancel{\sum_{C_2\subseteq Z} \Pi_Z(C_2)v(C_2)}\Big) \\
&= \sum_{Z\subseteq N\setminus\{i\}} c_{\text{Shapley}}(|N|,|Z|) \left(\sum_{C\subseteq Z} p_i\Pi_Z(C)v(C\cup\{i\}) - \sum_{C\subseteq Z} p_i\Pi_Z(C)v(C)\right) \\
&= p_i \times \sum_{Z\subseteq N\setminus\{i\}} c_{\text{Shapley}}(|N|,|Z|) \left(\sum_{C\subseteq Z} \Pi_Z(C)(v(C\cup\{i\}) - v(C))\right) \\
&= p_i \times \sum_{C\subseteq N\setminus\{i\}} (v(C\cup\{i\}) - v(C)) \left(\sum_{C\subseteq Z\subseteq N\setminus\{i\}} c_{\text{Shapley}}(|N|,|Z|) \times \Pi_Z(C)\right)
\end{aligned}$$

4 Equality Between EShap and ShapE

We prove in this section that EShap and ShapE are actually equal. We note that this is non-trivial, and in particular not a simple consequence of the linearity of the expected value, but critically relies on the combinatorial structure of the Shapley coefficients c_{Shapley}. For arbitrary score functions (e.g., Banzhaf), this equality fails, as shown in Sect. 5. Formally:

Proposition 1. *For any probabilistic game* $\mathcal{G} = (N, (p_i)_{i \in N})$, *any utility function* v *over* N, *and any player* $i \in N$, *we have:*

$$\mathsf{EShap}(v, \mathcal{G}, i) = \mathsf{ShapE}(v, \mathcal{G}, i)$$

Proof. To prove the equality of EShap and ShapE we have to show:

$$p_i \times \sum_{C \subseteq N \setminus \{i\}} (v(C \cup \{i\}) - v(C)) \left(\sum_{C \subseteq Z \subseteq N \setminus \{i\}} c_{\mathsf{Shapley}}(|Z| + 1, |C|) \times \Pi_{N \setminus \{i\}}(Z) \right)$$

$$\stackrel{?}{=} p_i \times \sum_{C \subseteq N \setminus \{i\}} (v(C \cup \{i\}) - v(C)) \left(\sum_{C \subseteq Z \subseteq N \setminus \{i\}} c_{\mathsf{Shapley}}(|N|, |Z|) \times \Pi_Z(C) \right)$$

For any fixed coalition C, it suffices to show that the coefficients of $(v(C \cup \{i\}) - v(C))$ in both expressions are equal, that is:

$$\underbrace{\sum_{C \subseteq Z \subseteq N \setminus \{i\}} c_{\mathsf{Shapley}}(|Z| + 1, |C|) \times \Pi_{N \setminus \{i\}}(Z)}_{\text{LHS}} \stackrel{?}{=} \underbrace{\sum_{C \subseteq Z \subseteq N \setminus \{i\}} c_{\mathsf{Shapley}}(|N|, |Z|) \times \Pi_Z(C)}_{\text{RHS}} \quad (1)$$

To show the equality of the above-mentioned coefficients, we view the expressions on the left-hand side (LHS) and right-hand side (RHS) as *polynomials over the* $(p_j)_{j \in N}$ *variables*. Consider the expansion of these polynomials into sums of monomials; it is clear that all monomials involved will be factors of $\prod_{j \in C} p_j$. We can thus rewrite LHS and RHS as sums of monomials with corresponding coefficients, in the form:

$$\text{LHS} = \sum_{C \subseteq X \subseteq N \setminus \{i\}} C^{(1)}_{C,X} \times \text{Prod}(X)$$

and

$$\text{RHS} = \sum_{C \subseteq X \subseteq N \setminus \{i\}} C^{(2)}_{C,X} \times \text{Prod}(X)$$

where $\text{Prod}(X) = \prod_{j \in X} p_j$, and $C^{(1)}_{C,X}$ and $C^{(2)}_{C,X}$ are the coefficients of $\text{Prod}(X)$ in LHS and RHS, respectively. We now show that $C^{(1)}_{C,X} = C^{(2)}_{C,X}$, for any fixed coalition C and any $X \supseteq C$.

Computing $C^{(1)}_{C,X}$.

$$\text{LHS} = \sum_{C\subseteq Z\subseteq N\setminus\{i\}} c_{\text{Shapley}}(|Z|+1,|C|)\Pi_{N\setminus\{i\}}(Z) = \sum_{C\subseteq X\subseteq N\setminus\{i\}} C^{(1)}_{C,X} \times \text{Prod}(X)$$

Let us expand $\Pi_{N\setminus\{i\}}(Z)$ as a sum of monomials over the $(p_j)_{j\in N}$:

$$\Pi_{N\setminus\{i\}}(Z) = \prod_{j\in Z} p_j \times \prod_{j\in N\setminus\{i\}\setminus Z} (1-p_j) = \sum_{Z\subseteq X\subseteq N\setminus\{i\}} (-1)^{|X|-|Z|} \times \text{Prod}(X)$$

Thus, for any X, the coefficient of $\text{Prod}(X)$ in LHS is:

$$\begin{aligned} C^{(1)}_{C,X} &= \sum_{C\subseteq Z\subseteq X} (-1)^{|X|-|Z|} \times c_{\text{Shapley}}(|Z|+1,|C|) \\ &= \sum_{k=|C|}^{|X|} (-1)^{|X|-k} \times \binom{|X|-|C|}{k-|C|} \times c_{\text{Shapley}}(k+1,|C|) \end{aligned}$$

We then compute:

$$\begin{aligned} &\binom{|X|-|C|}{k-|C|} \times c_{\text{Shapley}}(k+1,|C|) \\ &= \frac{(|X|-|C|)!}{(k-|C|)!\,(|X|-k)!} \times \frac{(k-|C|)!\,|C|!}{k!} \times \frac{1}{k+1} \\ &= \frac{|X|!\,(|X|-|C|)!\,|C|!}{k!\,(|X|-k)!\,|X|!} \times \frac{1}{k+1} \\ &= \frac{\binom{|X|}{k}}{\binom{|X|}{|C|}} \times \frac{1}{k+1} \end{aligned}$$

Thus:

$$\begin{aligned} C^{(1)}_{C,X} &= \sum_{k=|C|}^{|X|} (-1)^{|X|-k} \times \frac{\binom{|X|}{k}}{\binom{|X|}{|C|}} \times \frac{1}{k+1} \\ &= \frac{(-1)^{|X|}}{\binom{|X|}{|C|}} \sum_{k=|C|}^{|X|} (-1)^k \binom{|X|}{k} \times \frac{1}{k+1} \\ &= \frac{(-1)^{|X|}}{\binom{|X|}{|C|}} \sum_{k=|C|}^{|X|} (-1)^k \frac{|X|!}{k!\,(|X|-k)!} \times \frac{1}{k+1} \\ &= \frac{(-1)^{|X|}}{\binom{|X|}{|C|}(|X|+1)} \sum_{k=|C|}^{|X|} (-1)^k \frac{(|X|+1)!}{(k+1)!\,(|X|-k)!} \\ &= \frac{(-1)^{|X|}}{\binom{|X|}{|C|}} \times \frac{1}{|X|+1} \sum_{k=|C|}^{|X|} (-1)^k \binom{|X|+1}{k+1} \end{aligned}$$

Then:

$$\sum_{k=|C|}^{|X|}(-1)^k\binom{|X|+1}{k+1}=\sum_{j=|C|+1}^{|X|+1}(-1)^{j-1}\binom{|X|+1}{j}=-\sum_{j=|C|+1}^{|X|+1}(-1)^j\binom{|X|+1}{j}$$

$$=\sum_{j=0}^{|C|}(-1)^j\binom{|X|+1}{j}\quad\left[\text{Using the binomial expansion of }(1+x)^{|X|+1}\Big|_{x=-1}\right]$$

$$=\binom{|X|}{0}+\sum_{j=1}^{|C|}(-1)^j\left(\binom{|X|}{j-1}+\binom{|X|}{j}\right)\quad\left[\because\binom{n}{r}+\binom{n}{r-1}=\binom{n+1}{r}\right]$$

$$=\binom{|X|}{0}-\left(\binom{|X|}{0}+\binom{|X|}{1}\right)+\left(\binom{|X|}{1}+\binom{|X|}{2}\right)-\left(\binom{|X|}{2}+\binom{|X|}{3}\right)$$

$$+\cdots+(-1)^{|C|-1}\left(\binom{|X|}{|C|-2}+\binom{|X|}{|C|-1}\right)+(-1)^{|C|}\left(\binom{|X|}{|C|-1}+\binom{|X|}{|C|}\right)$$

$$=(-1)^{|C|}\binom{|X|}{|C|}$$

Therefore, we get:

$$C^{(1)}_{C,X}=\frac{(-1)^{|X|}}{\binom{|X|}{|C|}}\times\frac{1}{|X|+1}\times(-1)^{|C|}\binom{|X|}{|C|}=(-1)^{|X|+|C|}\frac{1}{|X|+1}$$

$$=(-1)^{|X|-|C|}\frac{1}{|X|+1}\quad[\because(|X|+|C|)\bmod 2=(|X|-|C|)\bmod 2]\qquad(2)$$

Computing $C^{(2)}_{C,X}$.

$$\text{RHS}=\sum_{C\subseteq Z\subseteq N\setminus\{i\}}c_{\text{Shapley}}(|N|,|Z|)\times\Pi_Z(C)=\sum_{C\subseteq X\subseteq N\setminus\{i\}}C^{(2)}_{C,X}\times\text{Prod}(X)$$

Let us expand $\Pi_Z(C)$ as a sum of monomials over the $(p_j)_{j\in N}$:

$$\Pi_Z(C)=\prod_{j\in C}p_j\times\prod_{j\in Z}(1-p_j)=\sum_{C\subseteq X\subseteq Z}(-1)^{|X|-|C|}\times\text{Prod}(X)$$

Thus, for any X, the coefficient of $\text{Prod}(X)$ in LHS is:

$$C^{(2)}_{C,X}=\sum_{X\subseteq Z\subseteq N\setminus\{i\}}(-1)^{|X|-|C|}\times c_{\text{Shapley}}(|N|,|Z|)$$

$$=(-1)^{|X|-|C|}\sum_{t=|X|}^{|N|-1}\binom{|N|-1-|X|}{t-|X|}\times c_{\text{Shapley}}(|N|,t)$$

We then compute:

$$\begin{aligned}
&\binom{|N|-1-|X|}{t-|X|} \times c_{\text{Shapley}}(|N|,t)\\
&= \frac{(|N|-1-|X|)!}{(t-|X|)!(|N|-1-t)!} \times \frac{t!(|N|-1-t)!}{(|N|-1)!} \times \frac{1}{|N|}\\
&= \frac{(|N|-1-|X|)! \times t! \times |X|!}{(t-|X|)! \times (|N|-1)! \times |X|!} \times \frac{1}{|N|}\\
&= \frac{\binom{t}{|X|}}{\binom{|N|-1}{|X|}} \times \frac{1}{|N|}
\end{aligned}$$

Thus:

$$\begin{aligned}
C^{(2)}_{C,X} &= (-1)^{|X|-|C|} \sum_{t=|X|}^{|N|-1} \frac{\binom{t}{|X|}}{\binom{|N|-1}{|X|}} \times \frac{1}{|N|}\\
&= (-1)^{|X|-|C|} \times \frac{1}{\binom{|N|-1}{|X|}} \times \frac{1}{|N|} \sum_{t=|X|}^{|N|-1} \binom{t}{|X|}\\
&= (-1)^{|X|-|C|} \times \frac{1}{\binom{|N|-1}{|X|}} \times \frac{1}{|N|} \times \binom{|N|}{|X|+1} \quad \text{[Hockey-stick identity]}\\
&= (-1)^{|X|-|C|} \frac{1}{|X|+1} \qquad (3)
\end{aligned}$$

From Eqs. (2) and (3) we have that $C^{(1)}_{C,X} = C^{(2)}_{C,X}$ for any $X \supseteq C$, which shows that LHS = RHS in Eq. (1), and concludes the proof. □

Example 1. Let us inspect a simple example with set of players $N = \{1,2,3\}$ associated with probabilities $p_1 = 0.3$, $p_2 = 0.6$, $p_3 = 0.7$. Define the utility function v such that: $v(\emptyset) = 0$, $v(\{1\}) = 1$, $v(\{2\}) = 2$, $v(\{3\}) = 3$, $v(\{1,2\}) = 7$, $v(\{1,3\}) = 9$, $v(\{2,3\}) = 11$, and $v(\{1,2,3\}) = 14$. We compute for player 1:

$$\begin{aligned}
&\mathsf{EShap}(v,\mathcal{G},1) = p_1 \Big[\Pi_{\{2,3\}}(\emptyset) c_{\text{Shapley}}(1,0)(v(\{1\}) - v(\emptyset))\\
&+ \Pi_{\{2,3\}}(\{2\}) \Big(c_{\text{Shapley}}(2,0)(v(\{1\}) - v(\emptyset)) + c_{\text{Shapley}}(2,1)(v(\{1,2\}) - v(\{2\})) \Big)\\
&+ \Pi_{\{2,3\}}(\{3\}) \Big(c_{\text{Shapley}}(2,0)(v(\{1\}) - v(\emptyset)) + c_{\text{Shapley}}(2,1)(v(\{1,3\}) - v(\{3\})) \Big)\\
&+ \Pi_{\{2,3\}}(\{2,3\}) \Big(c_{\text{Shapley}}(3,0)(v(\{1\}) - v(\emptyset)) c_{\text{Shapley}}(3,1)(v(\{1,2\}) - v(\{2\}))\\
&\quad + c_{\text{Shapley}}(3,1)(v(\{1,3\}) - v(\{3\})) + c_{\text{Shapley}}(3,2)(v(\{1,2,3\}) - v(\{2,3\})) \Big) \Big]\\
&= 0.891
\end{aligned}$$

$$\begin{aligned}
\mathsf{ShapE}(v,\mathcal{G},1) &= p_1\Bigg[c_{\text{Shapley}}(3,0)\Big(\Pi_{\emptyset}(\emptyset)(v(\{1\})-v(\emptyset))\Big)\\
&+c_{\text{Shapley}}(3,1)\Big(\Pi_{\{2\}}(\emptyset)(v(\{1\})-v(\emptyset))+\Pi_{\{2\}}(\{2\})(v(\{1,2\})-v(\{2\}))\Big)\\
&+c_{\text{Shapley}}(3,1)\Big(\Pi_{\{3\}}(\emptyset)(v(\{1\})-v(\emptyset))+\Pi_{\{3\}}(\{3\})(v(\{1,3\})-v(\{2\}))\Big)\\
&+c_{\text{Shapley}}(3,2)\Big(\Pi_{\{2,3\}}(\emptyset)(v(\{1\})-v(\emptyset))+\Pi_{\{2,3\}}(\{2\})(v(\{1,2\})-v(\{2\}))\\
&\quad+\Pi_{\{2,3\}}(\{3\})(v(\{1,3\})-v(\{3\}))+\Pi_{\{2,3\}}(\{2,3\})(v(\{1,2,3\})-v(\{2,3\}))\Big)\Bigg]\\
&=0.891
\end{aligned}$$

We then inherit the tractability results about EShap from [7] (Corollary 3.7):

Corollary 1. *Let $\mathcal{G} = (N,(p_i)_{i\in N})$ be a probabilistic game, and let v be a Boolean utility function over N in any class of Boolean functions whose probability can be computed in polynomial time (e.g., read-once functions, or functions given by a deterministic and decomposable circuits). Then* $\mathsf{ShapE}(v,\mathcal{G},i)$ *can also be computed in polynomial time.*

5 Inequality for Unnormalized Banzhaf Values

Note that Proposition 1 is specific to Shapley value, it does not hold for arbitrary other common score functions such as Banzhaf values:

Proposition 2. *Proposition 1 does not hold when the Shapley coefficient function is replaced with the Banzhaf coefficient function ($(k,\ell)\mapsto 1$).*

Proof. Consider a simple setting where N is formed of three players f, g, h with probabilities p_f, p_g, and 1, respectively, and v returns 1 if and only if at least two among the players $\{f,g,h\}$ are in the coalition, 0 otherwise. We compute $\mathsf{EBanz}(v,\mathcal{G},h)$ and $\mathsf{BanzE}(v,\mathcal{G},h)$ for the Banzhaf coefficient function and show they differ.

$$\begin{aligned}
\mathsf{EBanz}(v,\mathcal{G},h) &= \Pi_N(\{f,g,h\})\times \mathsf{Score}_{c_{\text{Banzhaf}}}(v,\{f,g,h\},h)\\
&+\Pi_N(\{f,h\})\times \mathsf{Score}_{c_{\text{Banzhaf}}}(v,\{f,h\},h)\\
&+\Pi_N(\{g,h\})\times \mathsf{Score}_{c_{\text{Banzhaf}}}(v,\{g,h\},h)\\
&= p_f p_g\times 2\times c(3,1)+(p_f(1-p_g)+p_g(1-f))\times c(2,1)
\end{aligned}$$

$$\mathsf{BanzE}(v,\mathcal{G},h) = c(3,2)\times(p_f(1-p_g)+p_g(1-p_f))+c(3,1)\times(p_f+p_g)$$

Let us fix $p_f = \frac{1}{4}$ and $p_g = \frac{1}{2}$. Then, for the Banzhaf coefficient function, $\mathsf{EBanz}(v,\mathcal{G},h)$ and $\mathsf{BanzE}(v,\mathcal{G},h)$ evaluate, respectively, to $\frac{1}{4}+\frac{1}{8}+\frac{3}{8}=\frac{3}{4}$ and to $\frac{1}{8}+\frac{3}{8}+\frac{1}{4}+\frac{1}{2}=\frac{5}{4}\neq\frac{3}{4}$. □

6 Equality for Normalized Banzhaf Values

In the previous section, we demonstrated that the equality $\mathsf{EShap} = \mathsf{ShapE}$ is specific to the classical Shapley value and does not extend to the Banzhaf index. However, a natural question arises: can this equality exist for other power indices that, similarly to Banzhaf values, can be expressed as Shapley-like values with a specific coefficient function? In this section, we show that it is indeed the case for the standard normalization of the Banzhaf value, sometimes called the Penrose–Banzhaf index [8], i.e., with coefficient function $c'(k, \ell) = 2^{-k+1}$. Note that, in a probabilistic setting, the number of available players is *not* constant, so the expected score EScore for this coefficient function is not a constant normalization of EBanz (however, ScoreE is a normalization of BanzE!). We show that Proposition 1 holds for this index too.

Though the details of the proof are different, we follow the same coefficient comparison strategy as in Sect. 4. First, we compute the coefficient $C^{(1)}_{C,X}$ of the monomial $\mathrm{Prod}(X)$ in the expansion of the LHS expression (expected score under the probabilistic model), using the modified coefficient $c'(k, \ell) = 2^{-k+1}$.

Computing $C^{(1)}_{C,X}$. The expression of $C^{(1)}_{C,X}$ for c' index is as follows:

$$
\begin{aligned}
C^{(1)}_{C,X} &= \sum_{C \subseteq Z \subseteq X} (-1)^{|X|-|Z|} \times c'(|Z|+1, |C|) \\
&= \sum_{k=|C|}^{|X|} (-1)^{|X|-k} \times \binom{|X|-|C|}{k-|C|} \times c'(k+1, |C|) \\
&= (-1)^{|X|} \sum_{k=|C|}^{|X|} (-1)^{-k} \times \binom{|X|-|C|}{k-|C|} \times 2^{-k} \\
&= (-1)^{|X|} \sum_{k=|C|}^{|X|} \left(-\frac{1}{2}\right)^{k} \times \binom{|X|-|C|}{k-|C|} \\
&= (-1)^{|X|} \sum_{j=0}^{|X|-|C|} \left(-\frac{1}{2}\right)^{j+|C|} \times \binom{|X|-|C|}{j} \qquad [j = k - |C|] \\
&= (-1)^{|X|-|C|} \times 2^{-|C|} \sum_{j=0}^{|X|-|C|} \left(-\frac{1}{2}\right)^{j} \times \binom{|X|-|C|}{j} \\
&= (-1)^{|X|-|C|} \times 2^{-|C|} \left(1 - \frac{1}{2}\right)^{|X|-|C|} \\
&= (-1)^{|X|-|C|} \times 2^{-|C|} \times 2^{|C|-|X|} \\
&= (-1)^{|X|-|C|} \times 2^{-|X|}
\end{aligned}
$$

Next, we compute the corresponding coefficient $C^{(2)}_{C,X}$ in the RHS expression, that is, the monomial coefficient in the Normalized Banzhaf index applied to the expected utility function.

Computing $C^{(2)}_{C,X}$. The expression of $C^{(2)}_{C,X}$ for c' index is as follows:

$$\begin{aligned}
C^{(2)}_{C,X} &= \sum_{X \subseteq Z \subseteq N \setminus \{i\}} (-1)^{|X|-|C|} \times c'(|N|,|Z|) \\
&= (-1)^{|X|-|C|} \sum_{t=|X|}^{|N|-1} \binom{|N|-1-|X|}{t-|X|} \times c'(|N|,t) \\
&= (-1)^{|X|-|C|} \sum_{t=|X|}^{|N|-1} \binom{|N|-1-|X|}{t-|X|} \times 2^{-|N|+1} \\
&= (-1)^{|X|-|C|} \times 2^{-|N|+1} \sum_{t=|X|}^{|N|-1} \binom{|N|-1-|X|}{t-|X|} \\
&= (-1)^{|X|-|C|} \times 2^{-|N|+1} \sum_{r=0}^{|N|-1-|X|} \binom{|N|-1-|X|}{r} \qquad [r = t - |X|] \\
&= (-1)^{|X|-|C|} \times 2^{-|N|+1} \times 2^{|N|-1-|X|} \\
&= (-1)^{|X|-|C|} \times 2^{-|X|}
\end{aligned}$$

Thus, $C^{(1)}_{C,X} = C^{(2)}_{C,X}$. Consequently, the expected index of players in a probabilistic game for c' is identical to the index of the game success-probability score function for c'.

Generalization. Motivated by the previous findings, we now investigate more generalized coefficient functions of the form $c(k,\ell) = a^{-k+m}$, where $a, m \in \mathbb{R}$ is a parameter. This allows us to analyze under what values of a the Proposition 1 holds.

We again follow the coefficient comparison approach and derive necessary conditions on a for the equality $\mathsf{EScore}_c = \mathsf{ScoreE}_c$.

$$\begin{aligned}
C^{1}_{C,X} &= \sum_{C \subseteq Z \subseteq X} (-1)^{|X|-|Z|} \times c(|Z|+1,|C|) \\
&= \sum_{k=|C|}^{|X|} (-1)^{|X|-k} \binom{|X|-|C|}{k-|C|} \times c(k+1,|C|) \\
&= \sum_{s=0}^{|X|-|C|} (-1)^{|X|-s-|C|} \binom{|X|-|C|}{s} \times c(s+|C|+1,|C|)
\end{aligned}$$

$$
\begin{aligned}
C^2_{C,X} &= \sum_{X \subseteq Z \subseteq N \setminus \{f\}} (-1)^{|X|-|C|} \times c(|N|, |Z|) \\
&= (-1)^{|X|-|C|} \sum_{t=|X|}^{|N|-1} \binom{|N|-1-|X|}{t-|X|} \times c(|N|, t) \\
&= (-1)^{|X|-|C|} \sum_{r=0}^{|N|-1-|X|} \binom{|N|-1-|X|}{r} \times c(|N|, r+|X|)
\end{aligned}
$$

For equality between $C^1_{C,X}$ and $C^2_{C,X}$, now we write:

$$
\begin{aligned}
&\sum_{s=0}^{|X|-|C|} (-1)^{|X|-s-|C|} \binom{|X|-|C|}{s} \times c(s+|C|+1, |C|) \\
&= (-1)^{|X|-|C|} \sum_{r=0}^{|N|-1-|X|} \binom{|N|-1-|X|}{r} \times c(|N|, r+|X|) \\
\Longleftrightarrow\ &\cancel{(-1)^{|X|-|C|}} \sum_{s=0}^{|X|-|C|} (-1)^{-s} \binom{|X|-|C|}{s} \times c(s+|C|+1, |C|) \\
&= \cancel{(-1)^{|X|-|C|}} \sum_{r=0}^{|N|-1-|X|} \binom{|N|-1-|X|}{r} \times c(|N|, r+|X|) \\
\Longleftrightarrow\ &\sum_{s=0}^{|X|-|C|} (-1)^{-s} \binom{|X|-|C|}{s} a^{-s-|C|-1+m} = \sum_{r=0}^{|N|-1-|X|} \binom{|N|-1-|X|}{r} a^{-|N|+m} \\
\Longleftrightarrow\ &a^{-|C|-1+m} \sum_{s=0}^{|X|-|C|} (-\frac{1}{a})^s \binom{|X|-|C|}{s} = a^{-|N|+m} \sum_{r=0}^{|N|-1-|X|} \binom{|N|-1-|X|}{r} \\
\Longleftrightarrow\ &a^{-|C|-1+\cancel{m}} \times (1-\frac{1}{a})^{|X|-|C|} = a^{-|N|+\cancel{m}} \times 2^{|N|-1-|X|} \\
\Longleftrightarrow\ &a^{|N|-1-|X|} \times (a-1)^{|X|-|C|} = 2^{|N|-1-|X|} \\
\Longleftrightarrow\ &(\frac{a}{2})^{|N|-1-|X|} \times (a-1)^{|X|-|C|} = 1
\end{aligned}
$$

For this equation to hold, the only possible value of a is 2, and m can take any arbitrary value.

7 Non-independent Players

We have assumed so far (see Sect. 3) that probabilistic games are *player-independent*, i.e., that the participation of a player i in a probabilistic game is independent of the participation of every other player. The proof of equality between EShap and ShapE crucially relies on the form of $\Pi_Z(C)$ for independent probability distributions; it is unclear whether it could be extended to (some) dependent settings. We leave this as exploration for future work.

However, we note that arbitrary dependencies between players can be captured in the utility function, on which we made no assumption. This observation is analogous to the observation made in [6] in the settings of probabilistic databases, where views defined by arbitrary queries over tuple-independent databases can represent any arbitrary correlations. In other words, any player-dependent probabilistic game can be transformed into an equivalent player-independent probabilistic game, and even into an equivalent non-probabilistic game.

Proposition 3. *Consider an* arbitrary *probabilistic game* $\mathcal{G} = (N, \Pr)$, *where* N *is a finite set of players and* $\Pr : 2^N \to [0,1]$ *is an arbitrary probability distribution over* 2^N. *Let* $v : 2^N \to \mathbb{R}$ *be some utility function. Then there exists a* player-independent *probabilistic game* $\mathcal{G}' = (N, (p'_i)_{i \in N})$ *over* N *and a utility function* $v' : 2^N \to \mathbb{R}$ *such that, for any* $Z \subseteq N$, $\mathbb{E}_{\mathcal{G}}(v(Z)) = \mathbb{E}_{\mathcal{G}'}(v'(Z))$.

Furthermore, one can choose p'_i *to be all equal to some constant* $\alpha > 0$, *including* $\alpha = 1$ *(which means the game becomes non-probabilistic and* $\mathbb{E}_{\mathcal{G}'}(v'(Z)) = v'(Z)$*).*

Proof. Let $Z \subseteq N$. We have:

$$\mathbb{E}_{\mathcal{G}}(v(Z)) = \sum_{C \subseteq N} \Pr(C) \times v(C \cap Z) = \sum_{C \subseteq Z} v(C) \left(\sum_{X \subseteq N - Z} \Pr(C \cup X) \right)$$

We need to define $v'(C)$ for any $C \subseteq N$ such that, for any $Z \subseteq N$:

$$\sum_{C \subseteq Z} v'(C) \prod_{j \in C} p'_j \prod_{j \in Z \setminus C} (1 - p'_j) = \sum_{C \subseteq Z} v(C) \left(\sum_{X \subseteq N - Z} \Pr(C \cup X) \right)$$

We pose $p'_i \stackrel{\text{def}}{=} \alpha$ for all $i \in N$, yielding:

$$\sum_{C \subseteq Z} v'(C) \alpha^{|Z|} = \sum_{C \subseteq Z} v(C) \left(\sum_{X \subseteq N - Z} \Pr(C \cup X) \right)$$

This holds if we define $\nu'(Z)$ inductively by:

$$\begin{cases} \nu'(\emptyset) \stackrel{\text{def}}{=} \nu(\emptyset) \\ \nu'(Z) \stackrel{\text{def}}{=} \alpha^{-|Z|} \sum_{C \subseteq Z} v(C) \left(\sum_{X \subseteq N - Z} \Pr(C \cup X) \right) - \sum_{C \subsetneq Z} v'(C) \quad \text{for } Z \neq \emptyset \end{cases}$$

□

This transformation, however, loses most of the structure of the game; for instance, if the utility function is a Boolean utility function given in a simple form, the transformed game will generally not be of the same nature and Corollary 1 cannot be applied.

8 Conclusion

We have proven that the Expected Shapley value (EShap) for player-independent probabilistic games equals the Shapley value of the expected utility game (ShapE), illustrating the robustness of Shapley's axioms under uncertainty. We contrasted this result with the unnormalized Banzhaf index, where the equality fails, and showed it is restored only after normalizing it.

Our findings help apply game-theoretic fairness principles to probabilistic reasoning confirming expected Shapley value (and Shapley value of the expected game) as a principled attribution tool in stochastic settings beyond the Boolean settings studied in the probabilistic database literature. Future directions include finding a complete characterization of the coefficient family that preserves the EScore = ScoreE equality and investigating the case of games that are not player-independent.

Miranda et al. [10] show that Shapley and normalized Banzhaf values can serve as probability transformations under imprecise probabilities, providing fairness and consistency under certain conditions. Exploring connections with our results is a direction for future work.

Acknowledgment. We are grateful to Benny Kimelfeld for suggesting investigating the connection between EShap and ShapE and to Stefano Moretti for discussions on this problem. This research is part of the DesCartes program and is supported by the National Research Foundation, Prime Minister's Office, Singapore under its Campus for Research Excellence and Technological Enterprise (CREATE) program. It is also supported by the French government under management of Agence Nationale de la Recherche as part of the PRAIRIE-PSAI project.

References

1. Banzhaf, J.F.: Weighted voting doesn't work: a mathematical analysis. Rutgers Law Rev. **19**, 317 (1964)
2. Bertossi, L.E., Kimelfeld, B., Livshits, E., Monet, M.: The Shapley value in database management. CoRR arxiv:2401.06234 (2024). https://doi.org/10.48550/ARXIV.2401.06234
3. Borkotokey, S., Gowala, S., Kumar, R.: The expected Shapley value on a class of probabilistic games. arXiv arxiv:2308.03489 (2023). http://arxiv.org/abs/2308.03489
4. Deutch, D., Frost, N., Kimelfeld, B., Monet, M.: Computing the shapley value of facts in query answering. In: Ives, Z.G., Bonifati, A., Abbadi, A.E. (eds.) SIGMOD '22: International Conference on Management of Data, Philadelphia, PA, USA, 12–17 June 2022, pp. 1570–1583. ACM (2022). https://doi.org/10.1145/3514221.3517912
5. Ghorbani, A., Zou, J.Y.: Data Shapley: equitable valuation of data for machine learning. In: Chaudhuri, K., Salakhutdinov, R. (eds.) Proceedings of the 36th International Conference on Machine Learning, ICML 2019, Long Beach, CA, USA, 9–15 June 2019. Proceedings of Machine Learning Research, vol. 97, pp. 2242–2251. PMLR (2019). http://proceedings.mlr.press/v97/ghorbani19c.html

6. Jha, A.K., Suciu, D.: Probabilistic databases with MarkoViews. Proc. VLDB Endow. **5**(11), 1160–1171 (2012). https://doi.org/10.14778/2350229.2350236. http://vldb.org/pvldb/vol5/p1160_abhayjha_vldb2012.pdf
7. Karmakar, P., Monet, M., Senellart, P., Bressan, S.: Expected Shapley-like scores of Boolean functions: complexity and applications to probabilistic databases. Proc. ACM Manag. Data **2**(2), 92 (2024). https://doi.org/10.1145/3651593
8. Kirsch, W., Langner, J.: Power indices and minimal winning coalitions. CoRR arxiv:0806.3906 (2008)
9. Lundberg, S.M., Lee, S.: A unified approach to interpreting model predictions. In: Guyon, I., von Luxburg, U., Bengio, S., Wallach, H.M., Fergus, R., Vishwanathan, S.V.N., Garnett, R. (eds.) Advances in Neural Information Processing Systems 30: Annual Conference on Neural Information Processing Systems 2017, Long Beach, CA, USA, 4–9 December 2017, pp. 4765–4774 (2017). https://proceedings.neurips.cc/paper/2017/hash/8a20a8621978632d76c43dfd28b67767-Abstract.html
10. Miranda, E., Montes, I.: Shapley and Banzhaf values as probability transformations. Int. J. Uncertain. Fuzziness Knowl. Based Syst. **26**(6), 917–947 (2018). https://doi.org/10.1142/S0218488518500411
11. Pongou, R., Tondji, J.: Valuing inputs under supply uncertainty: the Bayesian Shapley value. Games Econ. Behav. **108**, 206–224 (2018). https://doi.org/10.1016/J.GEB.2017.08.005
12. Roth, A.E., Verrecchia, R.E.: The Shapley value as applied to cost allocation: a reinterpretation. J. Account. Res. 295–303 (1979)
13. Shapley, L.S.: A value for n-person games. Ann. Math. Study **28**, 307–317 (1953)
14. Suciu, D., Olteanu, D., Ré, C., Koch, C.: Probabilistic Databases. Synthesis Lectures on Data Management, Morgan & Claypool Publishers (2011). https://doi.org/10.2200/S00362ED1V01Y201105DTM016

Upper Expected Meeting Times for Interdependent Stochastic Agents

Marco Sangalli(✉), Erik Quaeghebeur, and Thomas Krak

Uncertainty in AI, Eindhoven University of Technology, Eindhoven, The Netherlands
m.sangalli@tue.nl

Abstract. We analyse the problem of meeting times for interdependent stochastic agents: random walkers whose behaviour is stochastic but controlled by their selections from some set of allowed actions, and the inference problem of when these agents are all in the same state for the first time. We consider the case where we are epistemically uncertain about the selected actions of these agents, and show how their behaviour can be modelled using imprecise Markov chains. This allows us to use results and algorithms from the literature, to exactly compute bounds on their meeting time, which are tight with respect to our epistemic uncertainty models. After focussing on the two-agent case, we analyse and discuss how it can be extended to an arbitrary number of agents, and how the corresponding combinatorial explosion can be partly mitigated by exploiting symmetries inherent in the problem.

Keywords: Markov Chain · Upper Expectation · Meeting Time · Imprecise Probability

1 Introduction

Markov chains are a cornerstone of stochastic modelling, finding applications in fields as diverse as statistical physics [15], queuing theory [11], and network science [19]. A fundamental question in this context is the *hitting time*: the first moment at which a stochastic process enters a given set of states [16]. When considering multiple independent Markov chains evolving on the same finite state space, a natural extension is the *meeting time*, defined as the first moment at which all chains occupy the same state. Equivalently, this can be viewed as a hitting-time problem on the Cartesian product of their state spaces, with the target set being the diagonal [7,14,16].

In this work, we generalize this problem to that of computing the expected meeting time of what we call *interdependent stochastic agents*. Broadly, these are random walkers on some shared state space, whose behaviour is stochastic, but controlled by their selection of transition probabilities from some set representing their allowed actions. Crucially, we allow the selections that these agents make to depend on the state(s) of the other agent(s) in the system; this induces the interdependency.

K. Sauerwald and M. Thimm (Eds.): ECSQARU 2025, LNAI 16099, pp. 238–252, 2026.
https://doi.org/10.1007/978-3-032-05134-9_17

On top of this construction, we consider the case where we are *epistemically uncertain* about the selections that the agents use, and show that meaningful and conservative estimates for the expected meeting time can still be computed in this setting. We focus in particular on three such uncertainty models: the degenerate belief, which simply describes the case where we *do* know the selections exactly; the vacuous belief, in which we are fully ignorant; and the degenerate-vacuous mixture, which combines these other models and may be particularly useful in some practical settings.

We show how the vacuous belief model allows us to describe the joint behaviour of the agents as an *imprecise Markov chain* [4,8,10] on their product space. This allows us to leverage known results from the literature, and in particular iterative algorithms for computing upper- and lower expected hitting times [13], to exactly solve the expected meeting time problem in this setting.

We largely focus on the two-agent case, but show how the formalization can be naturally extended to an arbitrary number of agents using a k-fold product construction. Moreover, we discuss how we can partly mitigate the combinatorial explosion of this problem, by quotienting the (exponentially large) product space over the symmetries obtained by permuting the order of the agents.

The remainder of this paper is structured as follows. Section 2 reviews preliminary notions of precise and imprecise Markov chains, known theory about hitting- and meeting times, and presents an extension of Krak's characterizations and algorithms [12] to hold under weaker conditions than their original assumptions. Section 3 formalizes the setting of two interdependent stochastic agents with epistemic uncertainty models for their selections, and the characterization of meeting times in terms of the hitting times of an imprecise Markov chain on the product space. In Sect. 4 we extend the theory to an arbitrary number of interdependent stochastic agents, and Sect. 5 concludes the paper and gives directions for future work.

2 Preliminaries

This section introduces the basic concepts of stochastic processes and Markov chains [16], hitting and meeting times for Markov chains [6,7,16] and imprecise Markov chains [4,8,10,13].

2.1 Stochastic Processes and Markov Chains

Let us denote by $\mathbb{N}$ the set of positive integers and define $\mathbb{N}_0 := \mathbb{N} \cup \{0\}$. Let $\mathscr{Z}$ be a finite state space of cardinality $N \geq 2$. A discrete-time stochastic process on $\mathscr{Z}$ is a sequence of $\mathscr{Z}$-valued random variables $(Z_n)_{n\in\mathbb{N}_0}$, and we write $\mathbb{P}_Z$ for its associated probability measure. Throughout, we use the notations "(Z_n)" and "$\mathbb{P}_Z$" interchangeably to refer to this process.

The process (Z_n) is called a *Markov chain* if it satisfies the Markov property, i.e. if for every $n \in \mathbb{N}_0$ and every $z_0, \ldots, z_{n+1} \in \mathscr{Z}$, it holds that

$$\mathbb{P}_Z\big(Z_{n+1} = z_{n+1} \mid Z_0 = z_0, \ldots, Z_n = z_n\big) = \mathbb{P}_Z\big(Z_{n+1} = z_{n+1} \mid Z_n = z_n\big).$$

The chain (Z_n) is called (time-)*homogeneous* if the one-step transition probabilities do not depend on n. Equivalently, there exists a single matrix $T = (T(z,z'))_{z,z' \in \mathcal{Z}}$, with

$$T(z,z') = \mathbb{P}_Z\big(Z_{n+1} = z' \mid Z_n = z\big) \quad \text{for all } n \in \mathbb{N}_0,$$

and each row of T summing to unity. Similarly, a non-homogeneous Markov chain (Z_n) is identified by a family of transition matrices (T_n).

2.2 Hitting and Meeting Times in the Precise Setting

Hitting Times. Let (Z_n) be a homogeneous Markov chain on $\mathcal{Z}$ with transition matrix $T = (T(z,z'))_{z,z' \in \mathcal{Z}}$. For any target set $A \subset \mathcal{Z}$, define the *hitting time*

$$\tau_A := \inf\{n \geq 0 : Z_n \in A\} \in \mathbb{N}_0 \cup \{+\infty\}.$$

This random variable represents the number of steps the process needs to do to first reach A. Conditioned on the chain starting at $z \in \mathcal{Z}$, the *expected hitting time* is

$$h_A^T(z) := \mathbb{E}_{\mathbb{P}_Z}\big[\tau_A \mid Z_0 = z\big].$$

The quantity $h_A^T(z)$[1] represents the expected number of steps that the process (Z_n), starting in $z \in \mathcal{Z}$, takes before reaching the set A.

Theorem 1 ([16]). *Let $A \subset \mathcal{Z}$ and let (Z_n) be a homogeneous Markov chain with transition matrix T. The vector of expected hitting times $h_A^T = (h_A^T(z))_{z \in \mathcal{Z}}$ is the minimal non-negative solution to the following system of equations:*

$$\begin{cases} h_A^T(z) = 0 & \text{for all } z \in A, \\ h_A^T(z) = 1 + \sum_{z' \in \mathcal{Z}} T(z,z') h_A^T(z') & \text{for all } z \notin A, \end{cases} \tag{1}$$

which can be rewritten as

$$h_A^T = \mathbb{1}_{A^c} + \mathbb{1}_{A^c} \cdot T h_A^T, \tag{2}$$

where $\mathbb{1}$ is the indicator function and $\cdot$ represents the element-wise multiplication.

Meeting Times. Consider a joint stochastic process $(X_n, Y_n)_{n \in \mathbb{N}_0}$ on $\mathcal{Z}^2 := \mathcal{Z} \times \mathcal{Z}$. Define the *meeting time* for X_n and Y_n as

$$\mu := \inf\{n \geq 0 : X_n = Y_n\} \in \mathbb{N}_0 \cup \{+\infty\}.$$

If the joint process starts at $(X_0, Y_0) = (x, y)$ then the *expected meeting time* is

$$m(x,y) := \mathbb{E}_{\mathbb{P}_{(X,Y)}}\big[\mu \mid X_0 = x,\ Y_0 = y\big]. \tag{3}$$

[1] The superscript T does *not* denote matrix transpose; rather, it indicates the dependency of the hitting time on the transition matrix T.

The quantity $m(x, y)$ represents the expected number of steps that the two processes, when starting in x and y respectively, take before meeting. In the case where the joint process (X_n, Y_n) is obtained as the independent product of two homogenous Markov chains (X_n) and (Y_n) with transition matrices T and S, respectively, the expected meeting time has a particularly nice characterisation.

Theorem 2 **([6,7]).** *Let (X_n) and (Y_n) be two homogenous Markov chains with transition matrices T and S respectively. The matrix of expected meeting times $m = (m(x, y))_{x,y \in \mathcal{Z}}$ is the minimal non-negative solution to the following system of equations:*

$$\begin{cases} m(z, z) = 0 & \text{for all } z \in \mathcal{Z}, \\ m(x, y) = 1 + \sum_{x', y' \in \mathcal{Z}} T(x, x')S(y, y')m(x', y') & \text{for all } x \neq y, \end{cases} \tag{4}$$

which can be rewritten as

$$m = J + J \cdot \left(TmS^{\top}\right), \tag{5}$$

where J is a $N \times N$ matrix that has zeros on the main diagonal and ones everywhere else, and $S^{\top}$ is the transpose of S.

The meeting time problem can be reformulated as a hitting time problem on the product space $\mathcal{Z}^2$, with target set being $D := \{(z, z) \mid z \in \mathcal{Z}\}$ and transition probability from state (x, y) to state (x', y') being $T(x, x')S(y, y')$.

Using the operation of vectorization and the Kronecker product [7,20], denoted by the symbol $\otimes$, we may rewrite (5) as

$$\text{vec}(m) = \mathbb{1}_{D^c} + \mathbb{1}_{D^c} \cdot (T \otimes S)\,\text{vec}(m),$$

where the operator vec stacks the columns of m to make an N^2 long vector.

2.3 Imprecise Markov Chains

Let us consider a set of transition matrices $\mathcal{T}$ on the finite space $\mathcal{Z}$, with $|\mathcal{Z}| = N$. Throughout this paper, we assume that $\mathcal{T}$ is a non-empty, compact, and convex set with rows that are independently specified—a property known in the literature as having separately specified rows (SSR) [10,13]. The assumption of having separately specified rows is equivalent to defining N separate convex and compact sets of probability distributions, one for each state $z \in \mathcal{Z}$.

An imprecise Markov chain (IMC) can be viewed as a collection of Markov chains. A natural example is $\mathcal{P}^H_{\mathcal{T}}$, the collection of all homogeneous Markov chains whose transition matrix belongs to $\mathcal{T}$. We are interested in computing hitting times for imprecise Markov chains, so we introduce the following upper and lower expectation operators:

$$\overline{\mathbb{E}}_{\mathcal{T}}[\,\cdot\,] := \sup_{\mathbb{P} \in \mathcal{P}^H_{\mathcal{T}}} \mathbb{E}_{\mathbb{P}}[\,\cdot\,], \qquad \underline{\mathbb{E}}_{\mathcal{T}}[\,\cdot\,] := \inf_{\mathbb{P} \in \mathcal{P}^H_{\mathcal{T}}} \mathbb{E}_{\mathbb{P}}[\,\cdot\,].$$

These definitions allow us to define the upper and lower expected hitting time of a target set $A \subset \mathscr{Z}$ as

$$\overline{h}_A^{\mathcal{T}}(z) := \overline{\mathbb{E}}_{\mathcal{T}}[\tau_A \mid Z_0 = z] \quad \text{and} \quad \underline{h}_A^{\mathcal{T}}(z) := \underline{\mathbb{E}}_{\mathcal{T}}[\tau_A \mid Z_0 = z],$$

respectively.

There exists a characterization for upper expected hitting times similar to Eq. (2). Let $\overline{T} : \mathbb{R}^N \to \mathbb{R}^N$ be the (possibly) nonlinear map defined for all $f \in \mathbb{R}^N$ and all $z \in \mathscr{Z}$ as

$$[\overline{T}f](z) := \sup_{T \in \mathcal{T}} [Tf](z).$$

Then, we have that $\overline{h}_A^{\mathcal{T}} = \mathbb{1}_{A^c} + \mathbb{1}_{A^c} \cdot \overline{T}\, \overline{h}_A^{\mathcal{T}}$, with a similar characterization for the lower expected hitting times [13].

Reachability Condition. Given a set of transition matrices $\mathcal{T}$ we say that a set of states $\mathcal{C} \subseteq \mathscr{Z}$ is *upper reachable* [2,4] from $z \in \mathscr{Z}$ if there exists $n \in \mathbb{N}$ such that $[\overline{T}^n \mathbb{1}_{\mathcal{C}}](z) > 0$, i.e. there exists $n \in \mathbb{N}$ and $T \in \mathcal{T}$ such that $[T^n \mathbb{1}_{\mathcal{C}}](z) > 0$. We denote by $z \rightharpoonup \mathcal{C}$ if $\mathcal{C}$ is upper reachable from z. Analogously, the set $\mathcal{C} \subseteq \mathscr{Z}$ is *lower reachable* from $z \in \mathscr{Z}$ if there exists $n \in \mathbb{N}$ such that $[\underline{T}^n \mathbb{1}_{\mathcal{C}}](z) > 0$, i.e.[2] there exists $n \in \mathbb{N}$ such that for all $T \in \mathcal{T}$ it holds that $[T^n \mathbb{1}_{\mathcal{C}}](z) > 0$. We denote by $z \rightharpoondown \mathcal{C}$ if $\mathcal{C}$ is lower reachable from z.

Given a set of transition matrices $\mathcal{T}$ and a target set $A \subset \mathscr{Z}$, we say that the reachability condition (R1) holds if

$$(\mathrm{R1}): \quad \forall z \in A^c : z \rightharpoondown A$$

Under (R1), the upper expected hitting time $\overline{h}_A^{\mathcal{T}}(z)$ is finite for all $z \in A^c$ [12]. If (R1) does not hold, then there exists a non-empty set of states $\mathscr{A}_{\mathcal{T}} \subset A^c$ such that

$$\mathscr{A}_{\mathcal{T}} := \{z \in A^c \mid z \not\rightharpoondown A\}.$$

For all states $z \in \mathscr{A}_{\mathcal{T}}$ it naturally holds that $\overline{h}_A^{\mathcal{T}}(z) = +\infty$. This is due to the fact that for all $z \in \mathscr{A}_{\mathcal{T}}$ and all $n \in \mathbb{N}$, there exists $T \in \mathcal{T}$ such that $[T^n \mathbb{1}_A](z) = 0$. The set $\mathscr{A}_{\mathcal{T}}$ is often called the set of (lower) *absorbing states* of $\mathcal{T}$.

Let us denote with $\mathscr{U}_{\mathcal{T}}$ the set of all states of $A^c \setminus \mathscr{A}_{\mathcal{T}}$ that upper reach a state in $\mathscr{A}_{\mathcal{T}}$, i.e.

$$\mathscr{U}_{\mathcal{T}} := \{z \in A^c \setminus \mathscr{A}_{\mathcal{T}} \mid z \rightharpoonup \mathscr{A}_{\mathcal{T}}\}.$$

The following theorem characterizes upper hitting times for all states of $\mathscr{Z}$.

Theorem 3. *Let $\mathcal{T}$ be a set of transition matrices and let $\mathscr{A}_{\mathcal{T}}$ and $\mathscr{U}_{\mathcal{T}}$ be as defined above. Then, for all $z \in \mathscr{B}_{\mathcal{T}} := \mathscr{A}_{\mathcal{T}} \cup \mathscr{U}_{\mathcal{T}}$ it holds that $\overline{h}_A^{\mathcal{T}}(z) = +\infty$. Moreover, there exists a matrix $\tilde{T} \in \mathcal{T}$ such that*

$$\overline{h}_A^{\mathcal{T}}|_{A^c \setminus \mathscr{B}_{\mathcal{T}}} = (I - \tilde{T}|_{A^c \setminus \mathscr{B}_{\mathcal{T}}})^{-1} \boldsymbol{1},$$

where I denotes the identity matrix and $\boldsymbol{1}$ the vector of all ones.

[2] This equivalence is not entirely trivial, but we omit the full derivation due to page limit constraints.

Proof. It follows from Krak et al. [13, Theorem 12] that there always exists a matrix $\tilde{T} \in \mathcal{T}$ such that $\overline{h}_A^{\mathcal{T}} = h^{\tilde{T}}$, where $h^{\tilde{T}}$ is the minimal non-negative solution of the linear system $h^{\tilde{T}} = \mathbb{1}_{A^c} + \mathbb{1}_{A^c} \cdot \tilde{T} h^{\tilde{T}}$. If $z \in \mathscr{U}_{\mathcal{T}}$, the Markov chain $\mathbb{P}_{\tilde{T}}$ that starts in z has positive probability of hitting the absorbing set $\mathscr{A}_{\mathcal{T}}$ thus positive probability of never reaching A. This implies that the upper expected hitting time for all $z \in \mathscr{U}_{\mathcal{T}}$ is infinite.

Observe that, for all $z \in A^c \setminus \mathscr{B}_{\mathcal{T}}$, for all $T \in \mathcal{T}$, and for all $n \in \mathbb{N}$, it holds that $[T^n \mathbb{1}_{\mathscr{B}_{\mathcal{T}}}](z) = 0$. Therefore, we can restrict $\tilde{T}$ on $\tilde{\mathcal{Z}} := \mathcal{Z} \setminus \mathscr{B}_{\mathcal{T}}$ as the Markov chain $\mathbb{P}_{\tilde{T}}$ starting from any state in $\tilde{\mathcal{Z}}$ never leaves $\tilde{\mathcal{Z}}$. Thus, starting from any state in $\tilde{\mathcal{Z}} \setminus A$, the process eventually reaches A, and this yields the invertibility of $I - \tilde{T}|_{\tilde{\mathcal{Z}} \setminus A}$ [16]. We are then able to conclude that $h^{\tilde{T}}|_{\tilde{\mathcal{Z}} \setminus A} = (I - \tilde{T}|_{\tilde{\mathcal{Z}} \setminus A})^{-1} \mathbf{1}$ which is what we wanted. □

An analogous result holds for lower expected hitting times: in this case, the definitions of $\mathscr{A}_{\mathcal{T}}$ and $\mathscr{U}_{\mathcal{T}}$ are obtained by swapping upper and lower reachability in their respective constructions.

A Computational Method. Upper- and lower expected hitting times can be computed efficiently using iterative algorithms [12,13]. One such algorithm is the following: starting from any extreme point T_1 of (the convex set) $\mathcal{T}$, let h_n be the unique solution of the linear system $h_n = \mathbb{1}_{A^c} + \mathbb{1}_{A^c} \cdot T_n h_n$ and let T_{n+1} be an extreme point of $\mathcal{T}$ such that $\overline{T} h_n = T_{n+1} h_n$. Krak [12] showed that, under (R1), the sequence $(h_n)_{n \in \mathbb{N}}$ converges to $\overline{h}_A^{\mathcal{T}}$. We refer to this procedure as Krak's algorithm.

If there is a non-empty set $\mathscr{A}_{\mathcal{T}}$ then, as Theorem 3 shows, we may restrict our analysis to $A^c \setminus \mathscr{B}_{\mathcal{T}}$ as elsewhere the upper expected hitting time is either zero or infinite. For each $T \in \mathcal{T}$ consider the restriction of T on $\mathscr{B}_{\mathcal{T}}^c$

$$T|_{\mathscr{B}_{\mathcal{T}}^c} = \left(T(i,j)\right)_{i,j \in \mathscr{B}_{\mathcal{T}}^c} \in \mathbb{R}^{|\mathscr{B}_{\mathcal{T}}^c| \times |\mathscr{B}_{\mathcal{T}}^c|},$$

the submatrix of T indexed by $\mathscr{B}_{\mathcal{T}}^c$. Then, the set of matrices $\mathcal{T}|_{\mathscr{B}_{\mathcal{T}}^c}$ containing the restriction on $\mathscr{B}_{\mathcal{T}}^c$ of all matrices in $\mathcal{T}$, satisfies (R1)[3]. Therefore, we may apply Krak's algorithm to compute the upper expected hitting time for all nontrivial states of $\mathcal{Z}$.

Before applying Krak's algorithm, we need to first identify sets $\mathscr{A}_{\mathcal{T}}$ and $\mathscr{U}_{\mathcal{T}}$ (in this order). To obtain the former we make use of the following lemma.

Lemma 1 ([2,3,9]). *Let $\mathcal{C}$ be a subset of $\mathcal{Z}$ such that $[\overline{T}\mathbb{1}_{\{y\}}](x) = 0$ for all $x \in \mathcal{C}$ and $y \in \mathcal{Z} \setminus \mathcal{C}$. Let $(\mathcal{C}_n)_{n \in \mathbb{N}_0}$ be the nondecreasing sequence given by $\mathcal{C}_0 = \mathcal{C}$ and*

$$\mathcal{C}_{n+1} = \mathcal{C}_n \cup \{z \in \mathcal{Z} \setminus \mathcal{C}_n \mid [\underline{T}\mathbb{1}_{\mathcal{C}_n}](z) > 0\},$$

for all $n \in \mathbb{N}_0$. Let n^* be the first index for which $\mathcal{C}_{n^*} = \mathcal{C}_{n^*+1}$. Then, the set $\mathcal{C}_{n^*}$ contains all states of $\mathcal{Z}$ that lower reach $\mathcal{C}$.

[3] To compute the lower expected meeting time, we need to further restrict $\mathcal{T}$ excluding every matrix that has a positive probability of reaching $\mathscr{B}_{\mathcal{T}}$.

This lemma enables us to implement a straightforward algorithm to identify $\mathscr{A}_{\mathcal{T}}^{c}$ (and therefore $\mathscr{A}_{\mathcal{T}}$). This algorithm is a modification of Algorithm 2 in [2].

Algorithm 1: Finding the set $\mathscr{A}_{\mathcal{T}}$

$\mathcal{C} \leftarrow A$;
repeat
  $\mathcal{M} \leftarrow \varnothing$;
  foreach $z \in \mathcal{Z} \setminus \mathcal{C}$ **do**
    if $[\underline{T}\,\mathbb{1}_{\mathcal{C}}](z) > 0$ **then**
      $\mathcal{M} \leftarrow \mathcal{M} \cup \{z\}$;
  $\mathcal{C} \leftarrow \mathcal{C} \cup \mathcal{M}$;
until $\mathcal{M} = \varnothing$;
return $\mathscr{A}_{\mathcal{T}} = \mathcal{C}^{c}$;

Finding the set $\mathscr{U}_{\mathcal{T}}$ of states that upper reach $\mathscr{A}_{\mathcal{T}}$ is even more straightforward. First, we build the directed graph $G_{\overline{T}} = (\mathcal{Z}, E)$, where $(x, y) \in E$ if $[\overline{T}\mathbb{1}_{\{y\}}](x) > 0$. Then, for all $z \in A^{c} \setminus \mathscr{A}_{\mathcal{T}}$, we check (e.g. by performing a breadth-first search on $G_{\overline{T}}$) whether there exists a path in $G_{\overline{T}}$ from z to $\mathscr{A}_{\mathcal{T}}$. If such path exists then $z \in \mathscr{U}_{\mathcal{T}}$.

3 Upper and Lower Meeting Times for Interdependent Stochastic Agents

We now move on to the formalization of what we call *stochastic agents*. The basic idea is that we have agents—essentially random walkers on the state space $\mathcal{Z}$—whose behaviour can be influenced by making selections from some allowed set of possible actions.

Formally, for each $z \in \mathcal{Z}$, we consider a set $\mathcal{T}_z$ of probability mass functions on $\mathcal{Z}$, which we interpret as the set of allowed actions that an agent can select from, whenever they are in state z. We then say that a stochastic agent is a random walker on $\mathcal{Z}$ whose behaviour is determined by her specifying some selection that is compatible with these sets $\mathcal{T}_z$. Such a selection, say $T(z, \cdot) \in \mathcal{T}_z$, thus corresponds to a probability distribution that governs the stochastic behaviour of the agent: the probability that she will be in state z' at the next time point is given by $T(z, z')$.

To clean up the notation, we gather all these allowed actions in a set $\mathcal{T}$ of transition matrices, such that

$$\mathcal{T} = \left\{ T \text{ a trans. mat.} \,|\, T(z, \cdot) \in \mathcal{T}_z \text{ for all } z \in \mathcal{Z} \right\}, \tag{6}$$

where $T(z, \cdot)$ denotes the z row of the transition matrix T. In this way, any state-dependent selection can be expressed as a single element of $\mathcal{T}$.

Note that so far we have not specified how these selections are made and what they can depend on. Indeed, a simple example would be an agent who simply selects some $T \in \mathcal{T}$ and maintains this forever; the associated walker can then be represented by a homogeneous Markov chain with transition matrix T. Another example might be an agent whose selections depend on time: these selections $(T_n)_{n\in\mathbb{N}_0}$ then determine a non-homogeneous Markov chain that describes the stochastic evolution of the agent. However, the selections might also be functions of additional things.

In particular, we are interested in studying the multi-agent setting, in which the behaviour of agents is interdependent. We start the exposition here with the simplest case, in which we are only dealing with two agents. We say that they are *interdependent*, when the selection that an agent makes at some point in time, depends on the state of the other agent at that same point in time (and vice versa). For each state y that one agent can be in, the other agent needs to specify a selection $T^y(x,\cdot) \in \mathcal{T}_x$ for each state x that *they* can be in. Hence, the selection for this agent can be summarised as a collection $(T^y)_{y\in\mathcal{Z}}$ of transition matrices in $\mathcal{T}$. Similarly, we denote the selection of the other agent as $(S^x)_{x\in\mathcal{Z}}$.

Given the selections of the two agents, their joint behaviour can be modelled by a stochastic process (X_n, Y_n) on $\mathcal{Z}^2$, in which X_n and Y_n represent the states of the two agents at time n. This process is Markovian and homogeneous, and satisfies

$$\mathbb{P}_{(X,Y)}\big((X_{n+1}, Y_{n+1}) = (x', y') \mid (X_n, Y_n) = (x, y)\big) = T^y(x, x')S^x(y, y')\,, \tag{7}$$

where we write (T^y) and (S^x) for the selections driving X_n and Y_n, respectively.

To summarize the above construction, we have described a multi-agent setting, in which the behaviour of each agent is stochastic, but influenced by their selections from some set of allowed actions. There are potentially many interesting inference problems that we could consider, but here we focus on the *expected meeting time* for the two agents.

To conclude the formalization of the problem that we want to study, we now consider the case where we are *epistemically uncertain* about the selections of these agents. Clearly, this uncertainty affects our ability to compute these expected meeting times. However, depending on the exact uncertainty model that we use to represent these beliefs, we may still be able to make useful conclusions about this quantity of interest. In the remainder of this section, we consider this problem under various choices of such uncertainty models.

3.1 Degenerate Belief

Let us begin by considering what is arguably the simplest uncertainty model: the degenerate belief, in which we are certain that the two agents use selections $(T^y)_{y\in\mathcal{Z}}$ and $(S^x)_{x\in\mathcal{Z}}$, respectively.[4]

[4] Clearly, in this case we are not actually "uncertain" at all, but this framing allows us to represent all cases that we consider in a unified framework.

It follows immediately that this case is described exactly by the single joint process (X_n, Y_n) characterised in Eq. (7). Since this joint process is a homogenous Markov chain, it is determined by a transition matrix Δ on $\mathcal{Z}^2$. We see from the above that the $((x,y),(x',y'))$ entry, which represents the probability of transitioning from (x,y) to (x',y'), is given by

$$\Delta\big((x,y),(x',y')\big) = T^y(x,x')S^x(y,y'). \tag{8}$$

Moreover, the expected meeting time for the agents coincides with the expected hitting time of the Markov chain (X_n, Y_n) on target set $D = \{(z,z) \mid z \in \mathcal{Z}\}$. The corresponding matrix of expected meeting times m satisfies a system of equations analogous to (4), where each occurrence of T and S is replaced by T^y and S^x, respectively; using the definition of Δ yields

$$\begin{cases} m(x,x) = 0 & \text{for all } x \in \mathcal{Z}, \\ m(x,y) = 1 + \sum_{x',y' \in \mathcal{Z}} \Delta\big((x,y),(x',y')\big)m(x',y') & \text{for all } x \neq y. \end{cases} \tag{9}$$

So, in this case, we can compute the expected meeting times exactly, by solving this linear system of equations.

3.2 Vacuous Belief

The next uncertainty model that we consider is the *vacuous belief* over the space of all possible selections; this corresponds to the case in which we are fully ignorant about which selections the agents use.

We know from our discussion in Sect. 3.1 that any specific pair of selections, say $(T^y)_{y\in\mathcal{Z}}$ and $(S^x)_{x\in\mathcal{Z}}$, determines a homogenous Markov chain on $\mathcal{Z}^2$ that is characterized by a transition matrix Δ, as in Eq. (8). By following this construction for every possible pair of selections that the agents might choose, we induce a set of transition matrices on $\mathcal{Z}^2$:

$$\mathcal{T}^2 := \left\{ \Delta \in \mathbb{R}^{N^2 \times N^2} \,\middle|\, \Delta((x,y),(x',y')) := T^y(x,x')S^x(y,y') \right\},$$

where $N = |\mathcal{Z}|$ and we are varying all possible selections (T^y) and (S^x) in $\mathcal{T}$.

Each element Δ of $\mathcal{T}^2$ exactly corresponds to a pair of selections (T^y) and (S^x), which makes this set a convenient representation of the space over which we want to model our beliefs. In particular, each $\Delta \in \mathcal{T}^2$ induces a homogeneous Markov chain $\mathbb{P}_\Delta$, which we collect in the set $\mathcal{P}_{\mathcal{T}^2} = \{\mathbb{P}_\Delta \mid \Delta \in \mathcal{T}^2\}$. Our vacuous beliefs are now represented by the upper (and lower) expectation operators given by

$$\overline{\mathbb{E}}_{\mathcal{T}^2}[\,\cdot\,] := \sup_{\mathbb{P}\in\mathcal{P}_{\mathcal{T}^2}} \mathbb{E}_{\mathbb{P}}[\,\cdot\,], \qquad \text{and} \qquad \underline{\mathbb{E}}_{\mathcal{T}^2}[\,\cdot\,] := \inf_{\mathbb{P}\in\mathcal{P}_{\mathcal{T}^2}} \mathbb{E}_{\mathbb{P}}[\,\cdot\,]. \tag{10}$$

We immediately recognize the set $\mathcal{P}_{\mathcal{T}^2}$ as an *imprecise Markov chain* on the product space $\mathcal{Z}^2$, that is characterised by the set $\mathcal{T}^2$ of transition matrices. Moreover, our vacuous beliefs in Eq. (10) correspond simply to the upper- and lower expectation operators for this imprecise Markov chain.

This also means that we can leverage the known results from Sect. 2.3, provided that $\mathcal{T}^2$ satisfies the required regularity conditions; let us analyze how these carry over from the set $\mathcal{T}$ of allowed actions. If $\mathcal{T}$ is compact and with SSR[5], the same holds for $\mathcal{T}^2$. This follows from the fact that for any fixed x and y, rows $T^y(x,\cdot)$ and $S^x(y,\cdot)$ appear only in one row of Δ. Convexity does not carry over from $\mathcal{T}$ to $\mathcal{T}^2$. This is due to the fact that the map

$$(T^1,\ldots,T^N,S^1,\ldots,S^N) \longmapsto \Delta$$

is bilinear (i.e. linear in each family (T^y) or (S^x) separately) rather than affine, and only affine maps are guaranteed to preserve convexity [17]. Restoring convexity by replacing $\mathcal{T}^2$ with its convex hull will prove useful later.

Moving on, we can now characterise the upper expected meeting time as

$$\overline{m}^{\mathcal{T}^2}(x,y) := \overline{\mathbb{E}}_{\mathcal{T}^2}[\,\mu \mid (X_0,Y_0)=(x,y)] = \overline{h}_D^{\mathcal{T}^2}\big((x,y)\big). \tag{11}$$

Since the supremum in Eq. (11) is always achieved on a extreme point [1] of $\mathcal{T}^2$, and since $\mathcal{T}^2$ and its convex hull $\mathrm{co}(\mathcal{T}^2)$ share the same extreme points, the upper expected meeting time can be computed by optimizing over $\mathrm{co}(\mathcal{T}^2)$, obtaining the same maximal value.

Similarly as before, let us define the upper transition operator $\overline{\Delta} : \mathbb{R}^{N^2} \to \mathbb{R}^{N^2}$ for $\mathrm{co}(\mathcal{T}^2)$ as $[\overline{\Delta} f](z) := \sup_{\Delta\in\mathrm{co}(\mathcal{T}^2)}[\Delta f](z)$, for all $f \in \mathbb{R}^{N^2}$ and all $z \in \mathcal{Z}^2$. Then, $\overline{m}^{\mathcal{T}^2}$ is the minimal non-negative solution to

$$\mathrm{vec}(\overline{m}^{\mathcal{T}^2}) = \mathbb{1}_{D^c} + \mathbb{1}_{D^c}\cdot\overline{\Delta}\,\mathrm{vec}(\overline{m}^{\mathcal{T}^2}). \tag{12}$$

An analogous construction characterises lower expected meeting times.

Computing Upper Meeting Times. To compute upper (and lower) expected meeting times under our vacuous belief model, we may use Krak's algorithm [12] for upper (and lower) expected hitting times, restricted to $\mathscr{B}^c_{\mathcal{T}^2}$, as introduced at the end of Sect. 2.3. First of all, we need to identify the sets $\mathscr{A}_{\mathcal{T}^2}$ and $\mathscr{U}_{\mathcal{T}^2}$ that have infinite upper expected meeting time. To do so, we apply the algorithms from the end of Sect. 2.3 to the product space $\mathcal{Z}^2$, replacing $\mathcal{T}$ with $\mathrm{co}(\mathcal{T}^2)$.

The Corresponding Optimal Control Problem. We feel that it is relevant to note that while we phrased the problem here in terms of our epistemic uncertainty about the selections of the agents, our formalization has a natural other interpretation as an optimal control problem. That is, the agents might be strategically choosing their selections—or even have these selections imposed by some external controller—in such a way as to minimize or maximize their meeting time, subject to the constraints on the allowed actions $\mathcal{T}$. Finding the optimal pair of selections then amounts to finding the elements of $\mathcal{T}^2$ that attain the extremal values in Eq. (10). Indeed, Krak's algorithm [12] may be used precisely to find such an optimal control policy.

[5] Note that $\mathcal{T}$ always has SSR, when it is constructed as in Eq. (6).

Exploiting the Symmetry. We shall note that we can exploit the symmetry of the problem and restrict our analysis on the *symmetric product space* $\mathscr{Z}^2/S_2$, where S_2 is the symmetric group [18]. Explicitly, we identify each pair (x, y) with (y, x), as the two agents are indistinguishable, so that the space $\mathscr{Z}^2/S_2$ consists of all unordered pairs of states of $\mathscr{Z}$. As a consequence the optimal selections $(T^y)_{y\in\mathscr{Z}}$ and $(S^x)_{x\in\mathscr{Z}}$ coincide, i.e. $T^z = S^z$ for all $z \in \mathscr{Z}$. As we pass to the symmetric product space $\mathscr{Z}^2/S_2$, $\mathcal{T}^2$ naturally becomes the set of transition matrices over $\mathscr{Z}^2/S_2$. For brevity, we continue to denote it by $\mathcal{T}^2$; the intended domain—whether the full product space or its symmetric quotient—is always clear from context.

Example 1. The figure below shows the graph $G_{\overline{T}}$ that encodes all possible transitions on the state space $\mathscr{Z} = \{1, 2, 3, 4, 5\}$ (left) and the corresponding transitions on the symmetric product space $\mathscr{Z}^2/S_2$ (right). An arrow that connects node i to node j in the left graph indicates that $[\overline{T}\mathbb{1}_{\{j\}}](i) > 0$; an analogous interpretation applies for the right graph with $\overline{\Delta}$ in place of $\overline{T}$.

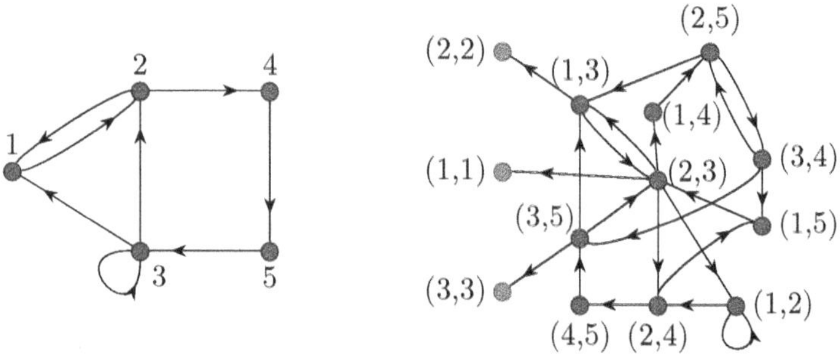

Depending on the choice of the set of allowed actions $\mathcal{T}$, some pair of states in $\mathscr{Z}$ may or may not have infinite upper expected meeting time. For example, if the set $\mathcal{T}$ is such that $[\underline{T}\mathbb{1}_{\{4\}}](2) = 0$, i.e. an agent in state 2 can choose not to go to state 4, then the pair $(1, 2)$ would become a lower absorbing state for $\mathscr{Z}^2/S_2$, i.e. $(1, 2) \in \mathscr{A}_{\mathcal{T}^2}$. In this case, every pair of states, e.g. $(2, 3)$, that has positive lower probability of eventually hitting $(1, 2)$ would be part of the set $\mathscr{U}_{\mathcal{T}^2}$ whose states also have infinite upper expected meeting time.

3.3 Degenerate-Vacuous Mixtures

The final uncertainty model that we consider is the *degenerate-vacuous mixture*. Note that this is a special case of the well-known *linear-vacuous mixture* [5], in which the linear component is represented by a degenerate (point mass) belief. Consequently, to characterize this model we need to specify both a pair of selections—which we conveniently represent through a single transition matrix $\Delta \in \mathcal{T}^2$—and some numerical parameter $\epsilon \in [0, 1]$. The associated upper expectation operator is then

$$\overline{\mathbb{E}}_{\epsilon,\Delta,\mathcal{T}^2}[\cdot] := (1-\epsilon)\mathbb{E}_{\mathbb{P}_\Delta}[\cdot] + \epsilon\overline{\mathbb{E}}_{\mathcal{T}^2}[\cdot], \tag{13}$$

and similarly for the lower expectation. Since for the particular case of meeting times, both terms on the right-hand side of this expression can be computed using the results in Sects. 3.1 and 3.2 respectively, it follows that we can also evaluate the upper (and lower) expected meeting times under this model.

We note that this uncertainty model may be particularly useful for conservatively evaluating performance in an "unreliable control" setting. That is, we might consider the degenerate component Δ to represent some optimal control, e.g. a minimizing pair of selections for the meeting time of the two agents, but in which these agents sometimes deviate from the intended control in a manner that is consistent with the allowed actions $\mathcal{T}$, yet otherwise completely unknown to us. The parameter ϵ measures this degree of unreliability, and the associated upper expected hitting time then provides a conservative estimate for the attained performance of this system.

4 Meeting Times for Multiple Interdependent Agents

In this section, we extend the meeting-time problem to multiple interdependent stochastic agents seeking to all gather at a single common location.

4.1 Imprecise Markov Chain Formulation for k Stochastic Agents

Consider $k \in \mathbb{N}, k > 2$ interdependent stochastic agents on the same state space $\mathcal{Z}$, with $|\mathcal{Z}| = N$, and with set of transition matrices $\mathcal{T}$. Each agent looks at the position of all other agents to determine which selection to make. For every agent $j \in [k] := \{1, \ldots, k\}$, her selections are identified with a collection of N^{k-1} transition matrices, $(T_j^{(z_i)_{i\in[k],i\neq j}})$ where $(z_i)_{i\in[k],i\neq j}$ represents the states of all other agents. To find the upper (and lower) expected meeting time of these stochastic agents, we consider the joint homogenous Markov chain $(Z^1, \ldots, Z^k)$ on $\mathcal{Z}^k = \mathcal{Z} \times \cdots \times \mathcal{Z}$, k times. Similarly as before, we define a set of transition matrices $\mathcal{T}^k$ on the space $\mathcal{Z}^k$ as follows

$$\mathcal{T}^k := \left\{ \Delta_k \in \mathbb{R}^{N^k \times N^k} \;\middle|\; \Delta_k((z_{1:k}), (z'_{1:k})) = \prod_{j=1}^{k} T_j^{(z_i)_{i\neq j}}(z_j, z'_j) \right\},$$

where, for each $j = 1, \ldots, k$, we vary over all possible selections of the k agents. Each matrix $\Delta_k \in \mathcal{T}^k$ is therefore defined using kN^{k-1} transition matrices on $\mathcal{Z}$.

As before, under the assumption that $\mathcal{T}$ is compact, convex and has SSR, the set $\mathcal{T}^k$ is compact and has separately specified rows. The upper (and lower) expected meeting time of k interdependent stochastic agents with set of transition matrices $\mathcal{T}$ can be seen as the upper (and lower) hitting time of an imprecise Markov chain on the space $\mathcal{Z}^k$ with set of transition matrices $\mathcal{T}^k$ and target set $D^k := \{(z, \ldots, z) \mid z \in \mathcal{Z}\}$. As in the case with two agents, by taking the convex hull of $\mathcal{T}^k$ and defining the corresponding upper (and lower) transition operator, we obtain a characterization of the upper (and lower) meeting time analogous to that in Eq. (12). Moreover, this also allows us to apply Krak's algorithm [12] to compute the upper (and lower) expected meeting time, as taking the convex hull leaves the upper (and lower) expected meeting time unchanged.

4.2 Symmetry Reduction

The state space $\mathcal{Z}^k$ grows exponentially with k. Exploiting the symmetry drastically reduces the number of states to consider as

$$|\mathcal{Z}^k/S_k| = \binom{N+k-1}{k} \ll N^k = |\mathcal{Z}^k|,$$

where S_k is the symmetric group of degree k. In other words, in the space $\mathcal{Z}^k/S_k$ all permutations of a k-tuple are identified. As in the case $k = 2$, every matrix $\Delta_k : \mathbb{R}^{|\mathcal{Z}^k/S_k|} \to \mathbb{R}^{|\mathcal{Z}^k/S_k|}$ is now defined using only N^{k-1} matrices from $\mathcal{T}$, as the k families of transition matrices coincide.

Moreover, if $2 \leq i < k$ stochastic agents are in the same state $z \in \mathcal{Z}$ their selected action that maximizes (or minimizes) the meeting time is the same for all i agents and depends only on the position of the other $k-i$ agents. Similarly, these other $k-i$ agents have the same optimal selection whether in z there are 1 or i distinct agents.

Hence, if we want to compute the expected meeting time of $k > N$ interdependent stochastic agents, we can reduce to the same problem with N such agents. From the optimal matrix Δ_N we can obtain the optimal selections for each agent, which we can then use to build the optimal matrix Δ_k. Therefore, the cost to compute upper (and lower) expected meeting times for $k > N$ interdependent stochastic agents is equivalent to that of N such agents, thus drastically reducing the computational burden for large values of k.

5 Conclusion and Future Work

In this work we considered the meeting-time problem for multiple interdependent stochastic agents, about whose selected actions we are epistemically uncertain. By establishing that these meeting times correspond to hitting the diagonal in the product space, and by focusing on specific uncertainty models for our beliefs about these agents' selected actions, we were able to recast the problem using the existing theory of imprecise Markov chains. We used their associated upper expectation operators to derive explicit characterizations for these quantities of interest, and leveraged Krak's iterative algorithm [12] to compute them. Finally, we showed that our approach extends naturally to an arbitrary number of agents via a k-fold product construction, and we exploited the problem's inherent symmetries to mitigate the exponential growth of the state space.

In future work, we hope to investigate more general interdependency mechanisms between these agents, provide a more in-depth characterisation of the joint imprecise process that describes their behaviour, and consider the case where agents may have different—possibly adversarial—objectives. It would also be interesting to generalize the problem to a continuous-time setting.

Acknowledgments. This work has been partly supported by the PersOn project (P21-03), which has received funding from the Nederlandse Organisatie voor Wetenschappelijk Onderzoek (NWO). Moreover, we are grateful to the three anonymous reviewers for their careful reading and thoughtful comments. Their input was essential in helping us strengthen the paper and present our ideas more clearly.

References

1. Bauer, H.: Minimalstellen von funktionen und extremalpunkte. Arch. Math. **9**, 389–393 (1958). https://doi.org/10.1007/BF01898615
2. Bock, J.: The limit behaviour of imprecise continuous-time markov chains. J. Nonlinear Sci. **27**(1), 159–196 (2016). https://doi.org/10.1007/s00332-016-9328-3
3. Bock, J.D., Erreygers, A., Persiau, F.: A convenient characterisation of convergent upper transition operators. In: Proceedings of the 14th International Symposium on Imprecise Probabilities: Theories and Applications (ISIPTA). Proceedings of Machine Learning Research, vol. 290 (2025). arXiv:2502.04509
4. de Cooman, G., Hermans, F., Quaeghebeur, E.: Imprecise markov chains and their limit behavior. Probab. Eng. Inf. Sci. **23**(4), 597–635 (2009). https://doi.org/10.1017/S0269964809990039
5. Destercke, S., Dubois, D.: Special cases. In: Augustin, T., Coolen, F.P.A., de Cooman, G., Troffaes, M.C.M. (eds.) Introduction to Imprecise Probabilities. Wiley Series in Probability and Statistics, Wiley (2014). https://doi.org/10.1002/9781118763117.ch4
6. Doeblin, W.: Exposé de la théorie des chaînes simples constantes de markov à un nombre fini d'états. Revue de Mathématiques de l'Union Interbalkanique **2**, 77–105 (1937)
7. George, M., Patel, R., Bullo, F.: The meeting time of multiple random walks. arXiv preprint arXiv:1806.08843 (2018)
8. Hartfiel, D.J., Seneta, E.B.: On the theory of markov set-chains. Adv. Appl. Probab. **26**(4), 947–964 (1994). https://doi.org/10.2307/1427899
9. Hermans, F., Cooman, G.: Characterisation of ergodic upper transition operators. Int. J. Approx. Reason. **53**(4), 573–583 (2012). https://doi.org/10.1016/j.ijar.2011.12.008
10. Hermans, F., Škulj, D.: Stochastic processes. In: Augustin, T., Coolen, F.P.A., de Cooman, G., Troffaes, M.C.M. (eds.) Introduction to Imprecise Probabilities, vol. 11. Wiley (2014). https://doi.org/10.1002/9781118763117.ch11
11. Kelly, F.P.: Reversibility and Stochastic Networks. Cambridge University Press, Cambridge (1979)
12. Krak, T.: Computing expected hitting times for imprecise markov chains. Space Technol. Proc. **8**, 185–205 (2021). https://doi.org/10.1007/978-3-030-80542-5_12
13. Krak, T., T'Joens, N., Bock, J.D.: Hitting times and probabilities for imprecise markov chains. In: Proceedings of the 14th International Symposium on Imprecise Probabilities: Theories and Applications (ISIPTA). Proceedings of Machine Learning Research, vol. 103, pp. 265–275 (2019)
14. Lindvall, T.: Lectures on the Coupling Method. Wiley-Interscience (1992)
15. Metropolis, N., Rosenbluth, A.W., Rosenbluth, M.N., Teller, A.H., Teller, E.: Equation of state calculations by fast computing machines. J. Chem. Phys. **21**(6), 1087–1092 (1953). https://doi.org/10.1063/1.1699114

16. Norris, J.R.: Markov Chains. Cambridge Series in Statistical and Probabilistic Mathematics, Cambridge University Press, Cambridge (1997). https://doi.org/10.1017/CBO9780511810633
17. Rockafellar, R.T.: Convex Analysis, Princeton Mathematical Series, vol. 28. Princeton University Press, Princeton (1970). https://doi.org/10.1515/9781400873173
18. Rotman, J.J.: An Introduction to the Theory of Groups, Graduate Texts in Mathematics, vol. 148. Springer (1995). https://doi.org/10.1007/978-1-4612-4176-8
19. Volchenkov, D., Blanchard, P.: Markov chain methods for analyzing complex transport networks. J. Stat. Phys. **132**(6), 1051–1069 (2008). https://doi.org/10.1007/s10955-008-9591-2
20. Zehfuss, G.: Ueber eine gewisse determinante. Zeitschrift für Mathematik und Physik **3**, 298–301 (1858)

Elicit and Weigh: A Voting-Based Approach to Optimal Weights in Imprecise Linear Pooling

Lea Bauer and Jonas Karge(✉)

TU Dresden, Dresden, Germany
lea.bauer@mailbox.tu-dresden.de, jonas.karge@tu-dresden.de

Abstract. Probabilistic opinion pooling aims to aggregate the probabilistic beliefs of multiple agents to reach a consensus. When dealing with high uncertainty contexts, agents' beliefs are often represented by *imprecise probabilities*, i.e. intervals of probability values. The most commonly used aggregation method for imprecise opinion pooling is *linear pooling*, which takes a weighted average of the input opinions. However, determining an optimal weight distribution for pooling is a complex challenge. In this work, we propose a novel elicitation method inspired by *epistemic voting* that provides probabilistic guarantees for agents to hold a correct belief. Furthermore, we show how to derive well-performing pooling weights from the elicited beliefs using existing results for the voting rule on which our elicitation method is based. Finally, we carry out parametric simulations that illustrate the whole process of elicitation and weighting and that show an increase in the quality of the aggregated opinions.

Keywords: Opinion Pooling · Imprecise Probabilities · Epistemic Voting

1 Introduction

The process of aggregating the probabilistic beliefs of multiple agents to reach a consensus is known as *probabilistic opinion pooling*. This approach is especially relevant in high-uncertainty contexts, such as forecasting critical climate tipping points [13]. In these cases, agents' beliefs are often best represented using *imprecise probabilities*, which express probability assignments as intervals rather than single values. When pooling imprecise probabilistic beliefs, numerous pooling functions have been proposed in the literature. Arguably, the most commonly used is *linear pooling* [18], which computes a weighted average of agents' input beliefs to produce a single collective belief. However, determining an *optimal* distribution of weights across agents when combining probabilistic beliefs remains a non-trivial problem [9].

In this paper, we take a novel approach to addressing the problem of identifying an optimal weight distribution by jointly considering the choice of weights

K. Sauerwald and M. Thimm (Eds.): ECSQARU 2025, LNAI 16099, pp. 253–266, 2026.
https://doi.org/10.1007/978-3-032-05134-9_18

and the method used to elicit agents' beliefs. *Elicitation methods* refer to processes designed to extract beliefs from experts. These methods are particularly useful in decision-making scenarios involving incomplete data or events characterized by severe uncertainty. A common approach in such cases is to elicit judgments from multiple experts to compensate for missing information [8].

The elicitation method we propose in this work is inspired by a recently introduced pooling method called *Voting for Bins* [3], which originates from the *epistemic voting* research program. In epistemic voting, elections aim to approximate a true state of the world, a concept supported by the *Condorcet Jury Theorem*, which provides probabilistic guarantees for correctly identifying the correct alternative. This connection also offers an interpretation of *optimal weights*: they correspond to a weight distribution in which the probabilistic linear pool best approximates the true probability of an event occurring, effectively representing the hidden ground truth. Building on this idea, we leverage information about the agents and their elicited beliefs, incorporating insights from epistemic voting theory to determine the optimal weight distribution.

Contributions. This paper makes four key contributions to *imprecise probabilistic opinion pooling*: First, we introduce a novel elicitation method based on plurality voting within an epistemic voting framework. Second, we establish a result analogous to the Condorcet Jury Theorem for plurality voting under the specific probabilistic assumptions considered in this work. Third, we demonstrate how the connection between elicitation and linear pooling enables the derivation of well-performing weights from elicited beliefs. Finally, we conduct a series of experiments simulating multiple rounds of elicitation under different parameter settings. By comparing the resulting linear pool with different weight distributions, we illustrate the elicitation and weighting procedure and show how the voting-based weights improve the overall quality of the linear opinion pool.

2 Preliminaries

In this section, we introduce the key terminology necessary to derive well-performing weights for linear imprecise pooling using our epistemic voting-based elicitation method.

To this end, we first provide an overview of imprecise probabilistic pooling, with a particular focus on linear pooling. We then discuss voting mechanisms in the context of the Condorcet Jury Theorem (CJT), a fundamental result in epistemic voting theory. Specifically, we present the classical CJT result and a prepare generalization thereof, which will play a central role in our analysis.

Imprecise Beliefs. Traditionally, an agent's probabilistic belief is represented by a single probability function, $\mathbb{P}$, which maps events to values in $[0, 1]$: capturing the agent's degree of belief in different propositions [13].

However, in many applications, expecting agents to assign precise probabilities is unrealistic—especially for events with significant uncertainty. To address this, the standard framework is extended to *Imprecise Probabilities* which are sets of probability functions [5].

A specific set of probability functions is denoted by $\mathcal{P}$. To express the range of values $\mathcal{P}$ assigns to a given event, we define the *imprecise degree of belief*:

Definition 1 (Imprecise Degree of Belief). *An agent's imprecise degree of belief in a proposition A is given by $\mathcal{P}(A) = \{\mathbb{P}(A) : \mathbb{P} \in \mathcal{P}\}$ [4].*

Following standard practice in imprecise pooling, we assume *convexity*, meaning that if an event is assigned different probabilities within $\mathcal{P}$, all intermediate values are also included. As a result, beliefs are represented by an interval $[a, b] \subseteq [0, 1]$, where a is the *lower probability* and b the *upper probability*.

Example 1. Consider an event A such as "it will rain tomorrow" and an agent a_1 who assesses the probability of A occurring. Suppose a_1 is rather confident that it will indeed rain tomorrow, but uncertain about the specific probability. We can then represent a_1's imprecise degree of belief as $\mathcal{P}(A) = [0.7, 0.9]$.

Imprecise Pooling. An imprecise pooling function, $\mathcal{F}$, aggregates a *profile* of probability function sets, where each agent i contributes a set $\mathcal{P}_i$. The function then maps this collection, $(\mathcal{P}_1, \dots, \mathcal{P}_n)$, to a single aggregated set of probability functions. When pooling is performed event-wise—i.e., with respect to a specific proposition A—the input consists of sets of imprecise degrees of belief, represented as probability intervals. The output is a single interval capturing the collective belief. Various pooling methods exist in the literature; in this work, we focus on *linear pooling*. Here, the input profile is defined in terms of the lower and upper probabilities of each agent's belief. Let λ_i denote the weight assigned to agent i's belief [12].

Definition 2 (Linear Pooling).
$\mathcal{F}([a_1, b_1], \dots, [a_n, b_n])(A) = [\sum_i \lambda_i a_i,\ \sum_i \lambda_i b_i]$.

Thus, linear pooling computes a weighted average of the lower and upper probabilities, producing an aggregated imprecise belief.

The Condorcet Jury Theorem. The CJT provides probabilistic guarantees for selecting the correct alternative in a voting scenario under certain conditions. Traditionally, CJT assumes that agents are: (1) equally competent (*homogeneity*), (2) more likely to vote correctly than incorrectly (*reliability*), (3) uninfluenced in their decisions (*independence*), and (4) required to choose exactly one of two alternatives (*dichotomy*) under majority voting [11]. Given these conditions, the classical CJT [6] states:

Theorem 1 (Marquis de Condorcet (1785)). *For an odd-numbered, homogeneous group of independent and reliable agents in a dichotomous voting setting, the probability that majority voting selects the correct alternative: (1) increases monotonically with the number of agents, and (2) converges to* 1 *as the number of agents approaches infinity.*

In practice, real-world settings rarely satisfy these idealized conditions. Consequently, CJT research explores generalizations that preserve asymptotic correctness under weaker assumptions. However, monotonicity no longer holds once agents with varying competencies (*heterogeneity*) are introduced [16].

In this work, we introduce a novel generalization of the CJT that accommodates heterogeneous agent competence, including unreliable voters, under *plurality voting*. To formalize this, we adopt the probabilistic framework presented in Karge et al. (2024) [10].

Formal Voting Framework. Intuitively, *plurality voting* is a system where each voter selects a single alternative from a finite set, and the option with the most votes wins. Formally, let $\mathcal{W} = \{\omega_1, \ldots, \omega_m\}$ be a set of m alternatives, and let $\mathcal{N}$ denote the set of agents. A *plurality voting instance* is given by $V \subseteq \mathcal{N} \times \mathcal{W}$, where $(a_i, \omega_j) \in V$ indicates that agent a_i votes for ω_j, with each agent selecting exactly one alternative. The *score* of an alternative $\omega \in \mathcal{W}$ is defined as: $\#_V\, \omega = |\{a_i \in \mathcal{N} \mid (a_i, \omega) \in V\}|$. The winner of V is the alternative with the highest score: $\#_V\, \omega > \max_{\omega' \in \mathcal{W} \setminus \{\omega\}} \#_V\, \omega'$.

The voting scenario is modeled as a random process that generates both the correct alternative, ω_*, and the voting outcome V. This process is governed by a joint probability distribution $\mathbb{P}$ over Bernoulli ($\{0,1\}$-valued) random variables $V_*^{\omega_1}, \ldots, V_*^{\omega_m}$ and $V_i^{\omega_1}, \ldots, V_i^{\omega_m}$ for all agents $i \in \{1, \ldots, n\}$ and alternatives $j \in \{1, \ldots, m\}$. The values of these variables represent the voting outcome as follows: $V_*^{\omega_j} = 1$ if ω_j is the true world state ($\omega_j = \omega_*$), and 0 otherwise. Likewise, $V_i^{\omega_j} = 1$ if agent a_i votes for ω_j, and 0 otherwise.

The Noise Model. To fully describe the probabilistic voting process underlying our generalization, we define the key probabilistic assumptions about agents, i.e. the *noise model*. As a first key assumption necessary to derive our CJT generalization, we formalize *independence*. For convenience, we denote the unknown correct alternative (or world state) as $[\omega_* = \omega_j]$ and any incorrect alternative as $\omega_\dagger$.

Definition 3 (Independence). *A joint distribution satisfies independence if, conditioned on the true world state, voting decisions are made independently across agents. Formally, for any $\omega, \omega_j \in \mathcal{W}$ and any sequence $v_1, \ldots, v_n \in \{0,1\}$,*

$$\mathbb{P}\Big(\bigwedge_{i=1}^{n} V_i^{\omega_j} = v_i \mid [\omega_*{=}\omega]\Big) = \prod_{i=1}^{n} \mathbb{P}\Big(V_i^{\omega_j} = v_i \mid [\omega_*{=}\omega]\Big) \text{ [11].}$$

Next, we introduce a key assumption regarding the agents' ability to identify the correct world state. An agent i votes for the correct and incorrect alternatives with probabilities $p_i^{\omega_*}$ and $p_i^{\omega_\dagger}$, respectively. The average probability of voting for ω across all agents is given by $\bar{p}^{\omega} = \frac{1}{n} \sum_{i=1}^{n} p_i^{\omega}$. To derive the asymptotic result, we need to guarantee that the agents are, at least on average, more likely to identify the correct alternative than any competing alternative.

Definition 4 (Δp-group reliability). *A joint probability distribution satisfies Δp-group reliability for some $\Delta p > 0$ if, on average, the probability of voting for the true world state exceeds that of any incorrect alternative by at least Δp. That is, for every n and $\omega_\dagger \in \mathcal{W} \setminus \{\omega_*\}$, $\bar{p}^{\omega_*} \geq \Delta p + \bar{p}^{\omega_\dagger}$.*

In order to complete our noise model, we recall our overall objective, i.e. to identify optimal weights for linear pooling by plurality voting. Therefore, our noise model is based on a noise model for which optimal weights for plurality voting have been identified. More specifically, our noise model is inspired by plurality voting in collective annotation tasks as presented by Qing et al., where the optimal weights were found to be $\lambda_i = \ln\left(\frac{(m-1)p_i^{\omega_*}}{1-p_i^{\omega_*}}\right)$ [17], giving more weight to more competent agents, but still including less reliable opinions. To simplify analysis, we adopt two key features from this model: First, as a competence bound, each agent i has a voting probability $p_i^{\omega_*} \in [\frac{1}{m}, 1]$, ensuring non-negative weights. Second, we adopt a uniform error distribution: The probability of voting for any incorrect alternative is uniform across all such alternatives: $p_i^{\omega_\dagger} = \frac{(1-\bar{p}^{\omega_*})}{(m-1)}$ [17]. Finally, since agents vote for a single alternative in plurality voting, we enforce: $p_i^{\omega_*} + \sum_{k=1}^{m-1} p_i^{\omega_\dagger} = 1$.

With the formal voting and probabilistic framework in place, we now examine how plurality voting under this model can be leveraged to elicit agents' beliefs and determine optimal weights for linear pooling.

3 Plurality Voting Based Elicitation

In decision-making scenarios where data is incomplete or events are characterized by significant uncertainty, it is common practice to elicit judgments from multiple experts to mitigate the missing information [8]. In the context of probabilistic expert elicitation, this process involves extracting knowledge from experts about uncertain events, such as the safety of nuclear facilities or the risk of terrorist attacks, and formulating this knowledge as a probability distribution [15]. Generally, elicitation is a complex task employed across various disciplines [15], and the quality of expert opinions can be enhanced by using structured elicitation methods [8].

In this paper, we propose a simple elicitation method based on plurality voting, grounded in a recently defined voting framework known as *Voting for Bins*. This approach serves two purposes: first, by reducing expert elicitation to plurality voting, we provide probabilistic guarantees regarding the experts' judgments; second, by directly connecting voting with the experts' beliefs, we can leverage optimal weights for plurality voting in linear pooling when aggregating their opinions.

Elicitation through Plurality Voting. To elicit experts' probabilistic beliefs about the likelihood of an event, we build upon a recently defined voting method for imprecise probabilistic beliefs, referred to as *Voting for Bins* [3]. The central idea is to partition the unit interval $[0, 1]$ into subintervals of equal width, called bins, where each bin contains probabilistic values that represent the likelihood of an event occurring. Assuming that exactly one bin holds the *true* probability for the event, and associating each bin with an alternative in a voting process, the correct bin represents the true alternative or ground truth. In the Voting for Bins framework, each agent votes for the bin that most closely aligns with their imprecise belief, enabling the application of probabilistic guarantees from the Condorcet Jury Theorem (CJT) to ensure the correct bin is the winner of the vote.

Building on this concept, we can formulate an elicitation method based on plurality voting as follows. Similar to the original Voting for Bins framework, we define a bin based on the unit interval and associate each bin with an alternative ω_j in the voting process [3]:

Definition 5 (Bin). *Each* $\omega_k \in \mathcal{W} = \{\omega_1, \ldots, \omega_m\}$ *represents a subinterval (bin) of the form* $[a_1, a_2)$*, obtained by partitioning the unit interval such that each* ω_k *has equal Lebesgue measure. The final subinterval is of the form* $[a_m, 1]$.

Note that the Lebesgue measure is the standard way of measuring the length of an interval. For any closed $[a, b]$, open (a, b), or half-open $(a, b]$ or $[a, b)$ interval, its Lebesgue measure is defined as the length $l = b - a$.

Definition 6 (Elicitation through Plurality Voting). *Suppose a set of* n *agents is faced with* m *bins, i.e., subintervals of the unit interval, where each agent chooses exactly one bin, i.e.,* $(a_i, \omega_j) \in V$ *for each agent, with exactly one* j *per agent.*

That is, contrary to the original Voting for Bins framework, the agents do not come with their imprecise beliefs and vote based on these beliefs; instead, they choose their beliefs through voting. This is illustrated in the following example:

Example 2. Let there be two bins, ω_1, ω_2 for some event A, with $\omega_1 = [0, 0.5)$ and $\omega_2 = [0.5, 1]$, reflecting the likelihood of A to occur, and two agents, a_1 and a_2. Suppose both agents believe that event A has a 0 to 50% probability of occurring. We then obtain $(a_1, \omega_1) \in V$ and $(a_2, \omega_1) \in V$, and the agents' beliefs are: $\mathcal{P}_1 = \mathcal{P}_2 = [0, 0.5)$.

Observe that the precision of the agents' beliefs directly corresponds to the number of bins in the plurality voting process. For example, if we had 20 bins instead of just two, the bins would be of the form $[0, 0.05)$, $[0.05, 0.1)$, ..., $[0.95, 1]$, each with size $l[0.95, 1] = 0.05$. Evidently, a larger number of bins—and thus, a more precise belief for each agent—is desirable, as more precise beliefs are more informative. However, since the number of bins corresponds to the number of alternatives in a voting process, a larger number of alternatives makes it generally less likely that the correct alternative will be identified through voting. To estimate the probability that the bin containing the correct probability value is chosen by more agents than any other bin, we derive a bound on this probability in the next section for our underlying noise model, and thus provide a measure of the expected quality of the chosen beliefs.

CJT for Plurality Voting. In this section, we aim at assessing the capacity of a group of agents to hold a correct belief based on our plurality voting-based elicitation method. This objective requires a bit of clarification: What does it mean exactly to hold a correct belief as an agent in our setting, and what probability can we assess? The first part of the question is quite straightforward: An agent holds a correct belief if the agent chooses the bin that contains the correct probabilistic value for an event to occur. The second part of the question is less straightforward. Given that we are in a voting setting based on the CJT, we can derive probabilistic guarantees about the correct alternative winning the election. Translated to our setting, this means that we can assess the probability of the correct bin being chosen as a belief by a number of agents greater than the number of agents choosing a particular wrong bin. In order to answer this second question, we will derive the minimal success probability for the correct alternative winning the plurality vote. The derivation of this minimal success probability parallels a similar proof of Karge and Rudolph (2022) [11].

We consider, agent by agent, the value $V_i^{\omega_*} - V_i^{\omega_\dagger}$. The "composite random variable" $V_i^{\omega_*} - V_i^{\omega_\dagger}$ can have two possible outcomes: 1, if agent a_i votes for ω_*, -1, if he votes for $\omega_\dagger$. To find good probability estimates, we use Hoeffding's inequality, which provides a tail estimate for the sum of independent random variables with the property of having zero probability outside a finite interval.

Lemma 1 (Hoeffding). *Let $X_1, \ldots, X_n$ be independent random variables satisfying $\mathbb{P}(l_i \leq X_i \leq u_i) = 1$ for reals l_i, u_i. Consider the sum of these random variables, $X = \sum_{i=1}^{n} X_i$. Then for every real number $t > 0$ holds*

$$\mathbb{P}(X - \mathbb{E}(X) \geq t) \leq e^{-\frac{2}{\sum_{i=1}^{n}(u_i - l_i)^2} t^2}.$$

We recall that the agent-wise distributions of $V_i^{\omega_*} - V_i^{\omega_\dagger}$ discussed above are of this type with $l_i = -1$ and $u_i = 1$. With that, we obtain a lower bound on the correct alternative receiving more votes than any competitor as follows:

$$\begin{aligned}
&\mathbb{P}(V^{\omega_*} > V^{\omega_\dagger}) \\
&\quad = \mathbb{P}(V^{\omega_*} - V^{\omega_\dagger} > 0) \\
&\quad = 1 - \mathbb{P}(V^{\omega_*} - V^{\omega_\dagger} \leq 0) \\
&\quad = 1 - \mathbb{P}((V^{\omega_*} - V^{\omega_\dagger}) - \mathbb{E}(V^{\omega_*} - V^{\omega_\dagger}) \leq -\mathbb{E}(V^{\omega_*} - V^{\omega_\dagger})) \\
&\quad = 1 - \mathbb{P}((V^{\omega_\dagger} - V^{\omega_*}) - \mathbb{E}(V^{\omega_\dagger} - V^{\omega_*}) \geq \mathbb{E}(V^{\omega_*}) - \mathbb{E}(V^{\omega_\dagger})) \\
&\quad \text{Observe that } \bar{p}^{\omega_\dagger} = \tfrac{1}{(m-1)}(1 - \bar{p}^{\omega_*}). \\
&\quad = 1 - \mathbb{P}((V^{\omega_\dagger} - V^{\omega_*}) - \mathbb{E}(V^{\omega_\dagger} - V^{\omega_*}) \geq n\bar{p}^{\omega_*} - n\tfrac{1}{(m-1)}(1 - \bar{p}^{\omega_*})) \\
&\quad \geq 1 - \mathbb{P}((V^{\omega_\dagger} - V^{\omega_*}) - \mathbb{E}(V^{\omega_\dagger} - V^{\omega_*}) \geq \tfrac{n(m\bar{p}^{\omega_*} - 1)}{m-1}) \\
&\quad \geq 1 - e^{-\frac{2}{4n}\left(\frac{n(m\bar{p}^{\omega_*} - 1)}{m-1}\right)^2} \\
&\quad \text{Hoeffding noting that } u_i - l_i = 2 \text{ for all } i \\
&\quad = 1 - e^{-\frac{1}{2}n\left(\frac{(m\bar{p}^{\omega_*} - 1)}{m-1}\right)^2}
\end{aligned} \qquad (1)$$

Then we obtain for the winning against all competitors:

$$\begin{aligned}\mathbb{P}((\omega_\dagger \in \mathcal{W} \setminus \{\omega_*\})V^{\omega_*} > V^{\omega_\dagger}) &\geq 1 - \sum_{i=1}^{m-1} (1 - \mathbb{P}(V^{\omega_*} > V^{\omega_i})) \\ &= 1 - \sum_{i=1}^{m-1} \left(1 - \left(1 - e^{-\frac{1}{2}n\left(\frac{(m\bar{p}^{\omega_*}-1)}{m-1}\right)^2}\right)\right) \\ &= 1 - (m-1)e^{-\frac{1}{2}n\left(\frac{(m\bar{p}^{\omega_*}-1)}{m-1}\right)^2} \qquad (2)\end{aligned}$$

This gives us an inequality (2), which is an expression that subtracts from 1 the product of a factor, where the right side of the product is an exponential that converges to 0 as n grows. Thus, the overall expression, the minimum probability of success for the correct alternative to receive the most votes, converges to 1. This, formulated as a CJT result, yields

Theorem 2. *Consider a plurality voting setting with $m > 1$ alternatives, satisfying independence (Definition 3) and Δp-group reliability (Definition 4) for some average probability across agents to approve the correct alternative, $\bar{p}^{\omega_*}$, such that for each agent i, $p_i^{\omega_*} \in \left[\frac{1}{m}, 1\right]$, and for each wrong alternative $\omega_\dagger$ it holds $p_i^{\omega_\dagger} = \frac{(1-\bar{p}^{\omega_*})}{(m-1)}$. Then the probability that plurality voting identifies the correct alternative converges to 1 as the number of agents goes to infinity.*

From inequality (2) we obtain not only the asymptotic CJT result, but also a worst-case estimate of the minimum success probability, P_{min}, for the bin containing the correct value to be chosen as an agent's belief more often than any other bin. Let us illustrate this for some example parameter values:

Example 3. Suppose we have $n = 100$ agents and $m = 20$ bins, such that the bins are of the form $[0, 0.05), [0.05, 0.1), ..., [0.95, 1]$. Suppose agents are asked about the probability of an event A such as "global sea level will rise at least 1.5 m by the year 2100, relative to the year 2000", and that the correct probability for this event is exactly 12%, then the bin $\omega_3 = [0.1, 0.15)$ is the one that contains the correct value. Obviously, this correct value is unknown to the agents, but let us say that on average the agents are rather inclined to choose the correct bin as their belief, i.e. $\bar{p}^{\omega_*} = 0.35$. From these parameters, by inequality (2), we obtain a minimum success probability for more agents choosing the correct bin than any other of $P_{min} = 0.87$.

4 Optimal Weights for Imprecise Linear Pooling

In the previous section, we focused on eliciting agents' beliefs. In this section, we assume agents already have imprecise beliefs and aim to aggregate them using *linear pooling*. A key challenge in linear pooling is optimally distributing weights across agents [9]. We connect the voting-based elicitation method with optimal weights, showing that the weights from plurality voting also perform well in linear pooling.

Optimal Weights. Optimal weights for belief aggregation refer to a distribution that best approximates the true state of the world. Therefore, to begin with, we must address two questions: First, what alternative weight distributions should we compare to the plurality voting distribution? Second, how do we measure how well the aggregated belief approximates the true state of the world?

For our experiments, we generate four different weight distributions in each round: uniform, bipartite, random, and optimal weights. Uniform weights treat every agent's belief equally, assigning each agent a weight of $\lambda_i = \frac{1}{n}$. Bipartite weights, as defined in the forecasting literature [13], for an even number of agents n, create two types of weights: lower and upper. Based on a variance σ^2, the lower weight is $\lambda_{lower} = \frac{1}{n} - \sigma^2 \times \frac{1}{n}$, and the upper weight is $\lambda_{upper} = \frac{1}{n} + \sigma^2 \times \frac{1}{n}$. Agents are split into two subsets based on their competencies $p_i^{\omega_*}$, with lower weights assigned to less competent agents and upper weights to more competent agents. In our simulations, the variance is set to 0.5. For example, if we have $n = 200$ agents, we get two groups of 100 agents each, where each agent in the higher competency group has a weight of 0.00625 and each agent in the lower competency group has a weight of 0.00375. Random weights are generated from a uniform distribution over [0,1] and normalized by dividing each weight by the sum of all weights, ensuring the total sum equals 1. The final set of weights are the optimal weights for plurality voting from Qing et al. [17].

Scoring Measures. To evaluate the quality of the pooled opinions from the input imprecise beliefs, we use *scoring rules*, which assign numerical values to probabilistic aggregates, providing an evaluation metric [7]. A common measure used in this context is the Kullback-Leibler (KL) divergence [14]. While often used informally to describe the distance between distributions, it's important to note that KL divergence is technically a measure of information gain, quantifying how one probability distribution diverges from a second, expected probability distribution. It is not a true metric distance because it is asymmetric. For discrete distributions, it is defined as:

Definition 7 (Discrete Kullback-Leibler divergence). *Let $p(x)$ be the true probability distribution and $q(x)$ a model distribution for a random variable $\mathcal{X}$. The KL divergence from q to p is defined as [1]:*

$$D(p\|q) = \sum_{x \in \mathcal{X}} p(x) \log \frac{p(x)}{q(x)}.$$

Example 4. Consider a biased coin with a 30% chance of landing heads ($p(X = 1) = 30\%, p(X = 0) = 70\%$). If an agent assumes the coin is fair ($q(X = 1) = q(X = 0) = 50\%$), the KL divergence between the true distribution and the agent's assumption is:

$$D(p\|q) = p(X = 1) \log \frac{p(X = 1)}{q(X = 1)} + p(X = 0) \log \frac{p(X = 0)}{q(X = 0)} = 0.087.$$

The Kullback-Leibler (KL) divergence [2] is commonly used to assess optimal weights for probabilistic opinion pooling, where the goal is to minimize the KL divergence between the pooled and true distributions [9]. In our case, we apply KL divergence to assess the quality of imprecise pooled beliefs. Compared to the discrete case, there are two key differences: first, the pooled opinions assess the likelihood of a single event with only two outcomes (event occurring or not); second, no standard, universally accepted definition of KL divergence exists for imprecise beliefs.

Therefore, we propose an extension to the discrete case definition. In our plurality voting setting, we compare two imprecise probability intervals: the true distribution (ground truth bin) containing the correct value p^* for the event and its complement, and the linear pool of the group of agents' imprecise beliefs. The true imprecise probability distribution is denoted as $p(x)$, and the model distribution as $q(x)$. Recall that, in imprecise probability theory, an agent's belief in proposition A is given by an interval $\mathcal{P}(A) = [a, b]$, and for its complement $\neg A$, it is $\mathcal{P}(\neg A) = [1 - b, 1 - a]$. To measure the KL divergence between these two imprecise distributions, we acknowledge that a single point-wise comparison is insufficient. To capture the divergence across the full plausible range, we compute the KL divergence for both the lower probability distributions ($D(\underline{p}||\underline{q})$) and the upper probability distributions ($D(\overline{p}||\overline{q})$) between the model and true distributions. The Imprecise Kullback-Leibler divergence is then obtained by averaging these two, providing a pragmatic measure of the overall discrepancy.

Definition 8 (Imprecise Kullback-Leibler divergence). *Let $p(x)$ be the true imprecise probability distribution of a random variable $\mathcal{X}$, and $q(x)$ the model distribution. The Imprecise Kullback-Leibler is defined as*

$$\mathcal{D}(p||q) = \frac{D(\underline{p}||\underline{q}) + D(\overline{p}||\overline{q})}{2}.$$

Example 5. Let $[0.2, 0.3)$ represent the aggregate obtained from linear pooling, and $[0.6, 0.7)$ represent the ground truth bin. From this, we obtain: $\mathcal{D}(\underline{p}||\underline{q}) = 0.404$, $D(\overline{p}||\overline{q}) = 0.316$, and $\mathcal{D}(p||q) = 0.36$.

Evaluating Weights through Simulations. The simulation procedure analyzes the impact of weights on pooling imprecise beliefs of multiple agents in an event. It assumes four input parameters: the number of alternatives m, the number of agents n, a minimum average competence $\bar{p}^{\omega_*}$, and a number of rounds r, which determines the repetitions for belief construction and weight generation fixed to $r = 100$ in our simulations. We pool beliefs about an event that is assumed to have a true probability p^* of occurring, generated from a uniform distribution over $[0, 1]$. Alternatives or bins are defined as disjoint subintervals of the unit interval, ensuring that the true probability belongs to exactly one alternative. The following steps are repeated for all r rounds: First, each agent's imprecise belief $\mathbb{P}_i$ is constructed using *Plurality Voting for Bins*, yielding beliefs corresponding to exactly one alternative. Then, weight distributions for uniform, bipartite, random, and optimal weights are generated. For each weight distribution, the aggregate $\mathcal{F}(\mathbb{P}_1, \mathbb{P}_2, \ldots, \mathbb{P}_n)$, the weighted linear pooling, is computed.

Next, the imprecise KL divergence is used to compute the scoring value, permitting comparisons between aggregates obtained from different weight distributions. After all r rounds, an average imprecise belief across all agents is computed. Additionally, for each weight distribution and pooling method, an average aggregate and scoring value are determined. Due to space constraints, we refer readers to the provided code repository[1]. Since uniform, bipartite, and optimal weights depend on the fixed input parameters n and $p_i^{\omega_*}$, they remain constant across all rounds. The only weight distribution that varies in each round is the random weights. However, new imprecise beliefs are generated in every round, ensuring that all weight distributions are applied to different belief sets.

As a further illustration for the imprecise KL divergence, we show in Fig. 1a the imprecise KL divergence, where we take as the true distribution the single point value 0.5 and as the model distribution we start with the interval [0.5, 0.5], where along the x-axis we subtract the indicated value from the lower probability and add it to the upper probability, thus obtaining a symmetric distance around the true value. As expected, the imprecise KL divergence is 0 when the true distribution matches the model distribution, and increases rapidly as the distance between the two increases.

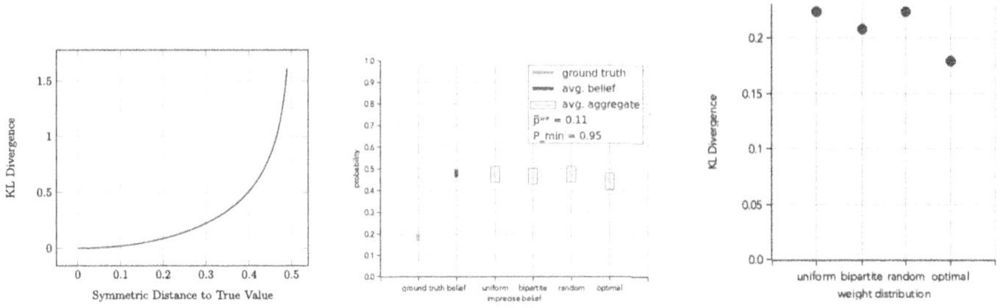

(a) Imprecise KL divergence. (b) $n = 2000, \bar{p}^{\omega *} = 0.11, m = 30$ (c) $n = 2000, \bar{p}^{\omega *} = 0.11, m = 30$

Fig. 1. Imprecise KL Divergence (left) and Weighted Linear Pooling Comparison (right)

In general, we consider pairs of plots for each parameter setting: As shown in Fig. 1b, we illustrate the generated ground truth bin as well as the average belief across all rounds of agents and the respective average aggregates for each weight distribution, to give the reader an intuitive understanding of the overall procedure for each parameter combination. Additionally, we compute the P_{min} value to assess of the overall quality of the beliefs. In Fig. 1c we see the second type of plot we consider for each parameter combination: the average KL divergence of each weight distribution across all rounds. For example, for these plots we consider $n = 2000$ agents with a small average probability of $\bar{p}^{\omega_*}$ to choose the

[1] For a detailed implementation and pseudocode of our algorithm, please refer to the GitHub repository at https://github.com/lea-bauer/weighted-pooling/.

correct bin, yielding an average belief that is a bit off the ground truth bin, given that there are $m = 30$ bins in total. From the different weight distributions we obtain average aggregates through the linear pool and respective scoring values where, in this case, the optimal weights from plurality voting perform the best as they minimize the imprecise KL divergence.

In the remaining plots (Fig. 2), we consider additional parameter combinations, ranging from a smaller number of agents ($n = 40$), fewer alternatives ($m = 10$), and less competent agents ($\bar{p}^{\omega_*} = 0.22$) to a larger number of agents ($n = 350$), many alternatives ($m = 100$), and more competent agents ($\bar{p}^{\omega_*} = 0.53$). Across all parameter settings, we could observe that the optimal weights from plurality voting outperform the alternative weight distributions here. However, due to space limitations, a more in-depth statistical analysis will be left to future work.

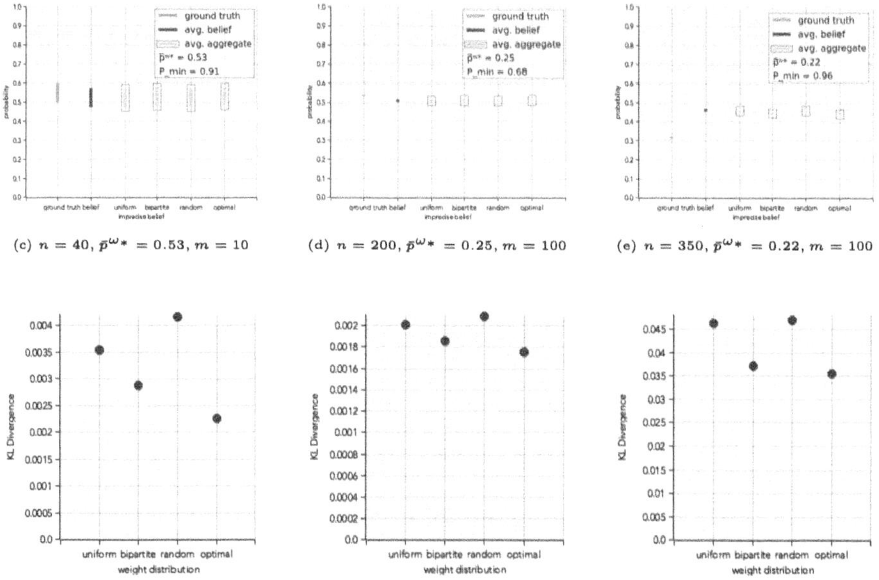

(c) $n = 40$, $\bar{p}^{\omega_*} = 0.53$, $m = 10$ (d) $n = 200$, $\bar{p}^{\omega_*} = 0.25$, $m = 100$ (e) $n = 350$, $\bar{p}^{\omega_*} = 0.22$, $m = 100$

(f) $n = 40$, $\bar{p}^{\omega_*} = 0.53$, $m = 10$ (g) $n = 200$, $\bar{p}^{\omega_*} = 0.25$, $m = 100$ (h) $n = 350$, $\bar{p}^{\omega_*} = 0.22$, $m = 100$

Fig. 2. Comparison of weighted linear pools for three different parameter settings in belief elicitation

5 Conclusion

This paper pursued two main objectives. First, we introduced a novel elicitation method for imprecise probabilistic beliefs based on plurality voting, inspired by the *Voting for Bins* approach. In this framework, agents select belief intervals according to their competencies. We established a probabilistic bound on the correctness of the chosen beliefs and proved an asymptotic version of the Condorcet Jury Theorem under the assumed noise model.

Second, by linking agents' competencies to their imprecise beliefs, we adapted results from epistemic voting to derive optimal weights for linear pooling. Finally, empirical simulations indicate that these voting-based weights outperform standard weighting schemes in aggregating imprecise beliefs.

Acknowledgments. This work is partly supported by BMFTR (Federal Ministry of Research, Technology and Space) in DAAD project 57616814 (SECAI, School of Embedded Composite AI, https://secai.org/) as part of the program Konrad Zuse Schools of Excellence in Artificial Intelligence.

Disclosure of Interests. The authors have no competing interests to declare that are relevant to the content of this article.

References

1. Entropy, Relative Entropy, and Mutual Information, chap. 2, p. 19. John Wiley and Sons, Ltd. (2005)
2. Abbas, A.E.: A kullback-leibler view of linear and log-linear pools. Decis. Anal. **6**(1), 25–37 (2009)
3. Bauer, L., Karge, J.: Multi-agent opinion pooling by voting for bins: simulations and characterization. In: International Conference on Practical Applications of Agents and Multi-Agent Systems, pp. 49–60. Springer, Heidelberg (2024)
4. Bradley, S.: How to choose among choice functions. Episteme **11**, 277–289 (2014)
5. Bradley, S., Steele, K.: Should subjective probabilities be sharp? Episteme **11**(3), 277–289 (2014)
6. Condorcet, M.J.A.N.C.: Essai sur l'application de l'analyse à la probabilité des décisions rendues à la pluralité des voix. Imprimerie Royale, Paris (1785)
7. Gneiting, T., Raftery, A.E.: Strictly proper scoring rules, prediction, and estimation. J. Am. Stat. Assoc. **102**(477), 359–378 (2007)
8. Hemming, V., Burgman, M.A., Hanea, A.M., McBride, M.F., Wintle, B.C.: A practical guide to structured expert elicitation using the idea protocol. Methods Ecol. Evol. **9**(1), 169–180 (2018)
9. Heskes, T.: Selecting weighting factors in logarithmic opinion pools. Adv. Neural Inf. Process. Syst. (1998)
10. Karge, J., Burkhardt, J.M., Rudolph, S., Rusovac, D.: To lead or to be led: a generalized condorcet jury theorem under dependence. In: AAMAS '24: Proceedings of the 2024 International Conference on Autonomous Agents and Multiagent Systems (2024)
11. Karge, J., Rudolph, S.: The more the Worst-Case-merrier: a generalized condorcet jury theorem for belief fusion. In: Proceedings of the 19th International Conference on Principles of Knowledge Representation and Reasoning, pp. 205–214 (2022)
12. Konek, J.: Ip scoring rules: foundations and applications. In: International Symposium on Imprecise Probabilities: Theories and Applications, pp. 256–264 (2019)
13. Kriegler, E., Hall, J.W., Held, H., Dawson, R., Schellnhuber, H.J.: Imprecise probability assessment of tipping points in the climate system. Proc. Natl. Acad. Sci. **106**(13), 5041–5046 (2009)

14. Kullback, S., Leibler, R.A.: On information and sufficiency. Ann. Math. Stat. **22**(1), 79–86 (1951)
15. O'Hagan, A., et al.: Uncertain judgements: eliciting experts' probabilities (2006)
16. Owen, G., Grofman, B., Feld, S.L.: Proving a distribution-free generalization of the Condorcet Jury Theorem. Math. Soc. Sci. **17**(1), 1–16 (1989)
17. Qing, C., Endriss, U., Fernández, R., Kruger, J.: Empirical analysis of aggregation methods for collective annotation. In: Proceedings of COLING 2014, the 25th International Conference on Computational Linguistics: Technical Papers, pp. 1533–1542. Dublin City University and Association for Computational Linguistics, Dublin (2014)
18. Stewart, R.T., Quintana, I.O.: Probabilistic opinion pooling with imprecise probabilities. J. Philos. Log. **47**, 17–45 (2018)

Conditionals, Inference, Change

Gärdenfors's Supplementary Postulates for Partial Product Contractions

Franz Baader[1(✉)] and Renata Wassermann[2]

[1] TU Dresden and Center for Scalable Data Analytics and AI (ScaDS.AI), Dresden, Germany
franz.baader@tu-dresden.de

[2] University of São Paulo and Center for AI (C4AI), São Paulo, Brazil

Abstract. In the area of belief change, contraction operations are used to modify a given belief set or belief base such that certain unwanted consequences no longer follow. In previous work we have introduced a framework for constructing contraction operations that generalizes the well-known partial meet contraction approach, called partial product contractions (PPCs). The main idea was to replace the remainders employed by partial meet contractions with optimal repairs, which were first considered in ontology engineering. We were able to characterize PPCs with variants of well-known rationality postulates, and provided a large number of concrete instances of the general framework. In the present work, we start to investigate whether the rather weak conditions imposed by our framework are sufficient to generalize further classical results from belief change to this setting. To this purpose, we consider Gärdenfors's supplementary postulates for belief contractions. We are able to show that, under two reasonable additional conditions, PPCs induced by maximizingly and transitively relational selection functions indeed satisfy these postulates, similarly to the classical case.

1 Introduction

Getting rid of knowledge that has undesired consequences has been investigated in the area of belief change under the name of *contraction* [1,13] and in ontology engineering under the name of *repair* [8,17,28,29]. In their seminal paper [1], Alchourrón, Gärdenfors, and Makinson introduce *partial meet contractions* and characterize them using certain *rationality postulates*, i.e., properties for which they argue that a reasonable contraction operation should satisfy them. Basically, this approach works on *belief sets*, i.e., deductively closed sets of formulas, considers all maximal subsets of a given belief set that do not contain the undesired consequence, called *remainders*, selects a subset of the set of remainders using a *selection function*, and then returns the *meet* (i.e., intersection) of the selected remainders as contraction. From a practical point of view, a disadvantage of working on belief sets is that the belief set returned by such a contraction operation may not be representable as the deductive closure of a finite *belief base*, even if the original belief set was finitely representable. To overcome this problem,

K. Sauerwald and M. Thimm (Eds.): ECSQARU 2025, LNAI 16099, pp. 269–284, 2026.
https://doi.org/10.1007/978-3-032-05134-9_19

Nebel [23] and Hansson [13] apply the partial meet approach directly to belief bases, i.e., remainders are now maximal subset of the base that do not imply the undesired consequence, and the contraction is again the intersection of a non-empty collection of these remainders. In ontology engineering, such remainders are called *optimal classical repairs* [8]. Both partial meet base contractions and optimal classical repairs have have been criticized for the fact that they are syntax-dependent and may remove too many consequences [2,8,15,22,27]. In the context of knowledge bases (KBs) expressed using certain Description Logics (DLs), *optimal repairs* yield a syntax-independent repair approach that does not lose consequences unnecessarily [4–7,19]

The original motivation for the new contraction approach presented in [9] was to leverage these advances on the side of ontology engineering to obtain a contraction approach that combines the advantages of belief set and belief base contractions without sharing their disadvantages. The main idea underlying this approach was to use, in the partial meet contraction approach, optimal repairs as remainders. However, instead of introducing this new approach in the specific instance of certain DL KBs, we consider in [9] a very general setup, where knowledge bases are not necessarily sets of formulas, the meet operation is replaced by an abstract product operation on KBs, and the repair goal may be different from non-entailment of an undesired consequence (such as forgetting [10,18,20,21] of certain parts of the signature). We were able to characterize the *partial product contractions* (PPCs) obtained this way using certain well-known rationality postulates and to describe a large variety of different instances of the general framework (see [9] and Sect. 2 for more details).

In the present work, we start to investigate whether the rather weak conditions imposed by our framework are sufficient to show that further classical results from belief change can be generalized to this setting. To this purpose, we consider Gärdenfors's *supplementary postulates* for belief contractions (*conjunctive overlap* and *conjunctive inclusion*), which were already investigated in the original AGM paper [1], but also considered in other settings (e.g., [11,15,16,26]). Although the supplementary postulates are typically studied in connection to belief sets, Ribeiro [24] presented a first characterization for belief bases. Basically, these postulates characterize a restriction of partial meet contractions where the selection functions are defined using a certain transitive relation on remainders. Under two additional assumptions (conditions (1) and (2)) we are able to show that Gärdenfors's supplementary postulates indeed hold for partial product contractions if we require the transitive relation defining the selection function to be also *maximizing*, a condition that has been introduced before [14,16]. We also give DL-based examples that show that the additional conditions are necessary.

2 The General Framework and $\mathcal{EL}$ Concepts as Instance

We briefly introduce the general framework and illustrate it using the instance of $\mathcal{EL}$ concepts since this instance (in different variants) will also be employed in the (counter)examples in the rest of the paper (see [9] for more details).

Partial Product Contractions. We assume that we are given a set of *knowledge bases* (KBs) and a reflexive and transitive *entailment relation* between knowledge bases. We write KBs as $\mathcal{K}$, possibly primed ($\mathcal{K}'$) or with an index ($\mathcal{K}_i$), and entailment as $\models$, i.e., $\mathcal{K} \models \mathcal{K}'$ means that $\mathcal{K}$ *entails* $\mathcal{K}'$, or equivalently that $\mathcal{K}'$ is *entailed by* $\mathcal{K}$. We call two KBs $\mathcal{K}, \mathcal{K}'$ *equivalent* (write $\mathcal{K} \equiv \mathcal{K}'$) if they entail each other. We say that $\mathcal{K}$ *strictly entails* $\mathcal{K}'$ ($\mathcal{K} \models_s \mathcal{K}'$) if $\mathcal{K} \models \mathcal{K}'$, but $\mathcal{K}' \not\models \mathcal{K}$.

We make no assumptions on the inner structure of knowledge bases, but we assume that we have operations *sum* ($\oplus$) and *product* ($\otimes$) available that are akin to conjunction and disjunction. For each finite, non-empty set of KBs $\mathfrak{K}$:

- $\oplus\mathfrak{K} \models \mathcal{K}$ for all $\mathcal{K} \in \mathfrak{K}$ and $\oplus\mathfrak{K}$ is the least KB satisfying this property, i.e., if $\mathcal{K}'$ is a KB satisfying $\mathcal{K}' \models \mathcal{K}$ for all $\mathcal{K} \in \mathfrak{K}$, then $\mathcal{K}' \models \oplus\mathfrak{K}$;
- $\mathcal{K} \models \otimes\mathfrak{K}$ for all $\mathcal{K} \in \mathfrak{K}$ and $\otimes\mathfrak{K}$ is the greatest KB satisfying this property, i.e., if $\mathcal{K}'$ is a KB satisfying $\mathcal{K} \models \mathcal{K}'$ for all $\mathcal{K} \in \mathfrak{K}$, then $\otimes\mathfrak{K} \models \mathcal{K}'$.

The goal of the contraction operation to be defined is to "repair" a certain defect of the given knowledge base, but this defect is not restricted to entailment of some unwanted consequence. Formally, we assume that we have additional syntactic entities called repair requests: given a KB $\mathcal{K}$, a *repair request* α determines a set of KBs $\text{Rep}(\mathcal{K}, \alpha)$ such that $\mathcal{K} \models \mathcal{K}'$ holds for every element $\mathcal{K}' \in \text{Rep}(\mathcal{K}, \alpha)$, and $\mathcal{K}' \in \text{Rep}(\mathcal{K}, \alpha)$ and $\mathcal{K}' \models \mathcal{K}''$ imply $\mathcal{K}'' \in \text{Rep}(\mathcal{K}, \alpha)$. We call the elements of $\text{Rep}(\mathcal{K}, \alpha)$ *repairs* of $\mathcal{K}$ for α. Two repair requests α and α' are *equivalent w.r.t.* $\mathcal{K}$ ($\alpha \equiv_{\mathcal{K}} \alpha'$) if $\text{Rep}(\mathcal{K}, \alpha) = \text{Rep}(\mathcal{K}, \alpha')$.

Note that this notion of repairs generalizes the classical no-entailment condition for contractions, where a repair request α is also a KB and contractions are required (by the *success* postulate) not to entail α. In this restricted setting, the set of repairs is defined as $\text{Rep}(\mathcal{K}, \alpha) = \{\mathcal{K}' \mid \mathcal{K} \models \mathcal{K}' \not\models \alpha\}$.

Finally, we assume the *optimal repair property*, which says that, for every pair $\mathcal{K}, \alpha$ consisting of a KB and a repair request (called a *repair problem*), there exists a finite set of KBs $\text{Orep}(\mathcal{K}, \alpha)$ satisfying

- $\text{Orep}(\mathcal{K}, \alpha) \subseteq \text{Rep}(\mathcal{K}, \alpha)$ (repair property),
- every element $\mathcal{K}'$ of $\text{Orep}(\mathcal{K}, \alpha)$ is *optimal*, i.e., there is no $\mathcal{K}'' \in \text{Rep}(\mathcal{K}, \alpha)$ such that $\mathcal{K}'' \models_s \mathcal{K}'$ (optimality),
- $\text{Orep}(\mathcal{K}, \alpha)$ *covers* all repairs, i.e., for every $\mathcal{K}'' \in \text{Rep}(\mathcal{K}, \alpha)$ there is $\mathcal{K}' \in \text{Orep}(\mathcal{K}, \alpha)$ such that $\mathcal{K}' \models \mathcal{K}''$ (coverage).

Note that $\text{Orep}(\mathcal{K}, \alpha)$ is unique up to equivalence and that coverage of $\text{Orep}(\mathcal{K}, \alpha)$ implies that this set is empty iff $\text{Rep}(\mathcal{K}, \alpha) = \emptyset$. As mentioned before, optimal repairs will play the role of remainders, and thus this equivalence says that there are remainders iff the repair goal can be achieved.

Given a set of KBs $\mathcal{K}$, a set of repair requests α inducing repair sets $\text{Rep}(\mathcal{K}, \alpha)$, and a reflexive and transitive binary relation $\models$ between KBs, we call $\models$ *partial product contraction (PPC) enabling* if all the properties introduced above are satisfied.

Let $\mathcal{K}$ be a KB and $\text{Orep}(\mathcal{K}, \alpha)$ for each repair request α the corresponding set of optimal repairs, which covers all repairs of $\mathcal{K}$ for α. A *selection function* γ

for $\mathcal{K}$ takes such sets of optimal repairs as input and must satisfy the following properties, for each repair request α:

- If $\mathrm{Orep}(\mathcal{K}, \alpha) \neq \emptyset$, then $\emptyset \neq \gamma(\mathrm{Orep}(\mathcal{K}, \alpha)) \subseteq \mathrm{Orep}(\mathcal{K}, \alpha)$.
- If $\mathrm{Orep}(\mathcal{K}, \alpha) = \emptyset$, then $\gamma(\mathrm{Orep}(\mathcal{K}, \alpha)) = \{\mathcal{K}\}$.
- If $\mathrm{Orep}(\mathcal{K}, \alpha)$ and $\mathrm{Orep}(\mathcal{K}, \alpha')$ are equal up to equivalence, then so are $\gamma(\mathrm{Orep}(\mathcal{K}, \alpha))$ and $\gamma(\mathrm{Orep}(\mathcal{K}, \alpha'))$.

Each selection function γ induces a *PPC operation* ctr_γ as follows:

$$\mathrm{ctr}_\gamma(\mathcal{K}, \alpha) := \otimes\gamma(\mathrm{Orep}(\mathcal{K}, \alpha)).$$

It was shown in [9] that, among all operations receiving as input a KB and a repair request and returning as output a KB, the PPC operations are exactly those operations that satisfy the postulates *logical inclusion*, *success*, *failure*, *vacuity*, *preservation*, and *relevance*.

$\mathcal{EL}$ Concepts as KBs. $\mathcal{EL}$ concepts are built inductively, starting with concept names A from a set N_C of such names, and using the concept constructors $\top$ (top concept), $C \sqcap D$ (conjunction), and $\exists r.C$ (existential restriction), where C, D are $\mathcal{EL}$ concepts and r belongs to a set N_R of role names. A general concept inclusion (GCI) of $\mathcal{EL}$ is of the form $C \sqsubseteq D$ for $\mathcal{EL}$ concepts C, D, and an $\mathcal{EL}$ TBox is a finite set of such GCIs. Given an $\mathcal{EL}$ concept C, its signature $\mathrm{Sig}(C)$ consists of the concept and role names occurring in C.

The semantics of $\mathcal{EL}$ is defined in a model-theoretic way, using the notion of an *interpretation* $\mathcal{I}$, which is a pair $\mathcal{I} = (\Delta^\mathcal{I}, \cdot^\mathcal{I})$, where the domain $\Delta^\mathcal{I}$ is a non-empty set and the interpretation function $\cdot^\mathcal{I}$ maps each concept name $A \in N_C$ to $A^\mathcal{I} \subseteq \Delta^\mathcal{I}$ and each role name $r \in N_R$ to a binary relation $r^\mathcal{I} \subseteq \Delta^\mathcal{I} \times \Delta^\mathcal{I}$. The interpretation of an $\mathcal{EL}$ concept is defined inductively as follows: $\top^\mathcal{I} := \Delta^\mathcal{I}$, $(C \sqcap D)^\mathcal{I} := C^\mathcal{I} \cap D^\mathcal{I}$, and $(\exists r.C)^\mathcal{I} := \{d \in \Delta^\mathcal{I} \mid \exists e \in \Delta^\mathcal{I}$ such that $(d, e) \in r^\mathcal{I}$ and $e \in C^\mathcal{I}\}$. A model $\mathcal{I}$ of the $\mathcal{EL}$ TBox $\mathcal{T}$ is an interpretation that satisfies all its GCIs, i.e., $C^\mathcal{I} \subseteq D^\mathcal{I}$ holds for all $C \sqsubseteq D \in \mathcal{T}$. Given $\mathcal{EL}$ concepts C, D and an $\mathcal{EL}$ TBox $\mathcal{T}$, we say that C is *subsumed by D w.r.t. $\mathcal{T}$* ($C \sqsubseteq^\mathcal{T} D$) if $C^\mathcal{I} \subseteq D^\mathcal{I}$ in all models $\mathcal{I}$ of $\mathcal{T}$. The $\mathcal{EL}$ concepts C, D are *equivalent w.r.t. $\mathcal{T}$* (written $C \equiv^\mathcal{T} D$) if $C \sqsubseteq^\mathcal{T} D$ and $D \sqsubseteq^\mathcal{T} C$. The $\mathcal{EL}$ TBox $\mathcal{T}$ is *cycle-restricted* if there is no $\mathcal{EL}$ concept C and $m \geq 1$ (not necessarily distinct) role names $r_1, \ldots, r_m$ such that $C \sqsubseteq^\mathcal{T} \exists r_1. \cdots \exists r_m.C$.

For a given cycle-restricted $\mathcal{EL}$ TBox $\mathcal{T}$, the following *instance* of the general framework was introduced in [2,9]: *KBs* are $\mathcal{EL}$ concepts, *entailment* is subsumption (i.e., $C \models D$ iff $C \sqsubseteq^\mathcal{T} D$), and *repair requests* are $\mathcal{EL}$ concepts with associated repair sets $\mathrm{Rep}^\mathcal{T}_{\mathrm{ent}}(C, D) := \{C' \mid C \sqsubseteq^\mathcal{T} C', C' \not\sqsubseteq^\mathcal{T} D\}$. As shown in [9], the entailment relation $\sqsubseteq^\mathcal{T}$ is PPC enabling for this repair setting. In fact, the *sum* is conjunction of concepts, and the *product* is the least common subsumer (lcs) w.r.t. the TBox $\mathcal{T}$, which exists according to [30] since the TBox is cycle-restricted. Cycle-restrictedness also ensures that the optimal repair property is satisfied. In [2], this was shown using results for optimal ABox repairs from [6]. A more generic argument, which can also be used for repair goals other than non-entailment follows from the following lemma (see Proposition 3 in [3]).

Lemma 1 **([3]).** *If $\mathcal{T}$ is a cycle-restricted $\mathcal{EL}$ TBox and C an $\mathcal{EL}$ concept, then* $\mathrm{Subs}^{\mathcal{T}}(C) := \{C' \mid C \sqsubseteq^{\mathcal{T}} C'\}$ *is finite up to equivalence.*

Since repairs of C are subsumers of C, the set of repairs is finite up to equivalence, and the optimal repairs are the ones that are the minimal elements w.r.t. subsumption of this finite set.

$\mathcal{EL}$ concept contraction was considered in [25] for the empty TBox and in [2] for cycle-restricted TBoxes. For the sake of simplicity, we use (variants of) $\mathcal{EL}$ concept contraction in our examples, but note that it is a special case of the practically more relevant ABox contractions considered as an instance of the general framework in [9].

3 The Supplementary Postulates

As mentioned above, in [9] it was shown that, for PPC enabling entailments, a contraction operation can be obtained by the partial product contraction approach iff it satisfies the rationality postulates *logical inclusion*, *success*, *failure*, *vacuity*, *preservation*, and *relevance*. We now investigate under what additional conditions Gärdenfors's supplementary postulates *conjunctive overlap* and *conjunctive inclusion* for belief contractions [1,12] also hold. In the setting considered in [1,12], KBs are set of formulas from a logic with conjunction, repair requests are formulas, and the repair goal is non-entailment of the repair request. The supplementary postulates put contraction w.r.t. $\alpha \wedge \beta$ in relation to contraction w.r.t. α and contraction w.r.t. β.

To generalize this setting to our framework, we first assume that repair requests are KBs and that the repair goal is non-entailment of the repair request. If we then use sum as stand-in for conjunction, we obtain the following identity, due to the fact that a KB entails a sum iff it entails all of it summands (see Lemma 3 in [9]):

$$\begin{aligned}\mathrm{Rep}(\mathcal{K}, \alpha \oplus \beta) &= \{\mathcal{K}' \mid \mathcal{K} \models \mathcal{K}' \wedge \mathcal{K}' \not\models \alpha \oplus \beta\} \\ &= \{\mathcal{K}' \mid \mathcal{K} \models \mathcal{K}' \wedge (\mathcal{K}' \not\models \alpha \vee \mathcal{K}' \not\models \beta)\} = \mathrm{Rep}(\mathcal{K}, \alpha) \cup \mathrm{Rep}(\mathcal{K}, \beta).\end{aligned}$$

In our general framework, where repair requests need not be KBs and the repair goals may be different from non-entailment, we now make the additional assumption that there is an operation $\boxplus$ on repair requests such that the following identity holds:

$$\mathrm{Rep}(\mathcal{K}, \alpha \boxplus \beta) = \mathrm{Rep}(\mathcal{K}, \alpha) \cup \mathrm{Rep}(\mathcal{K}, \beta). \tag{1}$$

Since union of sets is associative, commutative, and idempotent, the operation $\boxplus$ also satisfies these properties, up to equivalence $\equiv_{\mathcal{K}}$ of repair requests.

The following is an example of a repair setting where repair requests are not KBs, but (1) nevertheless holds.

Example 1. We consider forgetting for $\mathcal{EL}$ concepts (for simplicity in the case $\mathcal{T} = \emptyset$), where repair requests are finite sets of concept and role names, and repairs are defined as follows[1]:

$$\mathrm{Rep}_{\mathrm{for}}(C, \alpha) = \{C' \mid C \sqsubseteq^{\emptyset} C' \text{ and } \alpha \not\subseteq \mathrm{Sig}(C')\}.$$

[1] In [9], we used the condition $\alpha \cap \mathrm{Sig}(C') = \emptyset$, which corresponds to a package repair setting, whereas the condition introduced here corresponds to a choice repair setting.

Since it is well-known that, for $\mathcal{EL}$ concepts, $C' \sqsubseteq^\emptyset C''$ implies $\mathrm{Sig}(C') \supseteq \mathrm{Sig}(C'')$, such repair sets are closed under entailment. Since the empty TBox is cycle-restricted, the entailment relation $\sqsubseteq^\emptyset$ is known to have product (least common subsumer) and sum (conjunction). The optimal repair property is an easy consequence of Lemma 1.

If we define $\alpha \boxplus \beta := \alpha \cup \beta$, then (1) holds: for all concepts C' satisfying $C \sqsubseteq^\emptyset C'$ we have $C' \in \mathrm{Rep}_{\mathrm{for}}(C, \alpha \boxplus \beta)$ iff $\alpha \cup \beta \not\subseteq \mathrm{Sig}(C')$ iff $\alpha \not\subseteq \mathrm{Sig}(C')$ or $\beta \not\subseteq \mathrm{Sig}(C')$ iff $C' \in \mathrm{Rep}_{\mathrm{for}}(C, \alpha) \cup \mathrm{Rep}_{\mathrm{for}}(C, \beta)$.

In general, however, (1) need not hold.

Example 2. Consider $\mathcal{EL}$ concepts as KBs, subsumption w.r.t. the empty TBox as entailment, and finite sets of concept and role names as repair requests, and define $\mathrm{Rep}(C, \alpha) = \{C' \mid C \sqsubseteq^\emptyset C' \text{ and } \mathrm{Sig}(C') \subseteq \alpha\}$. Closure under entailment holds for the same reason as in the previous example.

We show that the repair sets defined here cannot satisfy (1) for any operation $\boxplus$ on repair requests. In fact, to satisfy the inclusion from right to left of (1) the sum operation on repair requests must satisfy $\alpha \cup \beta \subseteq \alpha \boxplus \beta$. But then one can easily generate an example where the other inclusion is not satisfied: $A \sqcap B \in \mathrm{Rep}(A \sqcap B, \{A\} \boxplus \{B\})$, but it belongs neither to $\mathrm{Rep}(A \sqcap B, \{A\})$ nor to $\mathrm{Rep}(A \sqcap B, \{B\})$.

In the following, we assume that the entailment relation is PPC enabling w.r.t. the repair sets at hand, and that contractions are built using the PPC approach. In addition, we assume that the identity (1) holds. The following lemma is an easy consequence of this identity.

Lemma 2. *Up to equivalence, the following inclusion holds:* $\mathrm{Orep}(\mathcal{K}, \alpha \boxplus \beta) \subseteq \mathrm{Orep}(\mathcal{K}, \alpha) \cup \mathrm{Orep}(\mathcal{K}, \beta)$.

Proof. Assume that $\mathcal{K}'' \in \mathrm{Orep}(\mathcal{K}, \alpha \boxplus \beta)$. Then $\mathcal{K}'' \in \mathrm{Rep}(\mathcal{K}, \alpha) \cup \mathrm{Rep}(\mathcal{K}, \beta)$ and there is no $\mathcal{K}' \in \mathrm{Rep}(\mathcal{K}, \alpha) \cup \mathrm{Rep}(\mathcal{K}, \beta)$ such that $\mathcal{K}' \models_s \mathcal{K}''$. If $\mathcal{K}'' \in \mathrm{Rep}(\mathcal{K}, \alpha)$, then $\mathcal{K}''$ is an optimal repair of $\mathcal{K}$ for α since there is no $\mathcal{K}' \in \mathrm{Rep}(\mathcal{K}, \alpha)$ such that $\mathcal{K}' \models_s \mathcal{K}''$. Consequently, coverage of $\mathrm{Orep}(\mathcal{K}, \alpha)$ implies that $\mathcal{K}''$ is equivalent to an element of $\mathrm{Orep}(\mathcal{K}, \alpha)$. If $\mathcal{K}' \in \mathrm{Rep}(\mathcal{K}, \beta)$, then the fact that $\mathcal{K}''$ is equivalent to an element of $\mathrm{Orep}(\mathcal{K}, \beta)$ can by shown in the same way □

The proof of this lemma actually shows the following stronger result.

Lemma 3. *Up to equivalence, the following holds:* $\mathrm{Orep}(\mathcal{K}, \alpha \boxplus \beta) \cap \mathrm{Rep}(\mathcal{K}, \alpha) \subseteq \mathrm{Orep}(\mathcal{K}, \alpha)$ *and* $\mathrm{Orep}(\mathcal{K}, \alpha \boxplus \beta) \cap \mathrm{Rep}(\mathcal{K}, \beta) \subseteq \mathrm{Orep}(\mathcal{K}, \beta)$.

The inclusion in the other direction in Lemma 2 does not hold in general, even if we use non-entailment as repair goal.

Example 3. As entailment we consider subsumption $\sqsubseteq^\mathcal{T}$ between $\mathcal{EL}$ concepts w.r.t. the following $\mathcal{EL}$ TBox $\mathcal{T} := \{\exists r.A \sqsubseteq P, \exists r.B \sqsubseteq P\}$, and repairs are defined by non-entailment of the repair request, which is an $\mathcal{EL}$ concept, i.e. $\mathrm{Rep}(C, \alpha) := \{C' \mid C \sqsubseteq^\mathcal{T} C' \wedge C' \not\sqsubseteq^\mathcal{T} \alpha\}$. Since the TBox $\mathcal{T}$ is cycle-restricted, the entailment relation $\models := \sqsubseteq^{\mathcal{T}}$ is known to be PPC-enabling w.r.t. this definition of repair sets [9]. As operation $\boxplus$ on repair requests, we use $\oplus$, which here is conjunction.

Let $C := \exists r.(A \sqcap B)$, $\alpha := P$, and $\beta := \exists r.A \sqcap \exists r.B$. Then, we obtain the following optimal repair sets (up to equivalence):

$$\begin{array}{l}\mathrm{Orep}(C,\alpha) = \{\exists r.\top\}, \quad \mathrm{Orep}(C,\beta) = \{\exists r.A, \exists r.B\},\\ \mathrm{Orep}(C,\alpha \boxplus \beta) = \mathrm{Orep}(C,\alpha \sqcap \beta) = \{\exists r.A, \exists r.B\}.\end{array}$$

Thus, the union of $\mathrm{Orep}(C,\alpha)$ and $\mathrm{Orep}(C,\beta)$ contains $\exists r.\top$, whereas $\exists r.\top$ does not belong to $\mathrm{Orep}(C,\alpha \boxplus \beta)$ since it is not optimal in the presence of the other two existential restrictions.

3.1 Conjunctive Overlap

The supplementary postulate *conjunctive overlap* can be formulated in our general setting as follows:

– $\mathrm{ctr}(\mathcal{K},\alpha \boxplus \beta) \models \mathrm{ctr}(\mathcal{K},\alpha) \otimes \mathrm{ctr}(\mathcal{K},\beta)$ (conjunctive overlap)

In the classical setting of [1], KBs are deductively closed sets of formulas (and thus entailment is the superset relation and product is intersection), repair requests are formulas, and $\boxplus$ is conjunction. Thus, *conjunctive overlap* is formulated as follows: $\mathrm{ctr}(\mathcal{K},\alpha \wedge \beta) \supseteq \mathrm{ctr}(\mathcal{K},\alpha) \cap \mathrm{ctr}(\mathcal{K},\beta)$.

As in this classical case, to ensure that *conjunctive overlap* is satisfied, we must make additional assumptions on the selection function (see, e.g., [16]). We say that the selection function γ is *transitively relational* if there is a transitive relation $\trianglelefteq$ on $\mathrm{Con}(\mathcal{K}) := \{\mathcal{K}' \mid \mathcal{K} \models \mathcal{K}'\}$ such that equivalent KBs are in this relation and

$$\gamma(\mathrm{Orep}(\mathcal{K},\alpha)) = \{\mathcal{K}'' \in \mathrm{Orep}(\mathcal{K},\alpha) \mid \mathcal{K}' \trianglelefteq \mathcal{K}'' \text{ for all } \mathcal{K}' \in \mathrm{Orep}(\mathcal{K},\alpha)\},$$

whenever $\mathrm{Orep}(\mathcal{K},\alpha) \neq \emptyset$. Note that the conditions imposed on selection functions in [9] require that non-emptiness of the optimal repair set implies that $\gamma(\mathrm{Orep}(\mathcal{K},\alpha))$ is non-empty as well. This is an additional condition that a transitive relation must satisfy to be able to induce a selection function. Invariance under equivalence is taken care of by our requirement that equivalent KBs are in the relation $\trianglelefteq$. For the sake of simplicity, we subsume this property under transitivity, i.e., whenever we say in the following that $\trianglelefteq$ is transitive, this also means that equivalent KBs are in the relation $\trianglelefteq$.

In addition, we assume that $\trianglelefteq$ is *weakly maximizing*, i.e., $\mathcal{K}' \models \mathcal{K}''$ implies $\mathcal{K}' \trianglerighteq \mathcal{K}''$. In the literature [16], the stronger property of being *maximizing* has been considered in this context. However, for showing the postulate *conjunctive overlap*, the weak version turns out to be sufficient. The relation $\trianglelefteq$ is *maximizing* if $\mathcal{K}' \models_s \mathcal{K}''$ implies $\mathcal{K}' \triangleright \mathcal{K}''$ (i.e., $\mathcal{K}' \trianglerighteq \mathcal{K}''$, but $\mathcal{K}'' \not\trianglerighteq \mathcal{K}'$).

Lemma 4. *Let $\trianglelefteq$ be a transitive relation on KBs such that equivalent KBs are in this relation. If $\trianglelefteq$ is maximizing, then it is also weakly maximizing.*

Proof. Assume that $\mathcal{K}' \models \mathcal{K}''$. If $\mathcal{K}' \equiv \mathcal{K}''$, then $\mathcal{K}' \trianglerighteq \mathcal{K}''$ due to the assumption that equivalent KBs are in the relation $\trianglelefteq$. Otherwise, $\mathcal{K}' \models_s \mathcal{K}''$, and thus maximizing yields $\mathcal{K}' \triangleright \mathcal{K}''$, which implies $\mathcal{K}' \trianglerighteq \mathcal{K}''$. □

We call a selection function *(weakly) maximizingly and transitively relational* if it is transitively relational w.r.t. a (weakly) maximizing relation $\trianglelefteq$. Due to the properties of the product, the postulate *conjunctive overlap* is an easy consequence of the following lemma.

Lemma 5. *Let γ by a weakly maximizingly and transitively relational selection function. Then, up to equivalence and under the assumption that* $\mathrm{Rep}(\mathcal{K}, \alpha) \neq \emptyset \neq \mathrm{Rep}(\mathcal{K}, \beta)$, *the following inclusion holds:*

$$\gamma(\mathrm{Orep}(\mathcal{K}, \alpha \boxplus \beta)) \subseteq \gamma(\mathrm{Orep}(\mathcal{K}, \alpha)) \cup \gamma(\mathrm{Orep}(\mathcal{K}, \beta)).$$

Proof. Note that non-emptiness of the repair sets implies that all optimal repair sets under consideration are also non-empty. Assume that $\mathcal{K}'' \in \gamma(\mathrm{Orep}(\mathcal{K}, \alpha \boxplus \beta))$. Then (up to equivalence) $\mathcal{K}'' \in \mathrm{Orep}(\mathcal{K}, \alpha) \cup \mathrm{Orep}(\mathcal{K}, \beta)$ and $\mathcal{L} \trianglelefteq \mathcal{K}''$ holds for all element $\mathcal{L}$ of $\mathrm{Orep}(\mathcal{K}, \alpha \boxplus \beta)$. Assume without loss of generality that $\mathcal{K}'' \in \mathrm{Orep}(\mathcal{K}, \alpha)$. To prove that $\mathcal{K}'' \in \gamma(\mathrm{Orep}(\mathcal{K}, \alpha))$, we consider an arbitrary element $\mathcal{K}'$ of $\mathrm{Orep}(\mathcal{K}, \alpha)$ and show that $\mathcal{K}' \trianglelefteq \mathcal{K}''$. If $\mathcal{K}'$ is also an element of $\mathrm{Orep}(\mathcal{K}, \alpha \boxplus \beta)$, then we have $\mathcal{K}' \trianglelefteq \mathcal{K}''$. Otherwise, $\mathcal{K}' \in \mathrm{Rep}(\mathcal{K}, \alpha)$ implies that $\mathcal{K}' \in \mathrm{Rep}(\mathcal{K}, \alpha \boxplus \beta)$, and thus there is $\mathcal{L} \in \mathrm{Orep}(\mathcal{K}, \alpha \boxplus \beta)$ such that $\mathcal{L} \models \mathcal{K}'$. But then $\mathcal{L} \trianglelefteq \mathcal{K}''$ and the weakly maximizing property yields $\mathcal{L} \trianglerighteq \mathcal{K}'$. Thus, transitivity of $\trianglelefteq$ implies $\mathcal{K}' \trianglelefteq \mathcal{K}''$. □

Theorem 1. *Assume that $\models$ is PPC enabling and that the identity (1) holds. If the selection function γ is weakly maximizingly and transitively relational, then the PPC operation* ctr_γ *satisfies the postulate* conjunctive overlap.

Proof. Note that the coverage property of optimal repairs implies that $\mathrm{Rep}(\mathcal{K}, \alpha) = \emptyset$ iff $\mathrm{Orep}(\mathcal{K}, \alpha) = \emptyset$. Thus, if $\mathrm{Orep}(\mathcal{K}, \alpha \boxplus \beta) = \emptyset$, then $\mathrm{Orep}(\mathcal{K}, \alpha) = \emptyset = \mathrm{Orep}(\mathcal{K}, \beta)$. In this case, $\mathrm{ctr}_\gamma(\mathcal{K}, \alpha \boxplus \beta) = \mathcal{K} = \mathrm{ctr}_\gamma(\mathcal{K}, \alpha) = \mathrm{ctr}_\gamma(\mathcal{K}, \beta)$, and thus *conjunctive overlap* clearly holds.

If all three sets of optimal repairs are non-empty, then *conjunctive overlap* is an immediate consequence of Lemma 5.

Now assume that $\mathrm{Orep}(\mathcal{K}, \alpha \boxplus \beta) \neq \emptyset \neq \mathrm{Orep}(\mathcal{K}, \alpha)$ and $\mathrm{Orep}(\mathcal{K}, \beta) = \emptyset$. In this case, $\mathrm{Rep}(\mathcal{K}, \alpha \boxplus \beta) = \mathrm{Rep}(\mathcal{K}, \alpha)$, and thus $\mathrm{Orep}(\mathcal{K}, \alpha \boxplus \beta) = \mathrm{Orep}(\mathcal{K}, \alpha)$ up to equivalence, which implies that $\mathrm{ctr}_\gamma(\mathcal{K}, \alpha \boxplus \beta) \equiv \mathrm{ctr}_\gamma(\mathcal{K}, \alpha)$. In addition, $\mathrm{Orep}(\mathcal{K}, \beta) = \emptyset$ implies that $\mathrm{ctr}_\gamma(\mathcal{K}, \beta) = \mathcal{K}$. Since $\mathcal{K} \models \mathrm{ctr}_\gamma(\mathcal{K}, \alpha)$, we thus have $\mathrm{ctr}_\gamma(\mathcal{K}, \alpha) \otimes \mathrm{ctr}_\gamma(\mathcal{K}, \beta) \equiv \mathrm{ctr}_\gamma(\mathcal{K}, \alpha)$, which shows that *conjunctive overlap* also holds in this case. The symmetric case where $\mathrm{Orep}(\mathcal{K}, \alpha) = \emptyset$ can be treated analogously. □

In a setting where KBs are $\mathcal{EL}$ concepts and entailment is subsumption, we can define transitive and weakly maximizing relations $\trianglelefteq$ as follows.

Example 4. Let $\mathcal{T}$ be a cycle-restricted $\mathcal{EL}$ TBox. Given a KB C together with concepts $D_1, \ldots, D_n$ such that $C \sqsubseteq^{\mathcal{T}} D_i$ for $i = 1, \ldots, n$, we define (for all C' with $C \sqsubseteq^{\mathcal{T}} C'$) the number $\kappa(C') := |\{D_i \mid C' \sqsubseteq^{\mathcal{T}} D_i \text{ for } i = 1, \ldots, n\}|$, which counts how many of the concepts D_i are still subsumers of C'. These numbers yield the following relation $\trianglelefteq$: $C'' \trianglelefteq C'$ iff $\kappa(C'') \leq \kappa(C')$.

We claim that the relation $\trianglelefteq$ is transitive and weakly maximizing. In fact, transitivity of $\trianglelefteq$ is obvious since the relation $\leq$ on natural numbers is transitive. To show the weakly maximizing property, assume that $C' \sqsubseteq^{\mathcal{T}} C''$. Then $C'' \sqsubseteq^{\mathcal{T}} D_i$ implies $C' \sqsubseteq^{\mathcal{T}} D_i$, and thus $\kappa(C') \geq \kappa(C'')$.

To be able to use this relation for defining a selection function γ, we must check whether $\mathrm{Orep}(C, \alpha) \neq \emptyset$ implies that the set

$$\{C'' \in \mathrm{Orep}(C, \alpha) \mid C' \trianglelefteq C'' \text{ for all } C' \in \mathrm{Orep}(C, \alpha)\}$$

is non-empty. This is clearly the case independently of what kind of repair requests are employed. In fact, a non-empty set $\mathrm{Orep}(C, \alpha)$ clearly contains an element with maximal κ-value since this set is finite.

3.2 Conjunctive Inclusion

The supplementary postulate *conjunctive inclusion* can be formulated in our general setting as follows:

- if $\mathrm{ctr}(\mathcal{K}, \alpha \boxplus \beta) \in \mathrm{Rep}(\mathcal{K}, \alpha)$, then $\mathrm{ctr}(\mathcal{K}, \alpha) \models \mathrm{ctr}(\mathcal{K}, \alpha \boxplus \beta)$ (conjunctive inclusion)

In the classical case, repairs are deductively closed sets of formulas not containing the repair request, and thus *conjunctive inclusion* can be formulated as follows: if $\alpha \notin \mathrm{ctr}(\mathcal{K}, \alpha \wedge \beta)$, then $\mathrm{ctr}(\mathcal{K}, \alpha) \supseteq \mathrm{ctr}(\mathcal{K}, \alpha \wedge \beta)$.

In our general setting, to draw conclusions from the left-hand side of this implication (which for a PPC contraction states that a product belongs to a repair set), it might be useful to have the following property connecting products with repair sets, where $\mathfrak{K}$ is a finite set of KBs that are entailed by $\mathcal{K}$:

$$\otimes\mathfrak{K} \in \mathrm{Rep}(\mathcal{K}, \alpha) \text{ iff } \mathcal{K}' \in \mathit{Rep}(\mathcal{K}, \alpha) \text{ for some } \mathcal{K}' \in \mathfrak{K}. \tag{2}$$

The implication from right to left always holds in our framework since repair sets are assumed to be closed under entailment. The other directions does not hold in general, but it holds if the repair goal is non-entailment.

Lemma 6. *Let* Rep$(\mathcal{K},\alpha)$ *be closed under entailment. Then* $\mathcal{K}' \in Rep(\mathcal{K},\alpha)$ *for some* $\mathcal{K}' \in \mathfrak{K}$ *implies* $\otimes\mathfrak{K} \in \text{Rep}(\mathcal{K},\alpha)$.

Proof. This is an immediate consequence of the fact that $\mathcal{K}' \models \otimes\mathfrak{K}$ for all $\mathcal{K}' \in \mathfrak{K}$. □

Lemma 7. *Let* $\text{Rep}(\mathcal{K},\alpha) = \{\mathcal{K}' \mid \mathcal{K} \models \mathcal{K}' \wedge \mathcal{K}' \not\models \alpha\}$ *and let* $\mathfrak{K}$ *be a finite set of KBs that are entailed by* $\mathcal{K}$. *Then* $\otimes\mathfrak{K} \in \text{Rep}(\mathcal{K},\alpha)$ *implies that there is a KB* $\mathcal{K}' \in \mathfrak{K}$ *such that* $\mathcal{K}' \in Rep(\mathcal{K},\alpha)$.

Proof. We show the contraposition. If $\mathcal{K}' \notin Rep(\mathcal{K},\alpha)$ for all $\mathcal{K}' \in \mathfrak{K}$, then $\mathcal{K}' \models \alpha$ for all $\mathcal{K}' \in \mathfrak{K}$. Due to the definition of the product, this implies $\otimes\mathfrak{K} \models \alpha$, and thus $\otimes\mathfrak{K} \notin \text{Rep}(\mathcal{K},\alpha)$. □

The following examples demonstrate that *conjunctive inclusion* need not hold if (2) is not satisfied, both in the weakly maximizing and in the maximizing case.

Example 5. We use $\mathcal{EL}$ concepts as knowledge bases and subsumption $\sqsubseteq^\emptyset$ w.r.t. the empty TBox as entailment between knowledge bases. Then, conjunction is the sum operation $\oplus$ and the least common subsumer is the product operation $\otimes$. As repair requests we also consider $\mathcal{EL}$ concepts and the repair goal is non-subsumption, but now w.r.t. the following TBox $\mathcal{T}$:

$$\{\exists r.A_1 \sqsubseteq P_1 \sqcap P_3, \exists r.A_2 \sqsubseteq P_1 \sqcap P_2, \exists r.A_3 \sqsubseteq P_2 \sqcap P_3\},$$

i.e., $\text{Rep}(C,\alpha) := \{C' \mid C \sqsubseteq^\emptyset C' \wedge C' \not\sqsubseteq^\mathcal{T} \alpha\}$. It is easy to see that these repair sets are closed under entailment $\sqsubseteq^\emptyset$ since $\sqsubseteq^\emptyset \subseteq \sqsubseteq^\mathcal{T}$. The optimal repair property is satisfied since (up to equivalence $\equiv^\emptyset$) a given $\mathcal{EL}$ concept has only finitely many subsumers w.r.t. $\sqsubseteq^\emptyset$. As operation $\boxplus$ on repair requests we also use conjunction. It is easy to see that we are in a PPC enabling setting and that (1) is satisfied. If we set $C := \exists r.(A_1 \sqcap A_2 \sqcap A_3)$, $\alpha := P_1 \sqcap P_2 \sqcap P_3$, $\beta := \exists r.A_2 \sqcap \exists r.A_3$, then

$$\text{Orep}(C,\alpha) = \{\exists r.A_1, \exists r.A_2, \exists r.A_3\},\ \text{Orep}(C,\beta) = \{\exists r.(A_1 \sqcap A_2), \exists r.(A_1 \sqcap A_3)\},$$
$$\text{Orep}(C,\alpha \boxplus \beta) = \{\exists r.(A_1 \sqcap A_2), \exists r.(A_1 \sqcap A_3)\}.$$

In fact, it is easy to see that the $\mathcal{EL}$ concepts C' satisfying $C \sqsubseteq^\emptyset C'$ are (up to equivalence) conjunctions of concepts of the form C, $\top$, $\exists r.\top$, $\exists r.A_i$ for $i \in \{1,2,3\}$, and $\exists r.(A_i \sqcap A_j)$ for $i,j \subseteq \{1,2,3\}$ with $i \neq j$. For such a concept C' not to entail $\alpha = P_1 \sqcap P_2 \sqcap P_3$ w.r.t. $\mathcal{T}$, there must be an $i \in \{1,2,3\}$ such C' does not entail P_i. Assume prototypically that $i = 1$ (the other cases are symmetric). Then C' entails neither $\exists r.A_1$ nor $\exists r.A_2$. The most specific concept entailed by C and satisfying this is $\exists r.A_3$. Regarding non-entailment of β by such a concept C', this is the case if C' does not entail $\exists r.A_2$ or it does not entail $\exists r.A_3$. Assume prototypically that $\exists r.A_2$ is not entailed by C'. The most specific concept entailed by C and satisfying this is $\exists r.(A_1 \sqcap A_3)$

If we take as relation $\trianglelefteq$ the universal relation on $\mathcal{EL}$ concepts, then $\trianglelefteq$ is clearly transitive and weakly maximizing. For this relation, the induced selection function γ always selects the whole set of optimal repairs. Consequently $\mathrm{ctr}(C, \alpha) = \mathrm{lcs}(\exists r.A_1, \exists r.A_2, \exists r.A_3) = \exists r.\top$ and $\mathrm{ctr}(C, \alpha \boxplus \beta) = \mathrm{lcs}(\exists r.(A_1 \sqcap A_2), \exists r.(A_1 \sqcap A_3)) = \exists r.A_1$. Thus, we have $\mathrm{ctr}(C, \alpha \boxplus \beta) \in \mathrm{Rep}(C, \alpha)$, but $\mathrm{ctr}(C, \alpha) = \exists r.\top \not\sqsubseteq^{\mathcal{T}} \exists r.A_1$, which shows that *conjunctive inclusion* is not satisfied. Note that (2) is not satisfied in this example. In fact, neither $\exists r.(A_1 \sqcap A_2)$ nor $\exists r.(A_1 \sqcap A_3)$ belongs to $\mathrm{Rep}(C, \alpha)$, but their product $\exists r.A_1$ does.

In this example, we could not have employed $\sqsubseteq^{\mathcal{T}}$ as entailment relation for comparing repairs. While (up to equivalence w.r.t. $\mathcal{T}$) the optimal repair sets would have been the same, the lcs of $\exists r.(A_1 \sqcap A_2)$ and $\exists r.(A_1 \sqcap A_3)$ w.r.t. $\mathcal{T}$ would be $P_1 \sqcap P_2 \sqcap P_3 \sqcap \exists r.A_1$ and thus not a repair for α. A modified version of Example 5 can be used to show that such a counterexample also exists if a maximizing (rather than just weakly maximizing) transitive relation is used.

Example 6. In this example, we basically employ the same setup as in the previous example, but restrict the set of KBs to consist of all existential restrictions subsuming $C := \exists r.(A_1 \sqcap A_2 \sqcap A_3)$ w.r.t. the empty TBox. Between these KBs we again use $\sqsubseteq^{\emptyset}$ as entailment relation. Up to equivalence, the set of KBs considered here consist of the concepts $\exists r.\sqcap M$ for $M \subseteq \{A_1, A_2, A_3\}$, where $\sqcap\emptyset = \top$ and otherwise $\sqcap M$ is the conjunction of the elements of M. For such concepts, we have $\exists r.\sqcap M \sqsubseteq^{\emptyset} \exists r.\sqcap N$ iff $M \supseteq N$, and thus sum corresponds to set union and product to set intersection, i.e., $\exists r.\sqcap M \oplus \exists r.\sqcap N = \exists r.\sqcap(M \cup N)$ and $\exists r.\sqcap M \otimes \exists r.\sqcap N = \exists r.\sqcap(M \cap N)$.

As repair requests we consider arbitrary $\mathcal{EL}$ concepts α, which define repair sets $\mathrm{Rep}(C, \alpha) := \{C' \mid C \sqsubseteq^{\emptyset} C' \wedge C' \not\sqsubseteq^{\mathcal{T}} \alpha\}$, where $\mathcal{T}$ is the TBox of Example 5. As in Example 5 it is easy to see that repair sets are closed under entailment and satisfy the optimal repair property. As operation $\boxplus$ on repair requests we again use conjunction, which ensures that (1) is satisfied. If we set $C := \exists r.(A_1 \sqcap A_2 \sqcap A_3)$, $\alpha := P_1 \sqcap P_2 \sqcap P_3$, and $\beta := \exists r.A_2 \sqcap \exists r.A_3$, then we obtain the same sets of optimal repairs as in Example 5.

Now, we define a maximizing and transitive relation $\trianglelefteq$ on knowledge bases: $\exists r.\sqcap M \trianglelefteq \exists r.\sqcap N$ iff $|M| \leq |N|$. This relation is clearly transitive since $\leq$ on natural numbers is transitive. If $\exists r.\sqcap N \sqsubset^{\emptyset} \exists r.\sqcap M$, then $N \supseteq M$, and thus $|N| \geq |M|$. Since $|N| = |M|$ would imply $N = M$, and thus $\exists r.\sqcap N \equiv^{\emptyset} \exists r.\sqcap M$, we actually have $|N| > |M|$, which implies $\exists r.\sqcap N \rhd \exists r.\sqcap M$.

For our optimal repair sets, the selection function induced by this relation $\trianglelefteq$ again selects all elements. We can now proceed as in Example 5 to show that *conjunctive inclusion* and (2) are not satisfied.

Now, we investigate whether the postulate *conjunctive inclusion* holds under the assumption that (1) and (2) are satisfied. We start with a lemma that looks similar to Lemma 5. Its proof is inspired by the proof of *condition* T in the proof of Observation 2.76 in [16]. For the case of belief set contraction, this lemma is crucial for showing *conjunctive inclusion*. Unfortunately, due to the fact that the inclusion $\text{Orep}(\mathcal{K},\alpha) \cup \text{Orep}(\mathcal{K},\beta) \subseteq \text{Orep}(\mathcal{K},\alpha \boxplus \beta)$ need not hold, we do not obtain a direct inclusion relation between the sets selected by γ.

Lemma 8. *Let γ be a weakly maximizingly and transitively relational selection function and assume that (1) and (2) hold. If $\text{Rep}(\mathcal{K},\alpha) \neq \emptyset \neq \text{Rep}(\mathcal{K},\beta)$ and $\text{ctr}(\mathcal{K},\alpha \boxplus \beta) \in \text{Rep}(\mathcal{K},\alpha)$, then for every element $\mathcal{Z}$ of $\gamma(\text{Orep}(\mathcal{K},\alpha))$ there exists an element $\mathcal{Z}'$ of $\gamma(\text{Orep}(\mathcal{K},\alpha \boxplus \beta))$ such that $\mathcal{Z}' \models \mathcal{Z}$.*

Proof. Since (2) holds, $\text{ctr}(\mathcal{K},\alpha \boxplus \beta) \in \text{Rep}(\mathcal{K},\alpha)$ implies that there is an $\mathcal{X} \in \gamma(\text{Orep}(\mathcal{K},\alpha \boxplus \beta))$ such that $\mathcal{X} \in \text{Rep}(\mathcal{K},\alpha)$. Lemma 3 yields $\mathcal{X} \in \text{Orep}(\mathcal{K},\alpha)$.

Now, assume that $\mathcal{Z} \in \gamma(\text{Orep}(\mathcal{K},\alpha))$. Then $\mathcal{Z} \in \text{Rep}(\mathcal{K},\alpha) \subseteq \text{Rep}(\mathcal{K},\alpha \boxplus \beta)$, and thus there is $\mathcal{Z}' \in \text{Orep}(\mathcal{K},\alpha \boxplus \beta)$ such that $\mathcal{Z}' \models \mathcal{Z}$. This implies $\mathcal{Z}' \trianglerighteq \mathcal{Z}$.

To show that $\mathcal{Z}'$ is selected by γ, we consider an arbitrary element $\mathcal{V}$ of $\text{Orep}(\mathcal{K},\alpha \boxplus \beta)$ and prove that $\mathcal{Z} \trianglerighteq \mathcal{V}$. Since $\mathcal{X} \in \text{Orep}(\mathcal{K},\alpha)$, we know that $\mathcal{Z} \trianglerighteq \mathcal{X}$. In addition, $\mathcal{V} \in \text{Orep}(\mathcal{K},\alpha \boxplus \beta)$ and $\mathcal{X} \in \gamma(\text{Orep}(\mathcal{K},\alpha \boxplus \beta))$ yield $\mathcal{X} \trianglerighteq \mathcal{V}$. Putting all inequalities together yields $\mathcal{Z}' \trianglerighteq \mathcal{Z} \trianglerighteq \mathcal{X} \trianglerighteq \mathcal{V}$, and thus $\mathcal{Z}' \trianglerighteq \mathcal{V}$ by transitivity. Since $\mathcal{V}$ was assumed to be an arbitrary element of $\text{Orep}(\mathcal{K},\alpha \boxplus \beta)$, this proves $\mathcal{Z}' \in \gamma(\text{Orep}(\mathcal{K},\alpha \boxplus \beta))$. □

In the proof of this lemma it is sufficient to know that $\trianglelefteq$ is weakly maximizing. If we make the stronger assumption that $\trianglelefteq$ is maximizing, then we obtain the following stronger lemma, which will allow us to prove *conjunctive inclusion*.

Lemma 9. *Assume in addition to the assumptions of the previous lemma that $\trianglelefteq$ is maximizing. Then for every element $\mathcal{Z}$ of $\gamma(\text{Orep}(\mathcal{K},\alpha))$ there exists an element $\mathcal{Z}'$ of $\gamma(\text{Orep}(\mathcal{K},\alpha \boxplus \beta))$ such that $\mathcal{Z}' \equiv \mathcal{Z}$.*

Proof. If none of the entailments $\mathcal{Z}' \models \mathcal{Z}$ in the previous lemma is strict, then we are done. We now show that assuming that one of these entailments is strict leads to a contradiction. Thus, assume that $\mathcal{Z}$ is an element of $\gamma(\text{Orep}(\mathcal{K},\alpha))$ such that there exists an element $\mathcal{Z}'$ of $\gamma(\text{Orep}(\mathcal{K},\alpha \boxplus \beta))$ satisfying $\mathcal{Z}' \models_s \mathcal{Z}$. Then the maximizing property yields $\mathcal{Z}' \triangleright \mathcal{Z}$. Since $\mathcal{Z}$ is selected, we also know that $\mathcal{Z} \trianglerighteq \mathcal{Z}_0$ holds for all $\mathcal{Z}_0 \in \text{Orep}(\mathcal{K},\alpha)$. In addition, $\mathcal{Z}_1 \trianglerighteq \mathcal{Z}'$ holds for all $\mathcal{Z}_1 \in \gamma(\text{Orep}(\mathcal{K},\alpha \boxplus \beta))$. Transitivity thus yields $\mathcal{Z}_1 \triangleright \mathcal{Z}_0$ for all $\mathcal{Z}_1 \in \gamma(\text{Orep}(\mathcal{K},\alpha \boxplus \beta))$ and all $\mathcal{Z}_0 \in \text{Orep}(\mathcal{K},\alpha)$.

The assumption $\text{ctr}(\mathcal{K},\alpha \boxplus \beta) \in \text{Rep}(\mathcal{K},\alpha)$ implies that there is an $\mathcal{X} \in \gamma(\text{Orep}(\mathcal{K},\alpha \boxplus \beta))$ such that $\mathcal{X} \in \text{Rep}(\mathcal{K},\alpha)$. Coverage yields an element $\mathcal{X}_0 \in \text{Orep}(\mathcal{K},\alpha)$ such that $\mathcal{X}_0 \models \mathcal{X}$, and thus $\mathcal{X}_0 \trianglerighteq \mathcal{X}$. However, we have shown in the previous paragraph that actually $\mathcal{X} \triangleright \mathcal{X}_0$ must hold. □

Theorem 2. *Assume that $\models$ is PPC enabling and that the identities (1) and (2) hold. If the selection function γ is maximizingly and transitively relational, then the partial product contraction operation ctr_γ satisfies the postulate* conjunctive inclusion.

Proof. As already pointed out in the proof of Theorem 1, the coverage property of optimal repairs implies that $\text{Rep}(\mathcal{K},\alpha) = \emptyset$ iff $\text{Orep}(\mathcal{K},\alpha) = \emptyset$. Thus, if $\text{Orep}(\mathcal{K},\alpha \boxplus \beta) = \emptyset$, then $\text{Orep}(\mathcal{K},\alpha) = \emptyset = \text{Orep}(\mathcal{K},\beta)$. In this case,

$\text{ctr}_\gamma(\mathcal{K}, \alpha \boxplus \beta) = \mathcal{K} = \text{ctr}_\gamma(\mathcal{K}, \alpha)$, and thus *conjunctive overlap* clearly holds. If all three sets of optimal repairs are non-empty, then *conjunctive inclusion* is an immediate consequence of Lemma 9.

Now assume that $\text{Orep}(\mathcal{K}, \alpha \boxplus \beta) \neq \emptyset \neq \text{Orep}(\mathcal{K}, \alpha)$ and $\text{Orep}(\mathcal{K}, \beta) = \emptyset$. In this case, $\text{Rep}(\mathcal{K}, \alpha \boxplus \beta) = \text{Rep}(\mathcal{K}, \alpha)$, and thus $\text{Orep}(\mathcal{K}, \alpha \boxplus \beta)$ and $\text{Orep}(\mathcal{K}, \alpha)$ are equal up to equivalence. This implies that $\text{ctr}(\mathcal{K}, \alpha) \equiv \text{ctr}(\mathcal{K}, \alpha \boxplus \beta)$ due to the properties required for selection functions, which shows that *conjunctive inclusion* also holds in this case. Finally, assume $\text{Orep}(\mathcal{K}, \alpha \boxplus \beta) \neq \emptyset \neq \text{Orep}(\mathcal{K}, \beta)$ and $\text{Orep}(\mathcal{K}, \alpha) = \emptyset$. In this case, the precondition $\text{ctr}(\mathcal{K}, \alpha \boxplus \beta) \in \text{Rep}(\mathcal{K}, \alpha)$ of *conjunctive inclusion* is false. Thus the postulate trivially holds. □

4 Conclusion

We have seen that, under reasonable additional assumptions, Gärdenfors's supplementary postulates can be shown to hold for the partial product contractions produced by the general framework of [9]. This clarifies what conditions are really needed for these postulates to hold. At the moment, it remains open whether the postulates in [9] together with *conjunctive overlap* and *conjunctive inclusion* characterize the partial product contractions obtained from all maximizingly and transitively relational selection functions. If one considers the proofs of such characterization theorems involving the supplementary postulates in the literature (see, e.g., [16], where quite a number of such theorems are shown), then one sees that they strongly make use of the "remainder variant" of the equation $\text{Orep}(\mathcal{K}, \alpha \boxplus \beta) = \text{Orep}(\mathcal{K}, \alpha) \cup \text{Orep}(\mathcal{K}, \beta)$, which holds for the remainders considered there, but not in our general setting (see Example 3). Also note that such proofs usually depend on the fact that KBs are sets of formulas of a logic in which certain Boolean operators are available. It needs to be seen whether the proof of an appropriate characterization theorem requires additional conditions on our framework, or whether the development of new proof approaches is sufficient.

Acknowledgements. Franz Baader was partially supported by DFG, Grant 389792660, within TRR 248 "Center for Perspicuous Computing", and by the German Federal Ministry of Education and Research (BMBF, SCADS22B) and the Saxon State Ministry for Science, Culture and Tourism (SMWK) by funding the competence center for Big Data and AI "ScaDS.AI Dresden/Leipzig". Renata Wassermann would like to thank the Center for Artificial Intelligence (C4AI-USP), supported by the São Paulo Research Foundation (FAPESP grant #2019/07665-4) and the IBM Corporation. Both authors thank the anonymous reviewers for their helpful comments.

References

1. Alchourrón, C.E., Gärdenfors, P., Makinson, D.: On the logic of theory change: partial meet contraction and revision functions. J. Symb. Log. **50**(2), 510–530 (1985). https://doi.org/10.2307/2274239

2. Baader, F.: Relating optimal repairs in ontology engineering with contraction operations in belief change. ACM SIGAPP Appl. Comput. Rev. **23**(3), 5–18 (2023). https://doi.org/10.1145/3626307.3626308
3. Baader, F.: An order-theoretic view on optimal repairs and complete sets of unifiers. LTCS-Report 25-02, Chair of Automata Theory, Institute of Theoretical Computer Science, Technische Universität Dresden, Dresden (2025). https://doi.org/10.25368/2025.143
4. Baader, F., Koopmann, P., Kriegel, F.: Optimal repairs in the description logic $\mathcal{EL}$ revisited. In: Gaggl, S.A., Martinez, M.V., Ortiz, M. (eds.) Logics in Artificial Intelligence - 18th European Conference, JELIA 2023, Proceedings. Lecture Notes in Computer Science, vol. 14281, pp. 11–34. Springer, Heidelberg (2023). https://doi.org/10.1007/978-3-031-43619-2_2
5. Baader, F., Koopmann, P., Kriegel, F., Nuradiansyah, A.: Computing optimal repairs of quantified ABoxes w.r.t. static $\mathcal{EL}$ TBoxes. In: Platzer, A., Sutcliffe, G. (eds.) Automated Deduction - CADE 28 - 28th International Conference on Automated Deduction, Proceedings. Lecture Notes in Computer Science, vol. 12699. Springer, Heidelberg (2021). https://doi.org/10.1007/978-3-030-79876-5_18
6. Baader, F., Koopmann, P., Kriegel, F., Nuradiansyah, A.: Optimal ABox repair w.r.t. static $\mathcal{EL}$ TBoxes: From quantified ABoxes back to ABoxes. In: The Semantic Web - 19th International Conference, ESWC 2022, Proceedings. LNCS, vol. 13261, pp. 130–146. Springer, Heidelberg (2022). https://doi.org/10.1007/978-3-031-06981-9_8
7. Baader, F., Kriegel, F.: Pushing optimal ABox repair from $\mathcal{EL}$ towards more expressive Horn-DLs. In: Kern-Isberner, G., Lakemeyer, G., Meyer, T. (eds.) Proceedings of the 19th International Conference on Principles of Knowledge Representation and Reasoning, KR 2022 (2022), https://proceedings.kr.org/2022/3/
8. Baader, F., Kriegel, F., Nuradiansyah, A., Peñaloza, R.: Making repairs in description logics more gentle. In: Thielscher, M., Toni, F., Wolter, F. (eds.) Principles of Knowledge Representation and Reasoning: Proceedings of the Sixteenth International Conference, KR 2018, pp. 319–328. AAAI Press (2018). https://aaai.org/ocs/index.php/KR/KR18/paper/view/18056
9. Baader, F., Wassermann, R.: Contractions based on optimal repairs. In: Marquis, P., Ortiz, M., Pagnucco, M. (eds.) Proceedings of the 21st International Conference on Principles of Knowledge Representation and Reasoning, KR 2024 (2024). https://doi.org/10.24963/KR.2024/9
10. Delgrande, J.P.: A knowledge level account of forgetting. J. Artif. Intell. Res. **60**, 1165–1213 (2017). https://doi.org/10.1613/JAIR.5530
11. Fuhrmann, A.: On the modal logic of theory change. In: Fuhrmann, A., Morreau, M. (eds.) The Logic of Theory Change, Workshop, Proceedings. Lecture Notes in Computer Science, vol. 465, pp. 259–281. Springer, Heidelberg (1989). https://doi.org/10.1007/BFB0018425
12. Gärdenfors, P.: Epistemic importance and minimal changes of belief. Aust. J. Philos. **62**(2), 136–157 (1984). https://doi.org/10.1080/00048408412341331
13. Hansson, S.O.: A dyadic representation of belief. In: Gärdenfors, P. (ed.) Belief Revision, Cambridge Tracts in Theoretical Computer Science, vol. 29, pp. 89–121. Cambridge University Press (1992)
14. Hansson, S.O.: Similarity semantics and minimal changes of belief. Erkenntnis **37**(3), 401–429 (1992). https://doi.org/10.1007/bf00666230
15. Hansson, S.O.: Changes of disjunctively closed bases. J. Logic Lang. Inf. **2**(4), 255–284 (1993). http://www.jstor.org/stable/40180034

16. Hansson, S.O.: A Textbook of Belief Dynamics - Theory Change and Database Updating, Applied logic series, vol. 11. Kluwer (1999)
17. Kalyanpur, A., Parsia, B., Sirin, E., Grau, B.C.: Repairing unsatisfiable concepts in OWL ontologies. In: Sure, Y., Domingue, J. (eds.) The Semantic Web: Research and Applications, 3rd European Semantic Web Conference, ESWC 2006, Proceedings. Lecture Notes in Computer Science, vol. 4011, pp. 170–184. Springer, Heidelberg (2006). https://doi.org/10.1007/11762256_15
18. Kern-Isberner, G., Bock, T., Beierle, C., Sauerwald, K.: Axiomatic evaluation of epistemic forgetting operators. In: Barták, R., Brawner, K.W. (eds.) Proceedings of the Thirty-Second International Florida Artificial Intelligence Research Society Conference, FLAIRS'19. pp. 470–475. AAAI Press (2019). https://aaai.org/ocs/index.php/FLAIRS/FLAIRS19/paper/view/18231
19. Kriegel, F.: Optimal fixed-premise repairs of $\mathcal{EL}$ TBoxes. In: Bergmann, R., Malburg, L., Rodermund, S.C., Timm, I.J. (eds.) KI 2022: Advances in Artificial Intelligence – 45th German Conference on AI, Proceedings. Lecture Notes in Computer Science, vol. 13404, pp. 115–130. Springer, Heidelberg (2022). https://doi.org/10.1007/978-3-031-15791-2_11
20. Lang, J., Liberatore, P., Marquis, P.: Propositional independence: formula-variable independence and forgetting. J. Artif. Intell. Res. **18**, 391–443 (2003). https://doi.org/10.1613/JAIR.1113
21. Lutz, C., Wolter, F.: Foundations for uniform interpolation and forgetting in expressive description logics. In: Walsh, T. (ed.) IJCAI 2011, Proceedings of the 22nd International Joint Conference on Artificial Intelligence, pp. 989–995. IJCAI/AAAI (2011). https://doi.org/10.5591/978-1-57735-516-8/IJCAI11-170
22. Matos, V.B., Guimarães, R., Santos, Y.D., Wassermann, R.: Pseudo-contractions as gentle repairs. In: Lutz, C., Sattler, U., Tinelli, C., Turhan, A., Wolter, F. (eds.) Description Logic, Theory Combination, and All That - Essays Dedicated to Franz Baader on the Occasion of His 60th Birthday. Lecture Notes in Computer Science, vol. 11560, pp. 385–403. Springer, Heidelberg (2019). https://doi.org/10.1007/978-3-030-22102-7_18
23. Nebel, B.: A knowledge level analysis of belief revision. In: Brachman, R., Levesque, H., Reiter, R. (eds.) First International Conference on Principles of Knowledge Representation and Reasoning - KR'89, pp. 301–311. Morgan Kaufmann, Toronto (1989)
24. Ribeiro, J.S.: Semantic constructions for belief base contraction: partial meet vs smooth kernel. In: Proceedings of the 21st International Conference on Principles of Knowledge Representation and Reasoning, pp. 620–630 (2024). https://doi.org/10.24963/kr.2024/58
25. Rienstra, T., Schon, C., Staab, S.: Concept contraction in the description logic $\mathcal{EL}$. In: Calvanese, D., Erdem, E., Thielscher, M. (eds.) Proceedings of the 17th International Conference on Principles of Knowledge Representation and Reasoning, KR 2020, pp. 723–732 (2020). https://doi.org/10.24963/kr.2020/74
26. Rott, H.: Preferential belief change using generalized epistemic entrenchment. J. Log. Lang. Inf. **1**(1), 45–78 (1992). https://doi.org/10.1007/BF00203386
27. Santos, Y.D., Matos, V.B., Ribeiro, M.M., Wassermann, R.: Partial meet pseudo-contractions. Int. J. Approx. Reason. **103**, 11–27 (2018). https://doi.org/10.1016/j.ijar.2018.08.006
28. Schlobach, S., Huang, Z., Cornet, R., Harmelen, F.: Debugging incoherent terminologies. J. Autom. Reason. **39**(3), 317–349 (2007). https://doi.org/10.1007/s10817-007-9076-z

29. Troquard, N., Confalonieri, R., Galliani, P., Peñaloza, R., Porello, D., Kutz, O.: Repairing ontologies via axiom weakening. In: McIlraith, S.A., Weinberger, K.Q. (eds.) Proceedings of the Thirty-Second AAAI Conference on Artificial Intelligence, (AAAI-18), pp. 1981–1988. AAAI Press (2018), https://www.aaai.org/ocs/index.php/AAAI/AAAI18/paper/view/17189
30. Zarrieß, B., Turhan, A.: Most specific generalizations w.r.t. general $\mathcal{EL}$-TBoxes. In: Rossi, F. (ed.) IJCAI 2013, Proceedings of the 23rd International Joint Conference on Artificial Intelligence, Beijing, China, 3–9 August 2013, pp. 1191–1197. IJCAI/AAAI (2013). http://www.aaai.org/ocs/index.php/IJCAI/IJCAI13/paper/view/6709

Explaining Changes in Total Preorders and Ranking Functions

Alexander Hahn[1](✉), Gabriele Kern-Isberner[1], Lars-Phillip Spiegel[2], and Christoph Beierle[2]

[1] TU Dortmund University, 44227 Dortmund, Germany
{alexander.hahn,gabriele.kern-isberner}@tu-dortmund.de
[2] FernUniversität in Hagen, 58097 Hagen, Germany
{lars-phillip.spiegel,christoph.beierle}@fernuni-hagen.de

Abstract. When observing a transition from one epistemic state to another from the outside, without knowing details about the underlying belief change mechanism, it is not obvious how the change was performed and which formal postulates were satisfied or violated in the process. In this paper, we explore whether and how an arbitrary transition between epistemic states, represented by total preorders or ranking functions, respectively, can be realized via different kinds of belief change operations. This corresponds to coming up with an explanation for the belief change, enabling the investigation of arbitrary epistemic belief changes from a formal perspective. We consider iterated belief change operations in the popular AGM framework, and also point out connections to Hansson's framework of descriptor revision.

Keywords: belief change · belief revision · epistemic state · total preorder · ranking function · conditional · descriptor revision · explanation

1 Introduction

In iterated belief revision, various forms of representations of epistemic states are often used to encode an agent's beliefs, conditional beliefs and any other information that may influence a belief change. Epistemic states can change in numerous ways, and when they do, we usually want the change to satisfy certain formal guarantees. Verifying this is not easy, however, when details about the belief change process are unknown, and one can only observe the end result.

In this paper, we explore whether and how the transition from one epistemic state to another can be realized via belief revision, or a series of belief change operations. Essentially, we investigate the question: "Given two epistemic states Ψ_1, Ψ_2, is there a revision operator $*$ and a suitable input φ such that $\Psi_1 * \varphi = \Psi_2$?". This corresponds to looking for an explanation for a perceived change in (conditional) beliefs.

K. Sauerwald and M. Thimm (Eds.): ECSQARU 2025, LNAI 16099, pp. 285–300, 2026.
https://doi.org/10.1007/978-3-032-05134-9_20

As representations of epistemic states, we consider total preorders and Spohn's ranking functions [25], which are both widely used in belief revision, and work with both propositional and conditional revision operators. First, we offer some constructive approaches based on the popular AGM framework and its extension for epistemic state change [1,6,21]. Afterwards, we consider Hansson's framework of descriptor revision [14], which can be considered an alternative to the AGM framework, and show that it offers an elegant way to describe (solutions for) our research question.

In Sect. 2, we provide formal preliminaries. In Sect. 3, we point out related work. Section 4 recalls basics of iterated belief change in more detail. In Sect. 5, we investigate transitions between total preorders, and Sect. 6 is about transitions between ranking functions. In Sect. 7, we explore connections to descriptor revision. Section 8 contains conclusions and ideas for future work.

2 Preliminaries

Let $\mathcal{L}$ be a finitely generated propositional language over the alphabet $\Sigma = \{a, b, c, \dots\}$. Formulas $A, B, C, \dots$ are formed using the standard connectives $\wedge, \vee, \neg$. For conciseness of notation, we will write AB instead of $A \wedge B$ for conjunctions, and overlining formulas will indicate negation, i.e. $\overline{A}$ means $\neg A$. The symbol $\top$ denotes an arbitrary propositional tautology, and $\bot$ denotes an arbitrary contradiction. The set of all *possible worlds* (propositional interpretations) over Σ is denoted by Ω, and $\omega \models A$ means that the propositional formula $A \in \mathcal{L}$ holds in the possible world $\omega \in \Omega$; then ω is called a *model* of A, and the set of all models of A is denoted by $\mathrm{Mod}(A)$. For propositions $A, B \in \mathcal{L}$, $A \models B$ holds iff $\mathrm{Mod}(A) \subseteq \mathrm{Mod}(B)$, as usual. Logical equivalence between formulas is denoted by $\equiv$. By slight abuse of notation, we will use ω both for the model and the corresponding conjunction of all positive or negated atoms. Since $\omega \models A$ means the same for both readings of ω, no confusion will arise.

We also consider *conditionals* $(B|A) \in (\mathcal{L}|\mathcal{L})$ which express statements like "If A then plausibly B". The formula A is called the *antecedent*, and B is called the *consequent* of the conditional $(B|A)$. A *conditional belief base* Δ is a finite set of conditionals. Semantics for conditionals and conditional belief bases are provided by *epistemic states* Ψ via an acceptance relation $\models$, i.e., $\Psi \models (B|A)$ means that $(B|A)$ is accepted in Ψ. For formulas A, we have $\Psi \models A$ iff $\Psi \models (A|\top)$. This allows us to subsume plausible propositional formulas in terms of conditionals. For sets of conditionals $\Delta \subseteq (\mathcal{L}|\mathcal{L})$, we have $\Psi \models \Delta$ if $\Psi \models \delta$ for all $\delta \in \Delta$. The set of all conditionals accepted by Ψ is denoted as $\mathcal{C}(\Psi)$, and the set of propositions accepted by Ψ is denoted as $\mathrm{Bel}(\Psi)$.

In this paper, we consider two types of (representations for) epistemic states: total preorders and ranking functions over Ω. *Total preorders* (TPOs) $\preceq\, \subseteq \Omega \times \Omega$ are total and transitive relations. As usual, $\omega_1 \prec \omega_2$ if $\omega_1 \preceq \omega_2$, but not $\omega_2 \preceq \omega_1$, and $\omega_1 \approx \omega_2$ if both $\omega_1 \preceq \omega_2$ and $\omega_2 \preceq \omega_1$. Total preorders represent plausibility orderings, with the most plausible worlds being located in the lowermost layer of $\preceq$ which we denote by $\min(\Omega, \preceq)$. More generally, if $\Omega' \subseteq \Omega$ is a subset of possible worlds, $\min(\Omega', \preceq)$ denotes the set of minimal worlds in Ω' according to $\preceq$. The preorder $\preceq$ is lifted to a relation between propositions in the usual way: $A \preceq B$ if there is $\omega \models A$ such that $\omega \preceq \omega'$ for all $\omega' \models B$. A conditional $(B|A)$ is accepted by $\preceq$, denoted by $\preceq \models (B|A)$, if $AB \prec A\overline{B}$.

Ordinal Conditional Functions [25] (OCFs, also called *ranking functions*) $\kappa : \Omega \to \mathbb{N} \cup \{\infty\}$ with $\kappa^{-1}(0) \neq \emptyset$ assign degrees of implausibility, or surprise, to possible worlds. κ is lifted to formulas by $\kappa(A) := \min\{\kappa(\omega) \mid \omega \models A\}$, with $\kappa(\bot) = \min(\emptyset) = \infty$ by convention. Conditionals are accepted by κ, written as $\kappa \models (B|A)$, if $\kappa(AB) < \kappa(A\overline{B})$. A proposition A is accepted by κ, denoted by $\kappa \models A$, if $\kappa(A) < \kappa(\overline{A})$. Note that these definitions are in full compliance with corresponding definitions for total preorders.

In general, an epistemic state represents an agent's complete information, knowledge, and beliefs about the world; therefore, an epistemic state is often considered as abstract and vague in nature. However, as in any logic-based setting, in our approach we can only work on a formal representation of an epistemic state (like a TPO or an OCF over interpretations of a given propositional signature). Therefore, instead of frequently having to talk about "a (fixed) representation Ψ of an epistemic state", we will often simply talk about "an epistemic state Ψ".

An epistemic state Ψ is called *TPO-representable* iff its (qualitative) conditional beliefs can be modeled via a total preorder, i.e. there exists a total preorder $\preceq$ such that $\Psi \models (B|A)$ iff $\preceq \models (B|A)$ for all $(B|A) \in (\mathcal{L}|\mathcal{L})$. The corresponding total preorder is then denoted as $\preceq_\Psi$. Clearly, OCFs and TPOs themselves are TPO-representable. Two TPO-representable epistemic states Ψ, Ψ' are called *(inferentially) equivalent*, in symbols $\Psi \cong \Psi'$, if they are represented by the same total preorder. In other words, equivalent epistemic states accept exactly the same conditionals. For TPO-representable epistemic states Ψ, we will use the notation $\Psi^{[i]}$ denote the set of worlds in the i-th layer of Ψ, and $\bigvee\Psi^{[i]}$ to denote the disjunction over these worlds $\Psi^{[i]}$. For OCFs κ, we have $\kappa^{[i]} = \{\omega \in \Omega \mid \kappa(\omega) = i\}$. And for TPOs $\preceq$, we assume $\mathrm{b}\preceq^{[i]} = \kappa_\preceq{}^{[i]}$ with $\kappa_\preceq(\omega) = \min\{\kappa(\omega) \mid \kappa \cong \preceq\}$.

A *uniform* epistemic state Ψ_u accepts only trivial conditionals, i.e. $\Psi_u \models (B|A)$ iff $A \models B$. For uniform TPOs $\preceq_u$ this means $\omega \approx_u \omega'$ for all ω, ω'; and for uniform OCFs κ_u we have $\kappa_u(\omega) = 0$ for all ω.

3 Related Work

The objective of our work is to investigate within the formal frameworks of total preorders resp. ranking functions whether an epistemic change can be explained.

Formal explanations for agents' beliefs after a qualitative belief change on epistemic level were also considered in [2]. However, the focus of the explanations in [2] lies on the initial epistemic state, not on the change itself.

In [5], explanations for observations are considered, that is, different types of belief changes are compared in order to pick a most plausible one. We do not try to explain observations, but rather try to construct suitable observations and change operators in order to achieve a transition from one specific epistemic state to another. We also do not rank or compare the explanations themselves.

Furthermore, our work is closely related to the concept of *epistemic state mappings*, as the approaches in this paper can be considered implementations of TPO-to-TPO resp. OCF-to-OCF mappings. Properties of such (and more general) epistemic state mappings have been investigated e.g. in [12].

Another area related to our work is given by logic-based approaches to planning. For instance, in the classical situation calculus [22], planning corresponds to finding a sequence of actions transforming an initial situation characterized by a set of formulas into a target situation satisfying a given goal formula. A similar relationship of our work exists to planning in the seminal STRIPS system and its successors [8,9].

4 Postulates for Iterated Belief Change

The term "belief revision" is used in the literature to refer to various kinds of belief change operations with different kinds of restrictions. It may be used as an umbrella term subsuming any type of belief change operation, or in a more restrictive way referring to only those operations that satisfy specific postulates.

In this paper, a *(belief) revision operator* $*$ is any operator that satisfies

(Success*) $\Psi * \Delta \models \Delta$.

Similarly, a *(belief) contraction operator* is any operator $-$ such that

(Success$^-$) $\Psi - \Delta \not\models \delta$ for all $\delta \in \Delta$.

Weak conditionals $(\!|B|A|\!)$ are a variant of the regular conditionals (see e.g. [7]). A weak conditional is accepted by an epistemic state Ψ if its verification is at least as plausible as its falsification, thus $\Psi \models (\!|B|A|\!)$ iff $\Psi \not\models (\overline{B}|A)$. The success condition for revision by sets of weak conditionals Δ^w is:

(|Success*|) $\Psi * \Delta^w \models \Delta^w$.

Another property that is sometimes postulated for belief change operations is that one should not make any changes if the success condition is already fulfilled. For revision, this can be formalized as follows:

(Stability*) If $\Psi \models \Delta$, then $\Psi * \Delta = \Psi$.

The AGM framework [1,15] is a seminal approach to propositional belief change, where beliefs are represented by deductively closed sets of propositional formulas. The DP framework [6] extends the AGM framework for iterated belief revision, employing total preorders as representations of epistemic states.

Proposition 1 ([6]). *A revision operator $*$ that assigns a posterior epistemic state $\Psi * A$ to a prior state Ψ and a proposition A is an* AGM revision operator *for epistemic states iff there exists a TPO $\preceq_\Psi$ on Ω with* $\mathrm{Mod}(\mathrm{Bel}(\Psi)) = \min(\Omega, \preceq_\Psi)$ *such that* $\mathrm{Mod}(\mathrm{Bel}(\Psi * C)) = \min(\mathrm{Mod}(C), \preceq_\Psi)$ *holds for every proposition C.*

In order to restrict iterated revision, Darwiche and Pearl [6] have proposed the following postulates for the revision of an epistemic state Ψ equipped with a total preorder $\preceq_\Psi$ with a proposition C:

(DP1) If $\omega_1, \omega_2 \models C$, then $\omega_1 \preceq_\Psi \omega_2$ iff $\omega_1 \preceq_{\Psi * C} \omega_2$.
(DP2) If $\omega_1, \omega_2 \models \overline{C}$, then $\omega_1 \preceq_\Psi \omega_2$ iff $\omega_1 \preceq_{\Psi * C} \omega_2$.
(DP3) If $\omega_1 \models C$ and $\omega_2 \models \overline{C}$, then $\omega_1 \prec_\Psi \omega_2$ implies $\omega_1 \prec_{\Psi * C} \omega_2$.
(DP4) If $\omega_1 \models C$ and $\omega_2 \models \overline{C}$, then $\omega_1 \preceq_\Psi \omega_2$ implies $\omega_1 \preceq_{\Psi * C} \omega_2$.

Any AGM revision operator for epistemic states that satisfies (DP1–4) will be called a *DP revision operator* in this paper. For iterated contraction, Konieczny and Pino Pérez [21] formulated a similar proposition and similar postulates.

Proposition 2 ([21]). *A contraction operator* $-$ *that assigns a posterior state* $\Psi - A$ *to a prior state* Ψ *and* $A \in \mathcal{L}$ *is an* AGM contraction operator *for epistemic states iff there exists a TPO* $\preceq_\Psi$ *on* Ω *with* $\mathrm{Mod}(\mathrm{Bel}(\Psi)) = \min(\Omega, \preceq_\Psi)$ *such that* $\mathrm{Mod}(\mathrm{Bel}(\Psi - C)) = \mathrm{Mod}(\mathrm{Bel}(\Psi)) \cup \min(\mathrm{Mod}(\neg C), \preceq_\Psi)$ *holds for every* $C \in \mathcal{L}$.

(KP1) If $\omega_1, \omega_2 \models C$, then $\omega_1 \preceq_\Psi \omega_2$ iff $\omega_1 \preceq_{\Psi - C} \omega_2$.
(KP2) If $\omega_1, \omega_2 \models \overline{C}$, then $\omega_1 \preceq_\Psi \omega_2$ iff $\omega_1 \preceq_{\Psi - C} \omega_2$.
(KP3) If $\omega_1 \models \overline{C}$ and $\omega_2 \models C$, then $\omega_1 \prec_\Psi \omega_2$ implies $\omega_1 \prec_{\Psi - C} \omega_2$.
(KP4) If $\omega_1 \models \overline{C}$ and $\omega_2 \models C$, then $\omega_1 \preceq_\Psi \omega_2$ implies $\omega_1 \preceq_{\Psi - C} \omega_2$.

Any AGM contraction operator for epistemic states that satisfies (KP1–4) will be called a *KP contraction operator* in this paper.

One concrete approach to revision of OCFs that we will consider in this paper are Kern-Isberner's *c-revisions* [16,17].

Definition 1 (c-revisions for OCFs; $CR(\kappa, \Delta)$**).** *Let* κ *be an OCF and let* $\Delta = \{(B_1|A_1), \ldots, (B_n|A_n)\}$*. Then a* c-revision $\kappa *^c \Delta$ *is an OCF of the form*

$$(\kappa *^c \Delta)(\omega) = \kappa_0 + \kappa(\omega) + \sum_{\substack{1 \leqslant i \leqslant n \\ \omega \models A_i \overline{B}_i}} \eta_i \tag{1}$$

with nonnegative integers η_i *for each* $(B_i|A_i)$*, called* impact factors, *satisfying*

$$\eta_i > \min_{\omega \models A_i B_i} \Big\{ \kappa(\omega) + \sum_{\substack{j \neq i \\ \omega \models A_j \overline{B}_j}} \eta_j \Big\} - \min_{\omega \models A_i \overline{B}_i} \Big\{ \kappa(\omega) + \sum_{\substack{j \neq i \\ \omega \models A_j \overline{B}_j}} \eta_j \Big\} \tag{2}$$

The constraints (2) *for* $1 \leqslant i \leqslant n$ *give rise to a constraint satisfaction problem (CSP) which is denoted by* $CR(\kappa, \Delta)$.

The constraints (2) ensure (Success*), and the integer κ_0 is a normalizing term, i.e., ensuring that $\kappa^{[0]} \neq \emptyset$. A solution of $CR(\kappa, \Delta)$ is a vector $\vec{\eta} \in \mathbb{N}^n$, which defines a c-revision $\kappa^*_{\vec{\eta}}$ according to (1) [20]. Each c-revision is a DP-revision operator [17,18].

C-Revisions can also be defined for weak conditionals $(\!|B_i|A_i|\!)$. To this end, the constraint (2) has to be modified by replacing ">" with "$\geqslant$" in order to ensure that $\kappa(A_i B_i) \leqslant \kappa(A_i \overline{B_i})$, which is equivalent to $(\!|$Success*$|\!)$ for OCFs [24].

5 Transitions Between Total Preorders

In this section, we explore how transitions between total preorders can be explained via belief revision. We first establish the following general negative result.

Proposition 3. *Let Ψ_1, Ψ_2 be epistemic states with $\Psi_1 \neq \Psi_2$. If $\mathcal{C}(\Psi_2) \subseteq \mathcal{C}(\Psi_1)$, then there is no Δ with $\Psi_1 * \Delta = \Psi_2$ for any revision operator $*$ satisfying (Success*) and (Stability*).*

Proof. Let Ψ_1, Ψ_2 with $\mathcal{C}(\Psi_2) \subseteq \mathcal{C}(\Psi_1)$ be as in the proposition. Towards a contradiction, assume there were some Δ, and some $*$ satisfying (Success*) and (Stability*), such that $\Psi_1 * \Delta = \Psi_2$. Due to (Success*) $\Psi_2 \models \Delta$ must hold, and therefore $\Delta \subseteq \mathcal{C}(\Psi_2)$. Then also $\Delta \subseteq \mathcal{C}(\Psi_1)$, and $\Psi_1 \models \Delta$. Thus with (Stability*) $\Psi_1 * \Delta = \Psi_1$, which contradicts the assumption $\Psi_1 \neq \Psi_2$. □

The core message of this proposition is that some epistemic state changes cannot be modeled by a single (DP-style) revision operation alone.

Example 1. Let $\Omega = \{a, \overline{a}\}$. Consider the two TPOs $a \prec_1 \overline{a}$ and $a \sim_2 \overline{a}$ representing two different epistemic states Ψ_1 and Ψ_2. Clearly, to go from Ψ_1 to Ψ_2, one needs to *forget* the conditional $(a|\top)$ in order to end up with the uniform TPO. However, (Success*) entails that the result of every non-trivial revision accepts at least one non-trivial conditional, and (Stability*) rules out $\Psi_1 * \emptyset = \Psi_2$.

It is easy to see that an analogous result to the one in Proposition 3 holds for the case $\mathcal{C}(\Psi_1) \subseteq \mathcal{C}(\Psi_2)$: it is impossible to expand the conditional beliefs of an epistemic state by a (KP-style) contraction.

In summary, in the AGM framework, one single change operation may not be enough to fully explain an epistemic belief change. However, every change can be explained by a series of change operations, as is shown next.

Proposition 4. *Let Ψ_1, Ψ_2 be epistemic states represented by total preorders, let $*$ be a DP revision operator, and let $-$ be a KP contraction operator. Then there is a series of belief changes via $*$ and $-$ (with formulas $A_1, \ldots, A_n \in \mathcal{L}$) such that $(((\Psi_1 * A_1) - A_2) \cdots * A_{n-1}) - A_n = \Psi_2$.*

Proof. We prove Proposition 4 by proving the correctness of the algorithm TPORTransition (Algorithm 1), which essentially constructs Ψ_2 top-down by iteratively revising and contracting Ψ_1. In the process, the list of change operations for transforming Ψ_1 into Ψ_2 is computed. This essentially yields the inputs $A_1, \ldots, A_n$ from the proposition above. Note that in the algorithm, multiple contractions may follow each other without a revision in between and vice versa. This does not break compatibility with the proposition since one can always perform revisions with $\top$ (or contractions with $\bot$) without changing the epistemic state.

Algorithm 1. TPORTransition

Input: TPO-representable epistemic states Ψ_1, Ψ_2
Parameters: DP revision operator $*$, KP contraction operator $-$
Output: list $\mathcal{O}$ containing change operators and corresponding input formulas

1: Let L_2 be the highest layer in Ψ_2.
2: Let $\mathcal{O}$ be an empty list.
3: Set $\Phi_0 := \Psi_1$.
4: **for** $i \in \{0, \ldots, L_2\}$ **do**
5: Set $A_i := \bigvee {\Psi_2}^{[L_2-i]}$.
6: Set $\Phi_{i+1} := \Phi_i * A_i$.
7: Append $(*, A_i)$ to the end of $\mathcal{O}$.
8: **for all** $\Omega_j \in \{{\Phi_{i+1}}^{[j]} \mid j > i\}$ **do**
9: **if** $\Omega_j \cap {\Psi_2}^{[L_2-i]} \neq \emptyset$ **then**
10: Set $C_{i,j} := \neg \bigvee(\Omega_j \cap {\Psi_2}^{[L_2-i]})$.
11: Set $\Phi_{i+1} := \Phi_{i+1} - C_{i,j}$.
12: Append $(-, C_{i,j})$ to the end of $\mathcal{O}$.
13: **end if**
14: **end for**
15: **end for**
16: Return $\mathcal{O}$.

We show that the algorithm satisfies the following invariant: After the for loop in iteration i (i.e. after Line 14) we have

$$ {\Phi_{i+1}}^{[0]} = {\Psi_2}^{[L_2-i]}, \ldots, {\Phi_{i+1}}^{[i]} = {\Psi_2}^{[L_2]} , \tag{3} $$

meaning that the bottom i layers in Φ_{i+1} correspond to the top i layers in Ψ_2.

First we consider $i = 0$. After Line 6, we have ${\Phi_1}^{[0]} = \min({\Psi_2}^{[L_2]}, \preceq_{\Psi_1})$ because of Proposition 1. With the repeated execution of Line 11, all remaining worlds from ${\Psi_2}^{[L_2]}$ are added to the lowest layer in Φ_1 (see Proposition 2). After Line 14, we therefore have ${\Phi_1}^{[0]} = {\Psi_2}^{[L_2]}$. The invariant (3) holds.

Now we prove the case of $i > 0$ via induction, i.e. we assume that the invariant holds for all previous iterations $0, \ldots, i-1$. After Line 6, we have ${\Phi_{i+1}}^{[0]} = \min({\Psi_2}^{[L_2-i]}, \preceq_{\Phi_i})$. Because of (DP2), the worlds from layer ${\Phi_i}^{[0]}$ were not split up, i.e. there exists a k with ${\Phi_{i+1}}^{[k]} = {\Phi_i}^{[0]} = {\Psi_2}^{[L_2-i+1]}$, and below this layer k in Φ_{i+1} there are only models of $A_i = \bigvee {\Psi_2}^{[L_2-i]}$, i.e. only worlds from ${\Psi_2}^{[L_2-i]}$. Above this layer k, we have ${\Phi_{i+1}}^{[k+1]} = {\Phi_i}^{[1]} = {\Psi_2}^{[L_2-i+2]}, \ldots, {\Phi_{i+1}}^{[k+i-1]} = {\Phi_i}^{[i-1]} = {\Psi_2}^{[L_2]}$, i.e. the top $i-1$ layers from Ψ_2, due to the induction hypothesis.

Again, with the repeated execution of Line 11 the remaining worlds from ${\Psi_2}^{[L_2-i]}$ are pulled into the bottom layer of Φ_{i+1}. Because of (KP1), the order of all other worlds is again not affected. Therefore, after Line 14, we have ${\Phi_{i+1}}^{[0]} = {\Psi_2}^{[L_2-i]}$. Moreover, all layers below the worlds from ${\Phi_i}^{[0]}$, i.e. all layers below what was previously layer k, have collapsed into a single layer. Hence, ${\Phi_{i+1}}^{[1]} = {\Phi_i}^{[0]} = {\Psi_2}^{[L_2-i+1]}, \ldots, {\Phi_{i+1}}^{[i]} = {\Phi_i}^{[i-1]} = {\Psi_2}^{[L_2]}$. □

Note that in Proposition 4 above, the change operations do not use conditional but propositional information as input, i.e. propositional revision and contraction are sufficient to achieve this result. The following example illustrates the algorithm TPORTransition (Algorithm 1).

Example 2. Consider the following input for the algorithm TPORTransition:

$$\Psi_1 : \quad \omega_1 \quad \prec_{\Psi_1} \quad \omega_2 \quad \approx_{\Psi_1} \quad \omega_3 \quad \prec_{\Psi_1} \quad \omega_4 \ ,$$
$$\Psi_2 : \quad \omega_2 \quad \approx_{\Psi_2} \quad \omega_4 \quad \prec_{\Psi_2} \quad \omega_3 \quad \prec_{\Psi_2} \quad \omega_1 \ .$$

Let $*, -$ be an arbitrary DP-revision resp. KP-contraction operator. We have $L_2 = 2$. In iteration $i = 0$, we have $\Phi_0 = \Psi_1$. We revise with $A_0 = \omega_1$ and obtain $\Phi_1 = \Phi_0 * \omega_1 = \Phi_0$ since ω_1 is already believed in Φ_0. Since there are no worlds from ${\Psi_2}^{[2]}$ above the lowermost layer in Φ_1, no contractions are performed. At this point, we have $\mathcal{O} = \{(*, \omega_1)\}$.

In iteration $i = 1$, we have $A_1 = \omega_3$. The revision yields the following TPO:

$$\Phi_2 : \quad \omega_3 \quad \prec_{\Phi_2} \quad \omega_1 \quad \prec_{\Phi_2} \quad \omega_2 \quad \prec_{\Phi_2} \quad \omega_4 \ .$$

Again, no contraction is performed since there is no ${\Psi_2}^{[1]}$-world above the lowermost layer in Φ_2. Now $\mathcal{O} = \{(*, \omega_1), (*, \omega_3)\}$.

In iteration $i = 2$, we revise with $A_2 = \omega_2 \vee \omega_4$. Now A_2 has multiple models in multiple layers of Φ_2, and our choice of $*$ influences the resulting TPO. However, the DP postulates guarantee that the relative ordering $\omega_3 \prec_{\Phi_2} \omega_1$ will remain intact. Assume that $*$ only pulls the minimal models of A_2 down and keeps the order between all other worlds[1]. Since ω_2 is the minimal model of A_2 in Φ_2, we obtain:

$$\Phi_3 : \quad \omega_2 \quad \prec_{\Phi_3} \quad \omega_3 \quad \prec_{\Phi_3} \quad \omega_1 \quad \prec_{\Phi_3} \quad \omega_4 \ .$$

Now there is $\omega_4 \in {\Psi_2}^{[0]}$ which is not yet in the lowermost layer in Φ_3. Therefore, a contraction with $C_{2,3} = \neg\omega_4$ is performed, altering Φ_3 as follows.

$$\Phi_3 : \quad \omega_2 \quad \approx_{\Phi_3} \quad \omega_4 \quad \prec_{\Phi_3} \quad \omega_3 \quad \prec_{\Phi_3} \quad \omega_1 \ .$$

After iteration 2, the algorithm terminates with the output $\mathcal{O} = \{(*, \omega_1), (*, \omega_3), (*, \omega_2 \vee \omega_4), (-, \neg\omega_4)\}$. Altogether, $(((\Psi_1 * \omega_1) * \omega_3) * \omega_2 \vee \omega_4) - \neg\omega_4 = \Psi_2$.

With the algorithm TPORTransition we have shown a constructive approach of realizing generic transitions between epistemic states using a series of propositional revisions and contractions. An alternative solution is to allow revision by a mix of conditionals and weak conditionals. When we use weak conditionals, we can restrict the result of a revision much more, since we can also specify which conditionals should *not* hold afterwards, allowing us to express an arbitrary transition between total preorders as a single change operation.

Proposition 5. *Let Ψ_2 be an epistemic state. Then there is a set Δ containing conditionals and weak conditionals such that $\Psi_2 = \Psi_1 * \Delta$ for every epistemic state Ψ_1 and every revision operator $*$ satisfying (Success*) and ⦇Success*⦈.*

[1] This operator called *natural revision* [3] is known to satisfy the DP postulates.

Proof. Let L_2 be the highest layer in Ψ_2. We choose the following conditionals:

$$\Delta^c = \left\{ \left(\bigvee {\Psi_2}^{[i]} \middle| (\bigvee {\Psi_2}^{[i]}) \vee (\bigvee {\Psi_2}^{[i+1]})\right) \;\middle|\; \leqslant i < L_2 \right\}$$

and the following weak conditionals:

$$\Delta^w = \left\{ \left\llparenthesis \neg\omega \middle| \bigvee {\Psi_2}^{[i]} \right\rrparenthesis \;\middle|\; \leqslant i \leqslant L_2,\ \omega \in {\Psi_2}^{[i]} \right\} .$$

Let $\Delta = \Delta^c \cup \Delta^w$ and let Ψ_1 be any epistemic state. We show that $\Psi_1 * \Delta$ is represented by the same total preorder as Ψ_2. For all conditionals $\delta = (\bigvee {\Psi_2}^{[i]} | (\bigvee {\Psi_2}^{[i]}) \vee (\bigvee {\Psi_2}^{[i+1]})) \in \Delta^c$ and every possible world $\omega \in \Omega$, ω verifies δ iff $\omega \in {\Psi_2}^{[i]}$, and ω falsifies δ iff $\omega \in {\Psi_2}^{[i+1]}$. Therefore, since $\Psi_1 * \Delta \models \delta$, there must be an $\omega \in {\Psi_2}^{[i]}$ such that $\omega \prec_{\Psi_1 * \Delta} \omega'$ for every $\omega' \in {\Psi_2}^{[i+1]}$. For all weak conditionals $\delta^w = \llparenthesis \neg\omega | \bigvee {\Psi_2}^{[i]} \rrparenthesis \in \Delta^w$, we have $\Psi_1 \models \delta^w$ iff $\Psi_1 \not\models (\omega | \bigvee {\Psi_2}^{[i]})$, which means that there must be an $\omega' \in {\Psi_2}^{[i]}$ such that $\omega' \preceq_{\Psi_1 * \Delta} \omega$. Since this holds for all possible worlds from ${\Psi_2}^{[i]}$, we have $\omega \approx_{\Psi_1 * \Delta} \omega'$ for all $\omega, \omega' \in {\Psi_2}^{[i]}$. Altogether, for every pair of worlds $\omega, \omega' \in \Omega$, we have $\omega \prec_{\Psi_1 * \Delta} \omega$ if $\omega \prec_{\Psi_2} \omega$, and $\omega \approx_{\Psi_1 * \Delta} \omega$ if $\omega \approx_{\Psi_2} \omega$. Hence $(\preceq_{\Psi_1 * \Delta}) = (\preceq_{\Psi_2})$. □

Note that the set Δ constructed in the proof of Proposition 5 only depends on Ψ_2 and not on Ψ_1. Hence, Δ fully specifies the new epistemic state, and does not really tell us anything about the specific change from Ψ_1 to Ψ_2. The proof of Proposition 4 also uses a very general construction that mostly relies on the information provided by Ψ_2, taking only marginal advantage of the structure of Ψ_1. Hence, for specific instances of Ψ_1 and Ψ_2, one may employ more refined techniques to find a shorter or more intuitive explanation for the epistemic state change. The core message of this section in light of our research question is that, even under unfavorable circumstances, we can always find *some* explanation.

6 Transitions Between Ordinal Conditional Functions

Now we investigate OCF transitions. We start with the following proposition stating that every OCF can be constructed via c-revision of the uniform OCF.

Proposition 6. *For every OCF κ there are a conditional belief base Δ and a c-revision operator $*^c$ such that $\kappa = \kappa_u *_c \Delta$.*

Proof (sketch). One can use very similar conditionals to the ones from Δ^c in the proof of Proposition 5: $\delta_i = (\bigvee {\kappa_2}^{[r_i]} Big | (\bigvee {\kappa_2}^{[r_i]}) \vee (\bigvee {\kappa_2}^{[r_{i+1}]}))$, with $r_0, \ldots, r_{m-1}$ being the non-empty ranks of κ_2 (excluding the highest rank $r_m = \max\{\kappa(\omega) \mid \omega \in \Omega\}$). Each such conditional δ_i is assigned the impact $\eta_i = r_{i+1}$. □

As a consequence of Proposition 6, there always is a "tabula rasa" solution for a mapping $\kappa_1 \mapsto \kappa_2$: first, all (non-trivial) conditional beliefs in κ_1 are forgotten, resulting in the uniform OCF, and then κ_2 is constructed from the uniform OCF.

Note that Definition 1 does not force c-revisions to satisfy (Stability*) in general. Therefore, Proposition 3 does not apply, and one could assume that c-revisions are powerful enough such that Proposition 6 could be extended to arbitrary prior OCFs. However, (Success*) still restricts the revision operator.

Lemma 1. *Let κ_1, κ_2 be OCFs. If there are $\omega, \omega' \in \Omega$ with $\kappa_1(\omega) < \kappa_1(\omega')$ but $\kappa_2(\omega) = \kappa_2(\omega') = 0$, then there is no c-revision $\kappa_1 *^c \Delta$ with $\kappa_1 *^c \Delta = \kappa_2$.*

Proof. Assume there were a set of conditionals Δ and a c-revision operator $*^c$ such that $\kappa_1 *^c \Delta = \kappa_2$. Due to (Success*), both ω and ω' may not falsify any conditionals from Δ, since they are minimal worlds in κ_2. Therefore, $(\kappa_1 *^c \Delta)(\omega) = \kappa_0 + \kappa_1(\omega)$ and $(\kappa_1 *^c \Delta)(\omega') = \kappa_0 + \kappa_1(\omega')$. Hence $(\kappa_1 *^c \Delta)(\omega) < (\kappa_1 *^c \Delta)(\omega')$, which contradicts the assumption that $\kappa_1 *^c \Delta = \kappa_2$. □

Lemma 1 essentially says that possible worlds which are in different layers in κ_1 can never end up together in layer 0 after a c-revision. The situation changes if we consider revision with weak conditionals as in Proposition 5.

Proposition 7. *Let κ_2 be an OCF. Then there is a set Δ containing conditionals and weak conditionals such that $\kappa_2 \cong \kappa_1 * \Delta$ for every OCF κ_1 and every OCF-revision operator $*$ satisfying (Success*) and ⦇Success*⦈.*

Note that in Proposition 7, we only have equivalence (and not necessarily equality) between κ_2 and $\kappa_1 * \Delta$ since the success conditions force $*$ to construct a specific order of worlds, but there is no information in Δ about the numerical ranks of the layers in κ_2. In order to strengthen Proposition 7 to achieve equality of κ_2 and $\kappa_1 * \Delta$, one needs to utilize revision operators which are flexible enough to allow shifting the worlds not just into the correct order, but each world to their specific ranks in κ_2. For this, we use c-revisions again.

Proposition 8. *Let κ_1, κ_2 be OCFs. Then there are a set Δ containing conditionals and weak conditionals, and a c-revision operator $*^c$, such that $\kappa_2 = \kappa_1 *^c \Delta$.*

Proof (sketch). We use essentially the same conditional construction as the one from the proof of Proposition 5, i.e., $\Delta = \Delta^c \cup \Delta^w$ with

$$\Delta^c = \left\{ \left(\bigvee {\kappa_2}^{[i]} \middle| (\bigvee {\kappa_2}^{[i]}) \vee (\bigvee {\kappa_2}^{[i+1]}) \right) \;\middle|\; \leqslant i < L_2 \right\}$$
$$\Delta^w = \left\{ \left(\neg\omega \middle| \bigvee {\kappa_2}^{[i]} \right) \;\middle|\; \leqslant i \leqslant L_2,\ \omega \in {\kappa_2}^{[i]} \right\} ,$$

and with $r_0 = 0 < r_1 < \cdots < r_{L_2} = \max\{r \mid {\kappa_2}^{[r]} \neq \emptyset\}$ being the non-empty ranks in κ_2. For each $\delta_i^c = \left(\bigvee {\kappa_2}^{[i]} \middle| (\bigvee {\kappa_2}^{[i]}) \vee (\bigvee {\kappa_2}^{[i+1]}) \right) \in \Delta^c$, we choose the impact $\eta_i^c = r_{i+1}$, and for each $\delta_i^w = \left(\neg\omega \middle| \bigvee {\kappa_2}^{[i]} \right) \in \Delta^w$, we choose $\eta_i^w = r_{L_1} - \kappa_1(\omega)$ with $r_{L_1} = \max\{r \mid {\kappa_1}^{[r]} \neq \emptyset\}$. This way, the impacts for the weak conditionals equalize the differences between the worlds, and the impacts for the regular conditionals shift the layers to the correct position. □

Alternatively, the information encoded in the impacts η_i could be included as additional quantitative information in the set Δ. By specifying quantified conditionals $(B|A)[m]$ with the acceptance condition $\kappa \models (B|A)[m]$ iff $\kappa(AB) + m = \kappa(A\overline{B})$ one can encode the desired ranks directly in Δ. As there are currently very few OCF-revision operators considering such inputs in the literature[2], we will leave a more detailed analysis of how this should be handled for future work.

7 Epistemic State Transitions with Descriptor Revision

Hansson's framework for *descriptor revision* [13,14] provides an alternative to the AGM-based approaches. The core building blocks in this framework are *atomic descriptors*, which are constructed using the symbol $\mathfrak{B}$ (called *belief predicate*) and propositions $A \in \mathcal{L}$, with $\mathfrak{B}A$ expressing that "A is believed". Descriptors can be constructed using the symbols $\neg, \vee, \wedge$ and by using sets of such constructions. Descriptor revision was instantiated to the case in which the underlying logic is the conditional logic $(\mathcal{L}|\mathcal{L})$ and ranking functions serve as a representation for epistemic states [10,11,23]. If Ξ is a descriptor over $(\mathcal{L}|\mathcal{L})$, we use $cond(\Xi)$ to denote the set of conditionals in Ξ, e.g. $cond(\neg\mathfrak{B}(B|A)) = \{(B|A)\}$.

When an agent performs a belief change, the change might not only affect explicit beliefs, but also implicit beliefs. Boutilier proposed that belief change should also minimize the effect on conditional beliefs [4]. However, Darwiche and Pearl [6] showed that a strict minimization may lead to counterintuitive results. They proposed axioms specifying a principle of conditional preservation (PCP) for specific cases, extended and generalized by Kern-Isberner [17].

Definition 2 (PCP for OCF changes, adapted from[19]). *A change of an OCF κ to an OCF κ° fulfils the* principle of conditional preservation with respect to the conditionals $\Delta = \{(B_1|A_1), \dots, (B_n|A_n)\}$, *if for every two multisets of propositional interpretations $\Omega_1 = \{\omega_1, \dots, \omega_m\}$ and $\Omega_2 = \{\omega'_1, \dots, \omega'_m\}$ with the same cardinality m such that the multisets Ω_1 and Ω_2 contain the same number of interpretations which verify, respectively falsify, each conditional $(B_i|A_i)$ in Δ, the OCFs κ and κ° are balanced in the following way:*

$$\sum_{i=1}^{m} \kappa(\omega_i) - \sum_{i=1}^{m} \kappa(\omega'_i) \quad = \quad \sum_{i=1}^{m} \kappa^\circ(\omega_i) - \sum_{i=1}^{m} \kappa^\circ(\omega'_i) \tag{4}$$

In the following, we use a central characterisation [16,19] of the principle of conditional preservation to obtain a characterisation of the principle of conditional preservation for descriptor revisions.

Definition 3 ($\kappa_{\vec{\gamma}}$). *Let κ be an OCF over Σ and $\Delta = \{(B_1|A_1), \dots, (B_n|A_n)\}$ be a set of conditionals. For $\vec{\gamma} = (\gamma_1^-, \gamma_1^+, \dots, \gamma_n^-, \gamma_n^+) \in \mathbb{Z}^{2n}$ we define $\kappa_{\vec{\gamma}}$ by*

$$\kappa_{\vec{\gamma}}(\omega) = \kappa_0 + \kappa(\omega) + \sum_{\substack{1 \leqslant i \leqslant n \\ \omega \models A_i B_i}} \gamma_i^+ + \sum_{\substack{1 \leqslant i \leqslant n \\ \omega \models A_i \overline{B}_i}} \gamma_i^- \tag{5}$$

[2] an exception being e.g. [17].

where κ_0 *is chosen such that* $\kappa_{\vec{\gamma}}$ *is a ranking function, i.e.,* $\kappa_{\vec{\gamma}}(\omega) \geqslant 0$ *for all* $\omega \in \Omega$ *and* $\kappa_{\vec{\gamma}}(\omega') = 0$ *for at least one* $\omega' \in \Omega$.

Thus, interpretations that verify and falsify the same conditionals are treated in the same way, and the two constants γ_i^+ and γ_i^- handle how interpretations that verify or falsify $(B_i|A_i)$ are shifted over the change process. The normalization constant κ_0 ensures that κ° is an OCF. If $\Delta = \{(B_1|A_1), \ldots, (B_n|A_n)\}$ and κ° is the result of a belief change of κ, then this change satisfies the *principle of conditional preservation* with respect to Δ if and only if there is a vector $\vec{\gamma} \in \mathbb{Q}^{2n}$ such that $\kappa^\circ = \kappa_{\vec{\gamma}}$ [19].

The principle of conditional preservation is a powerful basic principle of belief change, demanding a specific relation between the conditionals in the prior belief state Ψ, in the posterior state Ψ°, and in the descriptor Ξ. However, there is no possibility to express conditional preservation by the means of general descriptor revision [10], because the principle of conditional preservation is orthogonal to descriptor revision, giving rationale to the following definition.

Definition 4 (Conditional Descriptor Revision[10]). *Let* κ *be a ranking function. A descriptor revision of* κ *to* κ° *by a descriptor* Ξ *over* $(\mathcal{L}|\mathcal{L})$ *is called a* conditional descriptor revision *of* κ *to* κ° *by* Ξ *if the change from* κ *to* κ° *satisfies the principle of conditional preservation with respect to cond*(Ξ).

Conditional descriptor revision can be characterized as solutions of a constraint satisfaction problem (CSP).

Definition 5 ($\mathrm{CR_D}(\kappa, \Xi, \Delta)$**[10]).** *Let* κ *be an OCF,* $\Delta = \{(B_1|A_1), \ldots, (B_n|A_n)\}$*, and* Ξ *a descriptor with cond*$(\Xi) \subseteq \Delta$. *The CSP for* Ξ *in* κ *under* Δ*, denoted by* $\mathrm{CR_D}(\kappa, \Xi, \Delta)$*, on the constraint variables* $\gamma_1^-, \gamma_1^+, \ldots, \gamma_n^-, \gamma_n^+$ *is given by:*

1. *If* $\Xi = \mathfrak{B}(B_i|A_i)$ *is atomic,* $\mathrm{CR_D}(\kappa, \Xi, \Delta)$ *is given by, for* $i = 1, \ldots, n$:

$$\begin{aligned} \gamma_i^- - \gamma_i^+ > \min_{\omega \models A_i B_i} &\Big(\kappa(\omega) + \sum_{\substack{j \neq i \\ \omega \models A_j B_j}} \gamma_j^+ + \sum_{\substack{j \neq i \\ \omega \models A_j \overline{B}_j}} \gamma_j^-\Big) \\ - \min_{\omega \models A_i \overline{B}_i} &\Big(\kappa(\omega) + \sum_{\substack{j \neq i \\ \omega \models A_j B_j}} \gamma_j^+ + \sum_{\substack{j \neq i \\ \omega \models A_j \overline{B}_j}} \gamma_j^-\Big) \end{aligned} \quad (6)$$

2. $\mathrm{CR_D}(\kappa, \neg\alpha, \Delta) = \neg(\mathrm{CR_D}(\kappa, \alpha, \Delta))$.
3. $\mathrm{CR_D}(\kappa, \alpha \vee \beta, \Delta) = (\mathrm{CR_D}(\kappa, \alpha, \Delta)) \vee (\mathrm{CR_D}(\kappa, \beta, \Delta))$.
4. $\mathrm{CR_D}(\kappa, \alpha \wedge \beta, \Delta) = (\mathrm{CR_D}(\kappa, \alpha, \Delta)) \wedge (\mathrm{CR_D}(\kappa, \beta, \Delta))$.
5. $\mathrm{CR_D}(\kappa, \{\alpha_1, \ldots, \alpha_m\}, \Delta) = (\mathrm{CR_D}(\kappa, \alpha_1, \Delta)) \wedge \cdots \wedge (\mathrm{CR_D}(\kappa, \alpha_m, \Delta))$.

A vector $\vec{\gamma}$ fulfils a constraint $A \vee B$ if $\vec{\gamma}$ fulfils either A or B or both. Analogously, $\vec{\gamma}$ fulfils $A \wedge B$ if it fulfils both A and B. $\vec{\gamma}$ fulfils $\neg A$ if it does not fulfil A. Thus, $Sol(A \vee B) = Sol(A) \cup Sol(B)$, $Sol(A \wedge B) = Sol(A) \cap Sol(B)$ and

$Sol(\neg A) = \mathbb{Z}^{2n} \setminus Sol(A)$, where $Sol(C)$ denotes the solutions of a CSP C. This CSP is sound and complete, i.e., $\kappa_{\vec{\gamma}} \models \Xi$ iff $\vec{\gamma} \in Sol(\mathrm{CR_D}(\kappa, \Xi, \Delta))$ [10].

The set of OCFs induced by its solutions is denoted as

$$OCF(\mathrm{CR_D}(\kappa, \Xi, \Delta)) := \{\kappa_{\vec{\gamma}} \mid \vec{\gamma} \in Sol(\mathrm{CR_D}(\kappa, \Xi, \Delta))\}\ . \tag{7}$$

With a sufficiently specific description, we can actually point the CSP from Definition 5 towards a specific target OCF (up to inferential equivalence).

Proposition 9. *Let κ_1, κ_2 be OCFs. Then there is a descriptor Ξ such that*

- *$\kappa_2 \in OCF(\mathrm{CR_D}(\kappa_1, \Xi, cond(\Xi)))$, and*
- *every $\kappa \in OCF(\mathrm{CR_D}(\kappa_1, \Xi, cond(\Xi)))$ is inferentially equivalent to κ_2.*

Proof (sketch). Let ${\kappa_2}^{[r_0]}$ $\ldots, {\kappa_2}^{[r_L]}$ be the non-empty layers of worlds induced by κ_2, with r_L being the highest layer. Let $\Xi = \Xi^+ \cup \Xi^-$ with:

$$\Xi^+ = \left\{\mathfrak{B}\left(\bigvee {\kappa_2}^{[r_i]} \middle| (\bigvee {\kappa_2}^{[r_i]}) \vee (\bigvee {\kappa_2}^{[r_{i+1}]})\right) \;\middle|\; \leqslant i < L\right\}$$

$$\Xi^- = \left\{\neg\mathfrak{B}\left(\omega \middle| (\bigvee {\kappa_2}^{[r_i]})\right) \;\middle|\; \leqslant i \leqslant L, \omega \in {\kappa_2}^{[r_i]}\right\}$$

Then impacts computed in the proof for Proposition 8 are a solution to the constraints $\mathrm{CR_D}(\kappa_1, \Xi, cond(\Xi))$. Therefore, $\kappa_2 \in OCF(\mathrm{CR_D}(\kappa_1, \Xi, cond(\Xi)))$.

Furthermore, every $\kappa \in OCF(\mathrm{CR_D}(\kappa_1, \Xi, cond(\Xi)))$ is inferentially equivalent to κ_2 because, analogously to the proof of Proposition 5, the conditionals in Ξ restrict the solutions of $\mathrm{CR_D}(\kappa_1, \Xi, cond(\Xi))$ such that only one ordering of the possible worlds can accept all conditionals in $cond(\Xi^+)$, while not accepting any of the conditionals from $cond(\Xi^-)$. □

According to Proposition 9, we can use descriptor revision to explain a transition between OCFs as an alternative to the AGM-based methods described in Sect. 6. If the priori state in a transformation to κ_2 is the state κ_u of complete ignorance, the descriptor Ξ used in the proof of Proposition 9 for going from κ_1 to κ_2 can be simplified by dropping the descriptors in Ξ^- from it, i.e., $\kappa_2 \in OCF(\mathrm{CR_D}(\kappa_u, \Xi^+, cond(\Xi^+)))$.

8 Conclusions and Future Work

In this paper, we have investigated how a transition from a total preorder resp. ranking function to another can be explained as the result of a belief change process. In the AGM framework, a mix of techniques for describing beliefs is necessary to explain arbitrary changes. We have developed the algorithm TPORTransition, which can simulate any qualitative belief change via a series of revisions and contractions. To obtain the exact desired outcome in a single change operation, we have shown that revision with a mix of regular and weak conditionals can be utilized. Moreover, as an alternative to the AGM-based approaches, we have demonstrated how the problem of finding the transition from one epistemic state to another can be encoded as an instance of conditional descriptor revision.

Throughout the paper, we have refrained from judging or comparing different explanations to one another. For future work, it will be interesting to rank or even quantify the value of different explanations in search of an "optimal" explanation, e.g. in terms of conciseness of the conditionals used as input for the revision process. Furthermore, considering other instantiations and further aspects of the descriptor revision framework is interesting, as descriptor revision offers a way to describe any desired belief change outcome in a common framework.

Acknowledgments. We would like to thank the anonymous reviewers for their valuable comments that have helped us to improve this paper. This work was supported by the Deutsche Forschungsgemeinschaft (DFG, German Research Foundation), project number 512363537, grant KE 1413/15-1 awarded to Gabriele Kern-Isberner and grant BE 1700/12-1 awarded to Christoph Beierle. Alexander Hahn was supported by grant KE 1413/15-1, and Lars-Phillip Spiegel was supported by grant BE 1700/12-1.

Disclosure of Interests. The authors have no competing interests to declare that are relevant to the content of this article.

References

1. Alchourrón, C., Gärdenfors, P., Makinson, D.: On the logic of theory change: partial meet contraction and revision functions. J. Symb. Log. **50**(2), 510–530 (1985)
2. Booth, R., Nittka, A.: Reconstructing an agent's epistemic state from observations about its beliefs and non-beliefs. J. Log. Comput. **18**(5), 755–782 (2008). https://doi.org/10.1093/logcom/exm091
3. Boutilier, C.: Revision sequences and nested conditionals. In: Proceedings International Joint Conference on Artificial Intelligence (IJCAI'93), pp. 519–525 (1993)
4. Boutilier, C.: Iterated revision and minimal change of conditional beliefs. J. Phil. Logic **25**(3), 263–305 (1996). https://doi.org/10.1007/BF00248151
5. Boutilier, C.: A unified model of qualitative belief change: a dynamical systems perspective. Artif. Intell. **98**(1), 281–316 (1998). https://doi.org/10.1016/S0004-3702(97)00066-0
6. Darwiche, A., Pearl, J.: On the logic of iterated belief revision. Artif. Intell. **89**(1–2), 1–29 (1997). https://doi.org/10.1016/s0004-3702(96)00038-0
7. Eichhorn, C., Kern-Isberner, G., Ragni, M.: Rational inference patterns based on conditional logic. In: McIlraith, S., Weinberger, K. (eds.) Proceedings of the Thirty-Second AAAI Conference on Artificial Intelligence, (AAAI-18), pp. 1827–1834. AAAI Press (2018). https://doi.org/10.1609/aaai.v32i1.11558
8. Fikes, R.E., Nilsson, N.J.: STRIPS: a new approach to the application of theorem proving to problem solving. Artif. Intell. **2**(3–4), 189–208 (1971)
9. Fikes, R.E., Nilsson, N.J.: STRIPS, a retrospective. Artif. Intell. **59**, 227–232 (1993)

10. Haldimann, J., Sauerwald, K., von Berg, M., Kern-Isberner, G., Beierle, C.: Conditional descriptor revision and its modelling by a CSP. In: Faber, W., Friedrich, G., Gebser, M., Morak, M. (eds.) Logics in Artificial Intelligence - 17th European Conference, JELIA 2021, Virtual Event, 17–20 May 2021, Proceedings. Lecture Notes in Computer Science, vol. 12678, pp. 35–49. Springer, Heidelberg (2021). https://doi.org/10.1007/978-3-030-75775-5_4
11. Haldimann, J., Sauerwald, K., von Berg, M., Kern-Isberner, G., Beierle, C.: Towards a framework of Hansson's descriptor revision for conditionals. In: SAC'21: Proceedings of the 36th Annual ACM Symposium on Applied Computing, pp. 889–891. ACM, New York (2021). https://doi.org/10.1145/3297280.3297391
12. Haldimann, J.P., Beierle, C., Kern-Isberner, G.: Epistemic state mappings among ranking functions and total preorders. J. Appl. Logics - IfCoLog J. Logics Appl. **10**(2), 155–192 (2023)
13. Hansson, S.O.: Descriptor revision. Studia Logica **102**(5), 955–980 (2014). https://doi.org/10.1007/s11225-013-9512-5
14. Hansson, S.O.: Descriptor Revision. Springer, Heidelberg (2017). https://doi.org/10.1007/978-3-319-53061-1
15. Katsuno, H., Mendelzon, A.: Propositional knowledge base revision and minimal change. Artif. Intell. **52**, 263–294 (1991)
16. Kern-Isberner, G. (ed.): Conditionals in Nonmonotonic Reasoning and Belief Revision. LNCS (LNAI), vol. 2087. Springer, Heidelberg (2001). https://doi.org/10.1007/3-540-44600-1
17. Kern-Isberner, G.: A thorough axiomatization of a principle of conditional preservation in belief revision. Ann. Math. Artif. Intell. **40**(1–2), 127–164 (2004)
18. Kern-Isberner, G.: Axiomatizing a qualitative principle of conditional preservation for iterated belief change. In: Thielscher, M., Toni, F., Wolter, F. (eds.) Principles of Knowledge Representation and Reasoning: Proceedings of the Sixteenth International Conference, KR 2018, pp. 248–256. AAAI Press (2018)
19. Kern-Isberner, G., Bock, T., Sauerwald, K., Beierle, C.: Iterated contraction of propositions and conditionals under the principle of conditional preservation. In: Benzmüller, C., Lisetti, C.L., Theobald, M. (eds.) GCAI 2017, 3rd Global Conference on Artificial Intelligence, Miami, FL, USA, 18–22 October 2017. EPiC Series in Computing, vol. 50, pp. 78–92. EasyChair (2017). http://www.easychair.org/publications/paper/DTmX
20. Kern-Isberner, G., Sezgin, M., Beierle, C.: A kinematics principle for iterated revision. Artif. Intell. **314**, 103827 (2023). https://doi.org/10.1016/j.artint.2022.103827
21. Konieczny, S., Pino Pérez, R.: On iterated contraction: syntactic characterization, representation theorem and limitations of the Levi identity. In: Scalable Uncertainty Management - 11th International Conference, SUM 2017, Granada, Spain, 4–6 October 2017, Proceedings. Lecture Notes in Artificial Intelligence, vol. 10564. Springer, Heidelberg (2017)
22. McCarthy, J., Hayes, P.: Some philosophical problems from the standpoint of Artificial Intelligence. In: Meltzer, B., Michie, D. (eds.) Machine Intelligence 4. Edinburgh University Press, Edinburgh (1969)
23. Sauerwald, K., Haldimann, J., von Berg, M., Beierle, C.: Descriptor revision for conditionals: literal descriptors and conditional preservation. In: Schmid, U., Klügl, F., Wolter, D. (eds.) KI 2020: Advances in Artificial Intelligence - 43rd German Conference on AI, Bamberg, Germany, 21–25 September 2020, Proceedings. Lecture Notes in Computer Science, vol. 12325, pp. 204–218. Springer, Heidelberg (2020). https://doi.org/10.1007/978-3-030-58285-2_15

24. Sezgin, M.: A conditional perspective of belief revision. Ph.D. thesis, TU Dortmund University, Dortmund (2023). https://doi.org/10.17877/DE290R-24062
25. Spohn, W.: Ordinal conditional functions: a dynamic theory of epistemic states. In: Harper, W.L., Skyrms, B. (eds.) Causation in Decision, Belief Change, and Statistics, pp. 105–134. Springer, Netherlands (1988). https://doi.org/10.1007/978-94-009-2865-7_6

Implementing Lexicographic Inference Using Partial MaxSAT

Jonas Haldimann[1,2,(✉)], Aron Spang[3], Lars-Phillip Spiegel[3], and Christoph Beierle[3]

[1] TU Wien, 1040 Vienna, Austria
[2] University of Cape Town and CAIR, Cape Town, South Africa
jonas@haldimann.de
[3] FernUniversität in Hagen, 58097 Hagen, Germany
{aron.spang,lars-phillip.spiegel, christoph.beierle}@fernuni-hagen.de

Abstract. Lehman's lexicographic inference is one of the established inference operators for reasoning from conditional belief bases that satisfies many properties desirable for nonmonotonic reasoning. In contrast to its well investigated formal properties, implementations of lexicographic inference are rare. In this paper, we introduce the algorithm LEXinf for realizing lexicographic inference using a MaxSAT solver. We prove the correctness of the algorithm and demonstrate the feasibility and efficiency of our approach by implementing it using Python and the state-of-the-art solver Z3. We empirically evaluate the implementation and compare it to implementations of other inference operators.

Keywords: Nonmonotonic reasoning · Conditionals · Lexicographic inference · Implementation · Partial MaxSAT

1 Introduction

"What does a conditional belief base entail?" This question is asked in the title of the seminal paper by Lehmann and Magidor [27]. It has been studied extensively in the area of logic based knowledge representation and reasoning, leading to the proposal of different semantic and syntactic approaches for dealing with conditionals. A conditional is a statement of the form "If A, then usually B" that encodes a plausible but uncertain connection between the statements A and B. One of the established approaches for reasoning from conditional belief bases is Lehmann's *lexicographic inference* [28]. Lexicographic inference has some notable properties like extending rational closure [28], complying with syntax splittings and conditional syntax splittings [20,21], and avoiding the drowning problem [8,20].

While many properties of lexicographic inference are well-understood on the theoretical side, less attention has been given to implementations of this inference. In this paper we develop a new algorithm LEXinf for realizing lexicographic inference that is based on finding *minimal correction sets* (MCS). This allows us

K. Sauerwald and M. Thimm (Eds.): ECSQARU 2025, LNAI 16099, pp. 301–315, 2026.
https://doi.org/10.1007/978-3-032-05134-9_21

to use modern MaxSAT solvers for answering queries with lexicographic inference. We study and investigate LEXinf both from the theoretical as well as the practical side and formally prove the correctness of LEXinf.

We also present an implementation of the algorithm LEXinf in Python that uses the solver Z3 [10] for finding the MCS. The implementation is empirically evaluated and compared to an earlier, more straightforward implementation of lexicographic inference. This comparison demonstrates how our new approach outperforms previous implementations and allows for reasoning over much larger problems than could be handled before, with both signature and belief base size well over 100 and thus involving more than 2^{100} possible worlds.

In summary, the main contributions of this paper are the following:

- Introducing the algorithm LEXinf for lexicographic inference
- Proving the correctness of LEXinf
- Presenting an implementation of LEXinf in Python using the solver Z3
- Evaluating the implementation empirically and comparing it to other implementations

The remainder of the paper is structured as follows. In Sect. 2 we recall some necessary preliminaries before recalling lexicographic inference in Sect. 3. We present the algorithm LEXinf in Sect. 4, prove its correctness in Sect. 5, and describe its implementation and evaluation in Sect. 6 before concluding in Sect. 7.

2 Background

A *(propositional) signature* is a finite set Σ of propositional variables. For a signature Σ, we denote the propositional language over Σ by $\mathcal{L}_\Sigma$. Usually, we denote elements of signatures with lowercase letters $a, b, c, \dots$ and formulas with uppercase letters $A, B, C, \dots$. We may denote a conjunction $A \wedge B$ by AB and a negation $\neg A$ by $\overline{A}$ for brevity of notation. For a set S of formulas, $\overline{S} = \{\overline{F} \mid F \in S\}$ denotes the elementwise negation of S. The set of interpretations over a signature Σ is denoted as Ω_Σ. Interpretations are also called *worlds* and Ω_Σ is called the *universe*. An interpretation $\omega \in \Omega_\Sigma$ is a *model* of a formula $A \in \mathcal{L}_\Sigma$ if A holds in ω, denoted as $\omega \models A$. The set of models of a formula (over a signature Σ) is denoted as $Mod_\Sigma(A) = \{\omega \in \Omega_\Sigma \mid \omega \models A\}$. The Σ in $Mod_\Sigma(A)$ can be omitted if the signature is clear from the context. A formula A *entails* a formula B, denoted by $A \models B$, if $Mod(A) \subseteq Mod(B)$. Two formulas A, B are *equivalent*, denoted $A \equiv B$, if $Mod(A) = Mod(B)$. The symbol $\perp$ denotes a formula with no models, i.e., $Mod(\perp) = \emptyset$. By slight abuse of notation we sometimes interpret worlds as the corresponding complete conjunction of all elements in the signature in either positive or negated form.

A *conditional* $(B|A)$ connects two formulas A, B and represents the rule "If A then usually B", where A is the *antecedent* and B the *consequent* of the conditional. The conditional language over a signature Σ is denoted as $(\mathcal{L}|\mathcal{L})_\Sigma = \{(B|A) \mid A, B \in \mathcal{L}_\Sigma\}$. A *conditional belief base* is a finite set of conditionals. We use a three-valued semantics of conditionals in this paper [15]. For a world ω a conditional $(B|A)$ is either *verified* by ω if $\omega \models AB$, *falsified* by ω if $\omega \models A\overline{B}$, or *not applicable* to ω if $\omega \models \overline{A}$. Different falsification behaviours can be captured by formulas; for example $\mathsf{nf}((B|A)) = A \rightarrow B$ represents non-falsification of $(B|A)$ in the sense that the models of $\mathsf{nf}((B|A))$ are exactly the worlds that do not falsify $(B|A)$. We lift the function nf to sets of conditionals by $\mathsf{nf}(\Delta) = \{\mathsf{nf}(r) \mid r \in \Delta\}$. Popular models for conditional belief bases are ranking functions (also called ordinal conditional functions, OCF) [33] and total preorders (TPO) on Ω_Σ [13]; transformations among these and other semantics are studied in [6]. Semantic structures for conditionals have in common that they model a conditional $(B|A)$ if they consider its verification AB to be strictly more plausible, or less surprising, etc., than its falsification $A\overline{B}$; they model a belief base Δ if they model every conditional in Δ. A belief base Δ is *consistent* if it has a model. This notion of (strong) consistency used here requires models in which every world is at least somewhat plausible, coinciding, e.g., with the notion of consistency used in [16].

3 Lexicographic Inference

An inductive inference operator completes an explicitly given belief base to the inference relation representing all conditional beliefs an agent can derive [21]. Examples for inductive inference operators include p-entailment [24] which coincides with system P [1], system Z [16,31] which coincides with rational closure [27], system W [22,23], and lexicographic inference [28] which is the topic of this paper. Contrary to p-entailment and system Z, lexicographic inference is one of the few inductive inference operators that are known to satisfy syntax splitting for inductive inference operators [21], and also conditional syntax splitting [20] which has been shown to be the decisive property for avoiding the drowning problem [8,20]. Additionally, unlike system W and c-inference, lexicographic inference satisfies *Rational Monotony (RM)* [24]. Thus, lexicographic inference satisfies a combination of properties not found in other common inference operators.

Lexicographic inference is defined using the Z-partition, also called *tolerance partition* or *ordered partition*, of a belief base.

Definition 1 (tolerance, Z-partition $OP(\Delta)$ **[16]).** *Let* $\Delta = \{(B_1|A_1), \dots, (B_n|A_n)\}$ *be a belief base.*

- *A conditional* $(B|A)$ *is* tolerated *by* Δ *if there exists a world* $\omega \in \Omega_\Sigma$ *that verifies* $(B|A)$ *and does not falsify any conditional in* Δ, *i.e.,* $\omega \models AB$ *and* $\omega \models \bigwedge_{i=1}^{n}(\overline{A_i} \vee B_i)$.
- *The* Z-partition $OP(\Delta) = (\Delta^0, \dots, \Delta^k)$ *of a belief base* Δ *is the partition of* Δ *where each* Δ^i *is the (with respect to set inclusion) maximal subset of* $\bigcup_{j=i}^{k} \Delta^j$ *such that each of its elements is tolerated by* $\bigcup_{j=i}^{k} \Delta^j$.

It is well-known that $OP(\Delta)$ exists iff Δ is consistent; moreover, because the Δ^i are chosen inclusion-maximal, the Z-partition is unique [31].

In the following definition of lexicographic inference, we will use $\min_\prec S$ to denote the set of minimal elements in the set S with respect to the ordering $\prec$. Furthermore, for a belief base Δ with $OP(\Delta) = (\Delta^0, \dots, \Delta^k)$ we use

$$\xi^j(\omega) = \{(B|A) \in \Delta^j \mid \omega \text{ falsifies } (B|A)\}$$

to denote the set of conditionals in Δ^j that are falsified by the world ω.

The *lexicographic ordering* on vectors in $\mathbb{N}^n$ is defined by $(v_1, \ldots, v_n) <^{lex} (w_1, \ldots, w_n)$ iff there is a $k \in \{1, \ldots, n\}$ such that $v_k < w_k$ and $v_j = w_j$ for $j = k+1, \ldots, n$. Note that in this means that the elements at the end of the vectors are the most significant ones.

Definition 2 (**$<^{lex}_\Delta$, lexicographic inference** [28]). *The binary relation $\leqslant^{lex}_\Delta \subseteq \Omega \times \Omega$ on worlds induced by a belief base Δ with $|OP(\Delta)| = n$ is defined by, for any $\omega, \omega' \in \Omega$,*

$$\omega \leqslant^{lex}_\Delta \omega' \quad \text{if} \quad (|\xi^1_\Delta(\omega)|, \ldots, |\xi^n_\Delta(\omega)|) \leqslant^{lex} (|\xi^1_\Delta(\omega')|, \ldots, |\xi^n_\Delta(\omega')|).$$

The order $<^{lex}_\Delta$ is lifted to consistent formulas by letting, for $F, G \in \mathcal{L}$,

$$F <^{lex}_\Delta G \quad \text{if} \quad \min_{<^{lex}_\Delta} Mod(F) <^{lex}_\Delta \min_{<^{lex}_\Delta} Mod(G)$$

Then, for formulas A, B, A lexicographically entails *B given Δ, denoted as*

$$A \mathrel{|\!\sim}^{lex}_\Delta B, \quad \text{if} \quad A\overline{B} \equiv \bot \text{ or}$$
$$AB, A\overline{B} \not\equiv \bot \text{ and } AB <^{lex}_\Delta A\overline{B}.$$

Lexicographic inference exhibits a number of notable properties. It is a *rational* inference operator [28], i.e., it is preferential and additionally satisfies (Rational Monotony). Furthermore, it respects *Syntax Splittings*, and even *Conditional Syntax Splittings* [20]. Thus, it also avoids the drowning problem [8] that has been shown to be a violation of Conditional Syntax Splitting [20]. In comparison to other inference systems, lexicographic inference licences strictly more entailments than p-entailment, system Z, and system W [17].

Example 1. Let $\Delta = \{(b|p), (f|b), (\overline{f}|p), (w|b)\}$ over $\Sigma = \{b, p, f, w\}$. Does $A = p\overline{b} \vee pf\overline{w}$ lexicographically entail $B = \overline{b}$? The Z-partition of Δ is $OP(\Delta) = \{\Delta^0, \Delta^1\}$ with $\Delta^0 = \{(f|b), (w|b)\}$ and $\Delta^1 = \{(b|p), (\overline{f}|p)\}$, resulting in the ordering $<^{lex}_\Delta$ shown in Fig. 1. The minimal models of $AB \equiv p\overline{b}$ are $\min_{<^{lex}_\Delta}(AB) = \{\overline{b}p\overline{f}\overline{w}, \overline{b}p\overline{f}w\}$ and the minimal models of $A\overline{B} \equiv bpf\overline{w}$ are $\min_{<^{lex}_\Delta}(A\overline{B}) = \{bpf\overline{w}\}$. Therefore, $AB <^{lex}_\Delta A\overline{B}$ and hence $A \mathrel{|\!\sim}^{lex}_\Delta B$.

Alternatively, lexicographic inference can be characterized by comparing the worlds verifying and falsifying the query directly.

Proposition 1. *Let Δ be a consistent belief base and $A, B \in \mathcal{L}$. Then*

$$A \mathrel{|\!\sim}^{lex}_\Delta B \quad \text{iff} \quad \text{for every } \omega' \in Mod(A\overline{B}) \text{ there is an } \omega \in Mod(AB) \text{ such that } \omega <^{lex}_\Delta \omega'. \tag{1}$$

$\xi^0(\omega)$	$\xi^1(\omega)$	$<^{lex}_{\Delta}$ (↑)
0	2	$\overline{b}pf\overline{w}, \overline{b}pfw$
1	1	$bpf\overline{w}$
0	1	$bpfw, \overline{b}p\overline{f}\overline{w}, \overline{b}p\overline{f}w$
2	0	$bp\overline{f}\overline{w}, b\overline{p}\overline{f}\overline{w},$
1	0	$b\overline{p}\overline{f}w, b\overline{p}f\overline{w}, bp\overline{f}w$
0	0	$\overline{b}\overline{p}\overline{f}\overline{w}, \overline{b}\overline{p}fw, \overline{b}\overline{p}\overline{f}w, \overline{b}\overline{p}f\overline{w}, b\overline{p}fw$

Fig. 1. The order $<^{lex}_{\Delta}$ over worlds from Example 1. The corresponding values of $|\xi^0(\omega)|, |\xi^1(\omega)|$ are indicated on the left.

Proof. We prove both directions of the "iff".
Direction $\Rightarrow$ Assume that $A \mid\!\sim^{lex}_{\Delta} B$. Therefore, $AB <^{lex}_{\Delta} A\overline{B}$. Let $\omega' \in Mod\,(A\overline{B})$. Let $\omega'_{min} \in \min_{<^{lex}_{\Delta}} Mod\,(A\overline{B})$, we have $\omega'_{min} \leqslant^{lex}_{\Delta} \omega'$. Let $\omega \in \min_{<^{lex}_{\Delta}} Mod\,(AB)$. Because $AB <^{lex}_{\Delta} A\overline{B}$, we have $\omega <^{lex}_{\Delta} \omega'_{min}$. In summary, we found an $\omega \in Mod\,(AB)$ with $\omega <^{lex}_{\Delta} \omega'$.
Direction $\Leftarrow$ Assume that (1) holds. Let $\omega' \in \min_{<^{lex}_{\Delta}} Mod\,(A\overline{B})$. By (1) there is an $\omega \in Mod\,(AB)$ with $\omega <^{lex}_{\Delta} \omega'$. Let $\omega_{min} \in \min_{<^{lex}_{\Delta}} Mod\,(AB)$. We have $\omega_{min} \leqslant^{lex}_{\Delta} \omega <^{lex}_{\Delta} \omega'$ and therefore $AB <^{lex}_{\Delta} A\overline{B}$. Therefore, $A \mid\!\sim^{lex}_{\Delta} B$. □

We will use the characterization in Proposition 1 for developing an algorithm for lexicographic inference.

4 The Algorithm LEXinf

A straightforward implementation of lexicographic inference might answer a query "does A lexicographically entail B" (in the context of Δ) by first computing the ordering $<^{lex}_{\Delta}$ on Ω_{Σ}, and then using it to compare the models of AB and $A\overline{B}$. This is, however, not feasible for larger signatures as the number of worlds in Ω_{Σ} grows exponentially with the size of Σ.

Therefore, LEXinf takes a different approach which is based on the concept of *minimal correction sets* [26]. Given a set of formulas S as soft constraints and a set of formulas H as hard constraints the *extended partial maximum satisfiability problem EPMaxSAT(S, H)* is the optimization problem of finding sets of formulas in S satisfied by at least one interpretation $\omega \in Mod\,(H)$ and determining all subsets of S that are maximal with this property. This corresponds to finding all minimal subsets M of S for which $S \setminus M$ has a model in $Mod\,(H)$.

Definition 3 ($MCS(S, H)$). *Let $S = \{S_1, \ldots, S_s\} \subseteq \mathcal{L}$ be a set of formulas, called* soft constraints, *and let $H = \{H_1, \ldots, H_h\} \subseteq \mathcal{L}$ be a set of formulas, called* hard constraints. *A set $M \subseteq S$ such that there is an $\omega \in Mod\,(H)$ with $\omega \models S \setminus M$ and for every $M' \subseteq S$ with $M' \subsetneq M$ there is no $\omega' \in Mod\,(H)$ with $\omega' \models S \setminus M'$ is called a* minimal correction set (MCS) *with respect to (S, H), and $MCS(S, H)$ denotes the set of all MCS with respect to (S, H).*

Algorithm 1. LEXinf (Δ, A, B)

Input: consistent belief base Δ and formulas A, B
Output: *Yes* if $A \mathrel{|\!\!\sim}^{lex}_{\Delta} B$, and *No* otherwise

let $OP(\Delta) = (\Delta^0, \ldots, \Delta^k)$

function $recLinf(j, H^V, H^F)$
  $\mathcal{V} \leftarrow MCS(\mathsf{nf}(\Delta^j), H^V \cup \{AB\})$
  $\mathcal{F} \leftarrow MCS(\mathsf{nf}(\Delta^j), H^F \cup \{A\overline{B}\})$
  $v \leftarrow \min_{N^v \in \mathcal{V}} |N^v|$
  $f \leftarrow \min_{N^f \in \mathcal{F}} |N^f|$
  $\mathcal{V}^{min} \leftarrow \{N^v \in \mathcal{V} \text{ with } |N^v| = v\}$
  $\mathcal{F}^{min} \leftarrow \{N^f \in \mathcal{F} \text{ with } |N^f| = f\}$
  if $v < f$ **then**
    return *Yes*
  if $f < v$ **or** $j = 0$ **then**
    return *No*
  for all $N^f \in \mathcal{F}^{min}$ **do**
    $vFound \leftarrow False$
    $H^F_{new} \leftarrow (\mathsf{nf}(\Delta^j) \setminus N^f) \cup \overline{N^f}$
    for all $N^v \in \mathcal{V}^{min}$ **do**
      $H^V_{new} \leftarrow (\mathsf{nf}(\Delta^j) \setminus N^v) \cup \overline{N^v}$
      if $recLinf(j-1, H^V \cup H^V_{new}, H^F \cup H^F_{new}) = Yes$ **then**
        $vFound \leftarrow True$
    if $\neg vFound$ **then**
      return *No*
  return *Yes*
end function

if $A\overline{B} \equiv \bot$ **then**
  return *Yes*
else if $AB \equiv \bot$ **then**
  return *No*
else
  return $recLinf(k, \emptyset, \emptyset)$

We observe that MCS can be used as an approximation of the size-minimal subsets of falsified conditionals.

Proposition 2. *Let Δ be a set of conditionals and $F \in \mathcal{L}$. Let $\mathcal{X} = \{\xi(\omega) \mid \omega \in Mod(F)\}$, where $\xi(\omega) = \{(B|A) \in \Delta \mid \omega$ falsifies $(B|A)\}$, and let $\mathcal{X}^{min} = \arg\min_{M \in \mathcal{X}} |M|$. Then $M \in \mathcal{X}^{min}$ implies $\mathsf{nf}(M) \in MCS(\mathsf{nf}(\Delta), F)$.*

Proof. Proof by contradiction. Let $M \in \mathcal{X}^{min}$ and assume that $\mathsf{nf}(M)$ is not in $MCS(\mathsf{nf}(\Delta), F)$. By construction there is a world $\omega \in Mod(F)$ with $M = \xi(\omega)$ implying that $\omega \models \mathsf{nf}(\Delta \setminus M) = \mathsf{nf}(\Delta) \setminus \mathsf{nf}(M)$. Therefore, there is a subset M' of M with $\mathsf{nf}(M') \in MCS(\mathsf{nf}(\Delta), F)$. Let $\omega' \in Mod(\mathsf{nf}(M') \cup \{F\})$, such a world exists by the definition of MCS. We have $\xi(\omega') \subseteq M'$. Because $M \in \mathcal{X}^{min}$ is size-minimal, it must be that $|\xi(\omega')| = |M|$ implying that $\xi(\omega') = M' = M$. As $\mathsf{nf}(M') \in \mathit{MCS}(\mathsf{nf}(\Delta), F)$ this contradicts the assumption. $\square$

To decide if $A \mid\!\sim^{lex}_{\Delta} B$, we need to check if $AB <^{lex}_{\Delta} A\overline{B}$. The algorithm LEXinf is based on three central observations. First, it does not consider each world individually. Instead, worlds that falsify the same conditionals can be considered together, compactly represented as models of a logical formula. Second, for comparing formulas $AB, A\overline{B}$ with respect to $<^{lex}_{\Delta}$ it suffices to consider only the minimal models of AB and $A\overline{B}$. Third, for reaching a result quickly, the algorithm considers the last and thus most relevant sets of the tolerance partition first. With this, the approach of LEXinf is the following. To check if $AB <^{lex}_{\Delta} A\overline{B}$, it first finds the subsets N^v of Δ^k such that the non-falsification of $\Delta \setminus N^v$ is consistent with AB and whose size is minimal with this property; let the set of these subsets be $\mathcal{V}^{min}$. Each such subset N^v corresponds to the set $\mathit{Mod}\,(\mathsf{nf}(\Delta^k \setminus N^v) \cup \{AB\})$ of worlds that falsify a minimal number of conditionals in Δ^k. Then it finds the size-minimal subsets N^f of Δ^k for which non-falsification of $\Delta^k \setminus N^f$ is consistent with $A\overline{B}$; let the set of these subsets be $\mathcal{F}^{min}$. If the subsets in $\mathcal{V}^{min}$ are strictly smaller than the subsets in $\mathcal{F}^{min}$, or vice versa, we are finished and know that $AB <^{lex}_{\Delta} A\overline{B}$, or $AB \not<^{lex}_{\Delta} A\overline{B}$, respectively. Otherwise, i.e., if the sets in $\mathcal{V}^{min}$ and $\mathcal{F}^{min}$ have the same size, LEXinf continues the comparison with Δ^{k-1}, and so on.

The tolerance partition $OP(\Delta) = (\Delta^0, \dots, \Delta^k)$ is constructed in Line 1, this is realized by using the algorithm by Goldszmidt and Pearl [16].

To decide if $A \mid\!\sim^{lex}_{\Delta} B$, LEXinf (Algorithm 1) first checks corner cases where the query is contradictory or self-fulfilling (Lines 24–27). Then it uses *recLinf* to check if $AB <^{lex}_{\Delta} A\overline{B}$. The function *recLinf*

first calculates the sets $\mathcal{V}^{min}$ and $\mathcal{F}^{min}$ (cf. Lines 3–8) using MCS to find candidates for size-minimal sets of conditionals in Δ^j that are violated by the models of $H^V \cup \{AB\}$ or $H^N \cup \{A\overline{B}\}$, respectively. Then, it compares the size of the subsets in $\mathcal{V}^{min}$ and $\mathcal{F}^{min}$ in Lines 9–12. If it is possible to decide if $AB <^{lex}_{\Delta} A\overline{B}$ based on that, it terminates and returns the result. Otherwise, it recursively calls itself to continue the comparison on the earlier parts of the Z-partition.

Observe that when enumerating the minimal subsets of Δ^{k-1}, they not only need to be consistent with AB (or $A\overline{B}$, respectively), but also with one of the minimal subsets of Δ^k; otherwise the models would not be minimal with respect to $<^{lex}_{\Delta}$. Therefore, *recLinf* is called for each combination of minimal subsets from $\mathcal{V}^{min}$ and $\mathcal{F}^{min}$ in Lines 13–21. To keep track of the violated conditionals in the later parts of the partition, the sets H^V and H^F are passed to *recLinf* and extended for each recursive call. *recLinf* returns *Yes* if for each set in $\mathcal{F}^{min}$ it finds a set in $\mathcal{V}^{min}$ for which the recursive call succeeds. In the initial call of *recLinf* for Δ^k in Line 29 these sets are empty.

Example 2. Continue Example 1. For Δ as in Example 1, we want to check if $p\overline{b} \vee pf\overline{w} \mid\!\sim^{lex}_{\Delta} \overline{b}$ by calling $\mathsf{LEXinf}(\Delta, p\overline{b} \vee pf\overline{w}, \overline{b})$. The algorithm first determines $OP(\Delta)$ and passes the **if**s in Lines 24–27 before calling *recLinf*$(1, \emptyset, \emptyset)$:

recLinf $(1, \emptyset, \emptyset)$
We get $\mathcal{V}^{min} = \{\{p \to b\}\}$ and $\mathcal{F}^{min} = \{\{p \to \overline{f}\}\}$ with $v = f = 1$, triggering the following recursive call.
recLinf $(0, \{p \to \overline{f}, \neg(p \to b)\}, \{p \to b, \neg(p \to \overline{f})\})$
We have $\mathcal{V}^{min} = \{\emptyset\}$, $\mathcal{F}^{min} = \{b \to w\}$ with $v = 0$ and $f = 1$. Because $v < f$ this call returns *Yes*.
Thus, LEXinf returns *Yes*.

The idea behind LEXinf of using Partial MaxSAT encodings was inspired by the recent algorithm SWinf [7] for system W [23] that also makes use of minimal correction sets and SMT solvers. The avoidance of representing the semantic structure on possible worlds explicitly and using conditionals or formulas instead can also be oberved in algorithms for system Z [31] employing SAT encodings and SAT solvers [7,12], or for inferences connected to belief revision [32].

5 Correctness of LEXinf

For proving the correctness of LEXinf, we use the concept of *nf/f*-conditions, which are a set of formulas expressing a specific verification/falsification pattern of conditionals in a belief base Δ. If $OP(\Delta) = (\Delta^0, \dots, \Delta^k)$, an *nf/f*-condition for (Δ, j) contains either the material implication $A \to B$ or its negation $A \wedge \neg B$ for every conditional $(B|A) \in \Delta^{j+1}, \dots, \Delta^k$.

Definition 4 (*nf/f*-**condition for** (Δ, j), [7]). *Let $OP(\Delta) = (\Delta^0, \dots, \Delta^k)$, and let $j \in \{0, \dots, k\}$. A set of formulas H is a non-falsifying/falsifying condition (nf/f-condition) for (Δ, j) if there are, for $i \in \{j+1, \dots, k\}$ sets $\Delta^i_{nf}, \Delta^i_f \subseteq \Delta^i$ such that $\Delta^i = \Delta^i_{nf} \cup \Delta^i_f$ and $\Delta^i_{nf} \cap \Delta^i_f = \emptyset$, and*

$$H = \bigcup_{i \in \{j+1, \dots, k\}} \mathsf{nf}(\Delta^i_{nf}) \cup \overline{\mathsf{nf}(\Delta^i_f)}$$

To show the correctness of LEXinf, we first prove the correctness of the recursive function *recLinf* used in LEXinf.

Proposition 3 (correctness of *recLinf***).** *Let Δ be a consistent belief base with $OP(\Delta) = (\Delta^0, \dots, \Delta^k)$ and $A, B \in \mathcal{L}$ with $AB \not\equiv \bot, A\overline{B} \not\equiv \bot$. Let $j \in \{0, \dots, k\}$, and let H^V, H^F be nf/f-conditions for (Δ, j) such that $H^V \not\equiv \bot, H^F \not\equiv \bot$. If for every model $\omega \in Mod(H^V)$ and every $\omega' \in Mod(H^F)$, for $i \in \{j+1, \dots, k\}$, we have $|\xi^i(\omega)| = |\xi^i(\omega')|$, then recLinf$(j, H^V, H^F)$ returns* Yes *iff*

$$\begin{aligned} &\text{for every } \omega' \in Mod(H^F \wedge A\overline{B}) \\ &\qquad \text{there is an} \omega \in Mod(H^V \wedge AB) \quad \text{with} \omega <^{lex}_{\Delta} \omega'. \end{aligned} \tag{2}$$

Proof. Let

$$\mathcal{V} = MCS(\mathsf{nf}(\Delta^j), H^V \cup \{AB\}), \qquad \mathcal{F} = MCS(\mathsf{nf}(\Delta^j), H^F \cup \{A\overline{B}\}),$$
$$v = \min_{N^v \in \mathcal{V}} |N^v|, \qquad f = \min_{N^f \in \mathcal{F}} |N^f|,$$
$$\mathcal{V}^{min} = \{N^v \in \mathcal{V} \text{ with } |N^v| = v\}, \qquad \mathcal{F}^{min} = \{N^f \in \mathcal{F} \text{ with } |N^f| = f\}$$

as in Lines 3–8 in Algorithm 1. According to Lines 3 and 4, $\mathcal{V}^{min}$ contains the MCS with minimal size for $(\mathsf{nf}(\Delta^j), H^V \cup \{AB\})$ and $\mathcal{F}^{min}$ contains the MCS with minimal size for $(\mathsf{nf}(\Delta^j), H^F \cup \{A\overline{B}\})$. We proof the proposition by induction over j.

Base Case ($j = 0$): According to Lines 9–12, *recLinf* (j, H^V, H^F) returns *Yes* iff $v < f$. Hence, for the base case we need to show that $v < f$ iff (2) holds. We will show both directions of the *iff*.

Direction $\Rightarrow$ Assume that $v < f$. Let ω' be any model of $H^F \cup \{A\overline{B}\}$. Then $|\xi^j(\omega')| \geq f$. Let $N^v \in \mathcal{V}^{min}$. Because N^v is a minimal correction set, there must be a world $\omega \in Mod(H^V \cup \{AB\})$ that falsifies exactly the conditionals from Δ^j corresponding to the material implications in N^v. Therefore, $|\xi^j(\omega)| = v$ which implies that $|\xi^j(\omega)| < |\xi^j(\omega')|$. Because ω, ω' are models of H^V and H^F, respectively, we have $|\xi^i(\omega)| = |\xi^i(\omega')|$ for $i \in \{j+1, \ldots, k\}$. In summary, we have $\omega <^{lex}_{\Delta} \omega'$ and thus (2) holds.

Direction $\Leftarrow$ Assume that (2) holds. Let $N^f \in \mathcal{F}^{min}$. Because N^f is a minimal correction set, there must be a world $\omega' \in Mod(H^F \cup \{A\overline{B}\})$ that falsifies exactly the conditionals from Δ^0 corresponding to the material implications in N^f. Furthermore, $|\xi^0(\omega')| = f$. Because of (2), there is an $\omega \in Mod(H^V \cup \{AB\})$ with $\omega <^{lex}_{\Delta} \omega'$. Because ω, ω' are models of H^V and H^F, respectively, we have $|\xi^i(\omega)| = |\xi^i(\omega')|$ for $i \in \{1, \ldots, k\}$. Therefore, it must be that $|\xi^0(\omega)| < |\xi^0(\omega')|$. As ω is a model of $H^V \cup \{AB\}$, we have $v \leqslant |\xi^0(\omega)|$, and thus $v < f$.

Induction Step: Let $j > 0$ and assume that the proposition holds for $j' = j-1$. We show that *recLinf* (j, H^V, H^F) returns *Yes* iff (2) holds by showing both directions of the *iff*.

Direction $\Rightarrow$ Assume that *recLinf* (j, H^V, H^F) returns *Yes*. If *Yes* is returned in Line 10, then $v < f$. In this case we can show that (2) holds analogously to *Direction* $\Rightarrow$ in the base case. It cannot be that $v > f$, because then *recLinf* (j, H^V, H^F) would return *No* in Line 12. For the remainder of this *Direction* $\Rightarrow$, assume that $v = f$ and *Yes* is only returned in Line 22.

Let ω' be any model of $Mod(H^F \wedge A\overline{B})$. Let $N^v \in \mathcal{V}^{min}$. As above, because N^v is a minimal correction set, there must be a world $\omega \in Mod(H^V \cup \{AB\})$ with $|\xi^j(\omega)| = v$. Because ω, ω' are models of H^V and H^F, respectively, we have $|\xi^i(\omega)| = |\xi^i(\omega')|$ for $i \in \{j, \ldots, k\}$. There are three cases:

Case 1: If $|\xi^j(\omega)| < |\xi^j(\omega')|$, we have $\omega <^{lex}_{\Delta} \omega'$ immediately.

Case 2: If $|\xi^j(\omega)| = |\xi^j(\omega')|$, then $|\xi^j(\omega')| = v = f$ and thus $\xi^j(\omega')$ has a corresponding set $N^f = \mathsf{nf}(\xi^j(\omega'))$ in $\mathcal{F}^{min}$. The nested for loops starting in Lines 13 and 16, respectively, ensure that the algorithm only returns *Yes*, if for every $N^f \in \mathcal{F}^{min}$ there is a $N^{v\prime} \in \mathcal{V}^{min}$ for which *recLinf* $(j', H^V \cup H^V_{new}, H^F \cup H^F_{new})$ returns true with $H^V_{new} = (\mathsf{nf}(\Delta^j) \setminus N^v) \cup \overline{N^v}$ and $H^F_{new} = (\mathsf{nf}(\Delta^j) \setminus N^f) \cup \overline{N^f}$. Note that every $H^V \cup H^V_{new}$ and $H^F \cup H^F_{new}$ are *nf*/*f*-conditions for $(\Delta, j-1)$ with $H^V \cup H^V_{new} \not\equiv \bot$ and $H^F \cup H^F_{new} \not\equiv \bot$. Furthermore, $|\xi^j(\omega^a)| = v = f = |\xi^j(\omega^b)|$ for every $\omega^a \in Mod(H^V \cup H^V_{new}), \omega^b \in Mod(H^F \cup H^F_{new})$. Thus, we can apply the induction hypothesis and conclude that there is some $\omega'' \in Mod(H^V \cup H^V_{new} \cup \{AB\})$ with $\omega'' <^{lex}_{\Delta} \omega$.

Case 3: The case $|\xi^j(\omega)| > |\xi^j(\omega')|$ is not possible, because it would imply $v > f$.

Direction $\Leftarrow$ Assume that (2) holds. If $v < f$, then Line 10 returns *Yes* and we are finished. For the remainder of this *Direction* $\Leftarrow$ assume that $v \geq f$. Let $N^f \in \mathcal{F}^{min}$. As above, because N^f is a minimal correction set, there must be a world $\omega' \in Mod(H^F \cup \{A\overline{B}\})$ with $|\xi^j(\omega)| = f$. By (2) there is an $\omega \in Mod(H^F \cup \{AB\})$ with $\omega <^{lex}_{\Delta} \omega'$. Because $|\xi^i(\omega)| = |\xi^i(\omega')|$ for $i \in \{j, \ldots, k\}$, we have $|\xi^j(\omega)| \leqslant |\xi^j(\omega')|$ and thus $v \leqslant f$. Therefore, $v = f$ and Lines 11–12 are passed without effect.

We need to show that for every $N^f \in \mathcal{F}^{min}$ there is an $N^v \in \mathcal{V}^{min}$ for which the recursive call in Line 18 returns *Yes*. Let $N^f \in \mathcal{F}^{min}$. Let $H^F_{new} = (\mathsf{nf}(\Delta^j) \setminus N^f) \cup \overline{N^f}$. Let ω^f_{min} be a world that is minimal in $Mod(H^F \cup H^F_{new} \cup \{A\overline{B}\})$ with respect to $<^{lex}_{\Delta}$. By (2) there is an $\omega^v \in Mod(H^V \cap AB)$ with $\omega^v <^{lex}_{\Delta} \omega^f_{min}$. Let ω^v_{min} be the minimal world in $Mod(H^V \cap AB)$. We have $\omega^v_{min} \leqslant^{lex}_{\Delta} \omega^v <^{lex}_{\Delta} \omega^f_{min}$. The set $\mathsf{nf}(\xi^j(\omega^v_{min}))$ must an MCS $N^v \in \mathcal{V}^{min}$, otherwise ω^v_{min} would not be minimal. Let $H^V_{new} = (\mathsf{nf}(\Delta^j) \setminus N^v) \cup \overline{N^v}$. We have that ω^v_{min} is a model of $H^F \cup H^F_{new}$, and because $\omega^v_{min} <^{lex}_{\Delta} \omega^f_{min}$ it is smaller than any world in $Mod(H^F \cup H^F_{new} \cup \{A\overline{B}\})$ with respect to $<^{lex}_{\Delta}$. Therefore, condition (2) is satisfied for the recursive call $recLinf(j-1, H^V \cup H^V_{new}, H^F \cup H^F_{new})$. Note that $H^V \cup H^V_{new}$ and $H^F \cup H^F_{new}$ are *nf/f*-conditions for $(\Delta, j-1)$ with $H^V \cup H^V_{new} \not\equiv \bot$ and $H^F \cup H^F_{new} \not\equiv \bot$ because N^v and N^f are correction sets with the hard constraints H^V and H^F, respectively. Furthermore, $|\xi^j(\omega^a)| = v = f = |\xi^j(\omega^b)|$ for every $\omega^a \in Mod(H^V \cup H^V_{new})$ and every $\omega^b \in Mod(H^F \cup H^F_{new})$. Thus, we can apply the induction hypothesis and get that the recursive call returns *Yes*.

As such an N^v can be found for every N^f, the algorithm eventually reaches Line 22 and returns *Yes*. □

Now we are ready to show the correctness of LEXinf.

Proposition 4 (correctness of *LEXinf*). *Let Δ be a consistent belief base and $A, B \in \mathcal{L}$. Then LEXinf(Δ, A, B) returns* Yes *iff $A \mid\!\sim^{lex}_{\Delta} B$.*

Proof. Lines 24–27 of Algorithm 1 cover some corner cases. If $A \equiv \bot$ then $A \mid\!\sim^{lex}_{\Delta} B$ and the algorithm returns *Yes* in Line 25. If $AB \not\equiv \bot$ and $A\overline{B} \equiv \bot$ then also $A \mid\!\sim^{lex}_{\Delta} B$ and the algorithm returns *Yes* in line 25. If $A\overline{B} \not\equiv \bot$ and $AB \equiv \bot$ then $A \not\mid\!\sim^{lex}_{\Delta} B$ and the algorithm returns *No* in line 27. If $AB \not\equiv \bot$ and $A\overline{B} \not\equiv \bot$, the algorithm returns the result of $recLinf(k, \emptyset, \emptyset)$. Because $\emptyset$ is a *nf/f*-condition for (Δ, k), Proposition 3 asserts that $recLinf(k, \emptyset, \emptyset)$ returns *Yes* iff (2) holds for $j = k$ and $H^F = H^V = \emptyset$. By Proposition 1 this is equivalent to $A \mid\!\sim^{lex}_{\Delta} B$. □

After showing the formal correctness of the algorithm, we will describe our empirical evaluation of its implementation in the next section.

6 Implementation and Evaluation of LEXinf

We implemented the algorithm LEXinf in Python as an extension of the library InfOCF [5].

Table 1. Average runtimes of the two implementations LEXinf and LEXJ of lexicographic inference for different problem sizes in milliseconds. If for a certain combination of signature size $|\Sigma|$ and belief base size $|\Delta|$ all instances could be solved before hitting the timeout the average runtime for answering 1000 queries (10 queries over each of 100 belief bases) is given; otherwise the percentage of solved instances is indicated. Timeout was set at 5 min.

$\|\Sigma\|$	6	8	10	12	14	16	18	20	30	40	50
$\|\Delta\|$	6	8	10	12	14	16	18	20	30	40	50
LEXinf	18	22	25	28	32	35	36	40	58	81	116
solved | %	✓	✓	✓	✓	✓	✓	✓	✓	✓	✓	✓
LEXJ	7	34	218	1354	7907	39568	—	—	—	—	—
solved | %	✓	✓	✓	✓	✓	✓	33	0	0	0	0

$\|\Sigma\|$	60	60	60	60	80	80	80	80	100	100	100	100	120	120	120	120
$\|\Delta\|$	60	80	100	120	60	80	120	160	60	100	160	200	60	80	120	160
LEXinf	137	420	—	—	117	214	—	—	119	366	—	—	124	176	874	—
solved | %	✓	✓	98	96	✓	✓	97	80	✓	✓	86	58	✓	✓	✓	93
LEXJ	—	—	—	—	—	—	—	—	—	—	—	—	—	—	—	—
solved | %	0	0	0	0	0	0	0	0	0	0	0	0	0	0	0	0

Our implementation uses the optimizing features of the Z3 SMT solver [10] to find Pareto fronts [11] which, in our case, is equivalent to finding the sets of all maximally satisfiable subsets of non-falsifying formulas of the conditionals of a partition. The required sets of all MCS are then derived from the obtained maximally satisfiable subsets.

Regarding other implementations, it should be noted that the algorithms and implementation described in [14,29,30] deal with a closely related inference that does not, however, coincide with Lehmann's lexicographic inference. For evaluating our implementation, we compared LEXinf to the only other published implementation LEXJ [34] of Lehmann's lexicographic inference that we are aware of. LEXJ is implemented in Java and answers queries $A \mathrel{|\!\sim}^{lex}_{\Delta} B$ by first explicitly computing the order $<^{lex}_{\Delta}$ and then using it to check if $AB <^{lex}_{\Delta} A\overline{B}$.

For the evaluation, 100 belief bases and 1000 queries were generated through a randomized process for each combination of signature size $|\Sigma|$ ranging from 6 to 120 and size $|\Delta|$ of the belief base ranging from 6 to 160; a detailed description of this scheme and algorithms realizing it are given in [9]. To avoid trivial cases, only consistent belief bases were taken into account. For different $(|\Sigma|, |\Delta|)$-combinations, in summary, 2 700 belief bases and 27 000 queries were used in the evaluation; these belief bases and queries are available at the CLKR repository [4] at https://www.fernuni-hagen.de/wbs/clkr/ as *problem set* CLKR-PS005.

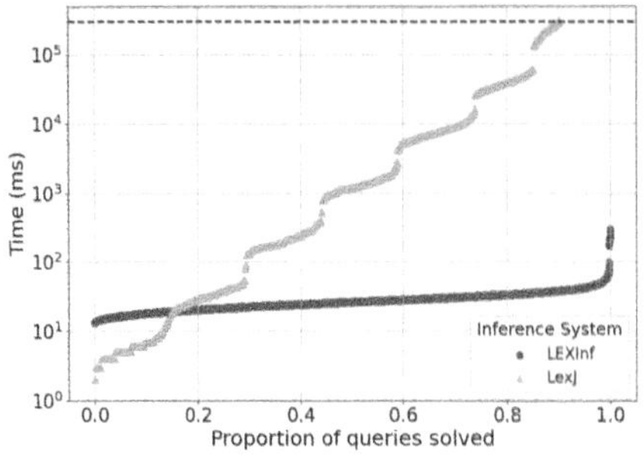

(a) $|\Sigma|, |\Delta| \leqslant 18$

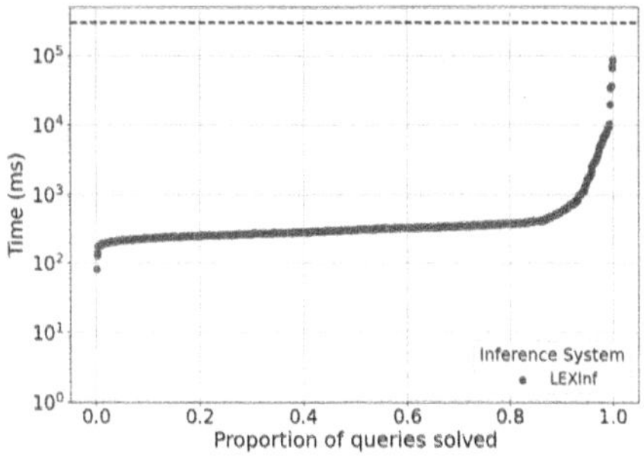

(b) $|\Sigma|, |\Delta| = 120$

Fig. 2. Cactus plots for LEXinf (•) and LEXJ (▲), plotting the proportion of queries solved against the time elapsed in milliseconds with one data point per query. The y-axes are scaled logarithmically and the dashed line (--) at the top represents the timeout of 300,000 ms. Plot (a) shows the aggregate of all problem Instances with $|\Sigma|, |\Delta| \leqslant 18$, i.e. those that were at least partially solved by LEXJ. Plot (b) shows LEXinf for the problem instance with $|\Sigma|, |\Delta| = 120$.

The evaluation was executed on an Intel i9-11950H CPU with 128GB DDR4-3200 working memory. Table 1 summarizes the average runtimes required for answering queries with LEXinf and LEXJ. Each column represents the tests for a certain combination of signature size $|\Sigma|$ and belief base size $|\Delta|$ as specified in the first two rows. If not all instances were solved for a combination of signature size and belief base size within the timeout of 5 min. (300,000 ms) per query, the table indicates the ratio of instances solved within this timeout. For LEXJ only instances with $|\Sigma|, |\Delta| \leqslant 16$ were solvable completely, while this implementation timed out for every tested instance with $|\Sigma|, |\Delta| > 18$.

Table 1 shows that our LEXinf implementation outperforms the LEXJ implementation for all but the smallest instances, and is several orders of magnitude faster for the instances with $|\Sigma|, |\Delta| = 16$. Moreover, LEXinf vastly increases the size of instances for which a lexicographic entailment query can be answered. Figure 2(a) shows a runtime comparison of LEXinf and LEXJ for $|\Sigma|, |\Delta| \leqslant 18$. The plot shows that LEXinf is less dependent on the size of the instance than LEXJ. The jumps in the LEXJ graph likely signify jumps in the size of the instance, leading to more possible worlds to be considered, while this has no visible impact on our LEXinf implementation. Figure 2(b) shows the runtime of LEXinf for the instance with $|\Sigma|, |\Delta| = 120$. Even for this large instance most of the queries can be solved very quickly, e.g., over 93% of the queries are solved in less than one second. Note that this instance, involving 2^{120} possible worlds, is far beyond the capabilities of LEXJ, and that it illustrates the scaling up of lexicographic inference by an order of magnitude.

7 Conclusions and Future Work

In this paper, we introduced the Partial MaxSAT-based algorithm LEXinf for realizing Lehmann's lexicographic inference [28] from conditional belief bases. After proving the correctness of the algoritmm, we presented an implementation of LEXinf. Its evaluation shows that it clearly outperforms previous imlementations of lexicographic inference. In particular, it scales up lexicographic inference into new problem dimensions. Besides p-entailment [24], system Z [16], c-inference [2], and system W [23], this makes lexicographic inference the only other inductive inference operator for which an implementation capturing belief bases with 100+ conditionals and involving more than 2^{100} possible worlds is available [3]. In future work, we will integrate LEXinf into the online reasoning platform InfOCF-Web [3,25], and we will investigate how the syntax splitting properties of lexicographic inference can be exploited for refining LEXinf such that local reasoning on subbases is used [20]. We plan to formally evaluate the algorithm with respect to time and space requirements, and finally, we are working on adapting the algorithm to also cover reasoning from weakly consistent belief bases [18,19].

Acknowledgments. This work was supported by the Austrian Science Fund (FWF) projects P30873, PIN8884924, and the FWF and netidee SCIENCE project T1349-N. Jonas Haldimann was supported by these grants. This work was supported by the Deutsche Forschungsgemeinschaft (DFG, German Research Foundation) - 512363537, grant BE 1700/12-1 awarded to Christoph Beierle. Aron Spang and Lars-Phillip Spiegel were supported by this grant.

Disclosure of Interests. The authors have no competiting interests to declare that are relevant to the content of this article.

References

1. Adams, E.: The logic of conditionals. Inquiry **8**(1–4), 166–197 (1965)
2. Beierle, C., Eichhorn, C., Kern-Isberner, G., Kutsch, S.: Properties and interrelationships of skeptical, weakly skeptical, and credulous inference induced by classes of minimal models. Artif. Intell. **297**, 103489 (2021). https://doi.org/10.1016/j.artint.2021.103489
3. Beierle, C., et al.: Scaling up reasoning from conditional belief bases. In: Scalable Uncertainty Management (SUM). LNCS, vol. 15350, pp. 29–44. Springer, Cham (2024). https://doi.org/10.1007/978-3-031-76235-2_3
4. Beierle, C., Haldimann, J., Schwarzer, L.: CLKR – conditional logic and knowledge representation. KI - Künstliche Intelligenz **38**, 61–67 (2024). https://doi.org/10.1007/s13218-024-00842-z
5. Beierle, C., Haldimann, J.P., Sanin, A., Spang, A., Spiegel, L.P., von Berg, M.: The InfOCF library for reasoning with conditional belief bases. In: 19th Edition of the European Conference on Logics in Artificial Intelligence (JELIA 2025) (2025)
6. Beierle, C., Kern-Isberner, G.: Semantical investigations into nonmonotonic and probabilistic logics. Ann. Math. Artif. Intell. **65**(2–3), 123–158 (2012). https://doi.org/10.1007/S10472-012-9310-1

7. Beierle, C., Spang, A., Haldimann, J.: A partial MaxSAT approach to non-monotonic reasoning with system W. In: Proceedings of the 37th International Florida Artificial Intelligence Research Society Conference (2024). https://doi.org/10.32473/FLAIRS.37.1.135330
8. Benferhat, S., Cayrol, C., Dubois, D., Lang, J., Prade, H.: Inconsistency management and prioritized syntax-based entailment. In: Proceedings of the Thirteenth International Joint Conference on Artificial Intelligence (IJCAI 1993), vol. 1, pp. 640–647. Morgan Kaufmann Publishers, San Francisco, CA, USA (1993)
9. von Berg, M., Sanin, A., Beierle, C.: An implementation of nonmonotonic reasoning with c-representations using an SMT solver. Int. J. Approx. Reason. **175**, 109285 (2024). https://doi.org/10.1016/j.ijar.2024.109285
10. Bjørner, N., de Moura, L., Nachmanson, L., Wintersteiger, C.M.: Programming Z3. Engineering Trustworthy Software Systems: 4th International School, SETSS 2018, Chongqing, China, 7–12 April 2018, Tutorial Lectures 4, pp. 148–201 (2019)
11. Bjørner, N., Phan, A.-D., Fleckenstein, L.: *νz* - an optimizing SMT solver. In: Baier, C., Tinelli, C. (eds.) TACAS 2015. LNCS, vol. 9035, pp. 194–199. Springer, Heidelberg (2015). https://doi.org/10.1007/978-3-662-46681-0_14
12. Casini, G., Meyer, T., Varzinczak, I.: Taking defeasible entailment beyond rational closure. In: Calimeri, F., Leone, N., Manna, M. (eds.) JELIA 2019. LNCS (LNAI), vol. 11468, pp. 182–197. Springer, Cham (2019). https://doi.org/10.1007/978-3-030-19570-0_12
13. Darwiche, A., Pearl, J.: On the logic of iterated belief revision. Artif. Intell. **89**(1–2), 1–29 (1997)
14. Everett, L., Morris, E., Meyer, T.: Explanation for KLM-style defeasible reasoning. In: Jembere, E., Gerber, A.J., Viriri, S., Pillay, A. (eds.) SACAIR 2021. CCIS, vol. 1551, pp. 192–207. Springer, Cham (2022). https://doi.org/10.1007/978-3-030-95070-5_13
15. de Finetti, B.: La prévision, ses lois logiques et ses sources subjectives. Ann. Inst. H. Poincaré **7**(1), 1–68 (1937). Engl. transl. Theory of Probability. Wiley (1974)
16. Goldszmidt, M., Pearl, J.: Qualitative probabilities for default reasoning, belief revision, and causal modeling. Artif. Intell. **84**(1–2), 57–112 (1996)
17. Haldimann, J., Beierle, C.: Properties of system W and its relationships to other inductive inference operators. In: Varzinczak, I. (ed.) FoIKS 2022. LNCS, vol. 13388, pp. 206–225. Springer, Cham (2022). https://doi.org/10.1007/978-3-031-11321-5_12
18. Haldimann, J., Beierle, C., Kern-Isberner, G., Meyer, T.: Conditionals, infeasible worlds, and reasoning with system W. In: FLAIRS 2023 (2023). https://doi.org/10.32473/flairs.36.133268
19. Haldimann, J., Beierle, C., Kern-Isberner, G., Meyer, T.: Reasoning with system W and infeasible worlds. Ann. Math. Artif. Intell. (2025). https://doi.org/10.1007/s10472-025-09982-w
20. Heyninck, J., Kern-Isberner, G., Meyer, T., Haldimann, J.P., Beierle, C.: Conditional syntax splitting for non-monotonic inference operators. In: Williams, B., Chen, Y., Neville, J. (eds.) Proceedings of the 37th AAAI Conference on Artificial Intelligence, vol. 37, pp. 6416–6424 (2023). https://doi.org/10.1609/aaai.v37i5.25789
21. Kern-Isberner, G., Beierle, C., Brewka, G.: Syntax splitting = relevance + independence: new postulates for nonmonotonic reasoning from conditional belief bases. In: KR-2020, pp. 560–571 (2020). https://doi.org/10.24963/kr.2020/56

22. Komo, C., Beierle, C.: Nonmonotonic inferences with qualitative conditionals based on preferred structures on worlds. In: Schmid, U., Klügl, F., Wolter, D. (eds.) KI 2020. LNCS (LNAI), vol. 12325, pp. 102–115. Springer, Cham (2020). https://doi.org/10.1007/978-3-030-58285-2_8
23. Komo, C., Beierle, C.: Nonmonotonic reasoning from conditional knowledge bases with system W. Ann. Math. Artif. Intell. **90**(1), 107–144 (2021). https://doi.org/10.1007/s10472-021-09777-9
24. Kraus, S., Lehmann, D., Magidor, M.: Nonmonotonic reasoning, preferential models and cumulative logics. Artif. Intell. **44**(1–2), 167–207 (1990)
25. Kutsch, S., Beierle, C.: InfOCF-web: an online tool for nonmonotonic reasoning with conditionals and ranking functions. In: IJCAI 2021, pp. 4996–4999. ijcai.org (2021). https://doi.org/10.24963/ijcai.2021/711
26. Larrosa, J., Rollon, E.: Towards a better understanding of (partial weighted) MaxSAT proof systems. In: Pulina, L., Seidl, M. (eds.) SAT 2020. LNCS, vol. 12178, pp. 218–232. Springer, Cham (2020). https://doi.org/10.1007/978-3-030-51825-7_16
27. Lehmann, D., Magidor, M.: What does a conditional knowledge base entail? Artif. Intell. **55**, 1–60 (1992)
28. Lehmann, D.: Another perspective on default reasoning. Ann. Math. Artif. Intell. **15**(1), 61–82 (1995)
29. Morris, M., Ross, T., Meyer, T.: Algorithmic definitions for KLM-style defeasible disjunctive datalog. South Afr. Comput. J. **32**(2) (2020). https://doi.org/10.18489/SACJ.V32I2.846
30. Park, D.: Scalable Defeasible Reasoning. Project report, University of Cape Town, South Africa (2021)
31. Pearl, J.: System Z: A natural ordering of defaults with tractable applications to nonmonotonic reasoning. In: Proceedings of the 3rd Conference on Theoretical Aspects of Reasoning About Knowledge (TARK 1990), pp. 121–135. Morgan Kaufmann Publ. Inc., San Francisco, CA, USA (1990)
32. Schwind, N., Konieczny, S., Lagniez, J., Marquis, P.: On computational aspects of iterated belief change. In: Bessiere, C. (ed.) Proceedings of the Twenty-Ninth International Joint Conference on Artificial Intelligence, IJCAI 2020, pp. 1770–1776. ijcai.org (2020). https://doi.org/10.24963/ijcai.2020/245
33. Spohn, W.: Ordinal conditional functions: a dynamic theory of epistemic states. In: Harper, W., Skyrms, B. (eds.) Causation in Decision, Belief Change, and Statistics, II, pp. 105–134. Kluwer Academic Publishers (1988)
34. Tönnies, D.: Implementierung und empirische Untersuchung lexikographischer Inferenz für das nichtmonotone Schließen. Bachelor thesis, FernUniversität in Hagen, Germany (2022). (in German)

Conditional Logics of Nondeterministic Change

Konstantinos Georgatos(✉)

Department of Mathematics and Computer Science, John Jay College City University of New York, 524 West 59th Street, New York, NY 10019, USA
kgeorgatos@jjay.cuny.edu

Abstract. We propose a novel approach to understanding conditional statements, viewing them as change descriptors within a standard nondeterministic framework. Our logical systems operate on a tree ordering, where the past is linear but the future is inherently uncertain and branching. We provide an axiomatization and demonstrate completeness for systems incorporating both a solely forward-looking conditional operator and a combination of backward and forward-looking operators. Additionally, we introduce and prove analogous results for the duals of these conditional operators, which naturally represent update operators by detailing the transformations leading to the current state.

Keywords: Conditional logic · Logics of change · Logics of update · Temporal logic

1 Introduction

A conditional statement "if a then b" asserts the truth of b given the truth of a. To evaluate such a statement, we must determine which cases where a is true are under consideration. The most straightforward approach is the maximal one, which considers all possible cases where a is true. This leads to the classical definition of material implication, where the conditional is interpreted as "either $\neg a$ is true or b is true."

However, this maximal interpretation rarely reflects natural language, leading to the well-known paradoxes of material implication ([13,14]). We typically use conditionals in a more informative sense where the set of considered cases where a is true is restricted. To formalize this, Stalnaker [20] introduced selection functions, which select the intended subset of cases where a holds. This selection is context-dependent, relying on the present case and the condition a. While various methods exist for generating these functions, such as Lewis's similarity-based sphere systems ([14]), most semantic accounts focus on the logical properties of

Support for this project was provided by the PSC-CUNY Award TRADB-55-370, jointly funded by The Professional Staff Congress and The City University of New York.

K. Sauerwald and M. Thimm (Eds.): ECSQARU 2025, LNAI 16099, pp. 316–330, 2026.
https://doi.org/10.1007/978-3-032-05134-9_22

the selection function itself. They often neglect the underlying structure of the states, presumably to maintain generality. A significant drawback of this focus is that it provides no method for computing a selection function in one state based on the function in another.

For example, Lewis's model considers a world x and orders all other worlds by their similarity to x. To evaluate the conditional $a > b$ (if a then b) at x, we examine the states where a is true that are minimal in this ordering—that is, the most similar states to x. This similarity ordering is inherently indexical, as it is relative to the prototype state x (serving as the basis of comparison) and can change radically if the prototype world changes.

An alternative to using similarity as a primitive concept is to use distinguishability ([5]). Here, a conditional is evaluated by selecting the worlds most indistinguishable from the present one, using the familiar indistinguishability relation from Kripke models. This approach is not indexical; instead, it relies on an underlying global relation of indistinguishability.

In a similar vein, this paper proposes using a tree ordering among states to provide semantics for conditional logics. Instead of an arbitrary accessibility relation of indistinguishability, we employ a tree ordering, analogous to the semantics of branching-time temporal logic ([17]). In this framework, trees encode the nondeterministic evolution of states, and conditionals describe the changes that occur along its paths. Branches represent maximal histories, and if a state t follows a state s, it signifies that s may transform into t. Branching at s indicates that the system can evolve in multiple ways, reflecting true nondeterminism or, equivalently, the different choices an agent might make.

Adopting the principle of minimization–a common thread in many semantic approaches to conditionals—we apply it to this procedural interpretation. To evaluate "if a then b" in a given state, we minimize over the transition relation, looking at the earliest future states where a holds. Since a tree ordering allows for multiple such minimal states, the conditional $a > b$ must be true in all of them. This interpretation embodies a principle of minimal change: the changes required to satisfy the condition are the smallest possible and are therefore assumed to occur first.

The temporal dimension of conditionals, particularly counterfactuals, has been studied extensively since Lewis ([15]). A common approach is to evaluate a counterfactual by "going back" to a time when its antecedent a was possible and then selecting histories that remain "closer" to the actual course of events. However, these studies typically interpret conditionals within an already developed temporal framework. They are hybrid approaches, combining a temporal frame for temporal operators with a separate semantic framework for conditionals (e.g., a selection function, a preferential ordering–see [1,9,10,16,21]). In contrast, our method interprets conditionals directly on the relation as minimization operators. We then study the axioms that these operators satisfy, thereby revealing the underlying causal or temporal structure of change itself.

Our system is particularly well-suited for modeling counterfactuals, especially historical ones. Consider the classic example:

(N) If Nixon had pressed the button, there would have been a nuclear war.

Lewis's analysis of (N) relies on finding the most similar world to our own where Nixon did press the button. However, (N) can be intuitively rephrased as:

(N′) At the last moment when it was possible for Nixon to press the button, if he had pressed it then, a nuclear war would have followed.

This revised form, N′, represents a nested conditional:

$$A >_1 (B >_2 C).$$

Here, $>_1$ identifies the most relevant past moment—the latest time when the event (e.g., Nixon pressing the button) was possible—by selecting a single path in the past. Although this moment is temporally the most recent, it is also the closest to the present in terms of difference. All earlier such moments lead up to this latest one and thus differ more from the present than the latest moment itself. Thus we do not measure time but *change*. On the other hand, $>_2$ represents the consequence (e.g., what would have happened if he had pressed the button), which can only be evaluated by considering an alternative set of possible paths, that is, a branching tree structure. By decomposing the counterfactual in this manner, our framework offers a more structured analysis, emphasizing its crucial role in understanding such statements.

In summary, the purpose of the present work is threefold:

- To introduce a global semantics for counterfactuals, where the properties of a specific world (the local view) are derived from a predefined global tree whose branches arise from nondeterministic changes.
- To demonstrate the inherent causal and temporal nature of counterfactuals, showing they can encode change directly without relying on external concepts like similarity or a separate temporal logic.
- To establish the conditional operator as a fundamental modality of minimization over a global relation, extending the core ideas of geodesic reasoning from an algebraic to a purely logical framework.

This paper is organized as follows: Sect. 2 introduces the syntax, semantics, and axiomatization of one-directional conditionals. Section 3 establishes completeness results for these conditionals. In Sect. 4, we define backward conditionals and their duals to capture bidirectional changes. Section 5 presents a comprehensive logical system encompassing all the connectives discussed. Finally, Sect. 6 explores the connections between these conditionals and temporal logic, and outlines related work and future research directions.

2 Syntax and Semantics

We assume a countable set Atom of atomic propositions. Our language $\mathcal{L}$ includes the constants $\top$ and $\bot$ (denoting truth and falsity, respectively) and is closed under the classical propositional connectives as well as the binary connective $>$ for conditionals. More formally, the *language* $\mathcal{L}$ is the smallest set $\mathcal{L}$ satisfying $\mathsf{Atom} \cup \{\top, \bot\} \subseteq \mathcal{L}$ and closed under the rule:

$$\frac{a, b \in \mathcal{L}}{\neg a,\ a \wedge b,\ a > b \in \mathcal{L}}.$$

Definition 1. *A* partially ordered frame *is a pair $(X, \leqslant)$ where X is a set of states and $\leqslant$ is a partial order; that is, $\leqslant$ is reflexive, transitive, and antisymmetric. A* tree frame *is a partially ordered frame whose order $\leqslant$ forms a tree, meaning that for every $y \in X$, the set $\{x \in X : x \leqslant y\}$ is linearly ordered.*

We interpret the language on tree frames as follows:

Definition 2. *A* model *is a triple $\mathcal{M} = \langle X, \leqslant, i\rangle$, where $(X, \leqslant)$ is a tree frame, and $i : \mathsf{Atom} \to \mathcal{P}(X)$ is an* initial interpretation *satisfying $i(\top) = X$ and $i(\bot) = \varnothing$.*

Definition 3. *Given a model $\mathcal{M} = \langle X, \leqslant, i\rangle$, the* satisfaction relation *$\models$ is a subset of $X \times \mathcal{L}$ defined recursively (we write $x \models_{\mathcal{M}} a$ instead of $(x, a) \in \models_{\mathcal{M}}$) as follows:*

$$\begin{array}{ll} x \models_{\mathcal{M}} A & \text{iff } x \in i(A),\ \text{where } A \in \mathsf{Atom} \\ x \models_{\mathcal{M}} a \wedge b & \text{iff } x \models_{\mathcal{M}} a \text{ and } x \models_{\mathcal{M}} b \\ x \models_{\mathcal{M}} \neg a & \text{iff } x \models_{\mathcal{M}} a \\ x \models_{\mathcal{M}} a > b & \text{iff for all } x' \text{ such that } x' \text{ is } a\text{-minimal at } x,\ x' \models_{\mathcal{M}} b \end{array}$$

*Here, a world y is a-*minimal *at x if $x \leqslant y$, $y \models a$, and for every x' with $x \leqslant x' < y$, we have $x' \models \neg a$. (We just write $\models$ instead of $\models_{\mathcal{M}}$, when the model is obvious.) We denote by $\min(x, a)$ the set of all a-minimal worlds at x. Thus, the clause for $x \models a > b$ can be equivalently expressed as $\min(x, a) \subseteq v(b)$, where $v(b) = \{z \in X : z \models b\}$.*

We also define the abbreviation

$$a >^{\exists} b := \neg(a > \neg b).$$

Accordingly,

$$x \models a >^{\exists} b \quad \text{iff there exists an } a\text{-minimal world } x' \text{ at } x \text{ such that } x' \models b.$$

The satisfaction condition for the conditional, based on the minimization operator, is meaningful only if the minimization is well-defined whenever the proposition is non-empty at every relevant state. To guarantee this, we impose the following assumption, known as the *global smoothness assumption*, which essentially corresponds to Lewis' limit assumption:

Global Smoothness Assumption:
For all $x \in X$ and $a \in \mathcal{L}$, if there exists $x' \geqslant x$ such that $x' \models a$, then there exists an a-minimal world at x below x'.

This assumption captures the intended interpretation of conditionals as specifying changes, ensuring the model explicitly reflects such changes. Note that this assumption differs from the corresponding one in linear frames (cf. [6]).

The axiom system **TC** consists of classical propositional rules and axioms plus the axiom schemes and rules of Table 1. Observe that axioms `C.C` through `CA` comprise the logic **VC** of counterfactuals by Lewis [14]. We introduce the axiom

$$a \vee b > b > c \leftrightarrow b > c \qquad \texttt{MC}$$

to express the principle of minimal change: at every branch, if a becomes true before b, then all conditionals based on b remain unchanged after a becomes true. This axiom can be equivalently reformulated as

$$a > a \wedge b > c \leftrightarrow a \wedge b > c \qquad \texttt{MC}'.$$

While `MC` holds for trees, it does not generally hold for arbitrary partial orders. A counterexample is presented in Fig. 1. In this example, w_1 is the minimal element and satisfies neither a nor b (the truth value of c is irrelevant). Similarly for the other elements in the structure. Observe that $w_1 \models b > c$, but $w_1 \not\models a \vee b > (b > c)$.

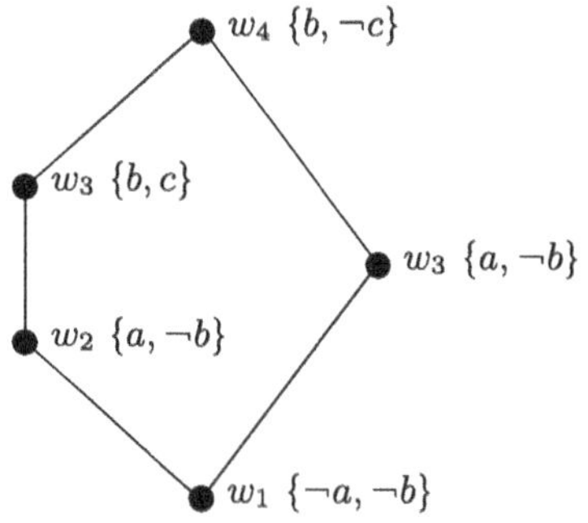

Fig. 1. A counterexample to `MC`

Notice that the axiom of Excluded Middle

$$a > b \vee a > \neg b \quad (\texttt{C.EM})$$

from the axiomatization of **LC** ([6]) and Rational Monotonicity

$$a > c \wedge \neg(a > \neg b) \rightarrow (a \wedge b > c) \quad (\texttt{RM})$$

from the theorems of **LC** that express linearity are not valid.

Lemma 1. *All axiom schemes and rules of* **TC** *are sound in partial order smooth models*

As usual, we will write $\vdash_{\mathbf{TC}} a$ iff a is a theorem of **TC** and let $a \vdash b$ if $\vdash a \rightarrow b$.

Table 1. System **TC**

Axioms

All axiom schemes and rules of Classical Logic

$a > b \wedge a > c \rightarrow a > b \wedge c$ (C.C)

$a > a$ (ID)

$a > b \rightarrow (a \rightarrow b)$ (MP)

$a \wedge b \rightarrow a > b$ (CS)

$a > b \wedge b > a \rightarrow (a > c \leftrightarrow b > c)$ (CSO)

$a > b \wedge a > c \rightarrow a \wedge b > c$ (ASC)

$a > b \wedge (a \wedge b > c) \rightarrow a > c$ (RT)

$a > c \wedge b > c \rightarrow (a \vee b > c)$ (CA)

$a \vee b > (b > c) \leftrightarrow b > c$ (MC)

$a > \bot \rightarrow \neg(a > \bot) > \bot$ (BTRANS)

$a > \bot \rightarrow c > (a > \bot)$ (BCOND)

Rules

$$\frac{a \leftrightarrow b}{a > c \leftrightarrow b > c} \text{ (RC.EA)}$$

$$\frac{b \rightarrow c}{a > b \rightarrow a > c} \text{ (RC.M)}$$

3 Step by Step Completeness

We construct our model through a step-by-step approach inspired by the method in [2], adapting Burgess' original completeness proof for temporal logic [4] with Since/Until operators, as well as its extensions to non-linear and branching models [22,23]. The key modification lies in the construction of minimal points, which ensures the global smoothness condition while preserving the tree structure. At each stage of the construction, we obtain a finite tree whose nodes are labeled with maximal consistent sets (*mcs*). Essentially, our model is built incrementally using fragments of the canonical model.

Definition 4. *An approximation N is a quadruple $\langle S, \leqslant, f, g\rangle$ where:*

1. *$(S, \leqslant)$ is a finite tree,*
2. *f is a mapping from S to the set of maximal consistent sets,*
3. *g is a function from $\{(s,t) \in S \times S : s < t\}$ to sets of formulas.*

The function g returns the formulas that should be common to all states between s and t at the final model. At each step of the construction leading to the final model, we ensure that the approximation satisfies all universal properties of the maximal consistent sets within its domain. We refer to this property as *coherency*.

Definition 5. *An approximation $\langle S, \leqslant, f, g\rangle$ is coherent if:*

1. *For all $s \leqslant t$, if $a > \bot \in f(s)$, then $a > \bot \in f(t)$,*
2. *Whenever s' immediately follows s, we have $f(s) \neq f(s')$, $f(s)Rf(s')$, and $g(s,s') = [f(s), f(s'))$,*
3. *For all $r < s < t$, it holds that $g(r,t) = g(r,s) \cap g(s,t)$.*

Here, R denotes the reachability relation defined by xRy if there exists $a \in \mathcal{L}$ such that $\{b : a > b \in x\} \subseteq y$, and $[x,y) = \{\neg b : a \vee b > a \in x, a \in c(x,y)\}$, where $c(x,y) = \{a : \text{if } a > c \in x \text{ then } c \in y\}$.

Definition 6. *Let $\langle S, \leqslant, f, g\rangle$ be an approximation.*

1. *A $>^{\exists}$-defect is a triple (s,a,b) where $s \in S$ and $a, b \in \mathcal{L}$ such that*

$$\neg a, \quad a >^{\exists} b \in f(s),$$

and there exists no $t \in S$ with $s \leqslant t$ satisfying

$$b \in f(t) \quad \text{and} \quad \neg a \in g(s,t).$$

2. *A $>$-defect is a quadruple (s,t,a,b) where $s,t \in S$, $a,b \in \mathcal{L}$, and $s \leqslant t$ such that*

$$\neg a, \neg b, a \vee b > a \in f(s),$$

and

$$b \in f(t), \quad \neg b \in g(s,t),$$

and there is no $u \in S$ with $s \leqslant u \leqslant t$ such that

$$a \in f(u), \quad \neg a \in g(s,u), \quad \text{and} \quad \neg b \in g(u,t).$$

Lemma 2 (Repair). *For every* $>^{\exists}$*-defect and* $>$*-defect of an approximation, there exists an extension of the approximation that eliminates this defect.*

Definition 7. *We construct the overall frame as a limit of a sequence of approximations. Let* $S = \{s_i : i \in \omega\}$ *be a fixed countable set from which the states of our model are drawn. The set of potential defects is*

$$(S \times \mathcal{L} \times \mathcal{L}) \cup (S \times S \times \mathcal{L} \times \mathcal{L}),$$

which is countable, and we fix an enumeration of it.

Each moment will be labeled with a mcs via a function f. *Let* Γ *be a consistent set of formulas, and choose an mcs* x_0 *such that* $\Gamma \subseteq x_0$. *Define the initial approximation*

$$N_0 = \langle S_0, \leqslant_0, f_0, g_0 \rangle,$$

where $S_0 = \{s_0\}$, $\leqslant_0 = \{(s_0, s_0)\}$, $f_0(s_0) = x_0$, *and* $g_0(s_0, s_0) = x_0$. *This forms a coherent approximation.*

At each subsequent step, we address the minimal defect in our enumeration that has not yet been repaired. To fix such a defect, we apply the repair lemma, extending the current approximation by introducing the least unused element s_i *from* S. *Once a defect is repaired, it does not reoccur. Prioritizing defects by minimality ensures that all defects will eventually be repaired, since only finitely many approximations can omit the treatment of any given defect.*

Finally, define the model

$$\mathcal{M} = \langle S, \leqslant, f, g, i \rangle,$$

where

$$i(A) = \{s \in S : A \in f(s)\},$$

and $\leqslant$, f, *and* g *are obtained as the unions of the respective relations and functions from all approximations in the sequence.*

Theorem 1. *For every formula* $a \in \mathcal{L}$, *we have*

$$a \in f(s) \quad \text{if and only if} \quad s \models_{\mathcal{M}} a.$$

Note that, during the construction of the final model in Definition 7, new states are only added as successors of the initial state s_0. In other words, for all states $s \in S$, we have $s_0 \leqslant s$. This observation leads to the following result:

Corollary 1. *The logic* ***TC*** *is strongly complete with respect to smooth models whose underlying tree structure has a root.*

4 Introducing Backward Linear Conditionals

Before combining branching forward and backward linear conditionals to express counterfactuals, as outlined in the introduction, we first present a logical system that includes only backward linear conditionals. Linear deterministic conditionals were introduced in [6], where completeness with respect to linear orderings was established. Here, we focus on how such conditionals are interpreted within the tree structures under consideration.

Backward linear conditionals, denoted by $>^-$, capture the reverse temporal direction, allowing us to express statements about the past. We interpret the formula $a >^- b$ as "if it was a, then b," reflecting a condition on preceding states.

The satisfaction clause for $>^-$ is defined as follows:

$$x \models a >^- b \quad \text{if and only if} \quad \text{for every } a\text{-maximal world } y \leqslant x, \quad y \models b,$$

where a world y is said to be *a-maximal at x* if $y \leqslant x$, $y \models a$, and for all x' with $y < x' \leqslant x$, $x' \models \neg a$. Due to linearity in the past, any a-maximal world at x is unique.

An additional interpretation of the backward conditional operator is noteworthy: the formula $\neg a >^- b$ can be understood to mean that b is a necessary precondition for the occurrence of a, or for the a-action, particularly when nondeterminism arises from agents' actions.

To support this framework, we introduce the mirror image of the global smoothness assumption for $>^-$:

Global Smoothness Assumption for $>^-$
For all $x \in X$ and for every formula $a \in \mathcal{L}$, if there exists some $x' \leqslant x$ such that $x' \models a$, then there exists an a-maximal world at x.

The backward linear conditional is interpreted over linear orderings. To recover forward branching, we introduce the dual connective to $>^-$, denoted by $\ominus$, which we call *retraction*. We interpret $a \ominus b$ as "a retracted to b." A retraction $a \ominus b$ holds at the latest state satisfying b that precedes an a state. In this sense, we can think of it as "dropping" the negation of b to reach a previous b state, motivating the term *retraction*.

Standard conditional logics typically focus on one direction of inference, capturing the conditional operator while omitting its dual. Since the conditional is defined via a universal quantification, its dual operator corresponds to an existential quantification. This means that the a-state to which we retract is not unique, introducing nondeterminism in the change.

Table 2. Logic **R.TC**

All Axioms and Rules of **LC**	
$(a >^- b) \ominus a \to b$	(CONV∘)
$a \to b >^- (a \ominus b)$	(CONV>)

We extend the language by adding the new connective $\ominus$ without any restrictions. Working within tree models, we define the satisfaction condition for $\ominus$ as follows:

Definition 8. *Satisfaction for retraction in a model $\mathcal{M}$ is defined by*

$$x \models a \ominus b \quad \textit{if and only if} \quad \textit{there exists } x' \textit{ such that } x \textit{ is } b\textit{-maximal at } x' \textit{ and } x' \models a.$$

Note that this definition relies on the Global Smoothness condition.

To axiomatize $>^-$, we employ the mirror versions of the axioms and rules presented in Table 1, modified appropriately for the opposite direction. Additionally, we include the excluded middle axiom `C.EM` introduced earlier. For instance, the axiom `MC` become

$$a \vee b >^- (b >^- c) \leftrightarrow b >^- c \quad \texttt{(P.MC)}.$$

To axiomatize $\ominus$, we add the axioms listed in Table 2.

Proposition 1. *The axioms listed in Table 2 are sound with respect to smooth models.*

The connection between the conditional operator $>^-$ and the retraction operator $\ominus$ mirrors the classical Ramsey rule:

Lemma 3 (Ramsey Rule). *For all $a, b, c \in \mathcal{L}$, the following equivalence holds:*

$$a \ominus b \vdash c \quad \textit{if and only if} \quad a \vdash b >^- c.$$

Proof. For the forward direction, assume $\vdash a \ominus b \rightarrow c$. Applying the rule $>^-$ RM, we derive

$$\vdash b >^- (a \ominus b) \rightarrow b >^- c.$$

Then, by the axiom `CONV`$\ominus$, it follows that

$$\vdash a \rightarrow b >^- c,$$

which implies $a \vdash b >^- c$.

Conversely, suppose $\vdash a \rightarrow b >^- c$. Using the rule `RU.M`, we obtain

$$\vdash a \ominus b \rightarrow (b >^- c) \ominus b.$$

Table 3. Logic **DTC**

Axioms and rules of **TC** for $>$	
Axioms and rules of **LC** for $>^{-}$	
$(a \vee b > (b >^{-} c) \leftrightarrow b >^{-} c)$	(MC1)
$\neg a \wedge (a > (\neg a >^{-} b)) \rightarrow (a \vee b > \neg a)$	(FB1)
$\neg(a \vee b > b) \wedge (b > \neg b >^{-} a >^{-} \neg a > c) \rightarrow (a \vee b > b) > c$	(FB2)
$a >^{-} (b > \bot) \rightarrow b > \bot$	(PB1)
All "mirror" axioms and rules of the above. For example:	
$a \vee b >^{-} (b > c) \leftrightarrow b > c$	(MC1-)

By the axiom CONV$>^{-}$, this yields

$$\vdash a \ominus b \rightarrow c,$$

and hence $a \ominus b \vdash c$.

Theorem 2 ([6]). *The system **R.TC** is strongly complete with respect to tree-ordered smooth models.*

5 Combining Forward and Backward Conditionals

In this section, we combine the two conditionals $>$ and $>^{-}$, representing forward (future) and backward (past) modalities, respectively. To proceed, we adopt the following assumption:

Dual Global Smoothness Assumption
For every $x \in X$ and $a \in \mathcal{L}$, if there exists $x' \geqslant x$ such that $x' \models a$, then there is an a-minimal world at x. Similarly, for every $x \in X$ and $a \in \mathcal{L}$, if there exists $x' \leqslant x$ with $x' \models a$, then there is an a-maximal world at x.

To axiomatize the interaction between $>$ and $>^{-}$, we combine the axioms **TC** for $>$ and **LC** for $>^{-}$, along with the excluded middle axiom C.EM introduced earlier. Additionally, we incorporate a set of combination axioms listed in Table 3.

The resulting system is called **DTC**. The completeness proof extends the model construction used for **TLC** to accommodate the backward operator; details are provided in the Appendix.

Corollary 2. ***DTC*** *is strongly complete with respect to tree-ordered smooth models.*

Table 4. Logic **UR.DTC**

All axioms and rules of **DTC**	
All axioms, rules of **R.TC** and their "mirrors"	
$a \circ b \rightarrow \neg(a >^{-} \bot)$	(U.COND)
$a \ominus b \rightarrow \neg(a > \bot)$	(R.COND)
$a \circ b \leftrightarrow (a \wedge b) \vee (\neg b \circ b \wedge (\neg b >^{-} (a \vee b >^{-} \neg b)))$	(U.CONV)
$a \ominus b \leftrightarrow (a \wedge b) \vee (\neg b \ominus b \wedge (\neg b > (a \vee b > \neg b)))$	(R.CONV)

Furthermore, we introduce dual operators for both conditionals. Alongside the previously defined operator $\ominus$, we add a new connective, *update*, denoted by $\circ$. We interpret $a \circ b$ as "a updated by b." Specifically, $a \circ b$ holds at a state s if there exists a prior a-state whose b-minimal successor is s. In other words, $a \circ b$ holds at s if s results from updating a state satisfying a with b. As in the case of the backward conditional, the connection between the conditional operator $>$ and the update operator $\circ$ is Ramsey rule:

Lemma 4 (Ramsey Rule). *For all $a, b, c \in \mathcal{L}$, the following equivalence holds:*

$$a \circ b \vdash c \quad \textit{if and only if} \quad a \vdash b > c.$$

We freely extend the language by adding the connective $\circ$ without restrictions. Satisfaction for the update operator in a model $\mathcal{M}$ is defined as follows:

$$x \models a \circ b \quad \text{iff} \quad \text{there exists } x' \text{ such that } x \text{ is } b\text{-minimal at } x' \text{ and } x' \models a.$$

To axiomatize $\circ$ and $\ominus$, we add the axioms listed in Table 4 to the system **DTC**, forming the extended system **UR.DTC**.

Proposition 2. *The Axioms of Table 4 are sound and complete with respect to smooth models.*

6 Conclusion

One of the significant contributions of the present work is the utilization of a single global tree to interpret conditionals. However, it is important to clarify this representation to avoid confusion with the single orderings employed in studies of nonmonotonic entailment, beginning with Shoham's preferential inference framework [19]. In the context of nonmonotonic entailment, a conditional statement of the form $a \mid\!\sim b$ is evaluated at worlds that satisfy a and are minimal with respect to a usually partial order. This partial order typically encodes notions such as similarity, typicality, normality, or other preference criteria [11,12]. Consequently, the evaluation of the conditional occurs at the most typical, normal, similar, or otherwise preferred worlds.

While these studies provide valuable insights into common-sense reasoning and the diverse interpretations that conditionals can have, along with their corresponding inference rules, it is crucial not to conflate the orderings used in preferential semantics with the tree ordering employed in our framework. Our tree ordering arises from the combination of a class of orderings defined for each individual state, whereas the semantics of nonmonotonic entailment select a single element of this class. Moreover, in our semantics, the context is dynamic and can change, while in preferential semantics, the ordering itself effectively represents the context.

The distinction between conditional logic and nonmonotonic entailment is perhaps most transparent when considered from a syntactic perspective. Although at first glance the postulates governing preferential relations resemble the axioms of conditional logic, they actually serve different roles. Nonmonotonic relations specify inferences between propositions within a language that is typically classical. In contrast, conditionals in conditional logic are part of the object language itself, allowing the expression of arbitrary nestings of conditionals. Boutilier ([3]) demonstrated that preferential entailment corresponds to the flat fragment of conditional logics. In particular, this fragment can be embedded within a modal logic framework, whereas it has been shown by Lewis ([14]) that conditional logic, in its full generality, cannot be adequately expressed using unary modal logic alone.

We have introduced a formal logic specifically designed to handle conditional statements that encapsulate dynamic changes within a nondeterministic setting. This framework draws a strong analogy to branching-time temporal logic, wherein the dimension of time serves as a structural tool represent the evolution of states over possible futures. Although the temporal operators $>$ and until are interdefinable in the linear case ([6]), this equivalence does not hold for trees. Notice that if we extend the conventional language of temporal logic by introducing a binary connective denoted by $\forall \mathsf{U}$ (as in [7]), whose satisfaction relation is defined as follows:

> $x \models_{\mathcal{M}} \forall(a \,\mathsf{U}\, b)$ if and only if for every branch starting from x, there exists a state y on that branch such that $y \models_{\mathcal{M}} b$ and for all states x' with $x \leqslant x' < y$, we have $x' \models_{\mathcal{M}} a$,

then conditionals cannot specify the existence of a minimal state on every branch, just as $\forall \, \mathsf{U}$ statements cannot express the absence of minimal states on some branches.

The close relationship between conditionals and updates was previously explored in [18]. There, the operators $\boxminus$ and $\Diamond$ correspond to our $>$ and $\circ$, respectively, as they are dual inverses. Additionally, two more modalities arise from duality in [18]: $\diamondminus$ and $\Box$, which correspond to $>^{-}$ and its dual in our framework.

Further, [18] argues that updates are the dual inverses of counterfactuals. Their counterfactuals, expressed as

"if A were the case, then B would be the case,"

correspond to what we refer to as past conditionals. In contrast, our work treats updates as the dual inverses of forward conditionals. This difference arises from one of the central aims of this paper: the dual inverses of accessibility relations are intimately connected to a form of the "Ramsey rule," and the interpretation of these operators depends on the chosen accessibility relation.

The work in [18] utilizes binary relations indexed by propositions, which effectively function as ternary relations (see also Sect. 3 in [8]). When inverting such a ternary relation, the perspective remains oriented forward rather than backward in time. Instead of maximizing from a past state, one minimizes from an opposite direction, reflecting the absence of an explicit notion of the past. More precisely, if xR_ay is interpreted as "y is a-minimal to x with respect to the ordering $\leqslant$," then the distinction between

$$x(R_a)^{-1}y \quad (\ x \text{ is } a\text{-minimal to } y \text{ with respect to } \leqslant\ )$$

and

$$x(R^{-1})_a y \quad (\ y \text{ is } a\text{-maximal to } x \text{ with respect to } \geqslant\ )$$

becomes indistinguishable within their framework.

It is important to note that not all conditionals conform to the form we have outlined. Some conditionals serve to reveal an agent's epistemic state—that is, what the agent knows or believes about the world—while others express notions of typicality or preferences.The update operators introduced in this work are not intended as belief update operators, nor retraction should be identified with the contraction operator of Belief revision. The logics developed here describe changes occurring in the external world itself. To accurately capture more complex belief updates, these conditional logics must be supplemented with an additional epistemic component, integrating aspects of the agent's knowledge or belief dynamics beyond what is addressed in this paper.

References

1. Alviano, M., Giordano, L., Dupré, D.T.: Temporal many-valued conditional logics: an abridged report. In: Porello, D., Vinci, C., Zavatteri, M. (eds.), Short Paper Proceedings of the 6th International Workshop on Artificial Intelligence and Formal Verification, Logic, Automata, and Synthesis, OVERLAY 2024, Bolzano, Italy, 28–29 November 2024, volume 3904 of CEUR Workshop Proceedings, pp. 33–40. CEUR-WS.org, 2024
2. Blackburn, P., de Rijke, M., de Venema, Y.: Modal Logic. Cambridge tracts in theoretical computer science. Cambridge University Press, Cambridge, 2002
3. Boutilier, C.: Conditional logics of normality: a modal approach. Artif. Intell. **68**(1), 87–154 (1994)

4. Burgess, J.P.: Axioms for tense logic. I. since and until. Notre Dame J. Form. Log. **23**(4), 367–374 (1982)
5. Georgatos, K.: Conditioning by minimizing accessibility. In: Bonanno, G., Löwe, B., van der Hoek, W. (eds.) LOFT 2008. LNCS (LNAI), vol. 6006, pp. 20–33. Springer, Heidelberg (2010). https://doi.org/10.1007/978-3-642-15164-4_2
6. Georgatos, K.: Conditional logics of deterministic change, 2025. To appear
7. Robert, I.: Goldblatt. Logics of time and computation. CSLI lecture notes, Center for the Study of Language and Information (1992)
8. Herzig, A.: Logics for belief base updating. In: Dubois, D., Prade, H. (eds.) Belief Change. HDRUMS, LNCS, vol. 3, pp. 189–231. Springer, Dordrecht (1998). https://doi.org/10.1007/978-94-011-5054-5_5
9. Hosokawa, Y.: From counterfactual conditionals to temporal conditionals. J. Log. Lang. Inf. **32**(4), 677–706 (2023)
10. Ju, F., Grilletti, G., Goranko, V.: A logic for temporal conditionals and a solution to the sea battle puzzle. In: Bezhanishvili, G., D'Agostino, G., Metcalfe, G., Studer, T. (eds.), Advances in Modal Logic 12, proceedings of the 12th conference on "Advances in Modal Logic," held in Bern, Switzerland, 27–31 August 2018, pp. 407–426. College Publications, 2018
11. Kraus, S., Lehmann, D., Magidor, M.: Nonmonotonic reasoning, preferential models and cumulative logics. Artif. Intell. **44**, 167–207 (1990)
12. Lehmann, D., Magidor, M.: What does a conditional knowledge base entail? Artif. Intell. **55**, 1–60 (1992)
13. Lewis, C.I.: Implication and the algebra of logic. Mind **21**(84), 522–531 (1912)
14. Lewis, D.: Counterfactuals. Harvard University Press, Cambridge, MA (1973)
15. Lewis, D.: Counterfactual dependence and time's arrow. Noûs **13**(4), 455–476 (1979)
16. Nute, D.: Historical necessity and conditionals. Noûs **25**(2), 161 (1991)
17. Prior, A.: Past, Present and Future. Oxford University Press, London (1967)
18. Ryan, M., Schobbens, P.-Y.: Counterfactuals and updates as inverse modalities. J. Log. Lang. Inform. **6**(2), 123–146 (1997)
19. Shoham, Y.: A semantical approach to non-monotonic logics. In: Proceedings of the Tenth International Joint Conference on Artificial Intelligence (IJCAI), pp. 1413–1419, 1987
20. Stalnaker, R.: A theory of conditionals. In: Rescher, N. (ed.) Studies in Logical Theory. Oxford University Press, Oxford (1968)
21. Thomason, R., Gupta, A.: A theory of conditionals in the context of branching time. Philos. Rev. **89**(1), 65–90 (1980)
22. Ming, X.: On some u, s-tense logics. J. Philos. Log. **17**(2), 181–202 (1988)
23. Zanardo, A.: A complete deductive-system for since-until branching-time logic. J. Philos. Log. **20**(2), 131–148 (1991)

Towards an Algebraic and Probabilistic Setting for Iterated Boolean Conditionals

Lydia Castronovo[1(✉)], Tommaso Flaminio[2], Lluis Godo[2], and Giuseppe Sanfilippo[3]

[1] Dipartimento di Scienze Matematiche e Informatiche, Scienze Fisiche e Scienze della Terra, Università degli Studi di Messina, Messina, Italy
lydia.castronovo@studenti.unime.it

[2] Artificial Intelligence Research Institute (IIIA - CSIC), Campus UAB, Bellaterra 08193, Spain
{tommaso,godo}@iiia.csic.es

[3] Department of Mathematics and Computer Science, University of Palermo, Palermo, Italy
giuseppe.sanfilippo@unipa.it

Abstract. The present paper is about iterated conditionals, i.e., expressions of the form $(a|b)|(c|d)$ that read as "if c holds conditionally to d, then a holds conditionally to b". Firstly, we introduce algebraic structures for iterated conditionals by repeating twice the construction of Boolean algebras of conditionals, where one can represent basic conditionals $(a|b)$ and their Boolean combinations. Then, from the probabilistic perspective, we show that relevant properties of a probability Q on these Boolean algebras of conditionals can be characterized in terms of satisfiability of known principles of its "canonical extensions" μ_Q to the algebra of iterated conditionals. Precisely, we show that Q satisfies a property called "separability" if and only if μ_Q satisfies a weak version of the Import-Export principle. Likewise, Q satisfies the McGee formula for the conjunction of basic conditionals if and only if a "conjunction rationality principle" holds for its canonical extension μ_Q on the algebra of iterated conditionals.

Keywords: Boolean Algebras · Conditional Probability · Import-Export Principle · Iterated Conditionals · McGee formula

1 Introduction

Conditional expressions are statements that read "if a is the case, then b is the case" and they play a fundamental role in the modeling of hypothetical situations and in reasoning under uncertainty.

The relation among conditionals, probability and conditional probability led to the formalization of several principles concerning the (inter)definability of the above three concepts, the best known being *Stalnaker's thesis*, see [22], that reads as follows:

K. Sauerwald and M. Thimm (Eds.): ECSQARU 2025, LNAI 16099, pp. 331–346, 2026.
https://doi.org/10.1007/978-3-032-05134-9_23

Stalnaker's thesis: The probability of a conditional is the conditional probability, whenever the antecedent has non-zero probability.

By the above, then, the conditional probability $P(a|b)$ quantifies the chances that the conditional event "if b, then a" holds.

As it is well known, Lewis's triviality results [5], together with its stronger version proved by Hájek in [15], rules out the possibility of defining a conditional "$(\cdot|\cdot)$" within the language of classical propositional logic that could, at the same time, satisfy Stalnaker's thesis and keeping probabilities non-trivial. Indeed, the unique probabilities that satisfy Stalnaker's thesis for conditionals that are classical logic definable are trivial, i.e., they are functions assigning at most four distinct values to events and they are therefore intuitively uninformative, as they cannot distinguish between many non-trivial propositions. Equivalently, for non-trivial probability functions, the thesis that the probability of a conditional is a conditional probability does not hold, making it untenable in many contexts.

A side effect of this impossibility is that objects like $(a|b)$ have to be considered outside the boundary of classical propositional logic and this makes them not easy to handle. To make these conditional operators less complex to deal with, they are sometimes given a bounded expressive power and, more precisely, they are formalised in a language that does not allow them to occur nested within a complex formula. In fact, besides the original semantics studied in [5,22] and the more recent algebraic setting of [3,20], conditional operators $(\cdot|\cdot)$ usually apply to unconditional formulas only. This limited language have been considered to study conditionals within the Boolean algebraic setting in [7,14,19,23], while the more recent [24] considers iterated conditionals of controlled, bounded, depth.

Besides the aforementioned approaches to (un)nested conditionals, it is worth mentioning the alternative yet well-known tradition that regards conditional objects as three-valued events, see for instance [1,4,6]. In this latter setting a conditional $(a|b)$ is true if a and b are both true, false when b is true and a is false, and it is *void* whenever the antecedent b turns out to be false. While we will mainly follow the algebraic setting developed in [7] (and then further studied also in [8,9]), it is worth to remark that also in the three-valued approach to conditionals, the issue of treating nested occurrences of the conditional operator is far from trivial and it can be regarded from several perspectives, see for instance the analysis proposed in [2,12,21] and references therein.

From a methodological viewpoint, we will follow the former algebraic approach to deal with iterated (nested) conditionals and the algebras that we employ to represent iterated conditionals are built from any Boolean algebra of plain events, by doubling the construction defined in [7] that defines Boolean algebras of conditionals. More precisely, given a Boolean algebra $\mathbf{A}$, its associated Boolean algebra of conditionals, denoted by $\mathcal{C}(\mathbf{A})$, contains all *basic* conditionals of the form $(a|b)$ for $a \in A$ and $b \in A \setminus \{\bot\}$ and their Boolean combinations. A nice property of the algebras $\mathcal{C}(\mathbf{A})$ is that, if we start with a (positive) probability P on $\mathbf{A}$, one can always extend it in a *canonical* way to a probability

μ_P on $\mathcal{C}(\mathbf{A})$ such that μ_P of a basic conditional $(a|b)$ coincides with the conditional probability $P(a|b)$, that is $\mu_P((a|b)) = P(a|b) = \frac{P(a \wedge b)}{P(b)}$, see [7,9] for more details.[1]

Since $\mathcal{C}(\mathbf{A})$ is itself a Boolean algebra, and moreover it is finite whenever so is $\mathbf{A}$, we can consider its Boolean algebra of conditionals $\mathcal{C}(\mathcal{C}(\mathbf{A}))$ that now contains *basic* iterated conditionals like $(a|b)|(c|d)$ for $a, c \in A$ and $b, d \in A\backslash\{\bot\}$ and their Boolean combinations as well (more details will be given in the next sections). An example of a linguistic expression that can be formalized as a basic iterated conditional $(a|b)|(c|d)$ is

$$\text{if } \overbrace{\underbrace{\text{the road is slippery}}_{c} \text{ if } \underbrace{\text{it rains}}_{d}}^{(c|d)}, \text{ then } \overbrace{\underbrace{\text{accidents occurs}}_{a} \text{ if } \underbrace{\text{cars go to fast}}_{b}}^{(a|b)}.$$

By doubling the construction that brings to Boolean algebras of conditionals, we have at our disposal a richer language in which it is possible to study, for instance, algebraic and probabilistic versions of the well-known Import-Export principle for iterated conditionals and their relation with properties of the so-called "canonical extensions" of probabilities on the algebras of conditionals and their iterated extension. Indeed, the main results of our paper will put in connection relevant properties of a probability Q defined on $\mathcal{C}(\mathbf{A})$ with known principles that can now be formalized within the richer language of $\mathcal{C}(\mathcal{C}(\mathbf{A}))$ and satisfied by Q's canonical extension μ_Q on $\mathcal{C}(\mathcal{C}(\mathbf{A}))$. More precisely, we show that the satisfaction of a weak version of the Import-Export principle by μ_Q characterizes the "separability" property of the probability Q. Likewise, we show that the validity by a probability Q of the McGee formula [18] for the conjunction of basic conditionals can also be characterized by the fact that μ_Q satisfies a principle that we call "conjunction rationality principle" on the algebra of iterated conditionals.

The present paper is organized as follows. In Sect. 2 we recall some preliminary notions on the construction of the algebra of conditionals $\mathcal{C}(\mathbf{A})$ and its atomic structure, the notion of canonical extension of a positive probability P on $\mathbf{A}$ and the "separability property" for a probability Q on $\mathcal{C}(\mathbf{A})$. In Sect. 3, we analyze the structure of the algebra of iterated conditionals $\mathcal{C}(\mathcal{C}(\mathbf{A}))$ by also describing its atoms and the different ways of obtaining a probability on $\mathcal{C}(\mathcal{C}(\mathbf{A}))$. In Sect. 4, starting from the well-known Import-Export principle, we formulate a weaker version of it and we use the latter to characterize the separable probabilities on $\mathcal{C}(\mathbf{A})$. Then, in Sect. 5 we introduce the "conjunction rationality" principle for the canonical extension of a positive probability Q on $\mathcal{C}(\mathbf{A})$ and we prove it is related to the McGee decomposition formula for the conjunction of two basic conditional given for Q. Finally in Sect. 6 we conclude and we point out future work.

---

[1] For the sake of a simpler notation, in the following we will simply write $\mu_P(a|b)$ for $\mu_P((a|b))$.

2 Preliminaries

Boolean algebras will be considered in their usual language $(\wedge, \vee, \bar{}, \bot, \top)$ of type $(2, 2, 1, 0, 0)$ where $\wedge$ and $\vee$ denote the lattice operations of meet and join respectively, $\bar{}$ indicates the operation of complementation (or negation), while $\bot$ and $\top$ are the constants for the bottom and the top elements respectively. For every Boolean algebra $\mathbf{B} = (B, \wedge, \vee, \bar{}, \bot, \top)$ we will denote by $\leqslant$ the lattice order of $\mathbf{B}$ so that for all $a, b \in B$, $a \leqslant b$ holds iff $a \wedge b = a$ or, equivalently, $a \vee b = b$. Moreover we will denote by B' the set $B \backslash \{\bot\}$.

Now, let $\mathbf{A}$ be a Boolean algebra. The *Boolean algebra of conditionals* of $\mathbf{A}$, denoted by $\mathcal{C}(\mathbf{A})$, is defined by firstly considering the Boolean algebra Free$(A \times A')$ freely generated by the set $A \times A' = \{(a, b) : a \in A, b \in A \backslash \{\bot\}\}$, and then imposing on it some suitable properties of conditionals. This second step is done by taking the quotient of Free$(A \times A')$ by the minimal congruence $\equiv$ that extends the following set of relations:

- $(b|b) \equiv \top$, for all $b \in A \backslash \{\bot\}$;
- $(a_1|b) \wedge (a_2|b) \equiv (a_1 \wedge a_2|b)$, for all $a_1, a_2 \in A$, $b \in A \backslash \{\bot\}$;
- $(a|b) \equiv (\overline{a}|b)$, for all $a \in A$, $b \in A \backslash \{\bot\}$;
- $(a|b) \equiv (a \wedge b|b)$, for all $a \in A$, $b \in A \backslash \{\bot\}$;
- $(a|b) \wedge (b|c) \equiv (a|c)$, for all $a \in A$, $b, c \in A \backslash \{\bot\}$ such that $a \leqslant b \leqslant c$.

In the above we have adopted the notational convention of writing $a|b$ for the pair $(a, b) \in A \times A'$. Sometimes, to ease the reading, we will also write ab instead of $a \wedge b$ and we will use the abbreviation $a \to b$ for the material conditional $\overline{a} \vee b$.

Then, in symbols, $\mathcal{C}(\mathbf{A}) = \text{Free}(A \times A')/_{\equiv}$. If $\mathbf{A}$ is finite, then so is $\mathcal{C}(\mathbf{A})$ and we will henceforth assume to work with finite algebras only. In particular the algebras we will consider are atomic with atoms $\mathsf{at}(\mathbf{A}) = \{\alpha_1, \ldots, \alpha_n\}$. In [7] the atoms of $\mathcal{C}(\mathbf{A})$ are characterized in terms of the atoms of $\mathbf{A}$ as follows: an element $\omega \in \mathcal{C}(\mathbf{A})$ is an atom iff there exists a permutation $\sigma = (i_1, \ldots, i_n)$ on the set of indices $\{1, \ldots, n\}$ in S_n,[2] and hence a linear sequence of pairwise different atoms of $\mathbf{A}$

$$(\alpha_{i_1}, \ldots, \alpha_{i_n}),$$

such that

$$\begin{aligned}\omega_\sigma &= (\alpha_{i_1}|\top) \wedge (\alpha_{i_2}|\overline{\alpha_{i_1}}) \wedge \ldots \wedge (\alpha_{i_{n-1}}|\overline{\alpha_{i_1}} \wedge \ldots \wedge \overline{\alpha_{i_{n-2}}}) \wedge (\alpha_{i_n}|\overline{\alpha_{i_1}} \wedge \ldots \wedge \overline{\alpha_{i_{n-1}}}) \\ &= (\alpha_{i_1}|\top) \wedge (\alpha_{i_2}|\overline{\alpha_{i_1}}) \wedge \ldots \wedge (\alpha_{i_{n-1}}|\overline{\alpha_{i_1}} \wedge \ldots \wedge \overline{\alpha_{i_{n-2}}}),\end{aligned} \tag{1}$$

since $(\alpha_{i_n}|\overline{\alpha_{i_1}} \wedge \ldots \wedge \overline{\alpha_{i_{n-1}}}) = (\alpha_{i_n}|\alpha_{i_n})$ and $(\alpha_{i_n}|\alpha_{i_n})$ is the top element of $\mathcal{C}(\mathbf{A})$. Because of this we can identify atoms of $\mathcal{C}(\mathbf{A})$ by shorter sequences $(\alpha_{i_1} \ldots, \alpha_{i_{n-1}})$ of $n-1$ pairwise different atoms of $\mathbf{A}$. To stress the identification of atoms of $\mathcal{C}(\mathbf{A})$ with sequences of atoms of $\mathbf{A}$, we will write ω_σ for the atoms

[2] Adhering to a standard notation we will henceforth denote by S_n the set of permutations over a set of n elements.

of $\mathcal{C}(\mathbf{A})$. Moreover, for every atom $\omega_\sigma \in \mathsf{at}(\mathcal{C}(\mathbf{A}))$ and every $j = 1, \ldots, n-1$, we write $\omega_\sigma[j]$ to denote the jth coordinate α_{i_j} of the sequence $(\alpha_{i_1}, \ldots, \alpha_{i_{n-1}})$ that uniquely determines ω_σ. Clearly, $\omega_\sigma[j] \in \mathsf{at}(\mathbf{A})$.

Every positive probability $P : \mathbf{A} \to [0,1]$ can be extended to a positive probability μ_P on $\mathcal{C}(\mathbf{A})$ by stipulating that for every atom $\omega_\sigma \in \mathsf{at}(\mathcal{C}(\mathbf{A}))$ defined as above,

$$\mu_P(\omega_\sigma) = P(\alpha_{i_1}) \cdot \frac{P(\alpha_{i_2})}{P(\overline{\alpha_{i_1}})} \cdot \ldots \cdot \frac{P(\alpha_{i_{n-1}})}{P(\overline{\alpha_{i_1}} \wedge \ldots \wedge \overline{\alpha_{i_{n-2}}})}.$$

By [7, Lemma 6.8] the above map μ_P is a probability distribution on $\mathsf{at}(\mathcal{C}(\mathbf{A}))$ and its associated probability on $\mathcal{C}(\mathbf{A})$, that we will still denote by the same symbol μ_P, is called the *canonical extension* of P to $\mathcal{C}(\mathbf{A})$.

Moreover, by [7, Theorem 6.13], for every $a, b \in A$, with $b \neq \bot$, $\mu_P(a|b) = \frac{P(a \wedge b)}{P(b)}$ and hence canonical extensions μ_P provide a *finitary* solution to what has been called the *strong conditional event problem* (see [13]) within the setting of Boolean algebras of conditionals. This reads as follows:

(SCEP) For every Boolean algebra $\mathbf{A}$, find another Boolean algebra $\mathbf{A}^*$ and a map $\rhd$: $\mathbf{A} \times \mathbf{A} \to \mathbf{A}^*$ such that $\mathbf{A}$ is subalgebra of $\mathbf{A}^*$ and, for every positive probability P on $\mathbf{A}$, there exists an extension P^* of P on $\mathbf{A}^*$ such that, for all $a, b \in A$ with $b \neq \bot$, $P^*(b \rhd a) = \frac{P(a \wedge b)}{P(b)}$.

The above (SCEP) can be further strengthened by requiring that *every* positive probability on the bigger algebra $\mathbf{A}^*$ behaves as a conditional probability on $\mathbf{A} \times \mathbf{A}'$. Call this stronger principle (SCEP)$^+$.

Although Boolean algebras of conditionals, and canonical extensions, provide a solution for the (SCEP), the stronger (SCEP)$^+$ fails in general in this setting. Indeed, [7, Example 6.3] shows that there are positive probability functions $Q : \mathcal{C}(\mathbf{A}) \to [0,1]$ that fail to model the axioms of conditional probability (see for instance [16]) and therefore they do not satisfy $Q(a|b) = \frac{Q(a \wedge b|\top)}{Q(b|\top)}$. However, it is relevant to observe that, by [7, Corollary 6.14], $Q : \mathcal{C}(\mathbf{A}) \to [0,1]$ is a conditional probability iff Q satisfies the next *separability* property.

(Sep) for all $a \leqslant b \leqslant c$ with $b \neq \bot$, $Q(a|c) = Q((a|b) \wedge (b|c)) = Q(a|b) \cdot Q(b|c)$.

We will call Q *separable* when it satisfies **(Sep)**. In other words, separable probabilities on $\mathcal{C}(\mathbf{A})$ behave as conditional probabilities on $\mathbf{A} \times \mathbf{A}'$.

3 Iterated Conditionals in $\mathcal{C}(\mathcal{C}(\mathbf{A}))$

In this section, we first analyze the algebraic structure $\mathcal{C}(\mathcal{C}(\mathbf{A}))$ of iterated conditionals, describing in particular its atoms and the general semantic for iterated conditionals. Then, we consider different ways of deriving probabilities on $\mathcal{C}(\mathcal{C}(\mathbf{A}))$ by also comparing the construction of the double canonical extension of a positive probability defined on $\mathbf{A}$, and of the canonical extension of a positive probability on $\mathcal{C}(\mathbf{A})$.

Mimicking the construction of $\mathcal{C}(\mathbf{A})$ from $\mathbf{A}$, being $\mathcal{C}(\mathbf{A})$ itself a Boolean algebra, it is possible to build its Boolean algebra of conditionals $\mathcal{C}(\mathcal{C}(\mathbf{A}))$, that is the Boolean algebra of iterated conditionals of $\mathbf{A}$. In $\mathcal{C}(\mathcal{C}(\mathbf{A}))$ we allow *basic iterated conditionals*, i.e. objects of the form $(a|b)|(c|d)$ with $a|b, c|d \in \mathcal{C}(\mathbf{A})$, $c|d \neq \bot_{\mathfrak{C}}$, which can be then freely combined using the usual Boolean operations.

Definition 1. *Given a Boolean algebra* $\mathbf{A}$ *and its Boolean algebra of conditionals* $\mathcal{C}(\mathbf{A})$, *we define the Boolean algebra of iterated conditionals of* $\mathbf{A}$ *as*

$$\mathcal{C}(\mathcal{C}(\mathbf{A})) = \mathrm{Free}(\mathcal{C}(\mathbf{A}) \times \mathcal{C}(\mathbf{A})')/_{\equiv}$$

where the congruence relation $\equiv$ *is defined as in the case of* $\mathcal{C}(\mathbf{A})$ *except that in the equations the conditions* $a, b, c \in \mathbf{A}$, $b, c \neq \bot$ *are replaced by* $a|b, c|d, e|f \in \mathcal{C}(\mathbf{A})$, $c|d, e|f \neq \bot$, *respectively.*

The following properties hold in $\mathcal{C}(\mathcal{C}(\mathbf{A}))$ by construction and by recalling how the congruence $\equiv$ is defined in the previous section.

Fact 1. *The following identities hold in every* $\mathcal{C}(\mathcal{C}(\mathbf{A}))$.

(i) $(a|b)|(a|b) = \top|\top$;
(ii) $((a|b)|(c|d)) \wedge ((a'|b')|(c|d)) = [(a|b) \wedge (a'|b')]|(c|d)$;
(iii) $\overline{(a|b)|(c|d)} = \overline{(a|b)}|(c|d) = (\overline{a}|b)|(c|d)$;
(iv) $[(a|b) \wedge (c|d)]|(c|d) = (a|b)|(c|d)$;
(v) *if* $(a|b) \leqslant (c|d) \leqslant (e|f)$, *then* $((a|b)|(c|d)) \wedge ((c|d)|(e|f)) = (a|b)|(e|f)$.

Now we want to give a characterization of the atoms of $\mathcal{C}(\mathcal{C}(\mathbf{A}))$ in terms of the atoms in $\mathcal{C}(\mathbf{A})$. A basic observation is that if $\mathbf{A}$ is finite, then $\mathcal{C}(\mathbf{A})$ is also finite, and thus $\mathcal{C}(\mathcal{C}(\mathbf{A}))$ is finite as well, and hence all of them are atomic.

We recall that, if $|\mathsf{at}(\mathbf{A})| = n$, the atoms of $\mathcal{C}(\mathbf{A})$ are determined by permutations in S_n and hence by sequences of length $n-1$ of pairwise different atoms of $\mathbf{A}$; as a consequence $|\mathsf{at}(\mathcal{C}(\mathbf{A}))| = n!$.

We also recall that the lattice order relation $\leqslant$ in $\mathcal{C}(\mathbf{A})$ is defined as

$$t \leqslant s \text{ iff } t \wedge s = t \text{ iff } t \vee s = s, \text{ for every } s, t \in \mathcal{C}(\mathbf{A}). \tag{2}$$

Remark 1. In [7, Proposition 4.7] it is shown that an atom $\omega_\sigma = (\alpha_{\sigma(1)}|\top) \wedge (\alpha_{\sigma(2)}|\overline{\alpha_{\sigma(1)}}) \wedge \cdots \wedge (\alpha_{\sigma(n-1)}|\overline{\alpha_{\sigma(1)}} \cdots \overline{\alpha_{\sigma(n-2)}})$ is below (i.e. it is a *model* for) a conditional $(a|b)$ w.r.t. the lattice order $\leqslant$ in $\mathcal{C}(\mathbf{A})$, i.e. $\omega_\sigma \leqslant (a|b)$ (also written as $\omega_\sigma \models (a|b)$), if and only if the following condition is satisfied:

$$\text{either “}\alpha_{\sigma(1)} \leqslant ab\text{”, or “}\alpha_{\sigma(1)} \leqslant \bar{b} \text{ and } \alpha_{\sigma(2)} \leqslant ab\text{”, or } \ldots$$
$$\text{or “}\alpha_{\sigma(1)} \leqslant \bar{b} \text{ and } \ldots \text{ and } \alpha_{\sigma(n-2)} \leqslant \bar{b} \text{ and } \alpha_{\sigma(n-1)} \leqslant ab\text{”.}$$

□

By repeating the same procedure as above, it follows that the atoms of $\mathcal{C}(\mathcal{C}(\mathbf{A}))$ will be determined by sequences of length $|\mathsf{at}(\mathcal{C}(\mathbf{A}))| - 1 = n! - 1$ of pairwise different atoms of $\mathcal{C}(\mathbf{A})$, that is, by sequences of the form $(\omega_{\sigma_1}, \omega_{\sigma_2}, \ldots, \omega_{\sigma_{n!-1}})$, where $\sigma_j \in S_n$ is a permutation and $\omega_{\sigma_j} \in \mathsf{at}(\mathcal{C}(\mathbf{A}))$ for all $j = 1, \ldots, n! - 1$.

Therefore, $|\mathsf{at}(\mathcal{C}(\mathcal{C}(\mathbf{A})))| = (n!)!$. In terms of the atoms of $\mathbf{A}$, an atom of $\mathcal{C}(\mathcal{C}(\mathbf{A}))$ can be represented by a sequence of sequences of atoms of $\mathbf{A}$, and it can be visualized as the matrix

$$M = \left(\omega_{\sigma_1}, \omega_{\sigma_2}, \ldots, \omega_{\sigma_{n!-1}}\right) = \begin{pmatrix} \omega_{\sigma_1}[1] & \omega_{\sigma_2}[1] & \ldots & \omega_{\sigma_{n!-1}}[1] \\ \omega_{\sigma_1}[2] & \omega_{\sigma_2}[2] & \ldots & \omega_{\sigma_{n!-1}}[2] \\ \vdots & \vdots & \ldots & \vdots \\ \omega_{\sigma_1}[n-1] & \omega_{\sigma_2}[n-1] & \ldots & \omega_{\sigma_{n!-1}}[n-1] \end{pmatrix}$$

Given a matrix M as the above, conforming to the previous notation, the corresponding atom ω_M of $\mathcal{C}(\mathcal{C}(\mathbf{A}))$ is the following conjunction of iterated conditionals:

$$\omega_M = (\omega_{\sigma_1}|\top) \wedge (\omega_{\sigma_2}|\overline{\omega_{\sigma_1}}) \wedge \cdots \wedge (\omega_{\sigma_{n!-1}}|\overline{\omega_{\sigma_1}} \cdots \overline{\omega_{\sigma_{n!-2}}}).$$

The next example hints on what these formal expressions look like in the iterated case of $\mathcal{C}(\mathcal{C}(\mathbf{A}))$.

Example 1. Let $\mathbf{A}$ be an algebra with 3 atoms $\alpha_1, \alpha_2, \alpha_3$. Then, the conditional algebra $\mathcal{C}(\mathbf{A})$ has $3! = 6$ atoms:

$$\begin{aligned} \omega_1 &= (\alpha_1|\top) \wedge (\alpha_2|\overline{\alpha}_1),\ \omega_2 = (\alpha_1|\top) \wedge (\alpha_3|\overline{\alpha}_1),\ \omega_3 = (\alpha_2|\top) \wedge (\alpha_1|\overline{\alpha}_2), \\ \omega_4 &= (\alpha_2|\top) \wedge (\alpha_3|\overline{\alpha}_2),\ \omega_5 = (\alpha_3|\top) \wedge (\alpha_1|\overline{\alpha}_3),\ \omega_6 = (\alpha_3|\top) \wedge (\alpha_2|\overline{\alpha}_3). \end{aligned}$$

Conforming to the notation introduced above, the atoms of $\mathcal{C}(\mathbf{A})$ are identified both with sequences $(\alpha_{i_1}, \alpha_{i_2}, \alpha_{i_3})$ of length 3 and with sequences $(\alpha_{i_1}, \alpha_{i_2})$ of length 2 (since the missing atom is univocally determined). For the sake of clarity, in this example we will consider sequences of length 3. For instance ω_1 will be identified with $(\alpha_1, \alpha_2, \alpha_3)$. Analogously, the conditional algebra $\mathcal{C}(\mathcal{C}(\mathbf{A}))$ has $6!$ atoms whose associated sequences have length 6 (instead of 5) and they are hence of the form

$$M = (\omega_{\sigma_1}, \omega_{\sigma_2}, \omega_{\sigma_3}, \omega_{\sigma_4}, \omega_{\sigma_5}, \omega_{\sigma_6})$$

where, for all $i = 1, \ldots, 6$, $\omega_{\sigma_i} \in \mathsf{at}(\mathcal{C}(\mathbf{A}))$.

For example, let us consider the matrix

$$M = \begin{pmatrix} \alpha_1 & \alpha_1 & \alpha_2 & \alpha_2 & \alpha_3 & \alpha_3 \\ \alpha_2 & \alpha_3 & \alpha_1 & \alpha_3 & \alpha_1 & \alpha_2 \\ \alpha_3 & \alpha_2 & \alpha_3 & \alpha_1 & \alpha_2 & \alpha_1 \end{pmatrix}$$

where the first column of M corresponds to ω_1, the second to ω_2 and so forth. Its corresponding atom in $\mathcal{C}(\mathcal{C}(\mathbf{A}))$ can be written as:

$$\begin{aligned} \omega_M &= (\omega_1|(\top|\top)) \wedge (\omega_2|\overline{\omega}_1) \wedge (\omega_3|\overline{\omega}_1 \wedge \overline{\omega}_2) \wedge (\omega_4|\overline{\omega}_1 \wedge \overline{\omega}_2 \wedge \overline{\omega}_3) \wedge \\ &\quad \wedge (\omega_5|\overline{\omega}_1 \wedge \overline{\omega}_2 \wedge \overline{\omega}_3 \wedge \overline{\omega}_4) = \\ &= (\omega_1|(\top|\top)) \wedge (\omega_2|\omega_2 \vee \omega_3 \vee \omega_4 \vee \omega_5 \vee \omega_6) \wedge \\ &\quad \wedge (\omega_3|\omega_3 \vee \omega_4 \vee \omega_5 \vee \omega_6) \wedge (\omega_4|\omega_4 \vee \omega_5 \vee \omega_6) \wedge (\omega_5|\omega_5 \vee \omega_6). \end{aligned}$$

To get more hints on the previous expression, let us observe that

$$\begin{aligned}\omega_5 \vee \omega_6 &= ((\alpha_3|\top) \wedge (\alpha_1|\overline{\alpha}_3)) \vee ((\alpha_3|\top) \wedge (\alpha_2|\overline{\alpha}_3)) = (\alpha_3|\top) \wedge (\alpha_1 \vee \alpha_2|\overline{\alpha}_3) = \\ &= (\alpha_3|\top) \wedge (\alpha_1 \vee \alpha_2|\alpha_1 \vee \alpha_2) = (\alpha_3|\top)\end{aligned}$$

and hence $(\omega_5|\omega_5 \vee \omega_6) = ((\alpha_3|\top) \wedge (\alpha_1|\overline{\alpha}_3))|(\alpha_3|\top) = (\alpha_1|\overline{\alpha}_3)|(\alpha_3|\top)$.

Moreover, recalling that for $a, b, c \in \mathbf{A}$

- if $a \leqslant b \leqslant d$ then $(a|b) \geqslant (a|d)$, and hence $\alpha_3 \leqslant \overline{\alpha}_2 = \alpha_1 \vee \alpha_3 \leqslant \top$ and it implies that $(\alpha_3|\overline{\alpha}_2) \geqslant (\alpha_3|\top)$,
- $(a \wedge b|\top) \leqslant (a|b) \leqslant (b \to a|\top)$ and hence $(\alpha_3|\overline{\alpha}_2) \leqslant (\overline{\alpha}_2 \to \alpha_3|\top)$

we have that

$$\begin{aligned}\omega_4 \vee \omega_5 \vee \omega_6 &= ((\alpha_2|\top) \wedge (\alpha_3|\overline{\alpha}_2)) \vee (\alpha_3|\top) \\ &= ((\alpha_2|\top) \vee (\alpha_3|\top)) \wedge ((\alpha_3|\overline{\alpha}_2) \vee (\alpha_3|\top)) \\ &= (\alpha_2 \vee \alpha_3|\top) \wedge (\alpha_3|\overline{\alpha}_2) \\ &= (\overline{\alpha}_2 \to \alpha_3|\top) \wedge (\alpha_3|\overline{\alpha}_2) = (\alpha_3|\overline{\alpha}_2).\end{aligned}$$

Then, $(\omega_4|\omega_4 \vee \omega_5 \vee \omega_6) = ((\alpha_2|\top) \wedge (\alpha_3|\overline{\alpha}_2))|(\alpha_3|\overline{\alpha}_2) = (\alpha_2|\top)|(\alpha_3|\overline{\alpha}_2)$.

Let us now consider

$$\omega_3 \vee \omega_4 \vee \omega_5 \vee \omega_6 = ((\alpha_2|\top) \wedge (\alpha_1|\overline{\alpha}_2)) \vee (\alpha_3|\overline{\alpha}_2) = (\alpha_2|\top) \vee (\alpha_3|\overline{\alpha}_2).$$

Therefore, $(\omega_3|\omega_3 \vee \omega_4 \vee \omega_5 \vee \omega_6) = ((\alpha_2|\top) \wedge (\alpha_1|\overline{\alpha}_2))|((\alpha_2|\top) \vee (\alpha_3|\overline{\alpha}_2))$.

We can also consider

$$\begin{aligned}\omega_2|\overline{\omega}_1 &= ((\alpha_1|\top) \wedge (\alpha_3|\overline{\alpha}_1))|((\alpha_2 \vee \alpha_3|\top) \vee (\alpha_1 \vee \alpha_3|\overline{\alpha}_1)) \\ &= ((\alpha_1|\top) \wedge (\alpha_3|\overline{\alpha}_1))|((\alpha_2 \vee \alpha_3|\top) \vee (\alpha_3|\overline{\alpha}_1)) \\ &= ((\alpha_1|\top) \wedge (\alpha_3|\overline{\alpha}_1))|((\alpha_2|\top) \vee (\alpha_3|\overline{\alpha}_1)).\end{aligned}$$

Finally, we come up with the following expression of the atom ω_M:

$$\begin{aligned}\omega_M = \; &((\alpha_1|\top) \wedge (\alpha_2|\overline{\alpha}_1))|(\top|\top) \quad \wedge \\ &((\alpha_1|\top) \wedge (\alpha_3|\overline{\alpha}_1))|((\alpha_2|\top) \vee (\alpha_3|\overline{\alpha}_1)) \quad \wedge \\ &((\alpha_2|\top) \wedge (\alpha_1|\overline{\alpha}_2))|((\alpha_2|\top) \vee (\alpha_3|\overline{\alpha}_2)) \quad \wedge \\ &(\alpha_2|\top)|(\alpha_3|\overline{\alpha}_2) \; \wedge (\alpha_1|\overline{\alpha}_3)|(\alpha_3|\top).\end{aligned}$$

□

Remark 2. Given an iterated conditional $(a|b)|(c|d) \in \mathcal{C}(\mathcal{C}(\mathbf{A}))$ and a matrix $M = (\omega_1, \ldots, \omega_n)$, we say the atom ω_M *models* $(a|b)|(c|d)$, written $\omega_M \models (a|b)|(c|d)$, if and only if $\omega_M \leqslant (a|b)|(c|d)$ and hence, recalling Remark 1, if and only if, $\exists j$ such that $M[j] = \omega_j \models (a|b) \wedge (c|d)$ and, $\forall k < j, M[k] = \omega_k \not\models (c|d)$.

Now, let us turn our attention on canonical extensions on $\mathcal{C}(\mathbf{A})$ and on $\mathcal{C}(\mathcal{C}(\mathbf{A}))$. Reproducing the results about the canonical extension of positive probabilities on $\mathbf{A}$ to probabilities on $\mathcal{C}(\mathbf{A})$, given a positive probability $Q : \mathcal{C}(\mathbf{A}) \to$

$[0,1]$ we can always define its canonical extension $\mu_Q : \mathcal{C}(\mathcal{C}(\mathbf{A})) \to [0,1]$ in such a way that, for every iterated conditional $(a|b)|(c|d) \in \mathcal{C}(\mathcal{C}(\mathbf{A}))$, we have

$$\mu_Q((a|b)|(c|d)) = \frac{Q((a|b) \wedge (c|d))}{Q(c|d)}.$$

In particular, if Q is the canonical extension μ_P of a positive probability P on $\mathbf{A}$, then μ_P on $\mathcal{C}(\mathbf{A})$ is again positive, and thus we can in turn canonically extend it to a probability μ_{μ_P} on $\mathcal{C}(\mathcal{C}(\mathbf{A}))$. In this case, [9, Theorem 8] (see also [8]) tells us that the expression for $\mu_P((a|b) \wedge (c|d))$ is

$$\mu_P((a|b) \wedge (c|d)) = P(abcd|b \vee d) + P(a|b)P(\bar{b}cd|b \vee d) + P(c|d)P(\bar{d}ab|b \vee d),$$

that coincides with the formula obtained by McGee [18] and Kaufmann [17]. Then, we get the following expression for the probability of an iterated conditional:

$$\mu_{\mu_P}((a|b)|(c|d)) = \frac{\mu_P((a|b)\wedge(c|d))}{\mu_P(c|d)} = \frac{P(abcd|b\vee d)+P(a|b)P(\bar{b}cd|b\vee d)+P(c|d)P(\bar{d}ab|b\vee d)}{P(c|d)}.$$

4 The Weak Import-Export Principle and the Separability Property

A well-known and widely discussed principle for conditional logics is that of *import-export* (also known under the name of *exportation*). This principle needs a nested occurrence of the conditional operator to be written and hence, while it cannot be expressed in a conditional algebra like $\mathcal{C}(\mathbf{A})$, it can be formalized in $\mathcal{C}(\mathcal{C}(\mathbf{A}))$. In the language of $\mathcal{C}(\mathcal{C}(\mathbf{A}))$ it hence reads as the following equation: for all $a, b, c \in A$ such that $b, c \neq \bot$,

(IE) $(a|c)|(b|\top) = (a|c \wedge b)|(\top|\top)$.

In what follows we will be interested in the next equation that is in fact a weak version of **(IE)** obtained by taking $c = \top$ in **(IE)**:

(wIE) $(a|\top)|(b|\top) = (a|b)|(\top|\top)$.

Besides being a weakening of the import-export principle, the identity **(wIE)** states a condition that appears to be reasonable to ask for iterated conditionals. Indeed, keeping the discussion at an informal level, the identification of every plain event $a \in A$ with its conditional representation $(a|\top) \in \mathcal{C}(\mathbf{A})$ ensures the two sides of **(wIE)** read the same. More precisely, omitting the trivial reading of those antecedents "given that the sure event $\top$ holds", **(wIE)** reads tautologically: "a given b equals a given b".

Although reasonable, **(wIE)** does not always hold in $\mathcal{C}(\mathcal{C}(\mathbf{A}))$ as the next result shows.

Proposition 1. *For every algebra* $\mathbf{A}$ *with more than two atoms, there are* $a, b \in A$ *with* $b \neq \bot$ *for which* **(wIE)** *does not hold in* $\mathcal{C}(\mathcal{C}(\mathbf{A}))$.

Proof. Let us consider the case of an algebra $\mathbf{A}$ with three atoms $\{\alpha, \beta, \gamma\}$. We take $a = \alpha$ and $b = \alpha \vee \beta$. Consider a matrix like the following

$$M_1 = \begin{pmatrix} \gamma \; \beta \ldots \\ \alpha \; \gamma \ldots \end{pmatrix}.$$

By Remark 2, $\omega_{M_1} \models (a|b)|(\top|\top)$ but $\omega_{M_1} \not\models (a|\top)|(b|\top)$. Similarly, a matrix like

$$M_2 = \begin{pmatrix} \gamma \; \alpha \ldots \\ \beta \; \gamma \ldots \end{pmatrix}$$

is such that $\omega_{M_2} \not\models (a|b)|(\top|\top)$ but $\omega_{M_2} \models (a|\top)|(b|\top)$.

Therefore, $(a|b)|(\top|\top)$ and $(a|\top)|(b|\top)$ are different elements of $\mathcal{C}(\mathcal{C}(\mathbf{A}))$, and hence **(wIE)** does not hold in this $\mathcal{C}(\mathcal{C}(\mathbf{A}))$. □

Although the weak import export principle **(wIE)** does not in general hold in the algebras $\mathcal{C}(\mathcal{C}(\mathbf{A}))$, however, it is interesting to observe that, if P is a positive probability on $\mathbf{A}$, then the double canonical extension $\mu_{\mu_P} : \mathcal{C}(\mathcal{C}(\mathbf{A})) \to [0, 1]$ is a *probabilistic model* for **(wIE)**, that is to say, for any $a \in A$ and $b \in A'$,

$$\mu_{\mu_P}((a|\top)|(b|\top)) = \mu_{\mu_P}((a|b)|(\top|\top)).$$

Still, μ_{μ_P} does not provide a model for the import-export principle **(IE)**.

Proposition 2. *For every positive probability function P on $\mathbf{A}$, μ_{μ_P} is a probabilistic model of* **(wIE)**, *but, in general, it is not a probabilistic model of* **(IE)**.

Proof. Let us consider the quantities $\mu_P((a|c) \wedge (b|\top))$ and $\mu_{\mu_P}((a|c \wedge b)|(\top|\top))$. By [17] and [21, §8], and recalling the last equation of the above Sect. 3,

$$\mu_{\mu_P}((a|c)|(b|\top)) = \frac{P(abc)+P(a|c)\cdot P(b\bar{c})}{P(b)}. \tag{3}$$

We distinguish two cases: (i) $bc = \bot$; (ii) $bc \neq \bot$.

Case (i). By (3), it follows that $\mu_{\mu_P}((a|c)|(b|\top)) = P(a|c)$, while $\mu_{\mu_P}((a|c \wedge b)|(\top|\top))$ is undefined, because $(a|c \wedge b) = (a|\bot) \notin \mathcal{C}(\mathbf{A})$.

Case (ii). By (3), it follows that

$$\begin{aligned} \mu_{\mu_P}((a|c)|(b|\top)) &= \frac{P(a|bc)P(c|b)P(b)+P(a|c)\cdot P(\bar{c}|b)P(b)}{P(b)} \\ &= P(a|c \wedge b)P(c|b) + P(a|c)P(\bar{c}|b) \end{aligned} \tag{4}$$

while

$$\mu_{\mu_P}((a|c \wedge b)|(\top|\top)) = P(a|c \wedge b).$$

Therefore, μ_{μ_P} does not model **(IE)** in general. However, let us take $c = \top$. As $P(\top|b) = 1$, $P(\bot|b) = 0$ and $P(a|\top \wedge b) = P(a|b)$, it holds that

$$\mu_{\mu_P}((a|\top)|(b|\top)) = P(a|b) = \mu_{\mu_P}((a|b)|(\top|\top)) = P(a|b)$$

and hence **(wIE)** is satisfied by μ_{μ_P}. □

Example 2. In this example we show what kind of consequences can be obtained when a positive probability P on $\mathbf{A}$ is such that μ_{μ_P} is a probabilistic model for **(IE)**. By using the fact in $\mathcal{C}(\mathcal{C}(\mathbf{A}))$ we have $\mu_P(t \wedge s) = \mu_{\mu_P}(t|s)\mu_P(s)$ for every $t, s \in \mathcal{C}(\mathbf{A})$, the following equalities always hold for any two events $a \in A$ and $c \in A'$:

$$\begin{aligned} P(a|c) &= \mu_P(a|c) = \mu_P((a|c) \wedge (a|\top)) + \mu_P((a|c) \wedge (\bar{a}|\top)) \\ &= \mu_{\mu_P}((a|c)|(a|\top))\mu_P(a|\top) + \mu_{\mu_P}((a|c)|(\bar{a}|\top))\mu_P(\bar{a}|\top) \\ &= \mu_{\mu_P}((a|c)|(a|\top))P(a) + \mu_{\mu_P}((a|c)|(\bar{a}|\top))P(\bar{a}). \end{aligned}$$

Now, if μ_{μ_P} is a probabilistic model for **(IE)** then it follows that $\mu_{\mu_P}((a|c)|(a|\top)) = \mu_{\mu_P}((a|ac)|(\top|\top)) = P(a|ac) = 1$ and $\mu_{\mu_P}((a|c)|(\bar{a}|\top)) = \mu_{\mu_P}((a|\bar{a}c)|(\top|\top)) = P(a|\bar{a}c) = 0$, and thus it results that

$$P(a|c) = 1 \cdot P(a) + 0 \cdot P(\bar{a}) = P(a),$$

which is in general not satisfactory. This derivation is actually another proof of one of the well-known Lewis' triviality results. However, as in general μ_{μ_P} is not a probabilistic model for (**IE**), Lewis' triviality result can be avoided by μ_{μ_P} in $\mathcal{C}(\mathcal{C}(\mathbf{A}))$.

Remark 3. We observe that in the particular cases in which $b \leqslant c$ or $c \leqslant b$, we have that μ_P satisfies **(IE)** ([11, Proposition 1]). If $b \leqslant c$ it holds that $\bar{c}b = \bot$ so that $P(\bar{c}|b) = 0$. Moreover, $a|(c \wedge b) = a|b$ and hence $P(a|c \wedge b) = P(a|b)$. Then, by (4), it holds that

$$\mu_{\mu_P}((a|c)|(b|\top)) = P(a|b) \cdot 1 + P(a|c) \cdot 0 = P(a|b) = \mu_{\mu_P}((a|c \wedge b)|(\top|\top)).$$

Likewise, if $c \leqslant b$, $P(a|c \wedge b) = P(a|c)$ and hence

$$\mu_{\mu_P}((a|c)|(b|\top)) = P(a|c)[P(c|b) + P(\bar{c}|b)] = P(a|c) = \mu_{\mu_P}((a|c \wedge b)|(\top|\top)).$$

Now we turn our attention on the satisfiability of **(wIE)** by the canonical extensions μ_Q on $\mathcal{C}(\mathcal{C}(\mathbf{A}))$ of a positive $Q : \mathcal{C}(\mathbf{A}) \to [0,1]$.

As we recalled in Sect. 2, the separability property for a probability $Q : \mathcal{C}(\mathbf{A}) \to [0,1]$ characterizes those functions that behave as conditional probabilities on $\mathbf{A}$. While separability seems to be non-characterizable in the language of $\mathcal{C}(\mathbf{A})$, the next result shows that, interestingly, it can be captured by requiring the canonical extension μ_Q of Q to model the equation **(wIE)** in $\mathcal{C}(\mathcal{C}(\mathbf{A}))$.

Theorem 1. *Let* $\mathbf{A}$ *be any finite Boolean algebra and let* $Q : \mathcal{C}(\mathbf{A}) \to [0,1]$ *be a positive probability function. Then,* Q *is separable iff* $\mu_Q((a|b)|(\top|\top)) = \mu_Q((a|\top)|(b|\top))$ *for every* $a \in \mathbf{A}$ *and* $b \in \mathbf{A}\backslash\{\bot\}$.

Proof. Let us start assuming that Q is separable. In such a case, we know that $Q(a \wedge b|\top) = Q((a|b) \wedge (b|\top)) = Q(a|b)Q(b|\top)$. Then, it follows that

$$\mu_Q((a|b)|(\top|\top)) = Q(a|b) = \frac{Q(a \wedge b|\top)}{Q(b|\top)} = \frac{Q((a|\top) \wedge (b|\top))}{Q(b|\top)} = \mu_Q((a|\top)|(b|\top)).$$

Conversely, let us suppose that $\mu_Q((a|\top)|(b|\top)) = \mu_Q((a|b)|(\top|\top))$ for every $a \in \mathbf{A}$ and $b \in \mathbf{A}\backslash\{\bot\}$. Now, let $P_Q : \mathbf{A} \to [0,1]$ be the probability on $\mathbf{A}$ defined by restricting Q to $\mathbf{A}$ (considered as a subalgebra of $\mathcal{C}(\mathbf{A})$), and consider $\mu_{P_Q} : \mathcal{C}(\mathbf{A}) \to [0,1]$, the canonical extension of P_Q to $\mathcal{C}(\mathbf{A})$. Then, for $a, b \in \mathbf{A}$,

$$\mu_{P_Q}(a|b) = \frac{P_Q(a \wedge b)}{P_Q(b)} = \frac{Q(a \wedge b|\top)}{Q(b|\top)} = \frac{Q((a|\top) \wedge (b|\top))}{Q(b|\top)}$$
$$= \mu_Q((a|\top)|(b|\top)) = \mu_Q((a|b)|(\top|\top)) = Q(a|b).$$

Therefore, Q and μ_{P_Q} coincide on the basic conditionals of the form $(x|y)$. Moreover, we know that μ_{P_Q} is a canonical extension and hence it is separable, i.e.

$$\mu_{P_Q}(a|c) = \mu_{P_Q}((a|b) \wedge (b|c)) = \mu_{P_Q}(a|b)\mu_{P_Q}(b|c)$$

for $a \leqslant b \leqslant c$, with $a, b, c \in \mathbf{A}$. But we found out that on basic conditionals, $\mu_{P_Q}(a|c) = Q(a|c)$, $\mu_{P_Q}(a|b) = Q(a|b)$, and $\mu_{P_Q}(b|c) = Q(b|c)$, and hence

$$Q(a|c) = Q(a|b)Q(b|c), \text{ for } a, b, c \in \mathbf{A} \text{ s.t. } a \leqslant b \leqslant c,$$

that is, Q is separable. □

5 On the McGee Formula and the Conjunction Rationality Principle

In this final section we consider probabilistic properties related to the conjunction of basic conditionals. Any canonical extension μ_P of a (positive) probability P on $\mathbf{A}$ satisfies the McGee formula for conjunction of basic conditionals, but this is not the case for any probability Q on $\mathcal{C}(\mathbf{A})$.

Definition 2. *A (positive) probability $Q : \mathcal{C}(\mathbf{A}) \to [0,1]$ satisfies the* McGee decomposition *formula (McD) when, for every $(a|b), (c|d) \in \mathcal{C}(\mathbf{A})$,*

$$Q((a|b) \wedge (c|d)) = Q(abcd|b \vee d) + Q(a|b)Q(\bar{b}cd|b \vee d) + Q(c|d)Q(\bar{d}ab|b \vee d).$$

By the very definition of the canonical extension μ_Q on $C(\mathcal{C}(\mathbf{A}))$ the following properties hold.

Lemma 1. *For any probability $Q : \mathcal{C}(\mathbf{A}) \to [0,1]$ the following identities hold:*

(i) $\mu_Q([(a|b)|(\top|\top)] \wedge [(c|d)|(\top|\top)]) = \mu_Q((a|b) \wedge (c|d)|(\top|\top)) = Q((a|b) \wedge (c|d))$.
(ii) If Q is separable, then $\mu_Q([(a|\top)|(b|\top)] \wedge [(c|\top)|(d|\top)]) = Q(abcd|b \vee d) + Q(a|b)Q(\bar{b}cd|b \vee d) + Q(c|d)Q(\bar{d}ab|b \vee d)$.

Proof. (i) Since $Q(x) = \mu_Q(x|(\top|\top))$ for any $x \in C(\mathcal{C}(\mathbf{A}))$, we simply have that $\mu_Q([(a|b)|(\top|\top)] \wedge [(c|d)|(\top|\top)]) = \mu_Q((a|b) \wedge (c|d)|(\top|\top)) = Q((a|b) \wedge (c|d))$, where the first equality follows from Fact 1 (ii).

(ii) Since μ_Q is a canonical extension, it satisfies McGee decomposition formula for a conjunction of basic (iterated) conditionals, and we have:

$$\begin{aligned}&\mu_Q([(a|\top)|(b|\top)] \wedge [(c|\top)|(d|\top)]) = \\ &= \mu_Q((abcd|\top)|(b \vee d|\top)) + \mu_Q((a|\top)|(b|\top)) \cdot \mu_Q((\bar{b}cd|\top)|(b \vee d|\top)) + \\ &\quad + \mu_Q((c|\top)|(d|\top)) \cdot \mu_Q((\bar{d}ab|\top)|(b \vee d|\top)).\end{aligned}$$

Now, if Q is separable, by Theorem 1, $\mu_Q((a|\top)|(b|\top)) = \mu_Q((a|b)|(\top|\top)) = Q(a|b)$. Therefore,

$$\begin{aligned}&\mu_Q([(a|\top)|(b|\top)] \wedge [(c|\top)|(d|\top)]) = \\ &= Q(abcd|b \vee d) + Q(a|b)Q(\bar{b}cd|b \vee d) + Q(c|d)Q(\bar{d}ab|b \vee d).\end{aligned}$$

□

Let us consider now the following principle at the level of iterated conditionals.

Definition 3. *A probability $Q : \mathcal{C}(\mathbf{A}) \to [0,1]$ satisfies the* conjunction rationality principle *(CRP) when, for all $a, b \in A$ and $c, d \in A'$:*

$$(CRP) \quad \mu_Q([(a|b)|(\top|\top)] \wedge [(c|d)|(\top|\top)]) = \mu_Q([(a|\top)|(b|\top)] \wedge [(c|\top)|(d|\top)])$$

Note that if Q satisfies (CRP) necessarily it must also be separable, since taking $c = d = \top$ above we get $\mu_Q((a|b)|(\top|\top)) = \mu_Q((a|\top)|(b|\top))$, and by Theorem 1, Q must be separable.

We can finally prove that (CRP) characterises in $\mathcal{C}(\mathcal{C}(\mathbf{A}))$ the satisfaction of McGee decomposition formula in $\mathcal{C}(\mathbf{A})$.

Theorem 2. *A probability $Q : \mathcal{C}(\mathbf{A}) \to [0,1]$ satisfies the* conjunction rationality principle *(CRP) iff Q satisfies the McGee decomposition (McD).*

Proof. If Q satisfies (CRP), Q is separable, and then by Lemma 1 above, $Q((a|b) \wedge (c|d)) = \mu_Q([(a|\top)|(b|\top)] \wedge [(c|\top)|(d|\top)]) = Q(abcd|b \vee d) + Q(a|b)Q(\bar{b}cd|b \vee d) + Q(c|d)Q(\bar{d}ab|b \vee d)$, hence Q satisfies (McD).

Conversely, since μ_Q is a canonical extension (and hence it satisfies McGee formula), we have:

$$\begin{aligned}&\mu_Q((a|\top)|(b|\top)) = \mu_Q([(a|\top)|(b|\top)] \wedge [(\top|\top)|(\top|\top)]) \\ &= \mu_Q((ab|\top)|(\top|\top)) + \mu_Q((a|\top)|(b|\top)) \cdot \mu_Q((\bar{b}|\top)|(\top|\top)) + 0 \\ &= Q(ab|\top) + \mu_Q((a|\top)|(b|\top)) \cdot Q((\bar{b}|\top))\end{aligned}$$

that is, $\mu_Q((a|\top)|(b|\top)) = Q(ab|\top)/Q(b|\top)$. On the other hand, if Q satisfies (McD), we have $Q(a|b) = Q((a|b) \wedge (\top|\top)) = Q(ab|\top) + Q(a|b) \cdot Q(\bar{b}|\top)$, hence $Q(a|b) = Q(ab|\top)/Q(b|\top)$, since we are assuming Q to be positive.

Therefore, it follows that $Q(a|b) = \mu_Q((a|\top)|(b|\top))$ and thus Q is separable because of (i) of Lemma 1. Then, we can finally conclude, by (ii) of the same lemma above, that:

$$\begin{aligned}&\mu_Q([(a|b)|(\top|\top)] \wedge [(c|d)|(\top|\top)]) = Q((a|b) \wedge (c|d)) \\ &= Q(abcd|b \vee d) + Q(a|b)Q(\bar{b}cd|b \vee d) + Q(c|d)Q(\bar{d}ab|b \vee d) \\ &= \mu_Q([(a|\top)|(b|\top)] \wedge [(c|\top)|(d|\top)]),\end{aligned}$$

that is, (CRP) is satisfied. □

6 Concluding Remarks

In this paper we have carried out an algebraic and probabilistic study of iterated conditionals, i.e. objects of the form $(a|b)|(c|d)$, by introducing algebras of iterated conditionals $\mathcal{C}(\mathcal{C}(\mathbf{A}))$. We have built such an algebra from the algebra of non-iterated conditionals $\mathcal{C}(\mathbf{A})$, by repeating the construction of the Boolean algebra of conditionals $\mathcal{C}(\mathbf{A})$ from the algebra of events $\mathbf{A}$, and we have analyzed it from an algebraic point of view, studying its atomic structure, and also from a probabilistic perspective. Indeed, we have shown that some properties of probabilities Q on the algebra of conditionals $\mathcal{C}(\mathbf{A})$ can be characterized in terms of satisfiability of specific principles of its canonical extensions μ_Q to the algebra of iterated conditionals. For instance, we have proved that a weaker version of the import-export principle, $(a|b)|(\top|\top) = (a|\top)|(b|\top)$, is satisfied by μ_Q if and only if Q is a separable probability.

As for future work we plan to further extend our analysis when, instead of starting from a positive probabilities on $\mathbf{A}$ and on $\mathcal{C}(\mathbf{A})$, we directly start from a conditional probability (in the axiomatic sense) on $\mathbf{A} \times \mathbf{A}'$ and on $\mathcal{C}(\mathbf{A}) \times \mathcal{C}(\mathbf{A})'$. Also we plan to explore the relationship, within $\mathcal{C}(\mathcal{C}(\mathbf{A}))$, between the general import-export principle and the p-validity of inference rules in nonmonotonic reasoning, as done in [10] within the framework of conditional random quantities.

Acknowledgments. The authors are grateful to the anonymous referees for their careful reading and valuable suggestions to clarify several parts of the present paper.

L. Castronovo and G. Sanfilippo acknowledge support by INdAM-GNAMPA research group. L. Castronovo acknowledges financial support under the National Recovery and Resilience Plan (NRRP), Mission 4, Component 2, Investment 1.1, Call for tender No. 1409 published on 14.9.2022 by the Italian Ministry of University and Research (MUR), funded by the European Union – NextGenerationEU – Project Title Quantum Models for Logic, Computation and Natural Processes (QM4NP) – CUP B53D23030160001 – Grant Assignment Decree No. 1371 adopted on 2023-09-01 by the Italian Ministry of University and Research (MUR).

Flaminio and Godo acknowledge the Spanish projects SHORE (PID2022-141529NB-C21) and LINEXSYS (PID2022-139835NB-C21) respectively, both funded by MCIU/AEI/10.13039/501100011033. Flaminio and Godo also acknowledge partial support by the H2020-MSCA-RISE-2020 project MOSAIC (Grant Agreement number 101007627).

G. Sanfilippo is also supported by the FFR2025 project of University of Palermo and by the MIUR-PRIN project 2022AP3B3B funded by Next Generation EU.

Disclosure of Interests. The authors have no competing interests to declare that are relevant to the content of this article.

References

1. de Finetti, B.: La Logique de la Probabilité. In Actes du Congrès International de Philosophie Scientifique, Paris, 1935, pp. IV 1–IV 9. Hermann et C.ie, Paris (1935)
2. Castronovo, L., Sanfilippo, G.: A probabilistic analysis of selected notions of iterated conditioning under coherence. Int. J. Approx. Reason. **165**, 109088 (2024)
3. Celani, S., Gruszczyński, R., Menchón, P.: Conditional algebras. Ann. Pure Appl. Log. **176**(5), 103556 (2025)
4. Dubois, D., Prade, H.: Conditional objects as nonmonotonic consequence relationships. IEEE Trans. Syst. Man Cybern. **24**, 1724–1740 (1994)
5. Lewis, D.: Probabilities of conditionals and conditional probabilities I-II. Philos. Rev. **85**(3) 297 (1976). Philos. Rev. 95 (4) 581–589, 1986
6. Égré, P., Rossi, L., Sprenger, J.: De Finettian logics of indicative conditionals Part I: trivalent semantics and validity. J. Philos. Log. **50**, 187–213 (2021)
7. Flaminio, T., Godo, L., Hosni, H.: Boolean algebras of conditionals, probability and logic. Artif. Intell. **286**, 103347 (2020)
8. Flaminio, T., Gilio, A., Godo, L., Sanfilippo, G.: Compound conditionals as random quantities and Boolean algebras. In: Kern-Isberner, G. Lakemeyer, G., Meyer, T. (eds.), Proceedings of the 19th International Conference on Principles of Knowledge Representation and Reasoning, KR 2022, pp. 141–151, 2022
9. Flaminio, T., Gilio, A., Godo, L., Sanfilippo, G.: On conditional probabilities and their canonical extensions to Boolean algebras of compound conditionals. Int. J. Approx. Reason. **159**, 108943 (2023)
10. Gilio, A., Over, D., Pfeifer, N., Sanfilippo, G.: On trivalent logics, probabilistic weak deduction theorems, and a general import-export principle. Artif. Intell. **337**, 104229 (2024)
11. Gilio, A., Sanfilippo, G.: Conditional random quantities and iterated conditioning in the setting of coherence. In: van der Gaag, L.C. (eds.) Symbolic and Quantitative Approaches to Reasoning with Uncertainty. ECSQARU 2013. LNCS, vol. 7958. Springer, Berlin, Heidelberg (2013). https://doi.org/10.1007/978-3-642-39091-3_19
12. Gilio, A., Sanfilippo, G.: On compound and iterated conditionals. Argumenta **6**(2), 241–266 (2021)
13. Goodman, I.R., Nguyen, H.T.: A theory of conditional information for probabilistic inference in intelligent systems: II. Product Space Approach Inf. Sci. **76**, 13–42 (1994)
14. Goodman, I.R., Nguyen, H.T.: Conditional objects and the modeling of uncertainty. In: Gupta, M.M., Yamakawa, T. (eds.) Fuzzy Computing. Theory, Hardware and Applications, North-Holland, Amsterdam, pp. 119–138 (1998)
15. Hájek, A.: Triviality Pursuit. Topoi **30**, 3–15 (2011)
16. Halpern, J.Y.: Reasoning About Uncertainty. MIT press, Cambridge (2003)
17. Kaufmann, S.: Conditionals right and left: probabilities for the whole family. J. Philos. Log. **38**, 1–53 (2009)
18. McGee, V.: Conditional probabilities and compounds of conditionals. Philos. Rev. **98**, 485–541 (1989)
19. Nguyen, H.T.: On conditional event algebra for probability reasoning in system design. In: Huynh, VN., Honda, K., Le, B., Inuiguchi, M., Huynh, H.T. (eds.) Integrated Uncertainty in Knowledge Modelling and Decision Making. IUKM 2025. LNCS, vol. 15585, pp. 3–13. Springer, Singapore (2025). https://doi.org/10.1007/978-981-96-4606-7_1

20. Rosella, G., Ugolini, S.: The algebras of Lewis's counterfactuals: axiomatizations and algebraizability The Review of Symbolic Logic. Forthcoming, 2025
21. Sanfilippo, G., Pfeifer, N., Over, D.E., Gilio, A.: Probabilistic inferences from conjoined to iterated conditionals. Int. J. Approx. Reason. **93**, 103–118 (2018)
22. Stalnaker, R.: Probability and conditionals. Philos. Sci. **37**, 64–80 (1970)
23. van Fraassen, B.C.: Probabilities of conditionals. In: Harper, W.L., Stalnaker, R., Pearce, G. (eds.) Foundations of Probability Theory, Statistical Inference, and Statistical Theories of Science, in: The University of Western Ontario Series in Philosophy of Science, vol. 1, pp. 261–308. D. Reidel, Dordrecht (1976)
24. Wójtowicz, A., Wójtowicz, K.: A minimal probability space for conditionals. J. Philos. Log. **52**, 1385–1415 (2023)

On Measuring the Possibility of Selection Function-Based Conditionals, General Updates, and Qualitative Capacities

Tommaso Flaminio[1], Lluis Godo[1], and Giuliano Rosella[2(✉)]

[1] Artificial Intelligence Research Institute (IIIA - CSIC), Campus de la UAB, Bellaterra, Spain
{tommaso,godo}@iiia.csic.es

[2] Department of Philosophy and Education, University of Turin, Turin, Italy
giuliano.rosella@unito.it

Abstract. This paper investigates updating methods for possibility measures and their logical representation through conditional operators. We introduce a general possible worlds semantics equipped with selection functions (or equivalently, Boolean algebras with binary conditional operators). This provides a unified framework for various conditionals, including those studied by Stalnaker and Lewis. Building on our recent triviality result—which shows standard conditionalization for possibility measures cannot be represented as the possibility of a given conditional—we explore how alternative updating methods for possibility measures can be represented as the possibility of conditionals within our framework. Specifically, we define novel updating methods for possibility measures based on these selection functions. These methods, unlike standard conditionalization, exhibit a direct correspondence with the possibility of conditionals. In particular, we prove the possibility of selection function-based conditionals directly aligns with updated qualitative capacities, as defined by Dubois et al. Furthermore, we delineate the specific conditions under which the possibility of such conditionals precisely coincides with a general update of the original possibility measure.

1 Introduction

Bayesian conditionalization is a prominent example of probability updating and, as such, it is used to describe how agents modify their prior epistemic state once they receive new information. The last decades have seen significant progress in understanding the interplay between numerical and logico-semantic perspectives on updating methods, particularly in the probabilistic setting (e.g., [10,13,14, 24]).

A central traditional finding here is Lewis's triviality theorem [24], which fundamentally shows that conditional probability $P(B \mid A)$ cannot be directly represented as the probability of a corresponding conditional operator $P(A \triangleright B)$ without trivializing the initial prior probabilities. A prominent line of research

K. Sauerwald and M. Thimm (Eds.): ECSQARU 2025, LNAI 16099, pp. 347–361, 2026.
https://doi.org/10.1007/978-3-032-05134-9_24

in this area has investigated how updating methods are semantically interpreted through conditional connectives, and conversely, what kinds of updating methods are associated with specific semantic conditional operators (see, e.g., [13,17,18, 21,27,28]). More recently, [16] introduced a general framework for probabilistic updating methods, including conditionalization and Lewis imaging (see [19]), revealing that only a specific subclass –those updates based on a mass shift from one world to another– can be represented by selection function-based conditional operators.

In the present paper, we extend this broad analytical perspective to the possibilistic framework. Our primary goal is to establish a general connection between updating methods for possibility measures (like conditionalization and imaging [10]) and their logical representation through conditionals. We thoroughly investigate the boundaries of these connections across a wide range of possibilistic updating methods and selection function-based conditionals, aiming to precisely ascertain which possibilistic updates are encoded by conditional logical operators and, conversely, which can be represented as the possibility of suitable conditionals. Our work is directly motivated by a recently proved Lewisian-like triviality result for possibilistic conditionalization [15], which demonstrates that conditional possibility cannot be represented as the possibility of conditionals without trivializing the initial possibility measures. Additionally, [15] provided an initial characterization of the necessity of Lewis's 'would'-counterfactuals and the possibility of 'might'-counterfactuals in terms of image-like updating methods for the underlying necessity or possibility measures. Given these initial findings, it remains an open question whether this possibilistic triviality extends to other updating methods beyond conditionalization, or if similar characterization results can encompass a broader class of conditionals and updating methods.

The present work aims to demonstrate that, indeed, only a specific, constrained class of updating methods can be represented by a particular class of conditionals. Conversely, we show that a large class of conditionals induce non-standard possibilistic updating methods that instead align with qualitative capacities [12], a concept generalizing possibility measures in a manner analogous to how Dempster-Shafer belief functions generalize probabilities. As a general methodology for our investigation, we employ a selection function tool, which provides both a semantics for a large class of conditionals and a general notion of updating methods. This tool allows us to generalize models for conditionals based on world orderings or spheres structures [5,23], while simultaneously encompassing methods for possibility measures, such as imaging and conditionalization [10].

The paper is structured as follows: Sect. 2 provides the basic formal tools and recapitulates and systematizes results concerning conditional logics and their semantics. Section 3 connects conditionals with the possibilistic framework, presenting initial results on representing possibility and necessity measures of conditionals. Section 4 characterizes the possibility of conditionals, showing that they can be represented by an image-like updating method delivering qualitative capacities. Section 5 presents the reversed representation result, demonstrating that only a certain constrained class of possibilistic updating methods, those where the mass shift is performed pointwise, can be characterized by the possibility of selection-function-based conditionals. Finally, Sect. 6 draws conclusions and outlines avenues for further work.

2 Preliminaries

The basic components of our framework are Boolean algebras, which we define as: $\mathbf{A} = (A, \wedge, \vee, \neg, \bot, \top)$ of type $(2, 2, 1, 0, 0)$. Their standard language includes $\wedge$ (meet) and $\vee$ (join) for lattice operations, $\neg$ for complementation (or negation), and the constants $\bot$ and $\top$ are the bottom and the top elements, respectively. In a Boolean algebra $\mathbf{A} = (A, \wedge, \vee, \neg, \bot, \top)$, a lattice order is definable as follows: for all $a, b \in A$, $a \leq b$ iff $a \wedge b = b$ (or equivalently $a \vee b = b$). Every finite Boolean algebra $\mathbf{A}$ is atomic; we denote the set of its atoms as $\mathrm{at}(\mathbf{A}) = \{\alpha_1, \ldots, \alpha_n\}$, using $\alpha, \beta, \gamma, \ldots$ to indicate individual atoms. Since every Boolean algebra $\mathbf{A}$ is isomorphic to the power set of the set of its atoms, $\wp(\mathrm{at}(\mathbf{A}))$, we shall henceforth identify elements of $\mathbf{A}$ with subsets of $\mathrm{at}(\mathbf{A})$. This allows us to write $|a|$ to denote the cardinality of the set of atoms below a. Conceptually, atoms represent classical valuations (possible worlds), and Boolean algebra elements represent classical propositions, with the order reflecting the satisfaction relation.

Recall that the usual semantics for modal logic is given in terms of Kripke frames, i.e. pairs (W, R) where W is a non-empty set of worlds and R is a binary *accessibility* relation on W, see [1] for further details. In what follows, we will consider Kripke frames based on $\mathrm{at}(\mathbf{A})$, i.e. taking $\mathrm{at}(\mathbf{A})$ as the set of worlds. As usual in modal logic, every binary relation R on $\mathrm{at}(\mathbf{A})$ defines a unary normal modal operator on $\mathbf{A}$ by the following stipulation: for all $x \in A$

$$\Box x = \bigvee \{\alpha \in \mathrm{at}(\mathbf{A}) \mid \bigvee R(\alpha) \leq x\}, \tag{1}$$

where $R(\alpha) = \{\alpha' \in \mathrm{at}(\mathbf{A}) \mid \alpha R \alpha'\}$.

Finally, let us recall some basic facts about *possibility theory*, a qualitative uncertainty model based on the use of a pair of dual measures to evaluate the degree of certainty and/or ignorance of events [9]. The basic building tool in possibility theory is the notion of *possibility distribution*. In our context of a finite Boolean algebra $\mathbf{A}$, a (normalized) possibility distribution on the set $\mathrm{at}(\mathbf{A})$ is a map $\pi : \mathrm{at}(\mathbf{A}) \to [0, 1]$ such that $\max_{\alpha \in \mathrm{at}(\mathbf{A})} \pi(\alpha) = 1$. A possibility distribution π defines a pair of dual *possibility* and *necessity* measures on $\mathbf{A}$ as maps $\Pi, N : \mathbf{A} \to [0, 1]$ as follows: for all $a \in A$,

$$\Pi(a) = \max_{\alpha \leq a} \pi(\alpha), \quad N(a) = 1 - \Pi(\neg a),$$

that satisfy the following relations: $\max(\Pi(a), \Pi(\neg a)) = 1$ and $\min(N(a), N(\neg a)) = 0$. Possibility measures are *maxitive*, i.e. $\Pi(a \vee b) = \max(\Pi(a), \Pi(b))$, while necessity measures are *minitive*, i.e. $N(a \wedge b) = \min(N(a), N(b))$.

3 Selection Functions and Conditionals

A selection function for $\mathbf{A}$ is a mapping $f : A\times \mathrm{at}(\mathbf{A}) \to A$ that associates to each pair of an atom and an element of A another element of A that we will identify with a set of atoms of $\mathbf{A}$ as observed above. Initially, we do not impose any further properties on this function. Intuitively, the selection function specifies the set of closest worlds (atoms) to a given world, relative to a certain element. For instance, $f(a,\alpha)$ represents the set of worlds closest to α, as determined by a. For every selection function $f : A \times \mathrm{at}(\mathbf{A}) \to A$, let us define a *selection function-based conditional* operator (or simply a *conditional* operator)

$$\rhd_f\colon A \times A \to A$$

as follows: for all $a, b \in A$ and for all $\alpha \in \mathrm{at}(\mathbf{A})$,

$$a \rhd_f b = \bigvee\{\alpha \in \mathrm{at}(\mathbf{A}) \mid f(a,\alpha) \leq b\}. \tag{2}$$

In other words,

$$\alpha \leq a \rhd_f b \text{ iff } f(a,\alpha) \leq b.$$

This algebraic setting has a very intuitive possible-worlds semantic counterpart: an atom α satisfying $a \rhd_f b$ can be regarded as the possible world α making $a \rhd_f b$ true. Consequently, given an intuitive interpretation of the selection function in terms of a closeness relation, the above condition is telling us that $a \rhd_f b$ is true at α if and only if all the closest a-worlds make b true.

This closeness relation, specified by f, is at this stage very general while it can be instantiated in different ways to represent, for instance, an order of similarity [23] or normality among worlds [5]. The logical properties of $\rhd_f$ will be induced by the constraints imposed on f, i.e., the type of closeness relation we aim to represent. Indeed, having imposed no specific properties on the selection function f does not inherently explain why the operator $\rhd_f$ defined as above should be considered a *conditional* operator[1]. For example, it might be desirable that $a \rhd_f a$ is always true, or that $\rhd_f$ satisfies the modus ponens inference rule, and so on. How properties of the selection function f result in properties of the corresponding operator has been discussed extensively in the literature, and already [24] contains a quite exhaustive taxonomic discussion. The following list, that has been presented in [16], recalls some of them.

(Emptyness): $f(\bot,\alpha) = \emptyset$ is expressed by the equation $\bot \rhd_f a = \top$;
(Normality): $a \in A \setminus \{\bot\}$, $f(a,\alpha) \neq \emptyset$ corresponds to the equation $d \rhd_f b \leq \neg(d \rhd_f \neg b)$ for $d \neq \bot$;
(Identity): for $a \in A$, $f(a,\alpha) \leq a$ corresponds to $a \rhd_f a = \top$;
(Centering-1): if $\alpha \leq a$, then $\alpha \in f(a,\alpha)$ and it corresponds to $a \rhd_f b \leq \neg a \vee b$;
(Centering-2): if $\alpha \leq a$, then $f(a,\alpha) \leq \alpha$ is expressed as $a \wedge b \leq a \rhd_f b$;

[1] It is worth noting that the operator $\rhd_f$ is inherently two-valued, as it is defined over a Boolean algebra. Therefore, it should be distinguished from the three-valued conditional operators often used in the context of conditional probability [13].

(Centering): if $\alpha \leq a$, $f(a, \alpha) = \{\alpha\}$ corresponds to the equation $a \wedge b \leq a \rhd_f b \leq \neg a \vee b$;

(Uniqueness): $|f(a, \alpha)| \leq 1$ is expressed by $(a \rhd_f \neg b) \vee (a \rhd_f b) = \top$;

(Well-order): if $f(a, \alpha) \leq b$ and $f(b, \alpha) \leq a$, then $f(a, \alpha) = f(b, \alpha)$ and it is written $(a \rhd_f b) \wedge (b \rhd_f a) \leq (a \rhd_f c) \leftrightarrow (b \rhd_f c)$;

(Nesting): $f(a \vee b, \alpha) \leq a$ or $f(a \vee b, \alpha) \leq b$ or $f(a \vee b, \alpha) = f(a, \alpha) \cup f(b, \alpha)$ is expressed by the complex conditional equation $((a \vee b) \rhd_f a) \vee ((a \vee b) \rhd_f b) \vee (((a \vee b) \rhd_f c) \leftrightarrow ((a \rhd_f c) \wedge (b \rhd_f c))) = \top$.

We may hence refer to $\rhd_f$ as to a *variably strict conditional*, and hence it obeys the logic C0 (see [22]) when f satisfies (i) identity, (ii) well-order, and (iii) nesting. The $\rhd_f$ is a *counterfactual conditional*, and hence it obeys the conditional logic C1 (see [22]), when f satisfies the following properties: (i) identity, (ii) well-order, (iii) nesting, and (iv) centering. Finally, we may use the term *Stalnaker conditional* for $\rhd_f$ when f satisfies (i) identity, (ii) well-order, (iii) nesting, (iv) centering, and (v) uniqueness, and hence it corresponds to Stalnaker's logic of conditionals [30].

4 Modalities, Conditionals and Possibility Functions

In this section, we will establish some key results concerning the relationship between normal modal operators and selection functions. These results will subsequently be employed as a tool to begin exploring the connection between selection function-based conditionals and possibility measures.

Consider a finite Boolean algebra $\mathbf{A}$ and a selection function $f : A \times \mathrm{at}(\mathbf{A}) \to A$; let the binary relation $R^f_a \subseteq \mathrm{at}(\mathbf{A}) \times \mathrm{at}(\mathbf{A})$ be defined as follows: for all $\alpha \in A$, $R^f_a(\alpha) = f(a, \alpha)$. In other words,

$$\alpha R^f_a \beta \text{ iff } \beta \in f(a, \alpha).$$

For each such R^f_a, let $\Box^f_a : A \to A$ be defined as in (1). Notice that, since $R^f_a(\alpha) = f(a, \alpha)$, comparing (1) with (2) we can immediately show the following result:

Fact 1. *For a finite Boolean algebra* $\mathbf{A}$ *and a selection function* $f : A \times \mathrm{at}(\mathbf{A}) \to A$*; for all* $a, b \in A$*, it holds that*

$$\alpha \leq a \rhd_f b \textit{ iff } \alpha \leq \Box^f_a(b).$$

In other words, for every $a \in A$, $a \rhd_f (\cdot)$ and $\Box^f_a(\cdot)$ are the same unary operator on A. This implies that selection function-based conditionals can also be equivalently defined in terms of a family of indexed normal modal operators, $\{\Box^f_a \mid a \in A\}$, where each operator behaves as a conditional with a fixed antecedent. Consequently, the structure $(\mathbf{A}, \{\Box^f_a\}_{a \in A})$ forms a *Boolean algebra with operators* in the sense of [1].

Following standard practice in modal logic, we define the corresponding dual operators $a \blacktriangleleft_f b$ and $\Diamond_a^f(b)$ respectively as $\neg(a \rhd_f \neg b)$ and $\neg\Box_a^f(\neg b)$, i.e.

$$a \blacktriangleleft_f b = \bigvee\{\beta \in \mathrm{at}(\mathbf{A}) \mid f(a,\alpha) \wedge b \neq \bot\},$$
$$\Diamond_a^f(b) = \bigvee\{\beta \in \mathrm{at}(\mathbf{A}) \mid R_a^f(\beta) \wedge b \neq \bot\}.$$

It readily follows that

$$\alpha \leq \Diamond_a^f(b) \text{ iff } \alpha \leq \neg\Box_a^f(\neg b) \text{ iff } \alpha \leq \neg(a \rhd_f \neg b) = a \blacktriangleleft_f b.$$

Treating a conditional (binary) operator as a family of indexed normal modal (unary) operators provides a valuable framework for gaining new insights into the properties of conditional operators. This approach allows us to leverage the well-established behavior of normal modal operators and to demonstrate relevant results that connect the properties of a selection function f (and consequently, the corresponding conditional $\rhd_f$) with the properties of the induced indexed modal operators. The following result has been proved in [16, Fact 3] and it contributes to this direction:

Lemma 1. *For a finite Boolean algebra* $\mathbf{A}$ *and selection function* $f : A \times \mathrm{at}(\mathbf{A}) \to A$ *the following holds for all* $a \in A$*:*

$$|f(a,\alpha)| = 1 \Leftrightarrow (\text{for all } x \in A,\ \Box_a^f x \leftrightarrow \Diamond_a^f x = \top).$$

We can now look into the relationship between conditionals and possibility measures using the introduced general framework. Let $\Pi : \mathbf{A} \to [0,1]$ be a possibility measure on a finite Boolean algebra $\mathbf{A}$ and consider a selection function $f : A \times \mathrm{at}(\mathbf{A}) \to A$. Then, given the above assumptions and definitions, it turns out that the possibility and necessity degrees of a conditional being true are as follows:

$$\Pi(a \rhd_f b) = \max_{\alpha \leq a \rhd_f b} \Pi(\alpha) = \max_{\alpha : f(a,\alpha) \leq b} \Pi(\alpha),$$
$$N(a \rhd_f b) = 1 - \Pi(\neg(a \rhd_f b)) = 1 - \Pi(a \blacktriangleleft_f \neg b)$$

That is, the possibility degree of a conditional $a \rhd_f b$ is given by the maximum of the possibilities of the atomic states (worlds, atoms) where the conditional is satisfied. Directly from Fact 1, we obtain the following.

Proposition 1. *For a finite Boolean algebra* $\mathbf{A}$*, a selection function* $f : A \times \mathrm{at}(\mathbf{A}) \to A$*, and possibility* $\Pi : \mathbf{A} \to [0,1]$ *the following relations hold for all* $a, b \in A$*:*

$$\Pi(a \rhd_f b) = \Pi(\Box_a^f(b)), \quad \Pi(a \blacktriangleleft_f b) = \Pi(\Diamond_a^f b)$$
$$N(a \rhd_f b) = N(\Box_a^f b), \quad N(a \blacktriangleleft_f b) = N(\Diamond_a^f b)$$

Proof. The claims are proved by the following series of identities.

- $\Pi(a \rhd_f b) = \max_{\alpha \leq a \rhd_f b} \Pi(\alpha) = \max_{\alpha \leq \Box_a^f b} \Pi(\alpha) = \Pi(\Box_a^f b)$
- $N(a \rhd_f b) = \min_{\alpha \not\leq a \rhd_f b} 1 - \Pi(\alpha) = \min_{\alpha \not\leq \Box_a^f b} 1 - \Pi(\alpha) = N(\Box_a^f b)$
- $\Pi(a \blacktriangleleft_f b) = \Pi(\neg(a \rhd_f \neg b)) = 1 - N(a \rhd_f \neg b) = 1 - N(\Box_a^f \neg b) = 1 - N(\neg\Diamond_a^f b) = \Pi(\Diamond_a^f b)$

- $N(a \blacktriangleleft_f b) = 1 - \Pi(\neg(a \blacktriangleleft_f b)) = 1 - \Pi(\neg(a \rhd_f \neg b)) = 1 - \Pi(\Box_a^f \neg b) = 1 - \Pi(\neg\Diamond_a^f b) = N(\Diamond_a^f b)$. □

As an immediate consequence of the above Proposition 1, we hence have that while the combination of a necessity N and the $\Box_f^a$ gives $N(a \rhd_f (\cdot))$ that is a necessity function and the combination of a possibility Π with the $\Diamond_f^a$ gives the map $\Pi(a \blacktriangleleft_f (\cdot))$ that still is a possibility function, the other resulting combinations $N(a \blacktriangleleft_f (\cdot)) = N(\Diamond_a^f(\cdot))$ and $\Pi(a \rhd_f (\cdot)) = \Pi(\Box_a^f(\cdot))$ do not give a necessity and a possibility, respectively. Indeed, for instance, $\Pi(a \rhd_f (\cdot)) = \Pi(\Box_a^f(\cdot))$ is not a possibility in general, since we only have the inequality $\Pi(a \rhd_f (b \vee c)) = \Pi(\Box_a^f(b \vee c)) \geq \Pi(\Box_a^f(b) \vee \Box_a^f(c)) = \max(\Pi(\Box_a^f(b)), \Pi(\Box_a^f(c))) = \max(\Pi(a \rhd_f b), \Pi(a \rhd_f c))$.

As we will clarify in the next section, these functions $N(a \blacktriangleleft_f (\cdot)) = N(\Diamond_a^f(\cdot))$ and $\Pi(a \rhd_f (\cdot)) = \Pi(\Box_a^f(\cdot))$ are related with the qualitative/possibilistic versions of Dempster-Shafer belief functions that have been introduced and studied by Dubois, Faux, Prade and Rico in a series of papers (see for instance [12,26]).

5 Possibility of Selection Function-Based Conditionals and Possibilistic Dempster-Shafer Theory

As we have observed at the end of the previous section, the combination of a possibility function Π with a conditional based on based on a selection function $\rhd_f$ is not a possibility function in general, and the combination of a necessity function N with a might conditional based on the selection function $\blacktriangleleft_f$ is not a necessity function either. Indeed, the resulting maps satisfy weaker conditions than possibility and necessity functions, respectively, that correspond to *qualitative capacities* as defined in [12].

To briefly introduce these functions within our setting, let us consider as usual a finite Boolean algebra $\mathbf{A}$, a selection function $f : A \times \mathrm{at}(\mathbf{A}) \to A$, and a possibility $\Pi : A \to [0, 1]$. For each $a \in A$, we can define a *possibilistic mass distribution* $m_a : A \to [0, 1]$ as follows:

$$m_a(b) = \bigvee_{\alpha : f(a,\alpha) = b} \Pi(\alpha).$$

Thus, m_a is indeed a possibility distribution over the entire domain A, since $\max_{b \in A} m_a(b) = 1$. Adapting the general way to define a Dempster-Shafer belief function from a mass assignment (cf. [8,29]) to the possibilistic case, given a possibilistic mass m_a, following [12], we define the *possibilistic belief* and the *possibilistic plausibility* functions as follows:

$$\Pi Bel_a(b) = \bigvee_{c \leq b} m_a(c) = \bigvee_{c \leq b} \bigvee_{f(a,\alpha) = c} \Pi(\alpha) = \bigvee_{f(a,\alpha) \leq b} \Pi(\alpha). \quad (3)$$

$$\Pi Pl_a(b) = \bigvee_{c \wedge b \neq \bot} m_a(c) = \bigvee_{c \wedge b \neq \bot} \bigvee_{\alpha : f(a,\alpha) = c} \Pi(\alpha) = \bigvee_{\alpha : f(a,\alpha) \wedge b \neq \bot} \Pi(\alpha). \quad (4)$$

The next remark points out some relevant differences between the usual Dempster-Shafer belief function theory and this qualitative/possibilistic version.

Remark 1. (1) Unlike the case of standard Dempster-Shafer belief and plausibility functions, their possibilistic variant ΠPl_a does not coincide with the conjugate of ΠBel_a defined as $(\Pi Bel_a)^c(b) = 1 - \Pi Bel_a(\neg b)$. Indeed, in the present case, we only have $\max(\Pi Bel_a(b), \Pi Pl_a(\neg b)) = 1$.

(2) For every Dempster-Shafer belief function $Bel : \mathbf{A} \to [0,1]$, there exists a unique mass assignment $m : \mathbf{A} \to [0,1]$ that is obtained from Bel by the so called *Möbius transform* and such that, for all $b \in A$, $Bel(b) = \sum_{a \leq b} m(a)$ (see [20]). As it has been observed in [12], it is not generally true that the possibilistic mass on A that determines ΠBel is unique. However, the least possibilistic mass assignment that determines ΠBel always exists and it is its (possibilistic) Möbius transform $\pi^{\#}$ so defined (see [12] for more details): for all $a \in A$,

$$\pi^{\#}(a) = \begin{cases} \Pi Bel(a) & \text{if } \Pi Bel(a) > \Pi Bel(a \wedge \neg\alpha) \text{ for all } \alpha \in \mathrm{at}(\mathbf{A}) \text{ and } \alpha \leq a, \\ 0 & \text{otherwise.} \end{cases}$$

As an almost direct consequence of the definitions, we have an initial result that links the above-defined functions and the possibility and necessity of selection function-based conditionals:

Proposition 2. *Consider a finite Boolean algebra* $\mathbf{A}$*, a selection function* $f : A \times \mathrm{at}(\mathbf{A}) \to A$*, and a possibility* $\Pi : A \to [0,1]$*, the following hold for all* $a, b \in A$*:*

$$\Pi(a \rhd_f (\cdot)) = \Pi(\Box^f_a(\cdot)) = \Pi Bel_a(\cdot);$$
$$N(a \blacktriangleleft_f (\cdot)) = N(\Diamond^f_a(\cdot)) = (\Pi Bel_a)^c(\cdot).$$

Proof. We only check the second property: $N(\Diamond^f_a(b)) = 1 - \Pi(\neg\Diamond^f_a(b)) = 1 - \Pi(\Box^f_a(\neg b)) = 1 - \Pi Bel_a(\neg b) = (\Pi Bel_a)^c(b)$.

Specifically, the possibility of a selection function-based conditional $a \rhd_f b$ is equal to the corresponding possibilistic belief degree of the consequent b, "imaged" on the antecedent a, i.e. $\Pi Bel_a(b)$.

Lemma 2. *Let* $\mathbf{A}$ *be a finite Boolean algebra, let* $f : A \times \mathrm{at}(\mathbf{A}) \to A$ *be a selection function, and let* $\Pi : A \to [0,1]$ *be a possibility measure. Let* $a \in A$ *and consider the following two conditions:*

(i) $|f(a,\alpha)| = 1$ *for any atom* α
(ii) $\Pi(a \rhd_f (\cdot)) : A \to [0,1]$ *is a possibility measure,*

Then (i) implies (ii).

Proof. By Lemma 1, (i) amounts to assume that $\Box^f_a x \leftrightarrow \Diamond^f_a x = \top$ holds for all $x \in A$. Then we have that $\Box^f_a$ distributes over disjunction, namely $\Box^f_a(c \vee b) = \Box^f_a c \vee \Box^f_a b$, and so, $\Pi(\Box^f_a(b \vee c)) = \Pi(\Box^f_a(b) \vee \Box^f_a(c)) = \max(\Pi(\Box^f_a(b), \Pi(\Box^f_a(c))$, and hence $\Pi(\Box^f_a(\cdot))$ is a possibility measure. $\square$

It is worth noticing that above (ii) does not imply (i), indeed, we show it by means of a counter-example.

Example 1. Let $\mathbf{A}$ be an algebra such that $\mathrm{at}(\mathbf{A}) = \{\alpha, \beta, \gamma, \delta\}$, and for a given $a \in A$ consider the selection function: $f : A \times \mathrm{at}(\mathbf{A}) \to A$ such that:

$$f(a,\beta) = \alpha \vee \beta, f(a,\alpha) = \alpha, f(a,\gamma) = \gamma, f(a,\delta) = \delta.$$

Let $\Pi : A \to [0,1]$ be the possibility function given by the distribution

$$\Pi(\alpha) = 0.9, \Pi(\beta) = 0.9, \Pi(\gamma) = 1, \Pi(\delta) = 0.5$$

Then, recalling that the mass function corresponding to Π and f is defined as $m_a(b) = \max_{u:f(a,u)=b} \Pi(u)$, we have:

$$m_a(\alpha) = 0.9, m_a(\alpha \vee \beta) = 0.9, m_a(\beta) = 0, m_a(\gamma) = 1, m_a(\delta) = 0.5,$$

and $m_a(x) = 0$ for any other $x \in A$. The corresponding possibilistic belief function, defined as $\Pi Bel_a(b) = \max_{u:f(a,u)\leq b} \Pi(u)$, is such that:

- $\Pi Bel(\alpha) = 0.9, \Pi Bel(\beta) = 0, \Pi Bel(\gamma) = 1, \Pi Bel(\delta) = 0.5$
- $\Pi Bel(\alpha \vee \beta) = \max(m(\alpha), m(\beta), m(\alpha \vee \beta)) = 0.9 = \max(\Pi Bel(\alpha), \Pi Bel(\beta))$
- $\Pi Bel(\gamma \vee b) = 1$, $\Pi Bel(\delta \vee \alpha \vee \beta) = 0.9$, ...etc.

So defined $\Pi Bel_a = \Pi(a \rhd_f (\cdot))$ is a possibility function while the values of $f(a,\cdot)$ are not all singletons. □

Although as we have seen (ii) does not imply (i), it does when we suitably modify (ii) as the next lemma shows.

Theorem 1. *Let $\mathbf{A}$ be a finite Boolean algebra, let $f : A \times \mathrm{at}(\mathbf{A}) \to A$ be a selection function, and let $\Pi : A \to [0,1]$ be a possibility measure. Then, the following conditions are equivalent:*

(i) $\Pi Bel^f_a = \Pi(a \rhd_f (\cdot)) : A \to [0,1]$ is a possibility function
(ii)' there exists a selection function f' such that $\Pi Bel^{f'}_a = \Pi Bel^f_a$ and $|f'(a,\alpha)| = 1$ for any atom α.

Proof. That (ii') implies (i) immediately follows by the above Lemma 2. Thus, let us prove that (i) implies $(ii)'$ and suppose ΠBel^f_a is a possibility measure. Then, by [10, Proposition 2], the focal elements of its Möbius transform $\pi_\#$ (recall Remark 1 (2)) are singletons. In fact, $\pi_\# : \mathrm{at}(\mathbf{A}) \to [0,1]$ is the possibility distribution underlying ΠBel^f_a, i.e. $\Pi Bel^f_a(\alpha) = \pi_\#(\alpha) = m_a(\alpha) = \max_{\beta:f(a,\beta)=\alpha} \Pi(\beta)$.

Suppose there exists β such that $f(a,\beta)$ is not an atom. By a cardinality argument, if we let $\Delta = \{\delta \in \mathrm{at}(\mathbf{A}) \mid \delta \not\leq f(a,\alpha)$ for all $\alpha \in \mathrm{at}(\mathbf{A})\}$ be the set of atoms not in the image of $f(a,\cdot)$, then necessarily $\Delta \neq \emptyset$. By definition, for every $\delta \in \Delta$, $m_a(\delta) = 0$, and hence $\pi_\#(\delta) = 0$ as well.

Since for all atoms α, $\pi_{\#}(\alpha) = m_a(\alpha)$ only depends on the possibility of those atoms $\beta \notin \Delta$ such that $f(a,\beta)$ is a singleton (atom), ΠBel_a^f only depends on them as well. In what follows, for any $a \in A$ and $\alpha \in \mathrm{at}(\mathbf{A})$, let $f_a^{-1}(b) = \bigvee\{\alpha \in \mathrm{at}(\mathbf{A}) \mid f(a,\alpha) = b\}$. Then we define:

$$f'(a,\alpha) = \begin{cases} f(a,\alpha), \text{ if } f(a,\alpha) \in \mathrm{at}(\mathbf{A})) \cup \{\perp\} \\ \gamma_\alpha, \quad \text{otherwise} \end{cases}$$

where γ_α is any atom such that $\gamma_\alpha \leq f(a,\alpha)$ and that $\Pi(f_a^{-1}(\gamma_\alpha)) = \Pi(f_a^{-1}(f(a,\alpha_\alpha)))$.

Claim. For all $a \in A$ and $\alpha \in \mathrm{at}(\mathbf{A})$, γ_α exists such that $\gamma_\alpha \leq f(a,\alpha)$ and that $\Pi(f_a^{-1}(\gamma_\alpha)) = \Pi(f_a^{-1}(f(a,\alpha_\alpha)))$.

Proof (Claim). Since $\Pi Bel_a^f(f(a,\alpha)) = \max_{\beta \leq f(a,\alpha)} \Pi Bel_a^f(\beta)$, there is $\gamma_a \leq f(a,\alpha)$ such that $\Pi Bel_a^f(f(a,\alpha)) = \Pi Bel_a^f(\gamma_a)$. Because γ_a is an atom, $\Pi Bel_a^f(\gamma_a) = m_a(\gamma_a)$ and, by definition of m_a, $m_a(\gamma_a) = \max_{\beta: f(a,\beta)=\gamma_a} \Pi(\beta) = \Pi(f_a^{-1}(\gamma_a)$. Therefore we have $\Pi Bel_a^f(f(a,\alpha)) = \Pi(f_a^{-1}(\gamma_a)$.

On the other hand, by definition of ΠBel_a^f, we have $\Pi Bel_a^f(f(a,\alpha)) = \max_{c \leq f(a,\alpha)} m(c) = \max_{c \leq f(a,\alpha)} \max_{\delta: f(a,\delta)=c} \Pi(\delta) = \max_{c \leq f(a,\alpha)} \max_{\delta \in f_a^{-1}(c)} \Pi(\delta) = \Pi(f_a^{-1}(f(a,\alpha))$. Therefore, we have proved that there exists an atom γ_a such that $\Pi(f_a^{-1}(\gamma_a) = \Pi(f_a^{-1}(f(a,\alpha))$.

Note that the last condition is equivalent to require $m_a(\gamma_\alpha) = \Pi(\bigvee\{\beta \mid f(a,\beta) = \gamma_\alpha\}) = \Pi(\bigvee\{\beta \mid f(a,\beta) = f(a,\alpha)\}) = m_a(f(a,\alpha))$.

Then $\Pi Bel_a^{f'} = \Pi Bel_a^f$. Indeed, $\Pi Bel_a^{f'}(\alpha) = \Pi Bel_a^f(\alpha) = 0$ when $\alpha \in \Delta$, and otherwise we have

$$\begin{aligned} \Pi Bel_a^{f'}(\alpha) &= \max_{\beta: \alpha \leq f'(a,\beta)} \Pi(\beta) = \max_{\beta: \alpha = f'(a,\beta)} \Pi(\beta) \\ &= \max_{\beta: f(a,\beta)=\alpha} \Pi(\beta) \vee \max_{\beta': \alpha < f(a,\beta), f(a,\beta)=f(a,\beta')} \Pi(\beta') = \\ &= \max_{\beta: f(a,\beta)=\alpha} \Pi(\beta) \vee \max_{\beta': \alpha < f(a,\beta')} \Pi(\beta') = \max_{\beta: \alpha \leq f(a,\beta))} \Pi(\beta) = \Pi Bel_a^f(\alpha). \end{aligned}$$

Moreover, since for all $\alpha \in \mathrm{at}(\mathbf{A})$, $f'(a,\alpha) \in \mathrm{at}(\mathbf{A})$ as well, f' satisfies unicity and (ii') holds. □

6 Dealing with General Updates

We now introduce a general framework for defining updating methods for possibilities. First, given a finite Boolean algebra $\mathbf{A}$ and a selection function $f : A \times \mathrm{at}(\mathbf{A}) \to A$, we define a *distribution function for* f as a map $\lambda : A \times \mathrm{at}(\mathbf{A}) \to [0,1]^{|\mathrm{at}(\mathbf{A})|}$ satisfying the following constraints:

(C1) $\lambda(a,\alpha)(\beta) = 0$ if $\beta \notin f(a,\alpha)$

(C2) $\bigvee_{\beta \in f(a,\alpha)} \lambda(a,\alpha)(\beta) = 1$

The scope of this constraint will become clearer later when we define the updating procedures for possibilities that employ λ. Now, consider a finite Boolean algebra $\mathbf{A}$, a possibility $\Pi : \mathbf{A} \to [0,1]$, a selection function $f : A \times \mathrm{at}(\mathbf{A}) \to A$, and distribution function $\lambda : A \times \mathrm{at}(\mathbf{A}) \to [0,1]^{|\mathrm{at}(\mathbf{A})|}$ for f. Given an element $a \in A \setminus \{\bot\}$, we can define Π_a^λ over $\mathrm{at}(\mathbf{A})$ as follows: for all $\beta \in \mathrm{at}(\mathbf{A})$

$$\Pi_a^\lambda(\beta) = \bigvee_{\alpha:\beta \in f(a,\alpha)} \lambda(a,\alpha)(\beta) \wedge \Pi(\alpha) \tag{5}$$

Specifically, $\Pi_a^\lambda(\cdot)$ is obtained by redistributing the original possibility mass of each atom α among all atoms in $f(a,\alpha)$. Coherently with what it has been proved in [15, Proposition 3.6], we are now going to prove that the constraints imposed on λ ensure that $\Pi_a^\lambda(\cdot)$ is indeed a possibility distribution.

$$\begin{aligned}
\max\nolimits_\beta \Pi_a^\lambda(\beta) &= \bigvee\nolimits_\beta \bigvee\nolimits_{\alpha:\beta \in f(a,\alpha)} \lambda(a,\alpha)(\beta) \wedge \Pi(\alpha) \\
&= \bigvee\nolimits_\alpha \bigvee\nolimits_{\beta \in f(a,\alpha)} \lambda(a,\alpha)(\beta) \wedge \Pi(\alpha) \\
&= \bigvee\nolimits_\alpha \Pi(\alpha) \\
&= 1
\end{aligned}$$

The possibility function determined by the above distribution will be denoted by the same symbol.

$$\Pi_a^\lambda(b) = \bigvee_{\beta \le b} \Pi_a^\lambda(\beta) = \bigvee_{\beta \le b} \left(\bigvee_{\alpha:\beta \in f(a,\alpha)} \lambda(a,\alpha)(\beta) \wedge \Pi(\alpha) \right). \tag{6}$$

$\Pi_a^\lambda(\cdot)$ represents an updated possibility distribution where the shift of possibility mass is performed according to the selection function f. This fact, together with the definition given in [10] and the results proved in [15] in the more specific context of sphere-based models, suggests to term these functions λ-*imaged* possibility functions.

Let us prove a general result concerning the relationship between the possibility of conditionals and updating methods, namely that the possibility of a conditional $a \rhd_f b$ (with f satisfying normality) will always be less than or equal to the corresponding λ-updated possibility of b given a:

Fact 2. *Consider a finite Boolean algebra* $\mathbf{A}$*, a selection function* $f : A \times \mathrm{at}(\mathbf{A}) \to A$ *satisfying normality, and a distribution mass* $\lambda : A \times \mathrm{at}(\mathbf{A}) \to [0,1]^{|\mathrm{at}(\mathbf{A})|}$*. For* $a \in A \setminus \{\bot\}$*, and for all* $b \in A$*,*

$$\Pi(a \rhd_f b) \le \Pi_a^\lambda(b)$$

Proof. (Sketch) We show that for any $\alpha \le a \rhd_f b$, the initial possibility mass of $\Pi(\alpha)$ contributes to the calculation of $\Pi_a^\lambda(b)$. Specifically, let us consider $\alpha \in \mathrm{at}(\mathbf{A})$ such that $\alpha \le a \rhd_f b$. This implies that $f(a,\alpha) \le b$. According to the definition of $\Pi_a^\lambda(\cdot)$, the possibility mass $\Pi(\alpha)$ is redistributed among the elements in $f(a,\alpha)$. However, since $f(a,\alpha) \leq b$, we know that for every $\beta \in f(a,\alpha)$, $\beta \leq b$. This implies that the mass $\Pi(\alpha)$ from every $\alpha \leq a \rhd_f b$ is redistributed among atoms that are below b. Consequently, this mass will be included in the maximisation that yields $\Pi_a^\lambda(b)$. Thus, we have $\bigvee_{\alpha \leq a \rhd_f b} \Pi(\alpha) \leq \Pi_a^\lambda(b)$, which is equivalent to $\Pi(a \rhd_f b) \leq \Pi_a^\lambda(b)$.

We now have all the necessary components to show the conditions under which the possibility of a conditional corresponds to an updated possibility.

Proposition 3. *Consider a finite Boolean algebra* $\mathbf{A}$*, a selection function* $f : A \times \mathrm{at}(\mathbf{A}) \to A$ *satisfying normality, a distribution function* $\lambda : A \times \mathrm{at}(\mathbf{A}) \to [0,1]^{|\mathrm{at}(\mathbf{A})|}$*, and a possibility* $\Pi : A \to [0,1]$*. The following are equivalent.*

1. *For all* $a \in A \setminus \{\bot\}$, $\Pi(a \rhd_f (\cdot)) = \Pi_a^\lambda(\cdot)$.
2. *There exits* f' *such that* $\Pi Bel_a^f(\cdot) = \Pi Bel_a^{f'}(\cdot)$ *and* f' *satisfies uniqueness.* □

Proof. (Sketch) (1 ⇒ 2). Assume that for all $a \in A \setminus \{\bot\}$, $\Pi(a \rhd_f (\cdot)) = \Pi_a^\lambda(\cdot)$. Then, by Proposition 2 $\Pi(a \rhd_f (\cdot)) = \Pi Bel_a^f(\cdot)$ is a possibility measure and hence, by Theorem 1 there exists f' that satisfies 2.

(2 ⇒ 1). Assume by way of contradiction that all selection functions f' for which $\Pi Bel_a^f(\cdot) = \Pi Bel_a^{f'}(\cdot)$ do not satisfy uniqueness. Then, by Theorem 1 $\Pi Bel_a^f(\cdot)$ is not a possibility function and hence, a fortiori, it cannot equate the possibility $\Pi_a^\lambda(\cdot)$.

The above proposition states that the possibility of a conditional $a \rhd_f b$ (whose underlying f satisfies normality) can be characterized as the possibility of b λ-updated on a (for some λ) if and only if the selection function underlying the conditional satisfies uniqueness, up to defining the same ΠBel_a^f. This implies that the possibility of a broad class of conditionals cannot be characterized as a λ-updated possibility, and, in turn, that only a restricted class of updated possibilities can be characterized in terms of the possibility of a corresponding selection function-based conditional.

Finally, we close this section with a result stating that, besides the analogy with the possibilistic imaging method of [10,15], the possibilistic λ-imaging is indeed so general to encompass all possible possibilistic update methods including, for instance, possibilistic conditionalization [4,6,7] and Jeffrey possibilistic conditionals [3] as particular cases. In this sense, we can say that this possibilistic λ-imaging is universal.

Theorem 2. *For any two possibility functions* Π_a, Π' *on* $\mathbf{A}$ *there exists a selection function* f *and a distribution mass* λ *for* f *such that* $\Pi_a^\lambda = \Pi'$.

Proof. Let α_0 be an atom such that $\Pi(\alpha_0) = 1$ and let $b_0 = \bigvee\{\beta \mid \Pi(\beta) > 0\}$. Let us define $f(a,\alpha) = \top$ for any $\alpha \in \mathrm{at}(\mathbf{A})$ and any $a \in A$, and define λ as follows: for any $\beta \in \mathrm{at}(\mathbf{A})$,

$$\lambda(a,\alpha)(\beta) = \begin{cases} \Pi'(\beta), & \text{if } \alpha = \alpha_0 \\ 0, & \text{otherwise.} \end{cases}$$

Note that, for any α, $\{\beta \mid \beta \in f(a,\alpha)\} = \mathrm{at}(\mathbf{A})$, and hence for any β we have:

$$\begin{aligned} \Pi_a^\lambda(\beta) &= \bigvee_{\alpha:\beta\in f(a,\alpha)} \lambda(a,\alpha)(\beta) \wedge \Pi(\alpha) \\ &= (\lambda(a,\alpha_0)(\beta) \wedge \Pi(\alpha_0)) \vee \bigvee_{\alpha\neq\alpha_0} \lambda(a,\alpha)(\beta) \wedge \Pi(\alpha) \\ &= (\lambda(a,\alpha_0)(\beta) \wedge \Pi(\alpha_0)) \vee 0 = \Pi'(\beta). \end{aligned}$$

□

7 Conclusions

This work introduces a general framework to connect numerical updating methods for possibility measures with their logical representations through conditional operators, both grounded on a semantics based on selection function models. We demonstrate that the possibility of a large class of conditional operators aligns with a corresponding updated qualitative imaged-like possibilistic Dempster-Shafer measure. Conversely, only a specific class of standard updated possibilistic measures can be characterized as the possibility of a corresponding conditional logical operator, constrained by their underlying selection function. The proposed framework is highly general and capable of defining all possible updated possibility measures, ensuring our results apply to all relevant updating procedures. These findings clarify the relationship between updated possibilities and conditionals, offering general characterization results and identifying meaningful connections. This dual insight interprets conditional operators as encoding updates, and updating methods as quantifying the possibility of specific conditional operators.

Our current research and results are primarily theoretical. Due to their novelty, comprehensive examples and direct applications of this framework remain limited; their identification presents a promising direction for future work. A particularly interesting line of application involves exploring how existing possibilistic updates, such as standard or Jeffrey-like conditioning (e.g., [2,11,25]), can be modeled as specific instances of our imaging-like updating. This would enable our framework to function as a tool for deriving and examining the numerical properties and logical representations of possibilistic updates. Moreover, our general equivalence results, linking updated possibilistic measures with the possibility of conditionals, can both facilitate the semantic representation of possibilistic updates through operations on epistemic states and help identify the possibilistic equivalent of an update operation on an epistemic state, with these operations being encoded by corresponding conditional operators.

The research reported in the present paper opens, in our opinion, at least two interesting lines for future work. The first one is to generalize these results beyond selection function-based conditional operators to encompass any logical operators. Such an investigation could significantly contribute to understanding the logic underlying updating methods in the possibilistic setting. A second direction involves leveraging our results to achieve a more syntax-oriented logical characterization of updating methods. While our framework currently expresses updated possibility based on semantic structures, it would be valuable to explore whether our findings can contribute to a more axiomatic characterization of updating methods.

We believe this framework is highly promising, significantly advancing our understanding of possibilistic updating methods and their underlying logic.

Acknowledgments. The authors are grateful to the anonymous referees for their careful reading and valuable suggestions to clarify several parts of the present paper. Flaminio and Godo acknowledge the Spanish projects SHORE (PID2022-141529NB-C21) and LINEXSYS (PID2022-139835NB-C21) respectively, both funded by MCIU/AEI/10.13039/501100011033. Flaminio and Godo also acknowledge partial support by the H2020-MSCA-RISE-2020 project MOSAIC (Grant Agreement number 101007627). Giuliano Rosella acknowledges financial support from the Italian Ministry of University and Research (MUR) through the PRIN 2022 grant n. 2022ARRY9N funded by the European Union (Next Generation EU).

References

1. Blackburn, P., de Rijke, M., Venema, Y.: Modal Logic. Cambridge University Press, Cambridge (2002)
2. Benferhat, S., Dubois, D., Prade, H., Williams, M.-A.: A general framework for revising belief bases using qualitative Jeffrey's rule. In: Rauch, J., Raś, Z.W., Berka, P., Elomaa, T. (eds.) ISMIS 2009. LNCS (LNAI), vol. 5722, pp. 612–621. Springer, Heidelberg (2009). https://doi.org/10.1007/978-3-642-04125-9_64
3. Benferhat, S., Tabia, K., Sedki, K.: Jeffrey's rule of conditioning in a possibilistic framework - an analysis of the existence and uniqueness of the solution. Ann. Math. Artif. Intell. **61**(3), 185–202 (2011)
4. Bouchon-Meunier, B., Coletti, G., Marsala, C.: Conditional possibility and necessity. In: Bouchon-Meunier, B., Gutiérrez-Ríos, J., Magdalena, L., Yager, R.R. (eds.) Technologies for Constructing Intelligent Systems 2. Studies in Fuzziness and Soft Computing, vol. 90, pp. 59–71. Springer, Heidelberg (2002). https://doi.org/10.1007/978-3-7908-1796-6_5
5. Burgess, J.P.: Quick completeness proofs for some logics of conditionals. Notre Dame J. Formal Logic **22**(1), 76–84 (1981)
6. Coletti, G., Vantaggi, B.: Comparative models ruled by possibility and necessity: a conditional world. Int. J. Approximate Reasoning **45**, 341–363 (2007)
7. Coletti, G., Petturiti, D., Vantaggi, B.: Independence in possibility theory under different triangular norms. In: van der Gaag, L.C. (ed.) ECSQARU 2013. LNCS (LNAI), vol. 7958, pp. 133–144. Springer, Heidelberg (2013). https://doi.org/10.1007/978-3-642-39091-3_12
8. Dempster, A.P.: Upper and lower probabilities induced by a multivalued mapping. Ann. Math. Stat. **38**(2), 325–339 (1967)
9. Dubois, D., Prade, H.: Possibility Theory. Plenum Press, New York (1988)
10. Dubois, D., Prade, H.: A survey of belief revision and updating rules in various uncertainty models. Int. J. Intell. Syst. **9**(1), 61–100 (1994)
11. Dubois, D., Prade, H.: A synthetic view of belief revision with uncertain inputs in the framework of possibility theory. Intl. J. Approximate Reasoning **17**(2–3), 295–324 (1997)

12. Dubois, D., Faux, F., Prade, H., Rico, A.: Qualitative capacities: basic notions and potential applications. Int. J. Approximate Reasoning **148**, 253–290 (2022)
13. Égré, P., Rossi, L., Sprenger, J.: Certain and Uncertain Inference with Indicative Conditionals. Aust. J. Philos. (forthcoming)
14. Flaminio, T., Godo, L., Hosni, H.: Boolean algebras of conditionals, probability and logic. Artif. Intell. **286**, 103347 (2020)
15. Flaminio, T., Godo, L., Rosella, G.: Possibility of conditionals and conditional possibilities: from the triviality result to possibilistic imaging. In: Proceedings of KR 2024, pp. 372–382 (2024)
16. Flaminio, T., Godo, L., Rosella, G.: Conditionals based on selection functions, modal operators and probabilities In: Proceedings of TARK 2025 (2025)
17. Flaminio, T.,Rosella, G., Subirana, L.: From conditionalization to imaging through the triviality glass. Submitted Manuscript (submitted)
18. van Fraassen, B.C.: Probabilities of conditionals. In: Harper, W.L., Hooker, C.A. (eds) Foundations of Probability Theory, Statistical Inference, and Statistical Theories of Science. The University of Western Ontario Series in Philosophy of Science, vol. 6a, pp. 261–308. Springer, Dordrecht (1976). https://doi.org/10.1007/978-94-010-1853-1_10
19. Gärdenfors, P.: Imaging and conditionalization. J. Philos. **79**, 747–760 (1982)
20. Grabisch, M.: Set functions, Games and Capacities in Decision-Making. Springer, Cham (2016)
21. Hájek, A.: Probabilities of conditionals - revisited. J. Philos. Log. **18**(4) (1989)
22. Lewis, D.: Completeness and decidability of three logics of counterfactual conditionals 1. Theoria **37**(1), 74–85 (1971)
23. Lewis, D.: Counterfactuals. Blackwell, Oxford (1973)
24. Lewis, D.: Probabilities of conditionals and conditional probabilities. Philos. Rev. **85**(3), 297–315 (1976)
25. Ma, J., Liu, W., Benferhat, S.: A belief revision framework for revising epistemic states with partial epistemic states. Intl. J. Approximate Reasoning **59**, 20–40 (2015)
26. Prade, H., Rico, A.: Possibilistic evidence. In: Liu, W. (ed.) ECSQARU 2011. LNCS (LNAI), vol. 6717, pp. 713–724. Springer, Heidelberg (2011). https://doi.org/10.1007/978-3-642-22152-1_60
27. Rosella, G., Flaminio, T., Bonzio, S.: Counterfactuals as modal conditionals, and their probability. Artif. Intell. **323**(C), 103970 (2023)
28. Santorio, P.: Probabilities of counterfactuals are counterfactual probabilities. J. Philos. (forthcoming)
29. Shafer, G.: A Mathematical Theory of Evidence. Princeton University Press (1976)
30. Stalnaker, R.: A theory of conditionals. In: Rescher, N. (ed.) Studies in Logical Theory. American Philosophical Quarterly Monograph Series 2, pp. 98–112. Blackwell, Oxford (1968)

Possibilistic Logic and Inference for Linear Systems

Armand Gaudillier[1(✉)], Khaled Belahcène[1], Wassila Ouerdane[1], and Sébastien Destercke[2]

[1] Université Paris-Saclay, CentraleSupelec, MICS, Paris, France
{armand.gaudillier,khaled.belahcene,wassila.ouerdane}@centralesupelec.fr
[2] Université de technologie de Compiègne, CNRS, Alliance Sorbonne Université, Heudiasyc, Compiègne, France
sebastien.destercke@hds.utc.fr

Abstract. In this work, we propose using possibility theory to represent a belief base and to reason over it, particularly in the presence of inconsistencies. We revisit semantics from the existing literature and introduce two additional properties that help to clarify how these semantics are interconnected. The framework is then restricted to hypotheses expressed as linear numerical inequalities, in order to benefit from the polynomial-time complexity of Linear Programming while maintaining possibilistic reasoning. Finally, we define certified inference syntaxes based on Farkas' Lemma, allowing a certificate to be provided for each inference.

Keywords: Possibility theory · Reasoning over uncertainty

1 Introduction

In many applications, involving e.g. Operations Research or Decision theory, knowledge is represented through linear inequalities. This allows both to seamlessly account for natively continuous phenomena and for computationally efficient inference procedures based on linear programming. When using a combination of linear inequalities to model a problem and infer, two issues may appear. Firstly, the validity of a linear inequality can be uncertain if it is a statement from a decision maker/user/expert. Secondly, the consistency of a linear inequality system can be lost, in which case the system has no solution. Without further information, this situation is tricky to solve, as it requires to remove one or more inequalities of the system to restore consistency. When inferring from a linear inequality system or trying to repair its consistency, it seems natural to give more priority to the most certain inequalities. An elegant way to do so is to combine linear inequalities with a framework to represent uncertainty, while trying to preserve computational tractability.

The paper studies what happens when *beliefs* are represented as linear inequations within the framework of Possibility theory. We use the term belief,

K. Sauerwald and M. Thimm (Eds.): ECSQARU 2025, LNAI 16099, pp. 362–375, 2026.
https://doi.org/10.1007/978-3-032-05134-9_25

as we assume that it comes from a subjective source such as a decision maker. Although Possibility theory took root in fuzzy sets [18], Possibilistic logic [8] is distinct from fuzzy logic: fuzzy logic deals with vague predicates with multiple truth degrees, while possibilistic logic still assumes two truth degrees, about which we are uncertain. Possibilistic logic amounts to associate each belief statement (hereafter, linear equalities) with a lower confidence degree, a.k.a. necessity measure. We therefore associate degree with the certainty of a belief; however, this is not the only possible interpretation—in [11], for instance, the degree reflects preference intensity. With this premise, Possibility theory proposes a framework to compute possibility distributions, define several measures on this distribution, and provide semantics to reason over a possibilistic base (a set of possibilistic belief statements), consistent or not. For an overview of Possibility theory, refer to [9,10], and to [5] for a focus on semantics to reason over inconsistency.

Our main concern, the combination of numerical models and Possibility theory, has rarely been studied. We believe that this combination is of interest, as it allows one to have in one hand the expressivity of numerical models, and on the other hand the degree of credibility and the semantics provided by the logical framework, which often results in higher interpretability. Furthermore, little attention has been paid to computational results within Possibility theory. [15] proposes algorithms and computational results when beliefs are expressed using propositional logic. In this paper, we define syntaxes for applying Possibility theory to beliefs expressed as numerical formulas and present computational results for the semantics.

The paper is organized as follows. In Sect. 2, we provide a brief introduction to the concepts of Possibility theory and the semantics of possibilistic logic, as discussed in the literature. Then, we establish properties holding between those semantics. In Sect. 3, we restrict our universe to beliefs expressed as linear inequalities. New syntaxes for inferring are developed and computational results are given. We end the paper with some conclusions in Sect. 4.

2 Possibilistic Logic: Semantics

This section is dedicated to introducing the key concepts and notation used throughout this work. Sections 2.1 and 2.2 provide the necessary background on Possibility theory and possibilistic logic. After that, Sect. 2.3 presents two new properties on semantics.

2.1 Preliminaries

Let us have Ω, the set of states of the world, with $\omega \in \Omega$, a state. A possibility distribution π is a mapping from Ω to $[0, 1]$. It represents the plausibility of each state of the world, the higher, the more plausible. $\pi(\omega) = 1$ means that the state is totally possible, $\pi(\omega) = 0$ that it is impossible.

A possibilistic belief base Γ is composed of a set of formulas, each associated with a level of belief. We assume formulas belong to a set $\mathcal{F}$ called the *hypothesis class*, e.g. propositional formulas over a given language, or linear comparisons between numerical values. For $\phi \in \mathcal{F}$, we note $[\![\phi]\!] \subseteq \Omega$ the subset of ω that satisfies ϕ. The associated level of belief for each ϕ is α, defined over a totally ordered space (possibly ordinal). It represents the priority of its associated formula, its credence, compared to the other formulas present in Γ.

Degrees of belief can be associated to various semantics. In the cardinal case, they can be linked to imprecise probabilities [7,17]. Given a formula ϕ, consider the lottery in which a gambler receives a unit gain if ϕ is satisfied and zero otherwise: α is then defined as the maximum purchase price that one would pay to enter this game. In particular, α is one iff the gambler is certain of a positive outcome, otherwise she would forfeit a sure gain or incur a sure loss. In other words, α is a lower bound on the necessity of ϕ ; the higher α, the lower the possibility of $\neg\phi$ (i.e. every ω not satisfying ϕ). In the ordinal case, α values simply translate various levels of certainty, i.e. the idea that some statements are "more certain" than others. The statement (ϕ, α) then claims that the worlds where ϕ is satisfied are fully possible and the worlds where ϕ is not are partially possible, at level $1 - \alpha$, as captured by Eq. (1).

$$\pi_{(\phi_j,\alpha_j)}(\omega) = \begin{cases} 1 & \text{if } \omega \in [\![\phi_j]\!], \\ 1-\alpha_j & \text{otherwise.} \end{cases} \tag{1}$$

Possibility theory opts for the *minimal specificity* criterion where the possibility level of a conjunction of formulas is aggregated using the minimum operator. Equation (1) is a result of this conservative approach, as π_Γ in Eq. (2).

$$\pi_\Gamma(\omega) = \min_{(\phi_j,\alpha_j)\in\Gamma} \pi_{(\phi_j,\alpha_j)}(\omega) \tag{2}$$

This definition extends the case where information is perfect: when levels are restricted to $\{0,1\}$, a new statement ϕ prunes the set of possible worlds by asserting all worlds that do not satisfy ϕ are completely impossible. Observe that, when $\alpha_1 > \alpha_2$, the statement (ϕ, α_1) subsumes the statement (ϕ, α_2).

Example 1. We have a bag. In the bag there could be nothing, a banana, an apple, or both. We note with a bar the negation of the corresponding boolean; $\Omega = \{ba, \bar{b}a, b\bar{a}, \bar{b}\bar{a}\}$. The user states that $(a \oplus b)$ with a certainty of 0.6 and $\oplus$ the logical XOR. Hence, $\Gamma^1 = \{(a \oplus b, 0.6)\}$. In other words, the necessity of having exactly one fruit in the bag is superior or equal to 0.6. Γ^1 induces a possibility distribution for all states of the world, as shown in Table 1 below. The states of the world not satisfying the formula in Γ^1 become less possible, as in Eq. (1). With $\Gamma^2 = \Gamma^1 \cup \{(b, 0.4)\}$, for $\bar{b}\bar{a}$ not satisfying both formulas, $\pi_{\Gamma^2}(\bar{b}\bar{a}) = \min(1-0.6, 1-0.4)$, as in Eq. (2).

Therefore, if ϕ_j has a strong credence, $\omega \notin [\![\phi_j]\!]$ will be deemed less possible. In contrast, if $\pi_\Gamma(\omega) = 1$, ω is totally possible. If such an ω does not exist, the base is inconsistent. The level of inconsistency is evaluated as in Eq. (3).

$$\text{Inc}(\Gamma) = 1 - \max_{\omega \in \Omega} \pi_\Gamma(\omega) \tag{3}$$

If the base is consistent, $\text{Inc}(\Gamma) = 0$. Otherwise, $\text{Inc}(\Gamma) \geq \alpha_{min}$ where $\alpha_{min} = \min \alpha_j$ s.t $(\phi_j, \alpha_j) \in \Gamma$. We can link inconsistency with the notion of (strict) α-cuts. α-cuts are sub-bases $\Gamma_{>\alpha}$ and $\Gamma_{\geq\alpha}$, defined in Eq. (4).

$$\begin{aligned} \Gamma_{>\alpha} &= \{(\phi_j, \alpha_j) \in \Gamma \text{ s.t } \alpha_j > \alpha\} \\ \Gamma_{\geq\alpha} &= \{(\phi_j, \alpha_j) \in \Gamma \text{ s.t } \alpha_j \geq \alpha\} \end{aligned} \tag{4}$$

Pairs with an α_j value (strictly or not) below the given threshold are simply not considered. This will prove useful when dealing with inconsistent bases and allows for a concise characterization of the inconsistency level:

$$\text{Inc}(\Gamma) = \alpha \iff \Gamma_{>\alpha} \text{ is consistent but not } \Gamma_{\geq\alpha} \tag{5}$$

Example 2 (Ex.1 Cont.). The user specifies that the necessity of the presence of an apple in the bag is at least 0.3. Hence, $\Gamma^3 = \Gamma^2 \cup \{(a, 0.3)\}$. Γ^3 is inconsistent, as shown in π_{Γ^3} in Table 1. Without specifying degrees of certainty, it would be asserting that there is exactly one fruit and that there are an apple and a banana—a contradiction. Without certainty degrees, resolving such an inconsistency would require removing one of the statements. Fortunately, each statement in Γ^3 is defined on an ordinal scale of certainty. A basic way to repair the belief base is to consider the degree of inconsistency, as defined in Eq. (3). As the most plausible world is $b\bar{a}$ with degree 0.7, $\text{Inc}(\Gamma^3) = 0.3$. In other words, the strict 0.3-cut of Γ, $(\Gamma^3)_{>0.3}$, is consistent. It amounts to ignoring formulas with level 0.3 or lower, which actually yields Γ^2.

In summary, Possibility theory offers three main advantages in handling uncertainty. Firstly, it captures standard set theory as a possibility is coherent whenever its maximum reaches one. Therefore, multiple elements can have possibility one, and this contrasts with probability theory, where the summation constraint implies that increasing the plausibility of one element necessarily decreases that of others, making it unsuitable for capturing set theory. Secondly, the coherence of the possibilistic base is not considered as an axiom. This differs e.g. from standard probabilities or even from lower previsions [17]. Thirdly, if we stick to an ordinal interpretation of α's forming a scale e.g. A, the operators (min, max) used throughout the reasoning process enable to associate with each deduction an α from A. This reduced the decision maker's cognitive load to understand to what extent a deduction is certain.

2.2 Possibilistic Semantics

With the basics of Possibility theory clearly defined, let us define the possibilistic inference ($\models_{pi}$) of a formula ϕ from π_Γ. When information is certain (i.e., all

α are one), inferring on Γ is equivalent to *skeptical* inference: checking that all totally possible states of the world satisfy ϕ. The possibilistic inference semantics (see Definition 1) extends this process to uncertain information, with a level in $[0, 1]$ and beliefs that are not necessarily consistent.

Definition 1 ([8], Possibilistic inference). $\Gamma \models_{pi} (\phi, \alpha)$ *iff* $\forall \omega, \pi_\Gamma(\omega) \leq \pi_{\{(\phi,\alpha)\}}(\omega)$

Example 3 (Ex.1 Cont.). It is possible to infer $\bar{a}$, i.e. the absence of an apple, from Γ^2. $\pi_{(\bar{a},\alpha)}$ is in Table 1. With $\alpha = 0.4$, $\forall \omega, \pi_{\Gamma^2}(\omega) \leq \pi_{\{(\bar{a},0.4)\}}(\omega)$. Hence, according to Definition 1, $(\bar{a}, 0.4)$ can be inferred from Γ^2. In other words, as it is 0.6-certain there is one fruit in the bag and it is 0.4-certain there is a banana, we can deduct it is 0.4-certain there is no apple.

Table 1. Possibility distributions induced by our different bases.

ω	π_{Γ^1}	π_{Γ^2}	π_{Γ^3}	$\pi_{(\bar{a},\alpha)}$
ba	0.4	0.4	0.4	$1-\alpha$
$\bar{b}a$	1	0.6	0.6	$1-\alpha$
$b\bar{a}$	1	1	0.7	1
$\bar{b}\bar{a}$	0.4	0.4	0.4	1

Possibilistic inference is similar to what is done in other kinds of logic. For example, Definition 1 can be rewritten as a refutation. Instead of checking the inclusion of all totally possible ω in $[\![\phi]\!]$, it is equivalent to verify that the intersection of totally possible ω and $[\![\neg\phi]\!]$ is empty. However, when $\text{Inc}(\Gamma) > 0$, any formula can be inferred at $\alpha = 1 - \text{Inc}(\Gamma)$ via Definition 1. Therefore, it is possible to infer both ϕ and $\neg\phi$ from the same base. Without degrees of certainty, this presents a problem, as there is no additional information to help resolve the contradiction. In contrast, the higher-order information provided by the valuation of beliefs with degrees of certainty can help address the problem, as the decision concerns (ϕ, α) and $(\neg\phi, \beta)$, a richer information. As decision is not the focus of this work, we leave this question open.

In order to prevent the apparition of a contradiction, two new types of inference will be introduced, specially built to deal with the inconsistent case. Definition 2 introduces the first semantics, the *non-trivial inference.*

Definition 2 ([8], Non-trivial inference). $\Gamma \models_{nt} (\phi, \alpha)$ *iff* $\pi_{\Gamma_{>\text{Inc}(\Gamma)}}(\omega) \leq \pi_{\{(\phi,\alpha)\}}(\omega)$*, with* $\pi_{\Gamma_{>\text{Inc}(\Gamma)}}$ *consistent by Equation* (5).

$\models_{nt}$ makes use of the possibility degrees as the formulas under $\text{Inc}(\Gamma)$ are ignored. Here, inference and decision are equivalent, as it is not possible to infer ϕ and $\neg\phi$ on a consistent base. However, the disadvantage of $\models_{nt}$ is the drowning effect: all information under $\text{Inc}(\Gamma)$ is lost, even though some of it might be consistent with the curated base $\Gamma_{>\text{Inc}(\Gamma)}$. Hence, the accepted inferences will be high in terms of certainty, but less pieces of information will be inferred. $\models_{pi}$ has a similar behaviour; observe how Definition 1 allows one to infer any formula at $\text{Inc}(\Gamma)$. If Γ is inconsistent, all the information under $\text{Inc}(\Gamma)$ is drowned and all the information is inferred at least at $\text{Inc}(\Gamma)$. In case of inconsistency, $\models_{pi}$ states that everything is possible while $\models_{nt}$ infers only the most plausible pieces of information.

Example 4 (Ex. 2 Cont.). The user states that the bag is green, noted g, with a certainty of 0.3. As Γ^3 is inconsistent, $\Gamma^4 = \Gamma^3 \cup \{(g, 0.3)\}$ is also inconsistent. When using $\models_{nt}$ to reason on Γ^4, the new statement will always be ignored, as its degree of certainty is equal to $\text{Inc}(\Gamma^4)$. It is not possible to infer any piece of information on g at an $\alpha > 0$. This is an issue because the statement does not cause any inconsistency; it is drowned. For the same example, $\models_{pi}$ infers $(g, 0.3)$ and $(\bar{g}, 0.3)$. This does not give more precision than $\models_{nt}$, both worlds are plausible at the same degree.

To avoid the drowning effect, the *safe* possibilistic inference is introduced in Definition 3.

Definition 3 (Safe inference). $\Gamma \models_s (\phi, \alpha)$ *iff* $\exists \Gamma^* \subseteq \Gamma$ *s.t* $\text{Inc}(\Gamma^*) = 0$ *and* $\Gamma^* \models_{pi} (\phi, \alpha)$

Γ^* is called an *argued reason* for ϕ if Γ^* supports the inference of (ϕ, α). This is similar to credulous inference; the states of the world satisfying Γ^* are possible, even if they do not satisfy Γ. While this definition of $\models_s$ is, to the best of our knowledge, original, it is strongly inspired by the notion of argued consequences proposed in [5]. Originally, the argued reasons supporting an argued consequence were required to be subset minimal. This requirement is unnecessary from a logical point of view, and simply translates a form of dialectical etiquette [6], where a locutor is expected to provide support for her claim which is minimally relevant. This is the same goal as expressed by the notion of *prime* implicant w.r.t. a mere implicant [2,16]. We choose to drop it from $\models_s$ to clearly delineate the deduction and explanation processes.

This semantics is much more expressive than $\models_{pi}$ and $\models_{nt}$, as it does not suffer from drowning. As Γ is inconsistent, it is possible to have an argued reason for ϕ and another for $\neg\phi$, each with a different degree of credence. In this case, the decision problem arises: which side will be recommended? It can be linked to *bipolar argumentation* [1], with the argued reasons as arguments for ϕ or $\neg\phi$. Another way to proceed is to choose an expressive semantic that guarantees the consistence of the set of inferred expressions. $\models_{ss}$ from [5] corresponds to these criteria. However, the study of this semantics is beyond the scope of this paper. In the next subsection, properties on the interaction of the semantics will be given.

2.3 Semantics and Nesting

These three semantics ($\models_{pi}, \models_{nt}, \models_s$) allow inference at different degrees of certainty. We may then wonder which is more informative than the others, for instance to select the more fitted to be used in a decision process. The literature is vague on this point, except for Proposition 1.

Proposition 1 ([5]). *if* $\Gamma \models_{nt} (\phi, \alpha)$, *then* $\Gamma \models_s (\phi, \beta), \beta \geq \alpha$

We propose to establish the same property between $\models_s$ and $\models_{pi}$.

Proposition 2. *if* $\Gamma \models_s (\phi, \beta)$, *then* $\Gamma \models_{pi} (\phi, \gamma), \gamma \geq \beta$

Proof. $\Gamma \models_s (\phi, \beta)$ iff $\exists \Gamma' \subseteq \Gamma$ s.t $\Gamma' \models_{pi} (\phi, \beta)$ and Γ' consistent. As $\Gamma' \subseteq \Gamma$, $\forall \omega, \pi_\Gamma(\omega) \leq \pi_{\Gamma'}(\omega) \leq \pi_{(\phi,\beta)}(\omega)$ (due to the min specificity principle). □

Remark that $\models_{pi}$ always infers with a higher or equal degree of certainty. However, $\models_{pi}$ and $\models_{nt}$ share the same behaviour.

Proposition 3. *Let us have* α *and* β, *maximal degrees that permit the inferences* $\Gamma \models_{nt} (\phi, \alpha)$ *and* $\Gamma \models_{pi} (\phi, \beta)$ *then* $\alpha = 0, \beta = \text{Inc}(\Gamma)$ *or* $\alpha = \beta$.

Proof. If there is no argued reason for ϕ strictly over $\text{Inc}(\Gamma)$, $\alpha = 0, \beta = \text{Inc}(\Gamma)$. Else, the argued reason will impact π_Γ s.t. $\models_{nt}$ and $\models_{pi}$ can infer ϕ at the degree of argued reason. □

$\models_{nt}$ and $\models_{pi}$ always reach the same conclusion, except that they have a different way of expressing ignorance. This is due to their similar sensitivity to the drowning effect. Naturally, $\models_s$, not suffering from such effect, is able to infer in cases where the argued reason is below the inconsistency level.

Having defined possibilistic logic and its semantics, we will now investigate the computational complexity and syntaxes for semantics of Definitions 1, 2 and 3, for the case where Ω and the *hypothesis class* are linear models and inequalities.

3 The Logic of Linear Comparison

In this section, we combine the expressive power and favourable computational properties of linear models with logical tools for reasoning over a belief base.

3.1 Restricting to Linear Inequalities

From now on, Ω is restricted to the Cartesian product of domains defined over a continuous space. We have $\Omega = (\mathbb{R}_+)^n \setminus \{0\}$. Therefore, each $\omega \in \Omega$ is a non-null n-dimensional vector in $\mathbb{R}_+$. Without loss of generality, each belief base is composed of a number of statements and n necessary statements with $\omega_i \geq 0$ of credence 1. The class of hypotheses $\mathcal{F}$ is also restricted to the *dual space* $\Omega^*_\geq$, so that each formula $\phi^{(j)}$ is associated with a n-dimensional vector $(\phi_1^{(j)}, \ldots, \phi_n^{(j)}) \in \mathbb{R}^n$ and a linear inequality of the form given in Eq. (6).

$$\sum_{i=1}^{n} \phi_i^{(j)} \omega_i \geq 0 \tag{6}$$

With this restriction, it is now possible to write $\neg\phi$ as $-\phi$.

Example 5. Several types of statement can be represented by linear inequalities. It depends from the subjacent use; for instance, in a case where a choice has to be made between several alternatives evaluated on several criteria, considering a weighted sum such that the score of each alternative is computed by $Score(x) = \sum_{i=1}^{n} x_i \omega_i$, with x_i the score of alternative x on criterion i. In this case, the linear inequalities can represent the preference of a criterion over another (e.g. $\phi^{(1)}, \phi^{(2)}$ or $\phi^{(4)}$) or the preference of an alternative over another (e.g. $\phi^{(3)}$). With this formalism and $\Omega = (\mathbb{R}^+)^3 \setminus \{0\}$, a possible base is $\Gamma = \{(\omega_1 \geq 0, 1), (\omega_2 \geq 0, 1), (\omega_3 \geq 0, 1), (\phi^{(1)}, 0.6), (\phi^{(2)}, 0.5), (\phi^{(3)}, 0.4), (\phi^{(4)}, 0.3)\}$ with $\phi^{(1)} = \omega_1 - \omega_2 \geq 0$, $\phi^{(2)} = \omega_3 - \omega_2 \geq 0$, $\phi^{(3)} = -2\omega_1 + 3\omega_2 - 3\omega_3 \geq 0$ and $\phi^{(4)} = \omega_3 - \omega_1 \geq 0$. If Γ is inconsistent, then no $\omega \neq 0$ is a solution of its system. Observe that the combination $7\phi^{(1)} + 2\phi^{(3)} + 4\phi^{(4)}$ ensures $-\omega_1 - \omega_2 - 2\omega_3 \geq 0$, while the non-negativity of $\omega_1, \omega_2, \omega_3$ entails $\omega_1 + \omega_2 + 2\omega_3 \geq 0$. Both cannot be satisfied if ω is non null. π_Γ is drawn with barycentric[1] coordinates in Fig. 1. The distribution shows that $\phi^{(4)}$ is drowned by the inconsistency, as its credence degree is below $\text{Inc}(\Gamma)$.

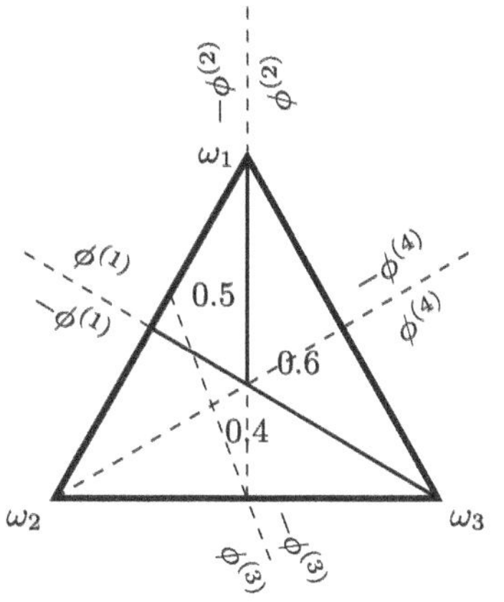

Fig. 1. The possibility distribution π_Γ.

With $\mathcal{F}$ and Ω specified, it is possible to give computational results for the various forms of possibilistic inference semantics.

3.2 Computational Results

According to Definition 1, to infer ϕ from a consistent Γ, the set of totally possible ω has to be included in $[\![\phi]\!]$. This is equivalent to proving that no totally possible ω is in $\Omega \setminus [\![\phi]\!]$. When Ω is a set of propositional variables and $\mathcal{F}$ the propositional formulas over them, ensuring that Γ is consistent is NP-complete,

[1] Without loss of generality, a normalization constraint $(\omega_1 + \omega_2 + \omega_3 = 1)$ is added.

and inference is computationally difficult [15]. With $\Omega = \mathbb{R}^n \setminus \{0\}$ and $\mathcal{F} = \Omega^*_{\geq}$, this check can be performed in polynomial time with linear programming (LP), yielding low complexity results for the various inference problems.

Proposition 4. *When $\Omega = \mathbb{R}_+{}^n \setminus \{0\}$ and $\mathcal{F} = \Omega^*_{\geq}$, checking whether a given possibilistic belief base is consistent is polytime.*

Proof. Consider the LP with decision variables in Ω consisting in maximizing $\phi^N := \sum_{i=1}^n \omega_i$ subject to all formulas in the base and the fundamental constraints $\omega_i \geq 0$. This LP is always feasible (because the null vector satisfies all constraints), can be solved in polynomial time [12,14], and the deduction is valid iff the optimum is strictly positive. □

As a corollary, finding the inconsistency level of a belief base is polytime.

Corollary 1. *When $\Omega = \mathbb{R}_+{}^n \setminus \{0\}$ and $\mathcal{F} = \Omega^*_{\geq}$, given a possibilistic belief base Γ, computing* $\mathrm{Inc}(\Gamma)$ *is polytime.*

Proof. Finding the inconsistency level can be performed with a binary search on α, by checking whether $\Gamma_{\geq\alpha}$ is consistent or not, as proposed in [15]. It requires $O(\log_2 |\Gamma|)$ calls to a polynomial algorithm, hence it is still polytime. □

For $\models_{pi}$, $\models_{nt}$ and $\models_s$, inference over a consistent belief base is polytime.

Corollary 2. *When $\Omega = \mathbb{R}_+{}^n \setminus \{0\}$ and $\mathcal{F} = \Omega^*_{\geq}$, given a possibilistic belief base Γ, a formula ϕ and a level $\alpha \in [0,1]$, if $\Gamma_{\geq\alpha}$ is consistent, then deciding whether $\Gamma \models_X (\phi, \alpha)$ is polytime whatever $X \in \{pi, nt, s\}$.*

Proof. For all three semantics, inferring (ϕ, α) amounts to checking whether $\Gamma_{\geq\alpha} \cup (-\phi, \alpha)$ is inconsistent. For $\models_{pi}$, it is direct via Corollary 1. As the base and all its sub-bases are consistent, it is also the case for $\models_{nt}$ and $\models_s$. □

Corollary 3. *When $\Omega = \mathbb{R}_+{}^n \setminus \{0\}$ and $\mathcal{F} = \Omega^*_{\geq}$, given a possibilistic belief base Γ, a formula ϕ and a level $\alpha \in [0,1]$, deciding whether $\Gamma \models_{nt} (\phi, \alpha)$ is polytime.*

Proof. Consistent case in Corollary 2. For the inconsistent case, computing $\mathrm{Inc}(\Gamma)$ is polytime. As $\Gamma_{>\mathrm{Inc}(\Gamma)}$ is always consistent, inferring with $\models_{nt}$ on an inconsistent base is polytime. □

When considering $\models_s$, the requirement to find a consistent sub-base makes the problem more computationally demanding. Fortunately, Proposition 5 ensures that it remains in NP.

Proposition 5. *When $\Omega = \mathbb{R}^n \setminus \{0\}$ and $\mathcal{F} = \Omega^*_{\geq}$, given a possibilistic belief base Γ, a formula ϕ and a level $\alpha \in [0,1]$, deciding whether $\Gamma \models_s (\phi, \alpha)$ is NP-complete.*

Proof. Membership: given a subset Γ^* of the belief base, checking whether Γ^* is consistent is polytime. If it is, then checking whether $\Gamma^* \models_{pi} (\phi, \alpha)$ is polytime. *Hardness:* reduction from VERTEX COVER [13]. From an instance $\langle V, E, K\rangle$ of VERTEX COVER, we build an instance $\langle \Gamma, (\phi, \alpha)\rangle$ of SAFE POSSIBILISTIC INFERENCE as follows. The parameter set is $\Omega := (R_+)^{E \cup V \cup \{\alpha,\beta\}}$. For each edge e and vertex $u \in e$, we denote ϕ_e^u the formula $\omega_e + \omega_\alpha \leq \omega_u$, and Γ the possibilistic belief base containing all these formulas with credence 1. Let $\phi^\#$ the formula $\sum_{v \in V} \omega_v + \omega_\beta \leq K\omega_\alpha$, and $\phi : \sum_{e \in E} \omega_e + \omega_\beta \leq K\omega_\alpha$. We claim $\Gamma, (\phi^\#, 1) \models_t (\phi, 1)$ iff there is a vertex cover of (V, E) of cardinality $\leq K$.

Indeed, suppose $U \subseteq V$ covers E with $|U| \leq K$, and consider the sub-base Γ_U containing all formulas ϕ_e^u for $e \in E$ and $u \in e \cap U$, with credence 1. First, the sub-base $\Gamma_U \cup \{(\phi^\#, 1)\}$ is consistent, because the interpretation where $\omega_e = 0$ for all edges in E, $\omega_u = \omega_\alpha$ for all vertices in U, $\omega_v = 0$ for all vertices in $V \setminus U$ and $\omega_\beta = 0$ satisfies all its formulas. Second, it allows to deduce ϕ with credence 1, because, for every interpretation of $\omega \in \Omega$ satisfying both Γ_U and $\phi^\#$, we have, by summation of all comparisons in Γ_U that $\sum_{e \in E} \omega_e \leq \sum_{u \in U} (\omega_u - \omega_\alpha) = \sum_{u \in U} \omega_u - |U|\omega_\alpha$. Moreover $\sum_{u \in U} \omega_u \leq \sum_{v \in V} \omega_v$ because all ω_u are non-negative and $U \subseteq V$. Thus, $\phi^\#$ yields $\sum_{e \in E} \omega_e + \omega_\beta \leq \sum_{v \in V} \omega_v + \omega_\beta \leq K\omega_\alpha$ and ϕ holds in every possible world.

Reciprocally, suppose there is a sub-base $\Gamma^* \subset \Gamma \cup \{(\phi^\#, 1)\}$ which is consistent and allows to derive ϕ. Suppose $\phi^\# \notin \Gamma^*$: there is no constraint bounding ω_β from above, and starting from any feasible model and letting $\omega_\beta \to +\infty$ yields a feasible model that does not satisfy ϕ at some point: a contradiction. For each edge $e \in E$, if Γ^* contained no formula ϕ_e^u for some $u_e \in e$, there would be no constraint bounding ω_e from above, leading to a similar contradiction. Thus, the set $U := \bigcup_{e \in E} \{u_e\}$ covers E, and because $\phi^\#$ holds, it cannot have cardinality above K. □

Remark that while $\models_s$ is harder than $\models_{nt}$, it allows to infer with more certainty, as in Proposition 1. At this point, no results have been given for $\models_{pi}$. It holds if Γ is inconsistent, allowing to infer *any* formula (and also its negation) at some level $\alpha > 0$. Computationally, this is a much more difficult problem.

Proposition 6. *When* $\Omega = {\mathbb{R}_+}^n \setminus \{0\}$ *and* $\mathcal{F} = \Omega^*_{\geq}$, *given a possibilistic belief base* Γ, *a formula* ϕ *and a level* $\alpha \in [0, 1]$, *deciding whether* $\Gamma \models_{pi} (\phi, \alpha)$ *is NP-hard.*

Proof (Sketch). Adaptation of the reduction from VERTEX COVER put forward in the proof of Proposition 5. Let $e^* = \{u^*, v^*\}$ an arbitrary edge in E, and consider a slightly modified belief base Γ', where the formulas $\phi_{e*}^{u^*}$ and $\phi_{e*}^{v^*}$ now have a slightly lower credence 0.9 instead of 1. The formula ϕ can be inferred with $\models_{pi}$ at level 0.9 iff there is a vertex cover, and at level 1 iff there is a vertex cover without e^*. □

$\models_{pi}$ reaches the same conclusion as $\models_{nt}$ but is more computationally difficult. Hence, using $\models_{pi}$ to infer on an inconsistent base is not pertinent. For this reason, no syntax will be provided for $\models_{pi}$ in the next section.

3.3 Certified Inference

The last section proposed a calculus for possibilistic logic based on LP. This is a satisfying solution from the computational point of view, allowing tractable inference. And even though NP-completeness is hardly scalable, it is sufficient to process small instances (which remain numerous in applications). Nevertheless, LP is certainly not human-friendly, and relying on a solver to check the validity of inference does not seem to fulfill the requirement of transparency. Thus, we propose to support inference with evidence allowing to check its adequacy. The main tool in this endeavour is Farkas' lemma: a system of linear inequalities over $\mathbb{R}^n$, $\phi^{(1)} \geq 0, \ldots, \phi^{(m)} \geq 0$ entails $\phi \geq 0$ if, and only if, ϕ is a convex combination of the $\phi^{(k)}$. Thus, deduction made under the assumptions of Corollary 2 can be supported with a certificate proving its soundness.

Reasoning w.r.t. Safe Inference. We propose a certificate for safe inference.

Definition 4. *When $\Omega = \mathbb{R}^n \setminus \{0\}$, a primal/dual (or p/d)-certificate is an ordered pair (ω^*, λ^*) where $\omega^* \in \Omega$ and λ^* is a tuple of non-negative numbers. Given a possibilistic belief base $\Gamma = \{(\phi^{(1)}, \alpha_1), \ldots, (\phi^{(m)}, \alpha_m)\}$, a formula ϕ and a level $\alpha \in [0, 1]$, we write $\Gamma \vdash_s^{(\omega^*, \lambda^*)} (\phi, \alpha)$ when all following conditions are satisfied:*

i) the length of λ^* is equal to m, the cardinality of Γ;
ii) for all $1 \leq k \leq m$, if $\lambda_k^* > 0$ then $\phi^{(k)}(\omega^*) \geq 0$;
iii) for all $1 \leq k \leq m$, if $\lambda_k^* > 0$ then $\alpha_k \geq \alpha$; and
iv) $\phi \geq \sum_{k=1}^m \lambda_k^* \phi^{(k)}$.

We write $\Gamma \vdash_s (\phi, \alpha)$ when there is a p/d-certificate (ω^*, λ^*) such that $\Gamma \vdash_s^{(\omega^*, \lambda^*)} (\phi, \alpha)$.

Proposition 7. *Syntactic deduction $\vdash_s$ is sound and complete w.r.t. $\models_s$.*

Proof. Define $\Gamma^* := \{(\phi^{(k)}, \alpha_k) : \lambda_k^* > 0\}$. Condition ii) ensures the consistency of Γ^*, as witnessed by the totally possible ω^*. Condition iii) ensures the credence level of Γ^* is at least α, warranting inference at this level. Condition iv) ensures the conclusion ϕ is in the convex span of the formulas in Γ^*. All these conditions are necessary for safe possibilistic inference, and together they are sufficient. □

Reasoning w.r.t. Non-Trivial Inference. There are two ways to perform non-trivial inference. Either to compute the inconsistency level $Inc(\Gamma)$ beforehand; maybe certify it with a primal/dual certificate (ω^*, λ^*) such that $\sum_k \lambda^* \phi^k = -\sum_k \omega_k$ (thus $\Gamma_{>Inc(\Gamma)}$ is consistent) and for all $1 \leq k \leq m$, if $\alpha_k > Inc(\Gamma)$ then $\phi^{(k)}(\omega^*) \geq 0$, and if $\alpha_k \leq Inc(\Gamma)$ then $\lambda_k = 0$ (thus $\Gamma_{\geq Inc(\Gamma)}$ is inconsistent); then perform inference with the consistent base (maybe supporting it with a dual certificate). Otherwise to perform safe inference restricted to a stratified consistent sub-base $\Gamma^* \subseteq \Gamma_{>Inc(\Gamma)}$.

Definition 5. *Under the same assumption as Definition 4, we write* $\Gamma \vdash_{nt}^{(\omega^*,\lambda^*)} (\phi,\alpha)$ *when conditions i), ii), iii) and iv) are satisfied, as well as:*

v) for all $1 \leq k \leq m$, *if* $\alpha > Inc(\Gamma)$ *then* $\phi^{(k)}(\omega^*) \geq 0$.

We write $\Gamma \vdash_{nt} (\phi,\alpha)$ *when there is a p/d-certificate* (ω^*,λ^*) *such that* $\Gamma \vdash_{nt}^{(\omega^*,\lambda^*)} (\phi,\alpha)$.

Proposition 8. *Syntactic deduction* $\vdash_{nt}$ *is sound and complete w.r.t.* $\models_{nt}$.

Proof. This is corollary of the fact non-trivial inference is simply safe inference restricted to the case where the sub-base $\Gamma^* \subseteq \Gamma_{>Inc(\Gamma)}$. Condition v) enforces this. □

As a direct consequence from Propositions 7 and 8, $\vdash_s$ and $\vdash_{nt}$ are not harder nor easier than their respective semantics, allowing NP-complete and polynomial-time inference. No syntax is given corresponding to $\models_{pi}$, as discussed at the end of Subsect. 3.2. On a consistent base, the syntaxes from Definitions 4 and 5 are equivalent. Let us illustrate these syntaxes with an example.

Example 6 (Ex.5 Cont.). We illustrate how inference based on different semantics produces different outcomes, with the goal of inferring $\phi := (6\omega_1 - 7\omega_2 + \omega_3 \geq 0)$ and $\phi' := (-2\omega_1 + \omega_2 + 2\omega_3 \geq 0)$.

Possibilistic inference $\models_{pi}$ allows to infer *any* formula ϕ from Γ with a level $\alpha = \text{Inc}(\Gamma)$. This is a much more nuanced version of the principle of explosion of classical logic which puts all formulas on the same level.

Non-trivial inference $\models_{nt}$ prescribes to ignore the less certain stratum at level 0.4 which provokes inconsistency. $\phi = 6\phi^{(1)} + \phi^{(2)}$, $(\omega^*,\lambda^*) = ((0.5, 0, 0.5), (6, 1, 0, 0))$ is a certificate in favour of ϕ with credence 0.5, since the minimum credence degree of a formula in the convex combination of ϕ is 0.5. In other words, λ^* provides the information that supports the inference. This is more convenient for a DM than a linear program; it can be seen as an early form of explanation: it is still hard to grasp for a non-specialist DM. The certificate can be long and has to be understood as a whole. However, it is not possible to infer ϕ' with the formulas in $\Gamma_{>0.4}$. $\phi^{(4)}$ would allow for it, but it is "drowned".

Safe inference $\models_s$ allows to make deductions based on any (maximally) consistent sub-base of Γ. With $\phi = 6\phi^{(1)} + \phi^{(2)}$, as with $\models_{nt}$. Here, it is possible to infer $\phi' = 2\phi^4 + (\omega_2 \geq 0)$. This is much more versatile than non-trivial inference, at the cost of solving a NP-complete problem.

4 Conclusion

In this paper, a possibilistic theoretical framework combining logical frameworks and numerical models has been presented, with the idea of benefitting from their respective qualities. Numerical models are expressive and computationally attractive, especially linear ones. Logical frameworks provide clear semantics and tools to infer, even in case of inconsistency. Possibility theory on its side is interesting for its simplicity as well as the fact that it includes both numerical sets and propositional logic as special cases.

While our focus was on logical inferences for linear systems, we provided some new insights about possibilistic logic inference tools (Sect. 2.3). We then proceeded to characterise the computational complexity of logical inference over linear systems, as well as providing completeness and soundness results relying on Farkas' criterion of contradiction, as used in several papers in the field of explainability [3,4]. Farkas' provides a certificate of infeasibility, which can be seen as an early form of explanation. A possible application for these tools is the Multi-Criteria Decision Aiding.

In the future, we would like to leverage our results to provide recommendation explanation under uncertain preferential information and model.

Acknowledgments. Armand Gaudillier and Khaled Belahcène are supported by the chair "Explainable artificial intelligence for the future of Industry" funded by the ANR.

Disclosure of Interests. The authors have no competing interests to declare that are relevant to the content of this article.

References

1. Amgoud, L., Cayrol, C., Lagasquie-Schiex, M.C., Livet, P.: On bipolarity in argumentation frameworks. Int. J. Intell. Syst. **23**(10), 1062–1093 (2008). https://doi.org/10.1002/int.20307
2. Amgoud, L., Cooper, M., Debbaoui, S.: Axiomatic characterisations of sample-based explainers. In: Proceedings of ECAI 2024, pp. 770–777 (October 2024). https://doi.org/10.48550/arXiv.2408.04903
3. Amoussou, M., Belahcène, K., Labreuche, C., Maudet, N., Mousseau, V., Ouerdane, W.: Questionable stepwise explanations for a robust additive preference model. Int. J. Approx. Reason. 108982 (2023). https://doi.org/10.1016/j.ijar.2023.108982
4. Belahcene, K., Labreuche, C., Maudet, N., Mousseau, V., Ouerdane, W.: Explaining robust additive utility models by sequences of preference swaps. Theor. Decis. **82**, 151–183 (2017). https://doi.org/10.1007/s11238-016-9560-1
5. Benferhat, S., Dubois, D., Prade, H.: An overview of inconsistency-tolerant inferences in prioritized knowledge bases. Fuzzy Sets Log. Reason. Knowl. **15**, 395–417 (1999). https://doi.org/10.1007/978-94-017-1652-9_25
6. Black, E., Maudet, N., Parsons, S.: Argumentation-based dialogue. In: Gabbay, D., Giacomin, M., Simari, G.R., Thimm, M. (eds.) Handbook of Formal Argumentation, vol. 2. College Publications (2021)
7. Dubois, D., Godo, L., Mántaras, R., Prade, H.: Qualitative reasoning with imprecise probabilities. J. Intell. Inf. Syst. **2**, 319–363 (1993). https://doi.org/10.1007/BF00961659
8. Dubois, D., Lang, J., Prade, H.: Possibilistic logic. In: Gabbay, D.M., Hogger, C.J., Robinson, J.A., Nute, D. (eds.) Handbook of Logic in Artificial Intelligence and Logic Programming, vol. 3, pp. 439–513. Oxford Univ. Press (1994)
9. Dubois, D., Prade, H.: Possibilistic logic: a retrospective and prospective view. Fuzzy Sets Syst. **144**, 3–23 (2004). https://doi.org/10.1016/j.fss.2003.10.011

10. Dubois, D., Prade, H.: Possibility theory and its applications: where do we stand? In: Kacprzyk, J., Pedrycz, W. (eds.) Springer Handbook of Computational Intelligence. Springer Handbooks, pp. 31–60. Springer, Berlin, Heidelberg (2015). https://doi.org/10.1007/978-3-662-43505-2_3
11. Kaci, S., Prade, H.: Mastering the processing of preferences by using symbolic priorities in possibilistic logic. In: Proceedings of the ECAI 2008, pp. 376–380 (2008). https://doi.org/10.3233/978-1-58603-891-5-376
12. Karmarkar, N.: A new polynomial-time algorithm for linear programming. Combinatorica **4**(4), 373–396 (1984). https://doi.org/10.1007/BF02579150
13. Karp, R.: Reducibility among combinatorial problems. In: Miller, R., Thatcher, J. (eds.) Complexity of Computer Computations, pp. 85–103. Plenum Press (1972). https://doi.org/10.1007/978-1-4684-2001-2_9
14. Khachiyan, L.: A polynomial algorithm for linear programming. Dokl. Akad. Nauk SSSR **224**(5), 1093–1096 (1979)
15. Lang, J.: Possibilistic logic: complexity and algorithms. In: Kohlas, J., Moral, S. (eds.) Handbook of Defeasible Reasoning and Uncertainty Management Systems, pp. 179–220. Springer-Science + Buisness Media, B.V., Berlin, Heidelberg (2000). https://doi.org/10.1007/978-94-017-1737-3_5
16. Marques-Silva, J., Gerspacher, T., Cooper, M., Ignatiev, A., Narodytska, N.: Explaining naive bayes and other linear classifiers with polynomial time and delay. In: Larochelle, H., Ranzato, M., Hadsell, R., Balcan, M., Lin, H. (eds.) Advances in Neural Information Processing Systems, vol. 33, pp. 20590–20600. Curran Associates, Inc. (2020). https://doi.org/10.48550/arXiv.2008.05803
17. Walley, P.: Statistical Reasoning with Imprecise Probabilities. Chapman & Hall, Boca Raton (1991)
18. Zadeh, L.: Fuzzy sets as a basis for a theory of possibility. Fuzzy Sets Syst. **1**, 3–28 (1978)

Argumentation

Assumption-Based Argumentation for General Extended Disjunctive Logic Programming with Negation as Failure in the Head

Toshiko Wakaki(✉)

Shibaura Institute of Technology, 307 Fukasaku, Minuma-ku, Saitama-city, Saitama 337–8570, Japan
twakaki@shibaura-it.ac.jp

Abstract. A general extended disjunctive logic program (GEDP) with negation as failure in the head may have *non-minimal* answer sets, while answer sets of an extended disjunctive logic program (EDLP) are minimal. So far, no work has been done to relate general extended disjunctive logic programming and assumption-based argumentation (ABA). In this paper, first, we propose a novel polynomial-time translation from a GEDP to an EDLP, with which there is a one-to-one correspondence between the consistent answer sets of the original GEDP and those of the translated EDLP. Second, based on the proposed translation as well as the work to relate EDLPs and ABA frameworks (ABFs), we show a one-to-one correspondence between the consistent answer sets of a consistent propositional GEDP and the consistent stable extensions of its associated ABF.

Keywords: Assumption-based argumentation · General extended disjunctive logic programs · Non-minimal answer sets · NAF in the head

1 Introduction

The most interesting property of general extended disjunctive logic programs (GEDPs) [9] with *negation as failure* (NAF) in the head is that they may have *non-minimal* answer sets, while answer sets of an extended disjunctive logic program (EDLP) [12] are minimal. A GEDP is useful for representing knowledge of various domains in which the principle of minimality is too strong, and its answer sets can be computed by the ASP system *clingo* [10][1].

On the other hand, in formal argumentation, numerous studies have been presented relating logic programming and assumption-based argumentation (ABA) [1–3, 7, 13–16]. As for the recent work, Wakaki [15,16] showed a correspondence

[1] https://potassco.org/.

K. Sauerwald and M. Thimm (Eds.): ECSQARU 2025, LNAI 16099, pp. 379–394, 2026.
https://doi.org/10.1007/978-3-032-05134-9_26

between the answer sets of an EDLP and the stable extensions of the associated assumption-based framework (ABF), while Rapberger et al. [13] showed a correspondence between the stable (resp. set-stable) models of a logic program (LP) whose each rule has either one atom or one NAF atom in the head and the stable [1] (resp. set-stable [4]) assumption sets of the associated *non-flat* ABF. However, neither classical negation nor disjunction in a rule head is allowed in LPs used by Rapberger et al. [13], while in EDLPs, they are allowed but NAF in the disjunctive head of a rule is not allowed. In contrast, the class of GEDPs includes the class of EDLPs as well as that of LPs used by Rapberger et al. [13].

Hence, the purpose of this study is to find the relationship between GEDPs and ABFs. Regarding GEDPs and EDLPs, the computational complexity of GEDPs is shown to remain in the same complexity class as EDLPs. Thus, Inoue and Sakama proposed a polynomial-time translation of any GEDP into an EDLP [9], where they claimed that with their translation, there is a one-to-one correspondence between the answer sets of the original GEDP and those of the translated EDLP. However, we found counterexamples against their claim, denoting that their translation can never yield *a one-to-one* correspondence between the answer sets of the respective programs.

Thus, in this paper, first we show the aforementioned counterexamples. Then, we propose a novel polynomial-time translation of a GEDP into an EDLP, which ensures a one-to-one correspondence between the *consistent* answer sets of the original GEDP and those of the translated EDLP. Second, based on the proposed translation of a GEDP into an EDLP as well as the recent work to relate EDLPs and ABFs [16], we show a one-to-one correspondence between the consistent answer sets of a consistent propositional GEDP and the consistent stable extensions of the ABF translated from the GEDP. Though our approach does not require such the translated ABF to be *flat*, it is shown that it is always *flat* due to its property.

The paper is organized as follows. Section 2 gives preliminaries. Section 3 presents the proposed translation of a GEDP into an EDLP and shows the correspondence between the answer sets of the respective LPs. Section 4 presents the relationship between GEDPs and ABFs. The last section concludes the paper.

2 Preliminaries

2.1 General Extended Disjunctive Logic Programs

We consider a *general extended disjunctive logic program* (GEDP) [8,9] in this paper. Since a rule with variables stands for the set of its ground instances, we can restrict our attention to (possibly infinite) ground logic programs.

A GEDP is a set of rules of the form:

$$L_1 \mid \ldots \mid L_k \mid \, not\; L_{k+1} \mid \ldots \mid not\; L_\ell \leftarrow L_{\ell+1}, \ldots, L_m, not\; L_{m+1}, \ldots, not\; L_n \quad (1)$$

where $n \geq m \geq \ell \geq k \geq 0$ and each L_i is a literal, that is, either an atom A or $\neg A$ preceded by classical negation $\neg$. "$|$" is the connective of a disjunction. "*not*" means *negation as failure* (NAF, for short) and *not* L is called a *NAF-literal*. The disjunction to the left of $\leftarrow$ is the *head* and the conjunction to the right of $\leftarrow$ is the *body* of the rule. *body*(r) denotes the body of a rule r. A rule with an empty head is called an *integrity constraint*. A GEDP is called an *extended disjunctive logic program* (EDLP) if it contains no NAF in the head of any rule (i.e., $k = \ell$). An EDLP is called a *normal disjunctive logic program* (NDP) if every L_i in the program is an atom; and an EDLP is called an *extended logic program* (ELP) if it contains no disjunction ($k = \ell \leq 1$). An ELP is called a *normal logic program* (NLP) [11] if "$\neg$" does not occur in it. Let Lit_P be the set of all ground literals in the language of a GEDP P. We say that a set of ground literals $S \subseteq Lit_P$ satisfies a ground rule of the form (1) iff $\{L_{\ell+1}, \ldots, L_m\} \subseteq S$ and $\{L_{m+1}, \ldots, L_n\} \cap S = \emptyset$ imply either $\{L_1, \ldots, L_k\} \cap S \neq \emptyset$ or $\{L_{k+1}, \ldots, L_\ell\} \not\subseteq S$.

The semantics of GEDPs is given by the *answer sets*.

Definition 1. [9] First, let P be a *not*-free GEDP (i.e. $k = \ell$ and $m = n$) and $S \subseteq Lit_P$. S is an *answer set* of P if S is a minimal set satisfying two conditions:

(i) S satisfies every rule in P, i.e., for each ground rule $L_1|\ldots|L_\ell \leftarrow L_{\ell+1}, \ldots, L_m$ from P, $\{L_{\ell+1}, \ldots, L_m\} \subseteq S$ implies $L_i \in S$ for some i ($1 \leq i \leq \ell$). In particular, for each ground rule $\leftarrow L_1, \ldots, L_m$ from P, $\{L_1, \ldots, L_m\} \not\subseteq S$ holds;
(ii) If S contains a pair of literals L and $\neg L$, then $S = Lit_P$.

Secondly, let P be any GEDP and $S \subseteq Lit_P$. The *reduct* P^S of P by S is the *not*-free EDLP P^S obtained as follows: a rule $L_1|\ldots|L_k \leftarrow L_{\ell+1}, \ldots, L_m$ is in P^S if there is a ground rule of the form (1) from P such that $\{L_{k+1}, \ldots, L_\ell\} \subseteq S$ and $\{L_{m+1}, \ldots, L_n\} \cap S = \emptyset$. Then S is an answer set of P if S is an answer set of P^S.

Every answer set of a GEDP P satisfies every ground rule from P [9]. An answer set S is *consistent* if $S \neq Lit_P$; otherwise S is *contradictory*. A GEDP P having a consistent answer set is *consistent*; otherwise P is *inconsistent*. When P is inconsistent, there are two different cases. If P has the single answer set Lit_P, P is *contradictory*; else if P has no answer set, P is called *incoherent*.

An answer set S of a GEDP P is *minimal* if there is no other answer set S' of P such that $S' \subset S$. Note that every answer set of any EDLP is minimal [12], but the minimality of answer sets no longer holds for GEDPs [9].

2.2 Assumption-Based Argumentation

A (propositional) *logic* for a propositional language $\mathcal{L}$ is a pair $\mathfrak{L} = (\mathcal{L}, \Vdash)$, where $\Vdash$ is a (Tarskian) consequence relation for $\mathcal{L}$ [6].

An *assumption-based framework* (or ABF) [7] is a tuple $\mathbf{ABF} = \langle \mathfrak{L}, \Gamma, \Lambda, - \rangle$, where $\mathfrak{L} = (\mathcal{L}, \Vdash)$, Γ (the strict assumptions) and Λ (the defeasible assumptions) are countable sets of $\mathcal{L}$-formulas, and $- : \Lambda \rightarrow \wp(\mathcal{L})$ is a contrariness operator, assigning a finite set of $\mathcal{L}$-formulas to every assumption in Λ, in which $\Lambda \neq \emptyset$ and $\wp(\cdot)$ denotes the powerset operator. We use $^{-}$ instead of $-$ as a contrariness operator when any assumption in Λ has a unique contrary [16]. In $\mathbf{ABF} =$

$\langle \mathfrak{L}, \Gamma, \mathcal{A}, ^- \rangle$, a set of assumptions $\Delta \subseteq \mathcal{A}$ is *closed* iff $\Delta = \{\alpha \in \mathcal{A} \mid \Gamma \cup \Delta \Vdash \alpha\}$. **ABF** is said to be *flat* iff every set Δ of defeasible assumptions is closed.

The usual semantics in abstract argumentation [5] is adapted to ABFs. In this subsection, we consider a propositional EDLP which includes no *integrity constraints*. The **ABF** translated from an EDLP [15,16] is defined as follows.

Definition 2. [15,16] $\mathfrak{L} = \langle \mathcal{L}_{\text{EDLP}}, \Vdash \rangle$ is the logic for the language $\mathcal{L}_{\text{EDLP}}$, where $\mathcal{L}_{\text{EDLP}}$ consists of disjunctions of propositional literals ($\ell_1|\ldots|\ell_n$, for $n \geq 1$), NAF-literals (*not* ℓ) and rules of an EDLP, while $\Vdash$ is constructed for $\mathcal{L}_{\text{EDLP}}$ by three inference rules: Modus Ponens (MP), Resolution (Res) and Reasoning by Cases (RBC) shown below.

$$[\mathsf{MP}] \quad \frac{\psi \leftarrow \phi_1, \ldots, \phi_n \qquad \phi_1 \quad \phi_2 \quad \cdots \quad \phi_n}{\psi}$$

$$[\mathsf{Res}] \quad \frac{\psi'_1|\ldots|\psi'_m|\ell_1|\ldots|\ell_n|\psi''_1|\ldots|\psi''_k \qquad not\,\ell_1 \quad \cdots \quad not\,\ell_n}{\psi'_1|\ldots|\psi'_m|\psi''_1|\ldots|\psi''_k}$$

$$[\mathsf{RBC}] \quad \frac{\begin{array}{cccc} \ell_1 & \ell_2 & & \ell_n \\ \vdots & \vdots & & \vdots \\ \psi & \psi & \cdots & \psi \end{array} \qquad \ell_1|\ldots|\ell_n}{\psi}$$

where $|$ is the connective of a disjunction, ℓ_i is a propositional literal, each $\phi_i \in \{\ell_i, not\ \ell_i\}$ is a literal or a NAF-literal, ψ, ψ_i are disjunctions of propositional literals using $|$, and $\psi \leftarrow \phi_1, \ldots, \phi_n$ is a rule of an EDLP. [MP] implies Reflexivity: [Ref] $\frac{\psi \leftarrow}{\psi}$. Note that $\Vdash$ denotes derivability using inference rules.

Definition 3. [15,16] The assumption-based framework (ABF) translated from an EDLP P is $\mathbf{ABF}(P) = \langle \mathfrak{L}, P, \mathcal{A}_P, ^- \rangle$, where $\mathfrak{L} = \langle \mathcal{L}_{\text{EDLP}}, \Vdash \rangle$, $\mathcal{A}_P = NAF_P = \{not\ \ell \mid \ell \in Lit_P\}$, and $\overline{not\ \ell} = \ell$ for every $not\ \ell \in \mathcal{A}_P$.

Let $P_{tr} = P \cup \{L \leftarrow p, \neg p \mid p \in Lit_P,\ L \in Lit_P\}$, where $Lit_P = Lit_{P_{tr}}$. Then, the ABF translated from an EDLP P_{tr} is $\mathbf{ABF}(P_{tr}) = \langle \mathfrak{L}, P_{tr}, \mathcal{A}_P, ^- \rangle$.

Note that $\mathbf{ABF}(P)$ translated from an EDLP P is always *flat* due to [16, Proposition 2]. The tree $\mathcal{T}_\Psi(K)$ defined below is used to define arguments in $\mathbf{ABF}(P)$.

Definition 4. [15,16] Let $\mathfrak{L} = \langle \mathcal{L}_{\text{EDLP}}, \Vdash \rangle$ and $\mathbf{ABF}(P) = \langle \mathfrak{L}, P, \mathcal{A}_P, ^- \rangle$ be the ABF translated from an EDLP P. Let $\mathcal{T}_\Psi(K)$ denote $P \cup K \Vdash \Psi$, where $K \subseteq \mathcal{A}_P$ is the support for a defeasible consequence $\Psi \in \mathcal{L}_{\text{EDLP}}$ w.r.t. P. In other words, $\mathcal{T}_\Psi(K)$ is a *tree with a root node labelled by* Ψ *(having a support* K*)* as follows.

1. The cases using no inference rules:
   (1) For $not\ \ell \in \mathcal{A}_P$, there is a one-node tree $\mathcal{T}_\Psi(K)$ whose root node is labelled by $\Psi = not\ \ell$ and $K = \{not\ \ell\}$.
   (2) For a rule $r \in P$, there is a one-node tree $\mathcal{T}_\Psi(K)$ whose root node is labelled by $\Psi = r$ and $K = \emptyset$.

2. The cases using inference rules:
   (1) **i.** For a rule $\psi \leftarrow \in P$, by [Ref], there is a tree $\mathcal{T}_\psi(K)$ whose root node N is labelled by ψ and N has a unique child node, namely a one-node tree $\mathcal{T}_r(\emptyset)$ where $r = \psi \leftarrow$. Then $K = \emptyset$.
   ii. For a rule $\psi \leftarrow \phi_1, \cdots, \phi_n$ in P, if for each ϕ_i $(1 \le i \le n)$, there exists a tree $\mathcal{T}_{\phi_i}(K_i)$ with the root node N_i labelled by ϕ_i, then by [MP], there is a tree $\mathcal{T}_\psi(K)$ with the root node N labelled by ψ and N has a child N_0 labelled by $r = \psi \leftarrow \phi_1, \cdots, \phi_n$ which is a one-node tree $\mathcal{T}_r(\emptyset)$ as well as n children N_i $(1 \le i \le n)$ where N_i is the root of a tree $\mathcal{T}_{\phi_i}(K_i)$. Then $K = \bigcup_i K_i$.
   (2) Let $\Phi = \psi'_1|\dots|\psi'_m|\ell_1|\dots|\ell_n|\psi''_1|\dots|\psi''_k$ and $\Psi = \psi'_1|\dots|\psi'_m|\psi''_1|\dots|\psi''_k$, where $\ell_i \in Lit_P$ $(1 \le i \le n)$. If there is a tree $\mathcal{T}_\Phi(K')$ with the root node N_0 labelled by Φ, then by [Res], there is a tree $\mathcal{T}_\Psi(K)$ with the root node N labelled by Ψ and N has a child N_0 as well as n children $N_1, \dots N_n$ each of which is a one-node tree $\mathcal{T}_{\phi_i}(\{\phi_i\})$ where $\phi_i = not\ \ell_i$ $(1 \le i \le n)$. Then $K = K' \cup \bigcup_{i=1}^n \{not\ \ell_i\}$.
   (3) Let $(\ell_i \dots \psi)^2$ denote the reasoning for the case ℓ_i and $\mathcal{T}_{\ell_i}(\emptyset)$ be a one-node tree whose root is labelled by ℓ_i. Suppose that
      - there is a tree $\mathcal{T}_\Phi(K')$ whose root node N_0 is labelled by $\Phi = \ell_1|\dots|\ell_n$;
      - for each ℓ_i $(1 \le i \le n)$, there exists reasoning for a case ℓ_i such that $(\ell_i \dots \psi)$, namely $P \cup \{\ell_i\} \cup K_i \Vdash \psi$ for $\exists K_i \subseteq \mathcal{A}_P$, which is represented by a tree $\mathcal{T}_\psi(K_i)$ constructed by newly introducing a tree $\mathcal{T}_{\ell_i}(\emptyset)$ in this definition.

   Then by [RBC], there is a tree $\mathcal{T}_\psi(K)$ with the root node N labelled by ψ and N has the child N_0 as well as n children $N_1, \dots N_n$ where each N_i $(1 \le i \le n)$ is the root of a tree $\mathcal{T}_\psi(K_i)$ for the case ℓ_i. Thus $K = K' \cup \bigcup_{i=1}^n \{K_i\}$. □

In $\mathbf{ABF}(P)$, arguments and *attacks* are defined as follows:

Definition 5. [15,16] Let $\mathbf{ABF}(P) = \langle \mathfrak{L}, P, \mathcal{A}_P, \overline{} \rangle$ be the ABF translated from an EDLP P, $\mathbb{L}_P = Lit_P \cup \mathcal{A}_P$, and $\phi \in \mathbb{L}_P$. Then in $\mathbf{ABF}(P)$,

- *an argument for a conclusion (or claim) ϕ supported by $K \subseteq \mathcal{A}_P$ ($K \vdash \phi$,* for short) is a (finite) tree $\mathcal{T}_\phi(K)$ whose root node is labelled by $\phi \in \mathbb{L}_P$.
- $K_1 \vdash \phi_1$ *attacks* $K_2 \vdash \phi_2$ iff $\phi_1 = \overline{\alpha}$ for some $\alpha \in K_2$.

In $\mathbf{ABF}(P)$, the semantics is given by not only *assumption* extensions[3] but also *argument* extensions defined as follows:

Definition 6. Let $\mathbf{ABF}(P) = \langle \mathfrak{L}, P, \mathcal{A}_P, \overline{} \rangle$ be the ABF translated from an EDLP P, AR be the set of all arguments generated from $\mathbf{ABF}(P)$, and $\mathcal{E} \subseteq AR$.

[2] This is depicted vertically in the inference rule of [RBC].

[3] Due to the space limitation, the details of *assumption* extensions [15,16] are omitted in this paper though *assumption* extensions are related to *argument* extensions.

$\mathcal{E}$ is *conflict-free* iff $\nexists A, B \in \mathcal{E}$ such that A *attacks* B. $\mathcal{E}$ *defends* an argument A iff each argument that attacks A is attacked by an argument in $\mathcal{E}$. Then, $\mathcal{E}$ is *admissible* iff $\mathcal{E}$ is conflict-free and defends all its elements. $\mathcal{E}$ is a *stable* argument extension iff it is conflict-free and attacks every argument in $AR \setminus \mathcal{E}$.

Let $\mathbb{L}_P = Lit_P \cup \mathcal{A}_P$. The *conclusion* of a set of arguments $\mathcal{E}$ is defined as

$$\text{Concs}(\mathcal{E}) = \{\phi \in \mathbb{L}_P \mid \phi \text{ is a conclusion (or claim) of an argument contained in } \mathcal{E}\}.$$

$\mathcal{E}$ is said to be *consistent* if Concs($\mathcal{E}$) is not contradictory w.r.t. $\neg$, i.e. $\nexists s \in \mathbb{L}_P$ s.t. $\{s, \neg s\} \subseteq \text{Concs}(\mathcal{E})$. Let $\mathsf{CN}_P : \wp(\mathbb{L}_P) \rightarrow \wp(\mathbb{L}_P)$ be a *consequence operator* such that for $X \subseteq \mathbb{L}_P$, $\mathsf{CN}_P(X) = \{\phi \in \mathbb{L}_P \mid P \cup X \Vdash \phi\}$. A set $X \subseteq \mathbb{L}_P$ is said to be *inconsistent* iff $\mathsf{CN}_P(X)$ is contradictory (i.e. contradictory w.r.t. $\neg$ or contradictory w.r.t. $\overline{}$). $X \subseteq \mathbb{L}_P$ is said to be *consistent* iff it is not inconsistent.

The following theorems hold for an EDLP P and $\mathbf{ABF}(P_{tr})$, and respectively, for a consistent EDLP P and $\mathbf{ABF}(P)$.

Theorem 1. *[15,16] Let P be an EDLP and $S \subseteq Lit_P$. Then, S is an answer set of P iff there is a stable argument extension $\mathcal{E}_{tr}$ of $\mathbf{ABF}(P_{tr})$ such that $S \cup \Delta_S = \text{Concs}(\mathcal{E}_{tr}) = \mathsf{CN}_{P_{tr}}(\Delta_S)$, where $\Delta_S = \{not\ \ell \mid \ell \in (Lit_P \setminus S)\}$ is a stable assumption extension of $\mathbf{ABF}(P_{tr})$.*

Theorem 2. *[15,16] Let P be a consistent EDLP, $S \subseteq Lit_P$ and $\mathbf{ABF}(P) = \langle \mathfrak{L}, P, \mathcal{A}_P, \overline{} \rangle$ be the ABF translated from P. Then S is an answer set of P iff there is a consistent stable argument extension $\mathcal{E}$ of $\mathbf{ABF}(P)$ such that $S \cup \Delta_S = \text{Concs}(\mathcal{E}) = \mathsf{CN}_P(\Delta_S)$, where $\Delta_S = \{not\ \ell \mid \ell \in (Lit_P \setminus S)\}$ is a consistent stable assumption extension of $\mathbf{ABF}(P)$.*

3 Translation from GEDPs to EDLPs

3.1 Inoue and Sakama's Method

Inoue and Sakama [8,9] proposed a polynomial-time translation of any GEDP into an EDLP. Their translation is as follows: Let P be any GEDP. The extended disjunctive logic program *edp*(P) [9, Section 6.1] is obtained from P by replacing each rule with NAF in the head in P of the form (1)

$$L_1 \mid \ldots \mid L_k \mid not\ L_{k+1} \mid \ldots \mid not\ L_\ell \leftarrow L_{\ell+1}, \ldots, L_m, not\ L_{m+1}, \ldots, not\ L_n \quad (1)$$

($n \geq m \geq \ell > k \geq 0$) with the rules without NAF in the head as follows:

$$\begin{aligned}
&\lambda_1 \mid \ldots \mid \lambda_k \mid \lambda_{k+1} \mid \ldots \mid \lambda_\ell \leftarrow L_{\ell+1}, \ldots, L_m, not\ L_{m+1}, \ldots, not\ L_n \\
&L_i \leftarrow \lambda_i \quad \text{for } i = 1, \ldots, k, \\
&\lambda_i \leftarrow L_i, L_{k+1}, \ldots, L_\ell \quad \text{for } i = 1, \ldots, k, \\
&\leftarrow \lambda_i, not\ L_j \quad \text{for } i = 1, \ldots, k \quad \text{and} \quad j = k+1, \ldots, \ell, \\
&\leftarrow \lambda_j, L_j \quad \text{for } j = k+1, \ldots, \ell.
\end{aligned}$$

Here, λ_i is a new atom not appearing elsewhere in P and is uniquely associated with each disjunct of a ground rule from P. Every rule without NAF in the head in P remains in *edp*(P). The following theorem is proved for their translation.

Theorem 3. [8,9] *Let P be a GEDP, and edp(P) its translated EDLP. A set S is an answer set of P iff a set Σ is an answer set of edp(P) such that $S = \Sigma \cap Lit_P$.*

Example 1. Consider the GEDP $P_1 = \{p \mid q \mid not\ r \mid not\ s \leftarrow,\quad p \mid r \leftarrow,\quad t \mid s \leftarrow\}$. It has four answer sets: $S_1 = \{q, r, s\}$, $S_2 = \{r, t\}$, $S_3 = \{p, t\}$, $S_4 = \{p, s\}$.

On the other hand, the EDLP $edp(P_1)$ consists of thirteen rules as follows:

$$\begin{array}{lllll} \lambda_1 \mid \lambda_2 \mid \lambda_3 \mid \lambda_4 \leftarrow & p \leftarrow \lambda_1 & q \leftarrow \lambda_2 & \lambda_1 \leftarrow p, r, s & \lambda_2 \leftarrow q, r, s \\ \leftarrow \lambda_1, not\ r & \leftarrow \lambda_1, not\ s & \leftarrow \lambda_2, not\ r & \leftarrow \lambda_2, not\ s & \leftarrow \lambda_3, r \\ \leftarrow \lambda_4, s & p \mid r \leftarrow & t \mid s \leftarrow, & & \end{array}$$

which has five answer sets Σ_j $(1 \leq j \leq 5)$ though P_1 has four answer sets S_i.

$$\Sigma_1 = \{q, r, s, \lambda_2\},\ \Sigma_2 = \{r, t, \lambda_4\},\ \Sigma_3 = \{p, t, \lambda_3\},\ \Sigma_4 = \{p, t, \lambda_4\},\ \Sigma_5 = \{p, s, \lambda_3\},$$
$$\begin{array}{ll} \text{where}\quad \Sigma_1 \cap Lit_{P_1} = S_1 = \{q, r, s\}, & \Sigma_2 \cap Lit_{P_1} = S_2 = \{r, t\}, \\ \Sigma_3 \cap Lit_{P_1} = \Sigma_4 \cap Lit_{P_1} = S_3 = \{p, t\}, & \Sigma_5 \cap Lit_{P_1} = S_4 = \{p, s\}. \end{array}$$

Notice that both Σ_3 and Σ_4 correspond to the same answer set S_3 of P_1. Hence, regarding this example, their translation yields a one-to-many correspondence.

Example 2. Consider the GEDP $P_2 = \{p \mid not\ p \leftarrow,\quad \neg p \mid not\ \neg p \leftarrow\}$ given in [9, Example 4.11]. It has four answer sets: $S_1 = \emptyset$, $S_2 = \{p\}$, $S_3 = \{\neg p\}$, $S_4 = Lit_{P_2}$, where S_1 is minimal, and others are non-minimal. Since P_2 has three consistent answer sets along with the contradictory answer set S_4, P_2 is consistent.

On the other hand, $edp(P_2)$ consists of ten rules as follows,

$$\begin{array}{lllll} \lambda_1 \mid \lambda_2 \leftarrow & p \leftarrow \lambda_1 & \lambda_1 \leftarrow p & \leftarrow \lambda_1, not\ p & \leftarrow \lambda_2, p \\ \lambda_3 \mid \lambda_4 \leftarrow & \neg p \leftarrow \lambda_3 & \lambda_3 \leftarrow \neg p & \leftarrow \lambda_3, not\ \neg p & \leftarrow \lambda_4, \neg p, \end{array}$$

which has three answer sets $\Sigma_j (1 \leq j \leq 3)$ though P_2 has four answer sets S_i.

$$\Sigma_1 = \{\lambda_2, \lambda_4\},\quad \Sigma_2 = \{\lambda_1, p, \lambda_4\},\quad \Sigma_3 = \{\lambda_2, \lambda_3, \neg p\},$$

where $\Sigma_1 \cap Lit_{P_2} = \emptyset = S_1$, $\Sigma_2 \cap Lit_{P_2} = \{p\} = S_2$, $\Sigma_3 \cap Lit_{P_2} = \{\neg p\} = S_3$.

This result indicates that the contradictory answer set S_4 of the consistent GEDP P_2 can never be captured by any answer set of the consistent EDLP $edp(P_2)$ due to the property of the answer sets of a consistent EDLP.

Thus, these examples show that their translation cannot yield a one-to-one correspondence between answer sets of any GEDP and those of the translated EDLP.

3.2 The Proposed Method

We propose a novel polynomial-time translation of a GEDP into an EDLP, with which there is a one-to-one correspondence between the consistent answer sets of the respective programs as proved in the subsequent theorem.

Definition 7. Let P be a GEDP. The extended disjunctive logic program *edlp*(P) is obtained from P by replacing each rule with NAF in the head in P of the form (1)

$$L_1 \mid \dots \mid L_k \mid \, not\ L_{k+1} \mid \dots \mid not\ L_\ell \leftarrow L_{\ell+1}, \dots, L_m, not\ L_{m+1}, \dots, not\ L_n \quad (1)$$

$(n \geq m \geq \ell > k \geq 0)$ with the rules without NAF in the head as follows:

$$\begin{aligned} L_1 \mid \dots \mid L_k \mid \lambda_{k+1} \mid \dots \mid \lambda_\ell &\leftarrow L_{\ell+1}, \dots, L_m, not\ L_{m+1}, \dots, not\ L_n, not\ \mu^r \quad (2)\\ \alpha^r &\leftarrow L_{k+1}, \dots, L_\ell \quad (3)\\ \mu^r &\leftarrow not\ \alpha^r \quad (4)\\ &\leftarrow \lambda_j, L_j \quad \text{for } j = k+1, \dots, \ell. \quad (5) \end{aligned}$$

Here, λ_j $(j = k+1, \dots .\ell)$, α^r and μ^r are newly introduced atoms not appearing elsewhere in P, and they are uniquely associated with each rule r with NAF in the head. Every rule without NAF in the head in P remains in *edlp*(P) as it is. We denote by Lit_P the set of all ground literals in the language of P, and Lit_P includes no new atoms $\lambda_j, \alpha^r, \mu^r$ (i.e. $\lambda_j \notin Lit_P, \alpha^r \notin Lit_P, \mu^r \notin Lit_P$).

In what follows, we show our theorem for the proposed translation. To prove it, we use a reduct P^S of a GEDP P by $S \subseteq Lit_P$ whose any rule is of the form:

$$L_1 \mid \dots \mid L_k \leftarrow L_{\ell+1}, \dots, L_m \quad (6)$$

corresponding to a rule (1) in P which satisfies two conditions (c1) and (c2):

$$\text{(c1) } \{L_{k+1}, \dots, L_\ell\} \subseteq S, \qquad \text{(c2) } \{L_{m+1}, \dots, L_n\} \cap S = \emptyset.$$

Then, given a set $S \subseteq Lit_P$, we denote by $r_i \in P$ $(1 \leq i \leq 3)$ a rule with NAF in the head such that r_1 satisfies both (c1) and (c2), r_2 satisfies (c1) but not (c2), and r_3 does not satisfy (c1). Using these rules, the following sets are defined:

$$\begin{aligned} \delta_1(S) &= \bigcup\nolimits_{r_1 \in P} \{\alpha^{r_1} \mid r_1 \text{ with NAF in the head satisfies both } (c1) \text{ and } (c2)\},\\ \delta_2(S) &= \bigcup\nolimits_{r_2 \in P} \{\alpha^{r_2} \mid r_2 \text{ with NAF in the head satisfies } (c1) \text{ but not } (c2)\},\\ \theta(S) &= \bigcup\nolimits_{r_3 \in P} \{\mu^{r_3} \mid \ r_3 \text{ with NAF in the head does not satisfy } (c1)\}, \end{aligned}$$

and $\delta(S) = \delta_1(S) \cup \delta_2(S)$. Besides, we denote by *edlp*(r) a set of rules (2)~(5) translated from each rule $r \in P$ of the form (1) according to Definition 7. Now, we are ready to show our theorem.

Theorem 4. *Let P be a GEDP, edlp(P) be its translated EDLP, and $S \subseteq Lit_P$. A set S is a consistent answer set of P iff there is a consistent answer set M of edlp(P) such that $M = S \cup \delta(S) \cup \theta(S)$ where $S = M \cap Lit_P$.*

Proof. ($\Rightarrow$) Let S be a consistent answer set of P and $M = S \cup \delta_1(S) \cup \delta_2(S) \cup \theta(S)$, where $M \subseteq Lit_{edlp(P)}$. Since S is consistent, M is consistent.

First, we show that M satisfies every rule in *edlp*$(P)^M$.

(1) For a rule $r_1 \in P$ satisfying both (c1) and (c2), P^S has the rule of the form (6) corresponding to r_1, which satisfies the following two conditions:

$$\{L_{k+1}, \ldots, L_\ell\} \subseteq S \subseteq M, \text{ and} \tag{7}$$

$$\{L_{m+1}, \ldots, L_n\} \cap S = \{L_{m+1}, \ldots, L_n\} \cap M = \emptyset. \tag{8}$$

Hence, corresponding to the rule r_1, *edlp*$(r_1)^M$ consists of rules:

$$L_1 \mid \ldots \mid L_k \mid \lambda_{k+1} \mid \ldots \mid \lambda_\ell \leftarrow L_{\ell+1}, \ldots, L_m \tag{9}$$

$$\alpha^{r_1} \leftarrow L_{k+1}, \ldots, L_\ell \tag{10}$$

and (5). W.r.t. them, first, since $S \subseteq M$ is an answer set of P^S, S satisfies the rule (6) constructed from r_1, which implies that if $\{L_{\ell+1}, \ldots, L_m\} \subseteq S \subseteq M$, then there is some literal $L_i \in S \subseteq M$ for $1 \leq \exists i \leq k$. Hence M satisfies the rule (9). Second, M satisfies the rule (10) because it holds that $\{L_{k+1}, \ldots, L_\ell\} \subseteq M$ due to (7) as well as $\alpha^{r_1} \in \delta_1(S) \subseteq M$. Finally, as for the rule (5) (i.e. $\leftarrow \lambda_j, L_j$), $\lambda_j \notin M$ holds for $j = k+1, \ldots, \ell$ due to $M = S \cup \delta_1(S) \cup \delta_2(S) \cup \theta(S)$. Therefore, $\{\lambda_j, L_j\} \not\subseteq M$ holds for $j = k+1, \ldots, \ell$, which means that M satisfies the rule (5). Hence, M satisfies every rule in *edlp*$(r_1)^M$.

(2) For a rule $r_2 \in P$ satisfying the condition (c1) but not (c2), (7) holds w.r.t. M, but (8) does not. Hence *edlp*$(r_2)^M$ consists of rules (3) and (5), that is, *edlp*$(r_2)^M = \{\alpha^{r_2} \leftarrow L_{k+1}, \ldots, L_\ell, \quad \leftarrow \lambda_j, L_j \text{ for } j = k+1, \ldots, \ell\}$. Then, M satisfies the rule (3), i.e. $\alpha^{r_2} \leftarrow L_{k+1}, \ldots, L_\ell$ due to (7) as well as $\alpha^{r_2} \in \delta_2(S) \subseteq M$. Besides, since $\lambda_j \notin M$ holds for $j = k+1, \ldots, \ell$, M also satisfies the rule (5). Hence, M satisfies every rule in *edlp*$(r_2)^M$.

(3) For a rule $r_3 \in P$ not satisfying the condition (c1), (7) does not hold w.r.t. M. Hence, *edlp*$(r_3)^M$ consists of rules (3), $\mu^{r_3} \leftarrow$ and (5), that is, *edlp*$(r_3)^M = \{\alpha^{r_3} \leftarrow L_{k+1}, \ldots, L_\ell, \quad \mu^{r_3} \leftarrow, \quad \leftarrow \lambda_j, L_j \text{ for } j = k+1, \ldots, \ell\}$). Then since $\{L_{k+1}, \ldots, L_\ell\} \not\subseteq M$ holds, M satisfies both the rule (3) and the rule (5) in *edlp*$(r_3)^M$. Since $\mu^{r_3} \in \theta(S) \subseteq M$ holds, M satisfies the rule: $\mu^{r_3} \leftarrow$. Hence, M satisfies every rule in *edlp*$(r_3)^M$.

Therefore, due to *(1)*, *(2)* and *(3)*, M satisfies every rule in *edlp*$(P)^M$.

Next, we need to prove that $M = S \cup \delta_1(S) \cup \delta_2(S) \cup \theta(S)$ is a minimal set satisfying the rules of *edlp*$(P)^M$, where $S = M \cap Lit_P$ is an answer set of P^S, i.e. a minimal set satisfying the rules of P^S. We thus need to verify that there is no M' such that: (i) $M' \subset M$, (ii) M' satisfies the rules of *edlp*$(P)^M$, and (iii) $S' \subset S$ for $S' = M' \cap Lit_P$. Suppose to the contrary that such a M' exists. Then the condition (iii) is satisfied only if there exists the rule (9) in *edlp*$(r_1)^M$ constructed from $r_1 \in P$ such that $L_i \in S$ and $L_i \notin S'$ for some i $(1 \leq i \leq k)$. In this case, since M' satisfies the rule (9) due to (ii), there exists some $\lambda_{j'} \in M'$ for $k+1 \leq j' \leq \ell$. Now, since M satisfies the rule (5) in *edlp*$(r_1)^M$, $\{\lambda_j, L_j\} \not\subseteq M$ holds for $j = k+1, \ldots, \ell$. However, $L_j \in M$ $(j = k+1, \ldots, \ell)$ holds due to (7). Thus, $\lambda_j \notin M$ holds for $j = k+1, \ldots, \ell$. Hence, regarding aforementioned $\lambda_{j'}$ $(k+1 \leq \exists j' \leq \ell)$, both $\lambda_{j'} \in M'$ and $\lambda_{j'} \notin M$ hold, which contradicts the condition (i). Therefore, M is a minimal set satisfying the rules of *edlp*$(P)^M$. Hence, M is an answer set of *edlp*$(P)^M$. Thus, M is an answer set of *edlp*(P).

($\Leftarrow$) Let M be a consistent answer set of $edlp(P)$ and $S = M \cap Lit_P$. Since M is consistent, $S = M \cap Lit_P$ is consistent. First, we show that such S satisfies every rule in P^S. Since the answer set M of $edlp(P)$ satisfies all rules in $edlp(P)^M$, M satisfies every rule in $edlp(r_1)^M$ for any $r_1 \in P$, i.e. rules (9), (10) and (5) corresponding to $r_1 \in P$. Then, for such a rule (9) in $edlp(r_1)^M$, if $\{L_{\ell+1}, \dots, L_m\} \subseteq S \subseteq M$ holds, there are two cases: (a) $L_i \in S \subseteq M$ holds for some $1 \leq i \leq k$; or (b) $\lambda_j \in M$ holds for some $k+1 \leq j \leq \ell$. Note that r_1 satisfies the condition (7) (i.e. (c1)), which implies $L_j \in M$ for $j = k+1, \dots, \ell$, while since M satisfies the rule (5) in $edlp(r_1)^M$, $\{\lambda_j, L_j\} \not\subseteq M$ holds for $j = k+1, \dots, \ell$. Thus, $\lambda_j \notin M$ for $j = k+1, \dots, \ell$ hold. Hence, the case (b) never exists. Then, due to the case (a), $L_i \in S$ holds for some $1 \leq i \leq k$. Hence S satisfies the rule (6) in P^S corresponding to r_1 in P. Now, since P^S has no rule (6) corresponding to r_2 as well as r_3 in P, it is proved that $S = M \cap Lit_P$ satisfies every rule in P^S.

Next, we need to prove that $S = M \cap Lit_P$ is an answer set of P, in other words, such S is a minimal set satisfying all rules in P^S. To this end, to the contrary, suppose that there is a set S' of literals from Lit_P such that (i) $S' \subset S$ and (ii) S' satisfies the rules of P^S. Then, two conditions (i) and (ii) are satisfied only if there is the rule (6) (i.e. $L_1 \mid \dots \mid L_k \leftarrow L_{\ell+1}, \dots, L_m$) in P^S constructed from some rule $r_1 \in P$ satisfying (c1) and (c2) such that $\{L_{\ell+1}, \dots, L_m\} \subset S'$ and for some two literal L_{i1} and L_{i2} ($1 \leq i1,\ i2 \leq k,\ i1 \neq i2$), $L_{i1} \in S' \subset S$ but $L_{i2} \in S \setminus S'$. Without loss of generality, we can assume that just one such rule exists in P^S. Now, let $M' = M \setminus \{L_{i2}\}$ and $S' = M' \cap Lit_P$. Corresponding to the aforementioned rule $r_1 \in P$, $edlp(r_1)^M$ consists of rules (9), (10) and (5). Then M' satisfies the rule (9) (i.e. $L_1 \mid \dots \mid L_k \mid \lambda_{k+1} \mid \dots \mid \lambda_\ell \leftarrow L_{\ell+1}, \dots, L_m$) because $\{L_{\ell+1}, \dots, L_m\} \subset S'$ and $L_{i1} \in S'$ ($1 \leq i1 \leq k$) holds. Besides, $\alpha^{r_1} \in M'$ holds since $\alpha^{r_1} \in M$ holds for this $r_1 \in P$. Hence M' satisfies the rule (10) due to $\{L_{k+1}, \dots, L_\ell\} \subseteq M'$ and $\alpha^{r_1} \in M'$. M' also satisfies the rule (5) due to $\lambda_j \notin M'$ since $\lambda_j \notin M$ for $j = k+1, \dots, \ell$. Thus M' satisfies every rule from $edlp(r_1)^M$. Hence, M' satisfies all rules in $edlp(P)^M$ where $M' \subset M$. This contradicts the fact that M is a minimal set satisfying all rules of $edlp(P)^M$ because M is an answer set of $edlp(P)^M$. Therefore, $S = M \cap Lit_P$ is an answer set of P. Obviously, for this answer set $S = M \cap Lit_P$ of P, $M = S \cup \delta_1(S) \cup \delta_2(S) \cup \theta(S)$ also holds according to the proof shown in the part of ($\Rightarrow$). □

Remark 1. $\alpha^r \in M$ (resp. $\mu^r \in M$) indicates that the rule $r \in P$ of the form (1) *satisfies* (resp. does *not satisfy*) condition (c1) for $S = M \cap Lit_P$.

Example 3. (Cont. Example 1) Consider the GEDP P_1 again. According to the proposed translation, $edlp(P_1)$ consists of seven rules as follows:

$$p \mid q \mid \lambda_3 \mid \lambda_4 \leftarrow not\ \mu \qquad \alpha \leftarrow r, s \qquad \mu \leftarrow not\ \alpha$$
$$\leftarrow \lambda_3, r \qquad \leftarrow \lambda_4, s \qquad p \mid r \leftarrow \qquad t \mid s \leftarrow .$$

It has four answer sets, M_i ($1 \leq i \leq 4$):

$$M_1 = \{q, r, s, \alpha\}, \quad M_2 = \{r, t, \mu\}, \quad M_3 = \{p, t, \mu\}, \quad M_4 = \{p, s, \mu\},$$

which correspond to answer sets S_i $(1 \le i \le 4)$ of P_1 such that $M_1 = S_1 \cup \delta_1(S_1)$ and $M_j = S_j \cup \theta(S_j)$ $(2 \le j \le 4)$, where $\delta_1(S_1) = \{\alpha\}$ and $\theta(S_j) = \{\mu\}$ with $\delta_2(S_1) = \theta(S_1) = \delta(S_j) = \emptyset$.

Example 4. (Cont. Example 2) Consider $P_2 = \{p \mid not\ p \leftarrow, \quad \neg p \mid not\ \neg p \leftarrow\}$. It has four answer sets: $S_1 = \emptyset$, $S_2 = \{p\}$, $S_3 = \{\neg p\}$, $S_4 = Lit_{P_2}$. Correspondingly,

$$\begin{aligned} edlp(P_2) = \{\ & p|\ \lambda_1 \leftarrow not\ \mu_1, & \alpha_1 \leftarrow p, \quad & \mu_1 \leftarrow not\ \alpha_1, & \leftarrow \lambda_1, p,\\ & \neg p|\ \lambda_2 \leftarrow not\ \mu_2, & \alpha_2 \leftarrow \neg p, \quad & \mu_2 \leftarrow not\ \alpha_2, & \leftarrow \lambda_2, \neg p\}. \end{aligned}$$

has three answer sets M_j $(1 \le j \le 3)$ as follows,

$$M_1 = \{\mu_1, \mu_2\}, \qquad M_2 = \{p, \alpha_1, \mu_2\}, \qquad M_3 = \{\neg p, \mu_1, \alpha_2\},$$

which correspond to the consistent answer sets S_i $(1 \le i \le 3)$ [4] of P_2 such that $M_1 = S_1 \cup \theta(S_1)$, $M_2 = S_2 \cup \delta_1(S_2) \cup \theta(S_2)$ and $M_3 = S_3 \cup \delta_1(S_3) \cup \theta(S_3)$, where $\theta(S_1) = \{\mu_1, \mu_2\}$, $\delta_1(S_2) = \{\alpha_1\}$, $\theta(S_2) = \{\mu_2\}$ and $\delta_1(S_3) = \{\alpha_2\}$, $\theta(S_3) = \{\mu_1\}$.

Example 5. Consider the GEDP $P_3 = \{p \mid not\ q \leftarrow, \quad q \mid not\ p \leftarrow\}$ given in [9, Example 6.2]. It has two answer sets, $S_1 = \{p, q\}$ and $S_2 = \emptyset$, where S_1 is non-minimal. Correspondingly, the translated EDLP $edlp(P_3)$ is as follows:

$$\begin{aligned} edlp(P_3) = \{\ & p|\lambda_1 \leftarrow not\ \mu_1, & \alpha_1 \leftarrow q, \quad & \mu_1 \leftarrow not\ \alpha_1, & \leftarrow \lambda_1, q,\\ & q|\lambda_2 \leftarrow not\ \mu_2, & \alpha_2 \leftarrow p, \quad & \mu_2 \leftarrow not\ \alpha_2, & \leftarrow \lambda_2, p\}. \end{aligned}$$

It has two answer sets, $M_1 = \{p, q, \alpha_1, \alpha_2\}$ and $M_2 = \{\mu_1, \mu_2\}$ such that $M_1 = S_1 \cup \delta_1(S_1)$ and $M_2 = S_2 \cup \theta(S_2)$, where $\delta_1(S_1) = \{\alpha_1, \alpha_2\}$ and $\theta(S_2) = \{\mu_1, \mu_2\}$ with $\delta_2(S_1) = \theta(S_1) = \delta(S_2) = \emptyset$.

Example 6. Consider the GEDP $P_4 = \{s \mid not\ p \leftarrow not\ q, \quad q \leftarrow, \quad p \mid r \leftarrow\}$. It has two answer sets, $S_1 = \{q, p\}$ and $S_2 = \{q, r\}$. Correspondingly,

$$edlp(P_4) = \{s \mid \lambda \leftarrow not\ q, not\ \mu, \quad \alpha \leftarrow p, \quad \mu \leftarrow not\ \alpha, \quad \leftarrow \lambda, p, \quad q \leftarrow, \quad p \mid r \leftarrow\}$$

has two answer sets, $M_1 = \{q, p, \alpha\}$ and $M_2 = \{q, r, \mu\}$ such that $M_1 = S_1 \cup \delta_2(S_1)$ and $M_2 = S_2 \cup \theta(S_2)$ for $\delta_2(S_1) = \{\alpha\}$, $\theta(S_2) = \{\mu\}$ and $\delta_1(S_1) = \theta(S_1) = \delta(S_2) = \emptyset$.

4 Assumption-Based Argumentation for General Extended Disjunctive Logic Programming

4.1 ABA for GEDPs Possibly Having Non-minimal Answer Sets

Based on the proposed translation of any GEDP into an EDLP, we show how ABA and general extended disjunctive logic programming are related.

The translated EDLP may include *integrity constraints* (e.g. rules of the form (5)). Nonetheless, it is well-known that any constraint with an empty head can be replaced with the semantically equivalent rule with a non-empty head under the answer set semantics as follows.

[4] For P_2, *clingo* [10] generates three models expressing its three consistent answer sets.

Definition 8. Let P be an EDLP and $\varphi \in Lit_P$. $ic(P)$ is the EDLP obtained from P by replacing every integrity constraint r in P of the form: $\leftarrow body(r)$ with the rule: $\varphi \leftarrow body(r), not\ \varphi$
where $\varphi \in Lit_P$ is an atom appearing nowhere in the program P.

Proposition 1. *Let P be an EDLP, $ic(P)$ be the EDLP and $S \subseteq Lit_P$. S is an answer set of P iff there is an answer set S of $ic(P)$, where $Lit_P = Lit_{ic(P)}$.*

The following theorem shows that there is a one-to-one correspondence between the consistent answer sets of a consistent (propositional) GEDP and the consistent stable extensions of the associated ABF.

Theorem 5. *Let P be a consistent propositional GEDP, $\mathfrak{L} = \langle \mathcal{L}_{\rm EDLP}, \Vdash \rangle$, $\mathscr{P} = ic(edlp(P))$ and $S \subseteq Lit_P$. S is a consistent answer set of P iff there is a consistent stable argument extension $\mathcal{E}$ of $\mathbf{ABF}(\mathscr{P}) = \langle \mathfrak{L}, \mathscr{P}, \mathcal{A}_{\mathscr{P}}, \bar{\ } \rangle$ such that $S \cup \Delta_S = \mathrm{Concs}(\mathcal{E}) = \mathsf{CN}_{\mathscr{P}}(\Delta_S)$ (in other words, $S = \mathrm{Concs}(\mathcal{E}) \cap Lit_P = \mathsf{CN}_{\mathscr{P}}(\Delta_S) \cap Lit_P$), where $\Delta_S = \{not\ \ell \mid \ell \in (Lit_{\mathscr{P}} \setminus S)\}$ is a consistent stable assumption extension of $\mathbf{ABF}(\mathscr{P})$.*

Proof. This is proved based on Theorem 4, Proposition 1 and Theorem 2. □

Example 7. (cont. Example 5) Corresponding to the GEDP P_3, $\mathscr{P}_3 = ic(edlp(P_3)) = (edlp(P_3) \setminus \{\leftarrow \lambda_1, q, \quad \leftarrow \lambda_2, p\}) \cup \{\varphi_1 \leftarrow \lambda_1, q, not\ \varphi_1, \quad \varphi_2 \leftarrow \lambda_2, p, not\ \varphi_2\}$ has also two answer sets, $M_1 = \{p, q, \alpha_1, \alpha_2\}$ and $M_2 = \{\mu_1, \mu_2\}$.
On the other hand, $\mathbf{ABF}(\mathscr{P}_3)$ has arguments and *attacks* as follows.

$A_1: \{not\ \mu_1, not\ \lambda_1\} \vdash p$, $A_2: \{not\ \mu_1, not\ p\} \vdash \lambda_1$, $A_3: \{not\ \mu_2, not\ \lambda_2\} \vdash \alpha_1$,
$A_4: \{not\ \alpha_1\} \vdash \mu_1$, $A_5: \{not\ \mu_1, not\ p, not\ \mu_2, not\ \lambda_2, not\ \varphi_1\} \vdash \varphi_1$,
$A_6: \{not\ \mu_2, not\ \lambda_2\} \vdash q$, $A_7: \{not\ \mu_2, not\ q\} \vdash \lambda_2$, $A_8: \{not\ \mu_1, not\ \lambda_1\} \vdash \alpha_2$,
$A_9: \{not\ \alpha_2\} \vdash \mu_2$, $A_{10}: \{not\ \mu_2, not\ q, not\ \mu_1, not\ \lambda_1, not\ \varphi_2\} \vdash \varphi_2$,
A_{n_i}: $\{not\ x\} \vdash not\ x$, where $x \in \{p, q, \lambda_1, \lambda_2, \mu_1, \mu_2, \alpha_1, \alpha_2, \varphi_1, \varphi_2\}$ for $11 \leq n_i \leq 20$.
$attacks = \{(A_1, A_2), (A_1, A_5), (A_1, A_{11}), (A_2, A_1), (A_2, A_8), (A_2, A_{10}), (A_2, A_{13}), (A_3, A_4), (A_3, A_{17}), (A_4, A_1), (A_4, A_2), (A_4, A_5), (A_4, A_8), (A_4, A_{10}), (A_4, A_{15}), (A_5, A_5), (A_5, A_{19}), (A_6, A_7), (A_6, A_{10}), (A_6, A_{12}), (A_7, A_3), (A_7, A_5), (A_7, A_6), (A_7, A_{14}), (A_8, A_9), (A_8, A_{18}), (A_9, A_3), (A_9, A_5), (A_9, A_6), (A_9, A_7), (A_9, A_{10}), (A_9, A_{16}), (A_{10}, A_{10}), (A_{10}, A_{20})$

Then, $\mathbf{ABF}(\mathscr{P}_3)$ has two stable argument extensions $\mathcal{E}_i$ $(i = 1, 2)$ such that

$$\mathcal{E}_1 = \{A_1, A_3, A_6, A_8, A_{13}, A_{14}, A_{15}, A_{16}, A_{19}, A_{20}\},$$
$$\mathcal{E}_2 = \{A_4, A_9, A_{11}, A_{12}, A_{13}, A_{14}, A_{17}, A_{18}, A_{19}, A_{20}\},$$

where $\mathrm{Concs}(\mathcal{E}_1) = \{p, \alpha_1, q, \alpha_2, not\ \lambda_1, not\ \lambda_2, not\ \mu_1, not\ \mu_2, not\ \varphi_1, not\ \varphi_2\}$, $\mathrm{Concs}(\mathcal{E}_2) = \{\mu_1, \mu_2, not\ p, not\ q, not\ \lambda_1, not\ \lambda_2, not\ \alpha_1, not\ \alpha_2, not\ \varphi_1, not\ \varphi_2\}$. Thus, $\mathrm{Concs}(\mathcal{E}_1) \cap Lit_{P_3} = \{p, q\} = S_1$ and $\mathrm{Concs}(\mathcal{E}_2) \cap Lit_{P_3} = \emptyset = S_2$ are obtained.

Example 8. Consider the GEDP $P_5 = \{p \mid not\ \neg q \leftarrow, \quad \neg q \mid r \leftarrow, \quad \neg r \leftarrow not\ q\}$. P_5 has the unique, consistent answer set $S = \{p, \neg q, \neg r\}$. Correspondingly,

$$\mathscr{P}_5 = ic(edlp(P_5)) = \{\ p \mid \lambda \leftarrow not\ \mu, \qquad \alpha \leftarrow \neg q, \qquad \mu \leftarrow not\ \alpha,$$
$$\varphi \leftarrow \lambda, \neg q, not\ \varphi, \qquad \neg q \mid r \leftarrow, \qquad \neg r \leftarrow not\ q\}$$

has the unique answer set $S' = \{p, \neg q, \neg r, \alpha\}$.

On the other hand, $\mathbf{ABF}(\mathscr{P}_5)$ has arguments and *attacks* as follows.

$$A_1: \{not\ \lambda,\ not\ \mu\} \vdash p,\quad A_2: \{not\ p,\ not\ \mu\} \vdash \lambda,\quad A_3: \{not\ r\} \vdash \alpha,$$
$$A_4: \{not\ \alpha\} \vdash \mu,\quad A_5: \{not\ p,\ not\ \mu, not\ r, not\ \varphi\} \vdash \varphi,\quad A_6: \{not\ r\} \vdash \neg q,$$
$$A_7: \{not\ \neg q\} \vdash r,\quad A_8: \{not\ q\} \vdash \neg r,\quad A_{n_i}: \{not\ x\} \vdash not\ x,$$

where $x \in \{p, \neg p, q, \neg q, r, \neg r, \lambda, \neg\lambda, \mu, \neg\mu, \alpha, \neg\alpha, \varphi, \neg\varphi\}$ for $9 \leq n_i \leq 22$.

$$\begin{aligned} attacks = \{&(A_1,A_2), (A_1,A_5), (A_1, A_9), (A_2, A_1), (A_2, A_{15}), (A_3, A_4), (A_3, A_{19}),\\ &(A_4, A_1), (A_4, A_2), (A_4, A_5), (A_4, A_{17}), (A_5, A_5), (A_5, A_{21}), (A_6, A_7),\\ &(A_6, A_{12}), (A_7, A_3), (A_7, A_5), (A_7, A_6), (A_7, A_{13}), (A_8, A_{14})\}. \end{aligned}$$

Then, $\mathbf{ABF}(\mathscr{P}_5)$ has two stable argument extensions $\mathcal{E}_i$ $(i = 1, 2)$ such that

$$\mathcal{E}_1 = \{A_1, A_3, A_6, A_8, A_{10}, A_{11}, A_{13}, A_{15}, A_{16}, A_{17}, A_{18}, A_{20}, A_{21}, A_{22}\},$$
$$\mathcal{E}_2 = \{A_4, A_7, A_8, A_9, A_{10}, A_{11}, A_{12}, A_{15}, A_{16}, A_{18}, A_{19}, A_{20}, A_{21}, A_{22}\},$$

where $\text{Concs}(\mathcal{E}_1) = \{p, \alpha, \neg q, \neg r, not\ \neg p, not\ q, not\ r, not\ \lambda, not\ \neg\lambda, not\ \mu, not\ \neg\mu\} \cup U$
$\text{Concs}(\mathcal{E}_2) = \{\mu, r, \neg r, not\ p, not\ \neg p, not\ q, not\ \neg q, not\ \lambda, not \neg\lambda, not \neg\mu, not\ \alpha\} \cup U$
for $U = \{not\ \neg\alpha, not\ \varphi, not\ \neg\varphi\}$.

Thus, $\text{Concs}(\mathcal{E}_1)$ is not contradictory w.r.t. $\neg$ though $\text{Concs}(\mathcal{E}_2)$ is contradictory.

Hence, for the consistent $\mathcal{E}_1$, $\text{Concs}(\mathcal{E}_1) \cap Lit_{P_5} = \{p, \neg q, \neg r\} = S$ is obtained.

4.2 ABA for GEDPs Having Minimal Answer Sets

There is a subclass of GEDPs whose program has always minimal answer sets. We denote by Π a GEDP whose rules are restricted to be either of the form (11) or (12), where $k, \ell, m, n \geq 0$ and A_i, B_j, C_s and D_t are literals:

$$A_1 \mid \ldots \mid A_k \leftarrow C_1, \ldots, C_m, not\ D_1, \ldots, not\ D_n \tag{11}$$
$$not\ B_1 \mid \ldots \mid not\ B_\ell \leftarrow C_1, \ldots, C_m, not\ D_1, \ldots, not\ D_n. \tag{12}$$

Proposition 2. *Every answer set of a GEDP* Π *is minimal.*

Proof. Since Π is N-acyclic[5], this follows from [9, Corollary 4.7]. □

Note that any logic program used in the work of Rapberger et al. [13] is the special case of Π because not only is every rule in their logic programs restricted to be the form (11) s.t. $k=1$ or the form (12) s.t. $\ell=1$ but also A_1, B_1, C_s and D_t are propositional atoms. Hence, Proposition 2 indicates that every answer set (i.e. stable model) of logic programs with NAF in the head used by Rapberger et al. [13] is always minimal.

For a GEDP Π, the following propositions hold by making use of the mapping *shift* of GEDPs to EDLPs as proposed by Inoue and Sakama [9].

[5] The notion of *N-acyclic* property for a GEDP is defined in [9, Section 4.1].

Proposition 3. *Given a GEDP* Π, *let* $S \subseteq Lit_{\Pi}$ *and* $shift(\Pi)$ *be the EDLP obtained from* Π *by replacing every rule of the form (12) with the rule:*

$$\leftarrow B_1, \ldots, B_\ell, C_1, \ldots, C_m, not\ D_1, \ldots, not\ D_n. \tag{13}$$

S is an answer set of a GEDP Π *iff S is an answer set of an EDLP* $shift(\Pi)$.

Proof. Since Π is N-acyclic, this follows from [9, Theorem 4.6]. □

Corollary 1 *A GEDP* Π *has a contradictory answer set iff* Π *is contradictory (i.e. inconsistent),*

Proof. Suppose that a GEDP Π has a contradictory answer set Lit_P. Then, the EDLP $shift(\Pi)$ has a unique contradictory answer set Lit_P due to Proposition 3, which means that Π has only the single answer set Lit_P. Hence, Π is contradictory. The converse holds obviously. □

Proposition 4. *Given a propositional GEDP* Π, *let* $S \subseteq Lit_{\Pi}$, $\mathfrak{L} = \langle \mathcal{L}_{\mathrm{EDLP}}, \Vdash \rangle$ *and* $\mathscr{P} = ic(shift(\Pi))$. *Then,*

(i) *S is an answer set of* Π *iff there is a stable argument extension* $\mathcal{E}_{tr}$ *of* $\mathbf{ABF}(\mathscr{P}_{tr}) = \langle \mathfrak{L}, \mathscr{P}_{tr}, \mathcal{A}_{\mathscr{P}}, \overline{} \rangle$ *such that* $S \cup \Delta_S = \mathrm{Concs}(\mathcal{E}_{tr}) = \mathsf{CN}_{\mathscr{P}_{tr}}(\Delta_S)$ *(or* $S = \mathrm{Concs}(\mathcal{E}_{tr}) \cap Lit_{\Pi}$*), where* $\Delta_S = \{not\ \ell \mid \ell \in (Lit_{\mathscr{P}} \setminus S)\}$.
(ii) *For a consistent* Π, *S is an answer set of* Π *iff there is a consistent stable argument extension* $\mathcal{E}$ *of* $\mathbf{ABF}(\mathscr{P}) = \langle \mathfrak{L}, \mathscr{P}, \mathcal{A}_{\mathscr{P}}, \overline{} \rangle$ *s.t.* $S \cup \Delta_S = \mathrm{Concs}(\mathcal{E}) = \mathsf{CN}_{\mathscr{P}}(\Delta_S)$ *(or* $S = \mathrm{Concs}(\mathcal{E}) \cap Lit_{\Pi}$*), where* $\Delta_S = \{not\ \ell \mid \ell \in (Lit_{\mathscr{P}} \setminus S)\}$.

Proof. (i) follows from Proposition 3, Proposition 1 and Theorem 1. Similarly, (ii) follows from Proposition 3, Proposition 1 and Theorem 2. □

Proposition 4 implies that there is a one-to-one correspondence between the stable models of a (special) propositional logic program Π used by Rapberger et al. [13] and the stable extensions of the ABF instantiated with the NLP $ic(shift(\Pi))$.

5 Conclusion

In the paper, first, we have shown that the translation of any GEDP into an EDLP proposed by Inoue and Sakama [8,9] cannot yield a one-to-one correspondence between the answer sets of the respective programs due to the existence of counterexamples against their claim. Hence, we have proposed a novel polynomial-time translation of a GEDP into an EDLP, with which there is a one-to-one correspondence between the consistent answer sets of an original GEDP and those of the translated EDLP as proved in Theorem 4. Note that, [9, Theorem 6.4] gives the complexity result about our translation because our translation is a polynomial-time translation from a GEDP into an EDLP, like the one by Inoue and Sakama [9]. Second, based on such the proposed translation as well as the existing work to relate EDLPs and ABFs [15,16], we have proved that there is a one-to-one correspondence between the consistent answer sets of a consistent propositional GEDP and the consistent stable extensions of the associated ABF in Theorem 5. To the best of our knowledge, this work is the first to relate ABA and general extended disjunctive logic programming with NAF in the head.

In the work of Rapberger et al. [13] to relate LP and ABA, they used logic programs with NAF in the head and non-flat ABFs. However, answer sets (i.e. stable models) of their logic programs with NAF in the head are *minimal* due to Proposition 2. In contrast, in this work, the correspondence between a propositional GEDP possibly having *non-minimal* answer sets and the associated ABF is shown, where the ABF is always ensured to be flat due to [16, Proposition 2].

This study shows the relationship between GEDPs and ABFs based on the proposed translation of a GEDP into an EDLP. Nevertheless, our future work is to investigate another approach to link GEDPs and ABFs by providing a new ABF translated from a GEDP such that its inference rules are directly applicable to rules of a GEDP as well as a disjunction of NAF-literals and literals. Moreover, the practical implementation of the proposed translation remains as our future work.

Acknowledgments. The author would like to thank Chiaki Sakama for his valuable comments and suggestions.

References

1. Bondarenko, A., Dung, P.M., Kowalski, R.A., Toni, F.: An abstract, argumentation-theoretic approach to default reasoning. Artif. Intell. **93**, 63–101 (1997)
2. Caminada, M., Schulz, C.: On the equivalence between assumption-based argumentation and logic programming. J. Artif. Intell. Res. **60**, 779–825 (2017)
3. Caminada, M., Schulz, C.: On the equivalence between assumption-based argumentation and logic programming (Extended Abstract). In: Proceedings of IJCAI 2018, pp. 5578–5582 (2018)
4. Cyras, K., Schulz, C., Toni, F.: Capturing bipolar argumentation in non-flat assumption-based argumentation. In: Proceedings of the 20th International Conference on Principles and Practice of Multi-Agent Systems (PRIMA 2017), pp. 386–402 (2017)
5. Dung, P.M.: On the acceptability of arguments and its fundamental role in nonmonotonic reasoning, logic programming and n-person games. Artif. Intell. **77**, 321–357 (1995)
6. Heyninck, J., Arieli, O.: On the semantics of simple contrapositive assumption-based argumentation frameworks. In: Proceedings of Computational Models of Argument (COMMA 2018), pp. 9–20 (2018)
7. Heyninck, J., Arieli, O.: An Argumentative characterization of disjunctive logic programming. In: Proceedings of EPIA-2019, LNAI, vol. 11805, pp. 526–538 (2019)
8. Inoue, K., Sakama, C.: On positive occurrences of negation as failure. In: Proceedings of the 4th International Conference on Principles of Knowledge Representation and Reasoning (KR 1994), pp. 293–304 (1994)

9. Inoue, K., Sakama, C.: Negation as failure in the head. J. Log. Program. **35**(1), 39–78 (1998)
10. Gebser, M., Kaminski, R., Kaufmann, B., Schaub, T.: Multi-shot ASP solving with clingo. Theory Pract. Logic Program. Theory Pract. Logic Program **19**(1), 27–82 (2019)
11. Gelfond, M., Lifschitz, V.: The stable model semantics for logic programming. In: Proceedings of ICLP/SLP-1988, pp. 1070–1080. MIT Press (1988)
12. Gelfond, M., Lifschitz, V.: Classical negation in logic programs and disjunctive databases. N. Gener. Comput. **9**, 365–385 (1991)
13. Rapberger, A., Ulbricht, M., Toni, F.: On the correspondence of non-flat assumption-based argumentation and logic programming with negation as failure in the head. In: Proceedings of the 22nd International Workshop on Non-Monotonic Reasoning (NMR 2024), pp. 112–121 (2024)
14. Wakaki, T.: Consistency in assumption-based argumentation. In: Proceedings of Computational Models of Argument (COMMA 2020), pp. 371–382. IOS Press (2020)
15. Wakaki, T.: Assumption-based argumentation for extended disjunctive logic programming. In: Proceedings of the 12th International Symposium on Foundations of Information and Knowledge Systems (FoIKS 2022), pp. 35–54 (2022)
16. Wakaki, T.: Assumption-based argumentation for extended disjunctive logic programming and its relation to nonmonotonic reasoning. Argument Comput. **15**(3), 309–353 (2024)

Winning by Numbers: Connecting Strong Admissibility to Optimal Play in Argumentation

Shawn Bowers[1(✉)], Martin Caminada[2], and Bertram Ludäscher[3]

[1] Gonzaga University, Spokane, USA
bowers@gonzaga.edu
[2] Cardiff University, Cardiff, UK
CaminadaM@cardiff.ac.uk
[3] University of Illinois, Urbana-Champaign,Champaign, USA
ludaesch@illinois.edu

Abstract. Strongly admissible labelings and min-max numberings offer well-founded explanations in formal argumentation. We establish a precise correspondence between min-max numberings and remoteness functions from combinatorial game theory, showing that min-max numbers characterize optimal play length, i.e., where players seek the fastest win or longest delay of loss. Our game–argumentation duality strengthens the theoretical and computational foundations for cross-fertilization between argumentation and game theory: game-theoretic provenance explanations apply to argumentation frameworks; pure strategy-based provenance aligns with strongly admissible labelings; and a linear-time algorithm for computing remoteness is sufficient to compute grounded labelings and min-max numbers.

Keywords: Formal Argumentation · Strongly Admissible Labelings · Provenance · Combinatorial Game Theory

1 Introduction

Formal argumentation is a key approach to reasoning with uncertainty. Strong admissibility [1,7] plays a central role for grounded semantics, much like admissibility does for preferred semantics, particularly in proof procedures. To show an argument is in a preferred extension, it suffices to show it is in an admissible set, without constructing the full extension. Similarly, to show that an argument is in the grounded extension it suffices to show it is in a strongly admissible set [7]. This strongly admissible set can then be presented directly or used as the basis for an interactive explanation as a discussion game [6].

Supported by the Joint Research and Innovation Seed Grants Program between University of Illinois and Cardiff University under *XAI-CA: Explainable AI via Computational Argumentation.*

K. Sauerwald and M. Thimm (Eds.): ECSQARU 2025, LNAI 16099, pp. 395–410, 2026.
https://doi.org/10.1007/978-3-032-05134-9_27

Strong admissibility has been defined in several different but equivalent ways [1,2,7]. We focus on its labeling-based form [7], where min-max numberings are central to defining and characterizing strong admissibility. In this paper, we deepen the connection between strong admissibility, min-max numberings, and optimal play in classical game theory, to further clarify the role of min-max numberings via connections to solving and explaining games.

Contributions. We establish a formal and precise correspondence between min-max numberings and remoteness functions [21] in combinatorial game theory, showing that min-max numbers are related to optimal play. Using this connection, we apply existing game-based provenance explanations [4,5] to argumentation frameworks. We also develop a new class of provenance based on pure strategies that align with strongly admissible labelings. Our results strengthen the connection between argumentation and game theory, providing a foundation for cross-fertilization between the two fields.

Outline. Section 2 recalls basic definitions in formal argumentation. Section 3 reviews relevant game theory concepts and develops provenance-based approaches for explaining games. Section 4 presents our duality results linking games and argumentation. Section 5 summarizes our contributions and suggests future work.

2 Preliminaries: AF Labelings and Min-Max Numbers

This section briefly recalls key concepts from formal argumentation. We assume finite argumentation frameworks (AFs) and games throughout the paper.

Definition 1 ([13]). An *argumentation framework* $F = (A, R)$ consists of a finite set of entities, called *arguments*, and a binary relation $R \subseteq A \times A$. An edge $(x, y) \in R$ means that x *attacks* y.

A labeling $\mathcal{L}ab : A \to \{\mathtt{in}, \mathtt{out}, \mathtt{undec}\}$ maps arguments to their status under a given semantics where in is *accepted*, out is *rejected*, and undec is *undecided.*

Definition 2 ([7]). $\mathcal{L}ab$ is an *admissible labeling* of F iff for each $x \in A$:

- if $\mathcal{L}ab(x) = \mathtt{in}$ then for each y that attacks x it holds that $\mathcal{L}ab(y) = \mathtt{out}$
- if $\mathcal{L}ab(x) = \mathtt{out}$ then there exists a y that attacks x such that $\mathcal{L}ab(y) = \mathtt{in}$

$\mathcal{L}ab$ is a *complete labeling* of F iff it is an admissible labeling and for each $x \in A$:

- if $\mathcal{L}ab(x) = \mathtt{undec}$ there is a y that attacks x such that $\mathcal{L}ab(y) = \mathtt{undec}$, and for each y that attacks x where $\mathcal{L}ab(y) \neq \mathtt{undec}$ it holds that $\mathcal{L}ab(y) = \mathtt{out}$.

We use $\mathtt{in}(\mathcal{L}ab)$ for $\{x \in A \mid \mathcal{L}ab(x) = \mathtt{in}\}$, $\mathtt{out}(\mathcal{L}ab)$ for $\{x \in A \mid \mathcal{L}ab(x) = \mathtt{out}\}$ and $\mathtt{undec}(\mathcal{L}ab)$ for $\{x \in A \mid \mathcal{L}ab(x) = \mathtt{undec}\}$. We can define partial orders on labelings (similar to subsets of extensions).

Definition 3 ([12]). Let $\mathcal{L}ab$ and $\mathcal{L}ab'$ be labelings of $F = (A, R)$: $\mathcal{L}ab \sqsubseteq \mathcal{L}ab'$ iff $\texttt{in}(\mathcal{L}ab) \subseteq \texttt{in}(\mathcal{L}ab')$ and $\texttt{out}(\mathcal{L}ab) \subseteq \texttt{out}(\mathcal{L}ab')$.

The grounded labeling can be defined as the ($\sqsubseteq$) smallest complete labeling.

Definition 4 ([7]). Let $\mathcal{L}ab$ be a complete labeling of $F = (A, R)$. $\mathcal{L}ab$ is the *grounded labeling* iff $\mathcal{L}ab$ is the (unique) smallest (w.r.t. $\sqsubseteq$) complete labeling.

Strongly admissible labelings can be defined using min-max numberings [7].

Definition 5 ([7]). Let $\mathcal{L}ab$ be an admissible labeling of $F = (A, R)$. A *min-max numbering* is a total function $\mathcal{MM}_{\mathcal{L}ab} : \texttt{in}(\mathcal{L}ab) \cup \texttt{out}(\mathcal{L}ab) \rightarrow \mathbb{N} \cup \{\infty\}$ such that for each $x \in \texttt{in}(\mathcal{L}ab) \cup \texttt{out}(\mathcal{L}ab)$:

- if $\mathcal{L}ab(x) = \texttt{in}$ then $\mathcal{MM}_{\mathcal{L}ab}(x) = 1 + max(\{\mathcal{MM}_{\mathcal{L}ab}(y) \mid y$ attacks x and $\mathcal{L}ab(y) = \texttt{out}\})$ (with $max(\emptyset)$ defined as 0)
- if $\mathcal{L}ab(x) = \texttt{out}$ then $\mathcal{MM}_{\mathcal{L}ab}(x) = 1 + min(\{\mathcal{MM}_{\mathcal{L}ab}(y) \mid y$ attacks x and $\mathcal{L}ab(y) = \texttt{in}\})$ (with $min(\emptyset)$ defined as ∞)

Theorem 1 ([7]). Every admissible labeling has a *unique* min-max numbering.

Min-max numbers can be used to define strongly admissible labelings as follows.

Definition 6 ([7]). A *strongly admissible labeling* $\mathcal{L}ab$ is an admissible labeling whose $\mathcal{MM}_{\mathcal{L}ab}$ yields natural numbers only (no argument is numbered ∞).

3 Combinatorial Games: Remoteness and Optimal Play

We recall basic notions and results from combinatorial game theory [17, 19–21]. A fundamental question addressed is: Who wins under optimal play? We show that solved games represent their own *provenance*, i.e., subgraphs that *explain* objective position values and the length of optimal play.

3.1 Playing Games, Winning Strategies, and Solving Games

Games. A *game* is a finite digraph $G = (V, E)$ consisting of *positions* V and *moves* $E \subseteq V \times V$. To play the game from a starting position $x_0 \in V$, players I and II take turns moving a pebble along the available edges E.

Plays. A *play* π starting at $x_0 \in V$ is a (finite or infinite) sequence of moves:

$$x_0 \xrightarrow{\text{I}} x_1 \xrightarrow{\text{II}} x_2 \xrightarrow{\text{I}} x_3 \xrightarrow{\text{II}} \cdots \qquad (\pi)$$

Player I starts. The *length* $|\pi|$ of a play is the length of the sequence. A play π is *complete* if it either ends after $|\pi| = k$ moves in a *terminal position* (a sink of G), or if $|\pi| = \infty$. The latter means π is a *draw* and the players are forever repeating moves (G is finite, so must have cycles). The player moving to a terminal node *wins*, so the opponent cannot move and *loses*. Players may play optimally, "good enough", or even blunder (e.g., turning a win into a draw or loss). To determine the objective *value* of a position, i.e., under optimal play, we need strategies.

Strategies. A (pure) *strategy* for $G = (V, E)$ is a function $S : V \to V$ such that $(x, S(x)) \in E$. S can be partial (e.g., for terminal positions). For strategy S_{I}, in position x, Player I chooses $S_{\mathrm{I}}(x)$ as the next position if it's I's turn (otherwise II moves according to S_{II}). Any pair S_{I}, S_{II} of strategy functions for I and II defines a unique play $\pi_{S_{\mathrm{I}},S_{\mathrm{II}}}$ from a starting position $x_0 \in V$:

$$x_0 \xrightarrow{\mathrm{I}} \underbrace{S_{\mathrm{I}}(x_0)}_{x_1} \xrightarrow{\mathrm{II}} \underbrace{S_{\mathrm{II}} \circ S_{\mathrm{I}}(x_0)}_{x_2} \xrightarrow{\mathrm{I}} \underbrace{S_{\mathrm{I}} \circ S_{\mathrm{II}} \circ S_{\mathrm{I}}(x_0)}_{x_3} \xrightarrow{\mathrm{II}} \cdots \qquad (\pi_{S_{\mathrm{I}},S_{\mathrm{II}}})$$

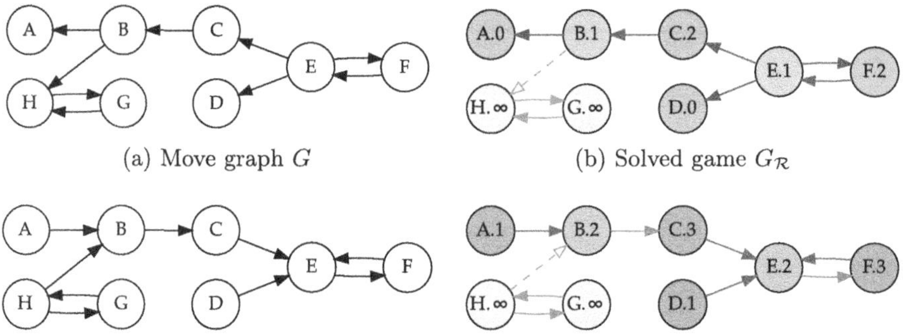

(a) Move graph G (b) Solved game $G_{\mathcal{R}}$

(c) Argumentation framework F (d) Grounded $\mathcal{L}ab$ of F with $\mathcal{MM}_{\mathcal{L}ab}$

Fig. 1. (a) Game $G = (V, E)$ and (b) $\mathcal{R}$-labeled solution $G_{\mathcal{R}}$. Node labels "$x.k$" mean $\mathcal{R}(x) = k$ and *optimal play* π_x from x has length $|\pi_x| = k$. $\mathcal{R}$'s parity determines val_G: x is `won` (odd/green), `lost` (even/red), or `drawn` (∞/yellow). (c) AF F is the dual of G. (d) The grounded labeling of F with min-max numbers $\mathcal{MM}_{\mathcal{L}ab}$ and $\mathcal{L}ab$: $x \in Ar$ is either `in` (blue), `out` (orange), or `undec` (yellow). (Color figure online)

Position Values. Position $x_0 \in V$ is `won` in $\leq k$ moves if there exists a strategy S_{I} for Player I such that for all strategies S_{II} of II there is an odd number $j < k$ and $S_{\mathrm{I}} \circ (S_{\mathrm{II}} \circ S_{\mathrm{I}})^{\frac{j-1}{2}}(x_0)$ exists, but is not defined for S_{II}. In other words, II cannot move. Such an S_{I} is a *winning strategy*. Conversely, x_0 is `won` for II in $\leq k$ moves if there is a strategy S_{II} such that for all strategies S_{I} there is an even number $j < k$ and $(S_{\mathrm{II}} \circ S_{\mathrm{I}})^{\frac{j}{2}}(x)$ exists, but is not defined for S_{I}: I cannot move!

Note that the objective *value* $\mathsf{val}_G(x_0)$ of position x_0 is *not* determined by an individual play π. Instead, the value of x_0 is `won` (`lost`) if Player I (II) can *force* a win, starting from x_0, no matter how the opponent moves. If neither player can force a win, then x_0 is `drawn` and optimal play is infinite (repeating moves).

Solved Games. Figure 1b shows the values $\mathsf{val}_G : V \to \{\texttt{won}, \texttt{lost}, \texttt{drawn}\}$ for all $x \in V$ using node colors, i.e., it shows a *solved game*. It is well known that the position values of a solved game satisfy the following two rules:[1]

- $\mathsf{val}_G(x) := \texttt{lost}$ if $\forall y$: $(x, y) \in E$ implies $\mathsf{val}_G(y) = \texttt{won}$. $(R_\forall)$
- $\mathsf{val}_G(x) := \texttt{won}$ if $\exists y$: $(x, y) \in E$ such that $\mathsf{val}_G(y) = \texttt{lost}$. $(R_\exists)$

3.2 Winning by Numbers: SMITH's Remoteness Function $\mathcal{R}$

A classic approach to solve games uses a *remoteness* function due to STEINHAUS and SMITH [21]. The remoteness $\mathcal{R}$ not only yields position values, but does so by defining for each $x \in V$ the length of optimal play from x.

Let $E^+(x) = \{y \mid (x, y) \in E\}$ denote the *followers* of x in $G = (V, E)$.

Definition 7 ([21])**.** The *remoteness* $\mathcal{R} : V \to \mathbb{N} \cup \{\infty\}$ is defined as:

$$\mathcal{R}(x) = \begin{cases} 0 & \text{if } x \text{ has } \textit{no} \text{ followers}, \\ 1 + \min\{\mathcal{R}(y) \mid y \in E^+(x), \mathcal{R}(y) \text{ is } \textit{even}\,\} & \ldots \text{ has an } \textit{even} \text{ follower}, \\ 1 + \max\{\mathcal{R}(y) \mid y \in E^+(x), \mathcal{R}(y) \text{ is } \textit{odd}\} & \ldots \text{ has } \textit{only odd} \text{ followers}, \\ \infty & \ldots \text{ otherwise}. \end{cases}$$

It is well-known that the parity of $\mathcal{R}$ determines the objective value of a position:

Theorem 2 ($\mathcal{R} \to \mathsf{val}_G$ [21])**.** For $G = (V, E)$, position $x \in V$ is $\texttt{won}$, $\texttt{lost}$, or $\texttt{drawn}$ if and only if $\mathcal{R}(x)$ is *odd*, *even*, or ∞, respectively.

This means "*remoteness is all you need*", i.e., $\mathcal{R}$ yields two connected insights: how long an optimal play from x will last and whether x is won, lost, or drawn.

Remoteness Algorithm. Definition 7 suggests a simple algorithm[2] to compute $\mathcal{R}$, which then can be used to solve for the values of a finite game G and identify optimal play in G: Label all terminal positions x with $\mathcal{R} = 0$. Then label all predecessors y of these x with $\mathcal{R} = 1$. Now delete all such numbered positions x and y from G and repeat after increasing $\mathcal{R}$ by 2, i.e., in the next round, $\mathcal{R}(x)$ will be 2 and 3 (instead of 0 and 1), etc. Repeat until there are no more terminal nodes. The remaining nodes receive $\mathcal{R} = \infty$.

In Fig. 2, succ and pred return the *successors* E^+ and *predecessors* E^- of positions, respectively. Lines 2–6 initialize: $\mathcal{R}$-values to ∞; $\mathsf{N_{succ}}$ to successor counts; T to the terminal nodes; del to false for each node; and the remoteness counter k to 0. Lines 7–20 repeat while there are terminal nodes x to process: in each round, these receive $\mathcal{R} = k$ (meaning *lost in* k), and their predecessors y get $\mathcal{R} = k + 1$ (i.e., *won in* $k + 1$), after which these nodes are deleted. Lines 13–16 compute the new terminal nodes after deletions; k is incremented by 2, and the loop starts over. It is easy to see that $\mathcal{R}$ can be computed in linear time:

[1] Indeed, one way to compute the solution is by iterating these rules, e.g., see [5].
[2] The authors of [3] attribute the method to VON NEUMANN and MORGENSTERN [17].

Theorem 3. SMITH's remoteness function $\mathcal{R}$ can be computed in $\mathcal{O}(|V|+|E|)$.

Proof. Consider the algorithm in Fig. 2. *Initialization:* Lines 2, 4, 5 are $\mathcal{O}(|V|)$ and Line 3 is $\mathcal{O}(|E|)$. *Main loop:* Each $x \in V$ can occur in T at most once, then it is deleted; so the loop in Line 7 executes at most $\mathcal{O}(|V|)$ times. *Predecessor processing* (Lines 11–17): When $x \in T$ is processed, each predecessor y corresponds to an edge $(y, x) \in E$, yielding $\mathcal{O}(|E|)$ *total* (i.e., over all loop iterations) for Lines 11, 12, 17. *Successor count updates* (Lines 13–16): For each y, we examine each of its predecessors z and the edge $(z, y) \in E$. Each of these is processed once (and then deleted with y). Lines 14–16 are $\mathcal{O}(1)$ per edge, so no edge is visited more than once in the main loop, resulting in a total cost of $\mathcal{O}(|V|+|E|)$.

Since on connected graphs $|E| \geq |V| - 1$, we have:

Corollary 4. On connected graphs, $\mathcal{R}$ can be computed in $\mathcal{O}(|E|)$.[3]

Algorithm: Computing **Remoteness** $\mathcal{R}$

```
   Input: Finite game graph G = (V, E)
   Result: Remoteness function R : V → ℕ ∪ {∞}
1  begin
2    R(x) := ∞ for each x ∈ V                      // drawn unless proven otherwise
3    N_succ[x] := |succ(x)| for each x ∈ V          // count successors
4    T := {x ∈ V | N_succ[x] = 0}                  // initial terminal nodes
5    del[x] := false for each x ∈ V                 // nothing deleted yet
6    k := 0                                         // initial remoteness
7    while T ≠ ∅ do                                 // until no more terminals
8      T_next := ∅                                  // prepare next terminal set
9      for x ∈ T do                                 // for each current terminal
10       R(x) := k                                  // even R(x) ⇒ x is lost
11       for y ∈ pred(x) and ¬del[y] do             // for each predecessor
12         R(y) := k + 1                            // odd R(y) ⇒ y is won
13         for z ∈ pred(y) and ¬del[z] do           // update predecessor counts:
14           N_succ[z] := N_succ[z] − 1             // ... z loses successor y
15           if N_succ[z] = 0 then                  // ... z becomes terminal
16             T_next := T_next ∪ {z}               // ... add to next iteration
17         del[y] := true                           // remove y from graph
18       del[x] := true                             // remove x from graph
19     T := T_next                                  // ready for new terminal set
20     k := k + 2                                   // ready for the next two levels
```

Fig. 2. Computing SMITH's remoteness function $\mathcal{R}$ [21] for finite games.

[3] FRAENKEL [14] sketches essentially the same algorithm, claiming it is $\mathcal{O}(|E|)$.

Example 1 ($\mathcal{R} \rightarrow \mathsf{val}_G$)**.** Consider the game G in Fig. 1a and its $\mathcal{R}$-labeled, colored solution $G_{\mathcal{R}}$ in Fig. 1b. Positions $\{\mathsf{A}, \mathsf{D}\}$ are terminal ($\mathcal{R} = 0$) and thus immediately lost (red). Positions $\{\mathsf{B}, \mathsf{E}\}$ are predecessors of $\{\mathsf{A}, \mathsf{D}\}$, so they are won (green) with $\mathcal{R} = 1$. After removing these four nodes, $\{\mathsf{C}, \mathsf{F}\}$ become the new terminal (lost) nodes, receiving $\mathcal{R} = 2$. After these have been removed, no more new terminal nodes are created and the algorithm terminates. H and G haven't been reached, so they are drawn (yellow), having infinite remoteness ($\mathcal{R} = \infty$).

Optimal Play. The $\mathcal{R}$-numbers of a solved game $G_{\mathcal{R}}$ allow to find optimal plays and winning strategies easily. Similar to how node colors indicate position values, *edge colors* (Fig. 1b) indicate which moves are *winning* (green), *delaying* a loss (red), or *drawing* (yellow). Another edge type are *blunders* (grey, dashed), e.g., $\mathsf{B} \rightarrow \mathsf{H}$: While $\mathsf{B} \rightarrow \mathsf{A}$ is a winning move,[4] the move to H blunders the win from B and gives the opponent a *draw* (via an infinite play $\mathsf{H} \rightleftharpoons \mathsf{G}$.) The optimal "countdown play" from E.1 is to D.0; the "count-up" move to C.2 is still winning, but requires a longer play.

Proposition 1 (Optimal Moves). All non-terminal positions x in $G_{\mathcal{R}}$ have at least one optimal (i.e., *countdown*) move to y, i.e., where $\mathcal{R}(y) = \mathcal{R}(x) - 1$. For drawn x, i.e., $\mathcal{R}(x) = \infty$, some y also has $\mathcal{R}(y) = \infty$ (keeping the draw).

Consider a game G and its $\mathcal{R}$-annotated solution $G_{\mathcal{R}}$. Using the latter, an *optimal play* π from any position $x \in V$ is found simply by following countdown moves.

Definition 8 ($\mathcal{R} \rightarrow$ **Optimal Strategies** [21])**.** Given a solved game $G_{\mathcal{R}}$, the strategy $S \colon V \rightarrow V$ is *optimal* if $S(x) = y$ implies $(x, y) \in E$ and $\mathcal{R}(y) = \mathcal{R}(x) - 1$.

If both players follow optimal strategies, they win in the fewest moves possible, delay inevitable defeat as long as possible, and avoid losing from drawn positions. Starting from x, this means that $\mathcal{R}(x)$ bounds the length of optimal play. Winning strategies (and winning moves) don't have to be optimal: e.g., in Fig. 1b, the move $\mathsf{E} \rightarrow \mathsf{C}$ is winning but not optimal.

3.3 Provenance: Explaining Position Values Through Subgraphs

The *provenance* $\mathcal{P}(x)$ of $x \in V$ is a subgraph of G that explains x's value (`won`, `lost`, or `drawn`) and possibly its remoteness $\mathcal{R}(x)$. Informally, $\mathcal{P}(x)$ is a subgraph rooted at x that contains some or all of the complete plays from x that are relevant for establishing x's value. We define different types of provenance: *potential*, *actual*, *primary*, and *pure*. Each type provides more specific (i.e., usually smaller) subgraphs that justify x's value (or remoteness).

Definition 9 (Potential Provenance). The *potential provenance* $\mathcal{P}_{\mathsf{pt}}(x)$ of a node $x \in V$ is the subgraph of nodes and edges reachable from x in $G = (V, E)$.

[4] $\mathsf{B} \rightarrow \mathsf{A}$ is also optimal because it counts down: $\mathcal{R}(\mathsf{A}) = \mathcal{R}(\mathsf{B}) - 1$.

$\mathcal{P}_{\mathsf{pt}}(x)$ might overestimate but never underestimate the subgraph needed to justify the value of x. If x is `won`, there exists a move to y that is `lost` for the opponent. However, x may also have moves that are *blunders*, i.e., to some y which is `won` or `drawn` for the opponent. Similarly, if x is `drawn`, it may have a follower y that blunders the draw and allows the opponent to win. *Actual provenance* $\mathcal{P}_{\mathsf{ac}}$ eliminates all blunders, i.e., contains only moves that can be used to determine position values. To this end, we first define edge types.

Definition 10 (Edge Types). Given $G_{\mathcal{R}} = (V, E)$ and position values val_G, the *edge types* $\tau : V \times V \to \{\texttt{won}, \texttt{lost}, \texttt{drawn}, \texttt{blunder}\}$ are defined by:

$$\tau(x, y) := \begin{cases} \texttt{won} & \text{if } \mathsf{val}_G(x) = \texttt{won} \text{ and } \mathsf{val}_G(y) = \texttt{lost} \\ \texttt{lost} & \text{if } \mathsf{val}_G(x) = \texttt{lost} \text{ and } \mathsf{val}_G(y) = \texttt{won} \\ \texttt{drawn} & \text{if } \mathsf{val}_G(x) = \texttt{drawn} \text{ and } \mathsf{val}_G(y) = \texttt{drawn} \\ \texttt{blunder} & \text{otherwise.} \end{cases}$$

Definition 11 (Actual Provenance). $\mathcal{P}_{\mathsf{ac}}(x)$, the *actual provenance* of x, is the subgraph of G reachable from x by following `won`, `lost`, and `drawn` edges.

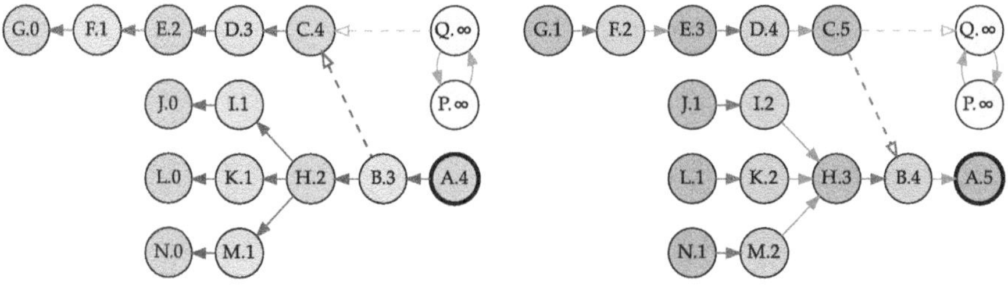

(a) A solved game (b) Grounded labeling of the dual AF

Fig. 3. (a) Optimal play *vs.* minimal-size explanation: The primary provenance $\mathcal{P}_{\mathsf{pr}}(\mathsf{A})$ excludes the dashed edge $\mathsf{B}{\to}\mathsf{C}$ and the subgraph $\mathsf{C} \rightsquigarrow \mathsf{G}$ as only countdown paths are in $\mathcal{P}_{\mathsf{pr}}$. The suboptimal $\mathsf{B}{\to}\mathsf{C} \rightsquigarrow \mathsf{G}$, however, is a minimal-size explanation of $\mathsf{val}(\mathsf{A})$. (b) The AF-dual of (a): $\{\mathsf{A}, \mathsf{C}, \mathsf{E}, \mathsf{G}\}$ is a *minimal strongly admissible set* witnessing $\mathcal{L}ab(\mathsf{A})$: it uses the subgraph $\mathsf{A}{\leftarrow}\mathsf{B}{\leftarrow}\mathsf{C} \leftsquigarrow \mathsf{G}$.

Since all blunders are removed, the remaining moves in $\mathcal{P}_{\mathsf{ac}}(x)$ are "good enough" to achieve the best outcome $\mathsf{val}(x)$, independent of what the opponent does. However, by playing suboptimal moves, a *mixed* strategy[5] may be required to win: In Fig. 1b, although the move $\mathsf{E} \to \mathsf{F}$ *is* winning, it requires the player to break out of the cycle *eventually* and move from E to either C or D to force a win. This is only possible with a mixed strategy, which allows a player to take one of many possible moves from a given position, but not with a pure strategy.

One solution to this problem is to exclude suboptimal winning moves from consideration. This idea gives rise to the notion of *primary provenance*. In the resulting subgraphs pure strategies are sufficient to explain position values.

[5] In that case, S is a *relation* and not necessarily a function.

Definition 12 (Primary Provenance). $\mathcal{P}_{\mathsf{pr}}(x)$ is the subset of $\mathcal{P}_{\mathsf{ac}}(x)$ that excludes suboptimal (i.e., non-countdown) winning moves.

Example 2. In Fig. 1b $\mathcal{P}_{\mathsf{pr}}(\mathsf{E})$ excludes both the "detour" through F, which was included in $\mathcal{P}_{\mathsf{ac}}(\mathsf{E})$, and the suboptimal path $\mathsf{E}{\to}\mathsf{C} \rightsquigarrow A$.

$\mathcal{P}_{\mathsf{pr}}$ only follows optimal winning moves, but includes suboptimal (not maximal) delaying moves. The rationale for this choice is that *all* followers of a losing position x must be explored to establish x as `lost`. Primary provenance avoids "detours" (e.g., through F above) and bases explanations on pure strategies. Finally, like actual provenance, $\mathcal{P}_{\mathsf{pr}}$ is easily computed using $\mathcal{R}$.

Optimal *vs.* Minimal Explanations. If we are interested in minimal-size explanations, by design, $\mathcal{P}_{\mathsf{pr}}$ may exclude smaller explanations (subgraphs) that are not countdown-optimal: e.g., in Fig. 3a, the primary provenance $\mathcal{P}_{\mathsf{pr}}(\mathsf{A})$ excludes the dashed edge $\mathsf{B}{\to}\mathsf{C}$ (it's not a countdown edge), and thus the subgraph $\mathsf{C} \rightsquigarrow \mathsf{G}$, as only countdown paths are in $\mathcal{P}_{\mathsf{pr}}$. However, the subgraph $\mathsf{B}{\to}\mathsf{C} \rightsquigarrow \mathsf{G}$ is a size-minimal explanation of $\mathsf{val}(\mathsf{A})$. Thus, $\mathcal{P}_{\mathsf{pr}}$ can be too selective to include all minimal explanations. The actual provenance $\mathcal{P}_{\mathsf{ac}}(\mathsf{A})$ does include the size-minimal subgraph ($\mathsf{B} \rightsquigarrow \mathsf{G}$), but unfortunately also includes the unfounded loop that primary provenance was meant to eliminate. What is needed is a new form of provenance that lies between actual and primary provenance.

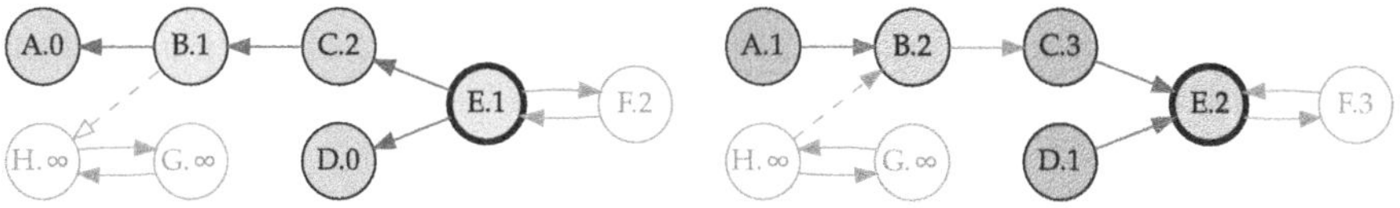

(a) The pure provenance of E (b) AF strongly-admissible set from E

Fig. 4. (a) The pure provenance $\mathcal{P}_{\mathsf{pu}}(\mathsf{E})$ of E (highlighted) does not include F, since $\mathsf{E}{\to}\mathsf{F}$ is not selected by any pure winning strategies (otherwise, it would result in infinite play from E), however, both the optimal move $\mathsf{E}{\to}\mathsf{D}$ (as in primary provenance) and the suboptimal move $\mathsf{E}{\to}\mathsf{C}$ (unlike in primary provenance) are included. (b) The corresponding explanation of E in the dual AF, where $\{\mathsf{A},\mathsf{C}\}$, $\{\mathsf{D}\}$, and $\{\mathsf{A},\mathsf{C},\mathsf{D}\}$ are corresponding strongly admissible sets.

Definition 13 (Pure-Strategy Provenance). $\mathcal{P}_{\mathsf{pu}}(x)$ is the subset of $\mathcal{P}_{\mathsf{ac}}(x)$ that excludes all y that cannot be reached from x via a pure (winning) strategy.

Example 3. Figure 4a depicts the pure provenance $\mathcal{P}_{\mathsf{pu}}(\mathsf{E})$ of E, which includes the subgraphs $\mathsf{E} \to \mathsf{C} \rightsquigarrow A$ and $\mathsf{E} \to \mathsf{D}$. Unlike with actual provenance, F is not included in $\mathcal{P}_{\mathsf{pu}}(\mathsf{F})$: no pure (winning) strategy can include $\mathsf{E}{\to}\mathsf{F}$ as it would result in infinite play from E (where a pure strategy allows only one move from a given position). The suboptimal move $\mathsf{E}{\to}\mathsf{C}$ is included in $\mathcal{P}_{\mathsf{pu}}(\mathsf{E})$ (and its associated subgraph) unlike with $\mathcal{P}_{\mathsf{pr}}(\mathsf{E})$.

Proposition 2. Let $G_{\mathcal{R}}$ be a solved game. For all positions $x \in V$:

$$\mathcal{P}_{\mathsf{pt}}(x) \supseteq \mathcal{P}_{\mathsf{ac}}(x) \supseteq \mathcal{P}_{\mathsf{pu}}(x) \supseteq \mathcal{P}_{\mathsf{pr}}(x)$$

This hierarchy allows users to employ the most suitable notion of provenance for their use cases. The potential provenance is easy to compute since it reduces to a simple reachability query. Similarly, actual and primary provenance are easily computed via $\mathcal{R}$ and regular path queries [5]. The pure provenance $\mathcal{P}_{\mathsf{pu}}(x)$, on the other hand, cannot be computed based on $\mathcal{R}$ alone.

4 Game–Argumentation Duality

It has been shown that grounded labelings of argumentation frameworks and solutions of games (computed via the well-founded semantics [15]) directly correspond to one another [4]. We revisit and expand this *Game–AF duality* here, as it allows us to transfer notions and results from one community to another.

4.1 Argumentation Frameworks as Combinatorial Games

To view an argumentation framework F as a game G_F (G for short), we reverse its attack edges, i.e., use the *attacked-by* relation.

Definition 14 (Dual Game). Let $F = (A, R)$ be an AF. The *dual game* $G = (A, R^{-1})$ of F has the same nodes, but *reversed* edges, i.e., the moves of G are the *attacked-by* relation: $R^{-1} = \{(y, x) \mid (x, y) \in R\}$.

Example 4. The game in Fig. 1a and the AF in Fig. 1c are dual to each other. They only differ in the interpretation of nodes (*positions vs. arguments*) and edges (*moves vs. attacks*). The duality carries over to the solved game $G_{\mathcal{R}}$ in Fig. 1b and its dual, the grounded labeling $\mathcal{MM}_{\mathcal{L}ab}$ in Fig. 1d: Positions that are `won` (green), `lost` (red), and `drawn` (yellow) correspond to arguments that are `out` (orange), `in` (blue), and `undec` (yellow), respectively. Positions have a *remoteness* $\mathcal{R}$, while arguments have similar *min-max numbers* from $\mathcal{MM}_{\mathcal{L}ab}$.

A Skeptic's Argumentation Game (SAG [4]). Consider argument E in Fig. 1c and 1d. To show that $x = \mathsf{E}$ is defeated (`out`), it suffices to find an attacker $y \in \{\mathsf{C}, \mathsf{D}, \mathsf{F}\}$ that is accepted (`in`). As it turns out (see below), this is equivalent to moving from x to a follower $y \in \{\mathsf{C}, \mathsf{D}, \mathsf{F}\}$ which is `lost`. More generally, if a player makes the move $x \to y$ in G, the intent is to demonstrate that x is `won` by selecting a y that is `lost` for the opponent. If, however, all moves from x end in a position that is `won` by the opponent, then x itself is `lost`. In the dual AF, this means that to show that x is `out`, one must find an attacker y that is `in`. If, however, all attackers y of x are `out`, then x itself is `in`. The first duality between G and F, illustrated by Fig. 1, is captured by the following theorem.

Theorem 5 (Duality $\mathcal{L}ab \cong \mathsf{val}$). Let $F = (A, R)$ be an AF, $\mathcal{L}ab$ its grounded labeling, and $G_{\mathcal{R}} = (A, R^{-1})$ the solved dual game. For all $x \in A$:

$$\mathcal{L}ab(x) = \mathtt{in/out/undec} \text{ iff } \mathsf{val}_G(x) = \mathtt{lost/won/drawn}, \text{ respectively.}$$

Proof. It is well-known [13] that the following rules, under the well-founded semantics (WFS) [15], compute the grounded solutions of AFs.

$$\begin{aligned} \mathtt{out}(x) &\leftarrow \mathtt{attacks}(y, x),\ \mathtt{in}(y). \\ \mathtt{in}(x) &\leftarrow \neg\,\mathtt{out}(x). \end{aligned} \qquad (P_{AF})$$

The following are equivalent under the reversed "*attacked-by*" direction of edges and thus also compute the grounded solutions.

$$\begin{aligned} \mathtt{out}(x) &\leftarrow \mathtt{attackedBy}(x, y),\ \mathtt{in}(y). \\ \mathtt{in}(x) &\leftarrow \neg\,\mathtt{out}(x). \end{aligned} \qquad (P_{AF}^{-1})$$

It is also well-known that the WFS of the following program solves games [15].

$$\begin{aligned} \mathtt{won}(x) &\leftarrow \mathtt{move}(x, y),\ \mathtt{lost}(y). \\ \mathtt{lost}(x) &\leftarrow \neg\,\mathtt{won}(x). \end{aligned} \qquad (P_G)$$

Since P_{AF}^{-1} and P_G are the same program (up to renaming), they have the same well-founded models (up to renaming/interpretation). Note that if x is $\mathtt{out}$ in the grounded labeling, a skeptic making the claim that x is defeated has a winning strategy, hence we call this the *Skeptics Argumentation Game* (SAG) [4].

Example 4 (*Continued*). Consider again the solved game in Fig. 1b and the grounded AF labeling in Fig. 1d. As in Theorem 5, each $\mathtt{won}$ (green) position in the game is $\mathtt{out}$ (orange) in the AF, each $\mathtt{lost}$ position is $\mathtt{in}$ (blue), and each $\mathtt{drawn}$ position (yellow) is $\mathtt{undec}$ (also yellow).

4.2 Remoteness *vs.* Min-Max Numbers

An argumentation framework F and its dual G each have an associated numbering, i.e., *min-max numbers* $\mathcal{MM}_{\mathcal{L}ab}$ for the grounded labeling of F and remoteness $\mathcal{R}$ for G, respectively. Figure 1 shows that these two numberings differ by 1. Another difference is that $\mathcal{R}$-values are derived directly from G, while min-max numbers are defined for (strongly) admissible labelings.

Theorem 6 (Duality $\mathcal{MM} \cong \mathcal{R} + 1$, Grounded $\mathcal{L}ab$). Let $F = (A, R)$ be an AF, $\mathcal{L}ab$ be the grounded labeling of F, $\mathcal{MM}_{\mathcal{L}ab}$ its min-max numbering, and $G_{\mathcal{R}} = (A, R^{-1})$ be the solved dual of F. For each $x \in A$:

- If $\mathcal{L}ab(x) \in \{\mathtt{in}, \mathtt{out}\}$ then $\mathcal{MM}_{\mathcal{L}ab}(x) = \mathcal{R}(x) + 1$;
- If $\mathcal{L}ab(x) = \mathtt{undec}$ then $\mathcal{MM}_{\mathcal{L}ab}(x) = \bot$ (undefined) and $\mathcal{R}(x) = \infty$.

Proof. By induction using Definitions 5 and 7.

Base Case: If x is unattacked, $\mathcal{L}ab(x)$ = in, $\mathcal{MM}_{\mathcal{L}ab}(x) = 1 + \max(\emptyset) = 1$, and $\mathcal{R}(x) = 0$ (since x is terminal in G), thus $\mathcal{MM}_{\mathcal{L}ab}(x) = \mathcal{R}(x) + 1$.

Rejected Case: Suppose $\mathcal{L}ab(x)$ is out and x has in-labeled attackers $y_1, \ldots, y_n$, then $\mathcal{MM}_{\mathcal{L}ab}(x) = \min(\{\mathcal{MM}_{\mathcal{L}ab}(y_1), \ldots, \mathcal{MM}_{\mathcal{L}ab}(y_n)\}) + 1$. Assume $\mathcal{MM}_{\mathcal{L}ab}(y_i) = \mathcal{R}(y_i) + 1$ for $1 \le i \le n$. Because $\mathcal{L}ab(y_i)$ is in, $\mathsf{val}(y_i)$ is lost and $\mathcal{R}(y_i)$ is even, thus $\mathcal{R}(x) = 1 + \min(\{\mathcal{R}(y_1), \ldots, \mathcal{R}(y_n)\})$. If $\mathcal{MM}_{\mathcal{L}ab}(y_k)$ has the smallest number of $y_1, \ldots, y_n$, then $\mathcal{MM}_{\mathcal{L}ab}(x) = \mathcal{MM}_{\mathcal{L}ab}(y_k) + 1$, $\mathcal{R}(x) = \mathcal{R}(y_k) + 1$, and since $\mathcal{MM}_{\mathcal{L}ab}(y_k) = \mathcal{R}(y_k) + 1$, $\mathcal{MM}_{\mathcal{L}ab}(x) = \mathcal{R}(x) + 1$.

Accepted Case: Suppose $\mathcal{L}ab(x)$ is in with attackers $y_1, \ldots, y_n$, which must be out, and $\mathcal{MM}_{\mathcal{L}ab}(x) = \max(\mathcal{MM}_{\mathcal{L}ab}(y_1), \ldots, \mathcal{MM}_{\mathcal{L}ab}(y_n)\} + 1$. Assume $\mathcal{MM}_{\mathcal{L}ab}(y_i) = \mathcal{R}(y_i) + 1$ for $1 \le i \le n$. Because $\mathcal{L}ab(y_i)$ is out, $\mathsf{val}(y_i)$ is won and $\mathcal{R}(y_i)$ is odd, thus $\mathcal{R}(x) = 1 + \max(\{R(y_1), \ldots, \mathcal{R}(y_n)\})$. If $\mathcal{MM}_{\mathcal{L}ab}(y_k)$ has the largest min-max number of $y_1, \ldots, y_n$, then $\mathcal{MM}_{\mathcal{L}ab}(x) = \mathcal{MM}_{\mathcal{L}ab}(y_k) + 1$, $\mathcal{R}(x) = \mathcal{R}(y_k) + 1$, and since $\mathcal{MM}_{\mathcal{L}ab}(y_k) = \mathcal{R}(y_k) + 1$, $\mathcal{MM}_{\mathcal{L}ab}(x) = \mathcal{R}(x) + 1$.

Undecided Case: If $\mathcal{L}ab(x)$ is undec, then by definition $\mathcal{MM}_{\mathcal{L}ab}(x) = \bot$, and since $\mathsf{val}(x)$ is drawn, $\mathcal{R}(x) = \infty$.

Example 4 (*Continued*). As shown in the solved game in Fig. 1b and the grounded solution of the dual AF in Fig. 1d, remoteness and min-max numbers differ by 1 when the values are natural numbers. This "off-by-1" nature of remoteness and min-max numbers follows from Theorem 6.

The $\mathcal{MM} \cong \mathcal{R} + 1$ correspondence also extends to admissible labelings. Let $G|_W = (W, E \cap (W \times W))$ denote the restriction of G to a set of nodes $W \subseteq V$.

Theorem 7 (Duality $\mathcal{MM} \cong \mathcal{R}$, Admissible $\mathcal{L}ab$). For $F = (A, R)$, its admissible labeling $\mathcal{L}ab$ with $W = \mathtt{in}(\mathcal{L}ab) \cup \mathtt{out}(\mathcal{L}ab)$, $\mathcal{MM}_{\mathcal{L}ab}$ the min-max numbering, $G = (A, R^{-1})$, and $\mathcal{R}_{G|_W}$ the remoteness function on $G|_W$. Then for all $x \in A$:

- If $\mathcal{MM}_{\mathcal{L}ab}(x) \neq \bot$ then $\mathcal{MM}_{\mathcal{L}ab}(x) = \mathcal{R}_{G|_W}(x) + 1$.

Proof. $\mathcal{MM}_{\mathcal{L}ab}$ is a unique numbering of F that only examines arguments labeled in or out by $\mathcal{L}ab$: for any x whose $\mathcal{L}ab(x)$ is undec, $\mathcal{MM}_{\mathcal{L}ab}(x) = \bot$. It follows that $\mathcal{MM}_{\mathcal{L}ab}$ returns the same numbers for $F|_W$ as for F. From Theorem 6, when x is in or out in the grounded labeling of $F|_W$, $\mathcal{MM}_{\mathcal{L}ab}(x) = \mathcal{R}_{G|_W}(x) + 1$. For those arguments x that are labeled undec in the grounded labeling of $F|_W$, $R_{G|_W}(x) = \infty$. Thus, it is enough to show that these same arguments have $\mathcal{MM}_{\mathcal{L}ab}(x) = \infty$. Note that such an x must have at least one move to a drawn position (undec attacker) and no moves to lost positions (in arguments) in $G|_W$ ($F|_W$, resp.). There are two cases to consider for such an argument x, which we show by contradiction: (1) If $\mathcal{L}ab(x)$ is out and $\mathcal{MM}_{\mathcal{L}ab}(x) \neq \infty$, x must have an in-labeled attacker y such that $\mathcal{MM}_{\mathcal{L}ab}(y) \neq \infty$. However, such a y implies $\mathcal{R}_{G|_W}(y) \neq \infty$ which means y cannot be `drawn`. (2) If $\mathcal{L}ab(x)$ is `in` and $\mathcal{MM}_{\mathcal{L}ab}(x) \neq \infty$, then all attackers y must have $\mathcal{MM}_{\mathcal{L}ab}(y) \neq \infty$. This means each such y cannot be `drawn` since $R_{G|_W}(y) \neq \infty$, and so $R_{G|_W}(x) \neq \infty$ implying x cannot be `drawn`.

The extension to admissible labelings is a direct consequence of the fact that, like the remoteness function, $\mathcal{MM}_{\mathcal{L}ab}$ computes the grounded solution of an AF restricted to the `in`/`out`-labeled arguments of $\mathcal{L}ab$.

Corollary 8 (Parity of $\mathcal{MM}$). Let $F = (A, R)$ be an AF, $\mathcal{L}ab_1$ an admissible labeling of F with $W = \mathtt{in}(\mathcal{L}ab_1) \cup \mathtt{out}(\mathcal{L}ab_1)$, $\mathcal{MM}_{\mathcal{L}ab_1}$ its min-max numbering, and $\mathcal{L}ab_2$ the grounded labeling of $F|_W$. For each $x \in A$:

- $\mathcal{MM}_{\mathcal{L}ab_1}(x)$ is *odd*/*even*/∞ iff $\mathcal{L}ab_2(x) =$ `in`/`out`/`undec`, respectively.

Given the connection between min-max numberings and remoteness, min-max numbers can be viewed as lengths given by optimal play. The following is immediate from Theorem 7.

Corollary 9 ($\mathcal{MM}$ *vs.* Optimal Play). Let $F = (A, R)$ be an AF, $\mathcal{L}ab$ be an admissible labeling of F with $W = \mathcal{L}ab(\mathtt{in}) \cup \mathcal{L}ab(\mathtt{out})$, and $\mathcal{MM}_{\mathcal{L}ab}$ its min-max numbering. If $\mathcal{MM}_{\mathcal{L}ab}(x) = n$, then the length of optimal play from x in the dual game $G|_W$ is $n - 1$, for all $x \in A$.

As a consequence of Theorems 2–6, the grounded labeling $\mathcal{L}ab$ and its min-max numbering $\mathcal{MM}_{\mathcal{L}ab}$ can be computed in linear time:

Corollary 10 (Computing Grounded $\mathcal{L}ab$). Let $F = (A, R)$ be an AF. The grounded labeling $\mathcal{L}ab$ of F can be computed in $\mathcal{O}(|A| + |R|)$.

Corollary 11 (Computing $\mathcal{MM}_{\mathcal{L}ab}$). Let $F = (A, R)$ be an AF and $\mathcal{L}ab$ its grounded labeling. $\mathcal{MM}_{\mathcal{L}ab}$ can be computed in $\mathcal{O}(|A| + |R|)$.

4.3 Strong Admissibility and Games

Close connections exist between strongly admissible labelings (as a form of explanation) and game provenance for explaining position values. As an example, min-max numberings can be used to check if a labeling is strongly admissible (Definition 6), and in a similar way, remoteness can be used to check if a subgraph of G corresponds to an admissible labeling.

Definition 15 (Admissible Subgraph). Let G be a game graph and val_G be a (potentially partial) `won`-`lost` labeling that satisfies the rules $R_\forall$ and $R_\exists$ (Sect. 3.1). G' is an *admissible subgraph* of G if it is an induced subgraph containing exactly the positions labeled as `won` or `lost` in val_G.

The following is immediate from Definition 6 and the duality of $\mathcal{MM}$ and $\mathcal{R}$.

Corollary 12 (Strongly Admissible Subgraphs). Let G' be an admissible subgraph of G. Then G' is a *strongly admissible subgraph* of G if its remoteness only yields natural numbers for all positions in G'.

Additionally, pure provenance of a `won` or `lost` position in a game represents a strongly admissible labeling of the dual AF. This follows because only position values with natural numbers are used to construct pure provenance.

Corollary 13 (Pure Provenance *vs.* Strong Admissibility). The pure provenance $\mathcal{P}_{\mathsf{pu}}(x)$ of a position in G is a strongly admissible subgraph of G.

4.4 Applying Game Provenance to Argumentation Frameworks

Game provenance can be directly applied to AFs based on the Game–AF duality.

Definition 16 (AF Potential Provenance). The *potential provenance* $\mathcal{P}_{\mathsf{pt}}(x)$ of argument x is the subgraph of arguments and attacks that reach x in F.

In games, the provenance of a node x is determined by what can be reached (via moves) from x, while in AFs (with edges reversed), x's provenance depends on the arguments that can reach it (i.e., attack x directly or indirectly). As in games, the potential provenance $\mathcal{P}_{\mathsf{pt}}(x)$ is an overestimate of the actual provenance (it includes attacks that correspond to blunders in SAG). The following defines the edge types of AFs for actual provenance.

Definition 17 (AF Edge Types). Let $F = (A, R)$ and $\mathcal{L}ab$ be its grounded labeling. The *edge types* $\tau : A \times A \rightarrow \{\texttt{out}, \texttt{in}, \texttt{undec}, \texttt{blunder}\}$ are defined by:

$$\tau(x, y) := \begin{cases} \texttt{out} & \text{if } \mathcal{L}ab(x) = \texttt{out} \text{ and } \mathcal{L}ab(y) = \texttt{in} \\ \texttt{in} & \text{if } \mathcal{L}ab(x) = \texttt{in} \text{ and } \mathcal{L}ab(y) = \texttt{out} \\ \texttt{undec} & \text{if } \mathcal{L}ab(x) = \texttt{undec} \text{ and } \mathcal{L}ab(y) = \texttt{undec} \\ \texttt{blunder} & \text{otherwise.} \end{cases}$$

Actual provenance for AFs is then defined as:

Definition 18 (AF Actual Provenance). $\mathcal{P}_{\mathsf{ac}}(x)$, the *actual provenance* of x, is the subgraph of F that reaches x by following `in`, `out`, and `undec` edges.

As in games, the actual provenance of an AF discards blunder attacks, but may include suboptimal attacks according to $\mathcal{MM}_{\mathcal{L}ab}$. The primary provenance of an AF removes suboptimal attacks:

Definition 19 (AF Primary Provenance). $\mathcal{P}_{\mathsf{pr}}(x)$ is the subset of $\mathcal{P}_{\mathsf{ac}}(x)$ that excludes `in` attacks $(x, y) \in R$ where $\mathcal{MM}_{\mathcal{L}ab}(x) \neq \mathcal{MM}_{\mathcal{L}ab}(y) - 1$.

Figure 3b highlights the suboptimal attack C→B within the actual provenance of A. Like games, the smaller explanations provided by primary provenance may not include all well-founded explanations of an argument, unlike in pure provenance:

Definition 20 (AF Pure Provenance). $\mathcal{P}_{\mathsf{pu}}(x)$ is the subset of $\mathcal{P}_{\mathsf{ac}}(x)$ that excludes arguments y that cannot reach x via a pure (winning) strategy in SAG.

Figure 4b gives the pure provenance of E, which discards the unfounded attack from F. Finally, from Corollary 13, the pure provenance $\mathcal{P}_{\mathsf{pu}}(x)$ of argument x is a strongly admissible set of F, which also provides the well-founded justification for the grounded label of x.

5 Conclusion

We established formal connections between min-max numberings in abstract argumentation and optimal play in combinatorial games. By linking min-max numbers to SMITH's remoteness function, provenance-based explanations can be directly applied to AFs. We also showed that pure strategy-based explanations provide a new class of provenance that bridges optimal and minimal approaches. Finally, we obtained new insights into min-max numberings via remoteness, including that parity determines argument labeling status and enables efficient computation of grounded labelings for admissible AF subgraphs.

Connections between game theory and argumentation have been studied extensively. Dung's seminal paper on argumentation frameworks [13] drew on n-player cooperative games from [17], while [16] uses similar game-theoretic concepts for defining argument strength. Two-player combinatorial games can be viewed as instances of n-person games in [18] where notions of independence and dominance apply. However, existing two-player dialog games for argumentation [7,10] operate on already-labeled AFs under specific semantics like strongly admissible and stable extensions, rather than establishing a direct correspondence between unlabeled frameworks and games that we develop here.

In future work, we aim to further explore the connections between games and argumentation. Since checking whether a strongly admissible labeling is minimal is co-NP-complete [8] for a given `in`-labeled argument, we conjecture that constructing minimal provenance explanations in games faces similar computational challenges. This contrasts with our remoteness-based provenance explanations, which can be computed efficiently. Building on approximation techniques [9,11], we will investigate tractable methods for computing approximately minimal explanations while preserving the theoretical guarantees of our duality framework.

References

1. Baroni, P., Giacomin, M.: On principle-based evaluation of extension-based argumentation semantics. Artif. Intell. **171**(10–15), 675–700 (2007). https://doi.org/10.1016/j.artint.2007.04.004
2. Baumann, R., Linsbichler, T., Woltran, S.: Verifiability of argumentation semantics. In: COMMA, pp. 83–94 (2016). https://ebooks.iospress.nl/volumearticle/45249

3. Boros, E., Gurvich, V., Makino, K., Vyalyi, M.: Computing remoteness functions of Moore, Wythoff, and Euclid's games. Int. J. Game Theory **53**(4), 1315–1333 (2024). https://link.springer.com/article/10.1007/s00182-024-00914-2
4. Bowers, S., Xia, Y., Ludäscher, B.: The skeptic's argumentation game or: well-founded explanations for mere mortals. In: SAFA 2024 (2024). https://ceur-ws.org/Vol-3757/paper8.pdf
5. Bowers, S., Xia, Y., Ludäscher, B.: On the structure of game provenance and its applications. In: Theory and Practice of Provenance (TaPP) at EuroS&PW (2024). https://doi.org/10.48550/arXiv.2410.05094
6. Caminada, M.: Argumentation semantics as formal discussion. In: Handbook of Formal Argumentation, vol. 1, pp. 487–518. College Publications (2018). https://orca.cardiff.ac.uk/id/eprint/99969/
7. Caminada, M., Dunne, P.: Strong admissibility revisited: theory and applications. Argum. Comput. **10**, 277–300 (2019). https://doi.org/10.3233/AAC-190463
8. Caminada, M., Dunne, P.: Minimal strong admissibility: a complexity analysis. In: COMMA, pp. 135–146 (2020). https://ebooks.iospress.nl/volumearticle/55365
9. Caminada, M., Harikrishnan, S.: An evaluation of algorithms for strong admissibility. In: SAFA, pp. 69–82 (2024). https://ceur-ws.org/Vol-3757/paper5.pdf
10. Caminada, M., Wu, Y.: An argument game for stable semantics. Logic J. IGPL **17**(1), 77–90 (2009). https://doi.org/10.1093/jigpal/jzn029
11. Caminada, M., Harikrishnan, S.: Tractable algorithms for strong admissibility. Argum. Comput. **16**(2), 212–236 (2025). https://doi.org/10.3233/AAC-230012
12. Caminada, M., Pigozzi, G.: On judgment aggregation in abstract argumentation. Auton. Agents Multi-Agent Syst. **22**(1), 64–102 (2011). https://link.springer.com/article/10.1007/s10458-009-9116-7
13. Dung, P.: On the acceptability of arguments and its fundamental role in nonmonotonic reasoning, logic programming and n-person games. Artif. Intell. **77**, 321–357 (1995). https://doi.org/10.1016/0004-3702(94)00041-X
14. Fraenkel, A.S.: Combinatorial game theory foundations applied to digraph kernels. Electron. J. Comb. **4**(2) (1997). https://doi.org/10.37236/1325
15. Gelder, A.V., Ross, K.A., Schlipf, J.S.: The well-founded semantics for general logic programs. J. ACM **38**(3), 620–650 (1991). https://doi.org/10.1145/116825.116838
16. Matt, P.-A., Toni, F.: A game-theoretic measure of argument strength for abstract argumentation. In: Hölldobler, S., Lutz, C., Wansing, H. (eds.) JELIA 2008. LNCS (LNAI), vol. 5293, pp. 285–297. Springer, Heidelberg (2008). https://doi.org/10.1007/978-3-540-87803-2_24
17. von Neumann, J., Morgenstern, O.: Theory of Games and Economic Behavior. Princeton University Press (1944)
18. Roth, A.E.: Subsolutions and the supercore of cooperative games. Math. Oper. Res. **1**(1), 43–49 (1976). https://doi.org/10.1287/moor.1.1.43
19. Roth, A.E.: Two-person games on graphs. J. Comb. Theory Ser. B **24**(2), 238–241 (1978). https://www.sciencedirect.com/science/article/pii/0095895678900266
20. Siegel, A.: Combinatorial Game Theory. Graduate Studies in Mathematics, vol. 146. American Mathematical Society (2013). https://doi.org/10.1090/gsm/146
21. Smith, C.A.: Graphs and composite games. J. Comb. Theory **1**(1), 51–81 (1966). https://doi.org/10.1016/S0021-9800(66)80005-4

First Steps Towards Forgetting in ASPIC$^+$

Hiba Abderrazik and Dragan Doder(✉)

Utrecht University, Utrecht, The Netherlands
d.doder@uu.nl

Abstract. Forgetting is a method used in several formalisms of knowledge representation and reasoning, which removes some elements from a framework while preserving the rest of the framework as much as possible. This paper investigates the process of forgetting in ASPIC$^+$, a structured argumentation framework. We explore possible effects of forgetting operators on several levels, namely: effects on (1) the underlying language, (2) arguments and their conclusions, and (3) the justification statuses of arguments' conclusions. We define the desired behaviour for forgetting formulas in a variant of ASPIC$^+$, drawing from both practical considerations and existing research on forgetting in other frameworks. Furthermore, for a specific modification of the standard ASPIC$^+$ framework, we managed to define two concrete forgetting operators, and evaluate them against the set of desiderata.

1 Introduction

Argumentation is the process of constructing and evaluating arguments and counterarguments to support or challenge claims. It was used to solve problems in various areas of AI, including reasoning with defeasible information [10], reasoning with inconsistency [18] decision making [1] and classification [2], and it is widely applied in areas such as sociology [16], health care [3,12], law [3,15] and police [17]. Argumentation distinguishes between abstract argumentation frameworks [8], which represent arguments and attack relations at a high level, and structured argumentation frameworks [6], which build arguments from explicit premises and rules. While structured frameworks such as assumption-based argumentation (ABA) [7] and ASPIC$^+$ [14] provide detailed constructions, their corresponding abstract frameworks can be obtained by focusing solely on the arguments and their attacks, disregarding their internal structure.

One particular recent line of research in computational argumentation is on forgetting. The concept of forgetting originated in classical logic [13] and later found significant applications in various fields of knowledge representation, and particularly in answer set programming [11]. Some approaches to forgetting in knowledge representation focus simply on elimination of some element (typically a formula) from a given framework, in a similar spirit as contraction operation in belief revision, while other focus on preservation of information after forgetting. The latter is typically used when we want to simplify a framework by eliminating

K. Sauerwald and M. Thimm (Eds.): ECSQARU 2025, LNAI 16099, pp. 411–423, 2026.
https://doi.org/10.1007/978-3-032-05134-9_28

auxiliary concepts, and possibly includes modification of the rest of the formalism in order to allow preservation of information [9]. Recently, the notion of forgetting has gained attention in abstract argumentation [4] and ABA [5]. To the best of our knowledge, there are no proposals on forgetting in another dominant structured framework, ASPIC$^+$.

In this paper, we conduct a preliminary research on forgetting formulas in a simple variant of ASPIC$^+$, with the aim to address above mentioned gap in the literature. The added complexity of ASPIC$^+$, which captures a wider range of attack relations than ABA, presents distinct challenges that have not yet been addressed. We first determine a set of desiderata suitable for evaluating forgetting operators in ASPIC$^+$. We start with two basic requirements, stating which parts of the framework must not appear after removal, and which parts must stay unaffected. We show compatibility of those two desiderata by providing a simple example of forgetting operator.

Then we focus on desiderata that formalize preservation properties after forgetting, namely steadiness of arguments' conclusions and their justification statuses. In an ASPIC$^+$ framework, that kind of steadiness cannot be expected after forgetting of any formula of the language. For example, if the formula can be used as a conclusion of one argument attacking another argument with the opposite conclusion, that attack cannot be preserved after removal of the formula from the language. Additional problems are related to the fact that forgetting a formula involved in a defeasible rule d might require replacement of that rule with another one, to allow "bridging" inferences toward conclusions that were originally obtained using d. This might in turn influence attacks targeting d, requiring further modification of the language that would target replacement rules. Finally, in the process of modifying or merging rules containing the formula to be forgotten, two different inferences can collapse to one same inference. To address this issue, we identify a reasonable minimality restriction on a set of inference rules in which such collapsing cannot occur. In addition, we conceptually modify the way defeasible rules are attacked in the framework after forgetting, addressing the above-mentioned need to redirect the attacks after a rule is replaced.

Finally, for frameworks which respect those restrictions, we define an operator that also satisfies proposed desiderata that formalize preservation properties, when applied to an irrelevant formula. For that, we formally define "irrelevance" of a formula in an argumentation theory.

2 Background

A Dung-style abstract argumentation framework (AF) is a directed graph $\langle \mathcal{A}, \mathcal{D} \rangle$, where $\mathcal{A}$ is a set of arguments and $\mathcal{D} \subseteq \mathcal{A} \times \mathcal{A}$ is a binary relation on $\mathcal{A}$, representing the attacks between arguments [8].

Extensions of an argumentation framework represent a set of arguments that can be accepted together. These extensions can be determined under different types of *semantics*. A set of arguments $S \subseteq \mathcal{A}$ attacks an argument A iff there is some argument $B \in S$ such that $(B, A) \in \mathcal{D}$. An argument $A \in \mathcal{A}$ is defended by a set $S \subseteq \mathcal{A}$ if, for every $B \in \mathcal{A}$, whenever B attacks A, S attacks B. Given an argumentation framework (AF), a set $E \subseteq \mathcal{A}$ is *conflict-free (cf)* iff there are no $A, B \in S$ such that $(A, B) \in \mathcal{D}$; A set E is *admissible (ad)* if it is conflict-free and defends all its members. E is a *complete extension (co)* if it is admissible and $A \in E$ iff A is defended by E; a *preferred extension (pr)* is a $\subseteq$-maximal complete extension; a *stable extension (stb)* is an admissible set that attacks every argument outside the set; and the *grounded extension (gr)* is a $\subseteq$-minimal complete extension. $\sigma(AF)$ denotes the set of all extensions of AF under a semantics $\sigma \in \{cf, ad, co, pr, gr, stb\}$.

ASPIC$^+$. Structured argumentation in ASPIC$^+$ relies on the following information [14]: a *logical language* $\mathcal{L}$ and a set of inference rules, which is split up in a *strict* ($\mathcal{R}_s$) and *defeasible* $\mathcal{R}_d$ inference rules. For the sake of simplicity, we assume in this paper that $\mathcal{L}$ is closed under ordinary negation $\neg$. For the same reason we use ASPIC$^+$ without a preference ordering on the arguments. Furthermore, we need a partial function n that specifies which well-formed formulas in $\mathcal{L}$ correspond to which defeasible rule in $\mathcal{R}_d$. $n(r)$, where $r \in \mathcal{R}_d$, essentially means that r is applicable. An argument then claiming $\neg n(r)$, indicating that a rule r is not applicable, attacks the inference step in r.

Definition 1 (Argumentation system). *An argumentation system (AS), is formally denoted by a triple $AS = (\mathcal{L}, \mathcal{R}, n)$, where*

- *$\mathcal{L}$ is a logical language closed under negation $\neg$;*
- *$\mathcal{R} = \mathcal{R}_s \cup \mathcal{R}_d$ is a finite set of strict ($\mathcal{R}_s$) and defeasible ($\mathcal{R}_d$) inference rules of the form $\varphi_1, \ldots, \varphi_n \rightarrow \varphi$ and $\varphi_1, \ldots, \varphi_n \Rightarrow \varphi$ respectively (where φ_i and φ are meta-variables ranging over formulas in $\mathcal{L}$) and $\mathcal{R}_s \cap \mathcal{R}_d = \emptyset$;*
- *n is a partial function such that $n : \mathcal{R}_d \longrightarrow \mathcal{L}$.*

The following definition uses the notion of a *knowledge base* in an $AS = (\mathcal{L}, \mathcal{R}, n)$, which is a set $\mathcal{K} \subseteq \mathcal{L}$ consisting of two disjoint subsets $\mathcal{K}_n$ (the *axioms* or necessary premises) and $\mathcal{K}_p$ (the ordinary premises).

Definition 2 (Argumentation theories). *An argumentation theory is a tuple $AT = (AS, \mathcal{K})$ where AS is an argumentation system and $\mathcal{K}$ is a knowledge base.*

An argument chains applications of rules from AS into directed, acyclic inference graphs, starting with elements from $\mathcal{K}$. The function `Prem` returns all formulas from $\mathcal{K}$ used to build the argument, referred to as *premises*, `Conc` returns its conclusion, `Sub` returns all its sub-arguments, `DefRules` returns all its defeasible rules and `TopRule` returns the last inference rule used in an argument.

Definition 3 (ASPIC$^+$ Argument). *An argument A on the basis of an argumentation theory AT with a knowledge base $\mathcal{K}$ and an AS $(\mathcal{L}, \mathcal{R}, n)$ is any structure obtained by applying one or more steps finitely many times:*

1. *φ if $\varphi \in \mathcal{K}$ with:* `Prem`$(A) = \{\varphi\}$, `Conc`$(A) = \varphi$, `Sub`$(A) = \{\varphi\}$, `DefRules`$(A) = \emptyset$, `TopRule`$(A) =$ *undefined.*

2. $A_1, \ldots, A_n \rightarrow \psi$ *if* $A_1, \ldots, A_n$ *are arguments such that there exists a strict rule* $\texttt{Conc}(A_1), \ldots, \texttt{Conc}(A_n) \rightarrow \psi$ *in* $\mathcal{R}_s$ *with:*
   $\texttt{Prem}(A) = \texttt{Prem}(A_1) \cup \cdots \cup \texttt{Prem}(A_n)$;
   $\texttt{Conc}(A) = \psi$;
   $\texttt{Sub}(A) = \texttt{Sub}(A_1) \cup \cdots \cup \texttt{Sub}(A_n) \cup \{A\}$;
   $\texttt{DefRules}(A) = \texttt{DefRules}(A_1) \cup \cdots \cup \texttt{DefRules}(A_n)$;
   $\texttt{TopRule}(A) = \texttt{Conc}(A_1), \ldots, \texttt{Conc}(A_n) \rightarrow \psi$.
3. $A_1, \ldots, A_n \Rightarrow \psi$ *if* $A_1, \ldots A_n$ *are arguments such that there exists a defeasible rule and* $\texttt{Conc}(A_1), \ldots, \texttt{Conc}(A_n) \Rightarrow \psi$ *in* $\mathcal{R}_d$ *with:*
   $\texttt{Prem}(A) = \texttt{Prem}(A_1) \cup \cdots \cup \texttt{Prem}(A_n)$;
   $\texttt{Conc}(A) = \psi$;
   $\texttt{Sub}(A) = \texttt{Sub}(A_1) \cup \cdots \cup \texttt{Sub}(A_n) \cup \{A\}$;
   $\texttt{DefRules}(A) = \texttt{DefRules}(A_1) \cup \cdots \cup \texttt{DefRules}(A_n) \cup \{ \texttt{Conc}(A_1), \ldots \texttt{Conc}(A_n) \Rightarrow \psi\}$;
   $\texttt{TopRule}(A) = \texttt{Conc}(A_1), \ldots, \texttt{Conc}(A_n) \Rightarrow \psi$.

Definition 4 (ASPIC$^+$ Attack). *Consider arguments A and B the basis of an argumentation theory AT with a knowledge base $\mathcal{K}$ and an argumentation system $(\mathcal{L}, \mathcal{R}, n)$. A attacks B iff A undercuts, rebuts or undermines B, where*

- *A undercuts argument B (on B') iff* $\texttt{Conc}(A) = \neg n(r)$ *for some* $B' \in \texttt{Sub}(B)$ *such that B''s top rule r is defeasible;*
- *A rebuts argument B (on B') iff* $\texttt{Conc}(A) = \neg\varphi$ *for some* $B' \in \texttt{Sub}(B)$ *of the form* $B_1^{''}, \ldots, B_n^{''} \Rightarrow \varphi$;
- *A undermines B (on φ) iff* $\texttt{Conc}(A) = \neg\varphi$ *for an ordinary premise φ of B.*

Abstract argumentation frameworks can be generated from ATs as follows.

Definition 5 (Argumentation frameworks). *An abstract argumentation framework (AF) corresponding to an argumentation theory (AT) is a pair $\langle \mathcal{A}, \mathcal{D} \rangle$ where $\mathcal{A}$ is the set of all arguments based on a given argumentation theory and $(X, Y) \in \mathcal{D}$ if X attacks Y.*

This allows us to define justification statuses of formulas for given σ. We say that a formula is sceptically justified if it is a conclusion of an argument that is present in all σ-extensions, and it is credulously justified if it is not sceptically justified and is the conclusion of an argument present in at least one σ-extension.

We introduce some additional notation used throughout the paper. Given a rule $r : \varphi_1, \ldots, \varphi_n \rightsquigarrow \varphi$, where $\rightsquigarrow$ denotes $\rightarrow$ if $r_i, r_j \in \mathcal{R}_s$, and $\Rightarrow$ otherwise, we define the antecedents of r as $ant(r) = \{\varphi_1, \ldots, \varphi_n\}$ and the consequent as $con(r) = \varphi$. The language $\mathcal{L}$ is partitioned as $\mathcal{L} = \mathcal{L}_0 \cup \mathcal{L}_r$, where $\mathcal{L}_0 = \mathcal{L} \setminus \{n(r) \mid r \in \mathcal{R}\}$ and $\mathcal{L}_r = \mathcal{L} \setminus \mathcal{L}_0$. Additionally, we restrict the use of literals in $\mathcal{L}_r$ solely to negations in the consequents of rules, consistent with ASPIC$^+$'s underlying intuition that certain language elements are introduced to enable undercutting attacks. We make this intuition explicit in our version of ASPIC$^+$. In other words, there cannot exist any rule r in the rule base of an argumentation theory such that it takes a formula in $\mathcal{L}_r$ as an antecedent.

For arguments in ASPIC$^+$ (see Definition 3), the direct subarguments of A in cases (2) and (3) are $\{A_1, \ldots, A_n\}$, corresponding to a rule $\texttt{Conc}(A_1), \ldots, \texttt{Conc}(A_n) \leadsto \psi$ in $\mathcal{R}$. The function $\texttt{DirSub}(A)$ returns all direct subarguments of A.

Given an argumentation theory $AT = ((\mathcal{L}, \mathcal{R}, n), \mathcal{K})$, its corresponding $AF = \langle \mathcal{A}, \mathcal{D} \rangle$, and $A \in \mathcal{A}$, we define $\texttt{Rules}(A) = \{\texttt{TopRule}(B) \mid B \in \texttt{Sub}(A)\}$ as the set of all rules used in A. We also define $\mathcal{A}^0 = \{A \in \mathcal{A} \mid \texttt{Conc}(A) \in \mathcal{L}_0\}$, the set of arguments concluding in $\mathcal{L}_0$, and $\mathcal{A}^l = \{A \in \mathcal{A} \mid \texttt{Conc}(A) \neq l\}$, the set of arguments with conclusions other than l.

3 Formula Forgetting Desiderata

In this section we construct a set of desiderata to define the desirable properties of forgetting operators in ASPIC$^+$. A forgetting operator $\texttt{f}$ accepts an AT F and a formula $l \in \mathcal{L}$ as its input and returns an AT $\texttt{f}(F, l)$, which is the ASPIC$^+$ framework after forgetting l.

Suppose that we want to forget a formula from the language. Consequently, it cannot occur in any other part of the framework. This property is referred to as deletion in related literature [5].

Desideratum 1. *Given an* $AT = ((\mathcal{L}, \mathcal{R}, n), \mathcal{K})$, *and a formula* $l \in \mathcal{L}$, *a forgetting operator* $\texttt{f}$ *satisfies (**fD**) formula deletion iff* $l \notin \mathcal{L}'$, *where* $\texttt{f}(AT, l) = ((\mathcal{L}', \mathcal{R}', n'), \mathcal{K}')$.

It follows that arguments using that formula can also no longer be built using the forgotten formula. However, any argument unrelated to the forgotten formula should still exist in the modified framework. In order to formalize that, we first define the notion of rules *related* to a formula.

Definition 6. *Given an* AT $F = ((\mathcal{L}, \mathcal{R}, n), \mathcal{K})$, *a rule* $r \in \mathcal{R}$ *is related to a formula* $l \in \mathcal{L}$ *iff* $l \in \{con(r)\} \cup ant(r)$; *or* r *undercuts* r' *and* r' *is related to* l.

Now we can formally define a desideratum for argument persistence, similar to the one introduced by [5].

Desideratum 2. *Given an* $AT = ((\mathcal{L}, \mathcal{R}, n), \mathcal{K})$, $l \in \mathcal{L}$, *and a resulting* $AT' = \texttt{f}(AT, l)$. *Let* $F = \langle \mathcal{A}, \mathcal{D} \rangle$ *and* $F' = \langle \mathcal{A}', \mathcal{D}' \rangle$ *be the corresponding* AF*s of* AT *and* AT' *respectively. A forgetting operator* $\texttt{f}$ *satisfies (**AP**) argument persistence iff* $\mathcal{A}' \supseteq \{A \in \mathcal{A} \mid l \notin \texttt{Prem}(A), r \text{ not related to } l \text{ for any } r \in \texttt{Rules}(A)\}$.

There is a basic forgetting operator we can introduce that minimises syntactic change and satisfies both (**fD**) and (**AP**). $\texttt{f}^1(F, l)$ removes l from F without adding or removing any other formulas, rules or premises.

Definition 7 (Formula forgetting operator f^1). *For any* AT $F = ((\mathcal{L}, \mathcal{R}, n), \mathcal{K})$ *and* $l \in \mathcal{L}$, *let* $\texttt{f}^1(F, l) := ((\mathcal{L} \setminus \{l\}, \mathcal{R}', n'), \mathcal{K} \setminus \{l\})$, *where* $\mathcal{R}' = \{r \in \mathcal{R} \mid r \text{ is not related to } l\}$ *and* $n'(d_i) = n(d_i)$ *for all* $d_i \in \mathcal{R}'$.

It is evident that $\mathtt{f}^1$ satisfies formula deletion (**fD**), since it explicitly constructs $\mathcal{L}' = \mathcal{L} \setminus \{l\}$ (Definition 7). Furthermore, since the operator does not remove any premises or rules other than those related to l, all other premises and rules are preserved post-forgetting. Since arguments are made up of premises and rules, all arguments unrelated to l can still be constructed in the new framework. Hence, $\mathtt{f}^1$ satisfies argument persistence (**AP**).

Proposition 1. *Given an* $AT = ((\mathcal{L}, \mathcal{R}, n), \mathcal{K})$ *and a formula* $l \in \mathcal{L}$. *Then* $\mathtt{f}^1(AT, l)$ *satisfies both (**fD**) and (**AP**).*

When forgetting formulas, it is important not only to remove certain elements but also to preserve key aspects of the framework. In particular, if we forget a formula l that is not in the knowledge base ($l \in \mathcal{L} \setminus \mathcal{K}$), we should aim to retain inferences where l functions as an intermediary between premises and conclusions. This aligns with the original approaches to forgetting as proposed in ASP [11] and ABA [5]. To achieve this, the overall inferences made via l should remain valid after forgetting, so that any conclusions in $\mathcal{A}^0$ that previously relied on l as an intermediate step are preserved in the updated framework.

Desideratum 3. *Given an* $AT = ((\mathcal{L}, \mathcal{R}, n), \mathcal{K})$, *a formula* $l \in \mathcal{L}$, *and a resulting* $AT' \in \mathtt{f}(AT, l)$. *Let* $F = \langle \mathcal{A}, \mathcal{D} \rangle$ *and* $F' = \langle \mathcal{A}', \mathcal{D}' \rangle$ *be the corresponding AFs of AT and AT′ respectively. A forgetting operator* $\mathtt{f}$ *satisfies (**CS**) conclusion steadiness iff* $\{\mathtt{Conc}(A) \mid A \in \mathcal{A}^l \cap \mathcal{A}^0\} = \{\mathtt{Conc}(B) \mid B \in \mathcal{A}'^0\}$.

Lastly, the requirement is that the acceptance status (credulous or sceptical) of conclusions, as determined by unaffected arguments, remains unchanged after forgetting a formula l. Thus, if a conclusion was credulously or sceptically accepted under semantics σ before forgetting l, and is unaffected by its removal, it should retain that status afterwards.

Desideratum 4. *Given an* $AT = ((\mathcal{L}, \mathcal{R}, n), \mathcal{K})$, *a formula* $l \in \mathcal{L}$, *a resulting* $AT' \in \mathtt{f}(AT, l)$ *and a semantics* σ. *Let* $F = \langle \mathcal{A}, \mathcal{D} \rangle$ *and* $F' = \langle \mathcal{A}', \mathcal{D}' \rangle$ *be the corresponding AFs of AT and AT′ respectively. Then a forgetting operator* $\mathtt{f}$ *satisfies (**JP**) justification persistence iff* $\forall x \in \mathcal{L} \setminus \{l\}$, *the justification status of* x *is the same in* F *as in* F'.

Proposition 2. $\mathtt{f}^1$ *does not satisfy (**CS**) and (**JP**).*

4 Forgetting Irrelevant Formulas

There are two main approaches to minimal change: minimizing changes to the framework"s structure, or minimizing semantic loss by preserving as many inferences and arguments as possible. Previously, we introduced the basic operator $\mathtt{f}^1$ to address structural minimality. In this section, we present the operator $\mathtt{f}^2$, which focuses on preserving information, such as rules and conclusions, when removing l. We show that if l is not relevant with respect to the considered set of rules (formally defined in Definition 14), then $\mathtt{f}^2$ satisfies both (**CS**) and (**JP**).

Consider an AT with rules $r_1 : x \rightsquigarrow l$ and $r_2 : l \rightsquigarrow y$, and suppose we wish to delete l from the language. Removing l requires eliminating any rule that references it, but the transitive inference from x to y should be preserved by introducing a new rule. If either original rule is defeasible (e.g., $r_1 : x \Rightarrow l$), the new rule ($x \Rightarrow y$) should likewise be defeasible, maintaining the level of uncertainty in the inference. Note that we are only considering formulas that serve as intermediate steps in derivations, and are not premises themselves. For clarity, in this section we assume that our operator $\mathtt{f}^2$ is defined only for $l \in \mathcal{L} \setminus \mathcal{K}$.

Generally, we want to merge rules where any occurrence of l in the antecedent of a rule is replaced with the antecedent of another rule where l is a consequence. By doing this, we retain the information that we could infer using l as an intermediate step, even after l is removed from the framework. Consider a rule base $\mathcal{R} = \mathcal{R}_d \cup \mathcal{R}_s$ with $r_i, r_j \in \mathcal{R}$. If $l = con(r_i) \in ant(r_j)$, then we can construct the merged rule $r_{i,j}$ as follows:

$$r_{i,j} = (ant(r_i) \cup ant(r_j)) \setminus \{l\} \rightsquigarrow con(r_j),$$

where $\rightsquigarrow$ denotes $\rightarrow$ if $r_i, r_j \in \mathcal{R}_s$, and $\Rightarrow$ otherwise. This way of merging rules was initially introduced in ASP [19] and later adapted into the *replace* operator in ABA [5]. We can construct the rule base after forgetting l as follows.

Definition 8 (Rule base after forgetting l). *Let $AT = ((\mathcal{L}, \mathcal{R}, n), \mathcal{K})$ and $l \in \mathcal{L} \setminus \mathcal{K}$. The rule base after forgetting l, $\mathcal{R}'$, is defined as*
$\mathcal{R}' = \mathcal{R} \setminus \{r_k \in \mathcal{R} \mid l \in \{con(r_k)\} \cup ant(r_k)\} \cup \{(ant(r_i) \cup ant(r_j)) \setminus \{l\} \rightsquigarrow con(r_j) \mid r_i, r_j \in \mathcal{R}, l = con(r_i) \in ant(r_j)\}$

An additional challenge arises in ASPIC$^+$ regarding the concept of forgetting, particularly due to the presence and vulnerability of defeasible rules. Suppose $r_i \in \mathcal{R}_d$ is combined with r_j to create a new defeasible rule $r_{i,j}$. Now, consider a rule that attacks the applicability of r_i, for instance, $r_3 : z \rightarrow \neg n(r_4)$ (Fig. 1a). Once l is forgotten, r_i no longer exists in the rule base. However, since $r_{i,j}$ implicitly depends on r_i, we should transfer this attack to $r_{i,j}$ (Fig. 1b).

Observe that B' no longer undercuts A' and C', while B undercuts A and C. Since B undercuts A and C on r_4, and in the updated framework $r_{1,4}$ is formed by merging r_1 and r_4, the intuitive expectation is that the undercutting attack should shift from r_4 to $r_{1,4}$, and similarly to $r_{2,4}$. However, it appears that the same rule $r_3 : z \rightarrow \neg n(r_4)$ can no longer undercut both arguments simultaneously, as the arguments in the new framework employ distinct rules $r_{1,4}$ and $r_{2,4}$ to reach the same conclusion w. After forgetting l, the goal is to construct the following arguments to retain the same information as in the previous framework, thereby minimizing the impact of forgetting l. In order to preserve the attack structure of the framework we must modify r_3 to somehow translate its previous undercutting attack on r_4 to the new rules $r_{1,4}$ and $r_{2,4}$.

We address this issue with the following approach. By redefining the naming function n as $n : \mathcal{P}(\mathcal{R}) \rightarrow \mathcal{L}_r$, we can map a set of rules to a single literal in $\mathcal{L}_r$, enabling us to attack a group of rules with one rule. With this new definition, we can specify $n(\{r_{1,4}, r_{2,4}\}) = a$, $n(\{r_{1,4}\}) = b$ and $n(\{r_{2,4}\}) = c$. This allows

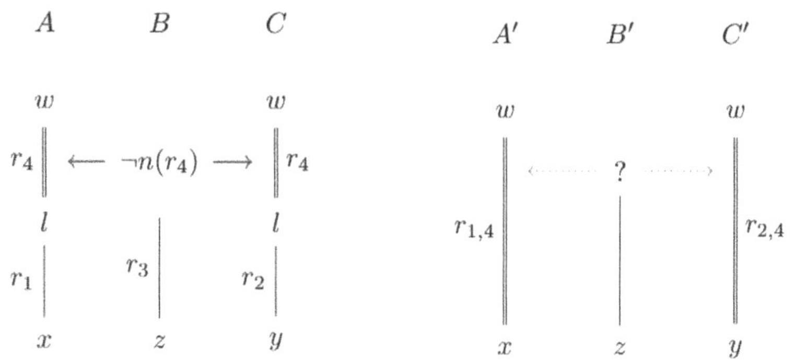

(a) *AT* before forgetting *l* (b) *AT* after forgetting *l*

Fig. 1. Merging rules to forget l

us to attack $r_{1,4}$ and $r_{2,4}$ together using a single rule $x \rightarrow \neg a$ if the attack was previously aimed at r_4, or attack them individually if r_1 or r_2 were targeted, with $y \rightarrow \neg b$ and $z \rightarrow \neg c$, respectively.

Definition 9 (Updated naming function). *Recall Definition 1 for an argumentation system* $AS = (\mathcal{L}, \mathcal{R}, n)$ *where* n *is a partial function such that* $n : \mathcal{R}_d \rightarrow \mathcal{L}$. *We now redefine* n *as a partial function* $n : \mathcal{P}(\mathcal{R}_d) \rightarrow \mathcal{L}_r$.

With this adjustment to our definition of n, we can now simply define the modified naming function after forgetting l.

Definition 10 (Naming function after forgetting l). *Let* $AT = ((\mathcal{L}, \mathcal{R}, n), \mathcal{K})$ *and* $l \in \mathcal{L} \backslash \mathcal{K}$. $\mathcal{R}'$ *is the rule base after forgetting* l *as constructed in Definition 8. The naming function after forgetting* l, n', *is defined as* $n'(R_i) = n(r_i)$, *where* $R_i = \{r_i \in \mathcal{R}'\} \cup \{r_{i,j} \in \mathcal{R}'\} \cup \{r_{j,i} \in \mathcal{R}'\}$.

Using Definitions 8 and 10 we can now define the following operator.

Definition 11 (Formula forgetting operator f^2). *Let* $AT = ((\mathcal{L}, \mathcal{R}_d \cup \mathcal{R}_s, n), \mathcal{K})$ *and* $l \in \mathcal{L} \setminus \mathcal{K}$. $f^2(AT, l) := ((\mathcal{L} \setminus \{l\}, \mathcal{R}', n'), \mathcal{K} \setminus \{l\})$ *with* $\mathcal{R}'$ *constructed as defined in Definition 8 and* n' *constructed as defined in Definition 10.*

In the original framework, the naming function n assigns only a single rule to each literal (i.e., each $n(r_i)$ is a singleton), never a set of rules. However, after forgetting, the updated naming function n' may assign a set of rules to a literal, e.g. $n'(\{r_i, r_{i,j}\})$. As a result, $\mathtt{f}^2$ cannot be applied again to its own output, since it requires each literal in $\mathcal{L}_r$ to be associated with a single rule. This limitation prevents repeated application of the operator.

Next, we evaluate $\mathtt{f}^2$ against our set of desiderata. By the same reasoning as $\mathtt{f}^1$, we can easily verify that $\mathtt{f}^2$ satisfies (**fD**) and (**AP**). In the remainder of this section we will show that $\mathtt{f}^2$ satisfies (**CS**) and, under specific conditions, (**JP**).

We demonstrate that $\mathtt{f}^2$ satisfies (**CS**) (and later (**JP**)) by construction. Let $AT = ((\mathcal{L}, \mathcal{R}, n), \mathcal{K})$ with corresponding AF $F = \langle \mathcal{A}, \mathcal{D} \rangle$ and $l \in \mathcal{L} \setminus \mathcal{K}$. We construct a mapping $\mathcal{M}$ recursively, ensuring that for each argument $A \in \mathcal{A}^l$, there exists an argument $\mathcal{M}(A) \in \mathcal{A}'^0$ where $\mathcal{A}'$ is the set of arguments in the corresponding AF for $\mathtt{f}^2(AT, l)$, such that (1) if $A \in \mathcal{A}^0$, then $\mathtt{Conc}(\mathcal{M}(A)) = \mathtt{Conc}(A)$; (2) if $A \notin \mathcal{A}^0$, then it holds that A undercuts some argument B iff $\mathcal{M}(A)$ undercuts $\mathcal{M}(B)$.

We consider the following cases for our mapping. Suppose argument A is a premise. In this case, we know $\mathtt{f}^2$ will not delete it since $l \notin \mathcal{K}$. Therefore, we can construct exactly the same argument $\mathcal{M}(A) = A$ in the new framework. Otherwise, suppose argument A is not a premise. Since the mapping is built recursively, we only need to focus on the top rule r and the conclusion $\mathtt{Conc}(A)$. From the definition of $\mathcal{A}^l$, it follows that $\mathtt{Conc}(A) \neq l$. There are two specific scenarios we need to address in order to construct an argument in $\mathcal{A}'^0$.

If l appears in the antecedents of r, then r will not exist in the updated framework $\mathtt{f}^2(AT, l)$. In this situation, we must identify another rule r' in the new framework to build $\mathcal{M}(A)$.

Otherwise, if the conclusion of A concerns the non-applicability of a rule r_i, i.e. $\mathtt{Conc}(A) \in \mathcal{A}^l \setminus \mathcal{A}^0$ and $\text{con}(r) = \neg n(r_i)$, we encounter a similar issue: if l appears in r_i, then r_i will no longer exist in the new framework. In this case, we must find a different top rule r' for the mapping of A that attacks a rule "equivalent" to r_i in the new framework.

From these scenarios, we can derive the following five cases.

Definition 12 (Mapping arguments after forgetting). *Let $AT = ((\mathcal{L}, \mathcal{R}, n), \mathcal{K})$ with $F = \langle \mathcal{A}, \mathcal{D} \rangle$, $l \in \mathcal{L} \setminus \mathcal{K}$ and $A \in \mathcal{A}^l$. The AT after forgetting l is defined by $\mathtt{f}^2(AT, l) = ((\mathcal{L}', \mathcal{R}', n'), \mathcal{K})$ with corresponding $F' = \langle \mathcal{A}', \mathcal{D}' \rangle$. We define a mapping $\mathcal{M} : \mathcal{A}^l \to \mathcal{A}'$ recursively, as follows:*

- $\mathcal{M}(A) = A$, *if* $\mathtt{Sub}(A) = \emptyset$
  Otherwise, if $\mathtt{TopRule}(A) = r_t$ *and* $\{A_1, \ldots, A_n\} = \mathtt{DirSub}(A)$, *then*
- $\mathcal{M}(A) = \mathcal{M}(A_1), \ldots, \mathcal{M}(A_n) \overset{r_t}{\rightsquigarrow} \mathtt{Conc}(A)$, *if* $l \notin ant(r_t)$ *and* $[\mathtt{Conc}(A) \neq \neg n(r_i)$or $l \notin \{con(r_i)\} \cup ant(r_i)]$
- $\mathcal{M}(A) = \mathcal{M}(A_1), \ldots, \mathcal{M}(A_n) \overset{r_t}{\rightsquigarrow} \neg n(R_i)$, *if* $l \notin ant(r_t)$ *and* $\mathtt{Conc}(A) = \neg n(r_i)$and $l \in \{con(r_i)\} \cup ant(r_i)$
- $\mathcal{M}(A) = \mathcal{M}(A_{11}), \ldots, \mathcal{M}(A_{1m}), \mathcal{M}(A_2), \ldots, \mathcal{M}(A_n) \overset{r_{s,t}}{\rightsquigarrow} \mathtt{Conc}(A)$, *if* $\mathtt{Conc}(A_1) = l$ and $[\mathtt{Conc}(A) \neq \neg n(r_i)$or $l \notin \{con(r_i)\} \cup ant(r_i)]$, *where* $\mathtt{TopRule}(A_1) = r_s$ *and* $\{A_{11}, \ldots, A_{1m}\} = \mathtt{DirSub}(A_1)$
- $\mathcal{M}(A) = \mathcal{M}(A_{11}), \ldots, \mathcal{M}(A_{1m}), \mathcal{M}(A_2), \ldots, \mathcal{M}(A_n) \overset{r_{s,t}}{\rightsquigarrow} \neg n(R_i)$, *if* $\mathtt{Conc}(A_1) = l$ and $\mathtt{Conc}(A) = \neg n(r_i)$and $l \in \{con(r_i)\} \cup ant(r_i)$, *where* $\mathtt{TopRule}(A_1) = r_s$ *and* $\{A_{11}, \ldots, A_{1m}\} = \mathtt{DirSub}(A_1)$

where $R_i = \{r_{x,y} \in \mathcal{R}' \mid i \in \{x, y\}\}$.

$\mathcal{M}$ preserves attack relations between arguments that do not conclude the forgotten literal l. Specifically, when mapping such arguments from the original framework to the modified one, $\mathcal{M}$ maintains each argument's conclusion, sub-argument structure, and rule composition. As a result, whenever an argument A undercuts, undermines or rebuts some B in the original system, its mapping $\mathcal{M}(A)$ will undercut, undermine or rebut $\mathcal{M}(B)$ in the new framework as well.

Theorem 1 (Attack preservation). *Consider an* $AT = ((\mathcal{L}, \mathcal{R}, n), \mathcal{K})$ *with* $F = \langle \mathcal{A}, \mathcal{D} \rangle$ *and* $A, B \in \mathcal{A}^l$. A ***attacks*** B *iff* $\mathcal{M}(A)$ ***attacks*** $\mathcal{M}(B)$.

In addition to the fact that $\mathcal{M}$ preserves the structure of the framework in terms of argument conclusions and attacks, it is crucial that the mapping neither discards nor introduces any new arguments. We want to ensure that each argument in $\mathcal{A}^l$ is mapped to exactly one argument in $\mathcal{A}'$ for $\mathtt{f}^2(AT, l)$, and that no other arguments exist in $\mathcal{A}'$ apart from those corresponding to an argument in $\mathcal{A}^l$. In other words, we must prove that $\mathcal{M}$ is bijective. This claim is paramount to demonstrating that both **(CS)** and **(JP)** are satisfied.

First, to prove the injectivity claim, we need to show that whenever $\mathcal{M}(A) = \mathcal{M}(B)$, then $A = B$. When we say two arguments are equal, we mean that they share the same direct sub arguments, the same top rule, and the same conclusion.

In order to ensure the desired properties when applying the mapping $\mathcal{M}$ in the context of forgetting within the ASPIC$^+$ framework, several restrictions are necessary. First, the restriction to ensure injectivity of $\mathcal{M}$ is that all rules must be minimal. We will first illustrate and then formally define the notion of minimality. The following examples show that redundant or non-minimal rules, as well as overlapping sets of premises, can lead to distinct arguments being mapped to the same argument after forgetting, breaking the injectivity of $\mathcal{M}$.

Example 1. Consider an AT containing the following rules: $r_1 : a, b \rightarrow l$, $r_2 : l \rightarrow c$, $r_3 : a \rightarrow l$, $r_4 : l, b \rightarrow c$ and the set of premises $\{a, b\}$. We can build two distinct arguments A and B using $\{r_1, r_2\}$ and $\{r_3, r_4\}$ respectively.

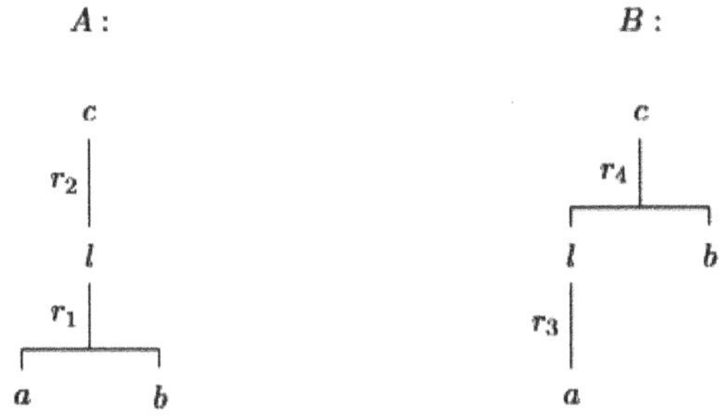

After forgetting l, A and B can be mapped to $\mathcal{M}(A) : a, b \overset{r_{1,2}}{\rightarrow} c$ and $\mathcal{M}(B) : a, b \overset{r_{3,4}}{\rightarrow} c$. This provides an example of two distinct arguments, A and B, in the original framework being mapped to the same argument in the modified framework, which directly challenges the injectivity claim we are trying to establish. Intuitively, it seems redundant to deduce l from both a and b, when a alone would suffice to deduce l.

Example 2. Consider an AT containing the following rules: $r_1 : a \rightarrow l$, $r_2 : b \rightarrow l$, $r_3 : l, a, b \rightarrow c$ and the set of premises $\{a, b\}$. We can build two distinct arguments A and B using $\{r_1, r_3\}$ and $\{r_2, r_3\}$ respectively.

Similar to Example 1, after forgetting l, A and B can be mapped to $\mathcal{M}(A)$: $a, b \overset{r_{1,3}}{\rightarrow} c$ and $\mathcal{M}(B) : a, b \overset{r_{2,3}}{\rightarrow} c$.

This is a different situation than Example 1, as there is no smaller set of premises from which to conclude l. However, it does not seem very "minimal", or intuitive, that r_3 requires a, b *and* l to conclude c, especially since l can already be derived from either a or b via r_1 and r_2 respectively. Thus, having l implicitly means that both a and b are available as well. More formally, we can express this as follows: Given two rules r and r', r is redundant if $con(r') \in ant(r)$ and $ant(r') \subseteq ant(r)$.

To address these counterexamples to the injectivity of $\mathcal{M}$ (Example 1, 2), we can introduce a minimality restriction on rules.

Definition 13 (Minimality of rules). *Given an* $AT = ((\mathcal{L}, \mathcal{R}, n), \mathcal{K})$, *let* $r \in \mathcal{R}$ *be a rule of the form* $\varphi_1, \ldots, \varphi_n \rightsquigarrow \varphi$, *with* $ant(r) = \{\varphi_1, \ldots, \varphi_n\}$ *and* $con(r) = \varphi$. *We say that r is minimal in AT iff there is no other rule* $r' \in \mathcal{R}$ *such that (1)* $con(r') = con(r)$ *and* $ant(r') \subset ant(r)$ *or (2)* $con(r') \in ant(r)$ *and* $ant(r') \subseteq ant(r)$.

We impose the requirement that all rules in our ASPIC$^+$ framework be minimal. Still, we can find a counterexample to the injectivity of $\mathcal{M}$. This time not because of the redundancy of individual rules, but because of how these rules can be combined in arguments.

Example 3. Consider an AT containing the following rules: $r_1 : a \rightarrow l$, $r_2 : l, b, c \rightarrow d$, $r_3 : c \rightarrow l$, $r_4 : a, b, l \rightarrow d$ and the set of premises $\{a, b, c\}$. We can build two distinct arguments A and B using $\{r_1, r_2\}$ and $\{r_3, r_4\}$ respectively.

Now consider the mapped arguments $\mathcal{M}(A) : a, b, c \overset{r_{1,2}}{\rightarrow} d$ and $\mathcal{M}(B)$: $a, b, c \overset{r_{3,4}}{\rightarrow} d$. It follows again that $\mathcal{M}(A) = \mathcal{M}(B)$ but $A \neq B$.

Here, an intuitive approach would be to assert that this construction renders l relevant with respect to $\mathcal{R}$. Specifically, given two subsets of $\mathcal{R}$, $P = \{r_1, r_2\}$ and $Q = \{r_3, r_4\}$, l serves as a distinguishing factor between these sets of rules. While the cumulative set of premises for both sets of rules is identical, as is the final conclusion, the different methods of deriving l create a distinction between these sets of rules, unlike their merged counterparts.

As a result, we introduce the restriction that only irrelevant literals may be forgotten. However, there is another situation in which a literal l can be considered relevant, namely when it is actively participating in an attack. Consider some arguments $A : x \rightarrow l \rightarrow y$ and $B : z \Rightarrow \neg l$ and let A' be the sub argument of A that attacks B. After applying $\mathcal{M}$ we would be left with the arguments $\mathcal{M}(A') : x \rightarrow y$ and $\mathcal{M}(B) : z \Rightarrow \neg l$. It is easy to see that although A' rebuts B, $\mathcal{M}(A')$ does not rebut $\mathcal{M}(B)$.

Definition 14 (Relevance of a formula). *Given an* $AT = ((\mathcal{L}, \mathcal{R}, n), \mathcal{K})$, *let* $l \in \mathcal{L} \setminus \mathcal{K}$ *be a literal. We say that* l *is relevant with respect to* $\mathcal{R}$ *if:*

1. *There exists a rule* $r \in \mathcal{R}$ *such that* $con(r) = \neg l$;
2. *There exist two pairs of rules* $r_1, r_2 \in \mathcal{R}$ *and* $r_3, r_4 \in \mathcal{R}$ *of the form:*

$$r_1 : \varphi_1, \ldots, \varphi_i, \ldots, \varphi_k \rightsquigarrow l \qquad r_3 : \varphi_1, \ldots, \varphi_i, \varphi_j, \ldots \varphi_n \rightsquigarrow l$$
$$r_2 : l, \varphi_{k+1}, \ldots, \varphi_j, \ldots, \varphi_n \rightsquigarrow \varphi \quad r_4 : l, \varphi_{i+1}, \ldots, \varphi_{j-1} \rightsquigarrow \varphi$$

Crucially, these restrictions (Definition 13, 14) fully align with the original intention of forgetting, which was introduced in ASP and other formalisms precisely to eliminate irrelevant information. Accordingly, we have defined rules and literals meeting these criteria as irrelevant of trivial within the ASPIC$^+$ framework, and permit forgetting only for such elements, ensuring that the core informational and argumentative structure of the framework is maintained. With these restrictions in place we can now ensure that if the top rules of two mapped arguments are equal, then the top rules of the original arguments must also be equal. This allows us to show that $\mathcal{M} : \mathcal{A}^l \rightarrow \mathcal{A}'$ is a bijective mapping.

Theorem 2 (Conclusion steadiness). *Given an* $AT = ((\mathcal{L}, \mathcal{R}, n), \mathcal{K})$ *such that every* $r \in \mathcal{R}$ *is minimal in* AT, *and a formula* $l \in \mathcal{L} \setminus \mathcal{K}$ *which is not relevant with respect to* $\mathcal{R}$. *Then* $\mathtt{f}^2(AT, l)$ *satisfies* ***(CS)***.

Given an $AT = ((\mathcal{L}, \mathcal{R}, n), \mathcal{K})$ with a corresponding AF F and $l \in \mathcal{L} \setminus \mathcal{K}$, we proceed in two steps to establish that $\mathtt{f}^2$ satisfies (**JP**). First, it is more straightforward to show that in the restricted framework F^l, which is a restriction of F omitting all arguments concluding the literal l, the justification status of each remaining conclusion is preserved relative to the original framework F. That is, every extension of F^l corresponds to an extension of F when arguments about l are ignored. The second step is to observe that $\mathcal{M}$ is an isomorphism between F^l and the framework F' derived from $\mathtt{f}^2(AT, l)$ (two AFs $F_1 = \langle \mathcal{A}_1, \mathcal{D}_1 \rangle$ and $F_2 = \langle \mathcal{A}_2, \mathcal{D}_2 \rangle$ are said to be *isomorphic* if there exists a bijective function $f : \mathcal{A}_1 \rightarrow \mathcal{A}_2$ such that $(A, B) \in \mathcal{D}_1$ iff $(f(A), f(B)) \in \mathcal{D}_2$). Because of this isomorphism, the preservation of justification statuses in F^l directly implies that F' also preserves the justification status of its conclusions.

Theorem 3 (Justification persistence). *Given an* $AT = ((\mathcal{L}, \mathcal{R}, n), \mathcal{K})$ *such that every* $r \in \mathcal{R}$ *is minimal in* AT, *a formula* $l \in \mathcal{L} \setminus \mathcal{K}$ *which is not relevant with respect to* $\mathcal{R}$, *and* $\sigma \in \{co, gr, pr, stb\}$. *Then* $\mathtt{f}^2(AT, l)$ *satisfies* ***(JP)*** *under* σ.

5 Conclusion

This paper addressed the challenge of forgetting formulas in the ASPIC$^+$ structured argumentation framework by identifying key desiderata and introducing forgetting operators that preserve essential reasoning properties. We demonstrated that, when only irrelevant literals are forgotten, our $\mathtt{f}^2$ operator maintains both conclusion steadiness and justification persistence, simplifying frameworks while preserving their core content.

A notable limitation is that $\mathtt{f}^2$ is not always applicable to its own output, restricting repeated forgetting operations. Investigating how to overcome this limitation presents a promising direction for future work, potentially leading to more flexible and robust forgetting mechanisms in structured argumentation.

References

1. Amgoud, L., Prade, H.: Using arguments for making and explaining decisions. Artif. Intell. **173**, 413–436 (2009)
2. Amgoud, L., Serrurier, M.: Agents that argue and explain classifications. Auton. Agent. Multi-Agent Syst. **16**(2), 187–209 (2008)
3. Atkinson, K., et al.: Towards artificial argumentation. AI Mag. **38**(3), 25–36 (2017)
4. Baumann, R., Gabbay, D., Rodrigues, O.: Forgetting an argument. In: Proceedings of the AAAI Conference on Artificial Intelligence, vol. 34, pp. 2750–2757 (2020)
5. Berthold, M., Rapberger, A., Ulbricht, M.: Forgetting aspects in assumption-based argumentation. In: Proceedings of the International Conference on Principles of Knowledge Representation and Reasoning, vol. 19, pp. 86–96 (2023)
6. Besnard, P., et al.: Introduction to structured argumentation. Argum. Comput. **5**(1), 1–4 (2014)
7. Bondarenko, A., Dung, P.M., Kowalski, R.A., Toni, F.: An abstract, argumentation-theoretic approach to default reasoning. Artif. Intell. **93**(1–2), 63–101 (1997)
8. Dung, P.M.: On the acceptability of arguments and its fundamental role in nonmonotonic reasoning, logic programming and n-person games. Artif. Intell. **77**(2), 321–357 (1995)
9. Eiter, T., Kern-Isberner, G.: A brief survey on forgetting from a knowledge representation and reasoning perspective. Künstliche Intell. **33**(1), 9–33 (2019)
10. Garcia, A., Simari, G.: Defeasible logic programming: an argumentative approach. Theory Pract. Logic Program. **4**(1–2), 95–138 (2004)
11. Gonçalves, R., Knorr, M., Leite, J.: The ultimate guide to forgetting in answer set programming. In: Fifteenth International Conference on the Principles of Knowledge Representation and Reasoning (2016)
12. Hunter, A., Williams, M.: Aggregating evidence about the positive and negative effects of treatments. Artif. Intell. Med. **56**(3), 173–190 (2012)
13. Lin, F., Reiter, R.: Forget it. In: Working Notes of AAAI Fall Symposium on Relevance, pp. 154–159 (1994)
14. Modgil, S., Prakken, H.: A general account of argumentation with preferences. Artif. Intell. **195**, 361–397 (2013)
15. Prakken, H., Sartor, G.: Law and logic: a review from an argumentation perspective. Artif. Intell. **227**, 214–245 (2015)
16. Proietti, C.: Understanding group polarization with bipolar argumentation frameworks. In: COMMA, pp. 41–52 (2016)
17. Schraagen, M., Odekerken, D., Testerink, B., Bex, F.: Argumentation-driven information extraction for online crime reports. In: CIKM Workshops (2018)
18. Simari, G., Loui, R.: A mathematical treatment of defeasible reasoning and its implementation. Artif. Intell. **53**(2–3), 125–157 (1992)
19. Zhang, Y., Foo, N.Y.: Solving logic program conflict through strong and weak forgettings. Artif. Intell. **170**(8–9), 739–778 (2006)

Strong Admissibility and Infinite Argumentation Frameworks

Martin Caminada[(✉)]

Cardiff University, Cardiff, UK
CaminadaM@cardiff.ac.uk

Abstract. Strong admissibility plays an important role in formal argumentation under the grounded semantics, especially when explaining the acceptance of an argument. However, strong admissibility has so far only been defined in the context of finite argumentation frameworks. In the current paper, we examine the case of infinite argumentation frameworks. In particular, we assess what the challenges are when moving from finite to infinite argumentation frameworks and we show that despite these challenges, strong admissibility can be meaningfully defined and applied in the context of *finitary* argumentation frameworks.

Keywords: Abstract Argumentation · Strong Admissibility · Infinite Argumentation Frameworks

1 Introduction

Formal argumentation has become one of the key approaches for symbolic reasoning under uncertainty [1]. Within formal argumentation, strong admissibility [2,4,6] plays a key role, especially in the context of grounded semantics. In essence, strong admissibility relates to grounded semantics in a similar way as admissibility relates to preferred semantics, especially when it comes to proof procedures. In order to show that an argument is in a preferred extension, it is not necessary to construct the entire preferred extension. Instead, it is sufficient to show that the argument is in an admissible set. Similarly, in order to show that an argument is in the grounded extension, it is not necessary to construct the entire grounded extension. Instead, it is sufficient to show that the argument is in a strongly admissible set [6]. Such a strongly admissible set can then either be presented in its original form, or be the basis for an interactive explanation in the form of a discussion game [5].

Strong admissibility has so far only been defined for finite argumentation frameworks [2,4,6,8,9]. This can be a limitation, especially when applying strong admissibility in the context of instantiated argumentation. For instance, when applying ASPIC$^+$ [14] with domain independent strict rules (that is, with strict rules based on classical logic entailment) the mere fact that there exist an infinite number of tautologies implies that there will be an infinite number of arguments.

K. Sauerwald and M. Thimm (Eds.): ECSQARU 2025, LNAI 16099, pp. 424–436, 2026.
https://doi.org/10.1007/978-3-032-05134-9_29

As such, it is worthwhile to explore how the concept of strong admissibility can be applied to infinite argumentation frameworks as well.

In the current paper, we examine the challenges when it comes to applying strong admissibility in the context of infinite argumentation frameworks. We show that for a particular class of infinite argumentation frameworks (called *finitary* argumentation frameworks [13]) it is still possible to apply strong admissibility, in both its set-based form and in its labelling-based form. We show that these forms are equivalent to each other and satisfy the same properties that have previously been proved in the context of finite argumentation frameworks.

The current paper is structured as follows. First, in Sect. 2, we provide some basic definitions and formal preliminaries. Then, in Sect. 3 we present some of the existing definitions of strong admissibility and examine why these are problematic in the context of infinite argumentation frameworks. Then, in Sect. 4 we examine how two of the definitions of strong admissibility (a set-based definition and a labelling-based definition) can still be used in the context of *finitary* argumentation frameworks, and that doing so results in properties similar as in the context of finite argumentation frameworks. We round off in Section 5 with a discussion of the obtained results.

2 Preliminaries

In the current section, we briefly restate some of the key concepts of abstract argumentation theory, in both its extension-based and labelling-based form.

Definition 1. *An* argumentation framework *is a pair* (Ar, att) *where* Ar *is a set of entities, called arguments, whose internal structure can be left unspecified, and att is a binary relation on* Ar. *For any* $A, B \in Ar$ *we say that* A attacks B *iff* $(A, B) \in att$.

Definition 2. *Let* (Ar, att) *be an argumentation framework,* $A \in Ar$ *and* $\mathcal{A}rgs \subseteq Ar$. *We define* A^+ *as* $\{B \in Ar \mid A \text{ attacks } B\}$, A^- *as* $\{B \in Ar \mid B \text{ attacks } A\}$, $\mathcal{A}rgs^+$ *as* $\cup\{A^+ \mid A \in \mathcal{A}rgs\}$, *and* $\mathcal{A}rgs^-$ *as* $\cup\{A^- \mid A \in \mathcal{A}rgs\}$. $\mathcal{A}rgs$ *is said to be* conflict-free *iff* $\mathcal{A}rgs \cap \mathcal{A}rgs^+ = \emptyset$. $\mathcal{A}rgs$ *is said to* defend A *iff* $A^- \subseteq \mathcal{A}rgs^+$. *The characteristic function* $F : 2^{Ar} \rightarrow 2^{Ar}$ *is defined as* $F(\mathcal{A}rgs) = \{A \mid \mathcal{A}rgs \text{ defends } A\}$.

Definition 3. *Let* (Ar, att) *be an argumentation framework.* $\mathcal{A}rgs \subseteq Ar$ *is said to be:*

- *an admissible set iff* $\mathcal{A}rgs$ *is conflict-free and* $\mathcal{A}rgs \subseteq F(\mathcal{A}rgs)$
- *a complete extension iff* $\mathcal{A}rgs$ *is conflict-free and* $\mathcal{A}rgs = F(\mathcal{A}rgs)$
- *a grounded extension iff* $\mathcal{A}rgs$ *is the (unique) smallest (w.r.t.* $\subseteq$*) complete extension*
- *a preferred extension iff* $\mathcal{A}rgs$ *is a maximal (w.r.t.* $\subseteq$*) complete extension*

The above definitions essentially follow the extension-based approach of [13].[1] It is also possible to define the key argumentation concepts in terms of argument labellings [3,7].

Definition 4. *Let (Ar, att) be an argumentation framework. An* argument labelling *is a function $\mathcal{L}ab : Ar \to \{\texttt{in}, \texttt{out}, \texttt{undec}\}$. An argument labelling $\mathcal{L}ab$ is called an* admissible labelling *iff for each $A \in Ar$ it holds that:*

- *if $\mathcal{L}ab(A) = \texttt{in}$ then for each B that attacks A it holds that $\mathcal{L}ab(B) = \texttt{out}$*
- *if $\mathcal{L}ab(A) = \texttt{out}$ then there exists a B that attacks A such that $\mathcal{L}ab(B) = \texttt{in}$*

$\mathcal{L}ab$ is called a complete labelling *iff it is an admissible labelling and for each $A \in Ar$ it also holds that:*

- *if $\mathcal{L}ab(A) = \texttt{undec}$ then there is a B that attacks A such that $\mathcal{L}ab(B) = \texttt{undec}$, and for each B that attacks A such that $\mathcal{L}ab(B) \neq \texttt{undec}$ it holds that $\mathcal{L}ab(B) = \texttt{out}$*

As a labelling is essentially a function, we sometimes write it as a set of pairs. Also, if $\mathcal{L}ab$ is a labelling, we write $\texttt{in}(\mathcal{L}ab)$ for $\{A \in Ar \mid \mathcal{L}ab(A) = \texttt{in}\}$, $\texttt{out}(\mathcal{L}ab)$ for $\{A \in Ar \mid \mathcal{L}ab(A) = \texttt{out}\}$ and $\texttt{undec}(\mathcal{L}ab)$ for $\{A \in Ar \mid \mathcal{L}ab(A) = \texttt{undec}\}$. As a labelling is also a partition of the arguments into sets of in-labelled arguments, out-labelled arguments and undec-labelled arguments, we sometimes write it as a triplet $(\texttt{in}(\mathcal{L}ab), \texttt{out}(\mathcal{L}ab), \texttt{undec}(\mathcal{L}ab))$.

Definition 5 **([10]).** *Let $\mathcal{L}ab$ and $\mathcal{L}ab'$ be argument labellings of an argumentation framework (Ar, att). We say that $\mathcal{L}ab \sqsubseteq \mathcal{L}ab'$ iff $\texttt{in}(\mathcal{L}ab) \subseteq \texttt{in}(\mathcal{L}ab')$ and $\texttt{out}(\mathcal{L}ab) \subseteq \texttt{out}(\mathcal{L}ab')$. $\mathcal{L}ab \sqcap \mathcal{L}ab'$ is defined as $(\texttt{in}(\mathcal{L}ab) \cap \texttt{in}(\mathcal{L}ab'), \texttt{out}(\mathcal{L}ab) \cap \texttt{out}(\mathcal{L}ab'), Ar \setminus ((\texttt{in}(\mathcal{L}ab) \cap \texttt{in}(\mathcal{L}ab')) \cup (\texttt{out}(\mathcal{L}ab) \cap \texttt{out}(\mathcal{L}ab'))))$. $\mathcal{L}ab \sqcup \mathcal{L}ab'$ is defined as $((\texttt{in}(\mathcal{L}ab) \setminus \texttt{out}(\mathcal{L}ab')) \cup (\texttt{in}(\mathcal{L}ab') \setminus \texttt{out}(\mathcal{L}ab)), (\texttt{out}(\mathcal{L}ab) \setminus \texttt{in}(\mathcal{L}ab')) \cup (\texttt{out}(\mathcal{L}ab') \setminus \texttt{in}(\mathcal{L}ab)), (\texttt{in}(\mathcal{L}ab) \cap \texttt{out}(\mathcal{L}ab') \cup (\texttt{out}(\mathcal{L}ab) \cap \texttt{in}(\mathcal{L}ab')) \cup (\texttt{undec}(\mathcal{L}ab) \cap \texttt{undec}(\mathcal{L}ab'))))$.*

Definition 6. *Let $\mathcal{L}ab$ be a complete labelling of an argumentation framework (Ar, att). $\mathcal{L}ab$ is said to be*

- *a grounded labelling iff $\mathcal{L}ab$ is the (unique) smallest (w.r.t. $\sqsubseteq$) complete labelling*
- *a preferred labelling iff $\mathcal{L}ab$ is a maximal (w.r.t. $\sqsubseteq$) complete labelling*

Given an argumentation framework (Ar, att) we define two functions Args2Lab and Lab2Args (to translate a conflict-free set of arguments to an argument labelling, and to translate an argument labelling to a set of arguments, respectively) such that $\texttt{Args2Lab}(\mathcal{A}rgs) = (\mathcal{A}rgs, \mathcal{A}rgs^+, Ar \setminus (\mathcal{A}rgs \cup$

[1] In [13] a preferred extension is defined as a maximal admissible set, instead of as a maximal complete extension, but as was first stated in [3], these two characterisations are equivalent.

$\mathcal{A}rgs^{+}$)) and $\texttt{Lab2Args}(\mathcal{L}ab) = \texttt{in}(\mathcal{L}ab)$. It has been proven [7] that if $\mathcal{A}rgs$ is an admissible set (resp. a complete, grounded or preferred extension) then $\texttt{Args2Lab}(\mathcal{A}rgs)$ is an admissible labelling (resp. a complete, grounded or preferred labelling), and that if $\mathcal{L}ab$ is an admissible labelling (resp. a complete, grounded or preferred labelling) then $\texttt{Lab2Args}(\mathcal{L}ab)$ is an admissible set (resp. a complete, grounded or preferred extension). Moreover, when the domain and range of Args2Lab and Lab2Args are restricted to complete extensions and complete labellings they become injective functions that are each other's reverses, which implies that the complete extensions (resp. the grounded extension and the preferred extensions) and the complete labellings (resp. the grounded labelling and the preferred labellings) are one-to-one related [7].

3 Strong Admissibility and Infinite Argumentation Frameworks

In the current section, we provide a brief overview of strong admissibility in its various forms, as well as of the challenges one encounters when trying to apply this concept in the context of infinite argumentation frameworks. Due to space limitations, we are unable to provide a general discussion of how strong admissibility is applied for finite argumentation frameworks. For this, we refer the reader to [6].

The concept of strong admissibility was first introduced by Baroni and Giacomin [2], using the notion of *strong defence.*

Definition 7 ([2]). *Let (Ar, att) be an argumentation framework, $A \in Ar$ and $\mathcal{A}rgs \subseteq Ar$. A is* strongly defended *by $\mathcal{A}rgs$ iff each attacker $B \in Ar$ of A is attacked by some $C \in \mathcal{A}rgs \setminus \{A\}$ such that C is strongly defended by $\mathcal{A}rgs \setminus \{A\}$.*

Baroni and Giacomin say that a set $\mathcal{A}rgs$ satisfies the strong admissibility property iff it strongly defends each of its arguments [2]. However, it is also possible to define strong admissibility in an equivalent way without having to refer to strong defence [6].

Definition 8 ([6]). *Let (Ar, att) be an argumentation framework. $\mathcal{A}rgs \subseteq Ar$ is* strongly admissible *iff every $A \in \mathcal{A}rgs$ is defended by some $\mathcal{A}rgs' \subseteq \mathcal{A}rgs \setminus \{A\}$ which in its turn is again strongly admissible.*

It is important to note that Definition 7 and Definition 8 have so far only been applied in the context of finite argumentation frameworks (that is, argumentation frameworks in which the number of arguments is finite). Unfortunately, these definitions cannot easily be applied in the context where the argumentation framework is infinite. To see why, consider the infinite argumentation framework $AF_1 = (Ar, att)$ where $Ar = \{A_1, A_2, A_3, \ldots\}$ and $att = \{(A_{i+1}, A_i) \mid i \geq 1\}$. This argumentation framework is shown in Fig. 1.

In argumentation framework AF_1 there exist precisely three admissible sets: $\emptyset$, $\{A_i \mid i \text{ is odd }\}$ and $\{A_i \mid i \text{ is even }\}$. The first set is the grounded extension.

Fig. 1. AF_1: each argument is attacked by its successor

The second and third set are the preferred extensions. However, when trying to apply either Definition 7 or Definition 8 to assess whether the latter two sets are strongy admissible, one stumbles upon a problem. Take for instance the set $\{A_i \mid i \text{ is odd }\}$. When applying Definition 7 to assess whether A_1 is strongly defended by $\{A_i \mid i \text{ is odd }\}$, we observe that A_1's attacker A_2 is attacked by $A_3 \in \{A_i \mid i \text{ is odd }\} \setminus \{A_1\}$. So we need to assess whether A_3 is strongly defended by $\{A_i \mid i \text{ is odd }\} \setminus \{A_1\}$. For this, we need to assess whether A_5 is strongly defended by $\{A_i \mid i \text{ is odd }\} \setminus \{A_1, A_3\}$, etc. The point here is that Definition 7 has a recursive nature, and for the argumentation framework AF_1 the recursion does not end. As such, one could either assume that for each odd j, A_j is strongly defended by $\{A_i \mid i \text{ is odd }\} \setminus \{A_k \mid k \text{ is odd and } k < j\}$, or that for each odd j, A_j is *not* strongly defended by $\{A_i \mid i \text{ is odd }\} \setminus \{A_k \mid k \text{ is odd and } k < j\}$. Both assumptions are consistent with Definition 7, yet only one of them can hold.

A similar problem occurs in the context of Definition 8. Here, in order to determine whether $\{A_i \mid i \text{ is odd }\}$ is a strongly admissible set, we have to determine whether A_1 is defended by some subset of $\{A_i \mid i \text{ is odd }\} \setminus \{A_1\}$ which in its turn is strongly admissible. In essence, Definition 8 is another example of a recursive definition of which the recursion does not end for argumentation framework AF_1.

A third definition of strong admissibility was provided in [6, Lemma 2, Theorem 1].[2]

Definition 9. *Let* (Ar, att) *be an argumentation framework and let* $\mathcal{A}rgs \subseteq Ar$. *Let* $H^0_{\mathcal{A}rgs} = \emptyset$ *and* $H^{i+1}_{\mathcal{A}rgs} = F(H^i_{\mathcal{A}rgs}) \cap \mathcal{A}rgs$ $(i \geq 0)$. *Args is strongly admissible iff* $\cup_{i=0}^{\infty} H^i_{\mathcal{A}rgs} = \mathcal{A}rgs$.

Definition 9 is not recursive. As such, it avoids the problem of potential infinite recursion. In particular, for AF_1 it can be observed that for any set $\mathcal{A}rgs$, $H^0_{\mathcal{A}rgs} = \emptyset$, $H^1_{\mathcal{A}rgs} = F(H^0_{\mathcal{A}rgs}) \cap \mathcal{A}rgs = \emptyset$, $H^2_{\mathcal{A}rgs} = F(H^1_{\mathcal{A}rgs}) \cap \mathcal{A}rgs = \emptyset$, etc. As such, the only set that is strongly admissible is the empty set, which as we observed before, is also the grounded extension.

Although Definition 9 allows one to unambiguously assess, even for infinite argumentation frameworks, whether a particular set is strongly admissible or not, it still has some issues. Consider the argumentation framework $AF_2 = (Ar, att)$ with $Ar = \{A_i \mid i \geq 1\} \cup \{B\}$ and $att = \{(A_i, A_{i+1}) \mid i \geq 1\} \cup \{(A_j, B) \mid j \text{ is even }\}$. This argumentation framework is shown in Fig. 2.

AF_2 only has one complete extension: $\{A_j \mid j \text{ is odd }\} \cup \{B\}$, which is also the grounded extension. Yet, this grounded extension is not strongly admissible, at least not according to Definition 9. This is because (when taking $\mathcal{A}rgs$ as

[2] It has been shown that Definition 7, Definition 8 and Definition 9 are equivalent to each other in the context of finite argumentation frameworks [6].

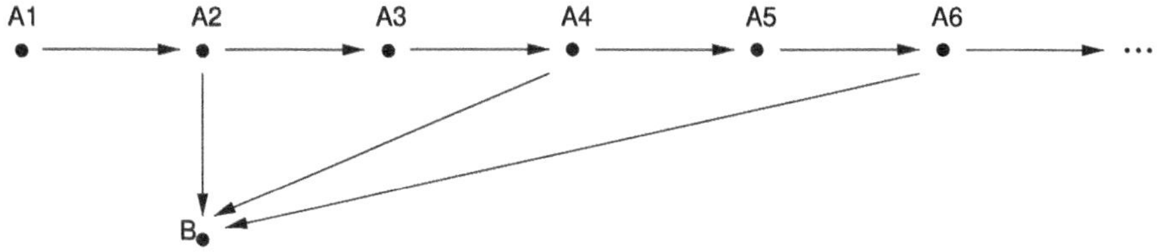

Fig. 2. AF_2: an argumentation framework that is not finitary in the sense of [13]

$\{A_j \mid j \text{ is odd }\} \cup \{B\}) \cup_{i=0}^{\infty} H^i_{Args}$ is $\{A_j \mid j \text{ is odd }\}$ instead of $\{A_j \mid j \text{ is odd }\}$ $\cup\{B\}$.[3] More seriously, even though B is in the grounded extension, there is no strongly admissible set that contains B, at least not according to Definition 9. This is a problem, as the whole idea of strong admissibility is to show that an argument is in the grounded extension by showing that it is in a strongly admissible set [9].[4] For finite argumentation frameworks, this property actually holds; in particular, it also holds that the grounded extension is always strongly admissible. For infinite argumentation frameworks, the property unfortunately does not always hold, as shown by the counter example of AF_2.

Strong admissibility, apart from its set-based form, has also been defined in a labelling-based form. This is done using the concept of a min-max numbering.

Definition 10 **([6]).** *Let $\mathcal{L}ab$ be an admissible labelling of an argumentation framework (Ar, att). A* min-max numbering *is a total function $\mathcal{MM}_{\mathcal{L}ab}$: $\texttt{in}(\mathcal{L}ab) \cup \texttt{out}(\mathcal{L}ab) \to \mathbb{N} \cup \{\infty\}$ such that for each $A \in \texttt{in}(\mathcal{L}ab) \cup \texttt{out}(\mathcal{L}ab)$ it holds that:*

- *if $\mathcal{L}ab(A) = \texttt{in}$ then $\mathcal{MM}_{\mathcal{L}ab}(A) = max(\{\mathcal{MM}_{\mathcal{L}ab}(B) \mid B$ attacks A and $\mathcal{L}ab(B) = \texttt{out}\}) + 1$ (with $max(\emptyset)$ defined as 0)*
- *if $\mathcal{L}ab(A) = \texttt{out}$ then $\mathcal{MM}_{\mathcal{L}ab}(A) = min(\{\mathcal{MM}_{\mathcal{L}ab}(B) \mid B$ attacks A and $\mathcal{L}ab(B) = \texttt{in}\}) + 1$ (with $min(\emptyset)$ defined as ∞)*

In the context of finite argumentation frameworks, it has been proven that every admissible labelling has a unique min-max numbering [6].

Definition 11. *A* strongly admissible labelling *is an admissible labelling whose min-max numbering yields natural numbers only (so no argument is numbered ∞).*

An important limitation is that min-max numberings have only been applied in the context of finite argumentation frameworks. Unfortunately, applying min-max numberings in the context of infinite argumentation frameworks is

---

[3] A similar problem was observed in [13] w.r.t. the inductive proof procedure for grounded semantics.

[4] In a similar way, one shows that an argument is in a preferred extension by showing that it is in an admissible set.

not straightforward. Consider again the example of AF_2 (Fig. 2). Here, there exists only one complete labelling. In this labelling (which is also the grounded labelling) every odd A_i is labelled `in`, every even A_i is labelled `out`, and B is labelled `in`. As for the min-max numbering of this labelling, it can be verified that each A_i will be numbered with i. However, when it comes to numbering B we encounter a problem. The attackers of B are the `out`-labelled arguments A_2, A_4, A_6, etc. These are respectively numbered 2, 4, 6, etc. As B itself is labelled `in`, we have to apply point 1 of Definition 10, which specifies that $\mathcal{MM}_{\mathcal{L}ab}(B) = max(\{2, 4, 6, \ldots\}) + 1$. However the maximum element of the set $\{2, 4, 6, \ldots\}$ is not defined. Therefore, the min-max number of B is not defined, at least not according to Definition 10.

4 Strong Admissibility and Finitary Argumentation Frameworks

In the current section, we show how the concept of strong admissibility can be applied in the context of infinite argumentation frameworks. However, we do have to restrict ourselves to argumentation frameworks that are *finitary* [13], meaning that although there can be an infinite number of arguments and an infinite number of attacks, each argument has to have a finite number of attackers.

Definition 12 ([13]). *An argumentation framework $AF = (Ar, att)$ is called* finitary *iff for each $A \in Ar$, the set $\{B \mid (B, A) \in att\}$ is finite.*

It turns out that for finitary argumentation frameworks, Definition 9 yields the same desirable properties as have previously been proved for finite argumentation frameworks [6].

Theorem 1. *Let (Ar, att) be a finitary argumentation framework and let $\mathcal{A}rgs \subseteq Ar$ be a strongly admissible set (in the sense of Definition 9). It holds that $\mathcal{A}rgs$ is an admissible set.*

Proof. We first observe that if $\mathcal{A}rgs'$ is an admissible set then (1) $F(\mathcal{A}rgs')$ is admissible, and (2) $\mathcal{A}rgs' \subseteq F(\mathcal{A}rgs')$. We proceed to show, by induction on i, that $H^i_{\mathcal{A}rgs}$ is admissible.

BASIS Let $i = 0$. In that case, $H^i_{\mathcal{A}rgs} = H^0_{\mathcal{A}rgs} = \emptyset$, which is admissible.
STEP Suppose that $H^i_{\mathcal{A}rgs}$ is admissible. From observation (1) it follows that $F(H^i_{\mathcal{A}rgs})$ is also admissible. We now have to prove that also $F(H^i_{\mathcal{A}rgs}) \cap \mathcal{A}rgs$ is admissible. We first observe that $F(H^i_{\mathcal{A}rgs}) \cap \mathcal{A}rgs$ is conflict-free, as $F(H^i_{\mathcal{A}rgs})$ is conflict-free by virtue of being admissible. Next, suppose towards a contradiction that $F(H^i_{\mathcal{A}rgs}) \cap \mathcal{A}rgs$ does not defend all of its arguments. This means that $F(H^i_{\mathcal{A}rgs}) \cap \mathcal{A}rgs$ contains an argument (say A) that has an attacker (say B) that is not attacked by any argument $C \in F(H^i_{\mathcal{A}rgs}) \cap \mathcal{A}rgs$. This is in spite of the fact that $F(H^i_{\mathcal{A}rgs})$ does contain at least one attacker of B (follows from observation (1)). It follows that all such attackers are not in $\mathcal{A}rgs$. But then all these attackers are also not in $H^i_{\mathcal{A}rgs}$, which means that $A \notin F(H^i_{\mathcal{A}rgs})$. Contradiction.

From the thus obtained fact that each $H^i_{\mathcal{A}rgs}$ is admissible, observation (2) allows us to infer that $H^i_{\mathcal{A}rgs} \subseteq H^{i+1}_{\mathcal{A}rgs}$ (for each $i \geq 0$). This implies that $\cup_{i=0}^{\infty} H^i_{\mathcal{A}rgs}$ is conflict-free (as any two attacking $A, B \in \cup_{i=0}^{\infty} H^i_{\mathcal{A}rgs}$ would also have to be in some $H^i_{\mathcal{A}rgs}$ ($i \geq 0$), which conflicts with $H^i_{\mathcal{A}rgs}$ being admissible and conflict-free). It also implies that $\cup_{i=0}^{\infty} H^i_{\mathcal{A}rgs}$ defends all of its arguments. This can be seen as follows. Let $A \in \cup_{i=0}^{\infty} H^i_{\mathcal{A}rgs}$. Then there exists a $H^i_{\mathcal{A}rgs}$ ($i \geq 0$) such that $A \in H^i_{\mathcal{A}rgs}$. The fact that $H^i_{\mathcal{A}rgs}$ is admissible means that for each attacker B of A, $H^i_{\mathcal{A}rgs}$ contains a C that attacks B. But then $\cup_{i=0}^{\infty} H^i_{\mathcal{A}rgs}$ contains the same C. As such, $\cup_{i=0}^{\infty} H^i_{\mathcal{A}rgs}$ defends all its arguments. This, together with the earlier observed fact that $\cup_{i=0}^{\infty} H^i_{\mathcal{A}rgs}$ is conflict-free, means that $\cup_{i=0}^{\infty} H^i_{\mathcal{A}rgs}$ is admissible. As $\cup_{i=0}^{\infty} H^i_{\mathcal{A}rgs} = \mathcal{A}rgs$, it therefore follows that $\mathcal{A}rgs$ is admissible.

Baroni and Giacomin prove that in the context of finite argumentation frameworks, the grounded extension is the unique biggest (w.r.t. $\subseteq$) strongly admissible set [2]. We proceed to prove that this result still holds in the context of finitary argumentation frameworks.

Theorem 2. *Let $AF = (Ar, att)$ be a finitary argumentation framework. The grounded extension of AF is the biggest (w.r.t. $\subseteq$) strongly admissible set (in the sense of Definition 9) of AF.*

Proof. We first show that the grounded extension is a strongly admissible set. Let GE be the grounded extension. From [13] it follows that $GE = \cup_{i=0}^{\infty} F^i$, where $F^0 = \emptyset$ and $F^{i+1} = F(F^i)$. It directly follows that for each $i \geq 0$, $F^i \subseteq GE$, so $F^i \cap GE = F^i$. This implies that for each $i \geq 0$, $H^i_{GE} = F^i$, so $\cup_{i=0}^{\infty} H^i_{GE} = \cup_{i=0}^{\infty} F^i = GE$, which means that GE is a strongly admissible set. We proceed to show that GE is also the *biggest* strongly admissible set. Let $\mathcal{A}rgs$ be an arbitrary strongly admissible set. From the fact that $\mathcal{A}rgs$ is strongly admissible, it follows that $\cup_{i=0}^{\infty} H^i_{\mathcal{A}rgs} = \mathcal{A}rgs$. Suppose $\mathcal{A}rgs \supseteq GE$. Then from $F^i \cap GE = F^i$ it follows that $F^i \cap \mathcal{A}rgs = F^i$. This implies that $H^i_{\mathcal{A}rgs} = F^i$, so $\cup_{i=0}^{\infty} H^i_{\mathcal{A}rgs} = \cup_{i=0}^{\infty} F^i = GE$. From the fact that $\mathcal{A}rgs$ is strongly admissible, it then follows that $\mathcal{A}rgs = GE$.

In addition to the grounded extension being the biggest strongly admissible set, it can be shown that the empty set is the smallest strongly admissible set.

Proposition 1. *Let $AF = (Ar, att)$ be a finitary argumentation framework. The empty set ($\emptyset$) is the smallest strongly admissible set (in the sense of Definition 9) of AF.*

Proof. This follows from the fact that the empty set is always strongly admissible in the sense of Definition 9, together with the fact that the empty set is a subset of each strongly admissible set.

It can be proved that the strongly admissible sets form a lattice[5] with the grounded extension as its top element (Theorem 2) and the empty set as its

[5] We recall that a *lattice* is a partial order such that each two elements have both a greatest lower bound and a least upper bound.

bottom element (Proposition 1). This has previously been proved in the context of finite argumentation frameworks [6], but we show that this result still holds in the context of finitary argumentation frameworks.

Proposition 2. *Let* $Args$ *and* $Args'$ *be sets of arguments such that* $Args \subseteq Args'$. *For every* $i \geq 0$ *it holds that* $H^i_{Args} \subseteq H^i_{Args'}$.

Proof. By induction on i.

BASIS Let $i = 0$. Then $H^0_{Args} = \emptyset = H^0_{Args'}$.

STEP Suppose that for some i it holds that $H^i_{Args} \subseteq H^i_{Args'}$. As F is a monotonic function, it follows that $F(H^i_{Args}) \subseteq F(H^i_{Args'})$. From the fact that $Args \subseteq Args'$ it then follows that $F(H^i_{Args}) \cap Args \subseteq F(H^i_{Args'}) \cap Args'$. That is, $H^i_{Args} \subseteq H^i_{Args'}$.

Lemma 1. *Let* $AF = (Ar, att)$ *be a finitary argumentation framework and let* $Args_1 \subseteq Ar$ *and* $Args_2 \subseteq Ar$. *If* $Args_1$ *and* $Args_2$ *are strongly admissible sets (in the sense of Definition 9), then* $Args_1 \cup Args_2$ *is also a strongly admissible set (in the sense of Definition 9).*

Proof. Suppose $Args_1$ and $Args_2$ are strongly admissible. That is, $\cup_{i=0}^{\infty} H^i_{Args_1} = Args_1$ and $\cup_{i=0}^{\infty} H^i_{Args_2} = Args_2$. We now proceed to prove that $\cup_{i=0}^{\infty} H^i_{Args_1 \cup Args_2} = Args_1 \cup Args_2$.

"$\subseteq$" By definition, it holds for each $i \geq 0$ that $H^i_{Args_1 \cup Args_2} \subseteq Args_1 \cup Args_2$, which implies that $\cup_{i=0}^{\infty} H^i_{Args_1 \cup Args_2} \subseteq Args_1 \cup Args_2$.

"$\supseteq$" Let $A \in Args_1 \cup Args_2$. Then either $A \in Args_1$ or $A \in Args_2$. Assume without loss of generality that $A \in Args_1$ (the case of $A \in Args_2$ is similar). From the fact that $Args_1 = \cup_{i=0}^{\infty} H^i_{Args_1}$ it follows that $A \in \cup_{i=0}^{\infty} H^i_{Args_1}$. This means there exists an $i \geq 0$ such that $A \in H^i_{Args_1}$. As $Args_1 \subseteq Args_1 \cup Args2$, we can apply Proposition 2 to obtain that $H^i_{Args_1} \subseteq H^i_{Args_1 \cup Args_2}$, so $A \in H^i_{Args_1 \cup Args_2}$. This directly implies that $A \in \cup_{i=0}^{\infty} H^i_{Args_1 \cup Args_2}$.

Lemma 2. *Let* $AF = (Ar, att)$ *be a finitary argumentation framework. Each set of arguments* $Args \subseteq Ar$ *has a unique biggest (w.r.t.* $\subseteq$*) strongly admissible (in the sense of Definition 9) subset.*

Proof. We first observe that there is always at least one strongly admissible set (the empty set). We also observe that every increasing sequence of strongly admissible sets $Args_1, Args_2, Args_3, \ldots$ has an upper bound ($\cup_{i=1}^{\infty} Args_i$ which is again strongly admissible; this follows from Lemma 1). This allows us to apply Zorn's lemma and obtain that there is at least one maximal strongly admissible set.[6] We now proceed to show that this maximal strongly admissible subset is

[6] Although not explicitly mentioned in [13], a similar form of reasoning is needed to prove that maximal admissible sets (i.e. preferred extensions) always exist, even for an infinite argumentation framework with an infinite sequences of ever increasing admissible sets.

unique. Let $\mathcal{A}rgs_1$ and $\mathcal{A}rgs_2$ be maximal strongly admissible subsets of $\mathcal{A}rgs$. Now consider $\mathcal{A}rgs_1 \cup \mathcal{A}rgs_2$. From Lemma 1 it follows that this is again a strongly admissible set. From the fact that $\mathcal{A}rgs_1$ and $\mathcal{A}rgs_2$ are *maximal* strongly admissible subsets, it follows that if $\mathcal{A}rgs_1 \subseteq \mathcal{A}rgs_1 \cup \mathcal{A}rgs_2$ then $\mathcal{A}rgs_1 = \mathcal{A}rgs_1 \cup \mathcal{A}rgs_2$, and that if $\mathcal{A}rgs_2 \subseteq \mathcal{A}rgs_1 \cup \mathcal{A}rgs_2$ then $\mathcal{A}rgs_2 = \mathcal{A}rgs_1 \cup \mathcal{A}rgs_2$, so we obtain that $\mathcal{A}rgs_1 = \mathcal{A}rgs_1 \cup \mathcal{A}rgs_2$ and $\mathcal{A}rgs_2 = \mathcal{A}rgs_1 \cup \mathcal{A}rgs_2$ so $\mathcal{A}rgs_1 = \mathcal{A}rgs_2$.

Theorem 3. *Let AF be a finitary argumentation framework. The strongly admissible sets (in the sense of Definition 9) of AF form a lattice (w.r.t. $\subseteq$).*

Proof. This can be proved in a similar way as Theorem 5 of [6], although the lemmas used in this proof would need to be replaced by Lemma 1 and Lemma 2, as the latter apply in the context of finitary argumentation frameworks instead of finite argumentation frameworks.

As for the labelling-based definition of strong admissibility, we observe that when restricting ourselves to finitary argumentation frameworks, the concept of a min-max numbering is always well-defined. This is because, in Definition 10, the maximal element of a set of numbers is always defined as long as this set is finite. Although the existing proofs in [6] were developed in the context of a finite argumentation framework, they do not actually rely on this, as long as the concept of a min-max numbering is well-defined. This means the existing proofs in [6] carry over to finitary argumentation frameworks in a straightforward way.

Theorem 4. *Let $AF = (Ar, att)$ be a finitary argumentation framework and let $\mathcal{L}ab$ be an admissible labelling of AF. $\mathcal{L}ab$ has a unique min-max numbering.*

Proof. Similar to the proof of Theorem 6 of [6].

Theorem 5. *Let $AF = (Ar, att)$ be a finitary argumentation framework.*

- *for every strongly admissible set $\mathcal{A}rgs$ of AF (in the sense of Definition 9), it holds that* `Args2Lab`$(\mathcal{A}rgs)$ *is a strongly admissible labelling*
- *for every strongly admissible labelling $\mathcal{L}ab$ of AF, it holds that* `Lab2Args`$(\mathcal{L}ab)$ *is a strongly admissible set (in the sense of Definition 9)*

Proof. Similar to the proof of Theorem 7 of [6].

We proceed to show that the grounded labelling is the biggest strongly admissible labelling and that the all-`undec` labelling[7] is the smallest strongly admissible labelling.

Theorem 6. *Let $AF = (Ar, att)$ be a finitary argumentation framework. The grounded labelling of AF is the biggest (w.r.t. $\sqsubseteq$) strongly admissible labelling of AF.*

[7] The all-`undec` labelling labels each argument `undec`.

Proof. Let $\mathcal{A}rgs$ be the grounded extension of AF and let $\mathcal{L}ab$ be $\texttt{Args2Lab}(\mathcal{A}rgs)$. From [7, Definition 9 and Theorem 6] it follows that $\mathcal{L}ab$ is the grounded labelling. From Theorem 5 and the fact that the grounded extension is strongly admissible (Theorem 2), it follows that $\mathcal{L}ab$ is a strongly admissible labelling. The next thing to show is that $\mathcal{L}ab$ is also the *biggest* (w.r.t. $\sqsubseteq$) strongly admissible labelling. Let $\mathcal{L}ab'$ be a strongly admissible labelling. Then Theorem 5 implies that $\mathcal{A}rgs' = \texttt{Lab2Args}(\mathcal{L}ab')$ is a strongly admissible set. As the grounded extension is the biggest strongly admissible set (Theorem 2), it holds that $\mathcal{A}rgs' \subseteq \mathcal{A}rgs$, so $\texttt{in}(\mathcal{L}ab') \subseteq \texttt{in}(\mathcal{L}ab)$. From [7, Lemma 1] it follows that $\texttt{out}(\mathcal{L}ab') \subseteq \texttt{out}(\mathcal{L}ab)$, so it follows that $\mathcal{L}ab' \sqsubseteq \mathcal{L}ab$. This, together with our initial assumption that $\mathcal{L}ab \sqsubseteq \mathcal{L}ab'$ implies that $\mathcal{L}ab' = \mathcal{L}ab$.

Proposition 3. *Let $AF = (Ar, att)$ be a finitary argumentation framework. The all-*`undec` *labelling of AF is the smallest (w.r.t. $\sqsubseteq$) strongly admissible labelling of AF.*

Proof. From Definition 4 it follows that the all-`undec` labelling is admissible. Its min-max numbering is empty, as there are no `in` or `out` labelled arguments to be numbered. This trivially implies that no argument is numbered ∞. Hence, the all-`undec` labelling is strongly admissible. It is also the *smallest* strongly admissible labelling, as for each strongly admissible labelling $\mathcal{L}ab'$ it holds that $\mathcal{L}ab \sqsubseteq \mathcal{L}ab'$, with $\mathcal{L}ab$ being the all-`undec` labelling.

We proceed to show that the strongly admissible labellings form a lattice with the grounded labelling as its top element (Theorem 6) and the all-`undec` labelling as its bottom element (Proposition 3). Notice that the mere fact that the strongly admissible sets form a lattice does by itself not directly imply that the strongly admissible labellings also form a lattice, as the relationship between strongly admissible sets and strongly admissible labellings is one-to-many instead of one-to-one.[8] Still, the proofs are very similar.

Lemma 3. *Let $AF = (Ar, att)$ be a finitary argumentation framework. If $\mathcal{L}ab_1$ and $\mathcal{L}ab_2$ are strongly admissible labellings, then $\mathcal{L}ab_1 \sqcup \mathcal{L}ab_2$ is also a strongly admissible labelling.*

Proof. Similar to the proof of Lemma 5 of [6]

Lemma 4. *Let $AF = (Ar, att)$ be a finitary argumentation framework. Each admissible labelling $\mathcal{L}ab$ of AF has a unique biggest (w.r.t. $\sqsubseteq$) strongly admissible sublabelling.*

Proof. Similar to the proof of Lemma 2, but with labellings instead of sets and $\subseteq$ replaced by $\sqsubseteq$ and $\cup$ replaced by $\sqcup$.

Theorem 7. *Let AF be a finitary argumentation framework. The strongly admissible labellings of AF form a lattice (w.r.t. $\sqsubseteq$).*

Proof. This can be proved similar to Theorem 5 of [6], with $\subseteq$ replaced by $\sqsubseteq$, $\cup$ replaced by $\sqcup$, $\cap$ replaced by $\sqcap$, and by using the labelling-specific results of Lemma 3 and Lemma 4 instead of their set-specific variants.

[8] We refer to [6] for an example.

5 Discussion

In essence, the current work generalises the results in [6], regarding both the well-definedness and the properties of strong admissibility, in both its set-based form and its labelling-based form. In particular, we have shown that for finitary argumentation frameworks, the concept of strong admissibility is well-defined (using Definition 9, as well as Definition 10 and Definition 11) and satisfies the same properties that were previously shown for finite argumentation frameworks.

As for the practical applicability of our results, we could look at the field of instantiated argumentation formalisms. For instance, in Assumption-Based Argumentation (ABA) [11] each argument is written as $Asms \vdash c$, where $Asms$ is a set of assumptions that allows one to infer conclusion c. This inference in essence takes the form of a tree of ABA rules (similar to how inferences work in for instance ASPIC$^+$) [14]. If one would take the set of ABA rules to coincide with all possible classical logic entailments (as was for instance done in [12]), one would obtain an infinite set of rules and an infinite set or arguments, as there would for instance be an argument $\emptyset \vdash t$ for each tautology t. However, as long as the set of assumptions is finite,[9] each argument will have a finite number of assumptions and a finite number of attackers. As such, the resulting argumentation framework is *finitary*, which means that we can apply the concept of strong admissibility as discussed in the current paper. That is, in order to show that an argument is in the grounded extension, we do not have to show the entire grounded extension (which would be infinite). Instead, it suffices to show that the argument is in a strongly admissible set.[10]

In terms of how the theory in the current paper relates to what was previously been developed regarding strong admissibility, we can make the following observations.

1. We have loosened the restriction on the argumentation frameworks under which the concept is defined (from *finite* argumentation frameworks to *finitary* argumentation frameworks).
2. Our theory is backwards compatible, meaning that for finite argumentation frameworks, a set of arguments is strongly admissible (Definition 9) iff it is strongly admissible according to the definitions that only work for finite argumentation frameworks (Definition 7 and Definition 8).
3. The strongly admissible sets (and labellings) form a lattice with the empty set (all-undec labelling) at the bottom and the grounded extension (grounded labelling) at the top.

One could imagine a further broadening of the concept of strong admissibility, which, instead of from finite to finitary, would go from finitary to unrestricted. Ideally, such a broadening would satisfy similar properties as those mentioned

[9] Additionally, we would also need to require that for each assumption the set of its contraries is finite.

[10] In essence, showing that an argument is in a strongly admissible set can be done by the kind of tree-based proof procedures that are also applied in ABA [6].

above. That is, such a theory would relate to finitary argumentation frameworks in a similar way as our theory relates to finite argumentation frameworks (point 2). How to construct such a theory is a topic for further research.

Acknowledgments. This publication is supported in part by the Joint Research and Innovation Seed Grants Program between Cardiff University and the University of Illinois System.

References

1. Baroni, P., Gabbay, D., Giacomin, M., van der Torre, L.: Handbook of Formal Argumentation, vol. 1. College Publications (2018)
2. Baroni, P., Giacomin, M.: On principle-based evaluation of extension-based argumentation semantics. Artif. Intell. **171**(10–15), 675–700 (2007)
3. Caminada, M.: On the issue of reinstatement in argumentation. In: Fisher, M., van der Hoek, W., Konev, B., Lisitsa, A. (eds.) JELIA 2006. LNCS (LNAI), vol. 4160, pp. 111–123. Springer, Heidelberg (2006). https://doi.org/10.1007/11853886_11
4. Caminada, M.: Strong admissibility revisited. In: Parsons, S., Oren, N., Reed, C., Cerutti, F. (eds.) Computational Models of Argument; Proceedings of COMMA 2014, pp. 197–208. IOS Press (2014)
5. Caminada, M.: Argumentation semantics as formal discussion. In: Handbook of Formal Argumentation, vol. 1, pp. 487–518. College Publications (2018)
6. Caminada, M., Dunne, P.: Strong admissibility revisited: theory and applications. Argum. Comput. **10**, 277–300 (2019)
7. Caminada, M., Gabbay, D.: A logical account of formal argumentation. Studia Logica **93**(2-3), 109–145 (2009)
8. Caminada, M., Harikrishnan, S.: An evaluation of algorithms for strong admissibility. In: Proceedings of SAFA 2024, pp. 69–82 (2024)
9. Caminada, M., Harikrishnan, S.: Tractable algorithms for strong admissibility. Argum. Comput. **16**, 212–235 (2025)
10. Caminada, M., Pigozzi, G.: On judgment aggregation in abstract argumentation. Auton. Agent. Multi-Agent Syst. **22**(1), 64–102 (2011)
11. Čyras, K., Fan, X., Schulz, C., Toni, F.: Assumption-based argumentation: disputes, explanations, preferences. In: Handbook of Formal Argumentation, vol. 1. College Publications (2018)
12. Dimopoulos, Y., Nebel, B., Toni, F.: On the computational complexity of assumption-based argumentation for default reasoning. Artif. Intell. **141**(1–2), 57–78 (2002)
13. Dung, P.: On the acceptability of arguments and its fundamental role in nonmonotonic reasoning, logic programming and n-person games. Artif. Intell. **77**, 321–357 (1995)
14. Modgil, S., Prakken, H.: The aspic+ framework for structured argumentation: a tutorial. Argum. Comput. **5**, 31–62 (2014)

Recognizing the Impact Among Relevant Elements for Reaching Stability in Incomplete Argumentation Frameworks

Anshu Xiong[1,2](✉) and Songmao Zhang[1]

[1] State Key Laboratory of Mathematical Sciences, Academy of Mathematics and Systems Science, Chinese Academy of Sciences, Beijing 100190, China
xionganshu21@mails.ucas.ac.cn, smzhang@math.ac.cn

[2] University of Chinese Academy of Sciences, Beijing 100049, China

Abstract. For Incomplete Argumentation Frameworks (IAFs), the notion of stability is of importance by indicating whether there is no need anymore to investigate the existence of currently uncertain elements. Further, the notion of relevance characterizes the actions required for the stability to occur in the future. In this study, we point out that the relevance of elements is not an independent matter, and the addition or removal of one relevant element may have impact on other relevant elements by leading them to turn irrelevant automatically. Based on this observation, we propose an impact-based method to resolve uncertainty in IAFs for reaching stability of a given set of arguments under five common semantics. This method iteratively performs the relevant action that has the largest impact until all relevant elements have become irrelevant. We give theoretical foundations of the method and effective ways to compute the impact under various semantics. Specifically, for admissible and stable semantics, we give characterizing conditions for directly identifying the impact of a relevant element, and then show that our impact-based method only has to decide the minimum number of uncertain elements in order to reach stability of the given set necessarily being an extension.

Keywords: Abstract argumentation · Incomplete knowledge · Stability · Relevance · Impact

1 Introduction

Dung's *Abstract Argumentation Framework* (AF) [10] is a groundbreaking theory for modeling argumentation, where attack relations among a group of arguments are represented and collectively accepted sets of arguments called *extensions* can be computed under various types of semantics. To further extend AF to model dynamic argumentation, *Incomplete Argumentation Framework (IAF)* [6] introduces qualitative uncertainty by additionally allowing uncertain arguments and attacks whose existence is unknown at the moment. Deciding the existence of all uncertain elements will yield various AFs called *completions* of the IAF.

K. Sauerwald and M. Thimm (Eds.): ECSQARU 2025, LNAI 16099, pp. 437–451, 2026.
https://doi.org/10.1007/978-3-032-05134-9_30

In order to characterize whether a problem of interest holds the same answer in all completions of an IAF, the notion of *stability* was initially proposed in [12,14] for acceptance of an argument, and also studied for verification of a set of arguments in [6,11], as well as all extensions under one semantics in our previous work [17]. An IAF being stable is of significance, as it means that there is no need anymore to investigate the existence of currently uncertain elements. To reach stability of acceptance of an argument from an unstable IAF, adding or removing an uncertain element is said to be *relevant* if such an action is required for the stability to occur in some situation in the future [14]. In our recent study [18], we extended the notion of relevance to verification of a set of arguments S, where the verifications status is distinguished between σ-*true*, which means that S is a σ-extension, or σ-$false$ with the opposite meaning. Further, we proposed *strong relevance* characterizing the necessity of uncertainty resolution in all situations.

One may naively assume that all relevant elements have to be decided so as to reach stability. We observe that the relevance of elements is not an independent matter, and the addition or removal of one relevant element may have *impact* on other relevant elements, i.e., leading them to turn *irrelevant* automatically. On the other hand, irrelevant elements can never become relevant. Therefore, as the relevant actions are taken one by one, the relevant elements become less and irrelevant ones become more. When all of the uncertain elements are irrelevant, the stable status is reached and vice versa.

Based on this observation, the task of reaching stability can be done by firstly resolving the necessary uncertainties by strong relevance, and then choosing some relevant element to add or remove, and computing the impact of the action so that the impacted elements become irrelevant automatically. Such a process is repeated until there are no relevant elements left. Furthermore, at each iteration, if we choose an action with the largest impact, i.e., making relevant elements changing to irrelevant as many as possible, then the number of uncertain elements needed to be decided for reaching stability can be reduced.

The main contribution of this paper lies in recognizing the impact among relevant actions and then proposing an impact-based method to resolve uncertainty in IAFs for reaching stability of a given set of arguments. We give theoretical foundations of the method and effective ways to compute the impact under various semantics. Specifically, for admissible and stable semantics, we give characterizing conditions for directly identifying the impact of a relevant action of an element, and then show that our impact-based method only has to decide existence of the minimum number of uncertain elements in order to reach *-true* stability. For complete, grounded and preferred semantics, unfortunately our method does not exhibit such least uncertainty resolution. This may come from considering the impact of a single action of a relevant element rather than the impact of a combination of actions.

2 Preliminaries

Argumentation Framework (AF). An *abstract argumentation framework* [10] is a directed graph $F = \langle \mathcal{A}, \mathcal{R} \rangle$ where $\mathcal{A}$ represents a set of considered arguments and $\mathcal{R} \subseteq \mathcal{A} \times \mathcal{A}$ the set of attacks between arguments in $\mathcal{A}$. We say that *a attacks b* if $(a, b) \in \mathcal{R}$, *a attacks* a set of arguments $S \subseteq \mathcal{A}$ if $\exists b \in S, (a, b) \in \mathcal{R}$, and the meaning of S *attacks* a is analogous. Let $S_F^+ = \{a \in \mathcal{A} \mid S \text{ attacks } a\}$ and $S_F^- = \{a \in \mathcal{A} \mid a \text{ attacks } S\}$, and S is *conflict-free* iff $S \cap S_F^+ = \emptyset$. We say that S *defends a* if all the attackers of a are attacked by S. *Semantics* σ is a function of which the input is an AF $F = \langle \mathcal{A}, \mathcal{R} \rangle$ and the output $\sigma(F)$ a set of subsets of $\mathcal{A}$, where every element of $\sigma(F)$ is called a *σ-extension* of F. The common semantics admissible, stable, complete, grounded and preferred semantics (abbr. ad, st, co, gr, pr) are originally proposed in [10] and defined as follows.

Definition 1. *Given an AF $F = \langle \mathcal{A}, \mathcal{R} \rangle$ and a set of arguments $S \subseteq \mathcal{A}$,*

1. $S \in \mathtt{ad}(F)$ *iff S is conflict-free and $\forall a \in S, S$ defends a;*
2. $S \in \mathtt{st}(F)$ *iff S is conflict-free and $S_F^+ = \mathcal{A} \setminus S$;*
3. $S \in \mathtt{co}(F)$ *iff $S \in \mathtt{ad}(F)$ and $\forall a \in \mathcal{A}$ s.t. S defends a, $a \in S$;*
4. $S \in \mathtt{gr}(F)$ *iff S is $\subseteq$-minimal in $\mathtt{co}(F)$; and*
5. $S \in \mathtt{pr}(F)$ *iff S is $\subseteq$-maximal in $\mathtt{ad}(F)$.*

Given a set of arguments S and semantics σ[1], we say that (the *verification status* of) S is *σ-true* (resp., *-false*) iff $S \in \sigma(F)$ (resp., $S \notin \sigma(F)$).

Now we recall the notion of IAF expanding AF with qualitative uncertainty.

Definition 2 (Incomplete Argumentation Framework). *[6] An incomplete argumentation framework (IAF) is a quadruple $\langle \mathcal{A}, \mathcal{A}^?, \mathcal{R}, \mathcal{R}^? \rangle$ where $\mathcal{A}$ and $\mathcal{A}^?$ are disjoint sets of arguments, and $\mathcal{R}$ and $\mathcal{R}^?$ are disjoint subsets of $(\mathcal{A} \cup \mathcal{A}^?) \times (\mathcal{A} \cup \mathcal{A}^?)$. $\mathcal{A}$ (resp., $\mathcal{R}$) represents arguments (resp., attacks) that are known to certainly exist, while $\mathcal{A}^?$ (resp., $\mathcal{R}^?$) contains additional arguments (resp., attacks) whose existence is yet uncertain. An IAF is called an AtIAF if it has no uncertain arguments.*

The *partial completions* [14] of an IAF I represent the possible IAFs that I can be specified to be, i.e., by remaining the certain parts and deciding some of the uncertain elements to be existent or not.

Definition 3 (Partial completion). *[14] Given an IAF $I = \langle \mathcal{A}, \mathcal{A}^?, \mathcal{R}, \mathcal{R}^? \rangle$, a partial completion is an IAF $I' = \langle \mathcal{A}', \mathcal{A}^{?'}, \mathcal{R}', \mathcal{R}^{?'} \rangle$, where $\mathcal{A} \subseteq \mathcal{A}' \subseteq \mathcal{A} \cup \mathcal{A}^?$, $\mathcal{R} \cap (\mathcal{A}' \cup \mathcal{A}^{?'}) \times (\mathcal{A}' \cup \mathcal{A}^{?'}) \subseteq \mathcal{R}' \subseteq \mathcal{R} \cup \mathcal{R}^?$, $\mathcal{A}^{?'} \subseteq \mathcal{A}^?$, and $\mathcal{R}^{?'} \subseteq \mathcal{R}^?$.*

We use $part(I)$ to denote the set containing all of the partial completions of I, and $cert(I) = \langle \mathcal{A}, \mathcal{R} \cap (\mathcal{A} \times \mathcal{A}) \rangle$ to denote the AF projected on the certain parts of

[1] In this paper we limit the semantics discussed to the five common semantics in Definition 1, and unless specifically stated otherwise the given semantics σ in context ranges over {ad, st, co, gr, pr}.

I. By partial completion, the notion of *completion* [6] can be alternatively defined as that an AF F is a completion of an IAF I iff $\exists I' \in part(I), F = cert(I')$.

Given an IAF $I = \langle \mathcal{A}, \mathcal{A}^?, \mathcal{R}, \mathcal{R}^? \rangle$ and a set of arguments $S \subseteq \mathcal{A} \cup \mathcal{A}^?$, similarly to notations for AF, we give the following notations:

- $S_I^+ = \{a \in \mathcal{A} \cup \mathcal{A}^? \mid \exists b \in S, (b, a) \in \mathcal{R}\}$;
- $S_I^- = \{a \in \mathcal{A} \cup \mathcal{A}^? \mid \exists b \in S, (a, b) \in \mathcal{R}\}$; and
- $S_I^\sim = \{a \in \mathcal{A} \cup \mathcal{A}^? \mid \forall b \in S, (b, a) \notin \mathcal{R} \cup \mathcal{R}^?\}$.

Further, in order to describe the changing of the IAF I concisely, given a set of uncertain attacks $\mathcal{R}_0 \subseteq \mathcal{R}^?$ or a set of uncertain arguments $\mathcal{A}_0 \subseteq \mathcal{A}^?$, let:

- $I + \mathcal{R}_0 = \langle \mathcal{A}, \mathcal{A}^?, \mathcal{R} \cup \mathcal{R}_0, \mathcal{R}^? \setminus \mathcal{R}_0 \rangle$, $I - \mathcal{R}_0 = \langle \mathcal{A}, \mathcal{A}^?, \mathcal{R}, \mathcal{R}^? \setminus \mathcal{R}_0 \rangle$; and
- $I + \mathcal{A}_0 = \langle \mathcal{A} \cup \mathcal{A}_0, \mathcal{A}^? \setminus \mathcal{A}_0, \mathcal{R}, \mathcal{R}^? \rangle$, $I - \mathcal{A}_0 = \langle \mathcal{A}, \mathcal{A}^? \setminus \mathcal{A}_0, \mathcal{R} \setminus \mathcal{R}', \mathcal{R}^? \setminus \mathcal{R}' \rangle$, where $\mathcal{R}' = \{(a, b) \in \mathcal{R} \cup \mathcal{R}^? \mid a \in \mathcal{A}_0 \text{ or } b \in \mathcal{A}_0\}$.

Now we introduce the notion of stability of verification of a set of arguments.

Definition 4 (Stability of verification). *[18] Given an IAF $I = \langle \mathcal{A}, \mathcal{A}^?, \mathcal{R}, \mathcal{R}^? \rangle$, a set of arguments $S \subseteq \mathcal{A} \cup \mathcal{A}^?$, semantics σ and a verification status $j \in \sigma \times \{true, false\}$, S is stable-j w.r.t. I iff S is j in every completion of I. We say that S is stable-σ w.r.t. I iff S is stable-σ-true or stable-σ-false w.r.t. I.*

The notions of *relevance* and *strong relevance* [17] respectively characterize which uncertainty is possible or necessary to be resolved to reach stability. An action (addition or removal) of an uncertain element e is said to be j-relevant for S if there is an unstable partial completion where e is the unique uncertain element and conducting the action on e can make S become j. And if conducting the opposite action makes S impossible to become stable-j, we say that the action of e is strongly j-relevant, i.e., it must be taken to reach j-stability of S.

Definition 5 (Relevance and strong relevance for verification). *[18] Given an IAF $I = \langle \mathcal{A}, \mathcal{A}^?, \mathcal{R}, \mathcal{R}^? \rangle$, a set of arguments $S \subseteq \mathcal{A} \cup \mathcal{A}^?$, a verification status j, and an uncertain element $e \in \mathcal{A}^? \cup \mathcal{R}^?$,*

- *addition (resp., removal) of e is j-relevant for S w.r.t. I, iff there exists an IAF $I' = \langle \mathcal{A}', \mathcal{A}^{?'}, \mathcal{R}', \mathcal{R}^{?'} \rangle \in part(I)$ s.t. $\mathcal{A}^{?'} \cup \mathcal{R}^{?'} = \{e\}$, and S is j in $cert(I' + \{e\})$ (resp., $cert(I' - \{e\})$) while S is not j in $cert(I' - \{e\})$ (resp., $cert(I' + \{e\})$);*
- *addition (resp., removal) of e is strongly j-relevant for S w.r.t. I, iff addition (resp., removal) of e is j-relevant for S w.r.t. I, and for each $I' \in part(I - \{e\})$ (resp., $part(I + \{e\})$), S is not stable-j w.r.t. I'.*

We use $RE^+(I, S, j)$ (resp., $RE^-(I, S, j)$) to denote the set containing all elements whose addition (resp., removal) is j-relevant for S w.r.t. I, and $SRE^+(I, S, j)$ (resp., $SRE^-(I, S, j)$) to denote the set containing all elements whose addition (resp., removal) is strongly j-relevant for S w.r.t. I.

Note that the addition and removal are dual actions in terms of relevance, that is, given semantics σ, $RE^{+}(I, S, \sigma\text{-}true) = RE^{-}(I, S, \sigma\text{-}false)$ and $RE^{-}(I, S, \sigma\text{-}true) = RE^{+}(I, S, \sigma\text{-}false)$ always hold. This says that for any uncertain element e, the -*true* relevance of its addition or removal coincides with the -*false* relevance of the opposite action. Hence, the whole elements with relevant actions for -*true* and -*false* stability essentially coincide. To characterize the relevance of an element e which can be an argument or attack, we say that e is σ-relevant for S w.r.t. I if $e \in RE^{+}(I, S, \sigma\text{-}true) \cup RE^{-}(I, S, \sigma\text{-}true)$, and use $RE(I, S, \sigma)$ to represent all the σ-relevant elements. And if $e \notin RE(I, S, \sigma)$, we say that e is σ-*irrelevant* for S w.r.t. I.

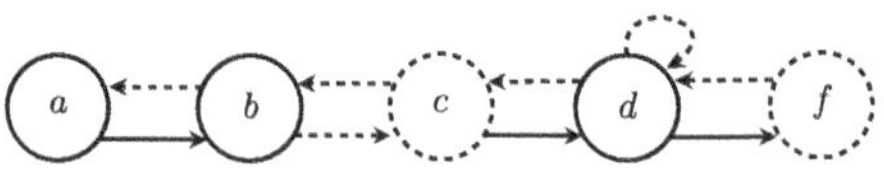

Fig. 1. An example IAF I_{ex} (uncertain arguments and attacks are depicted using dashed circles and lines, respectively)

Example 1. Consider the IAF I_{ex} in Fig. 1 and the set of arguments $S = \{b\}$. S is not stable-co w.r.t. I , since $S \in \mathsf{co}(cert(I_{ex} + \{(b, a), (d, d)\}))$ while $S \notin \mathsf{co}(cert(I_{ex} - \{(b, a)\}))$. One can see that $RE^{+}(I_{ex}, S, \mathsf{co}\text{-}true) = \{(b, a), (b, c), (d, c), (d, d), (f, d), c, f\}$ and $RE^{-}(I_{ex}, S, \mathsf{co}\text{-}true) = \{(b, c), (c, b), c\}$. In addition, $SRE^{+}(I_{ex}, S, \mathsf{co}\text{-}true) = \{(b, a)\}$ and $SRE^{-}(I_{ex}, S, \mathsf{co}\text{-}true) = \emptyset$.

3 The Impact-Based Method for Resolving Uncertainty

In this section, we give the impact-based method for resolving uncertainty to reach stability of verification of a set of arguments. Before doing that, we first give the theoretical foundations.

We start with a proposition formally showing that there is no need to resolve the uncertainty of irrelevant elements, since an uncertain element e being irrelevant is equivalent to that for every partial completion where the stability is reached, no matter what the decision of e is, the stability remains without the resolution of e. On the other hand, it is necessary to resolve the uncertainty of strongly relevant elements since if addition (resp., removal) of e is strongly relevant, then e must be present (resp., absent) in every stable partial completion.

Proposition 1. *Given an IAF $I = \langle \mathcal{A}, \mathcal{A}^{?}, \mathcal{R}, \mathcal{R}^{?} \rangle$, a set of arguments $S \subseteq \mathcal{A} \cup \mathcal{A}^{?}$, semantics σ, a verification status $j \in \sigma \times \{true, false\}$ and an uncertain element $e \in \mathcal{A}^{?} \cup \mathcal{R}^{?}$, the following results hold:*

1. *$e \notin RE(I, S, \sigma)$ iff $\forall I' \in part(I)$ s.t. S is stable-j w.r.t. I', $\forall I'' \in part(I)$ s.t. $I' = I'' + \{e\}$ or $I' = I'' - \{e\}$, S is stable-j w.r.t. I''; and*

2. *if* $e \in SRE^+(I,S,j)$ *(resp.,* $SRE^-(I,S,j)$*), then* $\forall I' = \langle \mathcal{A}', \mathcal{A}^{?'}, \mathcal{R}', \mathcal{R}^{?'} \rangle \in part(I)$ *s.t. S is stable-j w.r.t.* I', $e \in \mathcal{A}' \cup \mathcal{R}'$ *(resp.,* $e \notin \mathcal{A}' \cup \mathcal{A}^{?'} \cup \mathcal{R}' \cup \mathcal{R}^{?'}$*).*

In [18], we concluded that S being stable-σ is equivalent to that all the uncertain elements become σ-irrelevant, giving an alternative view of the stable status of verification of a set of arguments in IAFs.

Proposition 2. *[18] Given an IAF* $I = \langle \mathcal{A}, \mathcal{A}^?, \mathcal{R}, \mathcal{R}^? \rangle$*, a set of arguments* $S \subseteq \mathcal{A} \cup \mathcal{A}^?$ *and semantics* σ*, S is stable-*σ *w.r.t. I iff* $\forall e \in \mathcal{A}^? \cup \mathcal{R}^?$, $e \notin RE(I,S,\sigma)$.

Further, we observe that the set of relevant elements exhibits a monotonic decreasing property as uncertain elements are decided.

Proposition 3. *Given an IAF* $I = \langle \mathcal{A}, \mathcal{A}^?, \mathcal{R}, \mathcal{R}^? \rangle$*, a set of arguments* $S \subseteq \mathcal{A} \cup \mathcal{A}^?$*, semantics* σ *and a verification status* $j \in \sigma \times \{true, false\}$, $\forall I' \in part(I)$, $RE^+(I',S,j) \subseteq RE^+(I,S,j)$ *and* $RE^-(I',S,j) \subseteq RE^-(I,S,j)$.

In other words, along with uncertainty being resolved, it is impossible for the previously irrelevant elements to become relevant. On the other hand, the decision of some uncertain element may lead to other relevant elements becoming irrelevant. According to Proposition 1, 2 and 3, the process of resolving uncertainty to reach stability of verification can be conducted by firstly deciding all of the strongly relevant elements and then choosing a relevant element to decide, which could make other relevant elements irrelevant, until there are no relevant elements left in the current IAF.

In order to characterize the influence of the decision of an uncertain element e that could make others irrelevant, we define the notion of *σ-impact* as follows.

Definition 6 (Impact). *Given an IAF* $I = \langle \mathcal{A}, \mathcal{A}^?, \mathcal{R}, \mathcal{R}^? \rangle$*, a set of arguments* $S \subseteq \mathcal{A} \cup \mathcal{A}^?$*, semantics* σ*, an element* $e \in \mathcal{A}^? \cup \mathcal{R}^?$ *and an element* $e' \in RE(I,S,\sigma)$*, addition (resp., removal) of e has σ-impact on* e' *for S w.r.t. I iff* $e' \notin RE(I + \{e\}, S, \sigma)$ *(resp.,* $e' \notin RE(I - \{e\}, S, \sigma)$*). And let*
$impact^+(I,S,\sigma,e) = RE(I,S,\sigma) \setminus RE(I + \{e\}, S, \sigma)$*; and*
$impact^-(I,S,\sigma,e) = RE(I,S,\sigma) \setminus RE(I - \{e\}, S, \sigma)$.

Example 2. Continue with the IAF I_{ex} in Fig. 1 and $S = \{b\}$. After (b,c) is decided to be present, $(c,b), (d,c)$ and c turn to be co-irrelevant. We can see that $impact^+(I_{ex}, S, \mathsf{co}, (b,c)) = impact^-(I_{ex}, S, \mathsf{co}, c) = \{(b,c),(c,b),(d,c),c\}$, while $impact^+(I_{ex}, S, \mathsf{co}, (d,d)) = \{(d,d),(f,d),f\}$.

According to the definition of relevance, it can be derived that addition and removal of e cannot have impact on the same relevant element simultaneously. And, irrelevant elements have no impact on any relevant elements, which justifies that the resolution of irrelevant elements is useless for reaching stability, since deciding them cannot reduce any relevant elements. Further, if addition or removal of e is strongly relevant, despite the necessity of conducting the action for stability, it has no impact on any relevant elements except e itself.

Proposition 4. *Given an IAF* $I = \langle \mathcal{A}, \mathcal{A}^?, \mathcal{R}, \mathcal{R}^? \rangle$*, a set of arguments* $S \subseteq \mathcal{A} \cup \mathcal{A}^?$*, semantics* σ *and an element* $e \in \mathcal{A}^? \cup \mathcal{R}^?$*, the following results hold:*

1. $impact^+(I, S, \sigma, e) \cap impact^-(I, S, \sigma, e) = \emptyset$;
2. if $e \notin RE(I, S, \sigma)$, then $impact^+(I, S, \sigma, e) \cup impact^-(I, S, \sigma, e) = \emptyset$; and
3. for a verification status $j \in \sigma \times \{true, false\}$, if $e \in SRE^+(I, S, j)$ (resp., $SRE^-(I, S, j)$), then $impact^+(I, S, \sigma, e) = \{e\}$ (resp., $impact^-(I, S, \sigma, e) = \{e\}$).

Algorithm 1: Impact-based method for reaching stability

Input: An IAF $I = \langle \mathcal{A}, \mathcal{A}^?, \mathcal{R}, \mathcal{R}^? \rangle$, a set of arguments $S \subseteq \mathcal{A} \cup \mathcal{A}^?$, semantics σ and a verification status $j \in \sigma \times \{true, false\}$.

1 **while** *S is not stable-σ w.r.t. I* **do**
2 $\quad I \leftarrow (I + SRE^+(I, S, j) \cap \mathcal{A}^?) - SRE^-(I, S, j) \cap \mathcal{A}^?$
3 $\quad I \leftarrow (I + SRE^+(I, S, j) \cap \mathcal{R}^?) - SRE^-(I, S, j) \cap \mathcal{R}^?$
4 $\quad \Omega \leftarrow \{\langle \alpha, e \rangle \mid \alpha \in \{+, -\}, e \in RE^\alpha(I, S, j)\}$
5 $\quad$ choose $\langle \alpha, e \rangle$ from Ω s.t. $|impact^\alpha(I, S, \sigma)|$ is maximal in Ω
6 $\quad$ **if** *α is +* **then**
7 $\quad\quad I \leftarrow I + \{e\}$
8 $\quad$ **else**
9 $\quad\quad I \leftarrow I - \{e\}$
10
11 **end**
12 **return** I

Now we present the impact-based method in Algorithm 1 for resolving uncertainty to reach stability of verification of a set of arguments S in an IAF I. The main idea is to iteratively decide strongly relevant elements and then conduct the relevant action of an element which makes the most relevant elements irrelevant until S becomes stable. In each iteration in Algorithm 1, after performing the strongly relevant actions (lines 2–3), we identify all the relevant elements and compute the impact of their addition or removal, and perform the action that has the largest impact (lines 4–9). Since each iteration in Algorithm 1 performs a relevant action, in the end the stability is reached in the output IAF which is a partial completion of the input I, formally shown in the following proposition.

Proposition 5. *Given an IAF $I = \langle \mathcal{A}, \mathcal{A}^?, \mathcal{R}, \mathcal{R}^? \rangle$, a set of arguments $S \subseteq \mathcal{A} \cup \mathcal{A}^?$, semantics σ and a verification status $j \in \sigma \times \{true, false\}$ s.t. S is not stable-σ w.r.t. I, for the IAF I' output by Algorithm 1 with I, S, σ and j as input, S is stable-j w.r.t. I'.*

Example 3. Let us start Algorithm 1 with I_{ex} in Fig. 1, the set of arguments $S = \{b\}$, co semantics and co-*true* status as input. The execution of the algorithm is illustrated in Fig. 2. In Iteration 1, after adding the strongly relevant element (b, a), computing the impact shows that the addition of (b, c) has co-impact on $(c, b), (d, c), c$ besides itself, which is the largest impact, hence (b, c) is added. In

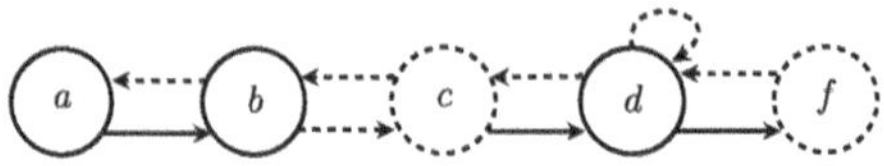

Iteration 1: $SRE^+ : (b,a);\ SRE^- : \emptyset$
$RE^+ : (b,c)[(c,b),(d,c),c],(d,d)[(f,d),f],(b,a),(d,c),(f,d),f;$
$RE^- : c[(b,c),(c,b),(d,c)],(c,b)$

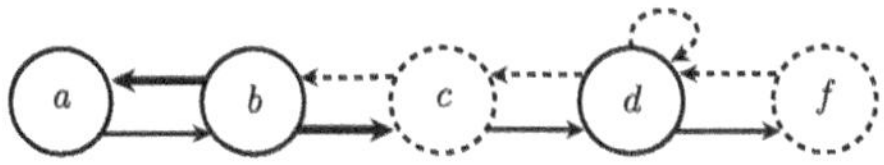

Iteration 2: $SRE^+ : \emptyset;\ SRE^- : \emptyset$
$RE^+ : (d,d)[(f,d),f],(f,d),f;\ RE^- : \emptyset$

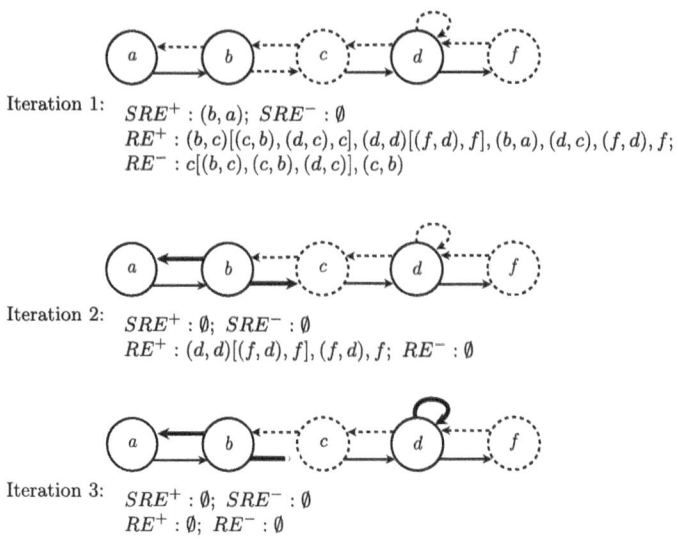

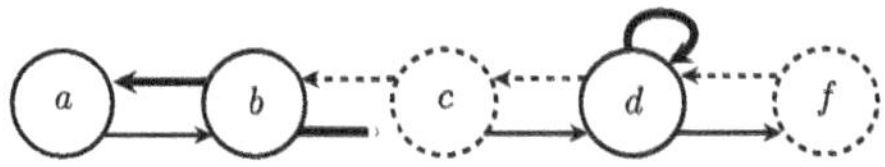

Iteration 3: $SRE^+ : \emptyset;\ SRE^- : \emptyset$
$RE^+ : \emptyset;\ RE^- : \emptyset$

Fig. 2. The execution of Algorithm 1 with I_{ex}, $\{b\}$, co and co-*true* as input. *The bracket following element e contains the elements on which e has* co*-impact except itself, and the bold arrows are the attacks added in the previous iteration.*

Iteration 2, there are no strongly relevant elements, and the addition of (d,d) is chosen and conducted, which has co-impact on the most relevant elements including (f,d) and f. Now the algorithm comes to Iteration 3 when there are no relevant elements in the current IAF, thus S becomes stable-co-*true*. One can see that although there are eight relevant elements at the beginning, our algorithm only has to decide three relevant elements to reach stability.

4 Effective Ways for Computing the Impact

In each iteration in Algorithm 1, computing the impact of every relevant element dominates the computational cost, where obtaining the impact of an action of one relevant element e requires identifying relevance again for each relevant element in the new IAFs where e is modified. In this section, we give results that can help optimize the impact computation. Specifically, under ad and st semantics, we will give ways to directly characterize the impact without depending on Definition 6. We will show that for -*true* stability under these two semantics, the IAF output by Algorithm 1 requires the minimal resolution of uncertain elements.

Firstly, following [13], we reduce an IAF to an AtIAF (recall that an AtIAF is an IAF without uncertain arguments by Definition 2) by introducing a new argument that issues uncertain attacks to the original uncertain arguments, and then making all the uncertain arguments to be existent.

Definition 7 (AtIAF-Transformation). *[13] Given an IAF $I = \langle \mathcal{A}, \mathcal{A}^?, \mathcal{R}, \mathcal{R}^? \rangle$, the AtIAF transformed from I is $I_{at} = \langle \mathcal{A} \cup \mathcal{A}^? \cup \{w\}, \emptyset, \mathcal{R}, \mathcal{R}^? \cup \{(w, a) \mid a \in \mathcal{A}^?\} \rangle$. And the mapping function $\psi_I : \mathcal{R}^? \cup \mathcal{A}^? \rightarrow \mathcal{R}^? \cup \{(w, a) \mid a \in \mathcal{A}^?\}$ is defined as: $\psi_I(e) = e$ if $e \in \mathcal{R}^?$, otherwise $\psi_I(e) = (w, e)$.*

One can see that ψ_I is a bijective function representing that the uncertainty of each uncertain argument a in I is replaced by the uncertainty of attack (w, a) in I_{at} whereas the uncertainty of attacks in I remains.

Through the transformation, the problem of recognizing the impact in IAFs can be reduced to the problem in AtIAFs, formally shown as follows.

Proposition 6. *Given an IAF $I = \langle \mathcal{A}, \mathcal{A}^?, \mathcal{R}, \mathcal{R}^? \rangle$, a set of arguments $S \subseteq \mathcal{A} \cup \mathcal{A}^?$, semantics σ, and two uncertain elements $e, e' \in \mathcal{A}^? \cup \mathcal{R}^?$, let I_{at} be the AtIAF transformed from I by Definition 7. The following results hold:*

1. *$e \in impact^+(I, S, \sigma, e')$ iff $\psi_I(e) \in impact^+(I_{at}, S \cup \{w\}, \sigma, \psi_I(e'))$ if $e' \in \mathcal{R}^?$, otherwise $\psi_I(e) \in impact^-(I_{at}, S \cup \{w\}, \sigma, \psi_I(e'))$; and*
2. *$e \in impact^-(I, S, \sigma, e')$ iff $\psi_I(e) \in impact^-(I_{at}, S \cup \{w\}, \sigma, \psi_I(e'))$ if $e' \in \mathcal{R}^?$, otherwise $\psi_I(e) \in impact^+(I_{at}, S \cup \{w\}, \sigma, \psi_I(e'))$.*

Proposition 6 specifies that solving the impact problem of an IAF can be done at its transformed AtIAF, and then the results are used reversely as solutions for the original IAF. Subsequently we limit our discussion to AtIAFs, where effective strategies for computing impact based on AtIAFs are given. Note that despite that the proposition gives a reduction to a specific AtIAF with a new argument not attacked by others, the results we will present are about general AtIAFs.

Secondly, we introduce an *equivalent* relation between two uncertain attacks, characterizing that the two attacks behave in the same way concerning the relevance of stability of S. For instance, given an uncertain attack (a, b) such that $a \notin S$ and $b \in S$, all the uncertain attacks from a to S are equivalent to (a, b), as they all represent the uncertainty about a being an attacker of S.

Definition 8. (Equivalence). *Given an AtIAF $I = \langle \mathcal{A}, \emptyset, \mathcal{R}, \mathcal{R}^? \rangle$, a set of arguments $S \subseteq \mathcal{A}$ and two attacks $(a_1, b_1) \neq (a_2, b_2) \in \mathcal{R} \cup \mathcal{R}^?$, (a_1, b_1) and (a_2, b_2) are equivalent for S w.r.t. I, denoted as $(a_1, b_1) \cong_I^S (a_2, b_2)$, iff*

1. *$a_1 = a_2 \notin S$ and $b_1, b_2 \in S$; or*
2. *$a_1, a_2 \in S$ and $b_1 = b_2 \notin S$.*

Given an uncertain $r \in \mathcal{R}^?$, let $\varphi_I^S(r) = \{r' \in \mathcal{R}^? \mid r' \cong_I^S r\} \cup \{r\}$, which contains r itself and all of the uncertain attacks equivalent to r for S w.r.t. I.

Obviously this equivalent relation satisfies symmetry and transitivity, hence it can be used to derive different equivalent classes of uncertain attacks for S, where each class contains all the attacks which are equivalent while the attacks in different classes are not. The following proposition tells that under all the common semantics except **gr**, every two equivalent attacks for the given S share the same relevance and have the same impact on other attacks besides their equivalent attacks. Further, addition of an attack with equivalent attacks can lead to all of its equivalent ones becoming irrelevant while removal of such an attack has no impact on any attacks.

Proposition 7. *Given an AtIAF* $I = \langle \mathcal{A}, \emptyset, \mathcal{R}, \mathcal{R}^? \rangle$*, a set of arguments* $S \subseteq \mathcal{A}$*, semantics* $\sigma \in \{\mathtt{ad}, \mathtt{st}, \mathtt{co}, \mathtt{pr}\}$*, a verification status* $j \in \sigma \times \{true, false\}$*, and two uncertain attacks* $r_1 \neq r_2 \in \mathcal{R}^?$ *such that* $r_1 \cong_I^S r_2$*,*

1. $r_1 \in RE^+(I, S, j)$ *iff* $r_2 \in RE^+(I, S, j)$*, and* $r_1 \in RE^-(I, S, j)$ *iff* $r_2 \in RE^-(I, S, j)$*;*
2. $\varphi_I^S(r_1) \subseteq impact^+(I, S, \sigma, r_1) = impact^+(I, S, \sigma, r_2)$ *if* $r_1 \in RE(I, S, \sigma)$*; and*
3. $impact^-(I, S, \sigma, r_1) \setminus \{r_1\} = impact^-(I, S, \sigma, r_2) \setminus \{r_2\} = \emptyset$*.*

Consequently, in order to decide the relevance and impact of those within a class of equivalent attacks, we just need to pick one to identify its relevance and compute its impact on other attacks except its equivalent attacks. The reason why such a property does not hold for gr is that the semantics requires *strong admissibility* [2,7], which means that the accepted set S can be constructed from an initial set of arguments which are not attacked by others, and then repeatedly merging the arguments defended by the current set until there are no arguments that can be merged. This makes the equivalent attacks behave differently in terms of relevance of stability of S.

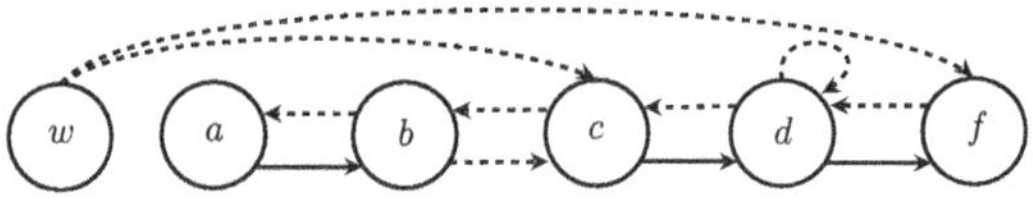

Fig. 3. The AtIAF I_{at} transformed from I_{ex} by Definition 7

Example 4. The AtIAF I_{at} in Fig. 3 is transformed from I_{ex} in Fig. 1 by Definition 7. From considering $S = \{b\}$ for I_{ex}, we consider $S' = \{b, w\}$ for I_{at} instead, and one can see that $(b, c) \cong_{I_{at}}^{S'} (w, c)$ and $impact^+(I_{at}, S', \mathtt{co}, (b, c)) \setminus \varphi_{I_{at}}^{S'}((b, c)) = \{(c, b), (d, c)\}$. Therefore, $impact^+(I_{ex}, S, \mathtt{co}, (b, c)) = impact^-(I_{ex}, S, \mathtt{co}, c) = \{(b, c), (c, b), (d, c), c\}$ according to Proposition 6 and 7.

Thirdly, using Proposition 7, we find ways to directly compute the impact and bypass identifying relevance under ad and st semantics in AtIAFs. Given a relevant attack $r = (a, b)$, note that if r is within S, i.e., $a, b \in S$, then it is trivial that adding r yields the $false$-stability and has impact on all the relevant attacks since all the common semantics satisfy conflict-freeness, whereas removing r has no impact on other attacks except itself.

For ad semantics, recall that in [18] we concluded that for any relevant attack $r = (a, b)$ not within S, either the attacker a or the target b is included in S. If

$a \in S$, its addition means that S certainly attacks b, which leads to all the attacks from b towards S irrelevant, as well as all its equivalent attacks by Proposition 7, whereas its removal has no impact on other attacks unless b certainly attacks S and r is the unique uncertain attack from S towards b. On the other hand, if $b \in S$, then its addition has no impact on others except its equivalent attacks unless a is impossible to be attacked by S, whereas its removal will lead to a not attacking S anymore when (a, b) is the unique attack from a to S, which leads to attacks that are used to defend S from a irrelevant.

Proposition 8. *Given an AtIAF $I = \langle \mathcal{A}, \emptyset, \mathcal{R}, \mathcal{R}^? \rangle$ and a set of arguments $S \subseteq \mathcal{A}$, for each attack $r = (a, b) \in RE(I, S, \texttt{ad})$,*

1. *if $a \in S$ and $b \notin S$, $impact^+(I, S, \texttt{ad}, r) = \{(b, s) \in RE(I, S, \texttt{ad}) \mid s \in S\} \cup \varphi_I^S(r)$; $impact^-(I, S, \texttt{ad}, r) = RE(I, S, \texttt{ad})$ if $b \in S_I^-$ and $|\varphi_I^S(r)| = 1$, otherwise $impact^-(I, S, \texttt{ad}, r) = \{r\}$; and*
2. *if $a \notin S$ and $b \in S$, $impact^+(I, S, \texttt{ad}, r) = RE(I, S, \texttt{ad})$ if $a \in S_I^\sim$, otherwise $impact^+(I, S, \texttt{ad}, r) = \varphi_I^S(r)$; $impact^-(I, S, \texttt{ad}, r) = \{(s, a) \in \mathcal{R}^? \mid s \in S\}$ if $|\varphi_I^S(r)| = 1$, otherwise $impact^-(I, S, \texttt{ad}, r) = \{r\}$.*

For st semantics, the relevant attacks not within S only contain those from S towards the arguments not included in S which are not attacked by S. We can see that for an attack $r = (a, b)$ where $a \in S$ and $b \notin S_I^+$, its addition cannot decide whether S attacks any other arguments except b, hence it has no impact on other attacks except its equivalent attacks. And its removal has no impact on other attacks unless r is the unique attack from S towards b.

Proposition 9. *Given an AtIAF $I = \langle \mathcal{A}, \emptyset, \mathcal{R}, \mathcal{R}^? \rangle$ and a set of arguments $S \subseteq \mathcal{A}$, for each attack $r \in RE(I, S, \texttt{st})$, $impact^+(I, S, \texttt{st}, r) = \varphi_I^S(r)$; $impact^-(I, S, \texttt{st}, r) = RE(I, S, \texttt{st})$ if $|\varphi_I^S(r)| = 1$, otherwise $impact^-(I, S, \texttt{st}, r) = \{r\}$.*

Fourthly, based on the above results, we further find that for *-true* stability under ad and st, the IAF obtained through Algorithm 1 actually becomes the stable partial completion that costs the least uncertainty resolution. Before proposing the formal result, we give a way for counting the number of actions required from an IAF to one of its partial completions.

Proposition 10. *Given an IAF $I = \langle \mathcal{A}, \mathcal{A}^?, \mathcal{R}, \mathcal{R}^? \rangle$, for any $I' \in part(I)$, I' can be represented as $I' = (((I + \mathcal{A}_1) - \mathcal{A}_2) + \mathcal{R}_1) - \mathcal{R}_2$ where $\mathcal{A}_1, \mathcal{A}_2 \subseteq \mathcal{A}^?$, $\mathcal{R}_1, \mathcal{R}_2 \subseteq \mathcal{R}^?$, and the four sets are unique in this regard. We use $numOfAct(I', I) = |\mathcal{A}_1 \cup \mathcal{A}_2 \cup \mathcal{R}_1 \cup \mathcal{R}_2|$ to denote the number of actions required to get I' from I.*

Note that such a representation of I' actually specifies that actions are taken in the order of addition of arguments, removal of arguments, addition of attacks and lastly removal of attacks. And, $\mathcal{A}_1 \cap \mathcal{A}_2 = \emptyset$, $\mathcal{R}_1 \cap \mathcal{R}_2 = \emptyset$, and attacks in $\mathcal{R}_1 \cup \mathcal{R}_2$ are not related to the arguments in $\mathcal{A}_2$ since those arguments are removed already and all of their related attacks are removed automatically. Hence removing one argument along with its related uncertain attacks is counted as one action in this way. The following proposition formally shows that the IAF output by Algorithm 1 always requires the minimal number of actions in all of the stable partial completions under ad and st semantics for *-true* stability.

Proposition 11. *Given an IAF $I = \langle \mathcal{A}, \mathcal{A}^?, \mathcal{R}, \mathcal{R}^? \rangle$, a set of arguments $S \subseteq \mathcal{A} \cup \mathcal{A}^?$, semantics $\sigma \in \{\mathtt{ad}, \mathtt{st}\}$, and a verification status $j = \sigma$-true satisfying that there is a completion C of I such that S is j in C, for the IAF I' output by Algorithm 1 with I, S, σ and j as input, $\forall I'' \in part(I)$ s.t. S is stable-j w.r.t. I'', $numOfAct(I', I) \leq numOfAct(I'', I)$.*

5 Related Works

Besides stability for verification studied in [6,11], the stability problem also concerns acceptance of an argument [5,12,14], which studies whether a given argument holds the same acceptance status in all completions of an IAF. Also focusing on a single argument, *functionality* studied in [1] presents a more strictly acceptable status, which specifies whether an argument can be firmly decided in every completion. In addition, in our previous work [17], we study the stability of semantics which characterizes whether every completion of a given IAF holds the same extensions, and similarly in [15], the stability of existence of nonempty extension is discussed. The relevance problem is firstly proposed in [14] for stability of acceptance problem, and then be extended to verification problem in our recent work [18]. One can see that the notion of impact proposed in this paper can be applied to these various kinds of stability problems.

Changing an argumentation setting to obtain a desired result about verification is also studied as *enforcement* [3] and *removal* [4] problem in dynamic AFs, which respectively study how to modify an AF to make a desired set of arguments S to become an extension or make S fail to be an extension. The two problems respectively correspond to reaching *-true* or *-false* stability in the IAF settings in our study. Specifically, the *minimal general strict enforcement* problem studied in [9,16] asks how to minimally modify the attacks of an AF to make S to become an extension. Focusing on the IAF settings, in this paper we study how to resolve fewer uncertain elements to make S to become an extension in all completions. The reduction method based on *MaxSAT* problem provided in [16] may help identify the precise complexity of finding stable partial completions with the minimal number of actions under $\mathtt{co}, \mathtt{gr}$ and $\mathtt{pr}$ semantics, which will be explored in our future work.

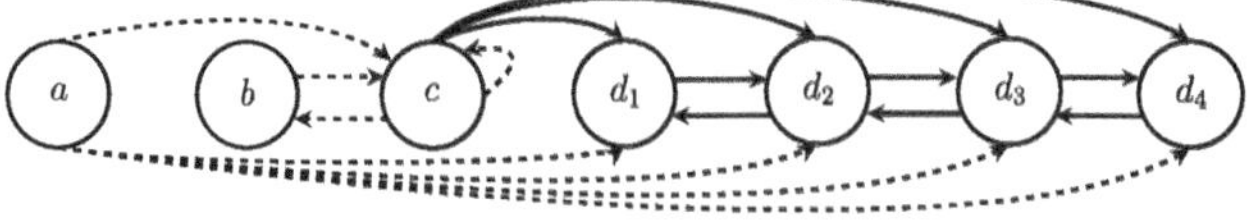

Fig. 4. An example IAF I'_{ex}

6 Discussion and Conclusions

One can see that the algorithmic complexity of Algorithm 1 depends on the complexity of (strong) relevance problem. For `ad`, `st` and `co` semantics, in [18] we found tractable methods to decide the related (strong) relevance problems, hence the complexity of Algorithm 1 under these three semantics is polynomial. However for `gr` and `pr` semantics, deciding relevance becomes intractable and it is worth exploring approximate ways for computing impact. Moreover, for both -*true* and -*false* stability under `co`, `gr` and `pr` semantics, as well as -*false* stability for `ad` and `st` semantics, Algorithm 1 does not guarantee to find the stable partial completion with the minimal number of actions. For example, let us consider the IAF I'_{ex} in Fig. 4 and the set of arguments $S = \{a, b\}$. For verification status $j \in \{\mathtt{co}, \mathtt{gr}, \mathtt{pr}\} \times true$, adding (a, c) has `co`-impact on the most relevant elements including $(b, c), (c, b)$ and (c, c), and the IAF output by the Algorithm 1 is $I_1 = I'_{ex} + \{(a, c), (a, d_1), (a, d_2), (a, d_3), (a, d_4)\}$ and $numOfAct(I_1, I'_{ex}) = 5$. However, S is also stable-j w.r.t. $I_2 = I'_{ex} + \{(c, c)\} - \{(a, c), (b, c), (c, b)\}$, whereas $numOfAct(I_2, I'_{ex}) = 4 < numOfAct(I_1, I'_{ex})$. The reason why our method does not find the optimal solution is that in each iteration we just consider the impact of a single action rather than all possible combinations of actions. For example, removing each one of $(a, c), (b, c), (c, b)$ or adding (c, c) has no impact on other elements so each of these actions does not get selected in the first iteration of Algorithm 1, but doing all of them can lead to the σ-*true*-stability, i.e., has impact on all of the other relevant elements. Nevertheless, computing the impact of all possible combinations of actions is obviously complex, and we also need to consider the compatibility of the combined actions. Continue with I'_{ex} as an example. Although adding (b, c), adding (a, d_1) and removing (a, d_2) are all `co`-*true*-relevant, taking the three actions simultaneously will result in that `co`-*true* stability can never be reached. Exploring the impact of a combination of multiple actions shall be within our future works.

Our study is a theoretical exploration of relevance and impact for stability of verification, and the results can be used in scenarios like agent negotiation. Consider a negotiation setting where each agent holds an AF derived from its own believes and opinions. An IAF can be obtained by merging different AFs of agents [6,8] (i.e., if an element is present in some AFs whereas absent in others, the element becomes uncertain). When all agents reach a consensus that some arguments must be collectively accepted or rejected, the merged IAF shall resolve some uncertain elements so that the stability of interest occurs. Such resolutions when reflected back mean that the agents have to change their original AFs by changing their belief. Our method can decide the uncertain elements as fewer as possible, hence help agents reduce their belief changes for reaching the consensus.

As a first attempt for IAFs, this paper explores the questions of how to reach stability of interest by deciding uncertain elements as fewer as possible, specifically focusing on the stability of a set of arguments. We propose the notion of impact and give an impact-based stability reaching method, along with effective ways for computing impact. Our method is shown to be able to find the optimal solution for -*true* stability under `ad` and `st` semantics. For future work, we will conduct comparison experiments to explore how much our method could save actions over the baseline approach that randomly selects an action on line 5 of Algorithm 1. Meanwhile, we will explore the impact of a group of elements as well as the complexity of finding the optimal solution under co, gr and pr. It is also necessary to design approximate methods for computing impact for gr and pr semantics, under which identifying relevance is intractable.

References

1. Alfano, G., Greco, S., Parisi, F., Trubitsyna, I.: Incomplete argumentation frameworks: properties and complexity. In: AAAI Conference on Artificial Intelligence, AAAI 2022, vol. 36, pp. 5451–5460 (2022)
2. Baroni, P., Giacomin, M.: On principle-based evaluation of extension-based argumentation semantics. Artif. Intell. **171**(10–15), 675–700 (2007)
3. Baumann, R., Brewka, G.: Expanding argumentation frameworks: enforcing and monotonicity results. In: Computational Models of Argument, COMMA 2010, pp. 75–86 (2010)
4. Baumann, R., Brewka, G.: Extension removal in abstract argumentation–an axiomatic approach. In: AAAI Conference on Artificial Intelligence, AAAI 2019, vol. 33, pp. 2670–2677 (2019)
5. Baumeister, D., Järvisalo, M., Neugebauer, D., Niskanen, A., Rothe, J.: Acceptance in incomplete argumentation frameworks. Artif. Intell. **295**, 103470 (2021)
6. Baumeister, D., Neugebauer, D., Rothe, J., Schadrack, H.: Verification in incomplete argumentation frameworks. Artif. Intell. **264**, 1–26 (2018)
7. Caminada, M., Dunne, P.: Strong admissibility revisited: theory and applications. Argum. Comput. **10**(3), 277–300 (2020)
8. Coste-Marquis, S., Devred, C., Konieczny, S., Lagasquie-Schiex, M.C., Marquis, P.: On the merging of Dung's argumentation systems. Artif. Intell. **171**, 730–753 (2007)
9. Coste-Marquis, S., Konieczny, S., Mailly, J.G., Marquis, P.: Extension enforcement in abstract argumentation as an optimization problem. In: Twenty-Fourth International Joint Conference on Artificial Intelligence, IJCAI 2015, pp. 2876–2882 (2015)
10. Dung, P.M.: On the acceptability of arguments and its fundamental role in nonmonotonic reasoning, logic programming and n-person games. Artif. Intell. **77**(2), 321–357 (1995)
11. Fazzinga, B., Flesca, S., Furfaro, F.: Revisiting the notion of extension over incomplete abstract argumentation frameworks. In: Twenty-Ninth International Joint Conference on Artificial Intelligence, IJCAI 2020, pp. 1712–1718 (2020)
12. Mailly, J.G., Rossit, J.: Stability in abstract argumentation. In: NMR 2020 Workshop Notes, pp. 93–99 (2020)
13. Mantadelis, T., Bistarelli, S.: Probabilistic abstract argumentation frameworks, a possible world view. Int. J. Approximate Reasoning **119**, 204–219 (2020)
14. Odekerken, D., Borg, A., Bex, F.: Justification, stability and relevance in incomplete argumentation frameworks. Argum. Comput. **15**(3), 251–308 (2024)
15. Skiba, K., Neugebauer, D., Rothe, J.: Complexity of nonempty existence problems in incomplete argumentation frameworks. IEEE Intell. Syst. **36**(2), 13–24 (2020)
16. Wallner, J.P., Niskanen, A., Järvisalo, M.: Complexity results and algorithms for extension enforcement in abstract argumentation. J. Artif. Intell. Res. **60**, 1–40 (2017)

17. Xiong, A., Zhang, H., Zhang, S.: Stability of extensions in incomplete argumentation frameworks. In: International Conference on Scalable Uncertainty Management, SUM 2024, pp. 470–485. Springer (2024)
18. Xiong, A., Zhang, S.: Relevance for stability of verification status of a set of arguments in incomplete argumentation frameworks. In: International Conference on Logic and Argumentation, CLAR 2025, pp. 343–360. Springer (2025)

Logic and Inconsistency

Privacy-Preserving Inconsistency Measurement

Carl Corea[1(✉)], Timotheus Kampik[2], and Nico Potyka[3]

[1] University of Koblenz, Koblenz, Germany
ccorea@uni-koblenz.de
[2] Umeå University, Sweden, SAP, Germany
tkampik@cs.umu.se
[3] Cardiff University, Cardiff, UK
PotykaN@cardiff.ac.uk

Abstract. We investigate a new form of (privacy-preserving) inconsistency measurement for multi-party communication. Intuitively, for two knowledge bases K_A, K_B (of two agents A, B), our results allow to quantitatively assess the degree of inconsistency for $K_A \cup K_B$ without having to reveal the actual contents of the knowledge bases. Using secure multi-party computation (SMPC) and cryptographic protocols, we develop two concrete methods for this use-case and show that they satisfy important properties of SMPC protocols—notably, *input privacy*, i.e., jointly computing the inconsistency degree without revealing the inputs.

1 Introduction

In multi-agent systems, agents may have to cooperate without being allowed to share their internal knowledge with each other. For example, revealing internal knowledge or beliefs of an agent may violate (external) privacy requirements, or agents are both cooperating and competing and do not want to reveal knowledge that may give others a competitive advantage.

In our work, we consider multi-agent systems where the agents carry internal knowledge or beliefs in form of propositional logic knowledge bases (KBs), and assume agents may not be allowed to reveal the contents (i.e., formulas) of their KBs to each other. Still, in order to assess the ability to cooperate, it may be necessary for the agents to verify whether, or to what extent, the knowledge bases are *consistent* with each other. Consider the following simplified example from the financial domain:

Example 1. Consider two agents A and B, with (own) propositional logic KBs K_A and K_B (with agents having knowledge on credit applications, and customers can have different statuses, creditworthiness, or be on a ban list), with:

$$K_A = \{\neg(\mathit{banList} \wedge \mathit{creditWorthy})\}$$
$$K_B = \{\mathit{platinumStatus};\ \mathit{platinumStatus} \rightarrow \mathit{creditWorthy};\ \mathit{banList}\}$$

K. Sauerwald and M. Thimm (Eds.): ECSQARU 2025, LNAI 16099, pp. 455–469, 2026.
https://doi.org/10.1007/978-3-032-05134-9_31

Clearly, $K_A \cup K_B$ is inconsistent (we will define inconsistency later), and knowing this may be crucial for the agents. But as stated, we assume A and B do not want to reveal the formulas in their KBs. To solve this issue, we present a novel approach for, what we call, *privacy-preserving inconsistency measurement.* The core idea is that we build on cryptographic protocols from the field of secure multi-party computation, which allow multiple agents to jointly compute a function $f(K_A, K_B)$ without revealing K_A and K_B. Here, we propose algorithms to compute (as f) different *inconsistency measures* [12] for $K_A \cup K_B$.

Our results allow the agents—in a privacy-preserving way—to know i) whether their knowledge is *consistent*, and ii) to what *degree* their knowledge disagrees (e.g., wrt. an inconsistency degree, the KBs may still be *sufficiently consistent* s.t. the alignment may be "good enough" for collaborating). Here, our contributions are as follows:

- We present a novel approach for privacy-preserving inconsistency measurement; specifically, for two KBs K_A, K_B, we show how to compute two specific inconsistency measures for $K_A \cup K_B$ without revealing K_A, K_B (Sect. 3). To this aim, we show how private set intersections of sets of KB interpretations can be computed to measure various aspects of (in)consistency.
- We evaluate the developed methods by showing important privacy- and runtime complexity properties (Sect. 4).

We discuss preliminaries in Sect. 2 and conclude in Sect. 5.

2 Preliminaries

2.1 Knowledge Bases, Inconsistency Measurement

In this work, we consider agents carrying internal knowledge in form of propositional logic knowledge bases. For this, let At be some fixed propositional signature and let $\mathcal{L}(\mathsf{At})$ be the corresponding propositional language constructed using the connectives $\wedge$, $\vee$, and $\neg$.

Definition 1. *A knowledge base K is a finite set of formulas $K \subset \mathcal{L}(\mathsf{At})$.*

For a set of formulas X, we denote the set of contained propositions as $\mathsf{At}(X)$. An interpretation ω on At is a function $\omega : \mathsf{At} \to \{0, 1\}$ (where 0 stands for false and 1 stands for true). Let $\Omega(\mathsf{At})$ denote the set of all interpretations for At. An interpretation ω *satisfies* (or is a *model* of) an atom $a \in \mathsf{At}$, denoted by $\omega \models a$, iff $\omega(a) = 1$. The satisfaction relation $\models$ is extended to formulas in the usual way. For $\Phi \subseteq \mathcal{L}(\mathsf{At})$ we also define $\omega \models \Phi$ if and only if $\omega \models \phi$ for every $\phi \in \Phi$. For a set of formulas X, the set of models is $\mathsf{Mod}(X) = \{\omega \in \Omega(\mathsf{At}) \mid \omega \models X\}$. If $\mathsf{Mod}(X) = \emptyset$ we write $X \models \perp$ and say that X is *inconsistent.*

An inconsistency *measure* $\mathcal{I}$ is a function that assigns a non-negative numerical value to a knowledge base. The concrete behaviour of inconsistency measures is driven by rationality postulates. In this work, we assume inconsistency measures $\mathcal{I}$ satisfy the basic property of *consistency* (for a KB K):

Consistency CO $\mathcal{I}(K) = 0$ iff $K \not\models \perp$

Numerous inconsistency measures have been proposed (see [12] for a survey). In this work, we consider the *drastic* inconsistency measure $\mathcal{I}_d$ [6] and the *contension* inconsistency measure $\mathcal{I}_c$ [5], which we define below. In order to define the contension measure we need some additional background on three-valued logic [9]. A three-valued interpretation is a function $\nu : \mathsf{At} \rightarrow \{0, 1, \mathsf{both}\}$, which assigns to every atom either 0, 1 or both, where 0 and 1 correspond to *false* and *true*, respectively, and both denotes a conflict. Assuming the *truth order* $\prec_T$ with $0 \prec_T \mathsf{both} \prec_T 1$, the function ν can be extended to arbitrary formulas as follows: $\nu(\alpha \wedge \beta) = \min_{\prec_T}(\nu(\alpha), \nu(\beta))$, $\nu(\alpha \vee \beta) = \max_{\prec_T}(\nu(\alpha), \nu(\beta))$, $\nu(\neg\alpha) = 1$ if $\nu(\alpha) = 0$, $\nu(\neg\alpha) = 0$ if $\nu(\alpha) = 1$, and $\nu(\neg\alpha) = \mathsf{both}$ if $\nu(\alpha) = \mathsf{both}$. We say an interpretation ν satisfies a formula α, denoted by $\nu \models^3 \alpha$, iff $\nu(\alpha) = 1$ or $\nu(\alpha) = \mathsf{both}$. We are now ready to define the considered inconsistency measures.

Definition 2 (Considered Inconsistency Measures). *Given a knowledge base* K*, define* $\mathcal{I}_d, \mathcal{I}_c$ *via:*

$$\mathcal{I}_d(K) = \begin{cases} 1 & \text{if } K \models \perp \\ 0 & \text{otherwise} \end{cases} \qquad \mathcal{I}_c(K) = \min\{|\nu^{-1}(\mathsf{both})| \mid \nu \models^3 K\}$$

Example 2. Consider $K_1 = \{a; a \rightarrow b; \neg b \wedge \neg a; c\}$, then we have that $\mathcal{I}_d(K_1) = 1$ and $\mathcal{I}_c(K_1) = 2$. (for $\mathcal{I}_c$, note that the three-valued interpretation ν_1 with $\nu_1(a) = \mathsf{both}$; $\nu_1(b) = \mathsf{both}$; $\nu_1(c) = 1$ is the only three-valued model that assigns both to a minimal number of atoms).

In this work—for two knowledge bases K_A, K_B of parties A, B, respectively—we compute $\mathcal{I}_d(K_A \cup K_B)$ and an upper-bound for $\mathcal{I}_c(K_A \cup K_B)$, without A and B having to reveal the contents of their knowledge bases to each other. To allude to some of our results, this will be achieved by comparing the *models* for the individual knowledge bases (also in a privacy-preserving way). For example, we can exploit that $\mathsf{Mod}(K_1) \cap \mathsf{Mod}(K_2) = \emptyset$ iff $K_1 \cup K_2 \models \perp$, which allows to verify consistency without revealing formulas. Intuitively, the interpretations should also not be revealed, which we will show how to handle. In the following subsections, we discuss important notions and methods from a security perspective.

2.2 Cryptographic Techniques

In this work, we consider (asymmetric) encryption schemes, or cryptosystems, that can securely encode and decode messages with algorithmic techniques.

Definition 3 (Cryptosystem, [11]). *Let* $\mathcal{M}$ *be a set of messages, called a* message space, *and let* $\rho \in \mathbb{N}$ *be a* security parameter. *Then, an encryption scheme is a tuple* $(\boldsymbol{K}, \boldsymbol{E}, \boldsymbol{D})$*, where*

- $\boldsymbol{K}$ *is a (key generation) function that takes the security parameter* ρ *and returns a key pair* (k_e, k_d) *for encryption/decryption, with* $k_e \in \mathcal{K}_e, k_d \in \mathcal{K}_d$ *(with* $\mathcal{K}_e, \mathcal{K}_d$ *being key spaces).*

- $\boldsymbol{E}$ *is an (encryption) function* $\boldsymbol{E}: \mathcal{K}_e \times \mathcal{M} \rightarrow \mathcal{C}$ *that returns a ciphertext for a plaintext* m*, where* $\mathcal{C}$ *is a ciphertext space.*
- $\boldsymbol{D}$ *is a (decryption) function* $\boldsymbol{D}: \mathcal{K}_d \times \mathcal{C} \rightarrow \mathcal{M}$ *that takes a ciphertext and outputs a plaintext* m*, s.t. if* $c = \boldsymbol{E}(k_e, m)$ *then* Probability$[\boldsymbol{D}(k_d, c) \neq m]$ *is negligible, i.e.,* Probability$[\boldsymbol{D}(k_d, c) \neq m] \leq 2^{-\rho}$.

We consider encryption functions that are probabilistic, i.e., $\mathbf{E}$ can return different ciphertexts even for two equal inputs (on the other hand, $\mathbf{D}$ is deterministic) [11]. To clarify, given two plaintexts $m_1 = m_2 = 1$ and a key pair k_e, k_d produced by the encryption scheme, we have that *Probability*$[\mathbf{E}(k_e, m_1) = \mathbf{E}(k_e, m_2)] \leq 2^{-\rho}$, but $\mathbf{D}(k_d, \mathbf{E}(k_e, m_1)) = \mathbf{D}(k_d, \mathbf{E}(k_e, m_2))$. This is also referred to as the encryption scheme being IND-CPA secure (ciphertext indistinguishability under chosen plaintext attacks) [3]. We use $\mathbf{E}(k_e, m_1) \equiv \mathbf{E}(k_e, m_2)$ to denote that two ciphertexts carry "semantically" the same value, even though the ciphertexts are not identical.

For the technical development of our techniques, we assume two communicating parties, where both parties act via a *honest-but-curious* adversarial model [3], i.e., parties do not deviate from the protocol but may try to infer additional information from t!+he data they obtain. We comment on the effects of a party taking on other adversarial models in Sect. 4.

2.3 Secure Multi-party Computation

An important cryptographic field we build on is that of secure multi-party computation (SMPC) [3]. The goal of SMPC approaches is to allow multiple parties $P_1, ..., P_n$ to compute a function f over their (respective) inputs $x_1, ..., x_n$, without revealing the inputs to the other parties. Any protocol performing this computation should satisfy the following properties:

Input Privacy (IP) Inputs should not be revealed during computation.
Correctness (Cor) The revealed output is the actual result of $f(x_1, ..., x_n)$.

We use the term "privacy-preserving" to denote that a computation satisfies IP.

To develop privacy-preserving inconsistency measurement techniques, we will devise protocols that can compute (various aspects of) intersections of sets of knowledge base models while satisfying IP, Cor. This type of protocol is referred to as private set intersection (PSI) (cf. Sect. 2.5). PSI protocols build on so-called homomorphic encryption schemes, which we introduce next.

2.4 Homomorphic Encryption

Homomorphic encryption [13] is a cryptographic method that allows certain mathematical operations to be performed directly on encrypted data. Specifically, we consider *fully homomorphic* encryption schemes [4], which allow addition and multiplications of numerical values while remaining encrypted.

Definition 4 (Homomorphic encryption scheme, [11]). *Let $\mathcal{M}$ be a message space, and let ρ be a security parameter. Then, a homomorphic encryption scheme is a quadruple $(\boldsymbol{K}, \boldsymbol{E}, \boldsymbol{D}, \circ)$ as follows:*

- *$\boldsymbol{K}, \boldsymbol{E}, \boldsymbol{D}$ are key-generation-, encryption- and decryption functions as before.*
- *$\circ$ is an operator for which it holds that for all messages $m_1, m_2 \in \mathcal{M}$: if $m_3 = m_1 \circ m_2$, and $c_1 = \boldsymbol{E}(k_e, m_1)$, and $c_2 = \boldsymbol{E}(k_e, m_2)$, then* Probability$[\boldsymbol{D}(k_d, c_1 \circ c_2) \neq m_3]$ *is negligible.*

In other words, a homomorphic encryption scheme is an encryption scheme with the property that the operation $\circ$ is correctly preserved when performing it on the encrypted ciphertexts themselves.

In the following, we assume encryption schemes that are fully homomorphic (i.e., where $\circ$ can be either addition $(+)$ or multiplication $(\times)$), s.t. for all $m_1, m_2 \in \mathcal{M}, k_e \in \mathcal{K}_e$ we have (cf. [13]):

$$\mathbf{E}(k_e, m_1) + \mathbf{E}(k_e, m_2) \equiv \mathbf{E}(k_e, m_1 + m_2), \quad m_1 + \mathbf{E}(k_e, m_2) \equiv \mathbf{E}(k_e, m_1 + m_2),$$
$$\mathbf{E}(k_e, m_1) \times \mathbf{E}(k_e, m_2) \equiv \mathbf{E}(k_e, m_1 \times m_2), \quad m_1 \times \mathbf{E}(k_e, m_2) \equiv \mathbf{E}(k_e, m_1 \times m_2).$$

Example 3. Let a key pair k_e, k_d produced by a fully homomorphic encryption scheme. For $m = 5$ and $c = \mathbf{E}(k_e, m) + 2$, we have $\mathbf{D}(k_d, c) = 7$.

Remark 1. We make the standard assumption that the size of the ciphertexts remains polynomially bounded (cf. the property of circuit-privacy in [1]). This ensures that the ciphertext obtained by performing an operation $\circ$ on two inputs is hard to distinguish from a ciphertext obtained by encrypting a plaintext m.

This extends to vectors via element-wise operations. A survey of fully homomorphic encryption schemes can be found in [13].

2.5 Private Set Intersection

PSI protocols [7] are subtypes of SMPC that allow to compute the intersection of two sets without revealing the rest of the sets. There are many applications for PSI, for example, finding (only) the common friends in the contact lists of two parties without disclosing the full contact lists to each other. As an example, consider the following baseline PSI protocol.

Example 4. Let two parties A, B each with a set containing exactly one integer, respectively, x and y. To compute PSI, A employs a fully homomorphic encryption scheme to generate a key pair k_e, k_d and sends $\mathbf{E}(k_e, x)$ to B. Then, B computes $c = r * (\mathbf{E}(k_e, x) - y)$ (which is a ciphertext, cf. Remark 1), where r is a random nonzero integer chosen by B. A now computes $\mathbf{D}(k_d, c)$: If the result is 0, x and y are identical, otherwise, $\{x\} \cup \{y\} = \emptyset$. In the latter case, A cannot infer any information about y (as r is chosen by B). In any case, B cannot infer anything about x (beyond the guarantees of the encryption scheme) as B only obtains ciphertext. The protocol can be performed symmetrically.

In this work, we consider versions of PSI protocols where only the size of the intersection is revealed. As we will show, inconsistency can then be characterized with various aspects of intersection sizes for sets of interpretations.

3 Approaches for Privacy-Preserving Inconsistency Measurement

For the remainder, we fix two parties A, B with respective knowledge bases K_A, K_B. Also, we fix a fully homomorphic encryption scheme $(\mathbf{K}, \mathbf{E}, \mathbf{D}, \circ)$ and a corresponding key-pair k_e, k_d. The goal of this section is then two-fold: first, we develop an SMPC protocol allowing to compute $\mathcal{I}_d(K_A \cup K_B)$; then, to allow for a more gradual measure, we develop an SMPC protocol allowing to compute an upper-bound for $\mathcal{I}_c(K_A \cup K_B)$ (both protocol satisfying IP and Cor). For the remainder, we assume the KBs K_A, K_B on their own are consistent (and the task is to assess the consistency of $K_A \cup K_B$).

From IP, it is immediate that no formulas must be revealed for the computations. Instead, in our protocols, the parties will exchange their respective models; as discussed, consistency can then be verified by checking whether $\mathsf{Mod}(K_A) \cap \mathsf{Mod}(K_B) \neq \emptyset$. An important remark here is that the interpretations/models should not be revealed in plain form. Otherwise, it would be possible to disjunctively write each interpretation as a conjunction of atoms, which would yield a formula in disjunctive normal form that is equivalent to the KB. Thus, we introduce PSI-based protocols that allow to *privately* compute the intersection of $\mathsf{Mod}(K_A)$ and $\mathsf{Mod}(K_B)$. For this, we need some further notation.

For any interpretation ω over At, we will encode ω as a bit sequence of 1s and 0s, which indicates the truth value of the atoms in alphabetical order.

Example 5. Let $\mathsf{At} = \{a, b, c\}$; then we write $\omega_1 = 101$ to encode $\omega_1(a) = 1$, and $\omega_1(b) = 0$, and $\omega_1(c) = 1$.

This encoding will be used in various encryption processes. For example, we can directly encrypt interpretations by encrypting the encoding—in the example, $\mathbf{E}(k_e, 101)$. A further remark is that this shorthand notation is useful for comparing interpretations via a bitwise comparison. For example, for two interpretations 11 and 10, a bitwise comparison 01 indicates that the first digit is identical and the second digit differs.

We are now ready to define a core protocol for comparing *two* interpretations. This core protocol will later be used in two subsequent protocols (for $\mathcal{I}_d, \mathcal{I}_c$).

3.1 General Protocol for Privacy-Preserving Comparison of (Two) Interpretations

Assume two parties A and B who each have one interpretation (ω_A, ω_B). For example, this interpretation could be derived from their knowledge bases under the closed-world assumption (if an atom is not entailed by the knowledge base, it is supposed to be false). Importantly, the two parties agree on a shared set of atoms At (needed to produce the encoding of the interpretations). We now want to verify if these interpretations are compatible. More precisely, Algorithm 1 specifies an SMPC protocol that takes as input two interpretations ω_A, ω_B and returns the number of atoms that they interpret differently. For the protocol, we recall the introduced encoding that allows to represent interpretations as binary numbers. For any binary number w, let $len(w)$ denote the number of digits of w, and w_i the ith bit of w.

Algorithm 1. (Alg1) Compute Number of Differing Truth Assignments Given Interpretations A, B

Input: Shared set of atoms At, Interpretations ω_A, ω_B (over At, in shorthand notation)
Output: Number of truth assignments differing between ω_A and ω_B
1: A generates key pair (k_e, k_d)
2: A generates a vector $v = \langle \omega_{A_1}, ..., \omega_{A_{len(\omega_A)}} \rangle$
3: A computes $v_{enc} = \langle \mathbf{E}(k_e, \omega_{A_1}), ..., \mathbf{E}(k_e \omega_{A_{len(\omega_A)}}) \rangle$
4: A sends v_{enc} to B
5: B generates a vector $v_B = \langle \omega_{B_1}, ..., \omega_{B_{len(\omega_B)}} \rangle$
6: B computes $v_{A \oplus B} = v_{enc} - v_B$ {"XOR" operation; B cannot read result}
7: B computes $n = \sum_{i=1}^{|v_{A \oplus B}|} (v_{A \oplus B}[i])^2$ {B cannot read result}
8: B sends n to A
9: A computes $n' = \mathbf{D}(k_d, n)$
10: **return** n'

Example 6. Assume two parties A, B with interpretations $\omega_A = 110$ and $\omega_B = 101$, respectively.

- A generates a key pair.
- A generates the vector $v = \langle 1, 1, 0 \rangle$, resp. $v_{enc} = \langle \mathbf{E}(k_e, 1), \mathbf{E}(k_e, 1), \mathbf{E}(k_e, 0) \rangle$.
- B generates the vector $v_B = \langle 1, 0, 1 \rangle$.
- B computes $v_{A \oplus B} = v_{enc} - v_B = \langle \mathbf{E}(k_e, 1) - 1, \mathbf{E}(k_e, 1) - 0, \mathbf{E}(k_e, 0) - 1 \rangle$ (note that each position is still a ciphertext that B cannot read).
- B computes $n = \sum_{i=1}^{|v_{A \oplus B}|} (v_{A \oplus B}[i])^2$ (sum of absolute values; result is a ciphertext).
- A receives n and returns $n' = \mathbf{D}(k_d, n) = 2$

In result, A can infer that ω_A, ω_B differ in two assignments, but, importantly, cannot infer at which assignments the interpretations differ. The protocol can be performed symmetrically to produce the result for B.

Theorem 1. *Algorithm 1 satisfies* IP, Cor.

Proof. The protocol adheres to IP *as no party learns anything beyond the Hamming distance, where the Hamming distance itself is the agreed-upon output (in particular, B works on ciphertexts only in line 6 and 7). The potential to infer complete input information in edge cases (e.g., output = 0 or* |At|*) is intrinsic to the meaning of the output and not an additional leakage under typical definitions. It is simply a characteristic of the output itself. For* Cor, *proceed by invariance: at each step, the algorithm accurately tracks the number of differing truth assignments between ω_A and ω_B. Initially, the vectors v and v_B represent the truth assignments of ω_A and ω_B, respectively. The XOR operation in $v_{A \oplus B}$ ensures* *that each entry reflects whether the corresponding truth assignments differ (1) or are identical (0), even under encryption. The summation step correctly accumulates the total number of differing assignments - squaring each $v_{A \oplus B}[i]$ does not change its value since $v_{A \oplus B}[i] \in \{0,1\}$. Finally, decryption reveals the correct count without altering the result. This invariant holds throughout the algorithm, ensuring its correctness.*

The presented core protocol allows to correctly compare the number of differing truth assignments for two interpretations, without revealing them. This core protocol will now be leveraged for computing further measures, specifically, by extending the protocol to take as input not only one interpretation, but two respective sets of interpretations/models by A and B.

3.2 Privacy-Preserving Computation of $\mathcal{I}_d$

We recall the definition of $\mathcal{I}_d$ and parties A, B with knowledge bases K_A, K_B. To compute $\mathcal{I}_d$, we build on the fact that $\mathsf{Mod}(K_A) \cap \mathsf{Mod}(K_B) = \emptyset$ iff $K_A \cup K_B \models \perp$. To leverage Algorithm 1 for computation, we create two bit sequences as follows: First, A, B agree on a shared set of atoms At. Then, both parties independently create a truth table showing satisfaction of their knowledge base, where the truth-assignments (rows) are in ascending binary order, ensuring equally ordered and exhaustive enumeration of all possible truth value combinations.

Example 7. Consider two agents A and B, each with their KBs K_A and K_B, respectively, with $K_A = \{a \wedge b\}$ and $K_B = \{\neg a\}$. Then, A and B construct the following truth tables:

A:

a	b	$\models K_A$
0	0	0
0	1	0
1	0	0
1	1	1

B:

a	b	$\models K_B$
0	0	1
0	1	1
1	0	0
1	1	0

Both parties then take the last column, which is a bit-sequence. In the example, we get the two sequences $S_A = 0001$ and $S_B = 1100$. It is important to note that (as the row index for both tables corresponds due to the ascending order), each index i over both sequences exactly encodes whether the ith assignment of truth values satisfies K_A, resp., K_B. We then leverage these sequences as input for Algorithm 1 to verify consistency. For this, we define a slight variation of Algorithm 1, denoted Algorithm 1^{binary}, where we change Lines 6 and 7 as follows: i) 6: B computes $v_{A \oplus B} = 1 - (v_{enc} * v_B)$; ii) 7: B computes $n = \prod_{i=1}^{|v_{A \oplus B}|} (v_{A \oplus B}[i])^2$.

This has the following impact on the algorithm output: For line 6, if the two multiplicants differ or are both 0 (corresponding to inconsistency or non-satisfaction), the entry computed in line 6 is 1 (indicating a distance). Otherwise, it is 0 (indicating correspondence and satisfaction). In result, if at least one row satisfies both knowledge bases, the result of Algorithm 1^{binary} is simply 0 (cf. line 7). If all rows differ, the returned value in this way is exactly 1, hiding the number of rows. This binary version of Algorithm 1 can be leveraged as follows.

Algorithm 2. (Alg2) Compute $\mathcal{I}_d(K_A \cup K_B)$

Input: Shared set of atoms At, knowledge bases K_A, K_B
Output: $\mathcal{I}_d(K_A \cup K_B)$
1: A, B create respective truth tables in ascending binary order (over At).
2: A, B obtain (via the last column) their private sequences S_A, S_B.
3: A, B compute $d =$ Algorithm 1^{binary} wrt. At, S_A, S_B
4: **return** d

Example 8. We recall the KBs and truth tables from Example 7, with the two sequences $S_A = 0001, S_B = 1100$ (this relates to lines 1–2 of Alg2). Then, Algorithm 1^{binary} is computed wrt. S_A, S_B and stored as d. Regarding that Algorithm, recall that if (the assignments) of at least one row match and satisfy both knowledge bases, $d = 0$, and $d = 1$ otherwise. In the example, indices 1,2,4 do not match, and, while the third index (i.e., the interpretation $\omega(a) = 1; \omega(b) = 0$) matches, this interpretation is not a model. In turn, the output is 1.

Theorem 2. *Algorithm 2 satisfies IP, Cor.*

Proof. The protocol adheres to IP as no party learns anything beyond a binary assessment of consistency, where the assessment itself is the agreed-upon output. Cor is established by maintaining an invariant: At each step, the algorithm correctly tracks whether there exists at least one model that satsifies both knowledge bases. In line one, both parties create sequences encoding satisfaction, where each index is in the same order and corresponds to the same truth value assignment(s). In line 6, for every such index, Algorithm 1^{binary} returns 0, if the values are both 1, and 1, otherwise. Then via multiplication, if there exists at least one 0, the product is also 0. This ensures that the algorithm will return 0 if there is at least one interpretation satisfying both K_A, K_B, and 1, otherwise.

3.3 Privacy-Preserving Approximation of $\mathcal{I}_c$

We continue with a gradual measure based on $\mathcal{I}_c$. For this, recall parties A, B with K_A, K_B. Then, consider Alg3, which works over *models* of K_A and K_B:

Algorithm 3. (Alg3) Compute Smallest Distinct Number of Mismatching Assignments for Any Pair in Two Sets of Models

Input: Shared set of atoms At, two sets of models: $\mathsf{Mod}(K_A)$, $\mathsf{Mod}(K_B)$
Output: Smallest number of different assignments over all combinations of models

```
A initializes an empty set S = {}
for all elementA ∈ Mod(K_A) do
    for all elementB ∈ Mod(K_B)) do
        Both A and B perform Algorithm 1 wrt. At, elementA, elementB.
        A stores the result in S
    end for
end for
return MIN(S)
```

Example 9. Assume two parties A,B (with K_A, K_B) and $\mathsf{Mod}(K_A) = \{111, 110\}$, $\mathsf{Mod}(K_B) = \{100, 101\}$.

–

Algorithm 3 will iterate over all combinations of models and yields: *Alg1* (111, 100) = 2; *Alg1* (111, 101) = 1; *Alg1* (110, 100) = 1; *Alg1* (110, 101) = 2.
– The returned result is MIN({1, 2}) = 1.

First, observe that the result of Example 9 can be interpreted s.t. no combination of models agree ($\mathsf{Mod}(K_A \cup K_B) = \emptyset$). We now show how the result of Algorithm 3 can be used to approximate the contension measure. The idea is that we use the results of Algorithm 3 to derive a set of *three-valued* interpretations $Mod_3(K_A \cup K_B)$ (to plug into $\mathcal{I}_c$). For this, the following will be useful.

Lemma 1. *Let F be a formula and let I be a three-valued interpretation that satisfies F. Let J be a three-valued interpretation obtained from I by changing the interpretation of a single atom to* both. *Then $I(F) = J(F)$ or $J(F) =$ both.*

Proof. We prove the claim by structural induction. We can assume w.l.o.g. that we change an atom that is contained in the formula F because changing the truth value of another atom cannot affect the interpretation by truth-functionality of the logical connectives.

For the base case, assume that F is an atom. If we change the interpretation of F to both, we have $J(F) =$ both.

Since all formulas can be expressed using only $\neg$ and $\wedge$, it is sufficient to consider these cases for the induction step.

Consider $F = \neg G$. If $I(\neg G) = 0$, then $I(G) = 1$ and by the induction assumption, we have $J(G) = 1$ or $J(G) =$ both. Thus, $J(\neg G) = 0 = I(\neg G)$ or $J(\neg G) =$ both. If $I(\neg G) = 1$, then $I(G) = 0$ and by the induction assumption, we have $J(G) = 0$ or $J(G) =$ both. Thus, $J(\neg G) = 1 = I(\neg G)$ or $J(\neg G) =$ both. If $I(\neg G) = B$, then $I(G) =$ both and by the induction assumption, we have $J(G) =$ both $= I(G)$.

Consider $F = G_1 \wedge G_2$. If $I(G_1 \wedge G_2) = 0$, then $I(G_1) = 0$ or $I(G_2) = 0$. Assume w.l.o.g. that $I(G_1) = 0$ (the case $I(G_2) = 0$ is analogous). By the induction assumption, $J(G_1) = 0$ or $J(G_1) =$ both. Hence, $J(G_1 \wedge G_2) = 0$ or $J(G_1 \wedge G_2) =$ both. If $I(G_1 \wedge G_2) = 1$, then $I(G_1) = 1$ and $I(G_2) = 1$. By the induction assumption, ($J(G_1) = 1$ or $J(G_1) =$ both) and ($J(G_2) = 1$ or $J(G_2) =$ both). Hence, $J(G_1 \wedge G_2) = 1$ or $J(G_1 \wedge G_2) =$ both. If $I(G_1 \wedge G_2) =$ both, then $I(G_1) =$ both or $I(G_2) =$ both. Assume w.l.o.g. that $I(G_1) =$ both (the case $I(G_2) =$ both is analogous). By the induction assumption, $J(G_1) =$ both. Hence, $J(G_1 \wedge G_2) =$ both.

Corollary 1. *Let I be a two-valued model of a knowledge base K and let J be a three-valued interpretation obtained from I by changing the interpretation of atoms to* both. *Then J is a three-valued model of K.*

Proof. For all formulas $F \in K$, we have $I(F) = 1$ by assumption. Note that two-valued interpretations are a special case of three-valued interpretations. When J changes the truth value of k atoms to both, it can be seen as a sequence $J_0, J_1, \ldots, J_k$ of three-valued models, $J_0 = I, J_k = J$ and J_i is obtained from J_{i-1}, $i = 1, \ldots, k$ by changing the interpretation of a single atom to both. Hence, Lemma 1 guarantees that $J_i(F) = 1$ or $J_i(F) = \mathsf{both}$ for all $i = 1, \ldots, k$. Hence, J satisfies K.

For two KBs K_1, K_2, we now use this result to define a function that can transform the two-valued interpretations $Mod(K_1), Mod(K_2)$ into a set of three-valued interpretations M_3 s.t. for every $m \in M_3 : m \models_3 K_1 \cup K_2$.

Definition 5. *Let two knowledge bases K_1, K_2 and let two interpretations i_1, i_2 over* At *s.t. $i_1 \models K_1$, $i_2 \models K_2$. Then, define a three-valued interpretation via the function $f(i_1, i_2)$, where*

$$f(i_1, i_2)(j) = \begin{cases} i_1(j), & \text{if } i_1(j) = i_2(j) \\ \mathsf{both}, & \text{otherwise} \end{cases}$$

Corollary 1 implies that a three-valued interpretation obtained via f is a three-valued model for $K_1 \cup K_2$. With a slight abuse of notation, we let:

$$f(Mod(K_1), Mod(K_2)) = \quad \{f(i_1, i_2) \mid i_1 \in Mod(K_1), i_2 \in Mod(K_2)\}.$$

We now show the relationship of Algorithm 3 to $\mathcal{I}_c$.

Proposition 1. *Let x be the inconcistency value computed by Algorithm 3. Then $x \geq \mathcal{I}_c(K_A \cup K_B)$.*

Proof. Corollary 1 guarantees that the 3-valued interpretations computed by Algorithm 3 are models of three-valued models of $K_A \cup K_B$. Since x is the minimal number of both found across these models, and $\mathcal{I}_c(K_A \cup K_B)$ is the minimal number across all models, we must have $x \geq \mathcal{I}_c(K_A \cup K_B)$.

However, Algorithm 3 can overestimate the inconsistency value.

Example 10. Let $K_A = \{a, a \rightarrow b_1 \wedge b_2\}$ and $K_B = \{a, a \rightarrow \neg b_1 \wedge \neg b_2\}$. Then $\mathsf{Mod}(K_A) = \{111\}$ and $\mathsf{Mod}(K_B) = \{100\}$. Hence, $f(\mathsf{Mod}(K_A), \mathsf{Mod}(K_B)) = \{1\mathsf{bothboth}\}$ and Algorithm 3 will return 2. However, both00, both01, both10, both11 are also three-valued models of $K_A \cup K_B$. Therefore $\mathcal{I}_c$ is 1.

While Algorithm 3 cannot compute the contension inconsistency value exactly, it will never underestimate the inconsistency (it gives an upper bound on the inconsistency value). Importantly, it will also never report a positive inconsistency value when the knowledge bases are, in fact, mutually consistent.

Proposition 2. *If $K_A \cup K_B$ is consistent, then Algorithm 3 will return 0.*

Proof. If $K_A \cup K_B$ is consistent, there must be an $i \in \mathsf{Mod}(K_A \cup K_B)$. Hence, Algorithm 3 will compute $f(i, i) = i$ and therefore return 0.

Let us note that Alg. 3 satisfies our privacy guarantee.

Theorem 3. *Algorithm 3 satisfies* IP.

Proof. The protocol adheres to IP *as no party learns the concrete models. A only learns the number of differing truth assignments but cannot map this to specific models.*

While Algorithm 3 satisfies IP, it reveals more than the output[1]: Clearly, a) B learns the number of models provided by A, and b) A learns all distinct differences in truth assignments over all model combinations. We therefore show a slight variation (Alg4) which allows to counteract this.

Algorithm 4. (Alg4) Compute Smallest Distinct Number of Mismatching Assignments for Any Pair in Two Sets of Models, Satisfying Con

---

Input: Shared set of atoms At, two sets of models: $\mathsf{Mod}(K_A)$, $\mathsf{Mod}(K_B)$
Output: Smallest number of different assignments over all combinations of models

1: A initializes $\mathsf{Mod}(K_A)$' as multiset of size $|2^{\mathsf{At}}|$, containing all and only elements of $\mathsf{Mod}(K_A)$
2: B initializes an empty list $S = <>$
3: **for all** elementA $\in \mathsf{Mod}(K_A)'$ **do**
4:     **for all** elementB $\in \mathsf{Mod}(K_B)$ **do**
5:         Both A and B perform **Algorithm 1** wrt. At, elementA, elementB.
6:         B stores the (encrypted) result in S
7:     **end for**
8: **end for**
9: B initializes an empty list $L = <>$
10: **for all** $i \in \{0, ..., |\mathsf{At}|\}$ **do**
11:     B computes $L_i \leftarrow \prod_{d \in S}(i - d)$
12: **end for**
13: **for all** $i \in \{0, ..., |\mathsf{At}|\}$ **do**
14:     B computes $p \leftarrow$ random prime number
15:     B computes $L_i \leftarrow (\prod_{0...i} L_i)^{p-1}$
16: **end for**
17: A decrypts L
18: **return** Index of the first element in L that is 0

In line 1, A creates a multiset with models of K_A of size $2^{|\mathsf{At}|}$ (possibly containing duplicates). This is a padding that ensures A does not reveal the number of models. Lines 2–8 are analogous to Alg3, using the padded multiset. Lines 9–12 are an encrypted computation by B. L is a list from 0 to $|\mathsf{At}|$, the possible range for $\mathcal{I}_c$. Then, we compute the distance between every L_i and all results in S: $i - d = 0$ must hold for at least one $d \in S$. We are only interested in the minimum of $0, ..., |\mathsf{At}|$ that is a match (lines 13–18), hence we obscure all left of the minimum by means of prime encryption and set all right of the

[1] This is also referred to as the SMPC properties of confidentiality (Con).

minimum to zero (numbers that are not zero are "meta-encrypted" and stay encrypted even after A decrypts the result). The smallest distinct number of mismatching assignments is the first index in L of an element that is 0. This solves the problems with Con exhibited in Alg3: i) B cannot know the number of A's models as A sends a padded multiset, ii) A does not learn all distinct differences in truth assignments over all combinations.

Example 11. Recall Example 9 with $\mathsf{Mod}(K_A) = \{111, 110\}$, $\mathsf{Mod}(K_B) = \{100, 101\}$. First, A will create a padded list of size $2^{|\mathsf{At}|}$, here: $\mathsf{Mod}(K_A)' = \{111, 110, 111, 110, 111, 110, 111, 110\}$. A and B perform lines 3–8 which yields a list of (encrypted) differences: Alg1 is performed for all (model, model)-tuples in $\mathsf{Mod}(K_A)' \times \mathsf{Mod}(_B)$, yielding the (encrypted) list $\{\mathbf{E}(k_e, 2), \mathbf{E}(k_e, 1), ...\}$. B then checks which of the potential distances in $\{0, 1, 2, 3\}$ exist in this list by executing lines 9–12, yielding the list $\langle 2, 0, 0, 2\rangle$ (again, encrypted). The multiplication of every element in the list with its predecessors and subsequent prime encryption (by B) in lines 13–14 results in the list $\langle \mathsf{enc}_p, 0, 0, 0\rangle$, where enc_p is the prime-encrypted 2. Finally, A decrypts the list. However, enc_p is useless (as it was meta-encrypted). A can only infer from $\langle \mathsf{enc}_p, 0, 0, 0\rangle$ that $\mathcal{I}_c = 1$ (index of the first 0).

While Alg4 comes with improvement wrt. Con, A has to create a padded multiset of exponential size. In the following we discuss this trade-off.

4 Discussion

We start by showing upper and lower bounds of runtime-complexity in Table 1.

Table 1. Runtime-complexity (upper ($\mathcal{O}$)/lower (Ω)) of the developed algorithms wrt. At; k = cost of key generation.

	$\mathcal{O}$	Ω
Algorithm 1	$\mathcal{O}(k + \|\mathsf{At}\|)$	$\Omega(k + \|\mathsf{At}\|)$
Algorithm 2	$\mathcal{O}(k + 2^{\|\mathsf{At}\|})$	$\Omega(k + 2^{\|\mathsf{At}\|})$
Algorithm 3	$\mathcal{O}(k + 2^{2^{\|\mathsf{At}\|}} * \|\mathsf{At}\|)$	$\Omega(k + \|\mathsf{At}\|)$
Algorithm 4	$\mathcal{O}(k + 2^{2^{\|\mathsf{At}\|}} * \|\mathsf{At}\|)$	$\Omega(k + 2^{\|\mathsf{At}\|} * \|\mathsf{At}\|)$

Proof.

- Alg.1: For $\mathcal{O}$, we proceed by line. Line 1 has cost k (see above). Line 2 and 3 perform constant operations over all $|\mathsf{At}|$ positions of the interpretation ($\mathcal{O}(|\mathsf{At}|)$). Line 4 is only part of the communication. Line 5 is analogous to line 2. Subtracting two vectors of length $|\mathsf{At}|$ (line 6) is $\mathcal{O}(|\mathsf{At}|)$. Note that $v_{A \oplus B}$ is also of size $|\mathsf{At}|$. Line 7 performs a constant operation over $|\mathsf{At}|$ positions. Line 8 is analogous to 4. Line 9 is constant. Thus we have $\mathcal{O}(k + 5 * |\mathsf{At}| + 1) = \mathcal{O}(k + |\mathsf{At}|)$. Ω is analogous

- Alg.2: Straightforward from Alg1 (Note that both parties construct a bit-sequence of length n, where n is $2^{|\mathsf{At}|}$).
- Alg.3: For $\mathcal{O}$ the outer loop iterates over all s models in $\mathsf{Mod}(K_A)$. The inner loop iterates over all t models in $\mathsf{Mod}(K_B)$. For each pair of models (each of length $|\mathsf{At}|$), Alg1 is called, which has a complexity of $\mathcal{O}(k + |\mathsf{At}|)$. For Ω in general the costs are $(k + s * t * |\mathsf{At}|)$ (assuming the key is only generated once), where k is the cost of generating the key pair. In the best case, both parties have 1 model each (recall the KBs are consistent per assumption). This relates to $\Omega(k + 1 * 1 * |\mathsf{At}|)$.
- Alg.4: For $\mathcal{O}$ lines 1–8 are analogous to Alg3 ($\mathcal{O}(k + 2^{2^{|\mathsf{At}|}} * |\mathsf{At}|)$). Note both parties could have up to $2^{|\mathsf{At}|}$ models, so S can have a size of $2^{|\mathsf{At}|}$. Line 9 is constant. Line 10 calls $|\mathsf{At}|$ times an operation that requires $2^{|\mathsf{At}|}$ subtractions. Lines 13–16 run $|\mathsf{At}|$ times. Line 17 is constant. So we have $\mathcal{O}(k + 2^{2^{|\mathsf{At}|}} * |\mathsf{At}| + 1 + |\mathsf{At}| * 2^{|\mathsf{At}|} + |\mathsf{At}|) = \mathcal{O}(k + 2^{2^{|\mathsf{At}|}} * |\mathsf{At}|)$. For Ω A pads to $2^{|\mathsf{At}|}$ models, so even if B has 1 model only, line 5 is called $2^{|\mathsf{At}|}$ times, where line 5's cost is $|\mathsf{At}|$. Lines 9–17 are anaologous to $\mathcal{O}$.

While Alg3 violates Con, it can approach polynomial scaling in best-cases. Alg4 retains its exponential component due to padding, trading off complexity and privacy requirements, depending on the use-case. Alg2 scales exponentially.

For the discussion of algorithms we have considered an *honest-but-curious* adversarial model. Threats in this setting are bounded by the compliance with IP. For adversarial models such as *malicious adversary* (participants may deviate from the protocol), the guarantees given by IP also hold. However, intuitively, such a threat model can affect the correctness of the results: A malicious adversary can deliberately provide altered models of his/her own knowledge base, e.g., flipping all bits (note that the ability of the adversary to manipulate ciphertexts is mitigated by IND-CPA security). Likewise, the adversary could provide models even if the KB is inconsistent. While preventing the adversary to provide fake models cannot be mitigated, various methods exist to prove the consistency of the own KB (without revealing it) via zero-knowledge proofs [2], which can be put before our algorithms if needed.

One should also be aware of risks by repeated queries. Given no restrictions wrt. the number of queries sent, A could reveal information about B's KB by altering the input for different queries. For this risk, it is important to consider what we actually reveal. Accordingly, we observe the worst-case probabilities with which one agent can successfully guess a model in another agents' KB.

Proposition 3 (Given without proof). *A can correctly guess a model in K_B with a probability of at least $\frac{1}{|\mathsf{Mod}(K_A)|}$ if K_A and K_B are consistent; if K_A and K_B are inconsistent, A can correctly guess with a probability of at least $\frac{1}{|\Omega(\mathsf{At})\setminus\mathsf{Mod}_{<\mathsf{Alg4}}|}$, where* $\mathsf{Mod}_{<\mathsf{Alg4}} := \{m | m \in \Omega(\mathsf{At}), \mathsf{Alg4}(\mathsf{Mod}(K_a), \{m\}) < \mathsf{Alg4}(\mathsf{Mod}(K_A), \mathsf{Mod}(K_B))\}$.

For both cases, A may straightforwardly reveal a formula equivalent to B's KB by measuring $g(\{m\}, \mathsf{Mod}(K_B))$ for all $m \in \Omega(\mathsf{At})$), where $g \in \{\mathsf{Alg2}, \mathsf{Alg3}, \mathsf{Alg4}\}$.

5 Conclusion

We have introduced novel methods for privacy-preserving inconsistency measurement. Leveraging SMPC and homomorphic encryption, the proposed algorithms enable agents to collaboratively evaluate the consistency of their KBs without revealing sensitive information. While the approach successfully implements input privacy, it also highlights trade-offs in runtime complexity and potential risks in adversarial settings. Overall, the framework advances the state of the art by enabling cooperative inconsistency measurement in privacy-critical settings. Future work can, e.g., focus on methods for privately computing interpolants/common knowledge or disagreement between more than two parties [8,10].

References

1. Armknecht, F., et al.: A guide to fully homomorphic encryption. Cryptology ePrint Archive (2015)
2. Bellare, M., Hoang, V.T., Rogaway, P.: Foundations of garbled circuits. In: Proceedings of the 2012 ACM Conference on Computer and Communications Security, pp. 784–796 (2012)
3. Cramer, R., et al.: Secure Multiparty Computation. Cambridge University Press (2015)
4. Gentry, C.: Fully homomorphic encryption using ideal lattices. In: Proceedings of the Forty-First Annual ACM Symposium on Theory of Computing, pp. 169–178 (2009)
5. Grant, J., Hunter, A.: Measuring consistency gain and information loss in stepwise inconsistency resolution. In: European Conference on Symbolic and Quantitative Approaches to Reasoning and Uncertainty, pp. 362–373. Springer (2011)
6. Hunter, A., Konieczny, S.: Measuring inconsistency through minimal inconsistent sets. KR **8**(358–366), 42 (2008)
7. Morales, D., Agudo, I., Lopez, J.: Private set intersection: a systematic literature review. Comput. Sci. Rev. **49**, 100567 (2023)
8. Potyka, N.: Measuring disagreement among knowledge bases. In: International Conference on Scalable Uncertainty Management, pp. 212–227. Springer (2018)
9. Priest, G.: The logic of paradox. J. Philos. Logic, 219–241 (1979)
10. Ribeiro, J.S., Sofronie-Stokkermans, V., Thimm, M.: Measuring disagreement with interpolants. In: Davis, J., Tabia, K. (eds.) SUM 2020. LNCS (LNAI), vol. 12322, pp. 84–97. Springer, Cham (2020). https://doi.org/10.1007/978-3-030-58449-8_6
11. Sen, J.: Homomorphic encryption-theory and application. Theory Pract. Cryptogr. Netw. Secur. Protoc. Technol. **31** (2013)
12. Thimm, M.: Inconsistency measurement. In: Ben Amor, N., Quost, B., Theobald, M. (eds.) SUM 2019. LNCS (LNAI), vol. 11940, pp. 9–23. Springer, Cham (2019). https://doi.org/10.1007/978-3-030-35514-2_2
13. Yi, X., Paulet, R., Bertino, E.: Homomorphic encryption. In: Homomorphic Encryption and Applications, pp. 27–46. Springer (2014)

Using Sentence Embeddings to Identify Conflicts in Propositional Logic

Anthony Hunter(✉)

Department of Computer Science, University College London, Gower Street, London, UK
anthony.hunter@ucl.ac.uk

Abstract. When using propositional logic, each atom is often associated with a sentence (a string of words) that gives the intended meaning of the atom, and so a propositional formula can be associated with a Boolean combination of these associated sentences. In this paper, we investigate the use of sentence embeddings to determine the similarity between pairs of sentences. Since different sentences can provide very similar information, we can enrich logical reasoning by treating atoms as "equal" when their associated sentences are very similar. We then use similarity between sentences to identify conflict. We can see some sets of formulae that are syntactically consistent, but via a similarity measure, are inconsistent. This means that we can use sentence embeddings to get a more intuitive understanding of conflict in real-world applications when a sentence is associated with each atom. We investigate notions of conflict based on this idea in this paper.

Keywords: Inconsistency · Conflict · Neuro-symbolic reasoning

1 Introduction

Different strings of words can convey the same information (e.g. *John is the father of Ann* and *John is Ann's dad*) or very similar information (e.g. *there will be a lot of showery weather today* and *today will be rainy*). This means that when we consider contradiction, a set of formulae may appear consistent, but if we then look at the associated string of words, they appear to be inconsistent. For example, if we associate $\mathtt{s}_1$ with *John is the father of Ann* and $\mathtt{s}_2$ with *John is Ann's dad*, then $\{\mathtt{s}_1, \neg\mathtt{s}_2\}$ is consistent in classical propositional logic, but when we look at their associated strings of words, the pair of formulae appear to contradict each other. So the aim of this paper is to provide tools with which to identify and analyse such implicit conflicts.

As a starting point for building these tools, we can harness a sentence embedding which gives a vector representation of a sentence, for example using Sentence BERT [17], PromptBERT [11], SKICSE [15], or Gemini Embeddings [12]. The similarity between a pair of sentences can then be calculated in terms of the similarity between their sentence embeddings [18]. See Table 1 for examples of similarity between sentences. We can then assume that two atoms can be treated as "equal" if the similarity between them is above a threshold. For example, according to Table 1, $\mathtt{s}_1$ and $\mathtt{s}_2$ is close to 1, and so if we treat them as equal, then we could for instance substitute $\mathtt{s}_1$ for $\mathtt{s}_2$, and thereby transform $\{\mathtt{s}_1, \neg\mathtt{s}_2\}$ into $\{\mathtt{s}_1, \neg\mathtt{s}_1\}$, and therefore obtain the contradiction.

K. Sauerwald and M. Thimm (Eds.): ECSQARU 2025, LNAI 16099, pp. 470–483, 2026.
https://doi.org/10.1007/978-3-032-05134-9_32

Table 1. Similarity between each pair of sentences (atoms) from $\mathtt{s}_1$ to $\mathtt{s}_4$ using the all-MiniLM-L6-v2 Sentence Transformer from sbert.net where $\mathtt{s}_1$ is *John is the father of Ann*, $\mathtt{s}_2$ is *John is Ann 's dad*, $\mathtt{s}_3$ is *There will be a lot of showery weather today*, and $\mathtt{s}_4$ is *Today will be rainy*. So $\mathtt{s}_1$ and $\mathtt{s}_2$ are very similar, and $\mathtt{s}_3$ and $\mathtt{s}_4$ are quite similar, whereas $\mathtt{s}_1$ and $\mathtt{s}_2$ are dissimilar to each of $\mathtt{s}_3$ and $\mathtt{s}_4$ and vice versa.

	$\mathtt{s}_1$	$\mathtt{s}_2$	$\mathtt{s}_3$	$\mathtt{s}_4$
$\mathtt{s}_1$	1	0.9472	0.0955	0.0829
$\mathtt{s}_2$	0.9472	1	0.1165	0.1154
$\mathtt{s}_3$	0.0955	0.1165	1	0.7143
$\mathtt{s}_4$	0.0829	0.1154	0.7143	1

Using the notion of a similarity measure between a pair of sentence embeddings, we have new notions of conflict. In other work [7], a general framework for *germane conflicts* was proposed that allows for the comparison of alternatives to minimally inconsistent subsets of a knowledgebase. In the following sections, we will briefly review germane conflicts, and then we will define two new notions of conflict, namely *match conflict* and *swap conflict*. These are based on the notion of quasi-equality, denoted $\simeq$, where $\alpha \simeq \beta$ means that the atoms α and β are similar according to the similarity measure (i.e. above a threshold). We then investigate these types of conflict as types of germane conflict. These different notions of conflict are intended to give different insights into implicit conflicts in real-world situations.

2 Preliminaries

Let $\mathcal{L}$ be the set of propositional formulae composed from the set of atoms $\mathcal{A}$ and the connectives $\wedge$, $\vee$, $\neg$. We use $\alpha, \beta, \gamma, \delta, \phi, \psi, \ldots$ for arbitrary formulae. A knowledgebase $K \subseteq \mathcal{L}$ is a finite set of formulae. We use $\mathcal{K}$ for the set of all knowledgebases. We let $\vdash$ denote the classical consequence relation, and $K \vdash \bot$ denotes that $K \in \mathcal{K}$ is inconsistent. If K is inconsistent, and there is no $K' \subseteq K$ s.t. $K' \vdash \bot$, then K is a **minimal inconsistent set**. $\mathsf{Atoms}(K)$ is the set of atoms appearing in the formulae in K. Let Cn be the consequence closure function (i.e. $\mathsf{Cn}(K) = \{\phi \mid K \vdash \phi\}$).

A (**letter-to-letter**) **substitution mapping** is a function $S : \mathcal{A} \rightarrow \mathcal{L}$ ($S : \mathcal{A} \rightarrow \mathcal{A}$), which can be extended to $S : \mathcal{L} \rightarrow \mathcal{L}$ inductively: $S(\neg\phi) = \neg S(\phi)$ and $S(\phi \bowtie \psi) = S(\phi) \bowtie S(\psi)$ for $\bowtie \in \{\wedge, \vee, \rightarrow\}$. For any substitution mapping S and knowledgebase K, $S(K)$ denotes the knowledgebase $\{S(\phi) \mid \phi \in K\}$. When we define a specific substitution, we assume $S(x_i) = x_i$ for all $x_i \in \mathcal{A}$ unless stated otherwise. Let $\mathcal{S}$ denote the set of all substitution mappings. For example, let $S(\mathtt{a}) = \mathtt{b}$ and $S(\mathtt{c}) = \mathtt{d}$, and let $K = \{\neg\neg\ \mathtt{a},\ \mathtt{a}\ \wedge \mathtt{c} \rightarrow\ \mathtt{e},\ \mathtt{d}\}$, and so, S is a letter-to-letter substitution mapping, and $S(K) = \{\neg\neg\mathtt{b}, \mathtt{b} \wedge \mathtt{d} \rightarrow \mathtt{e}, \mathtt{d}\}$.

3 Quasi-Equality Relations

We assume that an atom can be described by a string of words, and we use a similarity measure to capture semantic similarity between these atoms, based on the similarity of their associated strings of words: For a set of atoms $\mathcal{A}$, a **similarity measure** M is a function $M : \mathcal{A} \times \mathcal{A} \to [0, 1]$ that satisfies: (Identity of indiscernibles) $M(\alpha_1, \alpha_2) = 1$ when $\alpha_1 = \alpha_2$; and (Symmetry) $M(\alpha_1, \alpha_2) = M(\alpha_2, \alpha_1)$. The nearer two atoms are according to the similarity measure, the closer the information conveyed by their associate strings of words. For example, in Table 1, the similarity between atoms $\mathtt{s}_1$ and $\mathtt{s}_2$ is the similarity between the word embeddings for their associated strings.

Next, we introduce the notion of a quasi-equality relation between atoms α and β for representing and reasoning with (very) similar atoms, as follows.

Definition 1. *For $\alpha, \beta \in \mathcal{A}$, a* **quasi-equality relation** *is $\alpha \simeq \beta$ (in which case, we say that α and β are* **quasi-equivalent***). A* **quasi-equality set** *Q is a set of quasi-equality relations that is closed under (Reflexivity) $\alpha \simeq \alpha \in Q$ and (Symmetry) $\alpha \simeq \beta \in Q$ iff $\beta \simeq \alpha \in Q$. We use $\mathcal{Q}$ for the set of all quasi-equality sets.*

In the examples, we present each set of quasi-equality relations Q assuming that additional quasi-equality relations are obtained by reflexivity and symmetry.

We can use a similarity measure between atoms to determine whether a quasi-equality relation holds in a quasi-equality set Q. For instance, for a similarity measure M, and for a pair of atoms α and β, if $M(\alpha, \beta)$ is greater than a threshold, then $\alpha \simeq \beta$ is in Q. The choice of threshold depends on the application.

Example 1. Consider the four sentences in Table 1 where M is specified. Let $\mathcal{A} = \{\mathtt{s}_1, \mathtt{s}_2, \mathtt{s}_3, \mathtt{s}_4\}$. If the threshold is 0.9 (respectively 0.7) Q contains $\mathtt{s}_1 \simeq \mathtt{s}_2$ (respectively $\mathtt{s}_1 \simeq \mathtt{s}_2$, and $\mathtt{s}_3 \simeq \mathtt{s}_4$).

In Sects. 4 and 5, we use quasi-equality relations in two forms of consequence relation, which in turn we use as the basis of new definitions for conflict.

4 Germane Conflicts

A *germane conflict* is a set of formulae that is inconsistent, and furthermore, all the formulae in the set appear problematic. In inconsistency analysis of a knowledgebase, a germane conflict can be regarded as a basic unit of inconsistency in the knowledgebase. In [7], a framework of properties for germane conflicts was proposed. An arbitrary definition for germane conflicts can be assessed in terms of the set of desirable properties it satisfies. Some of the types of constraint on germane conflicts $\mathcal{C} \subseteq \mathcal{K}$ introduced in [7], with specific properties in each category, are the following:

Core Properties are the most basic ones, and so might normally be expected for a reasonable conflict definition:

- **Inconsistency**: If $K \in \mathcal{C}$, then K is inconsistent.
- **Inclusion**: If $K \in \mathcal{K}$ is inconsistent, then there is a $K' \in \mathcal{C}$ s.t. $K' \subseteq K$.
- **Non-Triviality**: There exists some inconsistent $K \in \mathcal{K} \setminus \mathcal{C}$.
- **Atom-indifference**: If $K \in \mathcal{C}$ and $S : \mathcal{A} \to \mathcal{A}$ is a bijective letter-to-letter substitution, then $S(K) \in \mathcal{C}$.

Set-theoretical Properties are based on set operations:

- **Minimality**: If $K \in \mathcal{C}$, then there is no $K' \in \mathcal{C}$ s.t. $K' \subset K$.

- **$\cup$-closure**: If $K, K' \in \mathcal{C}$, then $K \cup K' \in \mathcal{C}$.

Semantic-based Properties are based on semantics of the formulae, such as logical equivalence or implication:

- **Syntax-Robustness**: Given a knowledgebase $K \in \mathcal{C}$, if $\phi \in K$ is replaced by a logically equivalent $\phi' \in \mathcal{L}$, the resulting knowledgebase is also in $\mathcal{C}$.
- **No-Equivalences**: If $K \in \mathcal{C}$, then there are no formulae $\phi, \psi \in K$ s.t. ψ is logically equivalent to ϕ.
- **Non-Redundancy**: If $K \in \mathcal{C}$, then there are no formulae $\phi, \psi \in K$ s.t. ψ implies ϕ.
- **Tautology-Freeness**: If $K \in \mathcal{C}$, then there is no tautology $\phi \in K$.
- **Non-Quasi-Triviality**: There exists some inconsistent $K \in \mathcal{K} \setminus \mathcal{C}$ that has no tautologies.

Atoms-related Properties consider atoms in a formula and to substitutions applied to atoms or formulae:

- **Safe-Set-Freeness**: If $K \in \mathcal{C}$, then there is no safe set $K' \subset K$ (where K' is a safe set in K if K' is non-empty, consistent, and shares no atoms with $K \setminus K'$).
- **Substitution-Robustness**: If $K \in \mathcal{C}$, and S is a substitution, then $S(K) \in \mathcal{C}$.

Different notions of germane conflict can be obtained by assuming different combinations of the properties such as those listed here. For instance, minimal inconsistent sets are exactly those that satisfy the properties of inconsistency, inclusion, and minimality. Further types of germane conflict include iceberg inconsistencies [6].

5 Match Conflicts

The following consequence relation is for reasoning with a knowledgebase and a quasi-equality set.

Definition 2. *The* **match consequence relation**, *denoted* $\vdash_{\mathsf{ma}}$, *is defined as follows where* $K \in \mathcal{K}$, *and* $Q \in \mathcal{Q}$:

1. *If* $\alpha \in K$, *then* $(K, Q) \vdash_{\mathsf{ma}} \alpha$
2. *If* $(K, Q) \vdash_{\mathsf{ma}} \alpha$, *and* $\{\alpha\} \vdash \beta$, *then* $(K, Q) \vdash_{\mathsf{ma}} \beta$
3. *If* $(K, Q) \vdash_{\mathsf{ma}} \alpha \vee \gamma$ *and* $(K, Q) \vdash_{\mathsf{ma}} \neg\beta \vee \delta$ *and* $\alpha \simeq \beta \in Q$, *then* $(K, Q) \vdash_{\mathsf{ma}} \gamma \vee \delta$
4. *If* $(K, Q) \vdash_{\mathsf{ma}} \alpha$ *and* $(K, Q) \vdash_{\mathsf{ma}} \neg\beta$ *and* $\alpha \simeq \beta \in Q$, *then* $(K, Q) \vdash_{\mathsf{ma}} \bot$

If $(K, Q) \vdash_{\mathsf{ma}} \bot$, *then* K *is called a* **match conflict**, *or equivalently a* ma-*conflict.*

We explain the above definition as follows: Rule 1 is the reflexivity proof rule; Rule 2 allows classical inference from an individual formula; Rule 3 uses a quasi-equality relation to allow two syntactically different literals to be used with the resolution proof rule to obtain a resolvent; And Rule 4 uses a quasi-equality relation to allow two syntactically different literals to obtain contradiction. With this definition, any formula can be translated into classical conjunctive normal form using Rule 2, and then clauses can be obtained by applying conjunction elimination again using Rule 2. Then Rules 3 and 4 provide the ability to obtain a contradiction from those clauses.

Table 2. Similarity from $\mathtt{s}_1$ to each $\mathtt{s}_2$ to $\mathtt{s}_7$ using the all-MiniLM-L6-v2 Sentence Transformer from sbert.net where $\mathtt{s}_1$ is *It is a bird*, $\mathtt{s}_2$ is *It is a chicken*, $\mathtt{s}_3$ is *It is an eagle*, $\mathtt{s}_4$ is *It is a penguin*, $\mathtt{s}_5$ is *It is a house*, $\mathtt{s}_6$ is *It is a cat*, and $\mathtt{s}_7$ is *It is a dog*.

$\mathtt{s}_2$	$\mathtt{s}_3$	$\mathtt{s}_4$	$\mathtt{s}_5$	$\mathtt{s}_6$	$\mathtt{s}_7$
0.7395	0.7128	0.6411	0.4727	0.5630	0.5993

Example 2. Let $K = \{\mathtt{a} \land \neg\mathtt{b}\}$ and $Q = \{\mathtt{a} \simeq \mathtt{b}\}$. (1) By Rule 1, $(K, Q) \vdash_{\mathsf{ma}} \mathtt{a} \land \neg b$. (2) By Rule 2, $(K, Q) \vdash_{\mathsf{ma}} \mathtt{a}$ and $(K, Q) \vdash_{\mathsf{ma}} \neg\mathtt{b}$. (3) From step 2, and $\mathtt{a} \simeq \mathtt{b} \in Q$, by Rule 4, $(K, Q) \vdash_{\mathsf{ma}} \bot$.

Example 3. Let $K = \{\mathtt{c}, \neg(\mathtt{a} \land \mathtt{b}), \mathtt{d}\}$ and $Q = \{\mathtt{a} \simeq \mathtt{c}, \mathtt{b} \simeq \mathtt{d}\}$. (1) By Rule 1, $(K, Q) \vdash_{\mathsf{ma}} \neg(\mathtt{a} \land \mathtt{b})$. (2) By Rule 2, and step 1, $(K, Q) \vdash \neg\mathtt{a} \lor \neg\mathtt{b}$. (3) By Rule 1, $(K, Q) \vdash_{\mathsf{ma}} \mathtt{c}$. (4) From steps 2 and 3, and $\mathtt{a} \simeq \mathtt{c} \in Q$, using Rule 3, $(K, Q) \vdash_{\mathsf{ma}} \neg\mathtt{b}$. (5) By Rule 1, $(K, Q) \vdash_{\mathsf{ma}} \mathtt{d}$. (6) From steps 4 and 5, and $\mathtt{b} \simeq \mathtt{d} \in Q$, using Rule 4, $(K, Q) \vdash_{\mathsf{ma}} \bot$.

Example 4. Consider Table 2, where M is specified between $\mathtt{s}_1$ and each of $\mathtt{s}_2$ to $\mathtt{s}_7$. Let Q be the quasi-equality set with threshold of 0.7 and so Q contains $\mathtt{s}_1 \simeq \mathtt{s}_2$ and $\mathtt{s}_1 \simeq \mathtt{s}_3$. Also let $\mathtt{s}_8$ be *it flies*. Therefore $K_2 = \{\mathtt{s}_2, \mathtt{s}_1 \to \mathtt{s}_8, \neg\mathtt{s}_8\}$, and $K_3 = \{\mathtt{s}_3, \mathtt{s}_1 \to \mathtt{s}_8, \neg\mathtt{s}_8\}$, are match conflicts, whereas $K_4 = \{\mathtt{s}_4, \mathtt{s}_1 \to \mathtt{s}_8, \neg\mathtt{s}_8\}$, $K_5 = \{\mathtt{s}_5, \mathtt{s}_1 \to \mathtt{s}_8, \neg\mathtt{s}_8\}$, $K_6 = \{\mathtt{s}_6, \mathtt{s}_1 \to \mathtt{s}_8, \neg\mathtt{s}_8\}$, and $K_7 = \{\mathtt{s}_7, \mathtt{s}_1 \to \mathtt{s}_8, \neg\mathtt{s}_8\}$, are not match conflicts.

When there are no quasi-equality relations, except from reflexivity, the match consequence relation and classical consequence relation coincide for non-tautological inferences as shown in the following result.

Proposition 1. *Let $K \in \mathcal{K}$ and $\gamma \in \mathcal{L}$ such that γ is not a tautology. If $Q = \{\alpha \simeq \alpha \mid \alpha \in \mathcal{A}\}$, then $(K \cup \{\neg\gamma\}, Q) \vdash_{\mathsf{ma}} \bot$ iff $K \vdash \gamma$.*

Proof. Using Rules 1 and 2 of Definition 2, every formula in K can be rewritten in conjunctive normal form, and conjunction elimination applied. So K can be represented by the clauses that can be obtained in this way. Since Q contains all and only the quasi-equality relations according to the reflexivity property, Rules 3 and 4 are equivalent to the resolution proof rule in propositional logic. So any resolvent of the clauses corresponding to K can be obtained. So $(K \cup \{\neg\gamma\}, Q) \vdash_{\mathsf{ma}} \bot$ iff $K \cup \{\neg\gamma\} \vdash \bot$. Hence, the inferences from the $\vdash_{\mathsf{ma}}$ and the $\vdash$ consequence relations coincide.

The match consequence relation is monotonic in the knowledgebase and in the quasi-equality set.

Proposition 2. *For $K, K' \in \mathcal{K}$ and $Q, Q' \in \mathcal{Q}$ and $\gamma \in \mathcal{L}$, (i) if $K \subseteq K'$, and $(K, Q) \vdash_{\mathsf{ma}} \gamma$, then $(K', Q) \vdash_{\mathsf{ma}} \gamma$, and (ii) if $Q \subseteq Q'$, and $(K, Q) \vdash_{\mathsf{ma}} \gamma$, then $(K, Q') \vdash_{\mathsf{ma}} \gamma$.*

When we assume that the set of atoms is finite, then the match consequence relation is decidable.

Proposition 3. *For $K \in \mathcal{K}$, and $Q \in \mathcal{Q}$, and $\gamma \in \mathcal{L}$, determining whether or not $(K, Q) \vdash_{\mathsf{ma}} \gamma$ holds is decidable.*

Proof. If there is a $\delta \in K$ s.t. $\{\delta\} \vdash \gamma$ then we are done. If there is no $\delta \in K$ s.t. $\{\delta\} \vdash \gamma$, then we need to determine if there is a clause ϕ s.t. $(K, Q) \vdash_{\mathsf{ma}} \phi$ and $\{\phi\} \vdash \gamma$. Given that $\mathcal{A}$ is finite, there is a finite number of clauses in the language that are candidates for ϕ. So there is a finite number of these candidates that can be obtained from Rule 2 of Definition 2, and hence there is a finite number of them that can then be obtained by repeated applications of Rules 1 and 3 of Definition 2. So in a finite number of steps, we can determine if there is a clause ϕ s.t. $\{\phi\} \vdash \gamma$. Hence, there is a finite procedure for deciding if $(K, Q) \vdash_{\mathsf{ma}} \gamma$ holds.

By using the match consequence relation, each inconsistency in a knowledgebase is explainable in the form of a proof with the quasi-equality relations used.

6 Swap Conflicts

As an alternative to using the quasi-equality relations for extending the use of the resolution proof rule (i.e. the match consequence relation), we can use quasi-equality relations for directly exchanging symbols in formulae, using swaps as defined as follows.

For a pair of atoms α_1, α_2, a **swap** is denoted α_1/α_2. For each swap α_1/α_2, we call α_1 the **outgoing symbol** and α_2 the **incoming symbol**. A swap α_1/α_2 is **reflexive** iff $\alpha_1 = \alpha_2$. When a swap α_1/α_2 is applied to a formula ϕ, denoted $\phi[\alpha_1/\alpha_2]$, α_1 is substituted by α_2 throughout ϕ. For example, for formula $\neg(\mathsf{a} \wedge (\neg \mathsf{a} \vee c))$, and swap a/b, we have $\neg(\mathsf{a} \wedge (\neg \mathsf{a} \vee \mathsf{c}))[\mathsf{a}/\mathsf{b}]$ is $\neg(\mathsf{b} \wedge (\neg \mathsf{b} \vee \mathsf{c}))$.

Next, we introduce our second consequence relation that is defined as follows, using the above notion of swap.

Definition 3. *The* **swap consequence relation**, *denoted $\vdash_{\mathsf{sw}}$, is defined as follows where $K \in \mathcal{K}$, and $Q \in \mathcal{Q}$:*

1. *If $\phi \in K$, then $(K, Q) \vdash_{\mathsf{sw}} \phi$*
2. *If $(K, Q) \vdash_{\mathsf{sw}} \phi_1, \ldots (K, Q) \vdash_{\mathsf{sw}} \phi_n$, and $\{\phi_1, \ldots, \phi_n\} \vdash \psi$, then $(K, Q) \vdash_{\mathsf{sw}} \psi$*
3. *If $(K, Q) \vdash_{\mathsf{sw}} \phi$ and $\alpha \simeq \beta \in Q$, then $(K, Q) \vdash_{\mathsf{sw}} \phi[\alpha/\beta]$*

If $(K, Q) \vdash_{\mathsf{sw}} \bot$, then K is called a **swap conflict**, *or equivalently a* sw-*conflict.*

We explain the above definition as follows: Rule 1 is the reflexivity proof rule and so any formula in the knowledgebase is an inference of the swap consequence relation; Rule 2 allows classical inference from inferences of the swap consequence relation; And Rule 3 uses a quasi-equality relation for a substitution to give an inference of the swap consequence relation.

Example 5. If $K = \{\mathsf{a} \wedge \neg \mathsf{b}\}$ and $Q = \{\mathsf{a} \simeq \mathsf{b}\}$, then $(K, Q) \vdash_{\mathsf{sw}} \mathsf{a} \wedge \neg \mathsf{b}[\mathsf{a}/\mathsf{b}]$, and hence, $(K, Q) \vdash_{\mathsf{sw}} \mathsf{b} \wedge \neg \mathsf{b}$, and so, $(K, Q) \vdash_{\mathsf{sw}} \bot$.

Example 6. If $K = \{\mathsf{c}, \neg(\mathsf{a} \wedge \mathsf{b}), \mathsf{d}\}$ and $Q = \{\mathsf{a} \simeq \mathsf{c}, \mathsf{b} \simeq \mathsf{d}\}$, then $(K, Q) \vdash_{\mathsf{sw}} \neg(\mathsf{a} \wedge \mathsf{b})[\mathsf{a}/\mathsf{c}]$, which gives $(K, Q) \vdash_{\mathsf{sw}} \neg(\mathsf{c} \wedge \mathsf{b})$. Then $(K, Q) \vdash_{\mathsf{sw}} \neg(\mathsf{c} \wedge \mathsf{b})[\mathsf{b}/\mathsf{d}]$, which gives $(K, Q) \vdash_{\mathsf{sw}} \neg(\mathsf{c} \wedge \mathsf{d})$. Since, $\{\mathsf{c}, \neg(\mathsf{c} \wedge \mathsf{d}), \mathsf{d}\} \vdash \bot$, we have $(K, Q) \vdash_{\mathsf{sw}} \bot$.

Examples 7 and 8 show that there are inferences from the $\vdash_{\mathsf{sw}}$ consequence relation that are not inferences from the $\vdash_{\mathsf{ma}}$ consequence relation.

Example 7. If $K = \{\mathsf{a} \vee \neg\mathsf{b}\}$ and $Q = \{\mathsf{a} \simeq \mathsf{c}\}$, then $(K, Q) \vdash_{\mathsf{sw}} \mathsf{a} \vee \neg\mathsf{b}[\mathsf{a}/\mathsf{c}]$, and hence, $(K, Q) \vdash_{\mathsf{sw}} \mathsf{c} \vee \neg\mathsf{b}$, but $(K, Q) \not\vdash_{\mathsf{ma}} \mathsf{c} \vee \neg\mathsf{b}$.

The following result shows that all inferences from the $\vdash_{\mathsf{ma}}$ consequence relation are inferences from the $\vdash_{\mathsf{sw}}$ consequence relation.

Proposition 4. *For $K \in \mathcal{K}$, and $Q \in \mathcal{Q}$, if $(K, Q) \vdash_{\mathsf{ma}} \phi$, then $(K, Q) \vdash_{\mathsf{sw}} \phi$*

Proof. Each rule of $\vdash_{\mathsf{ma}}$ can be captured by $\vdash_{\mathsf{sw}}$: (Rule 1 of the match consequence relation) This is captured by Rule 1 of the swap consequence relation; (Rule 2 of the match consequence relation) This is captured by Rule 2 of the swap consequence relation using $n = 1$; (Rule 3 of the match consequence relation) This is captured by Rule 3 of the swap consequence relation by using the swap $[\alpha/\beta]$ for $\alpha \simeq \beta$, and then by Rule 2 of the swap consequence relation using $\{\beta \vee \gamma, \neg\beta \vee \delta\} \vdash \gamma \vee \delta$; and (Rule 4 of match consequence relation) This is captured by Rule 3 of the swap consequence relation by using the swap $[\alpha/\beta]$ for $\alpha \simeq \beta$, and then by Rule 2 of the swap consequence relation using $\{\beta, \neg\beta\} \vdash \bot$.

Example 8. If $K = \{\mathsf{a}, \neg\mathsf{c}\}$ and $Q = \{\mathsf{a} \simeq \mathsf{b}, \mathsf{b} \simeq \mathsf{c}\}$, then $(K, Q) \vdash_{\mathsf{sw}} \mathsf{a}[\mathsf{a}/\mathsf{b}]$, giving $(K, Q) \vdash_{\mathsf{sw}} \mathsf{b}$, and then $(K, Q) \vdash_{\mathsf{sw}} \mathsf{b}[\mathsf{b}/\mathsf{c}]$, giving $(K, Q) \vdash_{\mathsf{sw}} \mathsf{c}$, and now $\{\mathsf{c}, \neg c\} \vdash \bot$, and hence $(K, Q) \vdash_{\mathsf{sw}} \bot$. In contrast, $(K, Q) \not\vdash_{\mathsf{ma}} \mathsf{c}$, and $(K, Q) \not\vdash_{\mathsf{ma}} \bot$.

The difference between these consequence relations is that the match consequence relation only allows use of a quasi-equality relation at the point of applying the resolution rule, whereas the swap consequence relation is more liberal in that it can make a sequence of swaps on a formula, and in effect, it is propagating the similarity. For instance, in the above example, using $\mathsf{a} \simeq b$ and $\mathsf{b} \simeq c$, a becomes c, which is the same as assuming transitivity of the quasi-equality relation, and so $\mathsf{a} \simeq c$, is obtained from $\mathsf{a} \simeq b$ and $\mathsf{b} \simeq c$.

Proposition 5. *If Q^+ is Q closed under transitivity (i.e. Q^+ is the smallest set such that $Q \subseteq Q^+$ and for all $\alpha \simeq \beta, \beta \simeq \gamma \in Q^+$, then $\alpha \simeq \gamma \in Q^+$), and $K \in \mathcal{K}$, and $\gamma \in \mathcal{L}$, if $(K, Q^+) \vdash_{\mathsf{ma}} \gamma$, then $(K, Q) \vdash_{\mathsf{sw}} \gamma$.*

Proof. Let $\alpha \simeq \beta \in Q^+$ be obtained by transitivity from $\alpha \simeq \alpha, \ldots, \alpha_n \simeq \beta \in Q^+$. So Rule 3 (respectively Rule 4) of the match consequence relation using $\alpha \simeq \beta \in Q^+$ can be captured by using Rule 3 of the swap consequence relation with $[\alpha/\alpha_1]...[\alpha_n/\beta]$, and then Rule 2 of the swap consequence relation with $\{\beta \vee \gamma, \neg\beta \vee \delta\} \vdash \gamma \vee \delta$ (respectively $\{\beta, \neg\beta\} \vdash \bot$). So for any inference using Rules 2, 3 and 4 of the match consequence relation can be captured by Rules 2 and 3 of the swap consequence relation. Therefore, if $(K, Q^+) \vdash_{\mathsf{ma}} \gamma$, then $(K, Q) \vdash_{\mathsf{sw}} \gamma$.

Example 9. Continuing Example 8, $K = \{\mathsf{a}, \neg\mathsf{c}\}$ and $Q = \{\mathsf{a} \simeq \mathsf{b}, \mathsf{b} \simeq \mathsf{c}\}$. So $\mathsf{a} \simeq \mathsf{c} \in Q^+$, and hence, $(K, Q^+) \vdash_{\mathsf{ma}} \mathsf{c}$, and $(K, Q^+) \vdash_{\mathsf{ma}} \bot$

When there are no non-reflexive quasi-equality relations, then the swap and classical consequence relations coincide for non-tautological inferences.

Proposition 6. *Let $K \in \mathcal{K}$, and $Q \in \mathcal{Q}$, and $\gamma \in \mathcal{L}$ such that γ is not a tautology. If $Q = \{\alpha \simeq \alpha \mid \alpha \in \mathcal{A}\}$, then $(K, Q) \vdash_{\mathsf{sw}} \gamma$ iff $K \vdash \gamma$.*

Proof. When $Q = \{\alpha \simeq \alpha \mid \alpha \in \mathcal{A}\}$, each rule of $\vdash_{\mathsf{sw}}$ can be captured by the $\vdash$ consequence relation: (Rule 1 of swap consequence relation) This is captured by reflexivity of $\vdash$; (Rule 2 of swap consequence relation) This is captured by $\{\phi_1, \ldots, \phi_n\} \vdash \psi$; And (Rule 3 of swap consequence relation) Given Q, Rule 3 of swap consequence relation is a tautology (as it will be "If $(K, Q) \vdash_{\mathsf{sw}} \phi$ and $\alpha \simeq \alpha \in Q$, then $(K, Q) \vdash_{\mathsf{sw}} \phi[\alpha/\alpha]$") and hence it is trivially captured by $\vdash$. For the converse, when $Q = \{\alpha \simeq \alpha \mid \alpha \in \mathcal{A}\}$, the $\vdash$ consequence relation is captured by Rules 1 and 2 of swap consequence relation.

The swap consequence relation is monotonic in the knowledgebase and the quasi-equality set.

Proposition 7. *If $K, K' \in \mathcal{K}$ and $Q, Q' \in \mathcal{Q}$ and $\gamma \in \mathcal{L}$, (i) if $K \subseteq K'$, and $(K, Q) \vdash_{\mathsf{sw}} \gamma$, then $(K', Q) \vdash_{\mathsf{sw}} \gamma$, and (ii) if $Q \subseteq Q'$, and $(K, Q) \vdash_{\mathsf{sw}} \gamma$, then $(K, Q') \vdash_{\mathsf{sw}} \gamma$.*

When the set of atoms is finite, the swap consequence relation is decidable.

Proposition 8. *For $K \in \mathcal{K}$, and $Q \in \mathcal{Q}$, and $\gamma \in \mathcal{L}$, determining whether or not $(K, Q) \vdash_{\mathsf{sw}} \gamma$ holds is decidable.*

Proof. Let $K_Q = \{\phi[\alpha/\beta] \mid \phi \in K \text{ and } \alpha \simeq \beta \in Q\}$. So $(K, Q) \vdash_{\mathsf{sw}} \gamma$ iff $K_Q \vdash \gamma$. Since K_Q is finite, and $K_Q \vdash \gamma$ is decidable, then $(K, Q) \vdash_{\mathsf{sw}} \gamma$ is decidable.

As with using the match consequence relation, by using the swap consequence relation, each inconsistency in a knowledgebase is explainable in the form of a proof with the quasi-equality relations used. However, because using the swap consequence relation subsumes the match consequence relation with the transitive closure of the quasi-equality set (Proposition 5), the swap consequence relation may be regarded as too liberal. To address this, a variant of the swap consequence relation could be defined to limit the number of times that Rule 3 can be used.

7 Minimal Conflicts

We start by considering match conflicts and swap conflicts as germane conflicts. For $\sigma \in \{\mathsf{ma}, \mathsf{sw}\}$, let $\mathcal{C}^Q_\sigma = \{K \in \mathcal{K} \mid (K, Q) \vdash_\sigma \bot\}$ be the set of σ-conflicts for Q.

Proposition 9. *For $\sigma \in \{\mathsf{ma}, \mathsf{sw}\}$, $\mathcal{C}^Q_\sigma$ is the set of σ-conflicts for Q iff $\mathcal{C}^Q_\sigma$ satisfies the germane properties of inconsistency, inclusion and $\cup$-closure.*

Proof. ($\Rightarrow$) Let $\mathcal{C}^Q_\sigma$ be the set of σ-conflicts for Q. So $\mathcal{C}^Q_\sigma$ satisfies inconsistency and inclusion by definition. Since $(K, Q) \vdash_\sigma \bot$ and $(K', Q) \vdash_\sigma \bot$ implies $(K \cup K', Q) \vdash_\sigma \bot$, $\mathcal{C}^Q_\sigma$ satisfies $\cup$-closure. ($\Leftarrow$) Assume $\mathcal{C}^Q_\sigma$ satisfies inconsistency, inclusion and $\cup$-closure. From inconsistency, every $K \in \mathcal{C}^Q_\sigma$ is s.t. $(K, Q) \vdash_\sigma \bot$. From inclusion, for every K s.t. $(K, Q) \vdash_\sigma \bot$, there is a $K' \subseteq K$ s.t. $K' \in \mathcal{C}^Q_\sigma$. Hence with $\cup$-closure, for every K s.t. $(K, Q) \vdash_\sigma \bot$, $K \in \mathcal{C}^Q_\sigma$. So, $\mathcal{C}^Q_\sigma = \{K \in \mathcal{K} \mid (K, Q) \vdash_\sigma \bot\}$. So $\mathcal{C}^Q_\sigma$ is the set of σ-conflicts for Q.

We now consider minimal inconsistency. Since there are two sets to consider K and Q, the first definition is for minimizing K, the second definition is for minimizing Q, and the third is for ensuring each is minimal with respect to the other.

Definition 4. *Let* $\vdash_\sigma \subseteq \mathcal{K} \times \mathcal{Q} \times \mathcal{L}$ *be a consequence relation. For* $K \in \mathcal{K}$*, and* $Q \in \mathcal{Q}$*,*

- K *is a* **min σ-conflict** *for* Q *iff* $(K, Q) \vdash_\sigma \bot$ *and for all* $K' \subset K$*,* $(K', Q) \not\vdash_\sigma \bot$
- Q *is a* **min σ-equality** *for* K *iff* $(K, Q) \vdash_\sigma \bot$ *and for all* $Q' \subset Q$*,* $(K, Q') \not\vdash_\sigma \bot$

(K, Q) *is a* **pareto σ-conflict-pair** *iff* K *is a min* σ*-conflict for* Q *and* Q *is a min* σ*-equality for* K*.*

Example 10. For $\sigma \in \{\mathsf{ma}, \mathsf{sw}\}$, if $K = \{\mathsf{a}, \neg\mathsf{b}\}$ and $Q = \{\mathsf{a} \simeq \mathsf{b}\}$, then $(K, Q) \vdash_\sigma \bot$. So, K is a min σ-conflict for Q and Q is a min σ-equality for K, and therefore (K, Q) is a pareto σ-conflict-pair.

Example 11. For $\sigma \in \{\mathsf{ma}, \mathsf{sw}\}$, if $K = \{\mathsf{a}, \neg\mathsf{b}, \mathsf{c}\}$ and $Q = \{\mathsf{a} \simeq \mathsf{b}, \mathsf{c} \simeq d\}$, then $(K, Q) \vdash_{\mathsf{ma}} \bot$. But, K is not a min σ-conflict for Q and Q is not a min σ-equality for K, and therefore (K, Q) is not a pareto σ-conflict-pair. However, as Example 10 shows, there is a subset of K and a subset of Q that constitute a pareto σ-conflict-pair.

Example 12. For $\sigma \in \{\mathsf{ma}, \mathsf{sw}\}$, let $K = \{\neg\mathsf{b}, \mathsf{a} \vee \neg\mathsf{d}, \mathsf{e} \vee \mathsf{a}, \neg\mathsf{g}\}$ and $Q = \{\mathsf{a} \simeq \mathsf{b}, \mathsf{d} \simeq \mathsf{e}, \mathsf{a} \simeq \mathsf{g}\}$. So $(K, Q) \vdash_\sigma \bot$, but it is not a pareto σ-conflict-pair, whereas (K', Q') is a pareto σ-conflict-pair when $K' = \{\neg\mathsf{b}, \mathsf{a} \vee \neg\mathsf{d}, \mathsf{e} \vee \mathsf{a}\}$ and $Q' = \{\mathsf{a} \simeq \mathsf{b}, \mathsf{d} \simeq \mathsf{e}\}$.

The following result shows that for a knowledgebase and a quasi-equality set that is a pareto ma-conflict-pair, we can take a subset of each of them as a pareto sw-conflict-pair.

Proposition 10. *For* $K \in \mathcal{K}$*, and* $Q \in \mathcal{Q}$*, if* (K, Q) *is a pareto* ma*-conflict-pair, then there is* $K' \subseteq K$ *and* $Q' \subseteq Q$ *s.t.* (K', Q') *is a pareto* sw*-conflict-pair.*

Proof. Assume (K, Q) is a pareto ma-conflict-pair. So K is a min ma-conflict for Q and Q is a min ma-equality for K. From Proposition 4, K is a min ma-conflict for Q implies K is a sw-conflict for Q, but not necessarily that K is min sw-conflict for Q. Similarly, from Q is a min ma-equality for K, it is not necessarily the case that Q is a min sw-equality for K. Therefore, there is a $K' \subseteq K$ and $Q' \subseteq Q$ such that K' is a min sw-conflict for Q', and Q' is a min sw-equality for K', and hence (K', Q') is a pareto sw-conflict-pair.

When identifying pareto σ-conflict-pairs, there can be a trade-off of minimizing K against minimizing Q as illustrated below.

Example 13. Let $K = \{\neg\mathsf{d}, \mathsf{d} \vee \neg\mathsf{a}, \mathsf{a} \vee \mathsf{b}, \neg\mathsf{b} \vee \neg\mathsf{c}, \mathsf{c}, \neg\mathsf{e}, \neg f\}$, $K_1 = \{\neg\mathsf{d}, \mathsf{d} \vee \neg\mathsf{a}, \mathsf{a} \vee \mathsf{b}, \neg\mathsf{b} \vee \neg\mathsf{c}, \mathsf{c}\}$, $K_2 = \{\mathsf{a} \vee \mathsf{b}, \neg\mathsf{e}, \neg\mathsf{f}\}$, and $Q = \{\mathsf{a} \simeq \mathsf{e}, \mathsf{b} \simeq \mathsf{f}\}$. Therefore, $(K_1, \emptyset)$ and (K_2, Q) are both pareto σ-conflicts, for $\sigma \in \{\mathsf{ma}, \mathsf{sw}\}$.

We now focus on min σ-conflicts by characterizing them as germane conflicts as follows where $C_\sigma^{\bullet Q}$ is the set of min σ-conflicts for Q and $\sigma \in \{\mathsf{ma}, \mathsf{sw}\}$.

Proposition 11. *For $\sigma \in \{\mathsf{ma}, \mathsf{sw}\}$, $\mathcal{C}_\sigma^{\bullet Q}$ is the set of min σ-conflicts for Q iff $\mathcal{C}_\sigma^{\bullet Q}$ satisfies the germane properties of inconsistency, inclusion, and minimality.*

Proof. ($\Rightarrow$) Let $\mathcal{C}_\sigma^{\bullet Q}$ be the set of min σ-conflicts for Q. Since every $K \in \mathcal{C}_\sigma^{\bullet Q}$ is a min σ-conflict for Q, $\mathcal{C}_\sigma^{\bullet Q}$ satisfies inconsistency and minimality. Also, for every $K \in \mathcal{C}_\sigma^{Q}$, there is a $K' \subseteq K$ s.t. $K' \in \mathcal{C}_\sigma^{\bullet Q}$. So, $\mathcal{C}_\sigma^{\bullet Q}$ satisfies inclusion. ($\Leftarrow$) Assume $\mathcal{C}_\sigma^{\bullet Q}$ satisfies inconsistency, inclusion, and minimality. From inconsistency, every $K \in \mathcal{C}_\sigma^{\bullet Q}$ is s.t. $(K, Q) \vdash_\sigma \bot$. From inclusion, for every K s.t. $(K, Q) \vdash_\sigma \bot$, there is a $K' \subseteq K$ s.t. $K' \in \mathcal{C}_\sigma^{\bullet Q}$. Hence with minimality, for every K s.t. $(K, Q) \vdash_\sigma \bot$, if there is no K' s.t. $K' \subset K$ and $(K', Q) \vdash_\sigma \bot$, then $K \in \mathcal{C}_\sigma^{\bullet Q}$. Therefore, $\mathcal{C}_\sigma^{\bullet Q}$ is the set of min σ-conflicts for Q.

Proposition 12. *For $\sigma \in \{\mathsf{ma}, \mathsf{sw}\}$, if $\mathcal{C}_\sigma^{\bullet Q}$ is the set of min σ-conflicts for Q, then $\mathcal{C}_\sigma^{\bullet Q}$ satisfies the germane properties of no-equivalences, non-redundancy, tautology-freeness, non-triviality, non-quasi-triviality, and syntax-robustness, but not $\cup$-closure, atom-indifference, safe-set-freeness, nor substitution-robustness.*

Proof. Because $\mathcal{C}_\sigma^{\bullet Q}$ satisfies minimality, it satisfies no-equivalences, non-redundancy, tautology-freeness, non-triviality, and non-quasi-triviality. Because of Rule 2 for $\vdash_{\mathsf{ma}}$, and Rule 2 for $\vdash_{\mathsf{sw}}$, $\mathcal{C}_\sigma^{\bullet Q}$ satisfies syntax-robustness. Also, because $\mathcal{C}_\sigma^{\bullet Q}$ satisfies minimality, $\mathcal{C}_\sigma^{\bullet Q}$ does not satisfy $\cup$-closure. Because of Rules 3 and 4 for $\vdash_{\mathsf{ma}}$, and Rule 3 for $\vdash_{\mathsf{sw}}$, $\mathcal{C}_\sigma^{\bullet Q}$ does not satisfy atom-indifference, safe-set-freeness, nor substitution-robustness.

The above results show that min σ-conflicts are generalizations of minimal inconsistent sets, and so allow us to use quasi-equality directly in applications such as measures of inconsistency and computational models of argumentation. Using min σ-conflicts seems appropriate when Q is fixed in advance, by for example using a threshold on a similarity function. Whereas if we are not obliged to use all of Q, then using pareto σ-conflict-pairs may be more appropriate. For the former (i.e. using min σ-conflicts), we are making a commitment to all the quasi-equality relations in Q, and then seeking the minimal subsets of K that are σ-conflicts. For the latter (i.e. using pareto σ-conflict-pairs), we are not necessarily making a commitment to all the quasi-equality relations in Q (perhaps we believe there is some uncertainty whether the quasi-equality relations are correct), and so we want to minimize both the subsets of K and of Q when seeking conflicts in the form of σ-conflict-pairs.

8 Conflicts Based on Substitutions

We now compare using quasi-equality relations in conflict definitions (i.e. match conflicts and swap conflicts) with conflicts based on substitutions.

Proposition 13. *For $K \in \mathcal{K}$, and $Q \in \mathcal{Q}$, and $\sigma \in \{\mathsf{ma}, \mathsf{sw}\}$, if $(K, Q) \vdash_\sigma \bot$, then there is an atomic substitution mapping S s.t. $S(K)$ is inconsistent.*

Proof. Assume $(K, Q) \vdash_\sigma \bot$. To identify an atomic substitution mapping S, randomly select an atom in $\alpha \in \mathcal{A}$, and then for all $\beta \in \mathcal{A}$, let $S(\beta) = \alpha$. So for proof of inconsistency with the ma consequence relation, whenever Rule 3 or Rule 4 is applied, the resolution involves α and $\neg\alpha$, and therefore, there is a proof from $S(K)$ of $\bot$, and so $S(K)$ is inconsistent. Similarly, for proof of inconsistency with the sw consequence relation, whenever Rule 2 is applied, the proof step is $\{\phi_1, \ldots, \phi_n\} \vdash \phi_{n+1}$, and so there is a proof step $\{\phi'_1, \ldots, \phi'_n\} \vdash \phi'_{n+1}$ that can be used as part of a proof from $S(K)$ where each for $i \in \{1, \ldots, n+1\}$, ϕ'_i is the result of substituting α for each atom in ϕ_i. So there is a proof from $S(K)$ of $\bot$, and so $S(K)$ is inconsistent.

The above construction for the atomic substitution mapping is an extreme option that does not take the quasi-equality relations into account. However, we can construct a substitution mapping to take these relations into account. For instance, if for all $\alpha \simeq \beta, \gamma \simeq \delta \in Q$, both $\alpha \notin \{\gamma, \delta\}$ and $\beta \notin \{\gamma, \delta\}$ hold, then for all $\phi, \psi \in \mathcal{A}$, if $\phi \simeq \psi \in Q$, then let either $S(\phi) = \psi$ or $S(\psi) = \phi$ but not both. So if $(K, Q) \vdash_\sigma \bot$, then $S(K)$ is inconsistent.

Example 14. Let $K = \{\neg\mathtt{a}, \mathtt{b} \vee \neg\mathtt{c}, \mathtt{d} \vee \mathtt{e}, \neg\mathtt{f}\}$ and $Q = \{\mathtt{a} \simeq \mathtt{b}, \mathtt{c} \simeq \mathtt{d}, \mathtt{e} \simeq \mathtt{f}\}$. Therefore, $(K, Q) \vdash_{\mathsf{ma}} \bot$ and $(K, Q) \vdash_{\mathsf{sw}} \bot$. For all $\alpha \simeq \beta, \gamma \simeq \delta \in Q$, both $\alpha \notin \{\gamma, \delta\}$ and $\beta \notin \{\gamma, \delta\}$ hold. Therefore, there is a substitution S such that for all $\phi, \psi \in \mathcal{A}$, if $\phi \simeq \psi \in Q$, then either $S(\phi) = \psi$ or $S(\psi) = \phi$ but not both. For instance, let $S(\mathtt{a}) = \mathtt{b}$, $S(\mathtt{c}) = \mathtt{d}$, and $S(\mathtt{e}) = \mathtt{f}$. So $S(K)$ is inconsistent.

In the following example, we see that in order to have an inconsistent set after substitution, the substitution function is not injective.

Example 15. Let $K = \{\mathtt{a} \vee \mathtt{b} \vee \mathtt{c}, \neg\mathtt{e} \vee \mathtt{f}, \neg\mathtt{f} \vee \mathtt{a}, \neg\mathtt{h}, \neg\mathtt{c}, \neg\mathtt{d} \vee \mathtt{k}\}$ and $Q = \{\mathtt{a} \simeq \mathtt{e}, \mathtt{a} \simeq \mathtt{h}, \mathtt{b} \simeq \mathtt{d}, \mathtt{k} \simeq \mathtt{h}\}$. So $(K, Q) \vdash_\sigma \bot$ for $\sigma \in \{\mathsf{ma}, \mathsf{sw}\}$. Now we can specify a non-injective substitution function. Let $S(\mathtt{a}) = \mathtt{x}$, $S(\mathtt{b}) = \mathtt{x}$, $S(\mathtt{d}) = \mathtt{x}$, $S(\mathtt{e}) = \mathtt{x}$, $S(\mathtt{h}) = \mathtt{x}$, and $S(\mathtt{k}) = \mathtt{x}$. So $S(K)$ is inconsistent. In contrast, for any injective substitution function S' (e.g. $S'(\mathtt{a}) = \mathtt{p}$, $S'(\mathtt{b}) = \mathtt{q}$, $S'(\mathtt{d}) = \mathtt{r}$, $S'(\mathtt{e}) = \mathtt{s}$, $S'(\mathtt{h}) = \mathtt{t}$, and $S'(\mathtt{k}) = \mathtt{v}$), $S'(K)$ is consistent.

Proposition 14. *For $K \in \mathcal{K}$, and $\sigma \in \{\mathsf{ma}, \mathsf{sw}\}$, and atomic substitution mapping S, if $S(K)$ is inconsistent, then there is a $Q \in \mathcal{Q}$ s.t. $(K, Q) \vdash_\sigma \bot$.*

Proof. Assume that there is an atomic substitution mapping S for which $S(K)$ is inconsistent. Let $Q = \{\alpha \simeq \beta \mid S(\alpha) = \beta \text{ for } \alpha, \beta \in \mathcal{A}\}$. Also, let $\mathsf{Clauses}(S(K))$ be the set of clauses obtained by writing $S(K)$ into conjunctive normal form, and then exhaustively applying conjunction elimination. Since $S(K)$ is inconsistent, there is a proof of inconsistency by applying the resolution proof rule to the clauses in $\mathsf{Clauses}(S(K))$ until there is a proof of the empty clause (i.e. $\mathsf{Clauses}(S(K)) \vdash \bot$). We can therefore construct a proof of $\bot$ from K using the ma consequence relation as follows. For each application of the resolution proof rule in the proof from $S(K)$, there are clauses ϕ and ψ to which resolution is applied in the proof. Furthermore, there are formulae in ϕ' and ψ' such that $(K, Q) \vdash_{\mathsf{ma}} \phi'$ and $(K, Q) \vdash_{\mathsf{ma}} \psi'$ and $S(\phi') = \phi$ and $S(\psi') = \psi$. Therefore, there is an application of Rule 3 or Rule 4 of the $\vdash_{\mathsf{ma}}$ consequence relation. Therefore, if $S(K)$ is inconsistent, then there is a $Q \in \mathcal{Q}$ s.t. (K, Q) is a ma-conflict. Furthermore, by Proposition 4, (K, Q) is a sw-conflict.

It is possible for min σ-conflicts and minimal inconsistent sets to coincide (Examples 16 and 17) but this is not always possible (Example 18).

Example 16. Let $K = \{\mathtt{a}, \neg\mathtt{b}\}$ and $Q = \{\mathtt{a} \simeq \mathtt{b}\}$. So K is a min sw-conflict for Q, and K is a min ma-conflict for Q, and there is an atomic substitution S such that $S(K)$ is a minimal inconsistent set (e.g. $S(\mathtt{a}) = \mathtt{b}$).

Example 17. Let $K = \{\mathtt{a} \vee \mathtt{b} \vee \mathtt{c}, \neg\mathtt{e} \vee \mathtt{f}, \neg\mathtt{f} \vee \mathtt{h}, \neg\mathtt{h}, \neg\mathtt{c}, \neg\mathtt{d} \vee \mathtt{k}\}$ and $Q = \{\mathtt{a} \simeq \mathtt{e}, \mathtt{b} \simeq \mathtt{d}, \mathtt{k} \simeq \mathtt{h}\}$. So K is a min sw-conflict for Q, and K is a min ma-conflict for Q. Let $S(\mathtt{a}) = \mathtt{e}$, $S(\mathtt{b}) = \mathtt{d}$, and $S(\mathtt{k}) = \mathtt{h}$. So $S(K)$ is a minimal inconsistent set.

Example 18. Let $K = \{\mathtt{a}, \neg\mathtt{c}\}$ and $Q = \{\mathtt{a} \simeq \mathtt{b}, \mathtt{b} \simeq \mathtt{c}\}$. So K is a min sw-conflict for Q, but K is not a min ma-conflict for Q. There is an atomic substitution S such that $S(K)$ is a minimal inconsistent set, (e.g. $S(\mathtt{a}) = \mathtt{c}$).

The following are relationships between pareto σ-conflicts and substitution conflicts.

Proposition 15. *For $K \in \mathcal{K}$, and $Q \in \mathcal{Q}$, and $\sigma \in \{\mathsf{ma}, \mathsf{sw}\}$, if K is a min σ-conflict for Q, then there is an atomic substitution mapping S s.t. $S(K)$ is inconsistent.*

Proof. By Definition 4, K is a min σ-conflict for Q implies $(K, Q) \vdash_\sigma \bot$. So by Proposition 13, there is an atomic substitution mapping S s.t. $S(K)$ is inconsistent.

Proposition 16. *For $K \in \mathcal{K}$, and $\sigma \in \{\mathsf{ma}, \mathsf{sw}\}$, and atomic substitution mapping S, if $S(K)$ is a minimal inconsistent set, then there is a $Q \in \mathcal{Q}$ and $K' \subseteq K$ s.t. K' is a min σ-conflict for Q.*

Proof. Assume $S(K)$ is a minimal inconsistent set. By Proposition 14, there is a $Q \in \mathcal{Q}$ s.t. $(K, Q) \vdash_\sigma \bot$. So there is a $K' \subseteq K$ s.t. K' is a min σ-conflict for Q.

In this section, we have provided some insight into the match and swap conflicts by comparing them with substitution conflicts. Whilst one can replicate the other to some degree, the advantage of match conflicts, and swap conflicts, is that the use of the quasi-equality relations is made explicit. Furthermore, it allows for different quasi-equivalences to be used at different points in the proof of inconsistency, whereas in contrast, the use of substitution can involve substituting several atoms at the same time without it being clear how they are being used (as seen in Example 15).

9 Discussion

Inconsistency is a common issue in dealing with data and knowledge. Approaches to dealing with it include paraconsistent logics [2,5,16] , measures of inconsistency (for a review, see [19]), characterizations of notions of conflict [6,7,14], inconsistency management frameworks (e.g. [8]), and computational models of argument (e.g. [1,3,4]). However, none of these take the meaning of the atoms into account. To address this, in this paper, we have introduced the notion of quasi-equality based on similarity between

Table 3. Similarity between each pair of sentences (atoms) from $\mathtt{s}_1$ to $\mathtt{s}_4$ using the all-MiniLM-L6-v2 Sentence Transformer from sbert.net where $\mathtt{s}_1$ is *The car is red*,$\mathtt{s}_2$ is *The car is big*,$\mathtt{s}_3$ is *The car is red and big*,and $\mathtt{s}_4$ is *The car is red and the car is big*.

	$\mathtt{s}_1$	$\mathtt{s}_2$	$\mathtt{s}_3$	$\mathtt{s}_4$
$\mathtt{s}_1$	1.0000	0.5811	0.8715	0.8460
$\mathtt{s}_2$	0.5811	1.0000	0.8049	0.7981
$\mathtt{s}_3$	0.8715	0.8049	1.0000	0.9708
$\mathtt{s}_4$	0.8460	0.7981	0.9708	1.0000

atoms, and we have provided two consequence relations for extending classical reasoning with quasi-equality. We have defined a notion of conflict based on each consequence relation and shown how they are types of germane conflict.

Other approaches to defining notions of conflict often appear as intermediate tools for measuring inconsistency such as defining conflict in terms of prime implicates [10], localizing inconsistency in terms of atoms [9], localizing inconsistency using the $\star$-conflicts framework [6], and localizing inconsistency using various 3-valued logic [9, 13, 14]. But none of these approaches have considered similarity between atoms as part of a definition of conflict.

These new notions of germane conflict are potentially valuable in the development of new inconsistency measures, new methods of conflict resolution, and new forms of attack relationship in computational argumentation. For example, for logic-based argumentation, a common definition for an argument A attacking an argument B is when the claim of A is inconsistent with the premises of B [4]. With the notions of conflict introduced in this paper, we can define a more general notion of attack holding when there is a σ-conflict involving the claim of A and the premises of B.

A topic for future work is investigating the compromises arising from using quasi-equality as illustrated by the following example. Let $K = \{\mathtt{a} \vee \mathtt{b}, \neg\mathtt{c} \vee \mathtt{d}, \neg\mathtt{e}, \neg\mathtt{f}, \neg\mathtt{g}\}$, $K_1 = \{\mathtt{a} \vee \mathtt{b}, \neg\mathtt{f}, \neg\mathtt{g}\}$, $K_2 = \{\mathtt{a} \vee \mathtt{b}, \neg\mathtt{c} \vee \mathtt{d}, \neg\mathtt{e}, \neg\mathtt{f}\}$, $Q = \{\mathtt{a} \simeq \mathtt{f}, \mathtt{b} \simeq \mathtt{g}, \mathtt{b} \simeq \mathtt{c}, \mathtt{d} \simeq \mathtt{e}\}$, $Q_1 = \{\mathtt{a} \simeq \mathtt{f}, \mathtt{b} \simeq \mathtt{g}\}$, $Q_2 = \{\mathtt{a} \simeq \mathtt{f}, \mathtt{b} \simeq \mathtt{c}, \mathtt{d} \simeq \mathtt{e}\}$, $M(\mathtt{a}, \mathtt{f}) = 0.6$, $M(\mathtt{b}, \mathtt{g}) = 0.7$, $M(\mathtt{b}, \mathtt{c}) = 0.8$, and $M(\mathtt{d}, \mathtt{e}) = 0.8$. Here (K_1, Q_1) and (K_2, Q_2) are both pareto ma-conflicts, but the compromises (the list of similarities between atoms appearing in the quasi-equality relations) for Q_1 is $\langle 0.7, 0.6\rangle$ and for Q_2 is $\langle 0.8, 0.8, 0.6\rangle$. So, Q_1 uses fewer quasi-equality relations, but Q_2 uses better quasi-equality relations.

Another topic for future work is extending quasi-equality to arbitrary formulae. For example, for the four sentences in Table 3. As $\mathtt{s}_3$ and $\mathtt{s}_4$ have the same semantic content, and high similarity score, $\mathtt{s}_3 \simeq \mathtt{s}_4$. Also both $\mathtt{s}_3$ and $\mathtt{s}_4$ imply $\mathtt{s}_1$ and $\mathtt{s}_2$. Moreover, $\mathtt{s}_4$ is the same string as the string involving the conjunction of $\mathtt{s}_1$ and $\mathtt{s}_2$, and this has the same information as the string $\mathtt{s}_1 \wedge \mathtt{s}_2$, and so we may want $\mathtt{s}_4 \simeq \mathtt{s}_1 \wedge \mathtt{s}_2$.

Finally, a comparison of different embedding systems would be interesting since the similarities could differ and thereby reveal different conflicts. This then raises the question of how these different conflicts could be aggregated to give deeper insights into the nature of the knowledge.

Acknowledgments. The author is grateful to Glauber De Bona and to the anonymous reviewers for valuable feedback for improving the paper.

References

1. Atkinson, K., et al.: Towards artificial argumentation. AI Mag. **38**(3), 25–36 (2017)
2. Belnap, N.: A useful four-valued logic. In: Modern Uses of Multiple-valued Logic, pp. 8–37. Reidel (1977)
3. Besnard, P., et al.: Introduction to structured argumentation. Argument Comput. **5**(1), 1–4 (2014)
4. Besnard, P., Hunter, A.: A logic-based theory of deductive arguments. Artif. Intell. **128**, 203–235 (2001)
5. Carnielli, W., Coniglio, M.E., Marcos, J.: Logics of formal inconsistency. In: Handbook of Philosophical Logic, pp. 1–93. Springer (2007)
6. De Bona, G., Hunter, A.: Localising iceberg inconsistencies. Artif. Intell. **246**, 118–151 (2017)
7. De Bona, G., Hunter, A.: Germane conflicts: desirable properties for localising inconsistency. In: Proceedings of AAAI'25. AAAI Press (2025)
8. Eiter, T., Fink, M., Schüller, P., Weinzierl, A.: Finding explanations of inconsistency in multi-context systems. Artif. Intell. **216**, 233–274 (2014)
9. Grant, J., Hunter, A.: Semantic inconsistency measures using 3-valued logics. Int. J. Approximate Reasoning **156**, 38–60 (2023)
10. Jabbour, S., Ma, Y., Raddaoui, B., Sais, L.: On the characterization of inconsistency measures: a prime implicates based framework. In: Proceedings of ICTAI'14, pp. 146–153. IEEE Press (2014)
11. Jiang, T., et al.: PromptBERT: improving BERT sentence embeddings with prompts (2022). arXiv:2201.04337
12. Lee, J., et al.: Gemini embedding: generalizable embeddings from Gemini (2025). arXiv:2503.07891
13. Mu, K.: Formulas free from inconsistency: an atom-centric characterization in Priest's minimally inconsistent LP. J. Artif. Intell. Res. **66**, 279–296 (2019)
14. Mu, K.: The interior of inconsistency in a knowledge base. Int. J. Approximate Reasoning **166**, 109127 (2024)
15. Ou, F., Xu, J.: SKICSE: Sentence knowable information prompted by LLMs improves contrastive sentence embeddings. In: Proceedings of NAACL'24, pp. 141–146. Association for Computational Linguistics (2024)
16. Priest, G.: Paraconsistent logic. In: Gabbay, D.M., Guenthner, F. (eds.) Handbook of Philosophical Logic, vol. 6, pp. 287–393. Springer (2002)
17. Reimers, N., Gurevych, I.: Sentence-BERT: sentence embeddings using Siamese BERT-networks. In: Proceedings of EMNLP'19, pp. 3982–3992. Association for Computational Linguistics (2019)
18. Surdeanu, M., Valenzuela-Escácega, M.A.: Deep Learning for Natural Language Processing. Cambridge University Press (2024)
19. Thimm, M.: On the expressivity of inconsistency measures. Artif. Intell. **234**, 120–151 (2016)

Dynamic Logic for Quantum Probability

Tomoaki Kawano(✉)

Kanagawa University, Yokohama, Japan
tomoakikawano.tk@gmail.com

Abstract. Quantum logic (**QL**) has been developed using various methods. Among them, orthomodular lattices and binary relational models have been discussed as models that concisely express the logic of quantum mechanics. Although these models are compatible with mathematical logic, some elements are still missing. In this study, a new binary relational model that introduces the concept of inner product in a Hilbert space is proposed. We also propose dynamic extended quantum logic (**DEQL**), which is the logic based on the new model, and prove some of the usefulness of the model and logic.

1 Introduction

Quantum logic (**QL**) is the field of mathematical logic that deals with the peculiar propositions of quantum mechanics. In this field, quantum mechanics concepts are appropriately represented using modal symbols, predicate symbols, and other logical concepts.

In quantum mechanics, *Hilbert spaces* are used as the state space of particles, and a quantum state is represented by a vector or one-dimensional closed subspace of a specific Hilbert space. Therefore, models of quantum logic are also based on Hilbert spaces. It ranges from models using the Hilbert space itself to simple models using only some aspects of it. One of the trends of quantum logic, starting with the literature [5] is research that analyzes *lattices* formed by sets of observational propositions, which is related to the closed subspaces of a Hilbert space. Among such lattices, *orthomodular lattices* have attracted attention, and quantum logic that is based on orthomodular lattices is referred to as *orthomodular logic* (**OML**) [11].

There is also a study for propositions of quantum mechanics with *binary relational models*, which are compatible with lattices in some sense [7]. In the simplest binary relational model in quantum logic, each element represents a quantum state and the binary relation represents an *orthogonal relation* between states. A model that adds several vital concepts from quantum mechanics, such as *unitary transformations* and *projections* due to observations to this simple model is also analyzed in the context of *dynamic quantum logic* (**DQL**) [1–3].

However, in studies dealing with propositions of quantum mechanics using binary relations, research that directly handles values of the *inner product* of quantum states has not advanced. Basic quantum logic only deals with the concept of whether states are orthogonal or not. Concrete inner product values

K. Sauerwald and M. Thimm (Eds.): ECSQARU 2025, LNAI 16099, pp. 484–498, 2026.
https://doi.org/10.1007/978-3-032-05134-9_33

between quantum states are important in dealing with properties of Hilbert spaces and *quantum probabilities*. In quantum mechanics, the probability that proposition A holds in state (unit vector) Ψ is given as follows:

$$|\langle\Psi|P(\Psi, A)\rangle|^2,$$

where $P(\Psi, A)$ is the normalized vector after Ψ is projected onto the closed subspace that A is true, and $\langle\ |\ \rangle$ is the inner product. Several logics involving quantum probability values have been proposed [4,10,17]. Each of these studies has significant characteristics and uses formulas or models which include complex mathematical structures of Hilbert spaces. In other words, this direction of study directly uses the concept of Hilbert spaces as a model or formulas for logic. One advantage in this direction is that it allows detailed propositional analysis of quantum structures. However, it is also important to have a logic that briefly addresses only certain concepts of Hilbert spaces and use relatively simple abstract models. Therefore, this study proposes and discusses a developed relational model that includes the concepts of quantum probabilities but does not directly use Hilbert spaces. One advantage of using methods in this direction is that it is easy to divert methods and compare concepts with other existing logics.

In mathematical logic, probability has mainly been discussed using *probabilistic logic*, *many-valued logic*, or *fuzzy logic* [6,8,9,16,19]. However, applying these logics directly to the logic of probability in quantum mechanics is difficult because in quantum mechanics, the dedicated concept, such as *change in states* due to observation is related to probability. In quantum mechanics, when a physical quantity is observed, the state is projected onto the closed subspace in which the obtained result is true. This study constructs suitable models that combine dynamic concepts and inner products to address these problems. Literature [18] may be regarded as the most basic study in which inner product values are introduced as relations in binary relational models. Based on such a model, *extended quantum logic* (**EQL**) and its modal logical counterpart **MB** were constructed and discussed in [18]. In **EQL**, the truth value of a proposition was associated with the inner product value between states. In **MB**, although the truth value is binary, some modal symbols were introduced to represent propositions related to the value of the inner product. However, the following issues remain because only the fundamental properties of the inner product value and minimum required logical symbols were introduced in [18].

1. **EQL** and **MB** do not include the concept of change of states.
2. Some fundamental properties of quantum mechanics may not handled in these two logics. For example, the basic property of probability, "If the probability that A is true is α, then the probability that A is not true is $1-\alpha$" may not hold or cannot be expressed.

This study proposes a model that solves these problems. We construct a suitable frame capable of handling the important nature of the inner product and dynamism in a Hilbert space by combining **MB** and some notions of **DQL**. In addition to introducing the numerical relation of the inner product, a wide variety of *conditions* are added to the model. These conditions are fundamental from the Hilbert space and quantum physics perspective and could not be expressed in the previous frame [18]. In this study, the usefulness and validity of this new model will be demonstrated as follows:

1. The formulas of the new logic can express all important conditions added to frames.
2. Some properties important in the context of quantum logic are naturally derived from the added conditions. In other binary relational frames of logic (such as **OML**, **EQL** or **DQL**), these conditions had to be added explicitly as a definition.

In Sect. 2, the basics of **EQL** are reviewed. In Sect. 3, the basics of new logic *dynamic extended quantum logic* (**DEQL**) are argued. In Sect. 4, conditions on a frame of **DEQL** are defined, and some properties of the new frame are discussed. In Sect. 5, an axiomatization of new logic is discussed.

2 Extended Quantum Logic (EQL)

In this section, we review **EQL** defined in [18]. In [18], two logics, **EQL** and **MB** were constructed. **EQL** is a logic that deals with some of the properties of the inner product of elements of a Hilbert space, and **MB** is **EQL**'s modal logic counterpart. From an expressive point of view, **MB** is suitable for expressing detailed properties of inner products. Therefore, we construct an extension of **MB** in this study. For later discussion, the definition is slightly changed from those in [18], but the essence remains the same. The language of **MB** consists of the following vocabulary:

propositional variables: $p, q, \ldots$
propositional constants: $\top, \bot$
logical connectives: $\neg, \wedge, \Box^c_\alpha, \Box^o_\alpha$ $(\alpha \in I)$

where I is a subset of the unit interval $[0, 1]$. In [18], for simplicity, I is defined as a finite set. In this study, we define I as the set of all rational numbers included in $[0, 1]$. This definition is a setting for expressing conditions regarding the inner product. Expressing more detailed properties of the inner product requires some basic arithmetic operations, such as number division, and it takes it out of the scope of a finite set. Even in this situation, as I is within the range of a countable set, the number of modal symbols also becomes countable. Therefore, this definition of I is a definition that just rightly balances both expressive power and mathematical logic requirements. c stands for "closed", and o stands for "open". These meanings can be seen in the definition of the valuation of formulas in a frame, which will be discussed later. The set of formulas of **MB** is defined as follows:

$$A ::= p \mid \top \mid \bot \mid \neg A \mid A \wedge A \mid \Box^c_\alpha A \mid \Box^o_\alpha A (\alpha \in I)$$

Formulas are denoted $A, B, \ldots$, and finite sets of formulas are denoted $\Gamma, \Delta, \Sigma, \ldots$.

An *EQL-frame* (W, R) is defined as follows:

W: a non-empty set, an element of which is referred to as a pure quantum state.
R: an I-valued accessibility relation on W, i.e., $R : W \times W \to I$, satisfying the following conditions: $R(x, y) = 1$ if $x = y$ (reflexivity), $R(x, y) = R(y, x)(\forall x, y \in W)$ (symmetry).

Each element of W represents a unit vector (quantum state) on a certain Hilbert space. R is introduced to express numerical values of the absolute square value of the inner product between quantum states, which is related to quantum probability. (At the level of abstraction in this study, whether we regard R as the absolute value of the inner product or the absolute value of the square of the inner product does not affect the essential content of a frame.However, considering the conditions on a frame, the square representation allows I within the range of rational numbers.Therefore, we regard R as representing the square of the absolute value of inner product of states.) We write $x(\alpha)y$ for $R(x, y) = \alpha$. We write $x \perp y$ for $R(x, y) = 0$, and $x \not\perp y$ for not $x \perp y$. Traditionally, the symbol $\perp$ is used for orthogonality in quantum logic. The context can determine the difference between this symbol and a contradictory symbol. We write $x \perp X$ if $x \perp y$ for all $y \in X$, and write $X^{\perp}$ for the set $\{x | x \perp X\}$. A set $X \subseteq W$ is a $\perp$-*closed set* (or *testable set*) if $X^{\perp\perp} = X$. $\perp$-closed sets represent closed subspaces on a Hilbert space, which correspond to observation propositions of quantum mechanics. We write OC_M for the set of all $\perp$-closed sets of $M = (W, R)$ without an empty set.

Valuation V is defined as a map from propositional variables to the power set of W. V is extended recursively to the set of all formulas as follows:

$V(\top) = W$,
$V(\perp) = \emptyset$,
$V(A \wedge B) = V(A) \cap V(B)$,
$V(\neg A) = V(A)^c$,
$V(\Box^c_\alpha A) = \{x \in W |$ for all $y \in W$, if $\alpha \leq R(x, y)$, then $y \in V(A)\}$,
$V(\Box^o_\alpha A) = \{x \in W |$ for all $y \in W$, if $\alpha < R(x, y)$, then $y \in V(A)\}$.

Considering the meaning of the inner product, we can regard the meaning of the formula $\neg\Box^c_\alpha \neg A$ as follows:

$\neg\Box^c_\alpha \neg A$: If an observer tests whether A holds, the observer obtains "A is true" with probability α or higher.

In this way, rather than $\Box^c_\alpha$ itself, but rather complex formulas that have various meanings. Regarding o, the above "α or higher" can be replaced as "higher than α".

An *EQL-model* is defined as a tuple (W, R, V) where (W, R) is an EQL-frame. Formula A is *true* at x if $x \in V(A)$ and we write $x \models A$. A is *valid* in an EQL-frame (W, R) if for all V and $x \in W$, A is true at x. A is valid in EQL-frames if A is valid in all EQL-frames. **EQL** is defined as the set of all valid formulas in EQL-frames.

3 Dynamic Extended Quantum Logic

In this section, *dynamic extended quantum logic* (**DEQL**), the appropriate extension of **MB**, is constructed. As logical symbols, we add modal symbols for unitary transformations and projections based on the symbols that appear in **DQL** [1–3]. Because the projection is related to quantum probability, rational number symbols α are assigned to the modal symbols of the projection. However, since unitary transformations are a single concept, rational number symbols are not assigned, and those of **DQL** are used as they are.

To interpret the meaning of these new symbols, we add relations for these notions of the quantum mechanism to an EQL-frame. Furthermore, various conditions are added to express some essential properties of Hilbert spaces.

MB deals with the modal symbols for c and o, which are comparison operators. To improve expressiveness, a modal symbol representing *equality* is also added. Then, it is possible to handle not only the proposition including "with probability greater than or equal to α" but also the proposition including "with exact probability α". This concept is important for expressing conditions for frames. The set of formulas of **DEQL** is defined as follows:

$$A ::= p \mid \top \mid \bot \mid \neg A \mid A \wedge A \mid \Box^c_\alpha A \mid \Box^o_\alpha A \mid \Box^=_\alpha A \mid [A?]^c_\alpha A \mid [A?]^o_\alpha A \mid [A?]^=_\alpha A \mid [U_j]A$$

where α and I are the same as the previous section, $j \in J$ and J is a countable set. A *DEQL-frame* (dynamic EQL-frame) $(W, R, P, \mathcal{U})$ is defined as an extension of an EQL-frame (W, R). The following relations are added to an EQL-frame.

P : a set of binary relations $P_X \subseteq W \times W : X \in OC_M$ which represent change of state by projections onto X.
$\mathcal{U}$: a set of binary relations $U_j \subseteq W \times W : j \in J$ which represent change of state by unitary transformations.

We write $x(X)y$ for $(x, y) \in P_X$. V is also extended as follows:

$$V(\Box^=_\alpha A) = \{x \in W \mid \text{for all } y \in W, \text{ if } \alpha = R(x, y), \text{ then } y \in V(A)\},$$
$$V([A?]^c_\alpha B) = \{x \in W \mid \forall y \in W, \text{ if } x(A?)y \text{ and } \alpha \leq R(x, y), \text{ then } y \in V(B)\},$$
$$V([A?]^o_\alpha B) = \{x \in W \mid \forall y \in W, \text{ if } x(A?)y \text{ and } \alpha < R(x, y), \text{ then } y \in V(B)\},$$
$$V([A?]^=_\alpha B) = \{x \in W \mid \forall y \in W, \text{ if } x(A?)y \text{ and } \alpha = R(x, y), \text{ then } y \in V(B)\}.$$
$$V([U_j]A) = \{x \in W \mid \text{for all } y \in W, \text{ if } x(U_j)y, \text{ then } y \in V(A)\}.$$

We write $x(A?)y$ for $x(X)y$ and $V(A) = X$. This relation represents the change in the state due to projection when "A is true" is obtained.

A vector in the Hilbert space represents a quantum state, but the magnitude of the vector is generally not considered important. Vectors in the same one-dimensional space are often regarded as the same state. Then, as its representative element, the unit vector (vector of magnitude 1) is often used, and this study also adopts this perspective for W. However, this representation is somewhat incompatible with the concept of projection because, in general, after a vector is projected, the magnitude of the vector may change. R is defined as assuming the inner product value between unit vectors. Therefore, we adopt the view that a vector has magnitude 1 after being projected, together with the notion of one-dimensional space. For example, in a three-dimensional space $\mathbb{R}^3$, we take the view that after $(1/\sqrt{3}, 1/\sqrt{3}, 1/\sqrt{3})$ is projected onto $xy-$plane, $(1/\sqrt{2}, 1/\sqrt{2}, 0)$ is obtained (not $(1/\sqrt{3}, 1/\sqrt{3}, 0)$).

DEQL-model is defined as a tuple $(W, R, P, \mathcal{U}, V)$ where $(W, R, P, \mathcal{U})$ is a DEQL-frame and V is a valuation.

We use the following abbreviations. $A \rightarrow B = \neg A \vee B$, $A \leftrightarrow B = (A \rightarrow B) \wedge (B \rightarrow A)$, $\Box A = \Box_0^o A$, $\sim A = \Box \neg A$, $\Diamond_\alpha^c A = \neg \Box_\alpha^c \neg A$, $\Diamond_\alpha^o A = \neg \Box_\alpha^o \neg A$, $\Diamond_\alpha^= A = \neg \Box_\alpha^= \neg A$. $\langle A? \rangle_\alpha^c B = \neg [A?]_\alpha^c \neg B$, $\langle A? \rangle_\alpha^o B = \neg [A?]_\alpha^o \neg B$, $\langle A? \rangle_\alpha^= B = \neg [A?]_\alpha^= \neg B$, $[A?]B = [A?]_0^c B$, $\langle U_j \rangle B = \neg [U_j] \neg B$.

In this definition of V, $\Box_\alpha^c$ can be defined by $\Box_\alpha^o$ and $\Box_\alpha^=$ in the following sense:

For all A of **DEQL** and DEQL-model, $V(\Box_\alpha^c A) = V(\Box_\alpha^o A \wedge \Box_\alpha^= A)$.

However, since $\Box_\alpha^c$ is important as an expression, we use it as a primitive symbol in this study.

$\sim$ is called *quantum negation*. $\neg A$ represents that proposition A is not 100% true and $\sim A$ represents that proposition A is 100% false. As in the case of **OML**, $V(\sim A) = V(A)^\perp$ holds.

Considering the meaning of the inner product and projections, we can regard the meaning of the formula $[A?]_\alpha^c B$ as follows:

$[A?]_\alpha^c B$: In a situation where A can be obtained with probability α or higher, if A is actually obtained, then B is also true.

Regarding o and $=$, the above "α or higher" can be replaced as "higher than α" or "exactly α" respectively. The meaning of this formula itself is somewhat complex, but it is rarely used as a standalone formula; as we will see later, it is more of a part of a meaningful, compound formula.

In a DEQL-frame, $X \subseteq X^{\perp\perp}$ for all $X \subseteq W$. From the definition of R, $\Box_0^c A$ means that for all $x \in W$, $x \models A$. Therefore, $\Box_0^c(\sim\sim A \rightarrow A)$ means $V(A)$ is a $\perp$-closed set. We abbreviate $\Box_0^c(\sim\sim A \rightarrow A)$ as $T(A)$.

4 Conditions on Frames

In this section, conditions on a DEQL-frame are argued, and a more strict frame is defined. The conditions covered in this study and their meanings are listed below. The conditions (1., 2., 3., 4., 13., 14.) have already been discussed in the context of DQL, but because the definition of the frame is different, some of the content has changed slightly.

1. **Repeatability of projection**
   If $x(X)y$, then $y \in X$.
   This condition expresses the property that after a state is projected onto X, the state is included in X.
2. **Adequacy**
   If $x \in X$ and $X \in OC_M$, then $x(X)x$.
   This condition expresses the property that if a state is already included in the closed subspace X, projecting it onto X does not change the state.
3. **Partial functionality of projection**
   If $x(X)y$ and $x(X)z$, then $y = z$.
   This condition expresses the property that once the state and closed subspace are determined, the projection destination is uniquely determined.
4. **Non-orthogonality of projection**
   If $x(X)y$, then $0 < R(x, y)$.
   This condition expresses the property that when a state is projected onto a closed subspace that is orthogonal to it, it becomes a zero vector. (That is, after such a projection, the state is no longer a pure quantum state, and so such binary relations should not appear in the frame.)
5. **Identity**
   If $x(1)y$, then $x = y$.
   This condition expresses the property that if the inner product of two normalized elements is 1, then these two elements are in the same state.
6. **Possibility of projection**
   For all $y \in W$, not $x(X)y$ iff one of the following is true.
   (I).$x \in X^{\perp}$,
   (II).$X \notin OC_M$.
   This condition expresses the property that if the state is not orthogonal to X, it can be treated as a quantum state without becoming a zero vector even when projected onto X. Therefore, the relation that represents such a movement should be included in the frame.
7. **Proper probability**
   For all $x, y \in W$, if $x(X)y$, $x(\alpha)y$ and $\alpha \neq 1$, then there exists $z \in W$ such that $x(X^{\perp})z$ and $R(x, z) = 1 - \alpha$.
   In quantum mechanics, when we measure whether A is true or not, if the result that A is true is obtained, the state is projected onto the closed subspace where A is true, and if the result that A is not true is obtained, the state is projected onto the orthogonal space of the closed subspace where A is true. (Other observations than this concept can be considered in quantum mechanics. But in this study, we will only cover this basic observational concept.) Whether A is true or not is determined by probability, and the sum of the probability values must be 1.
8. **Proper projection**

For all $x, y \in W$, if $x(X)y$ and $x(\alpha)y$, then $\alpha = \max\{\beta | z \in X \text{ and } x(\beta)z\}$. This condition expresses the property that the state of the projection of state Ψ onto space X is an element in X that is "closest" to Ψ.

9. **Non-orthogonality of dense states**
   For all $x, y, z \in W$, if $x(\alpha)y$, $y(\beta)z$, $x(\gamma)z$ and $1 < \alpha + \beta$, then $0 < \gamma$. This condition expresses that if three states are close in the sense of inner product, no two states of these states will be orthogonal.
10. **Plane1**
    If $x(\alpha)y$, $x \neq y$ and $\alpha \neq 0$, then there exists $z \in W$ such that $x(0)z$ and $R(y, z) = 1 - \alpha$.
    This condition expresses that if a state exists and another state exists, the space is at least two-dimensional, so an orthogonal basis of the two-dimensional space exists.
11. **Plane2**
    For all $x, y, z \in W$ and $X \in OC_M$, if $x(\alpha)y$, $y(1 - \alpha)z$, $x \perp z$, $x \in X$ and $y \in X$, then $z \in X$.
    This condition expresses that when a state Ψ can be decomposed into two bases, then Ψ and these two bases are on one plane.
12. **Inner product and projection**
    For all $x, y, z \in W$ and $X \in OC_M$, if $x(\alpha)y$, $y \in X$, $x(\beta)z$ and $x(X)z$, then $z(\alpha/\beta)y$.
    This condition represents the change in the inner product value due to projection. The inner product value with a point contained in the closed subspace of the projection changes from α to α/β. This is a corollary of the following well-known theorem on Hilbert spaces:
    $P_X\Psi = \sum_{i=1}^{\infty}(e_i, \Psi)e_i$
    where $P_X\Psi$ is the projection of Ψ onto subspace X, and $\{e_1, e_2, ...\}$ is an orthonormal basis of X. The condition can be derived from this theorem by using the basic properties of the inner product. Therefore, we omit the proof here.
    The probability distribution after some measurement has been made is essential. In classical probability theory, such a notion occupies an important position with *conditional probability*. In the case of quantum mechanics, since the state changes depending on the observation, it is important to see how the probability distribution changes by projections. In other words, how the value of the inner product between states changes after projection must be investigated. However, this condition does not cover all cases. This condition only deals with changes in the inner product value with y included in X. This notion is related to the *commutativity* of propositions [7]. In quantum mechanics, if propositions X and Y are commutative, observing Y after X is observed and observing $X \cap Y$ are the same movement. Therefore, if X and Y are commutative, when we observe Y after X, only the states already included in X are relevant. Therefore, this condition is related to the change in the inner product value when two commutative propositions are observed in sequence. (Within the scope of the level of abstraction in this study, it is difficult to argue for general

law about changes of probabilities when X and Y are not commutative. When operators are not commutative, the analysis of stochastic processes becomes much more complex. That analysis would require another complex algebraic concept, and even if it were to be expressed in modal logic, it would require a considerably different and complex model. However, from a quantum mechanical point of view, the analysis of commutative operators alone is helpful in its way.)

13. **Unitary1**
    For all $x \in W$, $\exists y \in W$, $x(U_j)y$.
    This condition expresses that unitary transformations are total functions.
14. **Unitary2**
    If $x(U_j)y$ and $x(U_j)z$, then $y = z$.
    This condition expresses the functionality of unitary transformations.
15. **Invariance of inner product value**
    If $x(\alpha)y$, $y(U_j)z$ and $x(U_j)w$, then $z(\alpha)w$.
    This condition expresses that unitary transformations keep the inner product invariant.

An *SDEQL-frame* (strict DEQL-frame) is defined as a DEQL-frame that satisfies all of the above conditions. The logic **DEQL** is defined as the set of all valid formulas in SDEQL-frames.

A simple example of SDEQL-frame is given below:

$W = \{w, x, y, z\}$,
$R(w, x) = R(y, z) = 0, R(w, y) = R(w, z) = R(x, y) = R(x, z) = 0.5$,
$P_{\{w\}} = \{(w, w), (y, w), (z, w)\}$, $P_{\{x\}} = \{(x, x), (y, x), (z, x)\}$,
$P_{\{y\}} = \{(y, y), (w, y), (x, y)\}$, $P_{\{z\}} = \{(z, z), (w, z), (x, z)\}$,
$P_W = \{(w, w), (x, x), (y, y), (z, z)\}$,
$U_1 = \{(w, y), (y, w), (x, z), (z, x)\}$,
For all the other U_j, $U_j = \{(w, w), (x, x), (y, y), (z, z)\}$.

Intuitively, in this example, W correspond to the set of four one-dimensional closed subspaces of $\mathbb{C}^2$ generated by $(1, 0), (0, 1), (1/\sqrt{2}, 1/\sqrt{2})$, and $(1/\sqrt{2}, -1/\sqrt{2})$. U_1 represents Hadamard gate. For all the other U_j represent the identity map. In this way, it is not necessary to add all unitary transformations to the frame, but only those necessary depending on the notions to be analyzed.

We define that in a set of frames $\mathcal{F}$, formula A *defines* (or *expresses*) a condition c if the following conditions hold:

1. For all $F \in \mathcal{F}$, if c holds in F, then all assignments of A are valid in F,
2. If c does not hold in $F \in \mathcal{F}$, then there exists V and an assignment of A such that A is not true at some $x \in W \in F$.

This definition of definability is the same as general modal logic. For example, $\Box A \to \Box\Box A$ defines the *transitivity* of the relation. Because A here is variable, all *assignments* must be considered. For example, if $\Box p \to \Box\Box p$ is not valid in a frame F, then transitivity is broken in F even if the other assignment $\Box(q \wedge r) \rightarrow \Box\Box(q \wedge r)$ is valid in F. In this study, as the variables of numerical values $\alpha, \beta, \ldots$ are included, assignments for all of them also must be considered.

All the conditions introduced above can be defined by formulas. In the following theorem, if there is no special mention, $\mathcal{F}$ is the set of all DEQL-frames. However, in the case of 8.**Proper projection**, the set of all DEQL-frames that satisfy 3.**Partial functionality of projection** and 6.**Possibility of projection** are assumed for $\mathcal{F}$, which have already been proven to be expressed. This difference is not a problem because **DEQL** deals with SDEQL-frames where all the conditions are met.

Theorem 1. *Each of the conditions in the above list is defined by a formula under a specific $\mathcal{F}$. For 8, $\mathcal{F}$ is the set of all DEQL-frames satisfying 3 and 6. In other conditions, $\mathcal{F}$ is the set of all DEQL-frames.*

Proof. We omit the proof for cases where the proof is simple or almost the same as the **DQL** case.

1. **Repeatability of projection** $[A?]A$
2. **Adequacy** $T(A) \wedge A \wedge [A?]B \rightarrow B$
3. **Partial functionality of projection** $[A]^c_\alpha B \vee [A]^c_\alpha \neg B$
4. **Non-orthogonality of projection** $\Box B \rightarrow [A?]^c_\alpha B$
5. **Identity** $A \rightarrow \Box^c_1 A$
6. **Possibility of projection** $[A?]\bot \leftrightarrow ({\sim} A \vee \neg T(A))$
   Suppose that the condition holds in $M = (W, R, P, \mathcal{U})$. If $x \models [A?]\bot$ for V, there is no y that meets $y \in W$ and $x(A?)y$. From the condition, this is equivalent to $x \in V(A)^\perp$ or $V(A) \notin OC_M$. Therefore, $x \models {\sim} A \vee \neg T(A)$. Almost the same proof is applied in the opposite direction.
   Suppose that the right direction of the condition does not hold for x and X in $M = (W, R, P, \mathcal{U})$. That is, for all $y \in W$, not $x(X)y$, but both (I) and (II) are not true. Then, the following V makes $[p?]\bot \rightarrow ({\sim} p \vee \neg T(p))$ false at x. $V(p) = X$ (from the failure of (II), $X \in OC_M$). Almost the same proof is applied in the opposite direction.
7. **Proper probability** $\langle A? \rangle^=_\alpha \top \rightarrow \langle {\sim} A? \rangle^=_{1-\alpha} \top \quad (\alpha \neq 1)$
   Suppose that the condition holds in $M = (W, R, P, \mathcal{U})$ and $\langle A? \rangle^=_\alpha \top$ $(\alpha < 1)$ is true at $x \in W$ for V. Since $\langle A? \rangle^=_\alpha \top$ is true at x, there exists $y \in W$ such that $x(A?)y$ and $x(\alpha)y$. From the condition, there exists $z \in W$ such that $x({\sim} A?)z$ and $R(x, z) = 1 - \alpha$. Therefore, $\langle {\sim} A? \rangle^=_{1-\alpha} \top$ is true at x.
   Suppose that the condition does not hold for x, y, X and α in $M = (W, R, P, \mathcal{U})$. That is, $x(X)y$, $x(\alpha)y$ and $\alpha \neq 1$, but there is no $z \in W$ such that $x(X^\perp)z$ and $R(x, z) = 1 - \alpha$. Then, the following V makes $\langle p? \rangle^=_\alpha \top \rightarrow \langle {\sim} p? \rangle^=_{1-\alpha} \top$ false at x. $V(p) = X$.
8. **Proper projection** $\Diamond^c_\alpha A \rightarrow \langle A? \rangle^c_\alpha \top$
   Suppose that the condition holds in $M = (W, R, P, \mathcal{U})$ and $\Diamond^c_\alpha A$ is true at $x \in W$ for V. Then, there exists $y \in W$ such that $x(\beta)y$, $\alpha \leq \beta$ and $y \models A$. From the 6.**Possibility of projection**, there exists $z \in W$ such that $x(A?)z$ and $x(\gamma)z$. From the condition, $\beta \leq \gamma$. Therefore, $\langle A? \rangle^c_\alpha \top$ is true at x.

Suppose that the condition does not hold for x, y, X and α in $M = (W, R, P, \mathcal{U})$. That is, $x(X)y$, $x(\alpha)y$, but there exists $z \in W$ such that $x(\beta)z$, $z \in X$ and $\alpha < \beta$. From the 3.**Partial functionality of projection**, not $x(X)z$. Then, the following V and γ make $\Diamond^c_\gamma p \to \langle p?\rangle^c_\gamma \top$ false at x. $V(p) = X$, $\alpha < \gamma < \beta$.

9. **Non-orthogonality of dense states** $\Diamond^c_\alpha \Diamond^c_\beta A \to \Diamond^o_0 A \quad (1 < \alpha + \beta)$
   Suppose that the condition holds in $M = (W, R, P, \mathcal{U})$ and $\Diamond^c_\alpha \Diamond^c_\beta A$ $(1 < \alpha + \beta)$ is true at $x \in W$ for V. Then, there exist $y, z \in W$ such that $x(\alpha')y$ $(\alpha < \alpha')$, $y(\beta')z$ $(\beta < \beta')$ and $z \models A$. From the condition, $x(\gamma)z$ and $\gamma > 0$. Therefore, $x \models \Diamond^o_0 A$.
   Suppose that the condition does not hold for x, y and z in $M = (W, R, P, \mathcal{U})$. That is, $x(\alpha)y$, $y(\beta)z$, $x(\gamma)z$ and $1 < \alpha + \beta$, but $\gamma = 0$. Then, the following V makes $\Diamond^c_\alpha \Diamond^c_\beta p \to \Diamond^o_0 p$ false at x. $V(p) = \{z\}$.
10. **Plane1** $A \to \Box^=_\alpha \Diamond^=_{1-\alpha} \Diamond^=_0 A \quad (\alpha \neq 0, 1)$
   Suppose that the condition holds in $M = (W, R, P, \mathcal{U})$ and A is true at $x \in W$ for V. If there is no $y \in W$ such that $x(\alpha)y$, then $\Box^=_\alpha \Diamond^=_{1-\alpha} \Diamond^=_0 A$ is true at x. From the condition, if $x(\alpha)y$ and $\alpha \neq 0, 1$, there exists $z \in W$ such that $x \perp z$ and $R(y, z) = 1 - \alpha$. From $x \perp z$ and $R(y, z) = 1 - \alpha$, $z \models \Diamond^=_0 A$ and $y \models \Diamond^=_{1-\alpha} \Diamond^=_0 A$. Therefore, $x \models \Box^=_\alpha \Diamond^=_{1-\alpha} \Diamond^=_0 A$.
   Suppose that the condition does not hold for x, y, X and α in $M = (W, R, P, \mathcal{U})$. That is, $x \neq y$, $x(\alpha)y$ and $\alpha \neq 0.1$, but there is no $z \in W$ such that $x \perp z$ and $R(y, z) = 1 - \alpha$. Then, the following V makes $p \to \Box^=_\alpha \Diamond^=_{1-\alpha} \Diamond^=_0 p$ false at x. $V(p) = \{x\}$.
11. **Plane2** $T(A) \wedge A \wedge B \to \Box^=_\alpha (A \to \Box^=_{1-\alpha}(\sim B \to A)) \quad (\alpha \neq 0, 1)$
   Suppose that the condition holds in $M = (W, R, P, \mathcal{U})$ and $T(A) \wedge A \wedge B$ is true at $x \in W$ for V. Then, from the condition, for all $y, z \in W$, if $x(\alpha)y$, $y(1-\alpha)z$, $x \perp z$ and $y \models A$, then $z \models A$. If $z \models \sim B$, then $x \perp z$. Therefore, for all $y \in W$, if $x(\alpha)y$, then $y \models A \to \Box^=_{1-\alpha}(\sim B \to A)$. Therefore, $x \models \Box^=_\alpha (A \to \Box^=_{1-\alpha}(\sim B \to A))$
   Suppose that the condition does not hold for x, y, z, X and α in $M = (W, R, P, \mathcal{U})$. That is, $X \in OC_M$, $x(\alpha)y$, $y(1-\alpha)z$, $x \perp z$, $x \in X$ and $y \in X$, but $z \notin X$. Then, the following V makes $T(p) \wedge p \wedge q \to \Box^=_\alpha (p \to \Box^=_{1-\alpha}(\sim q \to p))$ false at x. $V(p) = X$, $V(q) = \{x\}$.
12. **Inner product and projection**
   $T(A) \wedge \Diamond^=_\alpha (A \wedge B) \to [A?]^=_\beta \Diamond^=_{\alpha/\beta}(A \wedge B)$
   Suppose that the condition holds in $M = (W, R, P, \mathcal{U})$ and $T(A) \wedge \Diamond^=_\alpha (A \wedge B) \wedge \langle A\rangle^=_\beta \top$ is true at x for V. From $x \models \Diamond^=_\alpha (A \wedge B)$, there exists $y \in W$ such that $y \models A \wedge B$ and $x(\alpha)y$. If there is no $z \in W$ such that $x(A?)z$ and $x(\beta)z$, then $[A?]^=_\beta \Diamond^=_{\alpha/\beta}(A \wedge B)$ is true at x. If $z \in W$ such that $x(A?)z$ and $x(\beta)z$ exist, from the condition, $z(\alpha/\beta)y$. Therefore, $z \models \Diamond^=_{\alpha/\beta}(A \wedge B)$, so $x \models [A?]^=_\beta \Diamond^=_{\alpha/\beta}(A \wedge B)$.
   Suppose that the condition does not hold for x, y, z, X, α and β in $M = (W, R, P, \mathcal{U})$. That is, $x, y, z \in W$, $X \in OC_M$, $x(\alpha)y$, $y \in X$, $x(\beta)z$ and $x(X)z$, but not $z(\alpha/\beta)y$. Then, the following V makes $T(p) \wedge \Diamond^=_\alpha (p \wedge q) \to [p?]^=_\beta \Diamond^=_{\alpha/\beta}(p \wedge q)$ false at x. $V(p) = X$, $V(q) = \{y\}$.

13. **Unitary1** $\neg[U_j]\bot$
14. **Unitary2** $[U_j]A \vee [U_j]\neg A$
15. **Invariance of inner product value** $\Diamond_\alpha^=\langle U_j\rangle A \to [U_j]\Diamond_\alpha^= A$

Suppose that the condition holds in $M = (W, R, P, \mathcal{U})$ and $\Diamond_\alpha^=\langle U_j\rangle A$ is true at $x \in W$ for V. Then, there exist $y, z \in W$ such that $x(\alpha)y$, $y(U_j)z$ and $z \models A$. From the condition, if $x(U_j)w$, then $z(\alpha)w$ and $w \models \Diamond_\alpha^= A$. Therefore, $x \models [U_j]\Diamond_\alpha^= A$.

Suppose that the condition does not hold for x, y, z, x, U_j and α in $M = (W, R, P, \mathcal{U})$. That is, $x(\alpha)y$, $y(U_j)z$ and $x(U_j)w$, but $z(\beta)w$ and $\alpha \neq \beta$. Then, the following V makes $\Diamond_\alpha^=\langle U_j\rangle p \to [U_j]\Diamond_\alpha^= p$ false at x. $V(p) = \{z\}$. □

The properties in the following theorems are important in frames of **OML** and **DQL**. To deal with these properties, in **OML** and **DQL**, there is no choice but to explicitly add them to the definition of a frame as frame conditions. In SDEQL-frames, these conditions can be derived as corollaries of the above natural conditions. Theorem 2 guarantees that all $x \in W$ in an SDEQL-frame $(W, R, P, \mathcal{U})$ represent quantum states. For details about *self-adjointness* and *orthomodularity*, see [1,2,7,12].

Theorem 2. *In an SDEQL-frame $(W, R, P, \mathcal{U})$, all singletons $\{w\} \subseteq W$ are $\bot$-closed.*

Proof. For the sake of a contradiction, suppose that $\{w\} \subseteq W$ is not $\bot$-closed. Then, there exists $x \in W$ such that $x \in \{w\}^{\bot\bot}$ and $x \neq w$. From 5.**Identity**, $1 > \alpha$ for $x(\alpha)w$. Because $x \in \{w\}^{\bot\bot}$, $\alpha > 0$ for $x(\alpha)w$. From 10.**Plane1**, there exists $y \in W$ such that $w \bot y$ and $x(1-\alpha)y$. However, $x \bot y$ because $y \in \{w\}^\bot$. This is a contradiction. □

We define that a DEQL-frame $(W, R, P, \mathcal{U})$ satisfies the *orthomodularity* if it satisfies the following condition:

For all $X, Y \in OC_M$, $X \cap (X^\bot \sqcup (X \cap Y)) \subseteq Y$,

where $X \sqcup Y = (X^\bot \cap Y^\bot)^\bot$.

We define that a DEQL-frame $(W, R, P, \mathcal{U})$ satisfies the *self-adjointness* if it satisfies the following condition:

For all $x, y, z \in W$ and $X \in OC_M$, if $x(X)y$ and $y \not\bot z$, then there exists $w \in W$ such that $z(X)w$ and $w \not\bot x$.

Note that in an SDEQL-frame $(W, R, P, \mathcal{U})$, if $x(X)y$ and $y \not\bot z$, there exists only one $w \in W$ such that $z(X)w$ because of 3.**Partial functionality** and 6.**Possibility of projection**.

Lemma 1. *All SDEQL-frames satisfy the self-adjointness.*

Proof. For the sake of contradiction, suppose that in an SDEQL-frame $(W, R, P, \mathcal{U})$, there exist $x, y, z, w \in W$ such that $x(X)y$, $y \not\bot z$, $z(X)w$ and $w \bot x$. On the one hand, from 12.**Inner product and projection** ($\alpha = 0$), $x(X)y$ and $x \bot w$, $y \bot w$. On the other hand, from 12.**Inner product and projection** ($\alpha > 0$), $z(X)w$ and $z \not\bot y$, $y \not\bot w$. This is a contradiction. □

Lemma 2. *For all SDEQL-frames and all* V, $V([A]B) = V(\sim (A \wedge \sim (A \wedge B)))$.

Proof. Using Lemma 1, the proof is almost the same as the one in [12]. □

Lemma 3. *If a DEQL-frame* $(W, R, P, \mathcal{U}))$ *satisfies the self-adjointness, then* $(W, R, P, \mathcal{U}))$ *satisfies the orthomodularity.*

Proof. Using Lemma 2, the proof is almost the same as the one in [12]. □

Theorem 3. *All SDEQL-frames satisfy the orthomodularity.*

Proof. The corollary of Lemma 1 and Lemma 3. □

5 Axiomatization

A Hilbert-style axiomatization **HDEQL**is defined by using the same method as shown in [18] and adding the formulas shown in Theorem 1 as axioms. In the following, $l \in \{c, o, =\}$.

1. All tautologies of propositional logic.
2. All axioms and rules for unitary transformations in **DQL**.
3. All axioms and rules for $\Box^{c}_{\alpha}, \Box^{o}_{\alpha}$, in **EQL**.
4. All formulas shown in Theorem 1.
5. $\Box^{=}_{\alpha}(A \to B) \to (\Box^{=}_{\alpha} A \to \Box^{=}_{\alpha} B)$
6. $A \to \Box^{=}_{\alpha} \Diamond^{=}_{\alpha} A$
7. $\Box^{c}_{\alpha} A \to \Box^{=}_{\beta} A \quad (\alpha \leqq \beta)$
8. $\Box^{o}_{\alpha} A \to \Box^{=}_{\beta} A \quad (\alpha < \beta)$
9. $\Box^{c}_{\alpha} A \leftrightarrow \Box^{o}_{\alpha} A \wedge \Box^{=}_{\alpha} A$
10. $[C?]^{l}_{\alpha}(A \to B) \to ([C?]^{l}_{\alpha} A \to [C?]^{l}_{\alpha} B)$
11. $[C?]^{c}_{\alpha} A \to [C?]^{c}_{\beta} A \quad (\alpha \leqq \beta)$
12. $[C?]^{o}_{\alpha} A \to [C?]^{o}_{\beta} A \quad (\alpha \leqq \beta)$
13. $\neg \langle C? \rangle^{o}_{1} A$
14. $[C?]^{c}_{\alpha} A \to [C?]^{o}_{\alpha} A$
15. $[C?]^{o}_{\alpha} A \to [C?]^{c}_{\beta} A \quad (\alpha < \beta)$
16. $[C?]^{c}_{\alpha} A \to [C?]^{=}_{\beta} A \quad (\alpha \leqq \beta)$
17. $[C?]^{o}_{\alpha} A \to [C?]^{=}_{\beta} A \quad (\alpha < \beta)$
18. $[C?]^{c}_{\alpha} A \leftrightarrow [C?]^{o}_{\alpha} A \wedge [C?]^{=}_{\alpha} A$
19. $\Box^{l}_{\alpha} A \to [C?]^{l}_{\alpha} A$

$$\frac{A}{[B?]^{c}_{\alpha} A} \qquad \frac{A}{[B?]^{o}_{\alpha} A} \qquad \frac{A}{[B?]^{=}_{\alpha} A} \qquad \frac{A \quad A \to B}{B}$$

Theorem 4 (Soundness theorem). *If A is provable in* **HDEQL**, *then A is valid in SDEQL-frame.*

Proof. By proving that all axioms and rules are valid. □

If we add $\Box A \rightarrow \Box\Box A$ as an axiom to the usual system of modal logic, we have a complete system with respect to the Kripke frames satisfying the transitive law [14,15]. Similarly, Theorem 1 would be considered evidence that **HDEQL** satisfies the completeness theorem. This statement is probably correct, but we need some ingenuity to prove the completeness theorem due to the nature of the newly added symbol =, which is also discussed a bit in [13]. Details are omitted here and left for another work.

Acknowledgements. This work was supported by JSPS KAKENHI Grant Number JP20K19740.

References

1. Baltag, A., Smets, S.: The logic of quantum programs. QPL **2004**, 39–56 (2004)
2. Baltag, A., Smets, S.: Quantum logic as a dynamic logic. Synthese **179**, 285–306 (2011)
3. Baltag, A., Smets, S.: The dynamic turn in quantum logic. Synthese **186**(3), 753–773 (2012)
4. Baltag, A., Bergfeld, J.M., Kishida, K., Sack, J., Smets, S.J.L., Zhong, S.: Quantum probabilistic dyadic second-order logic. In: Libkin, L., Kohlenbach, U., de Queiroz, R. (eds.) WoLLIC 2013. LNCS, vol. 8071, pp. 64–80. Springer, Heidelberg (2013). https://doi.org/10.1007/978-3-642-39992-3_9
5. Birkhoff, G., Neumann, J.: The logic of quantum mechanics. Ann. Math. **37**(4), 823–843 (1936)
6. Cattaneo, G., Dalla, C.M., L., Giuntini, R.: Fuzzy intuitionistic quantum logics. Stud. Logica. **52**, 419–444 (1993)
7. Chiara, M.L.D., Giuntini, R.: Quantum logics. In: Gabbay, D.M., Guenthner, F. (ed.): Handbook Of Philosophical Logic. 2nd Edition, vol. 6, no. 1, pp. 129–228 (2002)
8. Hähnle, R.: Advanced many valued logic. In: Gabbay, D. M., Guenthner, F. (ed.): Handbook of Philosophical Logic. 2nd Edition, vol. 2, pp. 297–396 (2002)
9. Halpern, J.Y.: An analysis of first-order logics of probability. Artif. Intell. **46**(3), 311–350 (1990)
10. Ilić Stepić, A., Ognjanović, Z., Perović, A.: Probability logics for reasoning about quantum observations. Log. Univers. **17**, 175–219 (2023)
11. Kalmbach, G.: Orthomodular logic. Math. Log. Q. **20**, 295–406 (1974)
12. Kawano, T.: Advanced Kripke frame for quantum logic. In: Proceedings of 25th Workshop on Logic, Language, Information and Computation, pp. 237–249 (2018)
13. Kawano, T.: Nested-sequent calculus for modal logic MB. Electr. Proc. Theor. Comput. Sci. **415**(10), 33–47 (2024)
14. Negri, S.: Proof analysis in modal logic. J. Philos. Log. **34**, 507–544 (2005)
15. Negri, S.: Proof theory for modal logic. Philos Compass **6**(8), 523–538 (2011)
16. Nilsson, N, J.: Probabilistic logic. Artif. Intell. **28**(1), 71–87 (1986)

17. Sernadas, A., Rasga, J., Sernadas, C., Alcácer, L., Henriques, A.B.: Probabilistic logic of quantum observations. Logic J. IGPL **27**(3), 328–370 (2018)
18. Tokuo, K.: Extended quantum logic. J. Philos. Log. **32**, 549–563 (2003)
19. Urquhart, A.: Basic many valued logic Logic. In: Gabbay, D. M., Guenthner, F. (ed.): Handbook Of Philosophical Logic. 2nd Edition, vol. 2, pp. 249–296 (2002)

A Kripke Semantics for Monadic BL Chains

Andrew Lewis-Smith[1(✉)] and Zhiguang Zhao[2]

[1] Middlesex University, London, UK
a.lewis-smith@mdx.ac.uk
[2] Taishan University, Tai'an, China

Abstract. We provide a generalisation of Kripke semantics for Monadic first-order Basic Logic of Chains (**MBLC**) of Petr Hájek and prove its soundness and completeness with respect to our semantics. This paper extends the insights of [10] from **BL** to the case of **MBLC**.

Keywords: Substructural logic · Kripke Semantics

1 Introduction

Hájek's basic logic (**BL**) occupies a central place in contemporary research on fuzzy and substructural logic. First-order **BL** ($\mathbf{BL}_{FO}$ hereon), like the propositional fragment, is primarily studied algebraically. **BL** is after all the logic of t-norms [6]. The papers of Jipsen and Montagna [8] and Bova and Montagna [1] suggest an alternative view of the situation: We can employ algebraic embedding results via *poset products* to construct generalisations of Kripke semantics appropriate to extensions of **GBL** [10] (and later [3]). This situates systems such as **GBL** and **BL** among constructive and intermediate logics, whose relational semantics are well-understood.

However, we need not restrict our attention to poset product representations of **GBL**-algebras. In fact, the vast majority of representation results in the literature on **BL** and $\mathbf{BL}_{FO}$ involve *ordinal sums* (and these served as the original inspiration for poset products; see [8]). The question arises what relational semantics might be obtained by ordinal sums as our starting point. Thus we extend our present programme of extracting relational semantics for substructural logics from poset products to ordinal sums, with the monadic fragment of $\mathbf{BL}_{FO}$ (hereon **MBLC**) as our present case study.

We emphasize that there are numerous advantages in identifying and studying relational semantics in fuzzy logics (and other systems) such as our proposal for **MBLC**. For one, relational semantics can make for interesting examples and counterexamples for logic as alternatives to e.g. counterexamples presented in matrix form. Similarly, having a relational semantics available makes it plausible to pursue semantically-based calculi, such as tableaux or labeled calculi, which exploit insights in the semantics to guide the decomposition of formulas

K. Sauerwald and M. Thimm (Eds.): ECSQARU 2025, LNAI 16099, pp. 499–511, 2026.
https://doi.org/10.1007/978-3-032-05134-9_34

in a principled way. Finally, relational semantics offer a different intuition on how the logic itself behaves: algebraic models (such as Hájek and his successors) for **BL** and **MBLC** are inherently static. The relational paradigm lends us a different view of logics as inherently dynamic objects (formulas progress in some value according to the behaviour of the poset); and perhaps it is only appropriate that many-valued and fuzzy logics have a means to represent many-values and change of valuation within a fixed structure.

The semantics we devise for **MBLC** is a departure from that of [10] and [9]. The present structures are defined over linear frames, with sloping functions similar to [9], but the worlds (and formulas) of the structure are valued in Wajsberg-hoops. Additionally, the interpretation of quantifiers require a monadic Heyting chain. This presents quite a bit more structure than is the case with [9]. Hence our designation Castaño-Cimadamore-Varela-Rueda, or **CCVR**-structure, as the present structures are derived from representation results via ordinal sums of Wajsberg hoops [2] as opposed to the poset product-based representations of Jipsen et al.

The structure of the paper is otherwise as with [10] or [9]. We give **MBLC**'s Hilbert system, followed by suitable definitions of algebras, validity, and our relational semantics. We prove **MBLC** sound and complete for our semantics, via an isomorphism between the ordinal sum construction and relational structures defined herein.

2 Proof Theory for MBLC

We consider briefly the proof theory of **MBLC**. We present the Hilbert-style system for the sake of clarity, but also to serve our later exposition and results (in particular our completeness proof).

The language has a countable number of unary predicate symbols and one individual variable, x, so that atomic formulas are of the form $P_i x$ where $i \in \mathbb{N}$ and $\mathbb{N}$ is the set of natural numbers. The formulas of **MBLC** are inductively defined from atomic formulas and $\bot$, using the binary connectives $\wedge, \vee, \otimes, \rightarrow$, and quantifiers $\forall x$ and $\exists x$ with x the fixed variable. We use $\phi \leftrightarrow \psi$ and $\top$ to abbreviate $(\phi \rightarrow \psi) \wedge (\psi \rightarrow \phi)$ and $\bot \rightarrow \bot$, respectively. We will refer to this language as $\mathbb{L}_{\otimes MFO}$, since it extends the language $\mathbb{L}_{MFO}$ of monadic first-order Gödel-Dummett logic (see Note 1) with a second form of conjunction, $\psi \otimes \chi$.

Below, we present the Hilbert system $\mathbf{MBLC}_H$ of [7].

- (BL1) $(\phi \rightarrow \psi) \rightarrow ((\psi \rightarrow \chi) \rightarrow (\phi \rightarrow \chi))$.
- (BL2) $(\phi \otimes \psi) \rightarrow \phi$.[1]
- (BL3) $(\phi \otimes \psi) \rightarrow (\psi \otimes \phi)$.
- (BL4) $(\phi \wedge \psi) \rightarrow (\psi \wedge \phi)$.
- (BL5a) $(\phi \rightarrow (\psi \rightarrow \chi)) \rightarrow ((\phi \otimes \psi) \rightarrow \chi))$.
- (BL5b) $((\phi \otimes \psi) \rightarrow \chi)) \rightarrow (\phi \rightarrow (\psi \rightarrow \chi))$.

[1] Here we do not put $(\phi \otimes \psi) \rightarrow \psi$ as an axiom because of the presence of (BL3) and (BL1).

- (BL6) $((\phi \to \psi) \to \chi) \to (((\psi \to \phi) \to \chi) \to \chi)$.
- (BL7) $\bot \to \phi$.
- ($\wedge$1) $(\phi \otimes (\phi \to \psi)) \to (\phi \wedge \psi)$.
- ($\wedge$2) $(\phi \wedge \psi) \to (\phi \otimes (\phi \to \psi))$.
- ($\vee$1) $(\phi \vee \psi) \to (((\phi \to \psi) \to \psi) \wedge ((\psi \to \phi) \to \phi))$.
- ($\vee$2) $(((\phi \to \psi) \to \psi) \wedge ((\psi \to \phi) \to \phi)) \to (\phi \vee \psi)$.
- (M1) $\forall\phi \to \phi$.
- (M2) $\forall(\phi \to \forall\psi) \leftrightarrow (\exists\phi \to \forall\psi)$.
- (M3) $\forall(\forall\phi \to \psi) \leftrightarrow (\forall\phi \to \forall\psi)$.
- (M4) $\forall(\exists\phi \vee \psi) \leftrightarrow (\exists\phi \vee \forall\psi)$.
- (M5) $\exists(\phi \otimes \phi) \leftrightarrow (\exists\phi \otimes \exists\phi)$.
- (Chain) $\forall x(\phi \vee \psi) \to (\forall x\phi \vee \forall x\psi)$.
- (R1) From $\vdash_{\mathbf{MBLC}_H} \phi, \vdash_{\mathbf{MBLC}_H} \phi \to \psi$ infer $\vdash_{\mathbf{MBLC}_H} \psi$.
- (R2) From $\vdash_{\mathbf{MBLC}_H} \phi$ infer $\vdash_{\mathbf{MBLC}_H} \forall x\phi$.

The system we obtained are referred to as $\mathbf{MBLC}_H$. When we wish to stress the precise system in which a formula ϕ is derivable we use the system as a subscript of the provability sign, e.g. $\vdash_{\mathbf{MBLC}} \phi$.

Note 1. Monadic Gödel-Dummett logic (**MGD**) results from **MBLC** by adding the axiom $(\phi \to (\phi \to \psi)) \to (\phi \to \psi)$.

3 Algebraic Semantics

We situate the algebraic semantics characterising **BL** in terms of the somewhat larger theory of residuated lattices.

Definition 1. $\mathbb{A} = \langle A, \wedge, \vee, \otimes, 1, \to\rangle$ *is called a* commutative residuated lattice *if*

- $\langle A, \wedge, \vee, \otimes, 1\rangle$ *is a commutative lattice-ordered monoid.*
- $x \otimes y \leq z$ *if and only if* $x \leq y \to z$.

Definition 2 (*BL*-algebras, *BL*-chains). *A* ***BL***-algebra is a bounded, commutative residuated lattice which satisfies the *divisibility property: if* $x \leq y$ *then* $y \otimes (y \to x) = x$*; pre-linearity:* $(x \to y) \vee (y \to x) = 1$*; bounded from below by* $\bot$*, i.e.* $\bot \leq x$ *for all* $x \in A$*, and integral in that* 1 *is the top element of the lattice, i.e.* $x \leq 1$ *for all* $x \in A$*. In this case we also denote* 1 *by* $\top$*. Finally, we note the condition of the divisibility property is equivalent to requiring that the residuated lattice satisfies the equation* $x \otimes (x \to y) = y \otimes (y \to x) = x \wedge y$*. A* ***BL****-chain is a totally-ordered* ***BL****-algebra.*

Definition 3 (Monadic *BL*-algebras). $\mathbb{A} = \langle A, \vee, \wedge, \otimes, \to, \exists, \forall, \bot, \top\rangle$ *is called a monadic BL-algebra (an* ***MBL****-algebra for short) if* $\langle A, \vee, \wedge, \otimes, \to, \bot, \top\rangle$ *is a* ***BL****-algebra,* $\forall$ *and* $\exists$ *are unary operations and the following identities are satisfied:*

1. *(M1)* $\forall x \to x = \top$.
2. *(M2)* $\forall(x \to \forall y) = \exists x \to \forall y$.
3. *(M3)* $\forall(\forall x \to y) = \forall x \to \forall y$.
4. *(M4)* $\forall(\exists x \vee y) = \exists x \vee \forall y$.
5. *(M5)* $\exists(x \otimes x) = \exists x \otimes \exists x$.

For brevity, if $\mathbb{A}$ *is a* ***BL****-algebra and we enrich it with a monadic structure, we denote the resulting algebra by* $\langle \mathbb{A}, \exists, \forall \rangle$. *We denote by* ***MBL*** *the variety of* ***MBL****-algebras. If in addition a* ***MBL****-algebra satisfies the chain condition:*

1. *(Chain)* $\forall(x \vee y) = \forall x \vee \forall y$,

then it is a ***MBL****-chain. The variety of* ***MBL****-chains is denoted as* **MBLC**.

Definition 4 (Hoop-algebra). *A* **Hoop***-algebra* $\mathbb{A} = (A, \otimes, \to, 1)$ *of type* $(2, 2, 0)$ *such that:*

1. $(A, \otimes, 1)$ *is a commutative monoid.*
2. $x \to x = 1$.
3. $(x \otimes y) \to z = x \to (y \to z)$.
4. $x \otimes (x \to y) = y \otimes (y \to x)$ *for all* $x, y, z \in A$.

Definition 5 (Wajsberg-hoop). *We say that a* **Hoop***-algebra* $\mathbb{A}$ *is a* **Wajsberg***-hoop if* $\mathbb{A}$ *satisfies:*

1. $(x \to y) \to y = (y \to x) \to x$ *for all* $x, y \in A$.

In **Wajsberg***-hoops, we can define* $\wedge$ *and* $\vee$ *as follows:*

- $x \wedge y := x \otimes (x \to y)$.
- $x \vee y := (x \to y) \to y$.

A **Wajsberg***-hoop is a* **Wajsberg***-chain if it is linearly ordered.*

4 Validity in MBLC

Definition 6 (Denotation functions). *Given a* **MBLC***-algebra* $\mathbb{A}_{\mathbf{MBLC}}$, *and an assignment from atomic formulas to elements of* $\mathbb{A}_{\mathbf{MBLC}}$:

$$Px \mapsto [\![Px]\!] \in \mathbb{A}_{\mathbf{MBLC}}$$

We thus refer to the denotation of an atomic formula Px *as* $[\![Px]\!]_{\mathbf{MBLC}}$.

We can extend that mapping to all formulas in the language of $\mathbb{L}_{\otimes MFO}$ *in a straightforward way:*

$$\begin{aligned}
[\![\phi \otimes \psi]\!]_{\mathbf{MBLC}} &:= [\![\phi]\!]_{\mathbf{MBLC}} \otimes [\![\psi]\!]_{\mathbf{MBLC}} \\
[\![\phi \wedge \psi]\!]_{\mathbf{MBLC}} &:= [\![\phi]\!]_{\mathbf{MBLC}} \wedge [\![\psi]\!]_{\mathbf{MBLC}} \\
[\![\phi \vee \psi]\!]_{\mathbf{MBLC}} &:= [\![\phi]\!]_{\mathbf{MBLC}} \vee [\![\psi]\!]_{\mathbf{MBLC}} \\
[\![\phi \to \psi]\!]_{\mathbf{MBLC}} &:= [\![\phi]\!]_{\mathbf{MBLC}} \to [\![\psi]\!]_{\mathbf{MBLC}} \\
[\![\forall x \phi]\!]_{\mathbf{MBLC}} &:= \forall [\![\phi]\!]_{\mathbf{MBLC}} \\
[\![\exists x \phi]\!]_{\mathbf{MBLC}} &:= \exists [\![\phi]\!]_{\mathbf{MBLC}}
\end{aligned}$$

Definition 7 (Validity). *A formula ϕ is valid in a* **MBLC**-*algebra if* $\top \leq [\![\psi]\!]$ *holds under all assignments in this* **MBLC**-*algebra. A formula is said to be* **MBLC**-valid *if it is valid in* all **MBLC**-*algebras (notation:* $\models_{\mathbf{MBLC}} \phi$*). The valid formulas, in the sense above, are precisely the ones provable in monadic first-order basic logic of chains [7]:*

Proposition 1. $\vdash_{\mathbf{MBLC}} \phi$ *iff* $\models_{\mathbf{MBLC}} \phi$.

Proof. See [7].

5 Kripke Semantics for MBLC

Note 2. The Kripke semantics for **MBLC** that we propose is something of a variant of our semantics introduced in [10] based on [1,8], but is more immediately derived from [2]. We first need to define a particular class of functions from the set of worlds W to **Wajsberg**-chains attached with a bottom from below.

Definition 8 (Sloping functions). *Let $\{\mathbb{A}_w\}_{w\in W}$ be a W-indexed family of* **Wajsberg**-*chains with almost disjoint domains except that they share the top element $\top$. We add the same new bottom element $\star$ to each $\mathbb{A}_w$ and get $\mathbb{A}_w \cup \{\star\}$. Let $\mathbb{W} = \langle W, \succeq\rangle$ be a linear order. A function $f\colon W \to \bigcup_{w\in W}(\mathbb{A}_w \cup \{\star\})$ is said to be a* sloping function for **MBLC** *(hereon* sloping function, *or* sloping*) if it is the $\top$-constant function or there are $w_f \in W$ and $a_f \in \mathbb{A}_{w_f} - \{\top\}$ such that*

$$f(w) = \begin{cases} \top \;\; if w \succ w_f \\ a_f \; if w = w_f \\ \star \;\; if w \prec w_f \end{cases}$$

Lemma 1. *If $f, g\colon W \to \bigcup_{w\in W}(\mathbb{A}_w \cup \{\star\})$ are sloping, then so are the following functions[2]:*

$$\begin{array}{ll} (f \wedge g)(w) & := f(w) \wedge_{\mathbb{A}_w \cup \{\star\}} g(w) \\ (f \vee g)(w) & := f(w) \vee_{\mathbb{A}_w \cup \{\star\}} g(w) \\ (f \otimes g)(w) & := f(w) \otimes_{\mathbb{A}_w \cup \{\star\}} g(w) \end{array}$$

$$(f \to g)(w) := \begin{cases} \top & if \;\; (w_f \succ w_g) or (w_f = w_g and a_f \leq a_g) or \\ & gisthe \top - constant function \\ g(w) & if \;\; w_f \prec w_g or fisthe \top - constant function \\ \top & if \;\; w \succ w_f = w_g and a_f > a_g \\ a_f \to_{\mathbb{A}_w} a_g & if \;\; w = w_f = w_g and a_f > a_g \\ \star & if \;\; w \prec w_f = w_g and a_f > a_g \end{cases}$$

where $\wedge, \vee, \otimes$ are extended to $\star$ such that $\star \wedge a = \star$, $\star \vee a = a$ and $\star \otimes a = \star$ for all $a \in \mathbb{A}_w \cup \{\star\}$.

Proof. The proof is similar to its counterpart in [10]. Let f, g be sloping functions. Let us consider each case:

[2] Here $\wedge_{\mathbb{A}_w \cup \{\star\}}$ means that the binary function corresponding to $\wedge$ is defined on $\mathbb{A}_w \cup \{\star\}$, and similarly for other functions indexed with **Wajsberg** chains.

- $f \wedge g$. When there are $\top$-constant functions, the proof is easy. Otherwise,

$$(w_{f\wedge g}, a_{f\wedge g}) := \begin{cases} (w_f, a_f) & \text{if} \quad w_f \succ w_g \\ (w_f, a_f \wedge a_g) & \text{if} \quad w_f = w_g \\ (w_g, a_g) & \text{if} \quad w_f \prec w_g \end{cases}$$

- $f \vee g$. When there are $\top$-constant functions, the proof is easy. Otherwise,

$$(w_{f\vee g}, a_{f\vee g}) := \begin{cases} (w_f, a_f) & \text{if} \quad w_f \prec w_g \\ (w_f, a_f \vee a_g) & \text{if} \quad w_f = w_g \\ (w_g, a_g) & \text{if} \quad w_f \succ w_g \end{cases}$$

- $f \otimes g$. When there are $\top$-constant functions, the proof is easy. Otherwise,

$$(w_{f\otimes g}, a_{f\otimes g}) := \begin{cases} (w_f, a_f) & \text{if} \quad w_f \succ w_g \\ (w_f, a_f \otimes a_g) & \text{if} \quad w_f = w_g \\ (w_g, a_g) & \text{if} \quad w_f \prec w_g \end{cases}$$

- $f \to g$. When f or g is the $\top$-constant function, it is obvious. Similarly for the cases where $w_f \neq w_g$ or ($w_f = w_g$ and $a_f \leq a_g$). When $w_f = w_g$ and $a_f > a_g$, then $w_{f\to g} = w_f = w_g$ and $a_{f\to g} = a_f \to_{\mathbb{A}_w} a_g$ (it is easy to see that $a_f \to_{\mathbb{A}_w} a_g < \top$).

In order to interpret **MBLC**, we still need the facilities to interpret the quantifiers. Indeed, we require that the underlying linear order to have two additional functions on it:

Definition 9 (Monadic Heyting chain). *A monadic Heyting chain is an algebra* $\mathbb{H} = \langle H, \wedge, \vee, \to, \bot, \top, \forall, \exists \rangle$ *such that* $\langle H, \wedge, \vee, \to, \bot, \top \rangle$ *is a linearly ordered Heyting algebra, and* $\forall$ *and* $\exists$ *satisfy the following conditions:*

(H1) $\forall a \leq a$, $a \leq \exists a$.
(H2) $\forall(a \wedge b) = \forall a \wedge \forall b$, $\exists(a \vee b) = \exists a \vee \exists b$.
(H3) $\forall \top = \top$, $\exists \bot = \bot$.
(H4) $\forall \exists a = \exists a$, $\exists \forall a = \forall a$.
(H5) $\exists(\exists a \wedge b) = \exists a \wedge \exists b$.

We define the order $\leq_{\mathbb{H}}$ *on* $\mathbb{H}$ *such that* $a \leq_{\mathbb{H}} b$ *iff* $a \wedge b = a$.

In what follows, we will use the elements of a monadic Heyting chain to be the 'possible worlds' of our relational semantics.

Definition 10 (CCVR-structure). *Let* $\mathbb{W} = \langle W, \succeq \rangle$ *be the unique poset such that*

- $W = \mathbb{H} - \{\top_{\mathbb{H}}\}$ *where* $\mathbb{H}$ *is a monadic Heyting chain and* $\top_{\mathbb{H}}$ *is the top element of* $\mathbb{H}$.
- *For any* $w, v \in W$, $w \preceq v$ *iff* $w \geq_{\mathbb{H}} v$.

That is to say, the order of $\mathbb{W}$ *is the reverse order of that of* $\mathbb{H} - \{\top_{\mathbb{H}}\}$. *In what follows, we use* $\leq$ *and* $\geq$ *to represent the order on algebras and* $\preceq$ *and* $\succeq$ *to represent the order on* $\mathbb{W}$. *Since* $\mathbb{H}$ *is a linear order, the Heyting algebra part is defined in the expected way. We denote* $\forall\mathbb{H} := \{\forall i \mid i \in \mathbb{H}\}$. *We also assume the following conditions when labelling all* $w \in W$ *with* **Wajsberg**-*chains:*

- *If* $\forall i < i$, $\mathbb{A}_{\forall i}$ *has a second largest element* $u_{\forall i}$.
- *If* $i < \exists i < \top_{\mathbb{H}}$, $\mathbb{A}_{\exists i}$ *has a least element* $0_{\exists i}$.
- *In the top element* w_1 *of* $\mathbb{W}$, $\mathbb{A}_{w_1}$ *has a bottom element.*

Let $\{\mathbb{A}_w\}_{w \in W}$ *be a* W*-indexed family of* **Wajsberg**-*chains as described in Definition 8. A* Castaño-Cimadamore-Varela-Rueda structure *for* $\{\mathbb{A}_w\}_{w \in W}$ *(or* **CCVR**-*structure) is a pair* $\mathbb{M} = \langle \mathbb{W}, \Vdash^{\mathrm{CCVR}} \rangle$ *where* $\Vdash^{\mathrm{CCVR}}$ *is an infix operator (on worlds and propositional variables) taking values in* $\bigcup_{w \in W}(\mathbb{A}_w \cup \{\star\})$, *i.e.* $(w \Vdash^{\mathrm{CCVR}} p) \in \mathbb{A}_w \cup \{\star\}$, *such that for any propositional variable* p *the function* $\lambda w.(w \Vdash^{\mathrm{CCVR}} p) \colon W \to \bigcup_{w \in W}(\mathbb{A}_w \cup \{\star\})$ *is a sloping function.*

Definition 11 (CCVR Kripke Semantics for $\mathbb{L}_{\otimes}$**).** *Given a* **CCVR**-*structure*

$$\mathbb{M} = \langle \mathbb{W}, \Vdash^{\mathrm{CCVR}} \rangle$$

the valuation function $w \Vdash^{\mathrm{CCVR}} p$ *on propositional variables* p *can be extended to all* $\mathbb{L}_{\otimes}$*-formulas as:*

$$
\begin{array}{lll}
w \Vdash^{\mathrm{CCVR}} \bot & := & \bot \\
w \Vdash^{\mathrm{CCVR}} \phi \wedge \psi & := & (w \Vdash^{\mathrm{CCVR}} \phi) \wedge_{\mathbb{A}_w \cup \{\star\}} (w \Vdash^{\mathrm{CCVR}} \psi) \\
w \Vdash^{\mathrm{CCVR}} \phi \vee \psi & := & (w \Vdash^{\mathrm{CCVR}} \phi) \vee_{\mathbb{A}_w \cup \{\star\}} (w \Vdash^{\mathrm{CCVR}} \psi) \\
w \Vdash^{\mathrm{CCVR}} \phi \otimes \psi & := & (w \Vdash^{\mathrm{CCVR}} \phi) \otimes_{\mathbb{A}_w \cup \{\star\}} (w \Vdash^{\mathrm{CCVR}} \psi) \\
w \Vdash^{\mathrm{CCVR}} \phi \to \psi & := & \begin{cases}
\top & \begin{array}{l} \mathit{if} \;\; w_\phi \succ w_\psi \; \mathit{or} \\ (w_f = w_g \; \mathit{and} \; a_f \leq a_g) \\ \mathit{or} \; \lambda w.(w \Vdash^{\mathrm{CCVR}} \psi) \; \mathit{is} \\ \mathit{the} \; \top - \mathit{constant function} \end{array} \\
w \Vdash^{\mathrm{CCVR}} \psi & \begin{array}{l} \mathit{if} \;\; w_\phi \prec w_\psi \; \mathit{or} \\ \lambda w.(w \Vdash^{\mathrm{CCVR}} \phi) \; \mathit{is\, the} \\ \top - \mathit{constant function} \end{array} \\
\top & \begin{array}{l} \mathit{if} \;\; w \succ w_\phi = w_\psi \\ \mathit{and} \; a_f > a_g \end{array} \\
(w \Vdash^{\mathrm{CCVR}} \phi) \to_{\mathbb{A}_w} (w \Vdash^{\mathrm{CCVR}} \psi) & \begin{array}{l} \mathit{if} \;\; w = w_\phi = w_\psi \\ \mathit{and} \; a_f > a_g \end{array} \\
\star & \begin{array}{l} \mathit{if} \;\; w \prec w_\phi = w_\psi \\ \mathit{and} \; a_f > a_g \end{array}
\end{cases} \\
w \Vdash^{\mathrm{CCVR}} \forall x \phi & := & \begin{cases}
w \Vdash^{\mathrm{CCVR}} \phi & \mathit{if} \; w_\phi \in \forall\mathbb{H} \; \mathit{or} \; \lambda w.(w \Vdash^{\mathrm{CCVR}} \phi) \; \mathit{is} \; \top - \mathit{constant} \\
\top & \mathit{if} \; w_\phi \notin \forall\mathbb{H} \; \mathit{and} \; w \succ \forall w_\phi \\
\star & \mathit{if} \; w_\phi \notin \forall\mathbb{H} \; \mathit{and} \; w \prec \forall w_\phi \\
u_{\forall i} & \mathit{if} \; w_\phi \notin \forall\mathbb{H} \; \mathit{and} \; w = \forall w_\phi
\end{cases} \\
w \Vdash^{\mathrm{CCVR}} \exists x \phi & := & \begin{cases}
w \Vdash^{\mathrm{CCVR}} \phi & \mathit{if} \; w_\phi \in \exists\mathbb{H} \; \mathit{or} \; \lambda w.(w \Vdash^{\mathrm{CCVR}} \phi) \; \mathit{is} \; \top - \mathit{constant} \\
\top & \mathit{if} \; w_\phi \notin \exists\mathbb{H} \; \mathit{and} \; (w \succ \exists w_\phi \neq \top_{\mathbb{H}} \; \mathit{or} \; \exists w_\phi = \top_{\mathbb{H}}) \\
\star & \mathit{if} \; w_\phi \notin \exists\mathbb{H} \; \mathit{and} \; w \prec \exists w_\phi \neq \top_{\mathbb{H}} \\
0_{\exists i} & \mathit{if} \; w_\phi \notin \exists\mathbb{H} \; \mathit{and} \; w = \exists w_\phi \neq \top_{\mathbb{H}}
\end{cases}
\end{array}
$$

Lemma 2. *For any formula* ϕ *the function* $\lambda w.(w \Vdash^{\mathrm{CCVR}} \phi) \colon W \to \bigcup_{w \in W}(\mathbb{A}_w \cup \{\star\})$ *is a sloping function.*

Proof. By induction on ϕ. The cases for $\psi \vee \xi, \psi \wedge \xi, \psi \otimes \xi$ and $\psi \to \xi$ follow directly from Definition 11 and Lemma 1. For the quantifiers cases, it is easy to see that the relevant function is a sloping function.

Lemma 3. *(The sloping functions are linearly ordered in CCVR's.) Let* $f, g : W \to \bigcup_{w \in W} (\mathbb{A}_w \cup \{*\})$ *be sloping for* **MBLC**. *Then:*

$$\forall v : (f(v) \geq g(v)) \vee \forall v : (g(v) \geq f(v)).$$

Proof. It suffices to see that $\forall v : (f(v) \geq g(v))$ iff f is the $\top$-constant function or $w_f \prec w_g$ or ($w_f = w_g$ and $a_f \geq a_g$).

Corollary 1 (Monotonicity). *The following (generalised) monotonicity property holds for all* $\mathbb{L}_{\otimes}$*-formulas* ϕ*, i.e.*

$$if w \preceq v then (w \Vdash^{\mathrm{CCVR}} \phi) \leq (v \Vdash^{\mathrm{CCVR}} \phi).$$

Proof. This follows from the observation that the valuations are sloping functions, which are in turn monotonic functions.

In what follows we define the validity concepts in **CCVR**-structures.

Definition 12.
- *We say that a formula* ϕ holds *in a* **CCVR**-*structure* $\mathbb{M}$ *(written* $\Vdash_{\mathbb{M}}^{\mathrm{CCVR}} \phi$*) if for all* $w \in W$ *we have*

$$(w \Vdash^{\mathrm{CCVR}} \phi) = \top$$

  Otherwise, we say that the formula fails $\mathbb{M}$ *(written* $\not\Vdash_{\mathbb{M}}^{\mathrm{CCVR}} \phi$*) and this means:*

$$\exists w \in W : (w \Vdash^{\mathrm{CCVR}} \phi) < \top$$

- *A formula* ϕ *is said to be valid under the* **CCVR**-*Kripke semantics (written* $\Vdash^{\mathrm{CCVR}} \phi$*) if* $\Vdash_{\mathbb{M}}^{\mathrm{CCVR}} \phi$ *for all* **CCVR**-*structures* $\mathbb{M}$.

6 CCVR Structures and Ordinal Sums of Monadic BL Chains

In what follows, we show the connection between **CCVR**-structures and ordinal sums of monadic BL chains.

Lemma 4. *Given a* **CCVR**-*structure*

$$\mathbb{M} = \langle \mathbb{W}, \Vdash^{\mathrm{CCVR}} \rangle$$

and the sloping functions $\mathsf{Slop}(\mathbb{M}) := \{f \mid f : W \to \bigcup_{w \in W} (\mathbb{A}_w \cup \{\star\}) is sloping\}$ *of* $\mathbb{M}$*, there is an isomorphism from* $\mathsf{Slop}(\mathbb{M})$ *to* $C_{\mathbb{H}} := \{(w, a) : w \in \mathbb{H} - \{\top_{\mathbb{H}}\}, a \in \mathbb{A}_w - \{\top_{\mathbb{A}_w}\}\} \cup \{(\top_{\mathbb{H}}, \top)\}$ *(here* $\top$ *is the shared top-element of all* *algebras $\mathbb{A}_w$) such that the total order on $C_{\mathbb{H}}$ is defined as the following lexicographic order:*

$$(i,a) \leq (j,b) \quad iff \quad i < j \quad or \quad (i = j \quad and \quad a \leq b)$$

We define on $C_{\mathbb{H}}$ the following operations:

$$(i,a) \wedge (j,b) = min\{(i,a),(j,b)\}$$

$$(i,a) \vee (j,b) = max\{(i,a),(j,b)\}$$

$$(i,a) \otimes (j,b) = \begin{cases} (i,a) & if \quad i < j \\ (i, a \otimes b) & if \quad i = j \\ (j,b) & if \quad i > j \end{cases}$$

$$(i,a) \to (j,b) = \begin{cases} (1,1) & if \quad (i,a) \leq (j,b) \\ (i, a \to b) & if \quad i = j \quad and \quad a > b \\ (j,b) & if \quad i > j \end{cases}$$

$$\forall(i,a) = \begin{cases} (i,a) & if \quad i \in \forall\mathbb{H} \\ (\forall i, u_{\forall i}) & if \quad i \notin \forall\mathbb{H} \end{cases}$$

$$\exists(i,a) = \begin{cases} (i,a) & if \quad i \in \forall\mathbb{H} \\ (\exists i, 0_{\exists i}) & if \quad i \notin \forall\mathbb{H} \quad and \quad \exists i \neq \top_{\mathbb{H}} \\ (\top_{\mathbb{H}}, \top) & if \quad i \notin \forall\mathbb{H} \quad and \quad \exists i = \top_{\mathbb{H}} \end{cases}$$

The operations $\wedge, \vee, \otimes, \to$ in $\mathsf{Slop}(\mathbb{M}) := \{f \colon W \to \bigcup_{w \in W}(\mathbb{A}_w \cup \{\star\}\}$ are defined as in Lemma 1. The quantifiers in $\mathsf{Slop}(\mathbb{M}) := \{f \colon W \to \bigcup_{w \in W}(\mathbb{A}_w \cup \{\star\}\}$ are defined as follows:

$$(\forall f)(w) := \begin{cases} f(w) & if\, w_f \in \forall\mathbb{H}\, or\, f\, is\, the\, \top - constant function \\ \top & if\, w_f \notin \forall\mathbb{H}\, and\, w \succ \forall w_f \\ \star & if\, w_f \notin \forall\mathbb{H}\, and\, w \prec \forall w_f \\ u_{\forall w_f} & if\, w_f \notin \forall\mathbb{H}\, and\, w = \forall w_f \end{cases}$$

$$(\exists f)(w) := \begin{cases} f(w) & if\, w_f \in \exists\mathbb{H}\, or\, f\, is\, the\, \top - constant function \\ \top & if\, w_f \notin \exists\mathbb{H}\, and\, (w \succ \exists w_f \neq \top_{\mathbb{H}}\, or\, \exists w_\phi = \top_{\mathbb{H}}) \\ \star & if\, w_f \notin \exists\mathbb{H}\, and\, w \prec \exists w_f \neq \top_{\mathbb{H}} \\ 0_{\exists w_f} & if\, w_f \notin \exists\mathbb{H}\, and\, w = \exists w_f \neq \top_{\mathbb{H}} \end{cases}$$

Proof. We map each $\top$-constant function to $(\top_{\mathbb{H}}, \top)$ and other sloping functions to (w_f, a_f). We denote this map as h. It is easy to see that h is well-defined and is a bijection. To show that h is an isomorphism, it suffices to show that h preserves operations, which is shown as follows:

– For the case of $\wedge$, let us consider $f, g \in \mathsf{Slop}(\mathbb{M})$.

- If both f and g are $\top$-constant functions, then $h(f) = h(g) = (\top_{\mathbb{H}}, \top)$, and so $f \wedge g = g$ and $(\top_{\mathbb{H}}, \top) \wedge (\top_{\mathbb{H}}, \top) = (\top_{\mathbb{H}}, \top \wedge \top) = (\top_{\mathbb{H}}, \top)$. Therefore, $h(f \wedge g) = h(g) = (\top_{\mathbb{H}}, \top) = (\top_{\mathbb{H}}, \top) \wedge (\top_{\mathbb{H}}, \top) = h(f) \wedge h(g)$.
- If f is the $\top$-constant function and g is not, then $f \wedge g = g$, $h(f) = (\top_{\mathbb{H}}, \top)$ and $h(g) = (w, a)$ for some $w \in \mathbb{H} - \{\top_{\mathbb{H}}\}$ and $a \in \mathbb{A}_w - \{\top_{\mathbb{A}_w}\}$. Since $w <_{\mathbb{H}} \top_{\mathbb{H}}$, we have that $(\top_{\mathbb{H}}, \top) \wedge (w, a) = (w, a)$. Then $h(f \wedge g) = h(g) = (w, a) = (\top_{\mathbb{H}}, \top) \wedge (w, a) = h(f) \wedge h(g)$.
- If g is the $\top$-constant function and f is not, the proof is similar.
- If neither f nor g are $\top$-constant functions, then there are $w_1, w_2 \in \mathbb{H} - \{\top_{\mathbb{H}}\}$ and $a_1, a_2 \in \mathbb{A}_w - \{\top_{\mathbb{A}_w}\}$ such that $h(f) = (w_1, a_1)$ and $h(g) = (w_2, a_2)$. Then $h(f) \wedge h(g) = (w_1, a_1) \wedge (w_2, a_2)$.
  - If $w_1 = w_2$, then $h(f) \wedge h(g) = (w_1, a_1 \wedge a_2)$, and $(f \wedge g)(w) := \begin{cases} \star & if\, w \prec w_1 \\ a_1 \wedge a_2 & if\, w = w_1 \\ \top & if\, w \succ w_1 \end{cases}$ so $h(f \wedge g) = (w_1, a_1 \wedge a_2) = h(f) \wedge h(g)$.
  - If $w_1 \neq w_2$, without loss of generality we assume that $w_1 \prec w_2$, then $h(f) \wedge h(g) = (w_1, a_1) \wedge (w_2, a_2) = (w_2, a_2)$, and $(f \wedge g)(w) := \begin{cases} \star \wedge \star = \star & if\, w \prec w_1 \\ a_1 \wedge \star = \star & if\, w = w_1 \\ \top \wedge \star = \star & if\, w_1 \prec w \prec w_2 \\ \top \wedge a_2 = a_2 & if\, w = w_2 \\ \top \wedge \top = \top & if\, w \succ w_2 \end{cases}$ therefore $h(f \wedge g) = (w_2, a_2) = h(f) \wedge h(g)$.

  Therefore in both cases we have $h(f \wedge g) = h(f) \wedge h(g)$.
- The case of $\vee$ is similar to the case of $\wedge$.
- For the case of $\otimes$, let us consider $f, g \in \mathsf{Slop}(\mathbb{M})$.
  - If both f and g are $\top$-constant functions, then $h(f) = h(g) = (\top_{\mathbb{H}}, \top)$, and it is easy to see that $f \otimes g = g$ and $(\top_{\mathbb{H}}, \top) \otimes (\top_{\mathbb{H}}, \top) = (\top_{\mathbb{H}}, \top \otimes \top) = (\top_{\mathbb{H}}, \top)$. Therefore, $h(f \otimes g) = h(g) = (\top_{\mathbb{H}}, \top) = (\top_{\mathbb{H}}, \top) \otimes (\top_{\mathbb{H}}, \top) = h(f) \otimes h(g)$.
  - If f is the $\top$-constant function and g is not, then $f \otimes g = g$, $h(f) = (\top_{\mathbb{H}}, \top)$ and $h(g) = (w, a)$ for some $w \in \mathbb{H} - \{\top_{\mathbb{H}}\}$ and $a \in \mathbb{A}_w - \{\top_{\mathbb{A}_w}\}$. Since $w <_{\mathbb{H}} \top_{\mathbb{H}}$, we have that $(\top_{\mathbb{H}}, \top) \otimes (w, a) = (w, a)$. Then $h(f \otimes g) = h(g) = (w, a) = (\top_{\mathbb{H}}, \top) \otimes (w, a) = h(f) \otimes h(g)$.
  - If g is the $\top$-constant function and f is not, the proof is similar.
  - If neither f nor g are $\top$-constant functions, then there are $w_1, w_2 \in \mathbb{H} - \{\top_{\mathbb{H}}\}$ and $a_1, a_2 \in \mathbb{A}_w - \{\top_{\mathbb{A}_w}\}$ such that $h(f) = (w_1, a_1)$ and $h(g) = (w_2, a_2)$. Then $h(f) \otimes h(g) = (w_1, a_1) \otimes (w_2, a_2)$.
    * If $w_1 = w_2$, then $h(f) \otimes h(g) = (w_1, a_1 \otimes a_2)$, and
    $$(f \otimes g)(w) := \begin{cases} \star & \text{if } w \prec w_1 \\ a_1 \otimes a_2 & \text{if } w = w_1 \\ \top & \text{if } w \succ w_1 \end{cases}$$
    so $h(f \otimes g) = (w_1, a_1 \otimes a_2) = h(f) \otimes h(g)$.
    * If $w_1 \neq w_2$, without loss of generality we assume that $w_1 \prec w_2$, then $h(f) \otimes h(g) = (w_1, a_1) \otimes (w_2, a_2) = (w_2, a_2)$, and

$$(f \otimes g)(w) := \begin{cases} \star \otimes \star = \star & \text{if } w \prec w_1 \\ a_1 \otimes \star = \star & \text{if } w = w_1 \\ \top \otimes \star = \star & \text{if } w_1 \prec w \prec w_2 \\ \top \otimes a_2 = a_2 & \text{if } w = w_2 \\ \top \otimes \top = \top & \text{if } w \succ w_2 \end{cases}$$

therefore $h(f \otimes g) = (w_2, a_2) = h(f) \otimes h(g)$.

Therefore in both cases we have $h(f \otimes g) = h(f) \otimes h(g)$.

- For the case of $\to$, let us consider $f, g \in \mathsf{Slop}(\mathbb{M})$.
  - If both f and g are $\top$-constant functions, then $f \to g$ is also the $\top$-constant function, so $h(f \to g) = h(f) = h(g) = (\top_{\mathbb{H}}, \top)$. Since $(\top_{\mathbb{H}}, \top) \to (\top_{\mathbb{H}}, \top) = (\top_{\mathbb{H}}, \top)$, we have $h(f \to g) = (\top_{\mathbb{H}}, \top) = (\top_{\mathbb{H}}, \top) \to (\top_{\mathbb{H}}, \top) = h(f) \to h(g)$.
  - If f is the $\top$-constant function and g is not, then $f \to g = g$, $h(f) = (\top_{\mathbb{H}}, \top)$ and $h(g) = (w, a)$ for some $w \in \mathbb{H} - \{\top_{\mathbb{H}}\}$ and $a \in \mathbb{A}_w - \{\top_{\mathbb{A}_w}\}$. Since $w <_{\mathbb{H}} \top_{\mathbb{H}}$, we have that $(\top_{\mathbb{H}}, \top) \to (w, a) = (w, a)$. Then $h(f \to g) = h(g) = (w, a) = (\top_{\mathbb{H}}, \top) \to (w, a) = h(f) \to h(g)$.
  - If g is the $\top$-constant function and f is not, then $f \to g = g$ is the $\top$-constant function, $h(g) = (\top_{\mathbb{H}}, \top)$ and $h(f) = (w, a)$ for some $w \in \mathbb{H} - \{\top_{\mathbb{H}}\}$ and $a \in \mathbb{A}_w - \{\top_{\mathbb{A}_w}\}$. Since $w <_{\mathbb{H}} \top_{\mathbb{H}}$, we have that $(w, a) \to (\top_{\mathbb{H}}, \top) = (\top_{\mathbb{H}}, \top)$. Then $h(f \to g) = h(g) = (\top_{\mathbb{H}}, \top) = (w, a) \to (\top_{\mathbb{H}}, \top) = h(f) \to h(g)$.
  - If neither f nor g are $\top$-constant functions, then there are $w_1, w_2 \in \mathbb{H} - \{\top_{\mathbb{H}}\}$ and $a_1, a_2 \in \mathbb{A}_w - \{\top_{\mathbb{A}_w}\}$ such that $h(f) = (w_1, a_1)$ and $h(g) = (w_2, a_2)$. Then $h(f) \to h(g) = (w_1, a_1) \to (w_2, a_2)$.
    * If $w_1 = w_2$ and $a_1 \leq a_2$, then $h(f) \to h(g) = (w_1, a_1) \to (w_2, a_2) = (\top_{\mathbb{H}}, \top)$, and $f \to g$ is the $\top$-constant function, so $h(f \to g) = (\top_{\mathbb{H}}, \top) = (w_1, a_1) \to (w_2, a_2) = h(f) \to h(g)$.
    * If $w_1 = w_2$ and $a_1 > a_2$, then $h(f) \to h(g) = (w_1, a_1) \to (w_2, a_2) = (w_1, a_1 \to a_2)$, and

      $$(f \to g)(w) := \begin{cases} \bot & \text{if } w \prec w_1 \\ a_1 \to a_2 & \text{if } w = w_1 \\ \top & \text{if } w \succ w_1 \end{cases}$$

      so $h(f \to g) = (w_1, a_1 \to a_2) = h(f) \to (g)$.
    * If $w_1 \prec w_2$, then $h(f) \to h(g) = (w_1, a_1) \to (w_2, a_2) = (w_2, a_2)$, and $f \to g = g$, therefore $h(f \to g) = h(g) = (w_2, a_2) = (w_1, a_1) \to (w_2, a_2) = h(f) \to h(g)$.
    * If $w_1 \succ w_2$, then $h(f) \to h(g) = (w_1, a_1) \to (w_2, a_2) = (\top_{\mathbb{H}}, \top)$, and $f \to g$ is the $\top$-constant function, so $h(f \to g) = (\top_{\mathbb{H}}, \top) = (w_1, a_1) \to (w_2, a_2) = h(f) \to h(g)$.

  Therefore in all four cases we have $h(f \to g) = h(f) \to h(g)$.
- For the case of $\exists$, let us consider $f \in \mathsf{Slop}(\mathbb{M})$.
  - If f is the $\top$-constant function, then $h(f) = (\top_{\mathbb{H}}, \top)$, and $\exists f$ is also the $\top$-constant function, so $h(\exists f) = (\top_{\mathbb{H}}, \top)$. Since $\top_{\mathbb{H}} = \forall \top_{\mathbb{H}}$, we have that $\top_{\mathbb{H}} \in \forall \mathbb{H}$, so $h(\exists f) = (\top_{\mathbb{H}}, \top) = \exists(\top_{\mathbb{H}}, \top) = \exists h(f)$.
  - If f is not the $\top$-constant function, then there are $w \in \mathbb{H} - \{\top_{\mathbb{H}}\}$ and $a \in \mathbb{A}_w - \{\top_{\mathbb{A}_w}\}$ such that $h(f) = (w_f, a_f)$. If $w_f \in \forall \mathbb{H}$, then $\exists f$ is

the same as f, therefore $h(\exists f) = h(f) = (w_f, a_f) = \exists(w_f, a_f) = \exists h(f)$. Otherwise, $w_f \notin \forall\mathbb{H}$, and we discuss in two cases:
  * If $\exists w_f = \top_{\mathbb{H}}$, then $\exists f$ is the $\top$-constant function, and therefore $h(\exists f) = (\top_{\mathbb{H}}, \top) = (\exists w_f, \top) = \exists(w_f, a_f) = \exists h(f)$.
  * If $\exists w_f \neq \top_{\mathbb{H}}$, then $h(\exists f) = (\exists w_f, 0_{\exists w_f}) = \exists(w_f, a_f) = \exists h(f)$.
- The case of $\forall$ is similar to the case of $\exists$.

7 Soundness and completeness of CCVR-semantics

We now prove the soundness of the Kripke semantics for **MBLC**.

Theorem 1 (Soundness). *If* $\vdash_{\mathbf{MBLC}} \phi$ *then* $\Vdash^{\mathrm{CCVR}} \phi$.

Proof. Suppose $\vdash \phi$ holds in **MBLC**. By the algebraic completeness result for **MBLC** algebras with respect to the Hilbert-style proof system $\mathbf{MBLC}_H$ (see Proposition 1), it follows that for all **MBLC**-algebras $\mathbb{G}$ and all mappings $h\colon Atom \to \mathbb{G}$ from atomic formulas to elements of $\mathbb{G}$, we have that $[\![\phi]\!]_h^{\mathbb{G}} = \top$.

Now for any **CCVR**-structure $\mathbb{M}$, by Lemma 4, $\mathsf{Slop}(\mathbb{M})$ is isomorphic to some $C_{\mathbb{H}}$. By ([2, Theorem 6.1]), $C_{\mathbb{H}}$ is a monadic BL chain, therefore we have $C_{\mathbb{H}} \models \phi$, so $\mathbb{M} \Vdash \phi$.

We now prove completeness of **MBLC** for the semantics presented above. Our proof is a departure from our earlier papers [10] and [9]. In the former, we simply embed our semantics into the poset products of Jipsen and Montagna, while in the latter case we exploit properties of **BL**-algebra representability (both in terms of poset products and ordinal sums) unique to that setting. Here, the result follows immediately by the representation of **MBLC**-algebras by ordinal sums and our isomorphism result in Lemma 4.

Theorem 2 (Completeness). *If* $\Vdash^{\mathrm{CCVR}} \phi$ *then* $\vdash_{\mathbf{MBLC}} \phi$.

Proof. Suppose $\vdash \phi$ fails in **MBLC**. By the algebraic completeness result for **MBLC**-algebras with respect to the Hilbert-style proof system $\mathbf{MBLC}_H$ (see Proposition 1), it follows that for some **MBLC**-algebra $\mathbb{G}$ and some mapping $h\colon Atom \to \mathbb{G}$ from atomic formulas to elements of $\mathbb{G}$, we have that $[\![\phi]\!]_h^{\mathbb{G}} \neq \top$. By ([2, Theorem 6.2]) we can take $\mathbb{G}$ to be some $C_{\mathbb{H}}$ as defined in Lemma 4. By Lemma 4, this $C_{\mathbb{H}}$ is isomorphic to the sloping function algebra $\mathsf{Slop}(\mathbb{M})$ of a **CCVR**-structure $\mathbb{M}$ where the valuation on $\mathbb{M}$ agrees with h so that $\mathbb{M} \nVdash \phi$.

8 Conclusion

In the preceding, we extracted a relational semantics from the ordinal sum representation of [2] for **MBLC**. By introducing generalisations of Kripke semantics adequate for **MBLC** (and neighbours, see [3,9,10]), we seek a new perspective on fuzzy logics such as **MBLC** as constructive or semi-constructive systems. Moreover, relational semantics typically come pregnant with connections to proof theory, decidability and model theory. We hope in the fullness of time to exploit the semantics developed here to develop semantically motivated calculi **MBLC** and similar systems. We also submit the question of how deep the analogy with intuitionistic systems runs (via Kripke semantics) has independent theoretical value.

There are several alternatives towards this end. One approach to consider are semantic tableaux and refutation systems: One can exploit the notion of unsatisfiability in our relational semantics to devise a proof system, as is done in classical modal or intuitionistic logic (see [12]). Another possibility is to consider labelled calculi, see e.g. [11] or [4]. Labelled calculi have been well-tested in cases of classical modal logics, extensions of classical modal systems, substructural cases, as well as logics over an intuitionistic or minimal base, although as yet untested on cases involving of divisibility ([($\wedge$1)] and [($\wedge$2)], page 2). Still another alternative are the multi-type calculi of e.g. [5]. These calculi seem well-adapted to systems defined over distributive structures, e.g. chains, having strong algebraic underpinnings.

References

1. Bova, S., Montagna, F.: The consequence relation in the logic of commutative GBL-algebras is PSPACE-complete. Theoret. Comput. Sci. **410**(12), 4 (2009). https://doi.org/10.1016/j.tcs.2008.10.024
2. Castaño, D., Cimadamore, C., Varela, J.P.D., Rueda, L.: Monadic BL-algebras: the equivalent algebraic semantics of Hájek's monadic fuzzy logic (2016). https://arxiv.org/abs/1609.05082
3. Fussner, W.: Poset products as relational models. Studia Logica **110**, 4 (2021). https://doi.org/10.1007/s11225-021-09956-z
4. Gabbay, D.: Labelled Deductive Systems. Oxford University Press (1996)
5. Greco, G., Liang, F., Moshier, M.A., Palmigiano, A.: Semi de Morgan logic properly displayed. Studia Logica **109** (2021). https://doi.org/10.1007/s005000000044
6. Hájek, P.: Basic fuzzy logic and BL algebras. Soft Comput. **2** (1998). https://doi.org/10.1007/s005000050043
7. Hájek, P.: Metamathematics of Fuzzy Logic, Trends in Logic, vol. 4. Klouwer (1998)
8. Jipsen, P., Montagna, F.: Embedding theorems for classes of GBL-algebras. J. Pure Appl. Algebra **214**(9), 4 (2010). https://doi.org/10.1016/j.jpaa.2009.11.015
9. Lewis-Smith, A.: A Kripke semantics for Hájek's BL. arXiv e-prints, pp. arXiv–2308 (2023)
10. Lewis-Smith, A., Oliva, P., Robinson, E.: A Kripke semantics for intuitionistic Łukasiewicz logic. Studia Logica **109**, 4 (2020). https://doi.org/10.1007/s11225-020-09908-z
11. Negri, S., Plato, J.V.: Proof Analysis: A Contribution to Hilbert's Last Problem. Cambridge University Press (2011)
12. Priest, G.: An Introduction to Non-Classical Logic: From If to Is. Cambridge University Press (2008)

Author Index

K. Sauerwald and M. Thimm (Eds.): ECSQARU 2025, LNAI 16099, pp. 513–514, 2026.
https://doi.org/10.1007/978-3-032-05134-9

The manufacturer's authorised representative in the EU is Springer Nature Customer Service Centre GmbH, Europaplatz 3, 69115 Heidelberg, Germany. If you have any concerns regarding our products, please contact ProductSafety@springernature.com

Printed and bound by CPI Group (UK) Ltd, Croydon, CR0 4YY

28/04/2026

02098524-0013